SIXTH CANADIAN EDITION

BASIC STATISTICS FOR BUSINESS & ECONOMICS

Douglas A. Lind

Coastal Carolina University and the University of Toledo

William G. Marchal

The University of Toledo

Samuel A. Wathen

Coastal Carolina University

Carol Ann Waite

Sheridan College

McGraw Hill Education

BASIC STATISTICS FOR BUSINESS & ECONOMICS
SIXTH CANADIAN EDITION

ISBN-13: 978-1-25-926893-9
ISBN-10: 1-25-926893-4

1 2 3 4 5 6 7 8 9 10 TCP 22 21 20 19 18

Printed and bound in Canada.

Care has been taken to trace ownership of copyright material contained in this text; however, the publisher will welcome any information that enables them to rectify any reference or credit for subsequent editions.

Portfolio Director, Business & Economics, International: *Nicole Meehan*
Portfolio Manager: *Sara Braithwaite*
Senior Marketing Manager: *Cathie Lefebvre*
Content Developer: *Amy Rydzanicz*
Senior Portfolio Associate: *Marina Seguin*
Supervising Editor: *Jeanette McCurdy*
Photo/Permissions Editor: *Nadine Bachan*
Copy Editor: *Valerie Adams*
Plant Production Coordinator: *Sheryl MacAdam*
Manufacturing Production Coordinator: *Emily Hickey*
Cover Design: *Lightbox Visual Communications Inc.*
Cover Image: © *Flatscreen | Dreamstime.com*
Interior Design: *Jennifer Stimson*
Page Layout: *MPS Ltd.*
Printer: *Transcontinental Printing Group*

CONTENTS

Contents   v

Chapter
10. Two-Sample Tests of Hypothesis 312

Chapter
11. Analysis of Variance 345

Chapter
12. Linear Regression and Correlation 375

Chapter
13. Multiple Regression and Correlation Analysis 424

PREFACE

Welcome to the Sixth Canadian Edition of *Basic Statistics for Business and Economics!* As the name implies, the objective of this textbook is to provide Canadian business students majoring in economics, finance, marketing, accounting, management, and other fields of business administration with an introductory survey of the many business applications of descriptive and inferential statistics.

Today's business environment requires people with skills to deal with numerical information from an increasingly wide variety of sources. We need to be critical consumers of the information presented by others, and we need to be able to reduce large amounts of data into meaningful formats, so that we can make effective interpretations, judgments, and decisions. *Basic Statistics for Business and Economics* introduces students to these business applications, while maintaining a student-oriented learning environment. Examples and problems are designed to teach the basics while remaining relevant to the real world.

FEATURES OF THE NEW CANADIAN EDITION

The Sixth Canadian Edition makes every effort to support student learning. We present the concepts clearly for students, and we support these concepts immediately with examples and exercises. Improvements you will find in this edition include the following:

- Updated Practice Tests at the end of each chapter to give students an idea of content that might appear on a test and how the test might be structured.
- Updated statistics throughout.
- Chapter-opening exercises in each chapter demonstrate how chapter content can be applied to a real-world situation.
- Updated multi-step questions.
- Chapter Exercises arranged in order of difficulty in each chapter.
- Excel 2013 software used for all Excel screenshots and computer commands.

Learning Objectives and Chapter-Opening Exercise

Each chapter begins with an exercise that opens the chapter and shows how the chapter content can be applied to a real-world situation. Chapters commence with a set of learning objectives designed to provide a focus for the chapter and motivate learning. These objectives indicate what students should be able to do after completing the chapter. Students can also locate learning objectives in the margin where they occur in the text.

Introduction to the Topic

Each chapter starts with a review of the important concepts of the previous chapter and provides a link to the material in the current chapter. This interconnected approach increases comprehension by providing continuity across concepts.

Example and Solution

After important concepts are introduced, we provide a straightforward, student-oriented example, including a full solution. Examples with solutions are a key learning tool, as they serve two purposes. First, they provide a "how to" illustration. Second, they show a relevant business or economics application that helps answer the question "What will I use this for?" All examples attempt to strike the appropriate balance, not only providing a realistic scenario or application, but also making the size and scale of the math reasonable for students in introductory courses.

Self-Review

Self-Reviews are interspersed throughout the chapter and are closely patterned after the preceding examples. These reviews help students monitor their progress, and provide immediate reinforcement for the particular techniques illustrated in the examples. The worked-out solutions are provided at the end of each chapter.

Statistics in Action

Statistics in Action boxes are scattered throughout the text. These boxes provide unique and interesting applications and historical insights into the field of statistics.

Key Ideas

Key ideas are boldfaced within the text to emphasize important concepts.

Formulas

Formulas used for the first time are boxed and numbered for reference. In addition, a formula card is available online, which lists these key formulas.

Exercises

Exercises can be found within the chapter and in the end-of-chapter material. Generally, the end-of-chapter exercises are the most challenging and integrative of the chapter concepts. The answers for most odd-numbered exercises appear at the end of the text.

Chapter Summary

Each chapter concludes with a Chapter Summary. This learning aid provides the opportunity to review material, and summarizes the learning objectives.

Data Set Exercises

The last exercises at the end of each chapter are based on large data sets. A complete listing of all the data sets used is available on page AP-1 of this text.

These data sets can be found on the McGraw-Hill online resource for *Basic Statistics*. They present real-world applications of statistics and more complex applications of the concepts.

Computer Commands

Computer examples using Excel and MegaStat can be found throughout the text. But the explanations of the computer input commands for each program are placed at the end of the chapter. This allows students to focus on the statistical techniques rather than ways to input data.

Answers to Self-Reviews

The worked-out solutions to the Self-Reviews are provided at the end of each chapter.

Practice Test

The Practice Test that appears at the end of each chapter is intended to give students an idea of content that might appear on a test and how the test might be structured. The Practice Test includes both objective questions and problems covering the material studied in the chapter.

Superior Learning Solutions and Support

The McGraw-Hill Education team is ready to help instructors assess and integrate any of our products, technology, and services into your course for optimal teaching and learning performance. Whether it's helping your students improve their grades, or putting your entire course online, the McGraw-Hill Education team is here to help you do it. Contact your Learning Solutions Consultant today to learn how to maximize all of McGraw-Hill Education's resources.

For more information, please visit us online: http://www.mheducation.ca/he/solutions

ACKNOWLEDGEMENTS

Comments and suggestions that have been invaluable to the development of the Sixth Canadian Edition were provided by a variety of reviewers, and a debt of gratitude is owed to the following educators:

Carolina Di Santo	*Niagara College*
Torben Drewes	*Trent University*
Bruno Fullone	*George Brown College*
Hayedeh Mottaghi	*Trent University*
Julie Orsini	*Durham College*
James Reimer	*Lethbridge College*
Glen Stirling	*Western University*
Kevin Willoughby	*Red Deer College*

I also wish to thank the staff at McGraw-Hill Education. This includes: Sara Braithwaite, Portfolio Manager; Amy Rydzanicz, Content Developer; Jeanette McCurdy, Supervising Editor; Cathie Lefebvre, Senior Marketing Manager; Valerie Adams, Copy Editor; and others who I do not know personally, but who made important contributions.

Carol Ann Waite

The Complete Course Solution

We listened to educators from around the world, learned about their challenges, and created a whole new way to deliver a course.

Connect2 is a collaborative teaching and learning platform that includes an instructionally designed complete course framework of learning materials that is flexible and open for instructors to easily personalize, add their own content, or integrate with other tools and platforms.

- Save time and resources building and managing a course.
- Gain confidence knowing that each course framework is pedagogically sound.
- Help students master course content.
- Make smarter decisions by using real-time data to guide course design, content changes, and remediation.

MANAGE — Dynamic Curriculum Builder

With one click you can launch a complete course framework developed by instructional design experts. Each Connect2 course is a flexible foundation for instructors to build upon by adding their own content or drawing upon the wide repository of additional resources.

- Easily customize Connect2 by personalizing the course scope and sequence.
- Get access to a wide range of McGraw-Hill Education content within one powerful teaching and learning platform.
- Receive expert support and guidance on how best to utilize content to achieve a variety of teaching goals.

MASTER — Student Experience

Improve student performance with instructional alignment and leverage Connect2's carefully curated learning resources. Deliver required reading through Connect2's award-winning adaptive learning system.

- Teach at a higher level in class by helping students retain core concepts.
- Tailor in-class instruction based on student progress and engagement.
- Help focus students on the content they don't know so they can prioritize their study time.

MEASURE — Advanced Analytics

Collect, analyze and act upon class and individual student performance data. Make real-time course updates and teaching decisions backed by data.

- Visually explore class and student performance data.
- Easily identify key relationships between assignments and student performance.
- Maximize in-class time by using data to focus on areas where students need the most help.

Course Map

The flexible and customizable course map provides instructors full control over the pre-configured courses within Connect2. Instructors can easily add, delete, or rearrange content to adjust the course scope and sequence to their personal preferences.

Implementation Guide

Each Connect2 course includes a detailed implementation guide that provides guidance on what the course can do and how best to utilize course content based on individual teaching approaches.

Instructor Resources

A comprehensive collection of instructor resources are available within Connect2. Instructor Support and Seminar Materials provide additional exercises and activities to use for in-class discussion and teamwork.

For more information, please visit www.mheconnect2.com

Barnes & Noble, Inc.

Electronic book readers (e-readers) allow users to browse, shop, download and read e-books, blogs, newspapers, and magazines all displayed in full colour. Assume that you know the number of units sold each day for the last month at the West Edmonton Mall. Describe a condition in which this information could be considered a sample. Illustrate a second situation in which the same data would be regarded as a population. (See Exercise 9.)

LEARNING OBJECTIVES

When you have completed this chapter, you will be able to:

LO1-1 Explain why knowledge of statistics is important.

LO1-2 Define statistics and provide an example of how statistics is used.

LO1-3 Differentiate between descriptive and inferential statistics.

LO1-4 Classify variables as qualitative or quantitative, and discrete or continuous.

LO1-5 Distinguish between nominal, ordinal, interval, and ratio levels of measurement.

LO1-6 Understand the values associated with the practice of statistics.

1.1 INTRODUCTION

More than 100 years ago, H. G. Wells, an English author and historian, suggested that one day quantitative reasoning will be as necessary for effective citizenship as the ability to read. He made no mention of business because the Industrial Revolution was just beginning. Mr. Wells could not have been more correct. Although "business experience," some "thoughtful guess-work," and "intuition" are key attributes of successful managers, today's business problems tend to be too complex for this type of decision making alone.

One of the tools used to make decisions is statistics. Statistics is used not only by business people, but we also apply statistical concepts in our lives. For example, to start the day, you turn on the shower and let it run for a few moments. Then you put your hand in the shower to sample the temperature and decide if you need to add more hot or cold water before you enter the shower. Then, later in the day, you are at Costco and wish to buy a frozen pizza. One of the pizza makers has a stand and offers you a sample. After sampling the pizza, you decide whether or not to purchase the pizza. In both the shower and the pizza examples, you make a decision and select a course of action based on a sample.

Businesses face similar situations. The Kellogg Company must ensure that the average amount of Raisin Bran in the 375 gram (g) box meets label specifications. To do so, it sets a "target" weight somewhat higher than the amount specified on the label. Each box is then weighed after it is filled. The weighing machine reports a distribution of the content weights for each hour as well as the number "kicked out" for being under the label specification during the hour. The Quality Control Department also randomly selects samples from the production line and checks the quality of the product and the weight of the contents in the box. If the average (mean) product weight differs significantly from the target weight or the percentage of kick-outs is too high, the process is adjusted.

As a student of business or economics, you will need basic knowledge and skills to organize, analyze, and transform data and to present the information. The purpose of this text is to develop your knowledge of basic statistical techniques and methods and how to apply them in order to develop your ability to make effective business and personal decisions.

LO1-1   1.2 WHY STUDY STATISTICS?

If you look through any college or university catalogue, you will find that statistics is required for many programs. Why is this so? As you investigate a future career in accounting, economics, human resources, finance, or other business area, you will also discover that statistics is required as part of these college programs. So why is an education in statistics a requirement in so many disciplines?

A major driver of the requirement for statistics knowledge is the technologies available for capturing data. Examples include the technology that Google uses to track how Internet users access websites. As people use Google to search the Internet, Google records every search and then uses these data to sort and prioritize the results for future Internet searches.

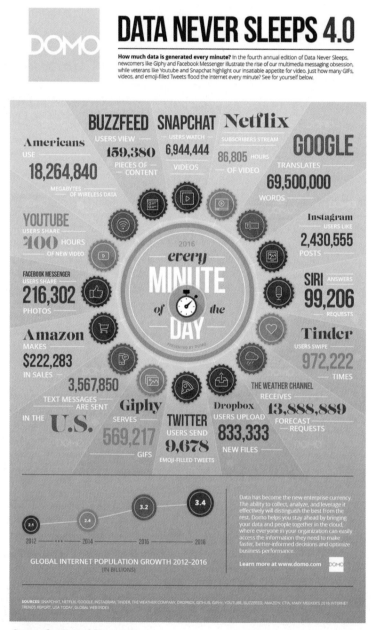

Source: Courtesy of Domo, Inc.

One recent estimate indicates that Google processes 20 000 terabytes of information per day. Big-box retailers like Costco, Walmart, Target, and others scan every purchase and use the data to manage the distribution of products, to make decisions about marketing and sales, and to track daily and even hourly sales. Police departments collect and use data to provide city residents with maps that communicate information about crimes committed and their location. Every organization is collecting and using data to develop knowledge and intelligence that will help people make informed decisions, and to track the implementation of their decisions. The graphic below shows the amount of data generated every minute (www.domo.com). A good working knowledge of statistics is useful for summarizing and organizing data to provide information that is useful and supportive of decision making. Statistics is used to make valid comparisons and to predict the outcomes of decisions.

In summary, there are at least three reasons for studying statistics: (1) data are collected everywhere and require statistical knowledge to make the information useful, (2) statistical techniques are used to make professional and personal decisions, and (3) no matter what your career, you will need a knowledge of statistics to understand the world and to be conversant in your career. An understanding of statistics and statistical methods will help you make more effective personal and professional decisions.

We call your attention to a feature called *Statistics in Action*. Read each one carefully to get an appreciation of the wide application of statistics in management, economics, nursing, law enforcement, sports, and other disciplines.

How are we to determine if the conclusions reported are reasonable? Was the sample large enough? How were the sampled units selected? To be an educated consumer of this information, we need to be able to read the charts and graphs and understand the discussion of the numerical information. An understanding of the concepts of basic statistics will be a big help.

A second reason for taking a statistics course is that statistical techniques are used to make decisions that affect our daily lives. That is, they affect our personal welfare. Here are two examples:

- Insurance companies use statistical analysis to set rates for home, automobile, life, and health insurance. Tables are available showing estimates that a 20-year-old female has about 61 years of life remaining, a 44-year-old man has about 25 years remaining, and a 50-year-old woman has about 26 years remaining. Life insurance premiums are established on the basis of these estimates of life expectancy. Tables can be found at statcan.gc.ca/tables-tableaux/sum-som/l01/cst01/health26-eng.htm.
- Medical researchers study the cure rates for diseases based on the use of different drugs and different forms of treatment. For example, what is the effect of treating a certain type of knee injury surgically or with physical therapy? If you take an aspirin each day, does that reduce your risk of a heart attack?

A third reason for taking a statistics course is that the knowledge of statistical methods will help you understand why decisions are made and give you a better understanding of how they affect you.

No matter what line of work you select, you will find yourself faced with decisions where an understanding of data analysis is helpful. To make an informed decision, you will need to be able to:

1. Determine whether the existing information is adequate or additional information is required.
2. Gather additional information, if it is needed, in such a way that it does not provide misleading results.
3. Summarize the information in a useful and informative manner.
4. Analyze the available information.
5. Draw conclusions and make inferences while assessing the risk of an incorrect conclusion.

The statistical methods presented in the text will provide you with a framework for the decision-making process.

In summary, there are at least three reasons for studying statistics: (1) data are everywhere; (2) statistical techniques are used to make many decisions that affect our lives; and (3) no matter what your career, you will make decisions that involve data. An understanding of statistical methods will help you make these decisions more effectively.

Statistics in Action

- *Canadian Business* publishes an annual list of the richest Canadians. As of July 2016, the Thomson family tops the list with a net worth of $36.8 billion, and Galen Weston is second, with a net worth of $13.7 billion (canadianbusiness.com).
- The estimated population in Canada is 36 286 400 as of July 1, 2016 (www.statcan.gc.ca/tables-tableaux/sum-som/l01/cst01/demo02a-eng.htm). The National Household Survey (2011) shows that 1 400 685 people had an Aboriginal identity (www12.statcan.gc.ca/nhs-enm/2011/as-sa/99-011-x/99-011-x2011001-eng.cfm).
- The Canadian Real Estate Association reports the average house prices nationally and in several urban centres across Canada. For example, the national average house price in April 2017 was estimated to be $559 317, which represents an increase of 10.4% from $506 596 in April 2016 (crea.ca).

LO1-2   1.3 WHAT IS MEANT BY STATISTICS?

How do we define the word *statistics*? This question can be rephrased in two, subtly different ways: what are statistics and what is statistics? To answer the first question, a statistic is a number used to communicate a piece of information. Examples of statistics are:

- The inflation rate is 2%.
- Your grade point average is 3.5.
- The price of a new Tesla Model S sedan starts at $86 000.

Each of these statistics is a numerical fact and communicates a very limited piece of information that is not very useful by itself. However, if we recognize that each of these statistics is part of a larger discussion, then the question "what *is* statistics" is applicable. Statistics is the set of knowledge and skills used to organize, summarize, and analyze data. The results of statistical analysis will start interesting conversations in the search for knowledge that will help us make decisions. For example:

- The inflation rate for the calendar year was 2%. By applying statistics we could compare this year's inflation rate to the past observations of inflation. Is it higher, lower, or about the same? Is there a trend of increasing or decreasing inflation? Is there a relationship between interest rates and government bonds?
- Your grade point average (GPA) is 3.5. By collecting data and applying statistics, you can determine the required GPA to be admitted to other colleges and universities such as the Master of Business Administration program (MBA) at Queen's University in Kingston, Ontario, or the University of Alberta in Edmonton, Alberta. You can determine the likelihood that you would be admitted to a particular program. You may be interested in interviewing for a management position at a large accounting firm. Is there a range of acceptable GPAs?
- You are budgeting for a new car. You would like to own an electric car with a small carbon footprint. The price for a new Tesla Model S sedan starts at $86 000 (www.tesla.com). By collecting additional data and applying statistics, you can analyze the alternatives. For example, another choice is a hybrid car that runs on both gas and electricity such as a Toyota Prius, which starts at $25 995 (www.toyota.ca) or a Chevrolet Volt, starting at $38 490 (www.chevrolet.ca). What are the differences in the cars' specifications? What additional information can be collected and summarized so that you can make a good purchase decision?
- Statistics Canada (Census Profile, 2016 Census) reports that 19.1% of the population in Canada is 65 years of age and over (www12.statcan.gc.ca/census-recensement/2016/dp-pd/prof/index.cfm?Lang=E).

Statistics The science of collecting, organizing, presenting, analyzing, and interpreting data to assist in making more effective decisions.

These are all examples of statistics. A collection of numerical information is called **statistics** (plural).

We frequently present statistical information in a graphical form. A graph is a visual way to convey information and can be used to capture reader attention. For example, Chart 1–1 shows

CHART 1–1 Average Canadian House Prices, June 2016

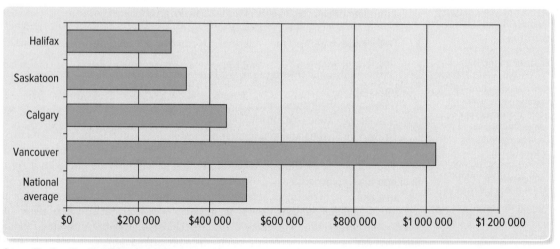

Source: The Canadian Real Estate Association; crea.ca

the average house prices in four Canadian cities in June 2016, compared with the national average (The Canadian Real Estate Association; crea.ca). It requires only a quick glance to see that Vancouver has the highest average house price in Canada.

These examples show that statistics is more than the presentation of numerical information. As the definition suggests, the first step in using statistics is to collect relevant data. After the data has been organized and presented, as in Chart 1–1, we can start to analyze and interpret them. Statistics is about collecting and processing information to create a conversation, to stimulate additional questions, and to provide a basis for making decisions.

In this book, you will learn the basic techniques and applications of statistics that you can use to support your decisions, both personal and professional. To start, we will differentiate between descriptive and inferential statistics.

LO1-3   1.4 TYPES OF STATISTICS

When we use statistics to generate information for decision making from data, we use either descriptive statistics or inferential statistics. Their application depends on the questions asked and the type of data available.

Descriptive Statistics

Masses of unorganized data—such as the census of population, the weekly earnings of thousands of computer programmers, and the individual responses of 2000 registered voters regarding their choice for prime minister—are of little value as is. However, descriptive statistics can be used to organize data into a meaningful form. The definition of statistics given earlier referred to "organizing, presenting, analyzing . . . data." This facet of statistics is usually referred to as **descriptive statistics**.

Descriptive statistics Methods of organizing, summarizing, and presenting data in an informative way.

The following are examples that apply descriptive statistics to summarize a large amount of data and provide information that is easy to understand.

The Canadian government reports that the population of Canada was 18 238 000 in 1961; 21 568 000 in 1971; 24 820 000 in 1981; 28 031 000 in 1991; 31 050 700 in 2001; 31 612 895 in 2006; 35 158 300 in 2013; and 36 286 400 as of July 1, 2016. This information is descriptive statistics. It is descriptive statistics if we calculate the percentage growth from one year to the next or from one decade to the next. However, it would *not* be descriptive statistics if we used the data to estimate the population of Canada in the year 2020 or the percentage growth from 2015 to 2025. Why? Because these statistics are not being used to summarize past populations but to estimate future populations.

The following are some other examples of descriptive statistics:

- The average hourly wage for employees in business, finance, and administrative occupations in Canada increased by 2.5% from June 2015 ($24.87) to June 2016 ($25.48) (statcan.gc.ca/tables-tableaux/sum-som/l01/cst01/labr69a-eng.htm).
- The class average of the first test in statistics over the last ten years has been between 63% and 72%.

Statistical methods and techniques to generate descriptive statistics are presented in Chapters 2 and 3. These include organizing and summarizing data with frequency distributions and presenting frequency distributions with charts and graphs. (These procedures are discussed in Chapter 2.) In addition, a number of statistical measures to summarize the characteristics of a set of data—such as the mean and standard deviation—are discussed in Chapter 3.

Inferential statistics The methods used to estimate a property of a population, based on a sample.

Inferential Statistics

Population The entire set of individuals or objects of interest or the measurements obtained from all individuals or objects of interest.

The second type of statistics is **inferential statistics**—also called **statistical inference**. Note the words *population* and *sample* in the definition of inferential statistics. We often make reference to the population of Canada or the fact that world population reached seven billion in 2011. However, in statistics the word *population* has a broader meaning. A **population** may consist of *individuals*—such as all persons living in Canada, or all students in Accounting 201, or all the chief executive officers (CEOs) from the Fortune 500 companies. But a population may also consist of *objects,* such as all SUVs (sport utility vehicles), or the accounts receivable at the end of the second quarter or all insurance claims filed by residents of Fort McMurray after the May 2016 wildfires. The *measurement* of concern might be population numbers by province, the grades on the first test of students in Accounting 201, or the dollar amount of the fire insurance claims as a result of the wildfires. Thus, a population in the statistical sense, does not always refer to people.

Sample A portion, or part, of the population of interest.

As there are times when we must make decisions based on a limited set of data, our interest regarding inferential statistics is in finding something about a population from results taken from a **sample** of that population. For example, a recent survey showed that only 46% of high school students can solve problems involving fractions, decimals, and percentages, and that only 77% of high school students can correctly total the cost of a salad, a burger, fries, and a cola on a restaurant menu. Since these are inferences about the population (all high school students) based on sample data, we refer to them as inferential statistics. You might think of inferential statistics as a "best guess" of a population value based on sample information.

Why take a sample instead of studying every member of the population? Samples are often used to obtain reliable estimates of population parameters. In the process, we make trade-offs between the time, money, and effort to collect the data and the error of estimating a population parameter. For example, the process of sampling SUVs is illustrated in the following graphic. We would like to know the mean or average fuel efficiency of all SUVs. To estimate the mean of the population, six SUVs are sampled and their mean fuel efficiency is tested. The mean fuel efficiency of the six is used to estimate fuel efficiency for the population.

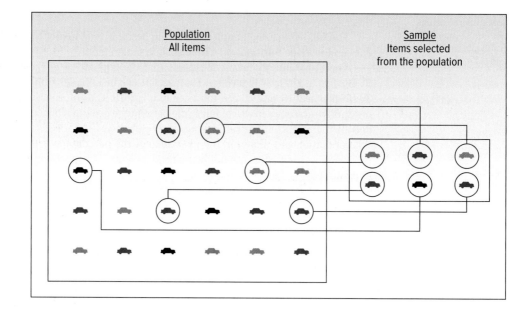

Note that inferential statistics is widely applied learn something about a population in business, agriculture, politics, and government, as shown in the following examples:

- Television networks constantly monitor the popularity of their programs by hiring Nielsen and other organizations to sample the preferences of TV viewers. For example, in a sample of 800 prime-time viewers, 320 or 40.0%, indicated that they watched *The Big Bang Theory* last week. These program ratings are used to set advertising rates or to continue or cancel programs (www.nielsen.com).
- An accounting firm is conducting an audit of M Studios. To begin, the accounting firm selects a random sample of 100 invoices (from a population of 2000 invoices) and

checks each for accuracy. There is at least one error on five of the invoices; hence the accounting firm estimates that 5% of the population of invoices contains at least one error.

- A random sample of 1260 marketing graduates showed their mean starting salary was $45 694. We therefore estimate the mean starting salary for all marketing graduates to be $45 694.

A feature of our text is self-review problems. There are a number of them interspersed throughout each chapter. The first self-review follows. Each tests your comprehension of the preceding material. The answer and method of solution are given at the end of the chapter. We recommend that you solve each one and then check your answer.

---

self-review 1–1

The answers are at the end of the chapter.
Brandon Foods asked a sample of 1960 consumers to try a newly developed chicken dinner called Chicken Delight. Of the 1960 sampled, 1176 said they would purchase the dinner if it is marketed.

(a) What would Brandon Foods report to its Board of Directors regarding the percentage of acceptance of Chicken Delight in the population?
(b) Is this an example of descriptive statistics or inferential statistics? Explain.

LO1-4   1.5 TYPES OF VARIABLES

Statistics in Action

Where did statistics get its start? In 1662, John Graunt published an article called "Natural and Political Observations Made upon Bills of Mortality." The author's "observations" were the result of his study and analysis of a weekly church publication called "Bill of Mortality," which listed births, christenings, and deaths and their causes. Graunt realized that the Bills of Mortality represented only a fraction of all births and deaths in London. However, he used the data to reach broad conclusions about the impact of diseases, such as the plague, on the general population. His logic is an example of statistical inference. His analysis and interpretation of the data are thought to mark the start of statistics.

There are two basic types of variables: (1) qualitative and (2) quantitative (see Chart 1–2). When the characteristic being studied is non-numeric, it is called a **qualitative variable** or an **attribute**. Examples of qualitative variables are gender, beverage preference, type of vehicle owned, country of birth and eye colour. When a variable is qualitative, we are usually count the number of observations for each category and determine what percent fall in each category. For example, if we observe the variable eye colour, what percent of the population has blue eyes and what percent has brown eyes? If the variable is type of vehicle, what percent of the total number sold last month were SUVs? Qualitative variables are often summarized in charts and bar graphs (see Chapter 2).

CHART 1–2 Summary of the Types of Variables

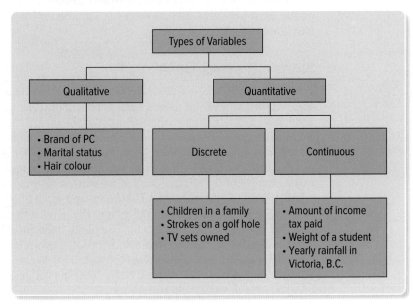

When the variable can be reported numerically, the variable is called a **quantitative variable**. Examples of quantitative variables are the balance in your chequing account, the ages of company CEOs, the life of a battery (such as 42 months), and the number of children in a family.

Quantitative variables are either discrete or continuous. **Discrete variables** can assume only certain values, and there are "gaps" between the values. Examples of discrete variables are the number of bedrooms in a house (1, 2, 3, 4, etc.), the number of cars arriving at a shopping centre in an hour (326, 421, etc.), and the number of students in each section of a statistics course (25 in section A, 42 in section B, and 18 in section C). We count, for example, the number of cars arriving at a shopping centre, and we count the number of statistics students in each section. Note that a home can have 3 or 4 bedrooms, but it cannot have 3.56 bedrooms. Thus, there is a "gap" between possible values. Typically, discrete variables result from counting.

Observations of a **continuous variable** can assume any value within a specific range. Examples of continuous variables are the air pressure in a tire, and the weight of a shipment of tomatoes. Other examples are the amount of raisin bran in a box and the duration of flights from Vancouver to Calgary. Grade point average (GPA) is also a continuous variable. We could report the GPA of a student as 3.2576952. The usual practice is to round up to two or three decimal places, such as 3.26 or 3.258 in this example. Typically, continuous variables result from measuring.

LO1-5   1.6 LEVELS OF MEASUREMENT

Data can be classified according to levels of measurement. The level of measurement determines how data should be summarized and presented. It will also indicate the type of statistical analysis that can be performed. Here are two examples of the relationship between measurement and how we apply statistics. There are six colours of candies in a bag of M&Ms. Suppose we assign brown a value of 1, yellow 2, blue 3, orange 4, green 5, and red 6. The colour of an M&M is a qualitative variable. If we add the assigned colour values and divide by the number of candies and report that the mean colour is 3.56, does this mean that the average colour is blue (3) or orange (4)? Of course not! So, how do we interpret this statistic? You would be correct in concluding that it has no meaning as a measure of M&M colour. As a qualitative variable, we can only report the count and percentage of each colour in a bag of M&Ms. As a second example, in a high school 400-metre track meet, there are eight competitors in the 400-metre run. We report the order of finish and that the mean finish is 4.5. What does the mean finish tell us? Nothing! In both of these instances, we have not used the appropriate statistics for the level of measurement.

There are four levels of measurement: nominal, ordinal, interval, and ratio. The lowest, or the most primitive, measurement is the nominal level. The highest is the ratio level of measurement.

Nominal Level Data

For the **nominal level** of measurement, observations of a qualitative variable are measured and recorded as labels or names, such as blue or red. The labels or names can only be classified and counted. There is no particular order to the labels. The classification of the six colours of M&M milk chocolate candies is an example of the nominal level of measurement. We simply classify the candies by colour. There is no natural order. That is, we could report the brown candies first, the orange first, or any of the colours first. Recording the variable gender is another example of the nominal level of measurement. Suppose we count the number of students entering a football game with a student ID and report how many are men and how many are women. We could report either the men or the women first. For data measured at the nominal level, we are limited to counting the number in each category of the variable, Sometimes, we convert these counts to percentages. Table 1–1 shows a breakdown of the program majors at a Canadian college. This is a nominal level variable because we record the information by program major and there is no natural order. We could list the program majors in alphabetical order or by number of students in each program.

TABLE 1–1 Business Administration Students by Major

Program	Number of Students	Code
Accounting	645	1
Marketing	746	2
Finance	343	3
Human Resources	461	4
General Business	485	5
Total	2680	

To process the data for a variable measured at the nominal level, we often numerically code the names or labels. That is, we assign students in the accounting major a code of 1, students in the marketing major a code of 2, students in the finance major a code of 3, and so on. This coding facilitates counting by a computer, but realize that the number assigned to each program major is still a name or label. Assigning these numbers to the various categories this does not give us licence to manipulate the numbers. To explain, $1 + 2$ does not equal 3; that is, the students in the accounting major plus the students in the marketing major does *not* equal the students in the finance major.

To summarize, the nominal level has the following properties:

1. The variable of interest is represented as names or labels.
2. There is no order. They can only be classified and counted.

Ordinal Level Data

The next higher level of data is the **ordinal level**. For this level of measurement, a qualitative variable or attribute is either ranked or rated on a relative scale. This type of scale is used when students rate professors on a variety of attributes. One attribute may be "Overall, how did you rate the quality of instruction in this class?" A student's response is recorded on a relative scale of inferior, poor, good, excellent, and superior. An important characteristic of using a relative measurement scale is that we cannot distinguish the magnitude of the differences between groups. We do not know if the difference between "Superior" and "Good" is the same as the difference between "Poor" and "Inferior."

Table 1–2 lists the frequencies of student ratings of instructional quality for Professor James Brunner in an Introduction to Finance course. The data are summarized based on the order of the scale used to rate the professor. That is, they are summarized by the number of students who indicated a rating of superior (6), good (28), and so on.

TABLE 1–2 Rating of a Finance Professor

Rating	Frequency
Superior	6
Good	28
Average	25
Poor	12
Inferior	3

Ordinal level data are also used to rank items in a list. An example can be found in Table 1–3, Provinces and Territories in Canada Listed by Total Area.

The rankings are an example of an ordinal scale because we know the order or ranks of the provinces and territories according to total area. For example, Nunavut is ranked first as Nunavut has the largest total area. Prince Edward Island—with the smallest total area—is ranked last at thirteenth. Nova Scotia is ranked lower than New Brunswick as the total area in Nova Scotia is less than the total area in New Brunswick. Note that British Columbia is ranked fifth, but we

TABLE 1–3 Provinces and Territories in Canada Listed by Total Area

Rank	Provinces and Territories	Province or Territory	Total Area (km²)
1	Nunavut	Territory	2 093 190
2	Quebec	Province	1 542 056
3	Northwest Territories	Territory	1 346 106
4	Ontario	Province	1 076 395
5	British Columbia	Province	944 735
6	Alberta	Province	661 848
7	Saskatchewan	Province	651 900
8	Manitoba	Province	647 797
9	Yukon	Territory	482 443
10	Newfoundland & Labrador	Province	405 212
11	New Brunswick	Province	72 908
12	Nova Scotia	Province	55 284
13	Prince Edward Island	Province	5 660

Source: Natural Resources Canada, GeoAccess Division. http://www.statcan.gc.ca/tables-tableaux/sum-som
/l01/cst01/phys01-eng.htm. Contains information licensed under the Open Government Licence – Canada.

cannot say that the total area in Nunavut is five times larger than the total area in British Columbia because the magnitude of the differences between total area is not the same.

In summary, the properties of an ordinal level of measurement are as follows:

1. Data recorded is based on a relative ranking or rating of items based on a defined attribute or qualitative variable.
2. Variables based on this level of measurement are only ranked or counted.

Interval Level Data

The **interval level** of measurement is the next highest level. It includes all the characteristics of the ordinal level, but in addition, the difference between values is a constant size. The Celsius temperature scale is an example of the interval level of measurement. Suppose the high temperatures on three consecutive winter days are 0, −2, and −3 degrees Celsius. These temperatures can be easily ranked, but we can also determine the difference between temperatures. This is possible because 1 degree Celsius represents a constant unit of measurement. Equal differences between two temperatures are the same, regardless of their position on the scale. That is, the difference between 10 degrees Celsius and 15 degrees is 5, and the difference between 30 and 35 degrees is also 5 degrees. It is also important to note that 0 is just a point on the scale. It does not represent the absence of the condition. Zero degrees Celsius does not represent the absence of heat, just that it is cold! A major limitation of a variable measured at the interval level is that we cannot make statements similar to "20 degrees Celsius is twice as warm as 10 degrees Celsius." The ratio is not reasonable. In short, if the distances between the numbers make sense, but the ratios do not, then you have an interval scale of measurement.

The properties of interval level data are as follows:

1. Data classifications are ordered according to the amount of the characteristic they possess.
2. Equal differences in the characteristic are represented by equal differences in the measurements.

Ratio Level Data

Almost all quantitative data are at the ratio level of measurement. The **ratio level** is the "highest" level of measurement. It has all the characteristics of the interval level, but in addition, the 0 point is meaningful, and the ratio between two numbers is meaningful. Examples of the ratio scale of measurement include wages, units of production, weight, changes in stock prices, distance between branch offices, and height. Money is a good illustration. If you have $0, then you have no money, and a wage of $50 per hour is two times that of $25 per hour. Weight is another example. If there is nothing on a scale, then the weight will be zero since there is a complete absence of weight. As well, a 1 kilogram (kg) bag of oranges is half as heavy as a bag of oranges that weighs 2 kg.

Table 1–4 illustrates the ratio scale of measurement for the variable income for four father-and-son combinations.

TABLE 1–4 Father–Son Income Combinations

Name	Father	Son
Lahey	$80 000	$40 000
Nale	90 000	30 000
Rho	60 000	120 000
Steele	75 000	130 000

Observe that the senior Lahey earns twice as much as his son does. In the Rho family, the son makes twice as much as the father does.

The difference between interval and ratio measurements can be confusing. The fundamental difference involves the definition of a true zero and the ratio between two values. If you have $50 and your friend has $100, then your friend has twice as much money as you do. If you spend your $50, then you have no money. This is an example of a true zero. As another example, a sales representative travels 150 kilometres (km) on Monday and 300 km on Tuesday. The ratio of the distances travelled on the two days is 2/1; converting the distances to metres or miles will not change the ratio. It is still 2/1. Suppose that on Wednesday, the sales representative works at home and does not travel. The distance travelled on Wednesday is zero, and this is a meaningful value. Hence, the variable distance has a true zero point.

In summary, the properties of ratio level data are as follows:

1. Data classifications are ordered according to the amount of the characteristics they possess.
2. Equal differences in the characteristic are represented by equal differences in the numbers assigned to the classifications.
3. The zero point is the absence of the characteristic and the ratio between two numbers is meaningful.

Chart 1–3 summarizes the major characteristics of the various levels of measurement.

CHART 1–3 Summary of the Characteristics for Levels of Measurement

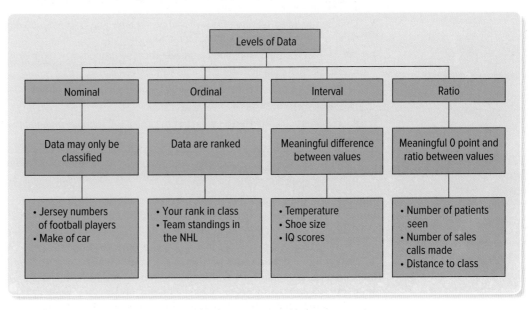

What is the level of measurement reflected by the following data?

(a) The ages of the persons in a sample of 50 adults who listen to one of the Oldies radio stations in Canada are as follows:

35	29	41	34	44	46	42	42	37	47
30	36	41	39	44	39	43	43	44	40
47	37	41	27	33	33	39	38	43	22
44	39	35	35	41	42	37	42	38	43
35	37	38	43	40	48	42	31	51	34

(b) In a survey of 200 luxury-car owners, 100 were from Victoria, 50 from Halifax, 30 from Calgary, and 20 from Winnipeg.

EXERCISES

The answers to the odd-numbered exercises are in Appendix A.1.

1. What is the level of measurement for each of the following variables?
   a. Student IQ (intelligence quotient) ratings.
   b. Distances students travel to class.
   c. Student scores on the first statistics test.
   d. A classification of students by province of birth.
   e. A ranking of students by letter grades.
   f. Number of hours students study per week.
   g. The political parties in Canada.
   h. Team standings in the National Hockey League (NHL).
   i. Jersey numbers in basketball.
   j. The number of car sales in the last six months.

2. What is the level of measurement for these items related to the newspaper business?
   a. The number of papers sold each Sunday during 2016.
   b. The number of employees in each of the departments, such as editorial, advertising, sports, and so on.
   c. A summary of the number of papers sold by county.
   d. The number of years with the paper for each employee.
   e. The number of male and female employees.
   f. The height of each employee.

3. Look in the latest edition of your local newspaper and find examples of each level of measurement. Write a brief memo summarizing your findings.

4. For each of the following, determine whether the group is a sample or a population:
   a. The participants in a study of a new diabetes drug.
   b. The drivers who received a speeding ticket in Halifax last month.
   c. Those on welfare in Victoria, B.C.
   d. The 30 stocks reported as a part of the Toronto Stock Exchange (TSX).

LO1-6   1.7 ETHICS AND STATISTICS

You have probably heard the old saying that there are three kinds of lies: lies, damn lies, and statistics. This saying is attributable to Benjamin Disraeli and is over a century old. It has also been said that "figures don't lie; liars figure." Both these statements refer to the misuse of statistics whereby data are presented in ways that are misleading.

Following recent events of Ponzi schemes—which swindled billions from investors—financial misrepresentations by Enron and other corporate disasters, business students need to understand that these events were based on the misrepresentation of business and financial data. In each case, people within each organization reported financial information to investors that indicated the companies were performing much better than the actual situation. When the true financial information was reported, the companies were worth much less than advertised. The result was that many investors lost all or nearly all of the money they put into these companies.

The article "Statistics and Ethics: Some Advice for Young Statisticians," in *The American Statistician* 57, no. 1 (2003), offers some guidance. The authors advise us to practise statistics with integrity and honesty and urge us to "do the right thing" when collecting, organizing, summarizing, analyzing, and interpreting numerical information. The real contribution of statistics to society is a moral one. Financial analysts need to provide information that truly reflects a company's performance so as to not mislead individual investors. Information regarding product defects that may be harmful to people must be analyzed and reported with integrity and honesty.

As you progress through this text, we will highlight ethical issues in the collection, analysis, presentation, and interpretation of statistical information. We also hope that as you learn about using statistics, you will become a more informed consumer of information. For example, you will question a report based on data that do not fairly represent the population, a report that does not include all relevant statistics, one that includes an incorrect choice of statistical measures, or a presentation that introduces the writer's bias in a deliberate attempt to mislead or misrepresent.

1.8 COMPUTER APPLICATIONS

Computers are now available to students at many colleges and universities. Spreadsheet programs, such as **Microsoft Excel**, and statistical software packages, such as MINITAB, are available in most computer labs. In this text, we use both **Excel** and an **Excel** add-in called MegaStat. This add-in gives **Excel** the capability to produce additional statistical reports and charts.

The following example shows the application of computers in statistical analysis. In Chapters 2 and 3, we illustrate methods for summarizing and describing data. An exercise used in those chapters refers to the list price of homes in Whistler, BC. The following **Excel** output reveals, among other things, that (1) 85 homes were listed, (2) the average (mean) list price was $735 511, and (3) the list prices ranged from $56 900 (minimum) to $1 999 999 (maximum). The full data set and others are available on this text's website.

	A	B	C	D	I	J	K	L
1								
2	List Price	Number of Bedrooms	Full Bathrooms	Square Feet	Style			
3	$ 56,900	1	1	587	Apartment		*List Price*	
4	58,000	1	1	273	Apartment			
5	60,000	1	1	592	Apartment		Mean	735511.4824
6	61,900	1	1	629	Apartment		Standard Error	65763.25643
7	61,900	1	1	589	Apartment		Median	499000
8	69,900	0	1	360	Studio		Mode	109000
9	76,900	1	1	621	Apartment		Standard Deviation	606307.2663
10	105,000	2	2	958	Apartment		Sample Variance	3.67609E+11
11	109,000	3	4	2495	Clubhouse		Kurtosis	-0.815430462
12	109,000	3	4	2560	Clubhouse		Skewness	0.693574656
13	109,000	3	4	2335	Clubhouse		Range	1943099
14	115,900	4	5	2499	Clubhouse		Minimum	56900
15	119,000	4	5	2732	Clubhouse		Maximum	1999999
16	124,000	1	1	397	Apartment		Sum	62518476
17	124,000	1	1	396	Apartment		Count	85
18	124,000	1	1	398	Apartment			
19	130,000	4	5	2732	Clubhouse			
20	139,900	4	5	1008	Clubhouse			
21	160,000	3	2	1245	Apartment			
22	189,000	0	1	363	Studio			
23	194,000	0	1	608	Studio			

Had we used a calculator to arrive at these measures and others needed to fully analyze the list prices, hours of calculations would have been required. The likelihood of an error in arithmetic is high when a large number of values are concerned. However, statistical software packages and spreadsheets can provide accurate information in seconds. We will see more such data in subsequent chapter exercises.

Chapter Summary

I. Statistics is the science of collecting, organizing, presenting, analyzing, and interpreting data to assist in making more effective decisions.

II. There are two types of statistics.

    A. Descriptive statistics are procedures used to organize and summarize data.

    B. Inferential statistics involve taking a sample from a population and making estimates about a population based on the sample results.

        1. A population is an entire set of individuals or objects of interest or the measurements obtained from all individuals or objects of interest.

        2. A sample is a part of the population.

III. There are two types of variables.

    A. A qualitative variable is non-numeric.

        1. Usually, we are interested in the number or percentage of the observations in each category.

        2. Qualitative data are usually summarized in graphs and bar charts.

    B. There are two types of quantitative variables and they are usually reported numerically.

        1. Discrete variables can assume only certain values, and there are usually gaps between values.

        2. A continuous variable can assume any value within a specified range.

IV. There are four levels of measurement.

    A. With the nominal level of measurement, the data are sorted into categories with no particular order to the categories.

    B. The ordinal level of measurement presumes that one classification is ranked higher than another.

    C. The interval level of measurement has the ranking characteristic of the ordinal level of measurement plus the characteristic that the distance between values is a constant size.

    D. The ratio level of measurement has all the characteristics of the interval level, plus there is a meaningful zero point, and the ratio of two values is meaningful.

Chapter Exercises

5. Explain the difference between qualitative and quantitative data. Give an example of qualitative and quantitative data.

6. Explain the difference between a sample and a population.

7. Explain the difference between a discrete variable and a continuous variable. Give an example of each not included in the text.

8. A company conducts a survey of a large number of college undergraduates for information on the following variables: the name of their cell phone provider (e.g., Rogers, Bell), the numbers of minutes used last month (e.g., 200, 400), and their satisfaction with the service (e.g., Terrible, Adequate, Excellent). What is the level of measurement for each of these three variables?

9. Electronic book readers allow users to browse, shop, download, and read e-books, blogs, newspapers, and magazines, all displayed in full colour. Assume that you know the number of units sold each day for the last month at the West Edmonton Mall. Describe a condition in which this information could be considered a sample. Illustrate a second situation in which the same data would be regarded as a population.

10. Using data from magazines or your local newspaper, give examples of nominal, ordinal, interval, and ratio levels of measurement.

11. A random sample of 300 executives out of 2500 employed by a large firm showed that 270 would move to another location if it meant a substantial promotion. On the basis of these findings, write a brief note to management regarding all executives in the firm.

12. A random sample of 500 customers is asked to comment on the take-out service at The Chicken Hut. Of the 500 customers surveyed, 400 said it was excellent, 32 thought it was fair, and the remaining customers had no opinion. On the basis of these sample findings, make an inference about the reaction of all customers to the take-out service.

13. The following table reports the number of tickets sold at an ice rink for sports activities for the months of January last year and January this year:

Company	Units	
	Last Year	**This Year**
Hockey (Men's Finals)	244 614	293 302
Hockey (Women's Finals)	175 850	160 594
Hockey–Men's	173 407	168 030
Hockey–Women's	165 668	204 528
Figure Skating–Seniors	100 790	98 428
Figure Skating–Juniors	82 644	75 890

    a. Compare the total sales in the two years. What would you conclude? Has there been an increase or decrease in sales?

    b. Compare the percentage change in sales for the six events. Has there been a change in the market for ticket sales?

Use the following information to answer Exercises 14 and 15.

Students in Statistics 101 who had a grade of less than 50% on their first test are required to take a three-hour upgrading class in order to continue in the course.

14. "Statistics 101":
    a. Is it a qualitative or quantitative variable?
    b. What is its level of measurement?

15. The variable "grade":
    a. Is it qualitative or quantitative?
    b. Is it discrete or continuous?
    c. What is its level of measurement?

Use the following information to answer Exercises 16 and 17.
Is there a relationship between box office sales and the associated box office budget (total amount available to spend making the picture)? Would you expect movies with large budgets to result in large box office revenues?

16. The variable "box office sales":
    a. Is it qualitative or quantitative?
    b. Is it discrete or continuous?
    c. What is its level of measurement?

17. The variable "box office budget":
    a. Is it qualitative or quantitative?
    b. Is it discrete or continuous?
    c. What is its level of measurement?

Use the following information to answer Exercises 18 and 19.
The Shell station on Portage Avenue in Winnipeg is studying the number of litres of fuel that are sold on each day of the week. Records are available for the past year.

18. Is the information collected from a sample or a population?

19. The variable "number of litres":
    a. Is it qualitative or quantitative?
    b. Is it discrete or continuous?
    c. What is its level of measurement?

Use the following information to answer Exercises 20 and 21.
PlayTime Toys Inc. employs 50 people in the Assembly Department. Of the employees, 40 belong to a union, and 10 do not. Five employees are selected at random to form a committee to meet with management regarding shift starting times.

20. Would the 50 employees be considered a population or a sample?

21. Would the five selected employees be considered a population or a sample?

Use the following information to answer Exercises 22 and 23.
A survey of students in the School of Business at Northern College revealed the following regarding the gender and majors of the students:

	Major			
Gender	**Accounting**	**Marketing**	**Finance**	**Total**
Male	250	215	220	685
Female	245	260	250	755
Total	495	475	470	1440

22. The variable "major":
   a. Is it qualitative or quantitative?
   b. What is its level of measurement?

23. The variable "gender":
   a. Is it qualitative or quantitative?
   b. What is its level of measurement?

24. For the following questions, would you collect information using a sample or a population? Why?
   a. Statistics 201 is a course taught at a college. Professor K. Khan has taught nearly 1500 students in the course over the past five years. You would like to know the average grade for the course.
   b. As part of a research project, you need to report the average profitability of the number one corporation in the Fortune 500 for the past 10 years.
   c. You are looking forward to graduation and your first job as a salesperson for one of the large pharmaceutical corporations. Planning for your interviews, you will need to know about each company's mission statement, profitability, products, and markets.
   d. You are shopping for a new MP3 player, such as the Apple iPod. The manufacturers advertise the number of music tracks that can be stored in the memory. Usually, the advertisers assume relatively short, popular music to estimate the number of tracks that can be stored. You, however, like tunes from Broadway musicals, and they are of much longer duration. You would like to estimate how many Broadway tunes will fit on your MP3 player.

25. For the following variables, classify each as discrete or continuous qualitative or quantitative, and determine the level of measurement:
   a. Salary.
   b. Gender.
   c. Sales volume of MP3 players.
   d. Soft drink preference.
   e. Temperature.
   f. GPA score.
   g. Student rank in class.
   h. Rating of a new movie.
   i. Number of home computers.

Data Set Exercises

Questions marked with 📈 have data sets available on McGraw-Hill's online resource for *Basic Statistics.*

26. Refer to the Real Estate Data—Whistler, BC, online, which reports information on listed homes for July 2016. Consider the variables: list price, number of bedrooms, full bathrooms, square feet, style, walk score, and pool.
   a. Which of the variables are qualitative, and which are quantitative?
   b. Determine the level of measurement for each of the variables.

27. Refer to the CREA (Canadian Real Estate Association) data online, which reports information on average house prices nationally and in a selection of cities across Canada. Consider the variables region and average house prices.
   a. Which of these variables are quantitative, and which are qualitative?
   b. Determine the level of measurement for each of the variables.

28. Refer to the Average Weekly Earnings data online, which reports information on the average weekly earnings by year and province. The variables are province, year, and average weekly earnings.
   a. Which of the variables are qualitative, and which are quantitative?
   b. Determine the level of measurement for each variable.

Practice Test

There is a practice test at the end of each chapter. The tests are mostly in two parts. The first part contains 10 to 15 objective questions, usually in a fill-in-the-blank format. The second part includes problems. The problems will require a calculator or computer. Check your answers against those provided in Appendix A.2 .

Part I Objective (Chapter 1 has Part 1 only)

1. The science of collecting, organizing, presenting, analyzing, and interpreting data to assist in making more effective decisions is referred to as _____.

2. Methods of organizing, summarizing, and presenting data in an enlightening way are called _____.

3. The methods used to estimate a value of a population on the basis of a sample are called _____.

4. A portion, or part, of the group of interest is referred to as a _____.

5. The entire set of individuals or objects of interest or the measurements obtained from all individuals or objects of interest is known as a _____.

6. With the _____ level of measurement, the data are sorted into categories with no particular order to the categories.

7. The _____ level of measurement has a significant zero point.

8. The _____ level of measurement presumes that one classification is ranked higher than another.

9. The _____ level of measurement has the characteristic that the distance between values is a constant size.

10. Is the number of bedrooms in a house a discrete or continuous variable? _____.

11. The jersey numbers on baseball uniforms are an example of the _____.

12. What level of measurement is used when students are classified by eye colour? _____.

Answers to Self-Reviews

1–1 **(a)** On the basis of the sample of 1960 customers, we estimate that, if it is marketed, 60% of all customers will purchase Chicken Delight $(1176/1960) \times 100 = 60\%$.

(b) Inferential statistics, because a sample was used to draw a conclusion about how all consumers in the population would react if Chicken Delight were marketed.

1–2 **(a)** Age is a ratio scale variable. A 40-year-old is twice as old as someone 20 years old.

(b) Nominal scale. We could arrange the cities in any order.

CHAPTER 2

Describing Data: Frequency Tables, Frequency Distributions, and Graphic Presentation

© Rob Daly/age fotostock

MERRILL LYNCH recently completed a study of online investment portfolios for a sample of clients. For the 70 participants in the study, organize these data into a frequency distribution. (See Exercise 45 and LO2-4.)

LEARNING OBJECTIVES

When you have completed this chapter, you will be able to:

LO2-1 Summarize qualitative variables with frequency and relative frequency tables.

LO2-2 Display a frequency table using a bar or pie chart.

LO2-3 Summarize quantitative variables with frequency and relative frequency distributions.

LO2-4 Display a frequency distribution using a histogram or frequency polygon.

LO2-5 Construct and interpret a cumulative frequency distribution.

LO2-6 Construct and describe a stem-and-leaf display.

2.1 INTRODUCTION

In this chapter, we will use data from the *Canadian Real Estate Association* (crea.ca) to present techniques that organize and show the variability of house prices from the resort municipality of Whistler, British Columbia.

Whistler is 120 km north of Vancouver, BC. There are approximately 10 500 permanent residents and about 2.7 million annual visitors (www.whistler.ca).

The data collected includes the following variables:

- **List price**—the amount the dwelling is listed for ($)
- **Number of bedrooms**—zero to seven bedrooms
- **Full bathrooms**—one to five bathrooms
- **Square feet**—the number of square feet in the dwelling
- **Style**—apartment, studio, clubhouse, house, townhouse
- **Walk score**—this number (from 0 to 100) indicates how close a dwelling is to local businesses (grocery stores, coffee shops, etc.) by walking
- **Pool**—yes or no

We will use these listings to develop some tables and charts that can be reviewed to see where the list prices tend to cluster, to see the variation in the list prices, and to note any trends. Learning these techniques may be useful to anyone who is employed in business.

LO2-1 2.2 CONSTRUCTING FREQUENCY TABLES

Frequency table A grouping of qualitative data into mutually exclusive classes showing the number of observations in each class.

Recall from Chapter 1 that techniques used to describe a set of data are called *descriptive statistics*. Descriptive statistics organize data to show the general pattern of the data and where values tend to concentrate, and to highlight extreme or unusual data values. The first technique we discuss is a **frequency table**.

In Chapter 1, we distinguished between qualitative and quantitative variables. To review, a qualitative variable is non-numeric; that is, it can only be classified into distinct categories. There is no particular order to these categories. Examples of qualitative data include political affiliation (Conservative, Liberal, Green Party, etc.), country of birth (Canada, United Kingdom, China, India, etc.), and method of payment for a purchase at Chapters (cash, debit, credit, or cheque). On the other hand, quantitative variables are numerical in nature. Examples of quantitative data relating to college and university students include the price of their textbooks, their age, and the number of credit hours they are registered in for this semester.

In the Whistler, BC, real estate data, there are seven variables for each listing: list price, number of bedrooms, full bathrooms, square feet, style, walk score, and pool. The list price, number of bedrooms, full bathrooms, square feet, and walk score are quantitative variables; style and pool are qualitative variables. Suppose that we wanted to summarize the listings by style.

To summarize this qualitative data, we classify the listings as apartment, clubhouse, house, studio, or townhouse, and count the number in each class. We use style to develop a frequency table with five mutually exclusive (distinctive) classes. This means that any one style cannot belong to more than one class. The style is an apartment or clubhouse or house or studio or townhouse—it cannot be both an apartment and a house. This frequency table is shown in Table 2–1. The number of observations in each class is called the **class frequency**. The total class frequency for the number of listings is 85.

TABLE 2–1 Frequency Table for the Whistler Real Estate Listings by Style

Dwelling Type	Number of Listings
Apartment	37
Clubhouse	9
House	16
Studio	5
Townhouse	18
Total	85

Relative Class Frequencies

You can convert class frequencies to **relative class frequencies** to show the fraction of the total number of observations in each class. A relative frequency captures the relationship between a class total and the total number of observations. In the Whistler Real Estate example, we may want to know the percentage of list prices that are apartments. To convert a frequency distribution to a **relative frequency distribution**, each of the class frequencies is divided by the total number of observations. For example, 37/85 (the fraction of apartments listed) is 0.4353. The relative frequency distribution is shown in Table 2–2.

TABLE 2–2 Relative Frequency Table of the Whistler Real Estate Listings by Style

Type	Number of Listings	Fraction	Relative Frequency	Percentage
Apartment	37	37/85	0.4353	43.53%
Clubhouse	9	9/85	0.1059	10.59%
House	16	16/85	0.1882	18.82%
Studio	5	5/85	0.0588	5.88%
Townhouse	18	18/85	0.2118	21.18%
	85		1.0000	100.00%

When rounding, the total of the relative frequencies may not be exactly 1.0000.

LO2-2 2.3 GRAPHIC PRESENTATION OF QUALITATIVE DATA

Bar Charts

Bar chart A graph that shows qualitative classes on the horizontal axis and the class frequencies on the vertical axis. The class frequencies are proportional to the heights of the bars.

The most common graphic form to present a qualitative variable is a **bar chart**. In most cases, the horizontal axis shows the variable of interest, and the vertical axis shows the frequency or fraction of each of the possible outcomes. A distinguishing feature of a bar chart is that there is a distance or gap between the bars. That is, because the variable of interest is qualitative, the bars are not adjacent to each other. Thus, a bar chart graphically describes a frequency table using a series of uniformly wide rectangles (bars), where the height of each bar is the class frequency.

We use the Whistler listings data from Table 2–1 to create the bar chart (Chart 2–1). The variable of interest is the style of dwelling listed (the horizontal axis), and the number of each style listed is the class frequency (the vertical axis). We label the horizontal with the five styles, and scale the vertical axis with the number of each style. The height of the bars corresponds to the number of dwellings listed in each category. So, for the style apartment, the height of the bar is 37. The variable style is of nominal scale, so the order of style (apartment, clubhouse, house, studio, or townhouse) on the horizontal axis does not matter. Listing the variable alphabetically, as shown in Chart 2–1, or in order of decreasing frequencies is also appropriate.

excel

CHART 2–1 Listings by Style for the Whistler Data.

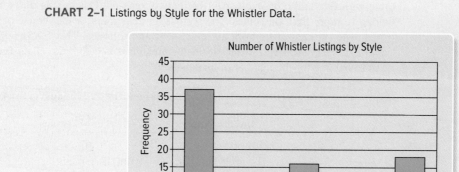

Computer commands to create this chart can be found at the end of the chapter.

Pie Charts

Pie chart A chart that shows the proportion or percentage that each class represents of the total number of frequencies.

Another useful type of chart for depicting qualitative information is a **pie chart**.

Construct a pie chart using the information in Table 2–3, which shows a breakdown of lottery proceeds from the Ontario Lottery and Gaming Corporation (OLG) (olg.ca). (See Chart 2–2.)

TABLE 2–3 OLG Lottery Proceeds

Use of Profits	Percentage Share (%)
Prizes	51.8
Province of Ontario	30.3
Retailers	7.1
Operating Expenses	8.4
Government of Canada	2.4
	100.0

excel

CHART 2–2 Pie Chart of OLG Use of Profits

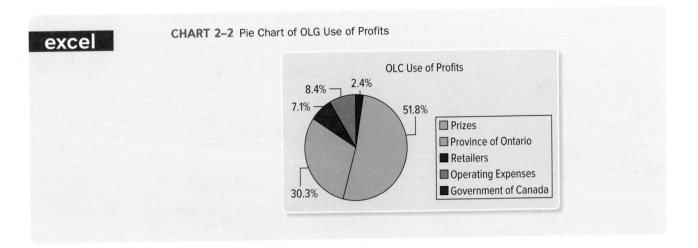

Each slice of the pie represents the relative frequency of each component as a percentage of the total profits, which makes it easy to compare them:

1. The largest expense of the OLG is for prizes.
2. Approximately 30% is transferred to the province of Ontario.
3. Operating expenses account for about 8% of the proceeds.

Computer commands to create this pie chart can be found at the end of the chapter.

Example	SkiLodges.com is test marketing its new website and is interested in how easy its web page design is to navigate. It randomly selected 200 regular Internet users and asked them to perform a search task on the website. Each person was asked to rate the ease of navigation as poor, good, excellent, or awesome. The results are shown in the following table:

Awesome	102
Excellent	58
Good	30
Poor	10

1. What level of measurement is used for ease of navigation?
2. Draw a bar chart for the survey results.
3. Draw a pie chart for the survey results.

Solution

The data are measured on an ordinal scale. That is, the scale ranks the ease of navigation from a low of "poor" to a high of "awesome." Also, the interval between each rating is unknown, so it is impossible, for example, to conclude that a rating of "good" is twice the value of a "poor" rating. We can use a bar chart to graph the data. The vertical axis shows the number of frequencies in each class, and the horizontal axis shows the values of the ease of navigation variable.

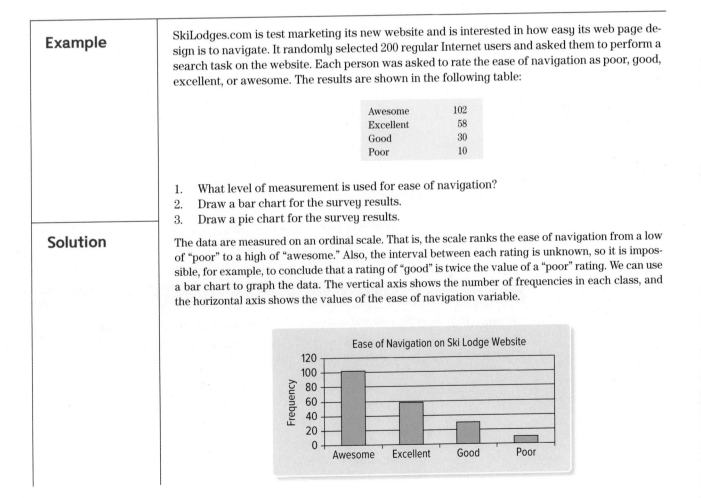

A pie chart can also be used to graph this data. We will need the proportion or percentages in each category. For this, we first total the frequency column and then calculate the percentages. For example, in the first class, 102/200 = 0.51 = 51%. The results are shown in the following table:

	Frequency	Percentage (%)
Awesome	102	51%
Excellent	58	29%
Good	30	15%
Poor	10	5%
Total	200	100%

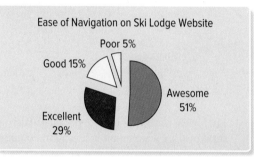

Note that the pie chart emphasizes that more than half of the respondents rate the relative ease of using the website as awesome.

self-review 2–1

The answers are at the end of the chapter.
DiCarlo's Café has been serving an Italian soda drink with a vanilla flavouring that is very popular with its customers. Joe DiCarlo is interested in customer preferences for some new flavours. He asks 100 of his regular customers to take a taste test and pick the one they like the best. The results are shown in the following table:

Flavour	Number
Vanilla	40
Cherry	25
Lemon	20
Orange	15
Total	100

(a) Is the data quantitative or qualitative? Why?
(b) What is the table called?
(c) Develop a bar chart to depict the information.
(d) Develop a pie chart using the relative frequencies.

EXERCISES

The answers to the odd-numbered exercises are in Appendix A.1.

1. A small business consultant is investigating the performance of several companies. The fourth-quarter sales for last year (in thousands of dollars) for the selected companies were as follows:

Corporation	Fourth-Quarter Sales ($ thousands)
Hoden Building Products	$ 1 645.2
J & R Printing Inc.	4 757.0
Long Bay Concrete Construction	8 913.0
Mancell Electric and Plumbing	627.1
Maxwell Heating and Air Conditioning	24 612.0
Mizelle Roofing & Sheet Metals	191.9

The consultant wants to include a chart in his report comparing the sales of the six companies. Use a bar chart to compare the fourth-quarter sales of these corporations, and write a brief report summarizing the bar chart.

2. In a marketing study, 100 consumers were asked to select the best digital music player from the iPod, the iRiver, and the Magic Star MP3. To summarize the consumer responses with a frequency table, how many classes would the frequency table have?

3. A total of 1000 residents in Manitoba were asked which season they preferred. The results were: 100 liked winters best, 300 liked spring, 400 liked summer, and 200 liked fall. If the data were summarized in a frequency distribution, how many classes would be used? What would be the relative frequencies for each class?

4. The National Household Survey conducted by Statistics Canada in 2011 reports that 851 560 people identified themselves as First Nations persons, 451 795 identified themselves as Métis, 59 445 identified themselves as Inuit, multiple Aboriginal identities were reported by 11 415, and Aboriginal identities not included elsewhere numbered 26 475 (www12.statcan.gc.ca/nhs-enm/2011/as-sa/99-011-x/99-011-x2011001-eng.cfm#a2).
   a. Construct a bar chart for the data.
   b. Create a table and add relative frequencies.
   c. Construct a pie chart for the data.

5. Wellstone Inc. produces and markets replacement covers for cell phones in a variety of colours. The company would like to allocate its production plans to five different colours: bright white, metallic black, magnetic lime, tangerine orange, and fusion red. The company set up a kiosk in the Qwanlin Mall for several hours and asked randomly selected shoppers which colour they preferred for a cell phone cover. The results follow:

Bright white	130
Metallic black	104
Magnetic lime	325
Tangerine orange	455
Fusion red	286

   a. Construct a bar chart for the table.
   b. Add relative frequencies to the table.
   c. Construct a pie chart for the data.

6. Shown below are the student loan amounts for 2018 for eight students in the business administration program. Develop a bar chart for the data, and summarize the results in a brief report.

Name	Amount ($)	Name	Amount ($)
Susan Chan	$6087	Daniel Ng	$3228
Sam Simone	4747	Erin Brooks	2828
Mary Suhanic	3272	Jasmine Smith	2492
Danielle Brothers	3284	Enrique Lopes	2347

LO2-3 2.4 CONSTRUCTING FREQUENCY DISTRIBUTIONS: QUANTITATIVE DATA

In Chapter 1 and earlier in this chapter, we distinguished between qualitative and quantitative data. In the previous section, using the real estate data listings from Whistler, BC, we summarized the qualitative variable, Style. We created frequency and relative frequency tables and depicted the results in bar and pie charts.

The real estate data also include several quantitative variables: the list price, the number of bedrooms, full bathrooms, and square feet. Suppose that we want to summarize the list prices and show what a typical list price is. We can do this and describe the list prices by using a **frequency distribution**.

How do we develop a frequency distribution? The following example shows the steps to construct a frequency distribution. Remember, our goal is to construct tables, charts, and graphs that will quickly reveal the concentration, extreme values, and shape of the data.

Frequency distribution
A grouping of data into mutually exclusive classes showing the number of observations in each class.

Example

Table 2–4 reports 85 house listings taken from the Canadian Real Estate Association for Whistler, BC. We want to summarize the quantitative variable list price with a frequency distribution and display the distribution with charts and graphs. With this information, the following questions can be easily answered: What is the typical list price? What is the highest or maximum list price? What is the lowest or minimum list price? Around what value do the list prices tend to cluster?

TABLE 2–4 Listings from Whistler, BC

1 195 000	1 499 000	160 000	839 000	1 450 000
1 229 000	519 000	219 000	1 395 000	124 000
1 350 000	989 000	429 000	365 000	124 000
1 559 000	1 850 000	469 000	399 000	369 000
1 559 000	1 995 000	499 000	599 000	379 000
1 599 000	1 358 000	859 000	849 000	56 900 → minimum
109 000	130 000	1 125 000	1 999 000	489 000
109 000	949 000	61 900	1 999 000	124 000
109 000	1 775 000	139 900	1 100 000	194 000
115 900	1 499 000	1 295 000	315 000	359 000
119 000	899 000	339 000	748 000	519 777
maximum ← 1 999 999	499 000	449 000	449 000	399 000
60 000	739 000	759 000	189 000	69 900
449 000	455 000	1 625 000	219 000	58 000
1 315 000	61 900	1 699 000	219 500	439 000
1 399 000	76 900	1 349 000	220 000	529 000
1 988 000	105 000	362 900	550 000	879 000

Source: The Canadian Real Estate Association; crea.ca.

Solution

Table 2–4 shows the list prices from Whistler. We refer to the unorganized information in Table 2–4 as **raw data** or **ungrouped data**. With a little searching, we can find the lowest list price ($56 900) and the highest list price ($1 999 999), but that is about all. It is difficult to determine a typical list price or to visualize where the list prices tend to cluster. The raw data are more easily interpreted if organized into a frequency distribution as follows.

Step 1: **Decide on the number of classes.** To begin, we need to decide the number of classes. The goal is to use just enough groupings or *classes* to reveal the shape of the distribution. Some judgment is needed here. Too many classes or too few classes might not reveal the basic shape of the set of data. In the real estate problem, for example, three classes would not give much insight into the pattern of the data (Table 2–5).

TABLE 2–5 An Example of Too Few Classes

List Price	Frequency
$0 to under $700 000	49
$700 000 to under $1400 000	21
$1400 000 to under $2100 000	15
	85

A useful recipe to determine the number of classes (k) is the "2 to the k rule." This guide suggests you select the smallest number (k) for the number of classes such that 2^k (in words, 2 raised to the power of k) is greater than the number of observations (n).

In the Whistler real estate example, there are 85 listings. So $n = 85$. If we try $k = 6$, which means we would use 6 classes, then $2^6 = 64$, less than 85. Hence, 6 is too few classes. If we let $k = 7$, then $2^7 = 128$, which is greater than 85. So, the suggested number of classes is 7.

Step 2: **Determine the class interval or width.** Generally, the *class interval* or *class width* is the same for all classes. The classes all taken together must cover at least the distance from the minimum value in the raw data up to the maximum value. Expressing these words in a formula:

$$i \geq \frac{Maximum\ value - Minimum\ value}{k}$$

where i is the class interval and k is the number of classes.

For the Whistler example, the minimum value is $56 900, and the maximum value is $1 999 999. If we need seven classes, the interval should be at least ($1 999 999 − 56 900)/7 = $277 586. In practice, this interval size is usually rounded up to some convenient number, such as a multiple of 10, 100 or 1000. The value of $300 000 might readily be used in this case.

In frequency distributions, equal class intervals are preferred. However, unequal class intervals may be necessary in certain situations to avoid a large number of empty, or almost empty, classes. Such is the case in Table 2–6. Real estate companies in the greater Vancouver region would likely use unequal-sized class intervals to report the list price on individual homes in their area. Using an equal-sized interval of, say, $250 000, about 100 classes would be required to describe all the listings. A frequency distribution with 100 classes would be difficult to interpret. In this case, the distribution is easier to understand in spite of the unequal classes. Note that the price of the homes reported is combined into larger intervals as the price increases to avoid empty classes. This also makes the information easier to understand.

TABLE 2–6 Listings in the Greater Vancouver Area

List Price ($)	
Under	$1 000 000
1 000 000 to under	1 500 000
1 500 000 to under	2 000 000
2 000 000 to under	2 500 000
2 500 000 to under	3 000 000
3 000 000 to under	4 000 000
4 000 000 to under	5 000 000
5 000 000 to under	7 500 000
7 500 000 to under	10 000 000
10 000 000 and over	

Step 3: **Set the individual class limits.** State clear class limits so you can put each observation into only one category. This means you must avoid overlapping or unclear class limits. For example, classes such as $300 000 to $600 000 and $600 000 to $900 000 should not be used because it is not clear whether the value of $600 000 is in the first or second class. Classes stated as $300 000 to $599 000 and $600 000 to 899 000 are frequently used but may also be confusing without the additional common convention of rounding all data at or above $599 500 up to the second class and data below $599 500 down to the first class. In this text, we will generally use the format $300 000 to under $600 000, $600 000 to under $900 000, and so on. With this format, it is clear that values can fall into one class only.

Because we round the class interval to get a convenient class size, we cover a larger than necessary range. For example, seven classes of width $300 000 in the Whistler real estate example result in a range 7($300 000) = $2 100 000. The actual range is $1 999 999 − $56 900 = $1 943 099. Comparing that value to $2 100 000, we have an excess of $156 901. Because we need to cover only the distance (*Maximum − Minimum*), it is natural to put approximately equal amounts of the excess in each of the two tails. Of course, we should also select convenient class limits. A guideline is to make the lower limit of the first class a multiple of the class interval. Sometimes, this is not possible, but the lower limit should at least be rounded. So, here are the classes we could use for these data:

$	0 to under	$300 000
	300 000 to under	600 000
	600 000 to under	900 000
	900 000 to under	1 200 000
	1 200 000 to under	1 500 000
	1 500 000 to under	1 800 000
	1 800 000 to under	2 100 000

Step 4: Tally the list prices into the classes. To begin, the first list price in Table 2–4 is $1 195 000. It is tallied in the "$900 000 to under $1 200 000" class. The second list price in the first column of Table 2–4 is $1 229 000. It is tallied in the "$1 200 000 to under $1 500 000" class. The other list prices are tallied in a similar manner. When all list prices are tallied, that table would appear as follows:

$	0	to under	$ 300 000	IIII LHI LHI LHI LHI LHI V
	300 000	to under	600 000	IIII LHI LHI LHI LHI III
	600 000	to under	900 000	III LHI
	900 000	to under	1 200 000	IIII V
	1 200 000	to under	1 500 000	III LHI LHI V
	1 500 000	to under	1 800 000	IIII LHI V
	1 800 000	to under	2 100 000	IIII LHI V

Step 5: Count the number of items in each class. The number of observations in each class is called the *class frequency*. There are 25 observations in the $0 to under $300 000 class, and in the $600 000 to under $900 000 class, there are 8 observations. Therefore, the class frequency is 25 in the first class and 8 in the third class. There are a total of 85 observations or frequencies in the set of data.

Often, it is useful to express the data in thousands, or some convenient units, rather than the actual data. Table 2–7, for example, reports the list prices in thousands of dollars, rather than in dollars.

TABLE 2–7 Frequency Distribution of Listings from Whistler, BC

List Price ($ thousands)	Frequency
$0 to under $300	25
300 to under 600	24
600 to under 900	8
900 to under 1 200	5
1 200 to under 1 500	11
1 500 to under 1 800	6
1 800 to under 2 100	6
Total	85

Now that we have organized the data into a frequency distribution, we can summarize the pattern in the list prices of the real estate example. Observe the following:

1. The list prices range from $0 to under $2 100 000.
2. The list prices are concentrated between $0 to under $600 000. A total of 49 list prices, or 57.6% of list prices, are within this range.
3. The largest concentration, or highest frequency, is in the first class, the $0 to under $300 000 range.
4. For each class, we can determine the **class midpoint**. It is halfway between the lower or upper limits of two consecutive classes. It is computed by adding the lower or upper limits of consecutive classes and dividing by 2. Refer to the second class. The lower limit is $300 000. In the third class, the lower limit is $600 000. The class midpoint is $450 000, found by ($300 000 + $600 000)/2. The midpoint best represents, or is typical of, the listings in that class.
5. The listings are classified using a class interval of $300 000. To determine the class interval subtract consecutive lower or upper class limits. For example, the lower limit of the second class is $300 000 and the lower limit of the third class is $600 000. Their difference is the class interval of $300 000. You can also determine the class interval by finding the difference between consecutive midpoints. The midpoint of the first class is $150 000 and the midpoint of the second class is $450 000. Their difference is $300 000.

By presenting this information, we can see a clearer picture of the distribution of list prices.

We admit that arranging the information on list prices into a frequency distribution does result in the loss of some detailed information. That is, by organizing the data into a frequency distribution, we cannot pinpoint the exact list price, such as $449 000 or $339 000. Or we cannot tell that the actual list price for the least expensive home was $56 900 and for the most expensive $1 999 999. However, the lower limit of the first class and the upper limit of the largest class convey essentially the same meaning. For example, we can tell that the highest list price is more than $1 800 000 but less than $2 100 000. The advantages of condensing the data into a more understandable form more than offset this disadvantage.

self-review 2–2

The commissions earned, in dollars, for the first quarter of last year by the 11 members of the sales staff at Master Chemical Company are as follows:

$1650	1475	1510	1670	1595	1760	1540	1495	1590	1625	1510

(a) What are the values such as $1650 and $1475 called?
(b) Using $1400 up to $1500 as the first class, $1500 up to $1600 as the second class, and so forth, organize the quarterly commissions into a frequency distribution.
(c) What are the numbers in the right column of your frequency distribution called?
(d) Describe the distribution of quarterly commissions, based on the frequency distribution. What is the largest amount of commission earned? What is the smallest? What is the typical amount earned?

A Software Example

As we mentioned in Chapter 1, there are many software packages that perform statistical calculations and output the results. Throughout this text, we will show the output from **Microsoft Excel** and from MegaStat, which is an add-in to **Microsoft Excel**.

The following is a frequency distribution, produced by MegaStat, showing the list prices of the real estate data. The form of the output is somewhat different than the frequency distribution of Table 2–7 created by hand, but the overall conclusions are the same. MegaStat steps to create this frequency distribution can be found at the end of the chapter.

excel

	List Price						Cumulative	
Lower		Upper	Midpoint	Width	Frequency	Percentage	Frequency	Percentage
0	<	300,000	150,000	300,000	25	29.4	25	29.4
300,000	<	600,000	450,000	300,000	24	28.2	49	57.6
600,000	<	900,000	750,000	300,000	8	9.4	57	67.1
900,000	<	1,200,000	1,050,000	300,000	5	5.9	62	72.9
1,200,000	<	1,500,000	1,350,000	300,000	11	2.9	73	85.9
1,500,000	<	1,800,000	1,650,000	300,000	6	7.1	79	92.9
1,800 000	<	2,100,000	1,950,000	300,000	6	7.1	85	100.0
					85	100.0		

self-review 2–3

Kristina had 73 customers in her retail bicycle store, Kristina's Bikes, last Sunday. The customers spent between $48.50 and $300. Kristina wants to construct a frequency distribution of the amount spent by her customers for that day.

(a) How many classes would you use?
(b) What class interval would you suggest?
(c) What actual classes would you suggest?

2.5 RELATIVE FREQUENCY DISTRIBUTION

It may be desirable, as we did earlier, to convert class frequencies to relative class frequencies to show the proportion of the total number of observations in each class. In our real estate example, we may want to know what percentage of the list prices are in the $600 000 to under $900 000 class. In another study, we may want to know what percentage of the employees used 5 up to 10 personal leave days last year. To convert a frequency distribution to a *relative* frequency distribution, each of the class frequencies is divided by the total number of observations. From the distribution of listings (Table 2–7, where the list price is reported in thousands of dollars), the relative frequency for the $300 to under $600 class is 0.2824, found by dividing 24 by 85. That is, 29.4% of the list prices are between $300 000 to under $600 000. The relative frequencies for the remaining classes are shown in Table 2–8.

TABLE 2–8 Relative Frequency Distribution for List Prices, Whistler, BC

List Price ($ thousands)	Frequency	Relative Frequency	Found by
$0 to under $300	25	0.2941	25/85
300 to under 600	24	0.2824	24/85
600 to under 900	8	0.0941	8/85
900 to under 1 200	5	0.0588	5/85
1 200 to under 1 500	11	0.1294	11/85
1 500 to under 1 800	6	0.0706	6/85
1 800 to under 1 200	6	0.0706	6/85
Total	85	1.0000	

self-review 2–4

Refer to Table 2–8, which shows the relative frequency for the real estate listings of homes in Whistler, BC.

(a) How many homes were listed for $600 000 to under $900 000?
(b) What percentage of homes were listed for $1 200 000 to under $1 500 000?
(c) What percentage of the homes were listed at $1 500 000 or more?

EXERCISES

7. A set of data consists of 38 observations. How many classes would you recommend for the frequency distribution?

8. A set of data consists of 45 observations between $0 and $29. What size would you recommend for the class interval?

9. A set of data consists of 230 observations between $235 and $567. What class interval would you recommend?

10. A set of data contains 53 observations. The lowest value is 42 and the largest is 129. The data are to be organized into a frequency distribution.

    a. How many classes would you suggest?
    b. What would you suggest as the lower limit of the first class?

11. The Wachesaw Manufacturing Co. produced the following number of units in the last 16 days:

27	27	27	28	27	25	25	28
26	28	26	28	31	30	26	26

    The information is to be organized into a frequency distribution.
    a. How many classes would you recommend?
    b. What class interval would you suggest?
    c. What lower limit would you recommend for the first class?

    d. Organize the information into a frequency distribution and determine the relative frequency distribution.

    e. Comment on the shape of the distribution.

12. The Quick Change Oil Company has a number of outlets. The numbers of oil changes at the Oak Street outlet in the past 20 days are as follows:

65	98	55	62	79	59	51	90	72	56
70	62	66	80	94	79	63	73	71	85

The data are to be organized into a frequency distribution.

    a. How many classes would you recommend?

    b. What class interval would you suggest?

    c. What lower limit would you recommend for the first class?

    d. Organize the information into a frequency distribution and determine the relative frequency distribution.

    e. Comment on the shape of the distribution.

13. The manager of the BiLo Supermarket gathered the following information on the number of times a customer visits the store during a month. The responses of 51 customers were as follows:

5	3	3	1	4	4	5	6	4	2	6	6	6	7	1
1	14	1	2	4	4	4	5	6	3	5	3	4	5	6
8	4	7	6	5	9	11	3	12	4	7	6	5	15	1
1	10	8	9	2	12									

    a. Starting with 0 as the lower limit of the first class and using a class interval of 3, organize the data into a frequency distribution.

    b. Describe the distribution. Where do the data tend to cluster?

    c. Convert the distribution to a relative frequency distribution.

14. The food services division at Cedar River Amusement Park is studying the amount families who visit the amusement park spend per day on food and beverages. A random sample of 40 families who visited the park yesterday revealed they spent the following amounts:

$77	18	63	84	38	54	50	59	54	56	36	26	50	34	44
41	58	58	53	51	62	43	52	53	63	62	62	65	61	52
60	60	45	66	83	71	63	58	61	71					

    a. Organize the data into a frequency distribution, using seven classes and 15 as the lower limit of the first class. What class interval did you select?

    b. Where do the data tend to cluster?

    c. Describe the distribution.

    d. Determine the relative frequency distribution.

LO2-4 2.6 GRAPHIC PRESENTATION OF A FREQUENCY DISTRIBUTION

Sales managers, stock analysts, hospital administrators, and other busy executives often need a quick picture of the trends in sales, stock prices, or hospital costs. These trends can often be depicted by the use of charts and graphs. Three charts that will help portray a frequency distribution graphically are the histogram, the frequency polygon, and the cumulative frequency polygon.

Histogram

Histogram A graph in which the classes are marked on the horizontal axis and the class frequencies on the vertical axis. The class frequencies are represented by the heights of the bars and the bars are drawn adjacent to each other.

A **histogram** for a frequency distribution based on quantitative data is similar to the bar chart showing the distribution of qualitative data. The classes are marked on the horizontal axis and the class frequencies on the vertical axis. The class frequencies are represented by the heights of the bars. However, there is one important difference based on the nature of the data. Quantitative data are usually measured using scales that are continuous, not discrete. Therefore, the horizontal axis represents all possible values, and the bars are drawn adjacent to each other to show the continuous nature of the data.

Example	Below is the frequency distribution of the 85 homes in Whistler, BC.

List Price ($ thousands)	Midpoint	Frequency
$0 to under $300	$ 150	25
300 to under 600	450	24
600 to under 900	750	8
900 to under 1 200	1 050	5
1 200 to under 1 500	1 350	11
1 500 to under 1 800	1 650	6
1 800 to under 2 100	1 950	6
Total		85

Construct a histogram. What observations can you reach based on the information presented in the histogram?

Solution	The class frequencies are scaled along the vertical axis (Y-axis) and either the class limits or the class midpoints along the horizontal axis (X-axis).

From Chart 2–3, we note that there are 25 listings in the $0 to under $300 000 class. Therefore, the height of the bar for that class is 25. There are 24 listings in the $300 000 to under $600 000 class; so, logically, the height of that bar is 24. The height of the bar represents the number of observations in the class.

excel CHART 2–3 Histogram of Real Estate Listings from Whistler, BC

This procedure is continued for all classes. The complete histogram is shown in Chart 2–3. Note that there is no space between the bars. This is a feature of the histogram. Why is this so? Because the variable plotted on the horizontal axis is a continuous variable. In a bar chart, the scale of measurement is often nominal, and the bars are separated. This is an important distinction between the histogram and the bar chart.

On the basis of the histogram in Chart 2–3, we conclude:

1. The lowest list price is between $0 to under $300 000. The highest list price is between $1 800 000 to under $2 100 000.
2. The largest class frequency is the $0 to under $300 000 class. A total of 25 of the 85 listings, or 29.41% are within this price range.
3. The list prices are concentrated between $0 to under $600 000. Forty-nine of the list prices, or 57.65% are within this range.
4. For each class, we can determine the the typical list price or class midpoint. It is halfway between the lower or upper limits of two consecutive classes. It is calculated by adding the lower or upper limits of consecutive classes and dividing by 2. Refer to Chart 2–3. The lower limit of the first class is $0 and the next class limit is $300 000. The class midpoint is $150 000, found by ($0 + $300 000)/2. The midpoint best represents, or is typical of, the list prices in that class. So, there are 25 listings with a typical price of $150 000.

Thus, the histogram provides an easily interpreted visual representation of a frequency distribution. We should also point out that we would have reached the same conclusions and the shape of the histogram would have been the same had we used a relative frequency distribution instead of the actual frequencies. That is, if we had used the relative frequencies of Table 2–8, we would have had a histogram of the same shape as Chart 2–3. The only difference is that the vertical axis would have been reported in percentage of listings instead of the number of listings.

MegaStat steps to create this histogram can be found at the end of the chapter.

Frequency Polygon

A **frequency polygon** also shows the shape of a distribution and is similar to a histogram. It consists of line segments connecting the points formed by the intersections of the class midpoints and the class frequencies. The construction of a frequency polygon is illustrated in Chart 2–4. We used the Whistler real estate listings. The midpoint of each class is scaled on the X-axis and the class frequencies on the Y-axis. Recall that the class midpoint is the value at the centre of a class and represents the typical values in that class. The class frequency is the number of observations in a particular class. The listings from the Whistler example are repeated below:

List Price ($ thousands)		Midpoint	Frequency
$0 to under	$300	$150	25
300 to under	600	450	24
600 to under	300	750	8
900 to under	1 200	1 050	5
1 200 to under	1 500	1 350	11
1 500 to under	1 800	1 650	6
1 800 to under	2 100	1 950	6
Total			85

As noted previously, the $0 up to $300 000 class is represented by the midpoint $150 000. To construct a frequency polygon, move horizontally on the graph to the midpoint $150, and then vertically up to 25, the class frequency, and place a dot. The X and the Y values of this point are called the *coordinates*. The coordinates of the next point are X = $450 and Y = 24. The process is continued for all classes. Then the points are connected in order. That is, the point representing the lowest class is joined to the one representing the second class and so on.

In Chart 2–4, note that to complete the frequency polygon, midpoints $–150 and $2250 are added to the X-axis to "anchor" the polygon at zero frequencies. These two values, $–150 and $2250, were derived by subtracting the class interval of $300 from the lowest midpoint ($150) and by adding $300 to the highest midpoint ($2150) in the frequency distribution.

excel

CHART 2–4 Frequency Polygon of Real Estate Listings Whistler, BC

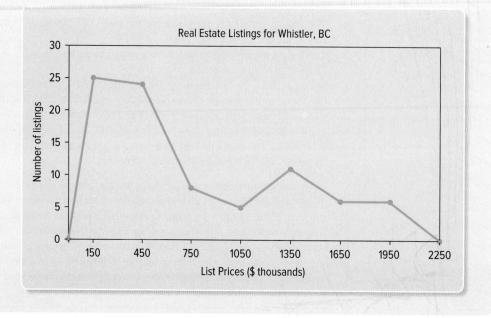

MegaStat steps to create this frequency polygon can be found at the end of the chapter.

Both the histogram and the frequency polygon allow us to get a quick picture of the main characteristics of the data (highs, lows, points of concentration, etc.). Although the two representations are similar in purpose, the histogram has the advantage of depicting each class as a rectangle, with the height of the rectangular bar representing the number in each class. The

CHART 2–5 Distribution of List Prices Last Year and This Year

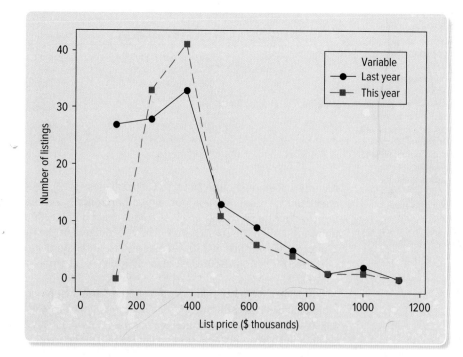

frequency polygon, in turn, has an advantage over the histogram. It allows us to compare directly two or more frequency distributions. Suppose that an office manager at a real estate company wants to compare the number of home listings in the same month last year. To do this, two frequency polygons are constructed, one on top of the other, as in Chart 2–5. But one thing is clear from the chart: the typical list price is lower for the same month last year.

The total numbers of listings for the two years are about the same, so a direct comparison is possible. If the difference in the total number of listings is large, then converting the frequencies to relative frequencies and graphing the two distributions would allow a clearer comparison.

self-review 2–5

The annual imports of a selected group of electronics suppliers are shown in the following frequency distribution:

Imports ($ millions)	Number of Suppliers
$2 to under $5	6
5 to under 8	13
8 to under 11	20
11 to under 14	10
14 to under 17	1

(a) Portray the imports as a histogram.
(b) Portray the imports as a relative frequency polygon.
(c) Summarize the important facets of the distribution (such as classes with the highest and lowest frequencies).

self-review 2–6

(a) Describe when it is preferable to use a bar   chart or a pie chart.
(b) Describe the differences between a bar chart and   a histogram.

EXERCISES

15. Molly's Candle Shop has several retail stores in coastal areas. Many of Molly's customers ask her to ship their purchases. The following chart shows the number of packages shipped per day for the last 100 days:

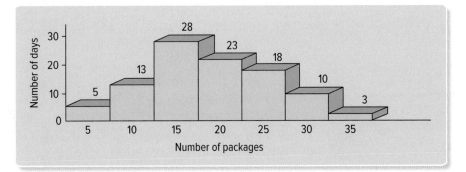

a. What is this chart called?
b. What is the total number of frequencies?
c. What is the class interval?
d. What is the class frequency for the 10 up to 15 class?
e. What is the relative frequency of the 10 up to 15 class?
f. What is the midpoint of the 10 up to 15 class?
g. On how many days were there 25 or more packages shipped?

16. The following chart shows the number of patients admitted daily to Memorial Hospital through the emergency room:

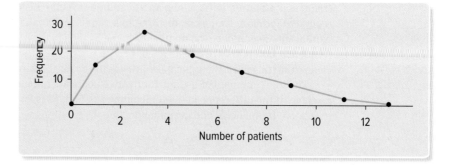

    a. What is the midpoint of the 2 up to 4 class?

    b. How many days were 2 up to 4 patients admitted?

    c. Approximately how many days were studied?

    d. What is the class interval?

    e. What is this chart called?

17. The following frequency distribution reports the number of frequent flier miles, reported in thousands, for employees of Brumley Statistical Consulting Inc. during the most recent quarter:

Frequent Flier Miles (thousands)	Number of Employees
0 to under 3	5
3 to under 6	12
6 to under 9	23
9 to under 12	8
12 to under 15	2
Total	50

    a. How many employees were studied?

    b. What is the midpoint of the first class?

    c. Construct a histogram.

    d. A frequency polygon is to be drawn. What are the coordinates of the plot for the first class?

    e. Construct a frequency polygon.

    f. Interpret the frequent flier miles accumulated using the two charts.

18. Stop-One.com, a large Internet retailer, is studying the lead time (elapsed time between when an order is placed and when it is filled) for a sample of recent orders. The lead times are reported in days.

Lead Time (days)	Frequency
0 to under 5	6
5 to under 10	7
10 to under 15	12
15 to under 20	8
20 to under 25	7
Total	40

    a. How many orders were studied?

    b. What is the midpoint of the first class?

    c. What are the coordinates of the first class for a frequency polygon?

    d. Draw a histogram.

    e. Draw a frequency polygon.

    f. Interpret the lead times using the two charts.

LO2-5 Cumulative Frequency Distributions

Consider once again the distribution of real estate listings from Whistler, BC. Suppose that we were interested in the number of homes listed for less than $600 000, or the value below which 40% of the homes were listed. These numbers can be approximated by developing a **cumulative**

frequency distribution, and portraying it graphically in a **cumulative frequency polygon**, or **ogive**. There are two types: the less-than cumulative frequency distribution and the more-than cumulative frequency distribution.

Example	The frequency distribution of the listings from Whistler, BC, is repeated below:

List Price ($)	Frequency
$0 to under $300 000	25
300 000 to under 600 000	24
600 000 to under 900 000	8
900 000 to under 1 200 000	5
1 200 000 to under 1 500 000	11
1 500 000 to under 1 800 000	6
1 800 000 to under 2 100 000	6
Total	85

Construct a less-than cumulative frequency polygon and use the results to answer the following two questions. Fifty percent of the homes were listed for less than what amount? Twenty-five of the dwellings were listed for less than what amount?

Solution

As the name implies, a cumulative frequency distribution and a cumulative frequency polygon require *cumulative frequencies*. To construct a cumulative frequency distribution, refer to the preceding table, and note that there were 25 homes listed for less than $300 000. Those 25 list prices plus the 24 in the next higher class, for a total of 49, were listed for less than $600 000. The cumulative frequency for the next higher class is 57, found by: $25 + 24 + 8$. This process is continued for all the classes. All the homes were listed for less than $2 100 000 (Table 2–9).

TABLE 2–9 Less-than Cumulative Frequency Distribution for Real Estate Listings from Whistler, BC

List Price ($ thousands)	Frequency	Cumulative Frequency	Found by
$0 to under $300	25	25	
300 to under 600	24	49	$25 + 24$
600 to under 900	8	57	$25 + 25 + 8$
900 to under 1 200	5	62	$25 + 24 + 8 + 5$
1 200 to under 1 500	11	73	$25 + 24 + 8 + 5 + 11$
1 500 to under 1 800	6	79	$25 + 24 + 8 + 5 + 11 + 6$
1 800 to under 2 100	6	85	$25 + 24 + 8 + 5 + 11 + 6 + 6$
Total	85		

To plot a less-than cumulative frequency distribution, scale the upper limit of each class along the *x*-axis and the corresponding cumulative frequencies along the *y*-axis. To provide additional information, you can label the vertical axis on the left in units and the vertical axis on the right in percentages. In the Whistler real estate example, the vertical axis on the left is labelled from 0 to 85 and on the right from 0 to 100%. The value of 50% corresponds to 1/2 or 42.5 listings.

To begin, the first plot is at $x = 300$ and $y = 25$. Twenty-five of the listings were less than $300 000. The list price on 49 of the dwellings was less than $600 000, so the next plot is at $x = \$600$ and $y = 49$. Continuing, the next plot is $x = 900$ and $y = 57$. This means that there are 57 listings less than $900 000. The points are plotted as follows:

Less than	300	25
Less than	600	49
Less than	900	57
Less than	1 200	62
Less than	1 500	73
Less than	1 800	79
Less than	2 100	85

Then, the points are connected to form the chart (Chart 2–6). To find the list price below which half (50%) the homes are listed, we draw a horizontal line from the 50% mark on the right-hand vertical axis over to the polygon, then drop down to the x-axis and read the list price. The value on the x-axis is about 500, so we estimate that 50% of the listings are less than $500 000. Note that the point (0, 0) is added to "anchor" the line at zero frequencies.

CHART 2–6 Less-than Cumulative Frequency Distribution for Real Estate Listings from Whistler, BC

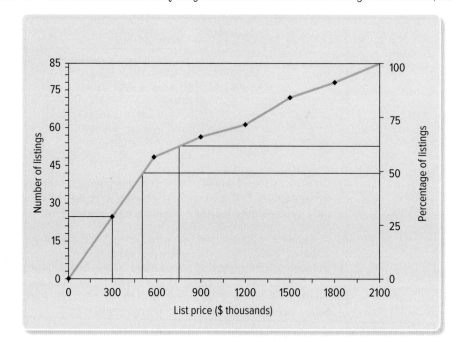

To find the price below which 25 of the homes are listed, we locate the approximate value of 25 on the left-hand vertical axis. Next, we draw a horizontal line from the value of 25 to the polygon, then drop down to the x-axis, and read the price. It is about 300, so we estimate that 25 of the homes were listed for less than $300 000. This corresponds to the frequency distribution that shows that 25 of the listings were less than $300 000. We can also make estimates of the percentage of homes that were listed less than a particular amount. To explain, suppose that we want to estimate the percentage of homes that were listed for less than $750 000. We begin by locating the value of 750 on the x-axis, move vertically to the polygon, and then move horizontally to the vertical axis on the right. The value is about 60%, so we conclude that 60% of the homes were listed for less than $750 000.

MegaStat steps to create this cumulative frequency diagram can be found at the end of the chapter.

TABLE 2–10 More-than Cumulative Frequency Distribution for Real Estate Listings from Whistler, BC

List Price ($ thousands)	Cumulative Frequency
$0 or more	85
300 or more	60
600 or more	36
900 or more	28
1 200 or more	23
1 500 or more	12
1 800 or more	6
2 100 or more	0

To construct a more-than cumulative frequency distribution, refer to Table 2–10 and note that there were 85 dwellings listed for $0 or more (all of the listings), 60 listed for $300 000 or more, and so on. To plot the distribution, we can use the same axes as the less-than cumulative frequency distribution. To begin the plotting, 85 listings were $0 or more, so the first point is $x = 0$ and $y = 85$. The coordinates for the next point are $x = 300$ and $y = 60$. The rest of the points are plotted, and then they are connected to form the chart (Chart 2–7).

CHART 2–7 More-than Cumulative Frequency Distribution for Real Estate Listings from Whistler, BC

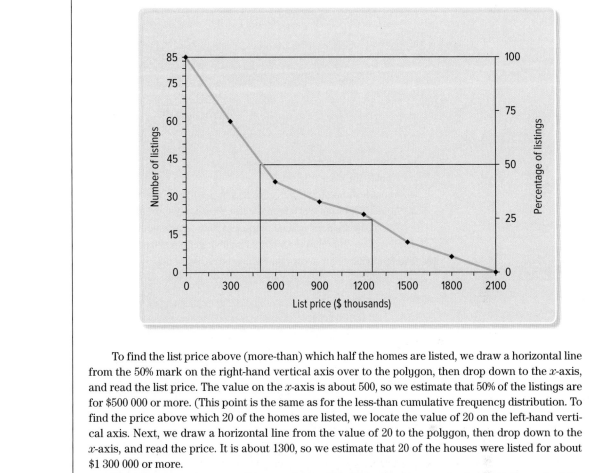

To find the list price above (more-than) which half the homes are listed, we draw a horizontal line from the 50% mark on the right-hand vertical axis over to the polygon, then drop down to the x-axis, and read the list price. The value on the x-axis is about 500, so we estimate that 50% of the listings are for $500 000 or more. (This point is the same as for the less-than cumulative frequency distribution. To find the price above which 20 of the homes are listed, we locate the value of 20 on the left-hand vertical axis. Next, we draw a horizontal line from the value of 20 to the polygon, then drop down to the x-axis, and read the price. It is about 1300, so we estimate that 20 of the houses were listed for about $1 300 000 or more.

MegaStat steps to create this cumulative frequency diagram can be found at the end of the chapter.

self-review 2-7

A sample of the hourly wages of 15 employees at Food City Supermarkets was organized into the following table:

Hourly Wages ($)	Number of Employees
$6 to under $8	3
8 to under 10	7
10 to under 12	4
12 to under 14	1

(a) What is the table called?
(b) Develop a less-than and more-than cumulative frequency distribution and portray the distribution in cumulative frequency polygons.
(c) On the basis of the cumulative frequency polygon, how many employees earn $9 per hour or less? Half of the employees earn an hourly wage of how much or more? Four employees earn how much or less?

EXERCISES

19. The following chart shows the hourly wages of a sample of certified welders:

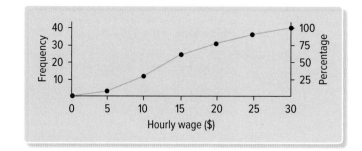

a. How many welders were studied?

b. What is the class interval?

c. About how many welders earn less than $10 per hour?

d. About 75% of the welders make less than what amount?

e. Ten of the welders studied made less than what amount?

f. What percentage of the welders make less than $20 per hour?

20. The following chart shows the selling price, in thousands of dollars, of houses sold last month in Corner Brook, Newfoundland:

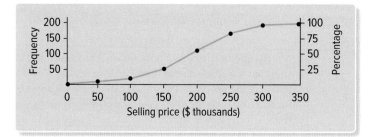

a. How many homes were studied?

b. What is the class interval?

c. One hundred homes sold for less than what amount?

d. About 75% of the homes sold for less than what amount?

e. Estimate the number of homes in the $150 000 up to $200 000 class.

f. About how many homes sold for less than $225 000?

Use the following information for Exercises 21 and 22.

The frequency distribution representing the number of frequent flier miles accumulated by employees at Brumley Statistical Consulting Company is repeated from Exercise 17.

Frequent Flier Miles (thousands)	Frequency
0 to under 3	5
3 to under 6	12
6 to under 9	23
9 to under 12	8
12 to under 15	2
Total	50

21. a. How many employees accumulated less than 3000 miles?

b. Convert the frequency distribution to a less-than cumulative frequency distribution.

c. Portray the cumulative distribution in the form of a less-than cumulative frequency polygon.

d. On the basis of the cumulative frequency polygons, about 75% of the employees accumulated how many miles or less?

22. a. Convert the frequency distribution to a more-than cumulative frequency distribution.
   b. Portray the cumulative distribution in the form of a more-than cumulative frequency polygon.
   c. About 40% of the employees accumulated more than how many miles?

Use the following information for Exercises 23 and 24.

The frequency distribution of order lead time at Stop-One.com from Exercise 18 is repeated below:

Lead Time (days)	Frequency
0 to under 5	6
5 to under 10	7
10 to under 15	12
15 to under 20	8
20 to under 25	7
Total	40

23. a. How many orders were filled in less than 10 days? In less than 15 days?
   b. Convert the frequency distribution to a less-than cumulative frequency distribution.
   c. Develop a less-than cumulative frequency polygon.
   d. About 60% of the orders were filled in less than how many days?
24. a. Convert the frequency distribution to a more-than cumulative frequency distribution.
   b. Develop cumulative frequency polygons.
   c. About 25% of the orders were filled in how many days or more?

LO2-6   2.7 STEM-AND-LEAF DISPLAYS

In the previous section, we showed how to organize data into a frequency distribution so that we could summarize the raw data into a meaningful form. The major advantage to organizing the data into a frequency distribution is that we get a quick visual picture of the shape of the distribution without doing any further calculation. That is, we can see where the data are concentrated and also determine whether there are any extremely large or small values. There are two disadvantages, however, to organizing the data into a frequency distribution: (1) we lose the exact identity of each value, and (2) we are not sure how the values within each class are distributed. To explain, the following frequency distribution shows the number of advertising spots purchased by the 45 members of the Greater Hilltown Automobile Dealers Association last year. We observe that 7 of the 45 dealers purchased between 90 to under 100 spots. However, are the spots purchased within this class clustered about 90, spread evenly throughout the class, or clustered near 99? We cannot tell.

Number of Spots Purchased	Frequency
80 to under 90	2
90 to under 100	7
100 to under 110	6
110 to under 120	9
120 to under 130	8
130 to under 140	7
140 to under 150	3
150 to under 160	3
Total	45

Stem-and-leaf display A statistical technique to present a set of data. Each numerical value is divided into two parts. The leading digit(s) becomes the stem and the trailing digit the leaf. The stems are located along the vertical axis, and the leaf values are stacked against each other along the horizontal axis.

One technique that is used to display quantitative information in a condensed form is the **stem-and-leaf display**. An advantage of the stem-and-leaf display over a frequency distribution is that we do not lose the identity of each observation. In the above example, we would not know the identity of the values in the 90 to under 100 class. To illustrate the construction of a stem-and-leaf display using the number of advertising spots purchased, suppose the seven observations in the 90 up to 100 class are: 96, 94, 93, 94, 95, 96, and 97. The **stem** value is the leading digit or digits, in this case 9. The **leaves** are the trailing digits. The stem is placed to the left of a vertical line and the leaf values to the right.

The values in the 90 up to 100 class would appear as follows:

9	6	4	3	4	5	6	7

Finally, we sort the values within each stem from smallest to largest. Thus, the second row of the stem-and-leaf display would appear as follows:

9	3	4	4	5	6	6	7

With the stem-and-leaf display, we can quickly observe that there were two dealers who purchased 94 spots and that the number of spots purchased ranged from 93 to 97. A stem-and-leaf display is similar to a frequency distribution with more information, that is, the data values are preserved.

The following example will explain the details of developing a stem-and-leaf display:

Example

Listed in Table 2–11 is the number of 30-second radio advertising spots purchased by each of the 45 members of the Greater Hilltown Automobile Dealers Association last year. Organize the data into a stem-and-leaf display. Around what values do the number of advertising spots tend to cluster? What is the fewest number of spots purchased by a dealer? The largest number purchased?

TABLE 2–11 Number of Advertising Spots Purchased by Members of the Greater Hilltown Automobile Dealers Association

96	93	88	117	127	95	113	96	108	94	148	156
139	142	94	107	125	155	155	103	112	127	117	120
112	135	132	111	125	104	106	139	134	119	97	89
118	136	125	143	120	103	113	124	138			

Solution

From the data in Table 2–11, we note that the smallest number of spots purchased is 88, so we will make the first stem value 8. The largest number is 156, so we will have the stem values begin at 8 and continue to 15. The first number in Table 2–11 is 96, which will have a stem value of 9 and a leaf value of 6. Moving across the top row, the second value is 93, and the third is 88. After the first three data values are considered, your chart is as follows:

Stem	Leaf
8	8
9	6 3
10	
11	
12	
13	
14	
15	

Organizing all the data, the stem-and-leaf chart looks as follows:

Stem	Leaf
8	8 9
9	6 3 5 6 4 4 7
10	8 7 3 4 6 3
11	7 3 2 7 2 1 9 8 3
12	7 5 7 0 5 5 0 4
13	9 5 2 9 4 6 8
14	8 2 3
15	6 5 5

The usual procedure is to sort the leaf values from the smallest to largest. The last line, the row referring to the values in the 150s, would appear as follows:

| 15 | 5 | 5 | 6 |

The final table would appear as follows, where we have sorted all of the leaf values:

Stem	Leaf
8	8 9
9	3 4 4 5 6 6 7
10	3 3 4 6 7 8
11	1 2 2 3 3 7 7 8 9
12	0 0 4 5 5 5 7 7
13	2 4 5 6 8 9 9
14	2 3 8
15	5 5 6

You can draw several conclusions from the stem-and-leaf display. First, the lowest number of spots purchased is 88 and the largest is 156. Two dealers purchased fewer than 90 spots, and three purchased 150 or more. You can observe, for example, that the three dealers who purchased 150 spots or more actually purchased 155, 155, and 156 spots. The concentration of the number of spots is between 110 and 130. There were nine dealers who purchased between 110 and 119 spots and eight who purchased between 120 and 129 spots. We can also tell that within the 120 to 129 group the actual number of spots purchased was spread evenly throughout. That is, two dealers purchased 120 spots, one dealer purchased 124 spots, three dealers purchased 125 spots, and two purchased 127 spots.

MegaStat steps to create this stem-and-leaf display can be found at the end of the chapter.

self-review 2–8

The price-earnings ratios for 21 stocks in the retail trade category are as follows:

| 8.3 | 9.6 | 9.5 | 9.1 | 8.8 | 11.2 | 7.7 | 10.1 | 9.9 | 10.8 | |
| 10.2 | 8.0 | 8.4 | 8.1 | 11.6 | 9.6 | 8.8 | 8.0 | 10.4 | 9.8 | 9.2 |

Organize this information into a stem-and-leaf display.

(a) How many values are less than 9.0?
(b) List the values in the 10.0 up to 11.0 category.
(c) What is the middle (median) value?
(d) What are the largest and the smallest price-earnings ratios?

EXERCISES

25. The first row of a stem-and-leaf chart appears as follows: 62 | 1 3 3 7 9. Assume whole number values.

  a. What is the "possible range" of the values in this row?

  b. How many data values are in this row?

  c. List the actual values in this row of data.

26. The third row of a stem-and-leaf chart appears as follows: 21 | 0 1 3 5 7 9. Assume whole number values.

  a. What is the "possible range" of the values in this row?

  b. How many data values are in this row?

  c. List the actual values in this row of data.

27. The following stem-and-leaf chart shows the number of units produced per day in a factory:

3	8
4	
5	6
6	0 1 3 3 5 5 9
7	0 2 3 6 7 7 8
8	5 9
9	0 0 1 5 6
10	3 6

    a. How many days were studied?
    b. How many observations are in the first class?
    c. What are the smallest and the largest values?
    d. List the actual values in the fourth row.
    e. List the actual values in the second row.
    f. How many values are less than 70?
    g. How many values are 80 or more?
    h. What is the middle value?
    i. How many values are between 60 and 89, inclusive?

28. The following stem-and-leaf chart reports the number of movies rented per day at Video Connection:

12	6 8 9
13	1 2 3
14	6 8 8 9
15	5 8 9
16	3 5
17	2 4 5 6 8
18	2 6 8
19	1 3 4 5 6
20	0 3 4 6 7 9
21	2 2 3 9
22	7 8 9
23	0 0 1 7 9
24	8
25	1 3
26	
27	0

    a. How many days were studied?
    b. How many observations are in the last class?
    c. What are the largest and the smallest values in the entire set of data?
    d. List the actual values in the fourth row.
    e. List the actual values in the next to the last row.
    f. On how many days were less than 160 movies rented?
    g. On how many days were 220 or more movies rented?
    h. What is the middle value?
    i. On how many days were between 170 and 210 movies rented?

29. A survey of the number of calls received by a sample of a regional phone company subscribers last week revealed the following information. Develop a stem-and-leaf chart. How many calls did a typical subscriber receive? What were the largest and the smallest number of calls received?

52	43	30	38	30	42	12	46	39
37	34	46	32	18	41	5		

30. Altar Banking Co. is studying the number of times its automatic teller, located in a Loblaws supermarket, is used each day. The following is the number of times it was used during each of the last 30 days. Develop a stem-and-leaf chart. Summarize the data on the number of times the automatic teller was used: How many times was the teller used on a typical day? What were the largest and the smallest number of times the teller was used? Around what values did the number of times the teller was used tend to cluster?

83	64	84	76	84	54	75	59	70	61
63	80	84	73	68	52	65	90	52	77
95	36	78	61	59	84	95	47	87	60

Chapter Summary

I. A frequency table is a grouping of qualitative data into mutually exclusive classes showing the number of observations in each class.

II. A relative frequency table shows the fraction or percentage of the number of observations in each class.

III. A bar chart is a graphic representation of a frequency table.

IV. A pie chart shows the proportion each distinct class represents of the total number of observations.

V. A frequency distribution is a grouping of data into mutually exclusive classes showing the number of observations in each class.

    A. The steps in constructing a frequency distribution are as follows:
        1. Decide on the number of classes.
        2. Determine the class interval.
        3. Set the individual class limits.
        4. Tally the raw data into the classes.
        5. Count the number of tallies in each class.

    B. The class frequency is the number of observations in each class.

    C. The class interval is the difference between the limits of two consecutive classes.

    D. The class midpoint is halfway between the limits of consecutive classes.

VI. A relative frequency distribution shows the percentage of observations in each class.

VII. There are three methods for graphically portraying a frequency distribution.

    A. A histogram portrays the number of frequencies in each class in the form of a rectangle.

    B. A frequency polygon consists of line segments connecting the points formed by the intersections of the class midpoints and the class frequency.

    C. A cumulative frequency polygon shows the number or percentage of observations below or above given values.

VIII. A stem-and-leaf display is an alternative to a frequency distribution.

    A. The leading digit is the stem, and the trailing digit is the leaf.

    B. The advantages of the stem-and-leaf chart over a frequency distribution include the following:
        1. The identity of each observation is not lost.
        2. The digits themselves give a picture of the distribution.
        3. The cumulative frequencies are also shown.

IX. There are many charts used in business.

    A. A line chart is ideal for showing the trend or sales of income over time.

    B. Bar charts are similar to line charts and are useful for showing changes in nominal scale data.

    C. Pie charts are useful for showing the percentages of the various components that make up the total.

Chapter Exercises

31. Describe the similarities and differences of quantitative and qualitative variables. Be sure to consider the following:
   a. What level of measurement is required for each variable type?
   b. Can both types be used to describe both samples and populations?

32. Alexandra Dawn will be building a new resort in Cape Breton. She must decide how to design the resort based on the type of activities that the resort will offer to its customers. A recent poll of 300 potential customers showed that 63 liked planned activities, 135 did not like planned activities, 78 were not sure, and 24 did not respond.
   a. Construct a bar chart to portray the survey results.
   b. Construct a pie chart for the survey results.
   c. If you were preparing a presentation, which graph would you prefer to show? Why?

33. A data set consists of 83 observations. How many classes would you recommend for a frequency distribution?

34. A data set consists of 145 observations that range from 56 to 490. What size class interval would you recommend?

35. A recent survey showed that a typical car owner spends $3487 per year on operating expenses. A breakdown of the various expenditure items is given below. Construct an appropriate chart to portray the data and summarize your findings in a report.

Expenditures	Amount ($)
Fuel	$ 603
Interest on Car Loan	279
Repairs	930
Insurance and Licence	1400
Depreciation	275
Total	$3487

36. The following table displays the average retail price of gasoline per litre, in July in St. John's, Newfoundland, over the last five years (statcan.gc.ca/tables-tableaux/sum-som/l01/cst01/econ154a-eng.htm). Develop a bar chart depicting this information.

Year	2012	2013	2014	2015	2016
Cost per litre	124.3	130.6	135.9	121.9	121.7

37. The business school at the local college reported the following percentage breakdown of expenses. Draw a pie chart showing the information.

Category	Percentage (%)
Professional development	32.3%
Equipment	23.5
Mileage	12.6
PAC meetings	12.1
Office supplies	10.9
Other	8.6

38. The Consumer Price Index increases from 2006 to 2015 (base year 2002 = 100) is shown in the following table (statcan.gc.ca/tables-tableaux/sum-som/l01/cst01/econ161a-eng.htm). Construct a line chart to depict the information.

Year	CPI
2015	126.6
2014	125.2
2013	122.8
2012	121.7
2011	119.9
2010	116.5
2009	114.4
2008	114.1
2007	111.5
2006	109.1

39. The following table shows the average weekly earnings of workers in Canada. Develop an appropriate chart to summarize the findings. The complete data set can be found on Connect "Average Weekly Earnings."

Year	Average Earnings ($)
2008	742.69
2009	770.30
2010	787.37
2011	808.69
2012	817.07
2013	833.71
2014	853.82
2015	868.41

40. The number of Olympic medals won by Canada in the last five Winter games is listed below. Develop an appropriate chart or graph, and write a brief report summarizing the information.

Year	Number of Medals
2014	25
2010	26
2006	24
2002	17
1998	15

41. A total of 42 students wrote the first test in statistics 101. Three students achieved a grade over 90%; 12 students were between 80 and 89; 16 students between 70 and 79; 8 between 60 and 69 and the rest achieved grades that were below 60. Develop a pie chart or a bar chart showing the grades. Write a brief report summarizing the information.

42. You are exploring the music in your iTunes library. The total play counts over the past year for the songs on your "smart playlist" are shown below. Make a frequency distribution of the counts and describe its shape. It is often claimed that a small fraction of a person's songs will account for most of their total plays. Does this seem to be the case here?

128	56	54	91	190	23	160	298	445	50	578	494	37	677
18	74	70	868	108	71	466	23	84	38	26	814	17	

43. Two thousand frequent business travellers are asked which western city they prefer: Vancouver, Calgary, Edmonton, or Saskatoon. One hundred liked Vancouver best, 450 liked Calgary, 1300 liked Edmonton, and the remainder preferred Saskatoon. Develop a frequency table and a relative frequency table to summarize this information. Report your findings.

44. Newcastle Inc. reported a total of $69.5 billion in sales revenue. Seventy-three percent of the total was paid out for operating expenses, 11% in dividends, 3% in interest, 8% profit, and 5% in a sinking fund to be used for future capital equipment. Develop a pie chart for the data. Write a brief report to summarize the information.

45. The following is the number of minutes to commute from home to work for a group of automobile executives:

28	25	48	37	41	19	32	26	16	23	23	29	36
31	26	21	32	25	31	43	35	42	38	33	28	

a. How many classes would you recommend?
b. What class interval would you suggest?
c. What would you recommend as the lower limit of the first class?
d. Organize the data into a frequency distribution.
e. Comment on the shape of the frequency distribution.

46. One of the most popular candies in North America is M&M's, which are produced by the Mars Company. For many years, M&M's plain candies were produced in six colours: red, green, orange, tan, brown, and yellow. Recently, tan was replaced by blue. Did you ever wonder how many candies were in a bag, or how many of each colour? Are there about the same number of each colour, or are there more of some colours than others? Here is some information for a 500-gram bag of M&M's plain candies. It contained a total of 544 candies. There were 135 brown, 156 yellow, 128 red, 22 green, 50 blue, and 53 orange. Develop a chart depicting this information and a brief report summarizing the information.

47. The following stem-and-leaf display shows the number of minutes of daytime TV viewing for a sample of college students:

```
 0 | 0 5
 1 | 0
 2 | 1 3 7
 3 | 0 0 2 9
 4 | 4 9 9
 5 | 0 0 1 5 5 6 6 7 7 9 9
 6 | 0 2 3 4 6 8
 7 | 1 3 6 6 7 8 9
 8 | 0 1 5 5 8
 9 | 1 1 2 2 3 7 9
10 | 0 2 2 3 6 7 8 9 9
11 | 2 4 5 7
12 | 4 6 6 8
13 | 2 4 9
14 | 5
```

a. How many college students were studied?
b. How many observations are in the second class?
c. What are the smallest and the largest values?
d. List the actual values in the fourth row.
e. How many students watched less than 60 minutes of TV?
f. How many students watched 100 minutes or more of TV?
g. What is the middle value?
h. How many students watched at least 60 minutes but less than 100 minutes?

48. The following data give the weekly amounts spent on groceries for a sample of households:

$271	363	159	76	227	337	295	319	250
279	205	279	266	199	177	162	232	303
192	181	321	309	246	278	50	41	335
116	100	151	240	474	297	170	188	320
429	294	570	342	279	235	434	123	325

a. How many classes would you recommend?
b. What class interval would you suggest?
c. What would you recommend as the lower limit of the first class?
d. Organize the data into a frequency distribution.

49. A chain of sport shops catering to beginner skiers, headquartered in Whistler, British Columbia, plans to conduct a study of how much a beginning skier spends on his or her initial purchase of equipment and supplies. On the basis of these figures, they want to explore the possibility of offering combinations, such as a pair of boots and a pair of skis, to induce customers to buy more. A sample of their cash register receipts revealed these initial purchases:

$140	82	265	168	90	114	172	230	142
86	125	235	212	171	149	156	162	118
139	149	132	105	162	126	216	195	127
161	135	172	220	229	129	87	128	126
175	127	149	126	121	118	172	126	

a. Determine a suggested class interval. Use five classes, and let the lower limit of the first class be $80.
b. What would be a better class interval?
c. Organize the data into a frequency distribution using a lower limit of $80.
d. Interpret your findings.

50. The Saskatoon Credit Union selected a sample of 40 student chequing accounts. Below are their end-of-the-month balances, in dollars:

$404	74	234	149	279	215	123	55	43	321
87	234	68	489	57	185	141	758	72	863
703	125	350	440	37	252	27	521	302	127
968	712	503	489	327	608	358	425	303	203

  a. Tally the data into a frequency distribution using $100 as a class interval and $0 as the starting point.
  b. Draw a cumulative frequency polygon.
  c. The bank considers any student with an ending balance of $400 or more a "preferred customer." Estimate the percentage of preferred customers.
  d. The bank is also considering a service charge to the lowest 10% of the ending balances. What would you recommend as the cutoff point between those who have to pay a service charge and those who do not?

51. Merrill Lynch recently completed a study of online investment portfolios for a sample of clients. The values of all the investments in thousands of dollars for the 70 participants in the study are listed below:

$669.9	7.5	77.2	7.5	125.7	516.9	219.9	645.2
301.9	235.4	716.4	145.3	26.6	187.2	315.5	89.2
136.4	616.9	440.6	408.2	34.4	296.1	185.4	526.3
380.7	3.3	363.2	51.9	52.2	107.5	82.9	63.0
228.6	308.7	126.7	430.3	82.0	227.0	321.1	403.4
39.5	124.3	118.1	23.9	352.8	156.7	276.3	23.5
31.3	301.2	35.7	154.9	174.3	100.6	236.7	171.9
221.1	43.4	212.3	243.3	315.4	5.9	1002.2	171.7
295.7	437.0	87.8	302.1	268.1	899.5		

  a. Organize the data into a frequency distribution. How many classes would you suggest? What value would you suggest for a class interval?
  b. Draw a histogram. Interpret your result.

52. The following chart summarizes the selling price of homes sold last month:

  a. What is the chart called?
  b. How many homes were sold during the last month?
  c. What is the class interval?
  d. About 75% of the houses sold for less than what amount?
  e. One hundred seventy-five of the homes sold for less than what amount?

53. David Wise handles his own investment portfolio and has done so for many years. Listed below is the holding time (rounded to the whole year) between purchase and sale for his collection of stocks:

8	8	6	11	11	9	8	5	11	4
8	5	14	7	12	8	6	11	9	7
9	15	8	8	12	5	9	8	5	9
10	11	3	9	8	6				

  a. How many classes would you recommend?
  b. What class interval would you suggest?
  c. What would you recommend as the lower limit of the first class?
  d. Organize the data into a frequency distribution.
  e. Comment on the shape of the distribution.

54. Speedy Swift is a package delivery service that serves several urban areas. To maintain customer loyalty, one of Speedy Swift's performance objectives is on-time delivery. To monitor its performance, each delivery is measured on the following scale: early (package delivered before the promised time), on-time (package delivered within 5 minutes of the promised time), late (package delivered more than 5 minutes past the promised time), lost (package never delivered). Speedy Swift has two prime objectives: (1) to deliver 99% of all packages either early or on-time and (2) to never lose a package. Speedy collected the following data for last month's performance:

Performance	Frequency
Early	22
On-time	67
Late	9
Lost	2

a. What scale is used to measure delivery performance? What kind of variable is delivery performance?

b. Construct a relative frequency table for delivery performance last month.

c. Construct a bar chart of the frequency table for delivery performance for last month.

d. Construct a pie chart of on-time delivery performance for last month.

e. Analyze the data, and write a short report of last month's delivery performance as it relates to the company's objectives.

55. The monthly issues of the *Journal of Finance* are available on the Internet. The table below shows the number of times an issue was downloaded over the last 33 months. Suppose that you wish to summarize the number of downloads with a frequency distribution.

312	2753	2595	6057	7624	6624	6362	6575	7760	7085	7272
5967	5256	6160	6238	6709	7193	5631	6490	6682	7829	7091
6871	6230	7253	5507	5676	6974	6915	4999	5689	6143	7086

a. How many classes would you recommend?

b. What class interval would you suggest?

c. What value would you use for the lower limit of the first class?

d. Using your responses to parts (a), (b), and (c), create a frequency distribution.

e. Describe the appearance of the frequency distribution.

56. A recent study of home technologies reported the number of hours of personal computer usage per week for a sample of 60 persons. People who worked out of their home and used the computer as a part of their work were excluded from the study.

9.3	5.3	6.3	8.8	6.5	0.6	5.2	6.6	9.3	4.3
6.3	2.1	2.7	0.4	3.7	3.3	1.1	2.7	6.7	6.5
4.3	9.7	7.7	5.2	1.7	8.5	4.2	5.5	5.1	5.6
5.4	4.8	2.1	10.1	1.3	5.6	2.4	2.4	4.7	1.7
2.0	6.7	1.1	6.7	2.2	2.6	9.8	6.4	4.9	5.2
4.5	9.3	7.9	4.6	4.3	4.5	9.2	8.5	6.0	8.1

a. Organize the data into a frequency distribution. How many classes would you suggest? What value would you suggest for a class interval?

b. Draw a histogram. Interpret your result.

57. A large pharmaceutical company with distribution centres in Canada and the United States has its call centre located in Mississauga, Ontario. There are 20 customer service representatives answering calls from 8 a.m. to 9 p.m. through the week, and from 9 a.m. to 5 p.m. on Saturdays. The call centre reported the number of calls waiting to be answered between the hours of 9 a.m. and 10 a.m. over a 50-day period as shown below. Summarize the data in a chart, and interpret.

47	1	8	46	76	26	4	3	39	45
4	21	80	63	100	65	91	29	7	15
7	52	87	39	106	25	55	2	3	8
14	38	59	33	76	71	37	51	1	24
35	86	185	13	7	43	36	20	79	9

58. The following stem-and-leaf display reports the number of orders received per day by a mail-order firm:

9	1
10	2
11	2 3 5
12	6 9
13	2
14	1 3 5
15	1 2 2 9
16	2 2 6 6 7 7 8
17	0 1 5 9 9
18	0 0 0 1 3 3 4 6 7 9 9
19	0 3 3 4 6
20	4 6 7 9
21	0 1 7 7
22	4 5
23	1 7

    a. How many days were studied?
    b. How many observations are in the fourth class?
    c. What are the smallest and the largest values?
    d. List the actual values in the sixth class.
    e. How many days did the firm receive less than 140 orders?
    f. How many days did the firm receive 200 or more orders?
    g. On how many days did the firm receive 180 orders?
    h. What is the middle value?

59. The following histogram shows the scores on the first statistics exam:

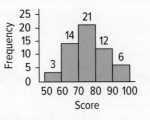

    a. How many students took the exam?
    b. What is the class interval?
    c. What is the class midpoint for the first class?
    d. How many students earned a score of less than 70?

60. The number of families who used the college's day care service was recorded during a 30-day period. The results are as follows:

31	49	19	62	24	45	23	51	55	60
40	35	54	26	57	37	43	65	18	41
50	56	4	54	39	52	35	51	63	42

    a. Construct a less-than cumulative frequency distribution.
    b. Sketch a graph of the less-than cumulative frequency polygon from part (a).
    c. How many days saw fewer than 30 families utilize the day care centre? Fewer than 40?
    d. How busy were the highest 80% of the days?
    e. Construct a more-than cumulative frequency distribution.
    f. Sketch a graph of the more-than cumulative frequency polygon from part (e).
    g. How many days saw more than 20 families utilize the day care centre? More than 50?

61. A social scientist is studying the use of iPods by college students. A sample of 45 students revealed they played the following number of songs yesterday:

4	6	8	7	9	6	3	7	7	6	7	1	4	7	7
4	6	4	10	2	4	6	3	4	6	8	4	3	3	6
8	8	4	6	4	6	5	5	9	6	8	8	6	5	10

Organize the above information into a frequency distribution.
    a. How many classes would you suggest?
    b. What is the most suitable class interval?
    c. What is the lower limit of the first class?
    d. Create the frequency distribution.
    e. Convert the frequency distribution to a less-than cumulative frequency distribution.
    f. Sketch a graph of the less-than cumulative frequency polygon from part (e).
    g. On the basis of the less-than cumulative frequency polygon, about 60% of students played less than what number of songs?
    h. Convert the frequency distribution to a more-than cumulative frequency distribution.
    i. Sketch a graph of the more-than cumulative frequency polygon from part (h).
    j. About 70% of students played more than how many songs?

62.

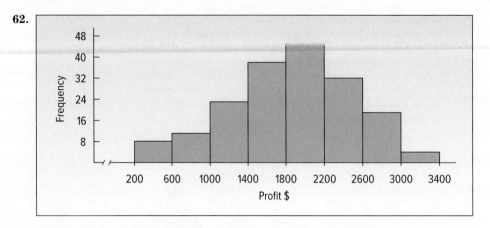

Use the above histogram to answer the following questions:
a. What is the total number of observations?
b. What is the class interval?
c. What is the relative frequency of the third class?
d. What percentage of observations had profits between $2200 and $3000?
e. In a frequency polygon, what would be the coordinates of the fifth class?

63. Bidwell Electronics Inc. recently surveyed a sample of employees to determine how far they lived from corporate headquarters. The results are shown below:

Distance (km)	Number
0 to under 5	4
5 to under 10	15
10 to under 15	27
15 to under 20	18
20 to under 25	6

a. Construct a less-than cumulative frequency distribution.
b. Sketch a graph of the less-than cumulative frequency polygon from part (a).
c. Use the graph in part (b) to estimate the number of employees reside less than 12 kilometres (km) and less than 18 km from the corporate headquarters.
d. Construct a more-than cumulative frequency distribution.
e. Sketch a graph of the more-than cumulative frequency polygon from part (d).
f. Estimate the percentage of employees who reside more than 17 km from the corporate headquarters.

Data Set Exercises

Questions marked with have data sets available on McGraw-Hill's online resource for *Basic Statistics*.

64. Refer to the Real Estate Data—Rockland Area online, which reports information on home listings.
  a. Select an appropriate class interval and organize the list prices into a frequency distribution.
    1. Around what values do the data tend to cluster?
    2. What is the largest list price? What is the smallest list price?
  b. Construct a histogram.
    1. Around what values do the data tend to cluster?
    2. What is the largest list price? What is the smallest list price?
  c. Draw less-than cumulative frequency polygon based on the frequency distribution developed in part (a).
    1. How many homes listed for less than $250 000?
    2. What percentage of the homes listed for less than $425 000?
  d. Develop a stem-and-leaf chart for the list price.
    1. Around what value are the list prices clustered?
    2. What is the smallest value? What is the largest value?

65. Refer to the Real Estate Data—Halifax Area online, which reports information on home listings.
   a. Organize the information on the total square feet into a frequency distribution. Select an appropriate class interval.
      1. What is a typical size? What is the range of square footage?
      2. Comment on the shape of the values. Does it appear that any of the square footages are out of line with the others?
   b. Draw a less-than and more-than cumulative frequency polygon based on the frequency distributions developed in part (a).
      1. Forty percent of the sizes are less than what square footage?
      2. About how many houses have a total area of less than 2000 square feet?
      3. What percentage of homes are greater than 1000 square feet?
   c. Develop a stem-and-leaf chart for the list price.
      1. Around what value are the list prices clustered?
      2. What is the smallest value? What is the largest value?
      3. Summarize the results in a brief report.
   d. Develop a stem-and-leaf chart for the total square feet.
      1. Around what value are the numbers of square feet clustered?
      2. What is the smallest value? What is the largest value?
      3. Summarize the results in a brief report.

Case

Rob Whitner is the owner of Whitner Autoplex. Rob's father founded the dealership in 1964, and for more than 30 years, they sold exclusively Pontiacs. In the early 1990s, Rob's father's health began to fail, and Rob took over more of the day-to-day operation of the dealership. At this same time, the automobile business began to change—dealers began to sell vehicles from several manufacturers—and Rob was faced with some major decisions. The first came when another local dealer, who handles Volvos, Saabs, and Volkswagens, approached Rob about purchasing his dealership. More recently, the local Chrysler dealership got into difficulty and Rob bought them out. So, now, on the same lot, Rob sells the complete line of Pontiacs, the expensive Volvos, Saabs, Volkswagens, and the Chrysler products, including the popular Jeep line. Whitner Pontiac employs 83, including 23 full-time salespeople. Because of the diverse product line, there is considerable variation in the selling price of the vehicles. A top-of-the-line Volvo sells for more than twice the price of a Pontiac Grand Am. Rob would like you to develop some tables and charts that he could review monthly and would like you to report where the selling prices tend to cluster, where the variation is in the selling prices, and to note any trends. The data are on Connect, Data Sets, and Whitner Autoplex.

Practice Test

Part I Objective

1. A grouping of qualitative data into mutually exclusive classes showing the number of observations in each class is known as a _____.

2. A grouping of quantitative data into mutually exclusive classes showing the number of observations in each class is known as a _____.

3. A graph in which the classes for qualitative data are reported on the horizontal axis and the class frequencies (proportional to the heights of the bars) on the vertical axis is called _____.

4. A _____ chart shows the proportion or percentage that each class represents of the total.

5. A graph in which the classes of a quantitative data set are marked on the horizontal axis and the class frequencies on the vertical axis is called a _____.

6. A set of data contained 70 observations. How many classes would you suggest to construct a frequency distribution? _____

7. The distance between successive lower class limits is called the _____.

8. The average of the respective class limits of two consecutive classes is the _____.

9. In a relative frequency distribution, the class frequencies are divided by _____.

10. A cumulative frequency polygon is created by line segments connecting the _____ and the corresponding cumulative frequencies.

Part II Problems

Consider these data on the selling prices of the latest model of cell phones in a local convenience store.

Selling Price			Frequency
$120 to under	$150		4
150 to under	180		18
180 to under	210		30
210 to under	240		20
240 to under	270		17
270 to under	300		10
300 to under	330		6

  a. How large is the class interval?
  b. What was the total number sold?
  c. How many cell phones sold for less than $210?
  d. What is the relative frequency for the "$210 up to 240" class?
  e. What is the midpoint of the "$150 up to 180" class?
  f. What were the maximum and minimum selling prices?
  g. Construct a histogram of these data.
  h. Make a frequency polygon of these data.

Computer Commands

1. Excel steps to create the bar chart are as follows:

  a. Open **Excel** and from McGraw-Hill's online resource select **Data Files**, and select **Table 2–1**.

  b. In cell *J3*, enter the label *Dwelling Type*. In cells *J4:J8*, enter the labels *Apartment, Clubhouse, House, Studio* and *Townhouse*. In cell *K3*, enter the label *Number of Listings*. In cells *K4:K8*, enter 37, 9, 16, 5 and 18. Select the range *J3:K8*.

  c. From the toolbar, Select **Charts**, and **Clustered Column**.

  d. Click the chart title and vertical axis to edit if required.

Note: the **Excel** chart type **Bar** will create a horizontal bar chart.

2. Excel steps to create the pie chart are as follows:

  a. Open **Excel** and from McGraw-Hill's online resource select **Data Files**, and select Table 2–3. Select the range *A3-B8*.

  b. From the toolbar, select **Charts**, and a pie chart subtype. Click the Chart Title to edit as required.

  c. To add the percentages and/or labels, right click any section of the pie, and click **Format Data Series** and **Data Labels**.

3. MegaStat steps to create the frequency distribution are as follows:

  a. Open **Excel** and from McGraw-Hill's online resource select **Data Files** and select **Table 2–4**.

  b. Click **MegaStat**, **Frequency Distributions**, and select **Quantitative**.

  c. In the dialog box, input the data range from *A2:A87*, select **Equal width intervals**, use *300000* as the interval width and *0* as the lower boundary of the first

interval. Remove the check mark in the histogram box, and click **OK**.

  d. The frequency distribution will appear on the **Output** sheet.

4. MegaStat steps to create the histogram are as follows:

  a. Open **Excel** and from McGraw-Hill's online resource select **Data Files** and select **Table 2–4**.

  b. Click **MegaStat**, **Frequency Distribution**, and select **Quantitative**.

  c. In the dialog box, input the data range from *A2:A87*, select **Equal width intervals**, use *300000* as the interval width and *0* as the lower boundary of the first interval.

  d. The check mark beside **Histogram** is the default. Click **OK**. The histogram will appear on the **Output** sheet.

  e. Note that MegaStat creates the histogram using percentages. To change to frequencies, right click inside the plot area of the histogram. Click **Select Data**. In the **Chart data range** box, select the *frequency* range, and click **OK**.

  f. Edit the titles as required.

5. MegaStat steps to create the frequency polygon are as follows:

  a. Open **Excel** and from McGraw-Hill's online resource select **Data Files** and select **Table 2–4**.

  b. Click **MegaStat**, **Frequency Distributions**, and select **Quantitative**.

  c. In the dialog box, input the data range from *A2:A87*, select **Equal width intervals**, use *60000* as the interval width and *120000* as the lower boundary of the first interval.

d. Check the box beside **Polygon**, and click **OK**. The frequency polygon will appear on the **Output** sheet.

e. Note that MegaStat creates the frequency polygon using percentages. To change to frequencies, right click inside the plot area of the chart. Click **Select Data**. In the **Chart data range** box, select the *frequency* range, and **OK**.

f. Edit the titles as required.

6. MegaStat steps to create the cumulative frequency diagram (less-than) are as follows:

    a. Open **Excel** and from McGraw-Hill's online resource select **Data Files** and select **Table 2–4**.

    b. Click **MegaStat, Frequency Distributions**, and select **Quantitative**.

    c. In the dialog box, input the data range from *A2:A87*, select **Equal width intervals**, use *60000* as the interval width, *120000* as the lower boundary of the first interval.

    d. Check mark beside **Ogive**, and click **OK**. The less-than ogive will appear on the **Output** sheet.

    e. Note that MegaStat creates a less-than ogive using cumulative percentages. To change to cumulative frequencies, select a data point, and right click inside the plot area of the ogive, Click **Select Data**. In the **Chart data range** box, select the *cumulative frequency* range, and click **OK**.

    f. Edit the titles as required.

7. MegaStat steps to create the cumulative frequency diagram (more-than) are as follows:

    a. Open **Excel** and from McGraw-Hill's online resource select **Data Files** and select **Table 2–4**.

    b. Click **MegaStat**, **Frequency Distributions**, and select **Quantitative**.

    c. In the dialog box, input the data range from *A2:A87*, select **Equal width intervals**, use *60000* as the interval width, *120000* as the lower boundary of the first interval.

    d. Check mark beside **Ogive**, and click **OK**. The less-than ogive will appear on the **Output** sheet.

    e. Note that MegaStat creates a less-than ogive using cumulative percentages. To change to a more-than cumulative diagram, change the values in the cumulative frequency column to more-than cumulative frequencies. Right click inside the plot area of the ogive. Click **Select Data**. In the **Chart data range** box, select the *cumulative frequency* range that you entered, and click **OK**.

    f. Edit the titles.

8. MegaStat steps to create the stem-and-leaf chart are as follows:

    a. Open **Excel** and from McGraw-Hill's online resource select **Data Files** and select **Table 2–11**.

    b. Click **MegaStat**, **Descriptive Statistics**, and select **Stem and Leaf Plot**. In the dialog box, enter the data range and select **OK**. The stem-and-leaf plot will appear on the **Output** sheet.

Pivot Tables

1. The Excel commands to use the PivotTable Wizard to create a frequency table, bar chart, and pie chart for the Orleans Real Estate data are as follows:

    a. Open **Excel**, and from McGraw-Hill's online resource select **Data Sets** and **Pivot Table Data—Orleans**.

    b. Click on a cell somewhere in the data set, such as cell *C6*.

    c. Click on the **INSERT** menu on the toolbar. Then click **PivotChart**.

    d. The following screen will appear:

The "*Select a table or range*," should appear as above, or select the data range as shown in the *Table/Range* row. Next, select "*Existing Worksheet*" and enter a cell location, such a *B76* and click **OK**.

    e. On the right-hand side of the spreadsheet, a *Pivot-Chart Fields* list will appear with a list of the data set variables. To summarize the "Type" variable, select the "Type" variable and it will appear in the lower left box called "AXIS (CATEGORY)". You will note that the frequency table is started in cell *B76* with the rows labelled with the values of the variable "Type." Next, return to the top box, and select and drag the "Type" variable to the "Σ VALUES" box. A bar chart will be created and a column of frequencies will be added to the table. Note that you can format the chart or table as needed.

    f. To edit size of the space between the bars, right click any bar and select "*Format Data Series*." Select "*Series Options*" and change the "*Gap Width*".

    g. To create the pie chart, the frequencies should be converted to relative frequencies. Click in the body of the PivotTable and the *PivotTable Fields* list will appear to the right. In the "Σ Values" box, click on the pull-down menu for "Count of Type" and select the *Value Fields Settings* option. You will see a number of different selections that can be used to summarize the variables in a PivotTable. Click on the tab "*Show Values As*" and, in the pull-down menu, select "*% of Grand Total*." Click **OK**. The frequencies will be converted to percentages.

To create the pie chart, select any cell in the Pivot-Table. Next, select the **INSERT** menu from the toolbar, and within the *Charts* group, select a pie chart from the *Insert Pie* drop-down menu. A pie chart appears. Click on the chart heading and label the chart as needed. To add the percentages, right click on the pie chart and a menu will appear. Click on "**Add Data Labels**."

2. The Excel commands to use the PivotChart Wizard to create frequency and relative frequency distributions for the Orleans Real Estate data are as follows:

a. Open **Excel**, and from McGraw-Hill's online resource select **Data Sets** and **Pivot Table Data—Orleans**.

b. Click on a cell somewhere in the data set, such as cell *C6*.

c. Click on the **INSERT** menu on the toolbar. Then click on **PivotChart**.

d. A screen will appear with a data range selected. Click on "*Select a table or range*," to edit the data range if required. Next, click on "*New Worksheet*" and click **OK**.

e. On the right-hand side of the spreadsheet, a *PivotTable Fields* list will appear with a list of the data set variables. To summarize the "List Price" variable, select the "List Price" variable, and drag it to the "AXIS CATEGORY" box. Then return to the top box, click on "List Price" again, and drag it to the "Σ VALUES" box. Staying in this box, click on the pull-down menu, and select the *Value Field Settings* option. You will see a number of different selections that can be used to summarize the variables in a PivotTable. In the "*Summarize Values By*" tab, select "Count" to create frequencies for the variable "List Price." Click **OK**. A PivotTable with frequencies will appear in the new worksheet.

f. In the PivotTable, the left column shows each value of the variable "List Price." We want to organize the frequency distribution with seven classes, starting at $120 000 and ending at $540 000 with a class interval of $60 000. To create classes for "List Price," select any cell in the column, and right click. A menu appears. Select "Group" from the menu to create the classes. First, uncheck both boxes. Then, in the dialogue box, enter the lower limit of the first class as the "Starting at" value. For the Orleans data, the value is 120000. Enter the upper limit of the last class as the "Ending at" value. For the Orleans data, the value is 540000. Then enter the class interval as the "By" value. For the Orleans data, the value is 60000. Click **OK**. A frequency distribution appears along with a bar chart. To eliminate the space between the bars, right click any bar and select "*Format Data Series*." Select "*Series Options*" and change the "*Gap Width*" to 0%.

g. To create a relative frequency distribution, point and click on one of the cells in the PivotTable, and the "PivotTable *Fields* list" appears to the right. Click and drag the variable "List Price" to the "Σ VALUES" box. A second "Count of List Price" appears. In the "Σ VALUES," click on the second "Count of List Price," and select the "Value Fields Setting." You will see a number of different selections that can be used to summarize the variables in a PivotTable. Click on the tab "*Show Values As*," and, in the pull-down menu, select "*% of Grand Total*." Click **OK**. The percentages will be added to the table. You can format the table by relabelling the column headings such as "Frequency" and "Percentages."

h. To add data labels to the histogram, select the histogram, right click, and select "**Add Data Labels**." Relabel the chart and axes as needed.

Answers to Self-Reviews

2–1

Flavour	Number	Relative Frequencies
Vanilla	40	0.40
Cherry	25	0.25
Lemon	20	0.20
Orange	15	0.15
Total	100	1.00

(a) Qualitative data, because the customers' response to the taste test is the flavour that they prefer.

(b) Frequency table. It shows the number of people who prefer each flavour.

(c)

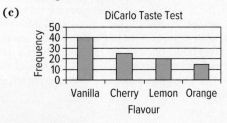

(d)

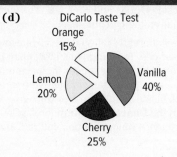

2–2 (a) The raw data.

(b)

Commission ($)		Number of Salespeople
$1400 up to	$1500	2
1500 up to	1600	5
1600 up to	1700	3
1700 up to	1800	1
Total		11

(c) Class frequencies.

(d) The largest concentration of commissions is $1500 up to $1600. The smallest commission is about $1400, and the largest is about $1800.

2–3 (a) $2^6 = 64 < 73 < 128 = 2^7$. So, 7 classes are recommended.

(b) The interval width should be at least $(300 - 48.50)/7 = 35.93$. Class intervals of 35 or 40 are reasonable.

(c) A class interval of 40, starting with $40, would require 7 classes.

2–4 (a) 8

(b) **12.94%**, found by: $(11/85) \times 100$

(c) **14.12%**, found by: $(12/85) \times 100$

2–5 (a)

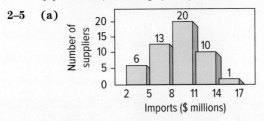

(b)

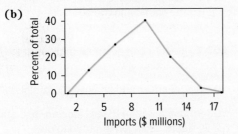

The points are: (3.5, 12), (6.5, 26), (9.5, 40), (12.5, 20), and (15.5, 2).

(c) The smallest annual sales volume of imports by a supplier is about $2 million, the highest about $17 million. The concentration is between $8 million and $11 million.

2–6 (a) Both a pie chart and a bar chart are useful in presenting quantitative data. However, a bar chart depicts frequencies, whereas a pie chart depicts relative frequencies (proportion of the whole).

(b) In both a bar chart and a histogram the height of the bar is proportional to the class frequencies. However, a bar chart is used to depict qualitative data and so, there is a distance or gap between the bars. A histogram is used to depict data; hence, the bars are drawn adjacent to each other to show the continuous nature of the data, so there is no gap or space between the bars.

2–7 (a) A frequency distribution.

(b)

Hourly Wages ($)	Less-than Cumulative Number	More-than Cumulative Number
$6 to under $8	3	15
8 to under 10	10	12
10 to under 12	14	5
12 to under 14	15	1
Total		

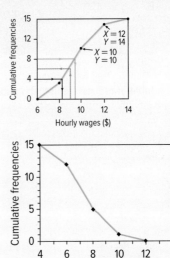

(c) About seven employees earn $9.00 or less. About half the employees earn $7.25 or more. About four employees earn $8.25 or less.

2–8

7	7
8	0 0 1 3 4 8 8
9	1 2 5 6 6 8 9
10	1 2 4 8
11	2 6

(a) 8
(b) 10.1, 10.2, 10.4, 10.8
(c) 9.5
(d) 7.7, 11.6

CHAPTER 3
Describing Data: Numerical Measures

Rachel Dewis/Getty Images

The housing market in Canada has been steadily increasing in recent years. Given a table of real estate listings, find the mean, median, and standard deviation of the list prices. (Exercise 119, LO3-1)

LEARNING OBJECTIVES

When you have completed this chapter, you will be able to:

LO3-1 Compute and interpret the mean, the median, and the mode.

LO3-2 Identify and compute a weighted mean.

LO3-3 Compute and interpret the geometric mean.

LO3-4 Compute and interpret the range, mean deviation, variance, and standard deviation.

LO3-5 Explain and apply Chebyshev's theorem and the Empirical Rule.

LO3-6 Compute and interpret the coefficient of skewness and the coefficient of variation.

LO3-7 Identify and compute measures of position.

LO3-8 Construct and analyze a box plot.

LO3-9 Compute the mean, median, and standard deviation of grouped data.

3.1 INTRODUCTION

Chapter 2 began our study of descriptive statistics. To summarize raw data into a meaningful form, we organized qualitative data into a frequency table and portrayed the results in a bar chart. In a similar way, we organized quantitative data into a frequency distribution and portrayed the results in a histogram. We also looked at other graphical techniques, such as pie charts to portray qualitative data and frequency polygons to portray quantitative data.

This chapter is concerned with two numerical ways of describing data, namely, **measures of location** and **measures of dispersion**. Measures of location are often referred to as *averages*. The purpose of a measure of location is to pinpoint the centre of a distribution of data. An average is a measure of location that shows the central value of the data. Averages appear daily on TV, on various websites, in the newspaper and in other journals. Here are some examples:

- The average amount of television watched by college-aged students.
- The average grade point average (GPA) required to be accepted at a college or university in Alberta.
- The average house price in Canada was $559 317 in April 2017 and $506 596 in April 2016 (crea.ca).

- The average weekly earnings in Canada in 2015 was $868.41 (www.statcan.gc.ca/tables-tableaux/sum-som/l01/cst01/health23-eng.htm).
- The average rainfall in Vancouver, British Columbia, is the lowest in July at 36.1 millimetres (mm) and the highest in November at 167.2 mm.

If we consider only the measures of location in a set of data, or if we compare several sets of data using central values, we may draw an erroneous conclusion. In addition to measures of location we should consider the **dispersion**—often called the *variation* or the *spread*—in the data. As an illustration, suppose the average annual income of executives for Internet-related companies is $80 000, and the average income for executives in pharmaceutical firms is also $80 000. If we looked only at the average incomes, we might wrongly conclude that the two salary distributions are the same. However, we need to examine the dispersion or spread of the distributions of salary. A look at the salary ranges indicates that this conclusion of equal distributions is not correct. The salaries for the executives in Internet-related firms range from $70 000 to $90 000, but salaries for the marketing executives in the pharmaceutical industry range from $40 000 to $120 000. Thus, we conclude that although the average salaries are the same for the two industries, there is much more spread or dispersion in salaries for the pharmaceutical executives. To describe the dispersion, we will consider the range, the mean deviation, the variance, and the standard deviation.

We begin by discussing measures of location. There is not just one measure of location; in fact, there are many. We will consider five: the arithmetic mean, the weighted mean, the median, the mode, and the geometric mean. The arithmetic mean is the most widely used and widely reported measure of location. We study the mean as both a population parameter and a sample statistic.

LO3-1 3.2 THE POPULATION MEAN

Many studies involve all the values in a population. For example, there are 12 sales associates employed at the Reynolds Road Carpet outlet. The mean amount of commission they earned last month was $2345. This is a population value because we consider the commissions of *all* the sales associates. Other examples of a population mean would be:

- The average house price in Calgary Alta. was $475 516 in April 2017.
- Caryn Tirsch's website on organic gardening had an average of 96.4 hits per day during the month of March last year compared to December where there were only 28.7 hits per day.
- The average number of hours of overtime worked last week by the six welders in the welding department of Butts Welding Inc. is 6.45 hours.

For raw data, that is, data that have not been grouped in a frequency distribution, the population mean is the sum of all the values in the population divided by the number of values in the population. To find the population mean, we use the following formula:

$$\text{Population mean} = \frac{\text{Sum of all the values in the population}}{\text{Number of values in the population}}$$

Instead of writing out in words the full directions for computing the population mean (or any other measure), it is more convenient to use the shorthand symbols of mathematics. The mean of a population using mathematical symbols is:

POPULATION MEAN	$\mu = \dfrac{\Sigma x}{N}$	[3–1]

where:

μ represents the population mean. It is the Greek lowercase letter "mu."

N is the number of items in the population.

x represents any particular value.

Σ is the Greek capital letter "sigma" and indicates the operation of adding.

Σx is the sum of the x values in the population.

Statistics in Action

The median age of a Canadian in July 2013 was 40.2 years. The median age for men was 39.4 years and for women, 41.1 years. The average hourly wage as of January 2013 was $24.03. The average number of persons per private household was 2.5 in 2011 compared with 3.5 in 1971. The average Canadian woman is 163 centimetres (cm) tall and weighs 65.8 kilograms (kg). The average Canadian man is 178 cm tall, and weighs 83.2 kg. The average age at which Canadian women marry for the first time is 28, and for a Canadian man, it is 30. The average Canadian couple will have 1.7 children. The average life expectancy of a Canadian male in 1951 was 66 years, whereas that of a female was 71 years. The average life expectancy for both males and females born in 2002 has increased by 11 years (Statistics Canada, www.statcan.gc.ca/).

Any measurable characteristic of a population is called a **parameter**. The mean of a population is a parameter.

Example	There are eight teams in the Eastern Atlantic Division of the NHL. Listed below is the number of points earned by each team in the 2015–2016 regular season (nhl.com).

Team	Points
Florida	103
Tampa Bay	97
Detroit	93
Boston	93
Ottawa	85
Montreal	82
Buffalo	81
Toronto	69

Is this a sample or a population? What is the arithmetic mean number of points earned?

Solution

This is a population if the researcher is considering only the teams in the Eastern Atlantic Division; otherwise, it is a sample. We add the number of points for each of the eight teams. The total number of points for the five teams is 703. To find the arithmetic mean, we divide this total by 8. Therefore, the arithmetic mean is 87.9, found by 703/8. Using formula (3–1):

$$\mu = \frac{103 + 97 + 93 + 93 + 85 + 82 + 81 + 69}{8} = \frac{703}{8} = 87.9$$

How do we interpret the value of 87.9? The typical number of points earned by a team in the Eastern Atlantic Division during the season was 87.9.

LO3-1 3.3 THE SAMPLE MEAN

As explained in Chapter 1, we often select a sample from a population to find something about a specific characteristic of the population. Smucker's quality control department, for example, needs to be assured that the amount of raspberry jam in the jar labelled as containing 310 mL actually contains that amount. It would be very expensive and time consuming to check every jar. Therefore, a sample of 20 jars is selected from the production line and the mean of the sample is determined, and that value is used to to estimate the amount in each jar.

For raw data, that is, ungrouped data, *the mean is the sum of all the sampled values divided by the total number of sampled values*. To find the mean for a sample:

$$\text{Sample mean} = \frac{\text{Sum of all the values in the sample}}{\text{Number of values in the sample}}$$

The mean of a sample and the mean of a population are computed in the same way, but the shorthand notation used is different. The formula for the mean of a *sample* is:

SAMPLE MEAN	$\bar{x} = \dfrac{\Sigma x}{n}$	[3–2]

where:
  $\bar{x}$ is the sample mean. It is read "x bar."
  n is the number in the sample.
  x represents any particular value.
  Σ is the Greek capital letter "sigma" and indicates the operation of adding.
  Σx is the sum of the x values in the sample.

Statistic A characteristic of a sample.

The mean of a sample, or any other measure based on sample data, is called a **statistic**. If the mean weight of the 20 jars of raspberry jam is 315 mL, this is an example of a statistic.

| **Example** | A leading communications company is studying the number of minutes used by clients in a particular cell phone rate plan. A random sample of 12 clients showed the following number of minutes used last month: |

| 90 | 77 | 94 | 89 | 119 | 112 |
| 91 | 110 | 92 | 100 | 113 | 83 |

What is the arithmetic mean number of minutes used?

| **Solution** | Using formula (3–2), the sample mean is: |

$$\text{Sample mean} = \frac{\text{Sum of all the values in the sample}}{\text{Number of values in the sample}}$$

$$\bar{x} = \frac{\sum x}{n} = \frac{90 + 77 + \cdots + 83}{12} = \frac{1170}{12} = 97.5$$

The arithmetic mean of the number of minutes used last month by the sample of cell phone users is 97.5 minutes.

excel

Computer commands to find the mean and to find descriptive statistics can be found at the end of the chapter.

Statistics in Action

Most colleges report the "average class size." This information can be misleading because average class size can be found in several ways. If we find the number of students *in each class* at a particular school, the result is the mean number of students per class. If we compiled a list of the class sizes for each student and find the mean class size, we might find the mean to be quite different. One school found the mean number of students in each of its 747 classes to be 40. But when it found the mean from a list of the class sizes of each student, it was 47. Why the disparity? Because there are fewer students in the small classes and a larger number of students in the larger class, which has the effect of increasing the mean class size when it is calculated this way.

3.4 THE PROPERTIES OF THE ARITHMETIC MEAN

The arithmetic mean is a widely used measure of central location or tendency. It has several important properties:

1. **To compute the mean, the data must be measured at the interval or ratio level.** Recall from Chapter 1 that ratio-level data include such data as ages, incomes, and weights, with the distance between numbers being constant.
2. **All the values are included in computing the mean.**
3. **The mean is unique.** That is, there is only one mean in a set of data. Later in the chapter, we will discover a measure of location that might appear twice, or more than twice in a set of data.
4. **The sum of the deviations of each value from the mean is zero.** Expressed symbolically:

$$\sum(x - \bar{x}) = 0$$

As an example, the mean of 3, 8, and 4 is 5. Then:

$$\sum(x - \bar{x}) = (3 - 5) + (8 - 5) + (4 - 5)$$
$$= -2 + 3 - 1$$
$$= 0$$

   Thus, we can consider the mean as a balance point for a set of data. To illustrate, we have a long board with the numbers 1, 2, 3, . . . , 9 evenly spaced on it. Suppose three bars of equal weight were placed on the board at numbers 3, 4, and 8, and the balance point was set at 5, the mean of the three numbers. We would find that the board balanced perfectly! The deviations below the mean (−3) are equal to the deviations above the mean (+3). Shown schematically:

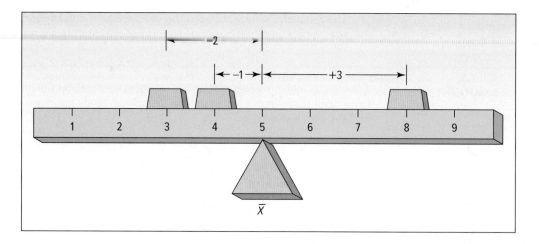

The mean does have a weakness. Recall that the mean uses the value of every item in a sample, or population, in its computation. If one or two of these values are either extremely large or extremely small, compared with the majority of the data, **the mean might not be an appropriate average to represent the data.** For example, suppose the annual incomes of a sample of real estate agents are $62 900, $61 600, $62 500, $60 800, and $1 200 000. The mean income is $289 560. Obviously, it is not representative of this group because all agents but one have an income in the $60 000 to $63 000 range. One income ($1.2 million) unduly affects the mean. It would be referred to as an *extreme value* or an *outlier*.

self-review 3–1

1. The annual incomes of a sample of middle-management employees at Costco are: $62 900, $69 100, $58 300, and $76 800.

   (a) Find the sample mean.
   (b) Is the mean you computed in (a) a statistic or a parameter? Why?
   (c) What is your best estimate of the population mean?

2. All the students in advanced Computer Science 411 are considered the population. Their course grades are 92, 96, 61, 86, 79, and 84.

   (a) Compute the mean course grade.
   (b) Is the mean you computed in (a) a statistic or a parameter? Why?

EXERCISES

The answers to the odd-numbered exercises are in Appendix A.1.

1. Compute the mean of the following population values: 6, 3, 5, 7, 6.
2. Compute the mean of the following population values: 7, 5, 7, 3, 7, 4.
3. **a.** Compute the mean of the following sample values: 5, 9, 4, 10.
   b. Show that $\sum (x - \bar{x}) = 0$
4. **a.** Compute the mean of the following sample values: 1.3, 7.0, 3.6, 4.1, 5.0.
   b. Show that $\sum (x - \bar{x}) = 0$
5. Compute the mean of the following sample values: 16.25, 12.91, 14.58.
6. Compute the mean hourly wage paid to carpenters who earned the following wages: $15.40, $20.10, $18.75, $22.76, $30.67, $18.00.

For Exercises 7–10, (a) compute the arithmetic mean and (b) indicate whether it is a statistic or a parameter.

7. There are 10 salespeople employed by Midtown Ford. The number of new cars sold last month by the respective salespeople was: 15, 23, 4, 19, 18, 10, 10, 8, 28, 19.
8. The accounting department at a mail-order company counted the following number of incoming calls per day to the company's toll-free number during the first seven days in May: 14, 24, 19, 31, 36, 26, 17.

9. The Cambridge Power and Light Company selected 20 residential customers at random. Following are the amounts, to the nearest dollar, the customers were charged for electrical service last month:

$54	48	58	50	25	47	75	46	60	70
67	68	39	35	56	66	33	62	65	67

10. The Human Resources Director at DuPont began a study of the overtime hours in the Inspection Department. A sample of 15 workers was selected at random, and records showed they worked the following number of overtime hours last month:

13	13	12	15	7	15	5	12
6	7	12	10	9	13	12	

11. AAA Heating and Air Conditioning completed 30 jobs last month with a mean revenue of $5430 per job. The president wants to know the total revenue for the month. On the basis of the limited information, can you compute the total revenue? What is it?

12. A pharmaceutical company hires business administration graduates to sell its products. The company is growing rapidly and dedicates only one day of sales training for new salespeople. The company's goal for new salespeople is $10 000 in sales per month. The goal is based on the current mean sales for the entire company, which is $10 000 per month. After reviewing the retention rates of new employees, the company finds that only 1 in 10 new employees stays longer than three months. Comment on using the current mean sales per month as a sales goal for new employees. Why do new employees leave the company?

LO3-2 3.5 THE WEIGHTED MEAN

The weighted mean is a convenient way to compute the arithmetic mean when there are several observations of the same value. To explain, suppose the nearby College Restaurant sold medium, large, and Biggie-sized soft drinks for $1.19, $1.29, and $1.59, respectively. Of the last 10 drinks sold, 2 were medium, 2 were large, and 6 were Biggie-sized. To find the mean price of the last 10 drinks sold, we could use formula (3–2).

$$\bar{x} = \frac{\$1.19 + \$1.19 + \$1.29 + \$1.29 + \$1.59 + \$1.59 + \$1.59 + \$1.59 + \$1.59 + \$1.59}{10}$$

$$= \frac{\$14.50}{10} = \$1.45$$

The mean selling price of the last 10 drinks is $1.45.

An easier way to find the mean selling price is to determine the weighted mean. That is, we multiply each observation by the number of times it happens. We will refer to the weighted mean as $\bar{x}_w$. This is read "x bar sub w."

$$\bar{x}_w = \frac{2(\$1.19) + 2(\$1.29) + 6(\$1.59)}{10}$$

$$= \frac{\$14.50}{10} = \$1.45$$

In this case, the weights are frequency counts. However, any measure of importance could be used as a weight.

In general, the weighted mean of a set of numbers designated $x_1, x_2, x_3, \ldots, x_n$, with the corresponding weights $w_1, w_2, w_3, \ldots, w_n$, is computed by:

WEIGHTED MEAN	$\bar{x}_w = \dfrac{w_1 x_1 + w_2 x_2 + w_3 x_3 + \cdots + w_n x_n}{w_1 + w_2 + w_3 + \cdots + w_n}$	[3–3]

This may be shortened to:

$$\bar{x}_w = \frac{\sum(wx)}{\sum w}$$

Note that the denominator of a weighted mean is always the sum of the weights.

Example	Professor Hunking just marked a quiz for his finance class. The grades follow. What is the mean grade on the quiz?

Grade on Quiz	4	5	6	7	8	9	10
Number of Students	1	2	7	7	9	10	6

Solution

To find the mean grade, we multiply each of the grades by the number of students earning that grade. Using formula (3–3), the mean grade is:

$$\bar{x}_w = \frac{1(4) + 2(5) + 7(6) + 7(7) + 9(8) + 10(9) + 6(10)}{42}$$

$$= \frac{327}{42} = 7.786$$

The weighted mean grade is rounded to 7.8.

---

self-review 3–2

Springers sold 95 Antonelli men's suits for the regular price of $400. For the spring sale the suits were reduced to $200 and 126 were sold. At the final clearance, the price was reduced to $100, and the remaining 79 suits were sold.

(a) What was the weighted mean price of an Antonelli suit?
(b) Springers paid $200 a suit for the 300 suits. Comment on the store's profit per suit if a sales-person receives a $25 commission for each one sold.

EXERCISES

13. In June, an investor purchased 300 shares of Oracle stock (an information technology company) at $20 per share. In August, she purchased an additional 400 shares at $25 per share. In November, she purchased an additional 400 shares, but the stock declined to $23 per share. What is the weighted mean price per share?

14. The Bookstall Inc. is a specialty bookstore concentrating on used books sold via the Internet. Paperbacks are $1 each, and hardcover books are $3.50. Of the 50 books sold last Tuesday morning, 40 were paperback, and the rest were hardcover. What was the weighted mean price of a book?

15. The Loris Healthcare System employs 200 persons on the nursing staff. Fifty are nurse's aides, 50 are practical nurses, and 100 are registered nurses. Nurse's aides receive $16 per hour, practical nurses $20 per hour, and registered nurses $28 per hour. What is the weighted mean hourly wage?

16. Andrews and Associates specialize in corporate law. They charge $100 per hour for research-ing a case, $75 per hour for consultations, and $200 per hour for writing a brief. Last week, one of the associates spent 10 hours consulting with her client, 10 hours researching the case, and 20 hours writing the brief. What was the weighted mean hourly charge for her legal services?

LO3-1   3.6 THE MEDIAN

Median The midpoint of the values after they have been ordered from the min-imum to the maximum, or the maximum to the minimum.

We have stressed that for data containing one or two very large or very small values, the arithme-tic mean may not be representative. The centre for such data can be better described using a measure of location called the **median**.

To illustrate the need for a measure of central location other than the arithmetic mean, suppose that you are seeking to buy a condominium in St. John's, Newfoundland. Your real estate agent says that the typical price of the units currently available is $210 000. Would you

Statistics in Action

One way to measure a goalie's success is his or her GAA (goals against average). For example, in the 2015–2016 regular hockey season, Henrik Lundqvist of the New York Rangers had a GAA of 2.48. The goals against average is calculated by taking the number of goals against, dividing it by the number of minutes played, and then multiplying the result by 60 (60 minutes is the length of three periods played in a hockey game). What this average does not consider is the team playing against the goalie and how many shots the opposition takes. So, perhaps a better measure of a goalie's success is the save percentage. Henrik Lundqvist's save percentage in the same season was 0.920. This means that if he faced 1000 shots, he would save 920 of them (nhl.com).

still want to look? If you had budgeted your maximum purchase price at $190 000, you might think they are out of your price range. However, checking the individual prices of the units might change your mind. They are $160 000, $165 000, $170 000, $180 000, and a deluxe penthouse costs $375 000. The arithmetic mean price is $210 000, as the real estate agent reported, but one price ($375 000) is pulling the arithmetic mean upward, causing it to be an unrepresentative average. It does seem that a price around $170 000 is a more typical or representative average, and it is. In such cases, the median provides a more valid measure of location.

The median price of the units available is $170 000. To determine this, we order the prices from minimum value ($160 000) to maximum value ($375 000) and select the middle value ($170 000). For the median, the data must be at least an ordinal level of measurement.

Prices Ordered from Low to High ($)		Prices Ordered from High to Low ($)
$160 000		$375 000
165 000		180 000
170 000	← Median →	170 000
180 000		165 000
375 000		160 000

Note that there are the same number of prices below the median of $170 000 as above it. **The median is, therefore, unaffected by extremely low or high prices**. Had the highest price been $190 000, or $300 000, or even $1 million, the median price would still be $170 000. Likewise, had the lowest price been $20 000 or $50 000, the median price would still be $170 000.

In the previous illustration, there is an *odd* number of observations (five). How is the median determined for an *even* number of observations? As before, the observations are ordered. Then we calculate the mean of the two middle observations. So, for an even number of observations, the median may not be one of the given values.

Example

The average list house price for a selection of Canadian locations in June 2016 is listed in the following table. Find the median list price.

Location	Price ($)
Yukon	$ 351 768
Vancouver	1 026 207
Calgary	466 717
Saskatoon	334 529
Ottawa	378 389
Montreal	353 535
Halifax	290 421
Saint John	179 633

Solution

Note that the number of list prices is even (eight). As before, the list prices are first ordered from low to high. Then the two middle list prices are identified. The arithmetic mean of the two middle observations gives us the median list price. Arranging from low to high:

Location	Price ($)
Saint John	$ 179 000
Halifax	290 421
Saskatoon	334 529
Yukon	351 768
Montreal	353 535
Ottawa	378 389
Calgary	466 717
Vancouver	1 026 207

$$\frac{351\ 768\ +\ 353\ 535}{2} = 352\ 652$$

The median is found by averaging the two middle values. Note that the median is not one of the values. As well, half of the list prices are below the median, and half are above it.

The major properties of the median are:

1. **It is not affected by extremely large or small values**. Therefore, the median is a valuable measure of location when such values do occur.
2. **It can be computed for ordinal-level data or higher**. Recall from Chapter 1 that ordinal-level data can be ranked from low to high.

excel   Computer commands to find the median and descriptive statistics can be found at the end of the chapter.

LO3-1   3.7 THE MODE

Mode The value of the observation that appears most frequently.

The **mode** is another measure of central location.

The mode is especially useful in summarizing nominal-level data. As an example of its use for nominal-level data, a company has developed five bath oils. The bar chart in Chart 3–1 shows the results of a marketing survey designed to find which bath oil consumers prefer. The largest number of respondents favoured Lamoure, as evidenced by the highest bar. Thus, Lamoure is the mode.

Chart 3–1 Number of Respondents Favouring Various Bath Oils

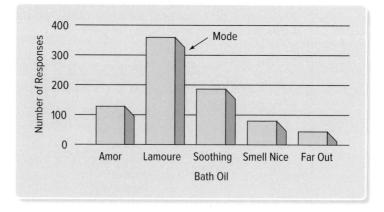

Example

The final grades of a statistics class at a community college are shown below. What is the modal grade?

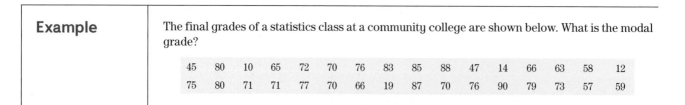

| 45 | 80 | 10 | 65 | 72 | 70 | 76 | 83 | 85 | 88 | 47 | 14 | 66 | 63 | 58 | 12 |
| 75 | 80 | 71 | 71 | 77 | 70 | 66 | 19 | 87 | 70 | 76 | 90 | 79 | 73 | 57 | 59 |

Solution	Organize the data from lowest to highest or vice-versa. A quick look at the grades reveals that 70 appears more often (three times) than any other grade. Therefore, the mode is 70.

Which of the three measures of location (mean, median, or mode) best represents the central location of these data? Is the mode the best measure of location to represent the final grades data? The mode assumes only the nominal scale of measurement, and the variable final grade is measured using the ratio scale. The mean is calculated to be 64.2, and the median is 70.5. Is the mean the best measure of location to represent these data? Probably not. There are several low values which are affecting the mean, making it low and not the best representative of the final grades data. What about the median? The median of 70.5 is the middle data point and is probably a more representative measure of an average of the final grades data.

excel   Computer commands to find the mode and descriptive statistics can be found at the end of the chapter.

In summary, we can determine the mode for all levels of data—nominal, ordinal, interval, and ratio. The mode also has the advantage of not being affected by extremely high or low values.

The mode does have disadvantages, however, that cause it to be used less frequently than the mean or median. For many sets of data, there is no mode because no value appears more than once. For example, there is no mode for this set of price data: $19, $21, $23, $20, and $18 because every value occurs once. Conversely, for some data sets there is more than one mode. Suppose the ages of a group are 22, 26, 27, 27, 31, 35, and 35. Both the ages 27 and 35 are modes. Thus, this grouping of ages is referred to as *bimodal* (having two modes). One would question the use of two modes to represent the location of this set of age data.

self-review 3–3

1. The average weekly earnings across Canada, 2015, are listed below:

Newfoundland and Labrador	$923.09
Prince Edward Island	$822.55
Nova Scotia	$823.81
New Brunswick	$810.92
Quebec	$812.94
Ontario	$900.34
Manitoba	$811.65
Saskatchewan	$897.31
Alberta	$943.68
British Columbia	$845.71
Yukon	$972.84
Northwest Territories	$1368.02
Nunavut	$1221.14

   (a) What is the median monthly income?
   (b) How many observations are below the median? Above it?
2. The numbers of work stoppages in the automobile industry for selected months are 6, 0, 10, 14, 8, and 0.
   (a) What is the median number of stoppages?
   (b) How many observations are below the median? Above it?
   (c) What is the modal number of work stoppages?

EXERCISES

17. What would you report as the modal value for a set of observations if there were a total of:
 a. 10 observations and no two values were the same?
 b. 6 observations and they were all the same?
 c. 6 observations and the values were 1, 2, 3, 3, 4, and 4?

For Exercises 18–20, (a) determine the median and (b) the mode.

18. The following is the number of oil changes for the last seven days at the Jiffy Lube located at the corner of Elm Street and Fortson Avenue:

| 41 | 15 | 39 | 54 | 31 | 15 | 33 |

19. The following is the percentage change in net income from last year to this year for a sample of 12 construction companies in Benton:

| 5 | 1 | −10 | −6 | 5 | 12 | 7 | 8 | 2 | 5 | −1 | 11 |

20. The following are the ages of the 10 people in the video arcade at the shopping mall at 10 a.m.:

| 12 | 8 | 17 | 6 | 11 | 14 | 8 | 17 | 10 | 8 |

21. Listed below is the average earnings ratio by gender for full-year, full-time workers from 2002 to 2011: (Source: Adapted from Statistics Canada. Go to Connect for complete file.)

Year	Women ($)	Men ($)	Earnings Ratio (%)
2002	29 300	46 700	62.8
2003	29 000	46 000	62.9
2004	29 400	46 200	63.5
2005	30 000	46 900	64.0
2006	30 500	47 100	64.7
2007	31 300	47 800	65.5
2008	31 700	49 300	64.3
2009	32 600	47 400	68.6
2010	32 600	47 800	68.1
2011	32 100	48 100	66.7

 a. What is the median earnings ratio?
 b. What is the modal earnings ratio?

22. Listed below is the number of hours that a sample of students spent travelling to college each week. What is the median number of hours spent travelling per week? What is the mode?

| 9.0 | 8.5 | 8.0 | 9.1 | 10.3 | 11.0 | 11.5 | 10.3 | 10.5 | 9.8 | 9.3 | 8.2 | 8.2 | 8.5 |

23. An accounting firm specializes in income tax returns for self-employed professionals, such as doctors, dentists, architects, and lawyers. The firm employs 11 accountants who prepare the returns. For last year, the number of returns prepared by each accountant was:

| 58 | 75 | 31 | 58 | 46 | 65 | 60 | 71 | 45 | 58 | 80 |

Find the mean, median, and mode for the number of returns prepared by each accountant. If you could report only one, which measure of location would you recommend reporting?

24. The demand for video games has exploded in the last several years. So, the owner of Matt Videos needs to hire several new technical people to keep up with the demand. Matt Videos gives each applicant a special test, designed by Dr. McGraw, who believes that the result of the test is closely related to the ability to create video games. For the general population, the mean on this test is 100. The applicants' scores are listed below:

| 95 | 105 | 120 | 81 | 90 | 115 | 99 | 100 | 130 | 10 |

The president, Matt Schauer, is interested in the overall quality of the job applicants based on this test. Compute the mean and the median score for the 10 applicants. What would you report to the president? Does it seem that the applicants are better than the general population?

AN EXCEL EXAMPLE

We can use **Excel** and **MegaStat** to find the measures of central location.

Example	Table 2–1 found in Chapter 2 shows the listings of 85 homes in Whistler, BC. Determine the mean, median and mode of the list prices.
Solution	The mean, median, and modal list prices are reported in the following **Excel** output. There are 85 listings, so calculations with a calculator would be tedious and prone to error.
	Note: Computer commands to produce this output can be found at the end of the chapter.

excel

List Price		List Price	
$ 56,900			
58,000		Mean	735511.4824
60,000		Standard Error	65763.25643
61,900		Median	499000
61,900		Mode	109000
69,900		Standard Deviation	606307.2663
76,900		Sample Variance	3.67609E+11
105,000		Kurtosis	-0.815430462
109,000		Skewness	0.693574656
109,000		Range	1943099
109,000		Minimum	56900
115,900		Maximum	1999999
119,000		Sum	62518476
124,000		Count	85
124,000			
124,000			
130,000			
139,900			
160,000			
189,000			
194,000			
219,000			
219,000			
219,500			
220,000			
315,000			
339,000			
359,000			
362,900			
365,000			
369,000			
379,000			

The mean list price is $735 511, the median is $499 000, and the mode is $109 000. What can we conclude from these values? The mean and the median are far apart in value. The mean is the higher of the two measures. This indicates that there are one or more high list prices that are affecting the mean. In this case, the median may be the more reasonable measure to represent a typical list price. We can also see from the output that the count is 85, indicating that the sample consisted of 85 listings. We will describe the meaning of the standard deviation, range, and other measures reported on the output later in this chapter and in later chapters.

3.8 THE RELATIVE POSITIONS OF THE MEAN, MEDIAN, AND MODE

Refer to the histogram in Chart 3–2. It is a symmetric distribution, which is also mound shaped. This distribution *has the same shape on either side of the centre*. If the histogram were folded in half, the two halves would be identical. **For any symmetric unimodal distribution, the mode, median, and mean are located at the centre and are always equal.** They are all equal to 20 years in Chart 3–2. We should point out that there are symmetric distributions that are not mound shaped.

CHART 3–2 A Symmetric Distribution

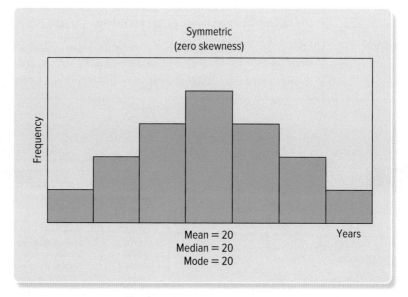

Note the smoothed frequency polygon drawn with the histogram. The number of years corresponding to the highest point of the curve is the *mode* (20 years). Because the distribution is symmetric, the *median* corresponds to the point where the distribution is cut in half (20 years). Also, because the arithmetic mean is the balance point of a distribution and the distribution is symmetric, the arithmetic mean is 20. Logically, any of the three measures would be appropriate to represent the distribution's centre.

If a distribution is nonsymmetric, or **skewed**, the relationship among the three measures changes. In a **positively skewed distribution**, as shown in Chart 3–3, the arithmetic mean is the largest of the three measures. Why? Because the mean is influenced more than the median or

CHART 3–3 A Positively Skewed Distribution

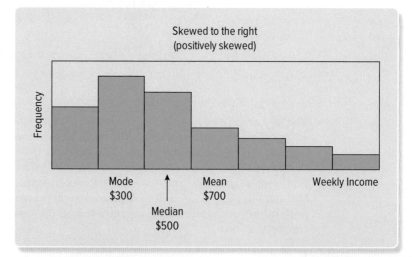

mode by a few extremely high values. The median is generally the next largest measure in a positively skewed frequency distribution. The mode is the smallest of the three measures.

If the distribution is highly skewed, such as the weekly incomes in Chart 3–3, the mean would not be a good measure to use. The median and mode would be more representative.

Conversely, in a distribution that is **negatively skewed**, as shown in Chart 3–4, the mean is the lowest of the three measures. The mean is, of course, influenced by a few extremely low observations. The median is greater than the arithmetic mean, and the modal value is the largest of the three measures. Again, if the distribution is highly skewed, such as the distribution of tensile strengths shown in Chart 3–4, the mean should not be used to represent the data.

CHART 3–4 A Negatively Skewed Distribution

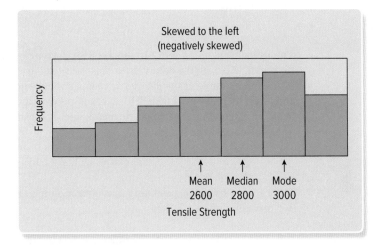

We will expand on the concept of skewness later in the chapter after learning about measures of dispersion.

---

self-review 3–4

The weekly sales from a sample of Hi-Tec electronic supply stores were organized into a frequency distribution. The mean of weekly sales was computed to be \$105 900, the median \$105 000, and the mode \$104 500.

(a) Sketch the sales in the form of a smoothed frequency polygon. Note the location of the mean, median, and mode on the X-axis.
(b) Is the distribution symmetric, positively skewed, or negatively skewed? Explain.

EXERCISES

25. The number of minutes that it takes an auditor to process an invoice is given in the table below:

| 7.8 | 8.2 | 7.6 | 7.2 | 6.6 | 6.6 | 6.1 | 5.8 | 5.9 | 5.7 | 6.3 | 6.8 |

    a. What is the arithmetic mean of processing time?
    b. Find the median and mode of the processing times.
    c. Are the data symmetric, positively skewed, or negatively skewed? Explain.

26. Big Orange Trucking is designing an information system for use in "in-cab" communications. It must summarize data from eight sites throughout a region to describe typical conditions. Compute an appropriate measure of central location for each of the three variables shown in the table below:

City	Wind Direction	Temperature (°C)	Pavement
Winnipeg	West	0	Dry
Grand Rapids	Northwest	−2	Wet
Garden Hill	Southwest	2	Wet
Brandon	South	1	Dry
Portage La Prairie	Southwest	2	Dry
Selkirk	South	2	Trace
The Pas	Southwest	3	Wet
Flin Flon	Southwest	3	Trace

LO3-3 3.9 THE GEOMETRIC MEAN

The geometric mean is useful in finding the average change of percentages, ratios, indexes, or growth rates over time. It has a wide application in business and economics because we are often interested in finding the percentage changes in sales, salaries, or economic figures, such as the gross domestic product (GDP), which compound or build on each other. The geometric mean of a set of n positive numbers is defined as the nth root of the product of the n values. The formula for the geometric mean is:

GEOMETRIC MEAN $$GM = \sqrt[n]{(x_1)(x_2) \cdots (x_n)}$$ [3–4]

The geometric mean will always be less than or equal to (never more than) the arithmetic mean. Also, all the data values must be positive.

As an example of the geometric mean, suppose you receive a 5% increase in salary this year and a 15% increase next year. The average percent increase is 9.886, not 10.0. Why is this so? We begin by calculating the geometric mean. Recall, for example, that a 5% increase in salary is 105% or 1.05. We will write it as 1.05.

$$GM = \sqrt{(1.05)(1.15)} = 1.09886$$

This can be verified by assuming that your monthly earning was $3000 to start and you received two increases of 5% and 15%.

$$
\begin{aligned}
\text{Raise } 1 &= \$3000(0.05) = \$150.00 \\
\text{Raise } 2 &= \$3150(0.15) = \underline{472.50} \\
\text{Total} & \qquad\qquad\qquad \$622.50
\end{aligned}
$$

Your total salary increase is $622.50. This is equivalent to:

$$\$3000.00(0.09886) = \$296.58$$

$$\$3296.58(0.09886) = \underline{325.90}$$

$$\$622.48 \text{ is about } \$622.50$$

The following example shows the geometric mean of several percentages:

Example	The return on investment earned by Atkins Construction Company for four successive years was: 30%, 20%, −40%, and 200%. What is the geometric mean rate of return on investment?
Solution	The number 1.3 represents the 30% return on investment, which is the "original" investment of 1.0 plus the "return" of 0.3. The number 0.6 represents the loss of 40%, which is the original investment of 1.0 reduced by 40% (−0.4). This calculation assumes the total return each period is reinvested or becomes the base for the next period. In other words, the base for the second period is 1.3, and the base for the third period is (1.3)(1.2) and so forth.

Then, the geometric mean rate of return is 29.4%, found by:

$$GM = \sqrt[n]{(X_1)(X_2) \cdots (X_n)} = \sqrt[4]{(1.3)(1.2)(0.6)(3.0)} = 1.294$$

The geometric mean is the fourth root of 2.808. So, the average rate of return (compound annual growth rate) is 29.4%.

Note also that if you compute the arithmetic mean [(30 + 20 − 40 + 200)/4 = 52.5], you would have a much larger number, which would overstate the true rate of return!

A second application of the geometric mean is to find an average percentage increase over a period. For example, if you earned $45 000 in 2004 and $100 000 in 2016, what is your annual rate of increase over the period? It is 6.88%. The rate of increase is determined from the following formula:

$$GM = \sqrt[n]{\frac{\text{Value at end of period}}{\text{Value at beginning of period}}} - 1 \qquad [3\text{–}5]$$

In the above box, n is the number of periods. An example will show the details of finding the average annual percentage increase.

Example	The average cost of a house in Canada grew from \$274 711 in 2009 to \$503 301 in 2016 (crea.ca). What was the average annual rate of percentage increase during the period?
Solution	There are seven years between 2016 and 2009, so $n = 7$. The formula (3–5) for the geometric mean as applied to this type of problem is: $$GM = \sqrt[n]{\frac{\text{Value at end of period}}{\text{Value at beginning of period}}} - 1$$ $$= \sqrt[7]{\frac{503\ 301}{274\ 711}} - 1 = 1.09035 - 1 = 0.09035$$ The final value is 0.09035. So, the annual rate of increase is 9.04%. This means that the average rate of average house price growth in Canada is 9.04% per year from 2009 to 2016.

self-review 3–5

1. The percentage increase in sales, for the last four years at Combs Cosmetics are: 4.91, 5.75, 8.12, and 21.60.
   (a) Find the geometric percentage increase.
   (b) Find the arithmetic percentage increase.
   (c) Is the arithmetic mean equal to or greater than the geometric mean?

2. Production of Cablos trucks increased from 23 000 units in 1996 to 120 520 units in 2016. Find the geometric mean annual percentage increase.

EXERCISES

27. Baxmedical stock has increased over the past five years by the following percentages: 8, 12, 14, 26, and 5. Compute the geometric mean of the percentage increases.

28. Enrollment in skating lessons at the Biway Community Centre has increased each year by the following percentages: 2, 8, 6, 4, 10, 6, 8, and 4. Compute the geometric percentage increase.

29. Listed below is the percentage increase in sales for the MG Corporation over the last five years. Determine the geometric mean percentage increase in sales over the period.

9.4	13.8	11.7	11.9	14.7

30. In 2003, the consumer price index (CPI) for Canada was 102.8, but in 2015, the CPI was 126.6. What was the geometric mean annual increase for the period? (See Connect for the data set.)

31. The population of Canada has increased from 21 961 999 in 1971 to an estimated 36 155 487 in 2016 (statcan.gc.ca/start-debut-eng.html). What was the geometric mean annual increase for the period?

32. Gas prices in St. John's, Newfoundland, have increased from 64.1 cents per litre for regular unleaded in 1990 to 121.7 cents per litre in 2016 (www40.statcan.gc.ca/l01/cst01/perecon154a-eng.htm). What was the geometric mean annual increase for the period?

33. In 2011, there were 42 million pager subscribers. By 2016, the number of subscribers increased to 70 million. What is the geometric mean annual increase for the period?

34. The average tuition fees for dentistry in Canada increased from $7863 for the 1999–2000 academic year to $21 021 in the 2016–2017 academic year (statcan.gc.ca/daily-quotidien/130912/dq130912b-eng.htm). What was the geometric mean annual increase for the period?

3.10 WHY STUDY DISPERSION?

A measure of location, such as the mean, median, or mode only describes the centre of the data. It is valuable from that standpoint, but it does not tell us anything about the spread of the data. For example, if your nature guide told you that the river ahead averaged 1 metre (m) in depth, would you want to wade across on foot without additional information? Probably not. You would want to know something about the variation in the depth. Is the maximum depth of the river 1.25 m and the minimum 0.5 m? If that is the case, you would probably agree to cross. What if you learned the river depth ranged from 0.5 m to 2 m? Your decision would probably be not to cross. Before making a decision about crossing the river, you want information on both the typical depth and the dispersion in the depth of the river.

A small value for a measure of dispersion indicates that the data are clustered closely, say, around the arithmetic mean. The mean is therefore considered representative of the data. Conversely, **a large measure of dispersion indicates that the mean is not reliable.** Refer to Chart 3–5. The 100 employees of Hammond Iron Works Inc., a steel fabricating company, are organized into a histogram based on the number of years of employment with the company. The mean is 4.9 years, but the spread of the data is from 6 months to 16.8 years. The mean of 4.9 years is not very representative of all the employees.

CHART 3–5 Histogram of Years of Employment at Hammond Iron Works Inc.

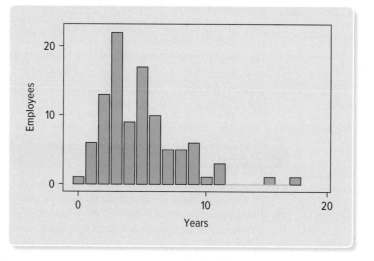

A second reason for studying the dispersion in a set of data is to compare the spread in two or more distributions. Suppose, for example, that the new Vision Quest LCD computer monitor is assembled in Kanata and also in Waterloo. The arithmetic mean hourly output in both the Kanata plant and the Waterloo plant is 50. On the basis of the two means, you might conclude that the distributions of the hourly outputs are identical. Production records for nine hours at the two plants, however, reveal that this conclusion is not correct (Chart 3–6). Kanata production varies from 48 to 52 assemblies per hour. Production at the Waterloo plant is more erratic, ranging from 40 to 60 per hour. Therefore, the hourly output for Kanata is clustered near the mean of 50; the hourly output for Waterloo is more dispersed.

CHART 3–6 Hourly Production of Computers at the Kanata and Waterloo Plants

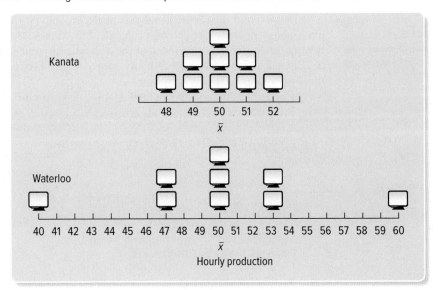

LO3-4 3.11 MEASURES OF DISPERSION

We will consider several measures of dispersion. The range is based on the maximum and the minimum values in the data set; that is, only two values are considered. The mean deviation, the variance, and the standard deviation use all the values in a data set and are all based on deviations from the arithmetic mean.

Range

The simplest measure of dispersion is the **range.** It is the difference between the maximum and minimum values in a data set. In the form of an equation:

RANGE	Range = Maximum value − Minimum value	[3–6]

You hear about a range every day. The weather forecast is given in high and low temperatures. In business, stock prices are quoted as highs and lows for the day, week, and so on. Also, the range is widely used in statistical process control (SPC) applications because it is very easy to calculate and understand.

Example	Refer to Chart 3–6. Find the range in the number of computer monitors produced per hour for the Kanata and the Waterloo plants. Interpret the two ranges.
Solution	The range of the hourly production at the Kanata plant is 4 computer monitors, found by the difference between the largest hourly production of 52 (maximum) and the smallest of 48 (minimum). The range in the hourly production for the Waterloo plant is 20 computer monitors, found by: 60 − 40. We, therefore, conclude that (1) there is less dispersion in the hourly production in the Kanata plant than in the Waterloo plant because the range of 4 computer monitors is less than a range of 20 computer monitors, and (2) the production is clustered more closely around the mean of 50 at the Kanata plant than at the Waterloo plant (because a range of 4 is less than a range of 20). Thus, the mean production in the Kanata plant (50 computer monitors) is a more representative measure of location than the mean of 50 computer monitors for the Waterloo plant.

Mean Deviation

Mean deviation The arithmetic mean of the absolute values of the deviations from the arithmetic mean.

A shortcoming of the range is that it is based on only two values, the maximum and the minimum; it does not take into consideration all of the values. The **mean deviation** does. For a number of observations, it is the mean of the absolute differences between each value and the mean of the values. It is a measure of the average distance between an observation and the mean of the observations. A definition follows:

In terms of a formula, the mean deviation, designated *MD*, is computed for a sample by:

MEAN DEVIATION	$MD = \dfrac{\sum |x - \bar{x}|}{n}$	[3–7]

where:

  x is the value of each observation.
  $\bar{x}$ is the arithmetic mean of the values.
  n is the number of observations in the sample.
  $\| \|$ indicates the absolute value.

Why do we ignore the signs of the deviations from the mean? If we did not, the positive and negative deviations from the mean would exactly offset each other, and the mean deviation would always be zero. Such a measure, zero, would be a useless statistic.

Example	The numbers of cappuccinos sold at the coffee shop in the Kings County Municipal Airport between 4 and 7 p.m. for a sample of five days last year were 20, 40, 50, 60, and 80. In the Sydney Airport, the number of cappuccinos sold at the coffee shop between 4 and 7 p.m. for a sample of five days last year were 20, 49, 50, 51, and 80. Determine the mean, median, range, and mean deviation for each location. Comment on the similarities and differences in these measures.
Solution	For the Kings County Municipal Airport the mean, median, and range are:

Mean	$(20 + 40 + 50 + 60 + 80)/5 = 50$ cappuccinos per day
Median	50 (the middle value when the data are ordered) cappuccinos per day
Range	$80 - 20 = 60$ cappuccinos per day

The mean deviation is the mean of the differences between individual observations and the arithmetic mean. For the Kings County Municipal Airport, the mean number of cappuccinos sold is 50. Next, we find the differences between each observation and the mean. Then, we sum these differences, ignoring the signs, and divide the sum by the number of observations. The result is the mean difference between the observations and the mean.

Number of Cappuccinos Sold	$x - \bar{x}$	Absolute Deviation
20	$(20 - 50) = -30$	30
40	$(40 - 50) = -10$	10
50	$(50 - 50) = 0$	0
60	$(60 - 50) = 10$	10
80	$(80 - 50) = 30$	30
		Total 80

$$MD = \frac{\sum |x - \bar{x}|}{n} = \frac{80}{5} = 16$$

The mean deviation is 16 cappuccinos. That is, the number of cappuccinos sold per day deviates, on average, by 16 from the mean of 50 cappuccinos per day. The summary of the mean, median, range, and mean deviation for the Sydney Airport follows. You should perform the calculations to verify the results.

Mean	50	cappuccinos per day
Median	50	cappuccinos per day
Range	60	cappuccinos per day
Mean Deviation	12.4	cappuccinos per day

Recall that in the previous chapter, we described data using graphical methods. In this chapter, we describe data using numerical measures. When we use numerical measures, it is very important to always report measures of location and dispersion.

Let us interpret and compare the results of our measures for the coffee shop locations. The mean and median of the two locations are exactly the same, 50 cappuccinos per day. Therefore, the location of both distributions is the same. The range for both locations is also the same, 60. However, recall that the range provides limited information about the dispersion of the distribution.

Note that the mean deviations are not the same because they are based on the differences between all observations and the arithmetic mean, which show the relative closeness or clustering of the data relative to the mean or centre of the distribution. Compare the mean deviation for the Kings County Municipal Airport of 16 to the mean deviation of the Sydney Airport of 12.4. On the basis of the mean deviation, we can say that the dispersion for the sales distribution of the Sydney Airport coffee shop is more concentrated near the mean of 50 than the Kings County Municipal Airport location.

The mean deviation has two advantages. First, it uses all the values in the computation. Recall that the range uses only the maximum and the minimum values. Second, it is easy to understand—it is the average amount by which values deviate from the mean. However, its drawback is the use of absolute values. Generally, absolute values are difficult to work with, so the mean deviation is not used as frequently as other measures of dispersion, such as the standard deviation.

self-review 3-6

The masses of a group of crates being shipped to Ireland are (in kilograms):

| 95 | 103 | 105 | 110 | 104 | 105 | 112 | 90 |

(a) What is the range of the masses?
(b) Compute the arithmetic mean mass.
(c) Compute the mean deviation of the masses.

excel

Computer commands to find the range and mean deviation can be found at the end of the chapter.

EXERCISES

For Exercises 35–38, calculate the (a) range, (b) arithmetic mean, and (c) mean deviation, and (d) interpret the range and the mean deviation.

35. There were five customer service representatives on duty at the Electronic Super Store during last Friday's sale. The number of HDTVs these representatives sold are: 5, 8, 4, 10, and 3.

36. The Business School at a local college offers eight sections of basic statistics. Following are the number of students enrolled in these sections: 34, 46, 52, 29, 41, 38, 36, and 28.

37. Dave's Automatic Door installs automatic garage door openers. The following list indicates the number of minutes needed to install a sample of 10 doors: 28, 32, 24, 46, 44, 40, 54, 38, 32, and 42.

38. A sample of eight companies in the aerospace industry was surveyed as to their return on investment last year. The results are (in percent): 10.6, 12.6, 14.8, 18.2, 12.0, 14.8, 12.2, and 15.6.

39. Ten randomly selected young adults living in British Columbia rated the taste of a newly developed sushi pizza topped with tuna, rice, and kelp on a scale of 1 to 50, with 1 indicating they did not like the taste and 50 that they did. The ratings were:

| 34 | 39 | 40 | 46 | 33 | 31 | 34 | 14 | 15 | 45 |

In a parallel study 10 randomly selected young adults in Manitoba rated the taste of the same pizza. The ratings were:

| 28 | 25 | 35 | 16 | 25 | 29 | 24 | 26 | 17 | 20 |

As a market researcher, compare the potential markets for sushi pizza.

40. A sample of the personnel files of eight sales employees at the Clean Carpet Company revealed that during the last six-month period they lost the following number of days due to illness:

| 2 | 0 | 6 | 3 | 10 | 4 | 1 | 2 |

A sample of eight warehouse employees of the same company during the same period revealed that they lost the following number of days due to illness:

| 2 | 0 | 1 | 0 | 5 | 0 | 1 | 0 |

As the director of human resources, compare the two sets of data. Is there a difference in the number of days lost due to illness in the two locations? What would you recommend?

Variance and Standard Deviation

Variance The arithmetic mean of the squared deviations from the mean.

Standard deviation The square root of the variance.

The **variance** and the **standard deviation** are also based on the differences between each observation and the mean. However, instead of using the absolute value of the deviations, the variance and the standard deviation square the deviations. So, the variance and standard deviation are based on squared deviations from the mean.

The variance is non-negative, and it has a value of zero only if all observations are the same.

Population Variance   The formulas for the population variance and the sample variance are slightly different. The population variance is considered first. (Recall that a population is the totality of all observations being studied.) The **population variance** is found by:

| **POPULATION VARIANCE** | $$\sigma^2 = \frac{\Sigma(x - \mu)^2}{N}$$ | [3–8] |

where:

σ^2 is the symbol for the population variance (σ is the lowercase Greek letter sigma). It is usually referred to as "sigma squared."
x is the value of each observation in the population.
μ is the arithmetic mean of the population.
N is the number of observations in the population.

Note the steps in computing the population variance:

1. Begin by finding the mean.
2. Find the difference between each observation and the mean.
3. Square the difference.
4. Sum all the squared differences.
5. Divide the sum of the squared differences by the number of observations in the population.

For populations whose values are near the mean, the variance will be small. For populations whose values are dispersed from the mean, the population variance will be large. So, you might think of the population variance as the mean of the squared difference between each value and the mean.

The variance has an important advantage over the range by using all the values in the population, whereas the range uses only the maximum and minimum. We overcome the issue of absolute values in the mean deviation by squaring the differences. Squaring the differences will always result in non-negative values.

Example	The ages of all the passengers in business class on the 1 p.m. flight to Edmonton today are 38, 26, 13, 41, and 22 years. Determine the population variance.	
Solution	We will consider the data as population data as we are studying the ages of all passengers in business class on the 1 p.m. flight to Edmonton today.	

Age (x)	x − μ	(x − μ)2	
38	+10	100	$\mu = \dfrac{\Sigma x}{N} = \dfrac{140}{5} = 28$
26	−2	4	
13	−15	225	
41	+13	169	$\sigma^2 = \dfrac{\Sigma(x - \mu)^2}{N} = \dfrac{534}{5} = 106.8$
22	−6	36	
140	0*	534	

*Sum of the deviations from mean must equal 0.

1. Begin by finding the mean. The calculations are shown above.
2. Next, we find the difference between each observation and the mean. That is shown in the second column. Note that the sum of the differences between the mean and the observations is 0.
3. The differences are squared in column 3.
4. The squared differences are totalled and are equal to 534.
5. Divide the squared differences by N, shown above.

The population variance of the ages is 106.8.

Like the range and the mean deviation, the variance can be used to compare the dispersion in two or more sets of observations. For example, the variance for the ages of the passengers in business class was just computed to be 106.8. If the variance in the ages of the passengers in coach is 342.9, we conclude that (1) there is less dispersion in the distribution of the ages of the passengers in business class than in the age distribution of the passengers in coach (because 106.8 is less than 342.9); and (2) the ages of the passengers in business class are clustered more closely about the mean of 28 years than the ages of those in coach. Thus, the mean age for the passengers in business class is a more representative measure of location than the mean for the passengers in coach.

Population Standard Deviation   Both the range and the mean deviation are easy to interpret. The range is the difference between the maximum and minimum values of a set of data, and the mean deviation is the mean of the absolute deviations from the mean. **However, the variance is difficult to interpret for a single set of observations.** The variance of 106.8 for the ages of the passengers in business class is not in terms of years, but rather "years squared."

There is a way out of this difficulty. **By taking the square root of the population variance, we can transform it to the same unit of measurement used for the original data.** The square root of 106.8 years-squared is 10.3 years. The units are now simply years. The square root of the population variance is the **population standard deviation**.

POPULATION STANDARD DEVIATION $\sigma = \sqrt{\dfrac{\Sigma(x - \mu)^2}{N}}$ [3–9]

self review 3 7   An office of Price Waterhouse Coopers LLP hired five accounting trainees this year. Their monthly starting salaries were: $3536, $3173, $3448, $3121, and $3622.

(a) Compute the population mean.

(b) Compute the population variance.

(c) Compute the population standard deviation.

(d) Another location hired six trainees. Their mean monthly salary was $3550, and the standard deviation was $250. Compare the two groups.

excel   Computer commands to find the population variance and the standard deviation can be found at the end of the chapter.

EXERCISES

41. Colton spent the following amounts in the cafeteria last week: $8, $3, $7, $3, and $4. Consider these five amounts a population.

  a. Determine the mean of the population.

  b. Determine the variance.

42. The number of customers ordering sandwiches from BagelStop between 8 and 9 am on six consecutive days was 13, 3, 8, 10, 8, and 6. Consider these six values a population.

  a. Determine the mean of the population.

  b. Determine the variance.

43. The annual report of Dennis Industries cited these primary earnings per common share for the past five years: $2.68, $1.03, $2.26, $4.30, and $3.58. If we assume these are population values, what is:

  a. The arithmetic mean primary earnings per share of common stock?

  b. The variance?

44. Referring to Exercise 43, the annual report of Dennis Industries also gave these returns on stockholder equity for the same five-year period (in percent): 13.2, 5.0, 10.2, 17.5, and 12.9.

  a. What is the arithmetic mean return?

  b. What is the variance?

45. Plywood Inc. reported these returns on stockholder equity for the past five years: 4.3, 4.9, 7.2, 6.7, and 11.6. Consider these as population values.

  a. Compute the range, the arithmetic mean, the variance, and the standard deviation.

  b. Compare the return on stockholder equity for Plywood Inc. with that for Dennis Industries cited in Exercise 44.

Statistics in Action

Patrick Kane of the Chicago Blackhawks played 82 games in the 2015–2016 regular season of the National Hockey League. He was the point leader with a total of 106, consisting of 46 goals and 60 assists. The second ranked points leader was Jamie Benn of the Dallas Stars. He also played 82 games and scored 41 goals and 48 assists for a total of 89 points (nhl.com).

46. The annual incomes of the five vice-presidents of TMV Industries are as follows: $125 000, $128 000, $122 000, $133 000, and $140 000. Consider this a population.

  a. What is the range?

  b. What is the arithmetic mean income?

  c. What is the population variance? The standard deviation?

  d. The annual incomes of officers of another firm similar to TMV Industries were also studied. The mean was $129 000 and the standard deviation $8612. Compare the means and dispersions in the two firms.

Sample Variance   The formula for the population mean is $\mu = \Sigma x / N$. We just changed the symbols for the sample mean—that is, $\overline{x} = \Sigma x / n$. Unfortunately, the conversion from the population variance to the sample variance is not as direct. It requires a change in the denominator. Instead of substituting n (number in the sample) for N (number in the population), the denominator is $n - 1$. Thus, the formula for the **sample variance** is:

SAMPLE VARIANCE, DEVIATION FORMULA	$s^2 = \dfrac{\sum(x - \bar{x})^2}{n - 1}$	[3–10]

where:

s^2 is the sample variance.

x is the value of each observation in the sample.

$\bar{x}$ is the mean of the sample.

n is the number of observations in the sample.

Why is this change made in the denominator? Although the use of n is logical since $\bar{x}$ is used to estimate μ, it tends to underestimate the population variance, σ^2. The use of $(n - 1)$ in the denominator provides the appropriate correction for this tendency. Because the primary use of sample statistics like s^2 is to estimate population parameters like σ^2, $(n - 1)$ is preferred to n in defining the sample variance. We will also use this convention when computing the sample standard deviation.

An easier way to compute the variance follows. This formula is much easier to use, even with a hand calculator because it avoids all but one subtraction. Hence, we recommend formula (3–11) for calculating a sample variance.

SAMPLE VARIANCE, DIRECT FORMULA	$s^2 = \dfrac{\sum x^2 - \dfrac{(\sum x)^2}{n}}{n - 1}$	[3–11]

Example	The hourly wages for a sample of part-time employees at Fruit Packers Inc. are: \$12, \$20, \$16, \$18, and \$19. What is the sample variance?
Solution	The sample variance is computed using two methods. On the left is the deviation method, using formula (3–10). On the right is the direct method, using formula (3–11).

$$\bar{x} = \frac{\sum x}{n} = \frac{\$85}{5} = \$17$$

Using squared deviations from the mean:

Hourly Wage (\$) x	\$ $x - \bar{x}$	\$^{2} $(x - \bar{x})^2$
12	−5	25
20	3	9
16	−1	1
18	1	1
19	2	4
85	0	40

$$s^2 = \frac{\sum(x - \bar{x})^2}{n - 1} = \frac{\$^2 40}{5 - 1}$$
$$= 10\,\$^2 \text{ (dollors squared)}$$

Using the direct formula:

Hourly Wage (\$) x	\$^{2} x^2
12	144
20	400
16	256
18	324
19	361
85	1485

$$s^2 = \frac{\sum x^2 - \dfrac{(\sum x)^2}{n}}{n - 1}$$
$$= \frac{1485 - \dfrac{(85)^2}{5}}{5 - 1} = \frac{40}{5 - 1}$$
$$= 10\,\$^2 \text{ (dollors squared)}$$

Sample Standard Deviation The sample standard deviation is used as an estimator of the population standard deviation. As noted previously, the population standard deviation is the square root of the population variance. Likewise, the *sample standard deviation is the square root of the sample variance*. The sample standard deviation is most easily determined by:

SAMPLE STANDARD DEVIATION, DIRECT FORMULA $s = \sqrt{\dfrac{\sum x^2 - \dfrac{(\sum x)^2}{n}}{n-1}}$ [3–12]

Example	The sample variance in the previous example involving hourly wages was computed to be 10^2. What is the sample standard deviation?
Solution	The sample standard deviation is $3.16, found by $\sqrt{10}$. Note again that the sample variance is in terms of dollars squared, but taking the square root of 10 gives us $3.16, which is in the same units (dollars) as the original data.

self-review 3–8

The years of service for a sample of seven employees at an insurance claims office are: 4, 2, 5, 4, 5, 2, and 6. What is the sample variance? Compute the sample standard deviation.

excel

Computer commands to find the sample variance and standard deviation can be found at the end of the chapter.

Statistics in Action

An average is a value used to represent all the data. However, often an average does not give the full picture of the set of data. Stockbrokers are often faced with this problem when they are considering two investments, where the mean rate of return is the same. They usually calculate the standard deviation of the rates of return to assess the risk associated with the two investments. The investment with the larger standard deviation is considered to have the greater risk. In this context, the standard deviation plays a vital part in making critical decisions regarding the composition of an investor's portfolio.

EXERCISES

For Exercises 47–52, do the following:
   a. Compute the sample variance.
   b. Determine the sample standard deviation.

47. The number of returns audited on each day last week are: 7, 2, 6, 2, and 3. Consider this sample data.

48. The following number of bags of cookies were removed from a production line in the last five hours to be tested for quality purposes: 11, 6, 10, 6, and 7.

49. Dave's Automatic Door, referred to in Exercise 37, installs automatic garage door openers. Based on a sample, following are the times, in minutes, required to install 10 doors: 28, 32, 24, 46, 44, 40, 54, 38, 32, and 42.

50. The sample of eight companies in the aerospace industry was surveyed as to their return on investment last year. The results are: 10.6, 12.6, 14.8, 18.2, 12.0, 14.8, 12.2, and 15.6.

51. The provincial Motel Owner Association conducted a survey regarding weekday motel rates in the northern part of the province. Listed below is the room rate for fishers for a sample of 10 motels:

$101	97	103	110	78	87	101	80	106	88

52. A consumer watchdog organization is concerned about credit card debt. A survey of 10 young adults with credit card debt of more than $2000 showed they paid an average of just over $100 per month against their balances. Listed below are the amounts each young adult paid last month:

$110	126	103	93	99	113	87	101	109	100

LO3-5 3.12 INTERPRETATION AND USES OF THE STANDARD DEVIATION

The standard deviation is commonly used as a measure to compare the spread in two or more sets of observations. For example, the price of two stocks may have about the same mean, but different standard deviations. The stock with the larger standard deviation has more variability in its mean price, and therefore, could be considered more risky.

Chebyshev's Theorem

Chebyshev's theorem For any set of observations (sample or population), the proportion of the values that lie within k standard deviations of the mean is at least $1 - 1/k^2$, where k is any value greater than 1.

We have stressed that a small standard deviation for a set of values indicates that these values are located close to the mean. Conversely, a large standard deviation reveals that the observations are widely scattered about the mean. The Russian mathematician P.L. Chebyshev (1821–1894) developed a theorem that allows us to determine the minimum proportion of the values that lie within a specified number of standard deviations of the mean. For example, according to **Chebyshev's theorem**, at least three of four values, or 75%, must lie between the mean plus 2 standard deviations and the mean minus 2 standard deviations. This relationship applies regardless of the shape of the distribution. Further, at least eight of nine values, or 88.9%, will lie between plus 3 standard deviations and minus 3 standard deviations of the mean. At least 24 of the 25 values, or 96%, will lie between plus and minus 5 standard deviations of the mean.

Example	The average biweekly amount contributed by the Dupree Paint employees to the company's profit-sharing plan is $51.54, and the standard deviation is $7.51. At least what percentage of the contributions lie within plus and minus 3.5 standard deviations of the mean?
Solution	About 92%, found by: $1 - 1/k^2 = 1 - 1/(3.5)^2 = 1 - 1/12.25 = 0.92$

The Empirical Rule

Empirical Rule For a symmetric, bell-shaped frequency distribution, approximately 68% of the observations will lie within plus and minus 1 standard deviation of the mean; about 95% of the observations will lie within plus and minus 2 standard deviations of the mean; and practically all (99.7%) will lie within plus and minus 3 standard deviations of the mean.

Chebyshev's theorem applies to any set of values; that is, the distribution of values can have any shape. However, for a symmetric, bell-shaped distribution, such as the one in Chart 3–7, we can be more precise in describing the dispersion about the mean. These relationships involving the standard deviation and the mean are described by the **Empirical Rule**, sometimes called the **Normal Rule**.

These relationships are portrayed graphically in Chart 3–7 for a bell-shaped distribution with a mean of 100 and a standard deviation of 10.

CHART 3–7 A Symmetric, Bell-Shaped Curve Showing the Relationships between the Standard Deviation and the Percentage of Observations

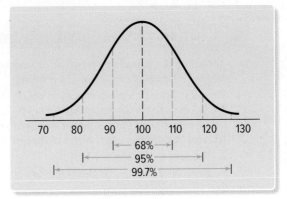

Applying the Empirical Rule, if a distribution is symmetric and bell-shaped, practically all of the observations lie between the mean plus and minus 3 standard deviations. Thus, if $\bar{x} = 100$ and $s = 10$, practically all the observations lie between $100 + 3(10)$ and $100 - 3(10)$, or 70 and 130. The estimated range is therefore 60, found by: $130 - 70$.

Conversely, if we know that the range is 60, we can approximate the standard deviation by dividing the range by 6. For this illustration: range $\div 6 = 60 \div 6 = 10$, the standard deviation.

Example	A sample of the rental rates at the College Park apartments approximates a symmetric, bell-shaped distribution. The sample mean is $1500; the standard deviation is $120. Using the Empirical Rule, answer these questions: 1. About 68% of the rental rates are between what two amounts? 2. About 95% of the rental rates are between what two amounts? 3. Almost all of the rental rates are between what two amounts?
Solution	1. About 68% are between $1380 ($1500 − $120) and $1620 ($1500 + $120). 2. About 95% are between $1260 ($1500 − 2[$120]) and $1740 ($1500 + 2[$120]). 3. Almost all (99.7%) are between $1140 ($1500 − 3[$120]) and $1860 ($1500 + 3[$120]).

Example	Professor Law calculated the following results for the first test in statistics: mean = 70%; standard deviation = 10%. The grades approximate a symmetric, bell-shaped distribution. Use the Empirical Rule to answer the following questions: 1. About what percentage of the grades fall between 60% and 80%? 2. About what percentage of grades fall between 50% and 90%? 3. About what percentage of grades fall between 40% and 100%?
Solution	1. About 68% are between 60% (70% − 10%) and 80% (70% + 10%). 2. About 95% are between 50% (70 − 2[10%]) and 90% (70% + 2[10%]). 3. Almost all (99.7%) are between 40% (70% − 3[10%]) and 100% (70% + 3[10%]).

self-review 3–9

The Superior Metal Company is one of several domestic manufacturers of PVC pipe. The quality control department sampled 600 10 m lengths. At a point 1 m from the end of the pipe, they measured the outside diameter. The mean was 1.2 m and the standard deviation 0.1 m.

(a) If the shape of the distribution is not known, at least what percentage of the observations will lie between 1.05 m and 1.35 m?

(b) If we assume that the distribution of diameters is symmetric and bell shaped, about 68% of the observations will be between what two values?

(c) If we assume that the distribution of diameters is symmetric and bell shaped, about 95% of the observations will be between what two values?

EXERCISES

53. According to Chebyshev's theorem, at least what percentage of any set of observations will be within 1.8 standard deviations of the mean?

54. The mean price of a group of sample observations is $500; the standard deviation is $40. According to Chebyshev's theorem at least what percentage of the prices will lie between $400 and $600?

55. The distribution of the weights of a sample of 1400 cargo containers is somewhat normally distributed. According to the Empirical Rule, what percentage of the weights will lie:

a. Between $\bar{x} - 2s$ and $\bar{x} + 2s$?

b. Between $\bar{x}$ and $\bar{x} + 2s$? Below $\bar{x} - 2s$?

56. The following figure portrays the appearance of a distribution of efficiency ratings for employees of Nale Nail Works Inc.:

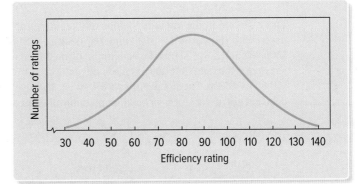

a. Estimate the mean efficiency rating.
b. Estimate the standard deviation to the nearest whole number.
c. About 68% of the efficiency ratings are between what two values?
d. About 95% of the efficiency ratings are between what two values?

LO3-6 3.13 RELATIVE DISPERSION

A direct comparison of two or more measures of dispersion—say, the standard deviation for a distribution of annual incomes and the standard deviation of a distribution of absenteeism for this same group of employees—is impossible. Can we say that the standard deviation of $1200 for the income distribution is greater than the standard deviation of 4.5 days for the distribution of absenteeism? Obviously not, because we cannot directly compare dollars and days absent from work. To make a meaningful comparison of the dispersion in incomes and absenteeism, we need to convert each of these measures to a *relative value*—that is, a percentage. Karl Pearson (1857–1936), who contributed significantly to the science of statistics, developed a relative measure called the **coefficient of variation** (CV). It is a very useful measure when:

Coefficient of variation
The ratio of the standard deviation to the arithmetic mean, expressed as a percentage.

1. The data are in different units (such as dollars and days absent).
2. The data are in the same units, but the means are far apart (such as the incomes of the top executives and the incomes of the unskilled employees).

In terms of a formula for a sample:

COEFFICIENT OF VARIATION $CV = \frac{s}{\bar{x}}(100) \leftarrow$ Multiplying by 100 converts the decimal to a percent [3–13]

Example	A study of the amount of bonus paid and the years of service of employees at Sea Pro Marine Inc. resulted in these statistics: the mean bonus paid was $200; the standard deviation was $40; the mean number of years of service was 20 years; and the standard deviation was 2 years. Compare the relative dispersion in the two distributions using the coefficient of variation.
Solution	The distributions are in different units (dollars and years of service). Therefore, they are converted to coefficients of variation.

For the bonus paid:
$$CV = \frac{s}{\bar{x}}(100)$$
$$= \frac{\$40}{\$200}(100)$$
$$= 20\%$$

For years of service:
$$CV = \frac{s}{\bar{x}}(100)$$
$$= \frac{2}{20}(100)$$
$$= 10\%$$

Interpreting, there is more dispersion relative to the mean in the distribution of bonus paid compared with the distribution of years of service (because 20% > 10%).

The same procedure is used when the data are in the same units but the means are far apart. (See the following example.)

Example	The variation in the annual incomes of executives at Nash-Rambler Products Inc. is to be compared with the variation in incomes of unskilled employees. For a sample of executives, $\bar{x} = \$500\,000$ and $s = \$50\,000$. For a sample of unskilled employees, $\bar{x} = \$32\,000$ and $s = \$3200$. We are tempted to say that there is more dispersion in the annual incomes of the executives because $\$50\,000 > \$3200$. The means are so far apart, however, that we need to convert the statistics to coefficients of variation to make a meaningful comparison of the variations in annual incomes.
Solution	For the executives: For the unskilled employees: $$CV = \frac{s}{\bar{x}}(100) \qquad\qquad CV = \frac{s}{\bar{x}}(100)$$ $$= \frac{\$50\,000}{\$500\,000}(100) \qquad = \frac{3200}{32\,000}(100)$$ $$= 10\% \qquad\qquad\quad = 10\%$$ There is no difference in the relative dispersion of the two groups.

Example	Sam Simone is a financial adviser based in Winnipeg, Manitoba. Sam is currently evaluating three stocks that are expected to continue with the same rate of return as in the last ten years. However, some of Sam's clients are risk adverse—meaning that they prefer to invest in stocks with low volatility. Which stock(s) should Sam recommend to his clients as having the least risk? MStudios mean = \$43.75; standard deviation = 10.50 CobdenIT mean = \$125.60; standard deviation = 19.75 Nine30 mean = \$10.75; standard deviation = 2.50
Solution	Calculate the CV for each stock. $$CV_{MStudios} = \frac{10.50}{43.75}(100) = 24.0\%$$ $$CV_{CobdenIT} = \frac{19.75}{125.60}(100) = 15.7\%$$ $$CV_{Nine30} = \frac{2.50}{10.75}(100) = 23.3\%$$ MStudios and Nine30 have approximately the same CV. The CV for CobdenIT is lower, and so has lower risk. CobdenIT is the stock that Sam should recommend to his clients.

self-review 3–10 A large group of new employees were given two experimental tests—a mechanical aptitude test and a finger dexterity test. The arithmetic mean score on the mechanical aptitude test was 200, with a standard deviation of 10. The mean and the standard deviation for the finger dexterity test were: $\bar{x} = 30$, $s = 6$. Compare the relative dispersion in the two groups.

EXERCISES

57. For a sample of students in a college studying Business Administration, the mean grade-point average is 3.10, with a standard deviation of 0.25. Compute the coefficient of variation.

58. Skipjack Airlines is studying the mass of luggage for each passenger. For a large group of domestic passengers, the mean is 21 kg, with a standard deviation of 5 kg. For a large group of overseas passengers, the mean is 35 kg, and the standard deviation is 7 kg. Compute the relative dispersion of each group. Comment on the difference in relative dispersion.

59. The research analyst for the Sidde Financial stock brokerage firm wants to compare the dispersion in the price-earnings ratios for a group of common stocks with the dispersion of their return on investment. For the price-earnings ratios, the mean is 4.9, and the standard deviation 1.8. The mean return on investment is 10% and the standard deviation 5.2%.

  a. Why should the coefficient of variation be used to compare the dispersion?

  b. Compare the relative dispersion for the price-earnings ratios and return on investment.

60. The spread in the annual prices of stocks selling for under $10 and the spread in prices of those selling for over $60 are to be compared. The mean price of the stocks selling for under $10 is $5.25

and the standard deviation $1.52. The mean price of those stocks selling for over $60 is $92.50 and the standard deviation $5.28.

a. Why should the coefficient of variation be used to compare the dispersion in the prices?

b. Compute the coefficients of variation. What is your conclusion?

LO3-6   3.14 SKEWNESS

Statistics in Action

Stephen Jay Gould (1941–2002) was a professor of zoology and professor of geology at Harvard University. In 1982, he was diagnosed with cancer and had an expected survival time of eight months. However, never to be discouraged, he showed through his research that the distribution of survival time was dramatically skewed to the right and that not only do 50% of similar cancer patients survive more than eight months but that the survival time could be years rather than months! On the basis of his experience, he wrote a widely published essay titled "The Median Is Not the Message."

Earlier in this chapter, we described measures of central location for a set of observations by reporting the mean, median, and mode. We also described measures that show the amount of spread or variation in a set of data, such as the range and the standard deviation. In addition, we introduced the concept of skewness, which is a measure of the shape of the data.

There are four shapes commonly observed: symmetric, positively skewed, negatively skewed, and bimodal. In a **symmetric** set of observations, the mean and median are equal and the data values are evenly spread around these values. The data values below the mean and median are a mirror image of those above. A set of values is **skewed to the right** or **positively skewed** if there is a single peak and the values extend much farther to the right of the peak than to the left of the peak. In this case, the mean is larger than the median. In a **negatively skewed** distribution, there is a single peak, but the observations extend further to the left, in the negative direction, than to the right. In a negatively skewed distribution, the mean is smaller than the median. Positively skewed distributions are more common. Salaries often follow this pattern. Think of the salaries of those employed in a small company of about 100 people. The president and a few top executives would have very large salaries relative to the other workers, and hence the distribution of salaries would exhibit positive skewness. A **bimodal distribution** will have two or more peaks. This is often the case when the values are from two or more populations. This information is summarized in Chart 3–8.

CHART 3–8 Shapes of Frequency Polygons

There are several formulas in the statistical literature used to calculate skewness. The simplest, developed by Professor Karl Pearson (1857–1936), is based on the difference between the mean and the median.

PEARSON'S COEFFICIENT OF SKEWNESS $sk = \dfrac{3(\bar{x} - \text{Median})}{s}$ [3–14]

According to this relationship, the coefficient of skewness can range from −3 up to 3. A value near −3, such as −2.57, indicates considerable negative skewness. A value such as 1.63 indicates moderate positive skewness. A value of 0, which will occur when the mean and median are equal, indicates the distribution is symmetric and that there is no skewness present.

Excel, with the Add-in **MegaStat**, calculates the coefficient of skewness using a formula that is slightly different from formula 3–14, that is based on the cubed deviations from the mean. The formula is:

$$sk = \frac{n}{(n-1)(n-2)}\left[\sum\left(\frac{x - \bar{x}}{s}\right)^3\right]$$

This formula offers an insight into skewness. The right-hand side of the formula is the difference between each value and the mean, divided by the standard deviation. That is the portion $(x - \bar{x})/s$ of the formula. This idea is called **standardizing.** We will discuss the idea of standardizing a value in more detail in Chapter 6 when we describe the normal probability distribution. At this point, observe that the result is to report the difference between each value and the mean in units of the standard deviation. If this difference is positive, the particular value is larger than the mean; if the variation is negative, the standardized quantity is smaller than the mean. When we cube these values, we retain the information on the direction of the difference. Recall that in the formula for the standard deviation (see formula 3–11), we squared the difference between each value and the mean, so the result was all non-negative values.

If the set of data values under consideration is symmetric, when we cube the standardized values and sum over all the values, the result would be near 0. If there are several large values, clearly separate from the others, the sum of the cubed differences would be a large positive value. Several values much smaller will result in a negative cubed sum.

The following example illustrates the idea of skewness:

Example	Following are the earnings per share, in dollars, for a sample of 15 software companies. The earnings per share are arranged from smallest to largest. $0.09 0.13 0.41 0.51 1.12 1.20 1.49 3.18 3.50 6.36 7.83 8.92 10.13 12.99 16.40 Compute the mean, median, and standard deviation. Find the coefficient of skewness using Pearson's estimate. What is your conclusion regarding the shape of the distribution?
Solution	These are sample data, so we use formula (3–2) to determine the mean: $$\bar{x} = \frac{\Sigma x}{n} = \frac{\$74.26}{15} = \$4.95$$ The median is the middle value in a set of data, arranged from smallest to largest. In this case, the middle value is $3.18, so the median earnings per share is $3.18. We use formula (3–12) to determine the sample standard deviation. $$s = \sqrt{\frac{\Sigma x^2 - \frac{(\Sigma x)^2}{n}}{n-1}} = \sqrt{\frac{749.372 - \frac{(74.26)^2}{15}}{15-1}} = \$5.22$$ Pearson's coefficient of skewness is 1.017, found by: $$sk = \frac{3(\bar{x} - \text{Median})}{s} = \frac{3(\$4.95 - \$3.18)}{\$5.22} = \$1.017$$ This indicates that there is moderate positive skewness in the earnings per share data.

We obtain a similar, but not exactly the same, value when using software. The details are shown below:

x	$\bar{x}$	$(x - \bar{x})$	S	$\left(\frac{x - \bar{x}}{s}\right)^3$
0.09	4.95067	−4.86067	5.22176	−0.80656
0.13	4.95067	−4.82067	5.22176	−0.78681
0.41	4.95067	−4.54067	5.22176	−0.65752
0.51	4.95067	−4.44067	5.22176	−0.61502
1.12	4.95067	−3.83067	5.22176	−0.39479
1.20	4.95067	−3.75067	5.22176	−0.37057
1.49	4.95067	−3.46067	5.22176	−0.29109
3.18	4.95067	−1.77067	5.22176	−0.03899
3.50	4.95067	−1.45067	5.22176	−0.02144
6.36	4.95067	1.40933	5.22176	0.01966
7.83	4.95067	2.87933	5.22176	0.16766
8.92	4.95067	3.96933	5.22176	0.43924
10.13	4.95067	5.17933	5.22176	0.97582
12.99	4.95067	8.03933	5.22176	3.64929
16.40	4.95067	11.44933	5.22176	10.54117
			Total	11.81004

$$sk = \frac{n}{(n-1)(n-2)}\left[\sum\left(\frac{x-\bar{x}}{s}\right)^3\right] = \frac{15}{(15-1)(15-2)}(11.81004) = 0.0734$$

We conclude that the earnings per share are somewhat positively skewed. The following summary, from Minitab, reports the descriptive measures, such as the mean, median, and standard deviation of the earnings per share data. Also included are the coefficient of skewness and a histogram with a bell-shaped curve superimposed.

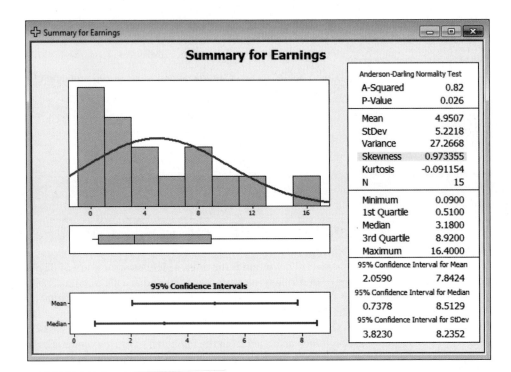

excel Computer commands to find the coefficient of skewness can be found at the end of the chapter.

self-review 3–11

A sample of five data entry clerks employed in the customer service department of a large pharmaceutical distribution company revised the following number of records last hour: 73, 98, 60, 92, and 84.

(a) Find the mean, median, and standard deviation.
(b) Compute the coefficient of skewness.
(c) What is your conclusion regarding the skewness of the data?

EXERCISES

For Exercises 61–64, do the following:

a. Determine the mean, median, and standard deviation.
b. Determine the coefficient of skewness.

61. The following values are the starting salaries, in thousands of dollars, for a sample of five accounting graduates who accepted positions in public accounting last year:

$36.0	26.0	33.0	28.0	31.0

62. Listed below are the salaries, in thousands of dollars, for a sample of 15 chief financial officers in the electronics industry:

$516.0	548.0	566.0	534.0	586.0	529.0
546.0	523.0	538.0	523.0	551.0	552.0
486.0	558.0	574.0			

63. Listed below are the commissions earned, in thousands of dollars, last year by the sales representatives at the Furniture Patch Inc.:

$3.9	5.7	7.3	10.6	13.0	13.6	15.1	15.8	17.1
17.4	17.6	22.3	38.6	43.2	87.7			

64. Listed below are the average commissions of top-producing financial advisors in the firm A2Z Securities:

$15 000	13 000	21 600	1250	12 000	382
396	5 667	389	382	456	3 000
432	23 429	13 000	10 000	385	490
750	382	1 500	16 000	10 500	
491	4 000	11 070	600	380	

LO3-7 3.15 MEASURES OF POSITION

The standard deviation is the most widely used measure of dispersion. However, there are other ways of describing the variation or spread in a set of data. One method is to determine the *location* of values that divide a set of observations into equal parts. These measures include **quartiles**, **deciles**, and **percentiles**.

Quartiles divide a set of observations into four equal parts. To explain further, think of any set of values arranged from the minimum to the maximum. Earlier in this chapter, we called the middle value of a set of data arranged from the minimum to the maximum the *median*. That is, 50% of the observations are larger than the median, and 50% are smaller. The median is a measure of location because it pinpoints the centre of the data. In a similar fashion, **quartiles** divide a set of observations into four equal parts. The first quartile, usually labelled Q_1, is the value below which 25% of the observations occur, and the third quartile, usually labelled Q_3, is the value below which 75% of the observations occur. Logically, Q_2 is the median. The values corresponding to Q_1, Q_2, and Q_3 divide a set of data into four equal parts.

Similarly, **deciles** divide a set of observations into 10 equal parts and **percentiles** into 100 equal parts. So, if you found that your GPA was in the 8th decile at your school, you could conclude that 80% of the students had a GPA lower than yours and 20% had a higher GPA. If your GPA was in the 92nd percentile, then 92% of students had a GPA less than yours, and only 8% of students had a GPA greater than your GPA. Percentile scores are frequently used to report results on such standardized tests as the SAT (Scholastic Assessment Test) and ACT (American College Testing), as well as the GMAT (Graduate Management Admission Test), which is used to judge entry into many business administration graduate programs, and the LSAT (Law School Admission Test), which is used to judge entry into law school.

Quartiles, Deciles, and Percentiles

To formalize the computational procedure, let L_p refer to the location of a desired percentile. So, if we wanted to find the 92nd percentile, we would use L_{92}, and if we wanted the median, the 50th percentile, then we would use L_{50}. For a number of observations, n, the location of the Pth percentile can be found using the formula:

LOCATION OF A PERCENTILE
$$L_p = (n+1)\frac{P}{100}$$
[3–15]

The following example will help to explain this further:

Example	Listed below are the commissions earned, in dollars, last month by a sample of 15 brokers at Salomon Smith Barney's office:

$2038	1758	1721	1637	2097	2047	2205	1787	2287
1940	2311	2054	2406	1471	1460			

Locate the median, the first quartile, and the third quartile for the commissions earned.

Solution	The first step is to organize the data from the smallest commission to the largest.

$1460	1471	1637	1721	1758	1787	1940	2038
2047	2054	2097	2205	2287	2311	2406	

The median value is the observation in the centre. The centre value or L_{50} is located at $(n + 1)(50/100)$, where n is the number of observations. In this case, that is position number 8, found by $(15 + 1)$ $(50/100)$. The eighth largest commission is $2038. So, we conclude this is the median and that half the brokers earned commissions more than $2038 and half earned less than $2038.

Recall the definition of *quartile*. Quartiles divide a set of observations into four equal parts. Hence, 25% of the observations will be less than the first quartile. Seventy-five percent of the observations will be less than the third quartile. To locate the first quartile, we use formula (3–15), where $n = 15$ and $P = 25$:

$$L_{25} = (n + 1)\frac{P}{100} = (15 + 1)\frac{25}{100} = 4$$

and to locate the third quartile, $n = 15$ and $P = 75$:

$$L_{75} = (n + 1)\frac{P}{100} = (15 + 1)\frac{75}{100} = 12$$

Therefore, the first and third quartile values are located at positions 4 and 12, respectively. The fourth value in the ordered array is $1721 and the 12th is $2205. These are the first and third quartiles.

In the above example the location formula yielded a whole number result. That is, we wanted to find the first quartile, and there were 15 observations, so the location formula indicated we should find the fourth ordered value. What if there were 20 observations in the sample, that is, $n = 20$, and we wanted to locate the first quartile? From the location formula (3–15):

$$L_{25} = (n + 1)\frac{P}{100} = (20 + 1)\frac{25}{100} = 5.25$$

We would locate the fifth value in the ordered array and then move 0.25 of the distance between the fifth and sixth values and report that as the first quartile. Like the median, the quartile does not need to be one of the actual values in the data set.

To explain further, suppose a data set contained the six values: 91, 75, 61, 101, 43, and 104. We want to locate the first quartile. We order the values from smallest to largest: 43, 61, 75, 91, 101, and 104. The first quartile is located at:

$$L_{25} = (n + 1)\frac{P}{100} = (6 + 1)\frac{25}{100} = 1.75$$

The position formula tells us that the first quartile is located between the first and second values and that it is 0.75 of the distance between the first and the second values. The first value is 43 and the second is 61. So, the distance between these two values is 18. To locate the first quartile, we need to move 0.75 of the distance between the first and second values, so $0.75(18) = 13.5$. To complete the procedure, we add 13.5 to the first value and report that the first quartile is 56.5.

We can extend the idea to include both deciles and percentiles. If we wanted to locate the 23rd percentile in a sample of 80 observations, we would look for the 18.63 position:

$$L_{23} = (n + 1)\frac{P}{100} = (80 + 1)\frac{23}{100} = 18.63$$

To find the value corresponding to the 23rd percentile, we would locate the 18th value and the 19th value and determine the distance between the two values. Next, we would multiply this difference by 0.63 and add the result to the smaller value. The result would be the 23rd percentile.

There are ways other than formula (3–15) to locate quartile values. For example, the method to find the position of the first quartile in **Excel** is $0.25n + 0.75$, and the position of the third quartile is $0.75n + 0.25$. Therefore, the quartile values found in **Excel** may be slightly different from the values found by formula (3–15).

Is the difference between methods important? No. In general, both methods calculate values that will support the statement that approximately 25% of the data values are less than the value of the first quartile, and approximately 75% of the data values are less than the value of the third quartile. When the sample size is large, the difference in the results from two or more methods is small.

---

excel

With a statistical software package, it is quite easy to sort the data from smallest to largest and to locate percentiles and deciles. Computer commands to find quartiles and percentiles can be found at the end of the chapter.

---

self-review 3–12

The quality control department of the Plainsville Peanut Company is responsible for checking the mass of the 500 grams (g) jar of peanut butter. The masses of a sample of nine jars produced last hour are:

490	495	496	498	500	500	501	504	505

(a) What is the median mass?
(b) Determine the masses corresponding to the first and third quartiles.

EXERCISES

65. The following data is the ages of a group of tourists horseback riding in Calgary, Alberta. Determine the median and the values corresponding to the first and third quartiles.

46	47	49	49	51	53	54	54	55	55	59

66. The following data is the number of seconds it took to save a large file. Determine the median and the values corresponding to the first and third quartiles.

5.24	6.02	6.67	7.30	7.59	7.99	8.03	8.35	8.81	9.45
9.61	10.37	10.39	11.86	12.22	12.71	13.07	13.59	13.89	15.42

67. The Thomas Supply Company Inc. is a distributor of small electrical motors. As with any business, the length of time customers take to pay their invoices is important. Listed below, arranged from smallest to largest, is the time, in days, for a sample of The Thomas Supply Company Inc. invoices:

13	13	13	20	26	27	31	34	34	34	35	35	36	37	38
41	41	41	45	47	47	47	50	51	53	54	56	62	67	82

    a. Determine the first and third quartiles.
    b. Determine the second decile and the eighth decile.
    a. Determine the 67th percentile.

68. Kevin Horn is the national sales manager for National Textbooks Inc. He has a sales staff of 40, who visit college and university professors. Each Saturday morning, he requires his sales staff to send him a report. This report includes, among other things, the number of professors visited during the previous week. Listed below, ordered from smallest to largest, are the number of visits last week.

| 38 | 40 | 41 | 45 | 48 | 48 | 50 | 50 | 51 | 51 | 52 | 52 | 53 | 54 | 55 | 55 | 55 | 56 | 56 | 57 |
| 59 | 59 | 59 | 62 | 62 | 62 | 63 | 64 | 65 | 66 | 66 | 67 | 67 | 69 | 69 | 71 | 77 | 78 | 79 | 79 |

   a. Determine the median number of calls.
   b. Determine the first and third quartiles.
   c. Determine the first decile and the ninth decile.
   d. Determine the 33rd percentile.

LO3-8 Box Plots

A **box plot** is a graphical display, based on quartiles, that helps us picture a set of data. To construct a box plot, we need only five statistics: the minimum value, Q_1 (the first quartile), the median, Q_3 (the third quartile), and the maximum value. The following example will help explain.

Example

Alexander's Pizza offers free delivery of its pizza within 15 km. Alex, the owner, wants some information on the time it takes for delivery. How long does a typical delivery take? Within what range of times will most deliveries be completed? For a sample of 20 deliveries, he determined the following information:

$$\text{Minimum value} = 13 \text{ minutes}$$
$$Q_1 = 15 \text{ minutes}$$
$$\text{Median} = 18 \text{ minutes}$$
$$Q_3 = 22 \text{ minutes}$$
$$\text{Maximum value} = 30 \text{ minutes}$$

Develop a box plot for the delivery times. What conclusions can you make about the delivery times?

Solution

The first step in drawing a box plot is to create an appropriate scale along the horizontal axis. Next, we draw a box that starts at Q_1 (15 minutes) and ends at Q_3 (22 minutes). Inside the box, we place a vertical line to represent the median (18 minutes). Finally, we extend horizontal lines from the box out to the minimum value (13 minutes) and the maximum value (30 minutes). These horizontal lines outside of the box are sometimes called "whiskers" because they look a bit like a cat's whiskers.

The box plot shows that the middle 50% of the deliveries take between 15 minutes and 22 minutes. The distance between the ends of the box, 7 minutes, is the **interquartile range.** The interquartile range is the distance between the first and the third quartiles. It shows the spread or dispersion of the middle 50% of deliveries.

   The box plot also reveals that the distribution of delivery times is positively skewed. How do we know this? In this case, there are actually two pieces of information that suggest that the distribution is positively skewed. First, the dashed line to the right of the box from 22 minutes (Q_3) to the maximum time of 30 minutes is longer than the dashed line from the left of 15 minutes (Q_1) to the minimum value of 13 minutes. To put it another way, the 25% of the data larger than the third quartile is more spread out than the 25% less than the first quartile. A second indication of positive skewness is that the median is not in the centre of the box. The distance from the first quartile to the median is smaller than the distance from the median to the third quartile. We know that the number of delivery times between 15 minutes and 18 minutes is the same as the number of delivery times between 18 minutes and 22 minutes.

Example	Refer to the Real Estate Data—Orleans in Connect. Develop a box plot for the variable list price. What can we conclude about the distribution of the list prices?
Solution	**Excel** and **MegaStat** were used to develop the following box plot. Computer commands to create this output can be found at the end of the chapter.

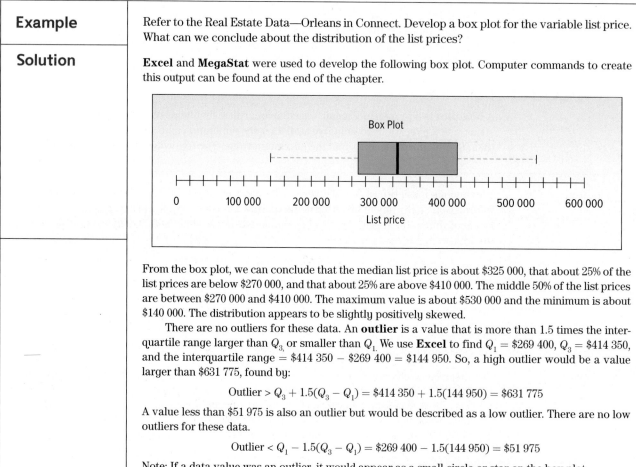

From the box plot, we can conclude that the median list price is about \$325 000, that about 25% of the list prices are below \$270 000, and that about 25% are above \$410 000. The middle 50% of the list prices are between \$270 000 and \$410 000. The maximum value is about \$530 000 and the minimum is about \$140 000. The distribution appears to be slightly positively skewed.

There are no outliers for these data. An **outlier** is a value that is more than 1.5 times the interquartile range larger than Q_3, or smaller than Q_1. We use **Excel** to find $Q_1 = \$269\ 400$, $Q_3 = \$414\ 350$, and the interquartile range = \$414 350 − \$269 400 = \$144 950. So, a high outlier would be a value larger than \$631 775, found by:

$$\text{Outlier} > Q_3 + 1.5(Q_3 - Q_1) = \$414\ 350 + 1.5(144\ 950) = \$631\ 775$$

A value less than \$51 975 is also an outlier but would be described as a low outlier. There are no low outliers for these data.

$$\text{Outlier} < Q_1 - 1.5(Q_3 - Q_1) = \$269\ 400 - 1.5(144\ 950) = \$51\ 975$$

Note: If a data value was an outlier, it would appear as a small circle or star on the box plot.

Example	The following is a box plot of list prices from the Real Estate Data—Whistler, BC2, Excel file found on Connect. Given that Q3 is about \$1 544 000 and the IQR is about \$1 300 250, find the approximate values of the three outliers (indicated by the small circles on the right side of the box plot.

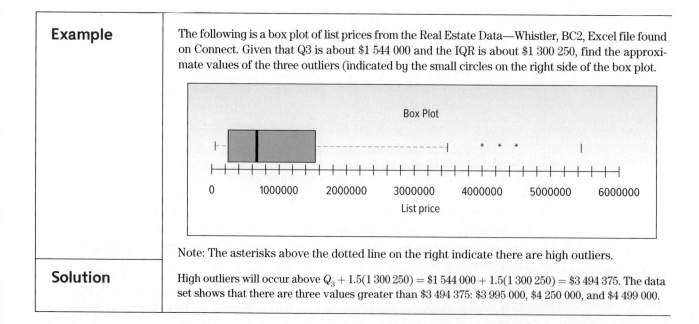

Note: The asterisks above the dotted line on the right indicate there are high outliers.

Solution	High outliers will occur above $Q_3 + 1.5(1\ 300\ 250) = \$1\ 544\ 000 + 1.5(1\ 300\ 250) = \$3\ 494\ 375$. The data set shows that there are three values greater than \$3 494 375: \$3 995 000, \$4 250 000, and \$4 499 000.

self-review 3–13   Refer to the following box plot:

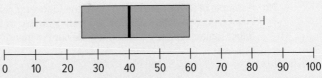

What are the median, minimum, and maximum values and the first and third quartiles? Would you agree that the distribution is symmetric?

EXERCISES

69. The box plot below shows the amount spent for books and supplies per year by students at community colleges:

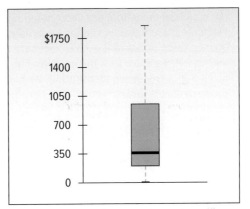

   a. Estimate the median amount spent.
   b. Estimate the first and third quartiles for the amount spent.
   c. Determine the interquartile range for the amount spent.
   d. Beyond what point is a value considered an outlier?
   e. Identify any outliers and estimate their value.
   f. Is the distribution symmetric or positively or negatively skewed?

70. Refer to the following box plot:

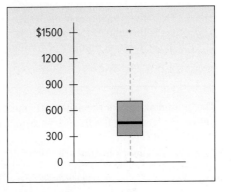

   a. Estimate the median.
   b. Estimate the first and third quartiles.
   c. Determine the interquartile range.
   d. Beyond what point is a value considered an outlier?
   e. Identify any outliers and estimate their value.
   f. Is the distribution symmetric or positively or negatively skewed?

71. In a study of the fuel efficiency of model year 2010 automobiles, the mean efficiency was 12 kilometres per litre (km/L), and the median was 11.7 km/L. The smallest value in the study was

5.5 km/L, and the largest was 22 km/L. The first and third quartiles were 7.8 km/L and 15.5 km/L, respectively. Develop a box plot and comment on the distribution. Is it a symmetric distribution?

72. A sample of 28 time-shares revealed the following daily charges, in dollars, for a one-bed suite. For convenience, the data are ordered from smallest to largest. Construct a box plot to represent the data. Comment on the distribution. Be sure to identify the first and third quartiles and the median.

$116	121	157	192	207	209	209
229	232	236	236	239	243	246
260	264	276	281	283	289	296
307	309	312	317	324	341	353

LO3-9   3.16 THE MEAN, MEDIAN, AND STANDARD DEVIATION OF GROUPED DATA

In most instances, measures of location, such as the mean, and measures of variability, such as the standard deviation, are determined by using the individual values. **Excel** makes it easy to calculate these values, even for large data sets. However, sometimes we are only given the frequency distribution and wish to estimate the mean or the standard deviation. In the following discussion, we show how the mean and the standard deviation can be estimated from data organized into a frequency distribution. We should stress that a mean or a standard deviation from grouped data is an *estimate* of the corresponding actual values.

The Arithmetic Mean of Grouped Data

To approximate the arithmetic mean of data organized into a frequency distribution, we begin by assuming the observations in each class are represented by the *midpoint* of the class. The mean of a sample of data organized in a frequency distribution is computed by:

ARITHMETICMEAN OF GROUPED DATA $\bar{x} = \dfrac{\sum fx}{n}$ [3–16]

where:

$\bar{x}$ is the designation for the sample mean.
x is the midpoint of each class.
f is the frequency in each class.
fx is the frequency in each class times the midpoint of the class.
$\sum fx$ is the sum of these products.
n is the total number of frequencies.

Example

The computations for the arithmetic mean of data grouped into a frequency distribution shown below are based on the list prices from the "Real Estate Data—Halifax Area" file on Connect. Recall, from Chapter 2, how a frequency distribution can be constructed. From the information given below, determine the arithmetic mean list price.

List Price ($ thousands)	Frequency
$0 to under $400	40
400 to under 800	42
800 to under 1 200	7
1 200 to under 1 600	7
1 600 to under 2 000	1
2 000 to under 2 400	0
2 400 to under 2 800	1
Total	98

Solution

The mean list price can be estimated from data grouped into a frequency distribution. To find the estimated mean, assume the midpoint of each class is representative of the data values in that class. Recall that the midpoint of a class is halfway between the lower class limits of two consecutive classes. To find the midpoint of a particular class, we add the lower limits of two consecutive classes and divide by 2. Hence, the midpoint of the first class is $200, found by: ($0 + $400)/2. We assume that the value of $200 is representative of the 40 values in that class. To put it another way, we assume the sum of the 40 values is $8000, found by 40($200). We continue the process of multiplying the class midpoint by the class frequency for each class and then sum these products. The results are summarized in Table 3–1.

Table 3–1 Calculation of the Mean for Grouped Data

List Price ($ thousands)	Frequency f	Midpoint ($) x	fx ($)
$0 to under $400	40	$ 200	$ 8 000
400 to under 800	42	600	25 200
800 to under 1 200	7	1 000	7 000
1 200 to under 1 600	7	1 400	9 800
1 600 to under 2 000	1	1 800	1 800
2 000 to under 2 400	0	2 200	0
2 400 to under 2 800	1	2 600	2 600
Total	98		$54 400

Solving for the arithmetic mean using formula (3–16), we get:

$$\bar{x} = \frac{\Sigma fx}{n} = \frac{\$54\,400}{98} = \$555.102$$

So, we conclude that an estimate of the mean list price is $555 102.

The Median of Grouped Data

Recall that the **median** is defined as the midpoint of the observations after they have been ordered from the lowest to the highest. If the data are grouped, some of the raw data values may not be available, and so we cannot necessarily determine the exact value of the median. But we can estimate the median by first finding the position of the median (which class it falls in) and then calculating an estimate of the median within this median class.

MEDIAN, GROUPED DATA
$$\text{Median} = L + \frac{\frac{N}{2} - f_c}{f}(i) \qquad [3\text{–}17]$$

where:

L is the lower limit of the median class.
N is the size of the population.
f is the frequency of the median class.
fc is the cumulative frequencies up to but excluding the median class.
i is the class width of the median class.

In the following example, the raw data are given:

Example

Professor Law lists the following quiz marks for his class of 30 students. Determine the median quiz mark:

Quiz Mark	10	9	8	7	6	5	4	3	2	1	0
Number of Students	2	3	5	12	4	2	1	0	1	0	0

Solution

1. Arrange the data from the lowest mark (?) to the highest mark (10) as follows.

Quiz Mark	0	1	2	3	4	5	6	7	8	9	10
Number of Students	0	0	1	0	1	2	4	12	5	3	2

2. Find the position of the median mark by using formula (3–15):

$$L_p = (n + 1)\frac{P}{100} = (30 + 1)\frac{50}{100} = 15.5$$

Therefore, the median quiz mark will be the 15.5th observation. Finally, count the number of students until the 15.5th observation is reached. The table below shows the cumulative number of observations until the 15.5th observation:

Quiz Mark	Number of Students	f_c	
0	0	0	
1	0	0	
2	1	1	
3	0	1	
4	1	2	
5	2	4	
6	4	8	
7	12	20	← median class
8	5	25	
9	3	28	
10	2	30	

3. The value of the median falls in the class where the number of students is 12 and the quiz mark is 7. Therefore, the median quiz mark is 7. Since the raw data values are listed, we are able to determine the exact value of the median.

The next example does not have the raw data listed. Instead, the data are grouped into a frequency distribution.

Example

The frequency distribution from the "Real Estate Data—Halifax Area" file, on Connect, is shown below. Compute the median of the list prices.

List Price ($ thousands)	Frequency
$0 to under $400	40
400 to under 800	42
800 to under 1 200	7
1 200 to under 1 600	7
1 600 to under 2 000	1
2 000 to under 2 400	0
2 400 to under 2 800	1
Total	98

Solution

1. The data are arranged from lowest to highest in the frequency distribution.

2. Find the position of the median list price by using formula (3–15):

$$L_p = (n + 1)\frac{P}{100} = (98 + 1)\frac{50}{100} = 49.5$$

Therefore, the median list price will be in the class where the 49.5th observation is found. Count the number of list prices until the 49.5th observation is reached. The table below shows the cumulative number of observations until the 49.5th observation:

List Price ($ thousands)	Frequency f	f_c	
$0 to under $400	40	40	
400 to under 800	42	82	← median class
800 to under 1 200	7	89	
1 200 to under 1 600	7	96	
1 600 to under 2 000	1	97	
2 000 to under 2 400	0	97	
2 400 to under 2 800	1	98	
Total	98		

3. Find the value of the median by using formula (3–17):

$$\text{Median} = L + \frac{\frac{N}{2} - f_c}{f}(i) = 400 + \frac{\frac{98}{2} - 40}{42}(400) = 485.7143$$

Therefore, an estimate of the median list price is $485 714. Since the original observations are not available, we can only estimate the median. *Note:* the median of the raw data from Table 3–1 is $450 200. The estimate is $35 514 larger, which is a 7.9% difference.

Standard Deviation of Grouped Data

Recall that for *ungrouped* data, one formula for the sample standard deviation is:

$$s = \sqrt{\frac{\sum x^2 - \frac{(\sum x)^2}{n}}{n - 1}}$$ [3–12]

If the data of interest are in *grouped* form (in a frequency distribution), the sample standard deviation can be approximated by substituting $\sum fx^2$ for $\sum x^2$ and $\sum fx$ for $\sum x$. The formula for the *sample standard deviation* then converts to:

STANDARD DEVIATION, GROUPED DATA
$$s = \sqrt{\frac{\sum fx^2 - \frac{(\sum x)^2}{n}}{n - 1}}$$ [3–18]

where:

    s is the symbol for the sample standard deviation.
    x is the midpoint of a class.
    f is the class frequency.
    n is the total number of sample observations.

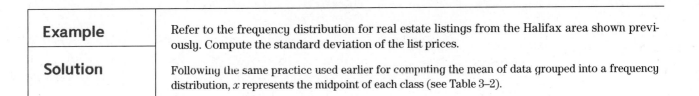

Example

Refer to the frequency distribution for real estate listings from the Halifax area shown previously. Compute the standard deviation of the list prices.

Solution

Following the same practice used earlier for computing the mean of data grouped into a frequency distribution, x represents the midpoint of each class (see Table 3–2).

Table 3–2 Calculation of Standard Deviation for Grouped Data

List Price ($ thousands)	Frequency f	Midpoint ($) x	fx ($)	fx^2
$0 to under $400	40	$200	$8 000	1 600 000
400 to under 800	42	600	25 200	15 120 000
800 to under 1 200	7	1 000	7 000	7 000 000
1 200 to under 1 600	7	1 400	9 800	13 720 000
1 600 to under 2 000	1	1 800	1 800	3 240 000
2 000 to under 2 400	0	2 200	0	0
2 400 to under 2 800	1	2 600	2 600	6 760 000
Total	98		$54 400	47 440 000

To find the standard deviation:

Step 1: Each class frequency is multiplied by its class midpoint. That is, multiply f times x. Thus, for the first class, 40($200) = $8000. For the second class, fx = 42($600) = $25 200, and so on.

Step 2: Calculate fx^2. This could be written as $fx \times x$. For the first class, it would be (8000)(200) = 1 600 000, and so on.

Step 3: Sum the fx and fx^2 columns. The totals are $54 400 and 47 440 000. We have omitted the units involved with the fx^2 column, but it is "dollars squared."

These values are used in the following formula (3–18):

$$s = \sqrt{\frac{\sum fx^2 - \frac{(\sum fx)^2}{n}}{n-1}} \quad \sqrt{\frac{47\ 440\ 000 - \frac{(54\ 400)^2}{98}}{98-1}} = 421.613$$

The mean and standard deviation calculated from grouped data into a frequency distribution are usually close to the values calculated from raw data. The grouping results in some loss of information. For the list prices, the mean price reported in the **Excel** output is $567 497 and the standard deviation is $416 469. The respective values estimated from data grouped into a frequency distribution are $555 102, and $421 613. The difference in the means is $12 395, which is a 2.18% difference. The difference in the standard deviation is −1.24%. On the basis of the percentage differences, the estimated values for the mean and standard deviation are close to the actual values.

self-review 3–14 The net incomes of a sample of large importers of antiques were organized into the following table:

Net Income ($ millions)	Number of Importers
$2 to under $6	1
6 to under 10	4
10 to under 14	10
14 to under 18	3
18 to under 22	2

(a) What is the table called?
(b) Based on the distribution, what is the estimate of the arithmetic mean net income?
(c) Based on the distribution, what is the estimate of the median net income?
(d) Based on the distribution, what is the estimate of the standard deviation?

EXERCISES

73. When we compute the mean of a frequency distribution, why do we refer to this as an *estimated* mean?

74. Determine the mean, median, and standard deviation of the following frequency distribution:

Class	Frequency
0 to under 5	2
5 to under 10	7
10 to under 15	12
15 to under 20	6
20 to under 25	3

75. Determine the mean, median, and standard deviation of the following frequency distribution:

Class	Frequency
20 to under 30	7
30 to under 40	12
40 to under 50	21
50 to under 60	18
60 to under 70	12

76. SCCoast, an Internet service provider, developed the following frequency distribution on the age of Internet users. Find the mean, median, and standard deviation.

Age (years)	Frequency
10 to under 20	3
20 to under 30	7
30 to under 40	18
40 to under 50	20
50 to under 60	12

77. The following frequency distribution reports the amount, in thousands of dollars, owed by a sample of 50 public accounting firms. Find the mean, median, and standard deviation.

Amount ($ thousands)	Frequency
$20 to under $30	1
30 to under 40	15
40 to under 50	22
50 to under 60	8
60 to under 70	4

78. Advertising expenses are a significant component of the cost of goods sold. Listed below is a frequency distribution showing the advertising expenditures for 60 manufacturing companies. Estimate the mean, median, and standard deviation of advertising expense.

Advertising ($ millions)	Expenditure	Number of Companies
$25 to under	$35	5
35 to under	45	10
45 to under	55	21
55 to under	65	16
65 to under	75	8
Total		60

3.17 ETHICS AND REPORTING RESULTS

In Chapter 1, we discussed the ethical and unbiased reporting of statistical results. While you are learning about how to organize and interpret data using statistics, it is also important to understand statistics so that you can be an intelligent consumer of information.

In this chapter, we learned how to compute descriptive statistics. Specifically, we showed how to compute and interpret measures of location for a data set: the mean, median, and mode. We also discussed the advantages and disadvantages for each statistic. For example, if a real estate developer tells a client that the average home in a particular subdivision sold for $350 000, we assume that $350 000 is a representative selling price for all the homes. But suppose that the client also asks what the median sales price is; the median is $200 000. Why was the developer only reporting the mean price? This information is extremely important to a person's decision making when buying a home. Knowing the advantages and disadvantages of the mean, median, and mode is important as we report statistics and we use statistical information to make decisions.

We also learned how to compute measures of dispersion: range, mean deviation, variance, and standard deviation. Each of these statistics also has advantages and disadvantages. Remember that the range provides information about the overall spread of a distribution. However, it does not provide any information about how the data are clustered or concentrated around the central location of the distribution. As we learn more about statistics, we need to remember that when we use statistics we must maintain an independent and principled point of view. Any statistical report requires objective and honest communication of the results.

Chapter Summary

I. A measure of location is a value used to describe the centre of a set of data.

  A. The arithmetic mean is the most widely reported measure of location.

    1. It is calculated by adding the values of the observations and dividing by the total number of observations.

      a. The formula for a population mean of ungrouped or raw data is:

$$\mu = \frac{\Sigma x}{N} \qquad [3\text{--}1]$$

      b. The formula for the mean of a sample is:

$$\bar{x} = \frac{\Sigma x}{n} \qquad [3\text{--}2]$$

      c. The formula for the sample mean of data in a frequency distribution is:

$$\bar{x} = \frac{\Sigma fx}{n} \qquad [3\text{--}16]$$

    2. The major characteristics of the arithmetic mean are:

      a. At least the interval scale of measurement is required.

      b. All the data values are used in the calculation.

      c. A set of data has only one mean. That is, it is unique.

      d. The sum of the deviations from the mean equals 0.

  B. The weighted mean is found by multiplying each observation by its corresponding weight.

    1. The formula for the weighted mean is:

$$\bar{x}_w = \frac{w_1 x_1 + w_2 x_2 + w_3 x_3 + \cdots + w_n x_n}{w_1 + w_2 + w_3 + \cdots + w_n} \qquad [3\text{--}3]$$

  C. The median is the value in the middle of a set of ordered data.

    1. To find the median, sort the observations from minimum to maximum, and identify the middle value.

    2. The major characteristics of the median are:

      a. At least the ordinal scale of measurement is required.

      b. It is not influenced by extreme values.

      c. Fifty percent of the observations are larger than the median.

      d. It is unique to a set of data.

3. The formula for the median of grouped data is:

$$\text{Median} = L + \frac{\frac{N}{2} - f_c}{f}(i)$$

[3–17]

D. The mode is the value that occurs most often in a set of data.
    1. The mode can be found for nominal-level data.
    2. A set of data can have more than one mode.

E. The geometric mean is the nth root of the product of n values.
    1. The formula for the geometric mean is:

$$GM = \sqrt[n]{(x_1)(x_2)(x_3) \cdots (x_n)}$$

[3–4]

    2. The geometric mean is also used to find the rate of change from one period to another.

$$GM = \sqrt[n]{\frac{\text{Value at end of period}}{\text{Value at beginning of period}}} - 1$$

[3–5]

    3. The geometric mean is always equal to or less than the arithmetic mean.

II. The dispersion is the variation or spread in a set of data.

    A. The range is the difference between the maximum and minimum values in a set of data.
        1. The formula for the range is:

$$\text{Range} = \text{Maximum Value} - \text{Minimum Value}$$

[3–6]

        2. The major characteristics of the range are:
            a. Only two values are used in its calculation.
            b. It is influenced by extreme values.
            c. It is easy to compute and to understand.

    B. The mean absolute deviation is the sum of the absolute values of the deviations from the mean divided by the number of observations.
        1. The formula for the mean absolute deviation is:

$$MD = \frac{\sum |x - \bar{x}|}{n}$$

[3–7]

        2. The major characteristics of the mean absolute deviation are:
            a. It is not unduly influenced by large or small values.
            b. All observations are used in the calculation.
            c. The absolute values are difficult to work with.

    C. The variance is the mean of the squared deviations from the arithmetic mean.
        1. The formula for the population variance is:

$$\sigma^2 = \frac{\sum (x - \mu)^2}{N}$$

[3–8]

        2. The formula for the sample variance is:

$$s^2 = \frac{\sum (x - \bar{x})^2}{n - 1}$$

[3–10]

        3. The major characteristics of the variance are:
            a. All observations are used in the calculation.
            b. The units are somewhat difficult to work with; they are the original units squared.

    D. The standard deviation is the square root of the variance.
        1. The major characteristics of the standard deviation are:
            a. It is in the same units as the original data.
            b. It is the square root of the average squared deviation from the mean.
            c. It cannot be negative.
            d. It is the most widely reported measure of dispersion.
        2. The formula for the sample standard deviation is:

$$s = \sqrt{\frac{\sum x^2 - \frac{(\sum x)^2}{n}}{n - 1}}$$

[3–12]

3. The formula for the standard deviation of grouped data is

$$s = \sqrt{\frac{\sum fx^2 - \frac{(\sum fx)^2}{n}}{n-1}}$$

[3–18]

III. We interpret the standard deviation using two measures.

  A. Chebyshev's theorem states that regardless of the shape of the distribution, at least $1 - 1/k^2$ of the observations will be within k standard deviations of the mean, where k is greater than 1.

  B. The Empirical Rule states that for a bell-shaped distribution about 68% of the values will be within 1 standard deviation of the mean, about 95% within 2 standard deviations, and virtually all within 3 standard deviations.

IV. The coefficient of variation is a measure of relative dispersion.

  A. The formula for the coefficient of variation is:

$$CV = \frac{s}{\bar{x}}(100)$$

[3–13]

  B. It reports the variation relative to the mean.

  C. It is useful for comparing distributions with different units.

V. The coefficient of skewness is a measure of the symmetry of a distribution.

  A. In a positively skewed set of data the long tail is to the right.

  B. In a negatively skewed distribution the long tail is to the left.

  C. There are two formulas for the coefficient of skewness.
    1. The formula developed by Pearson is:

$$sk = \frac{3(\bar{x} - \text{Median})}{s}$$

[3–14]

    2. The coefficient of skewness computed by statistical software is:

$$sk = \frac{n}{(n-1)(n-2)}\left[\sum\left(\frac{x - \bar{x}}{s}\right)^3\right]$$

VI. Measures of location also describe the shape of a set of observations.

  A. Quartiles divide a set of observations into four equal parts.
    1. Twenty-five percent of the observations are less than the first quartile, 50% are less than the second quartile (the median), and 75% are less than the third quartile.
    2. The interquartile range is the difference between the third and first quartiles.

  B. Deciles divide a set of observations into 10 equal parts and percentiles into 100 equal parts.

  C. A box plot is a graphic display of a set of data.
    1. A box is drawn enclosing the regions between the first and third quartiles.
      a. A line is drawn inside the box at the median value.
      b. Dotted line segments are drawn from the third quartile to the largest value to show the highest 25% of the values and from the first quartile to the smallest value to show the lowest 25% of the values.
    2. A box plot is based on five statistics: the maximum and minimum values, the first and third quartiles, and the median.

Chapter Exercises

79 The accounting firm of Crawford and Associates has five senior partners. Yesterday, the senior partners saw 6, 4, 3, 7, and 5 clients, respectively.
  a. Compute the mean number and the median number of clients seen by a partner.
  b. Is the mean a sample mean or a population mean?
  c. Verify that $\Sigma(x - \mu) = 0$.

80. Owens Orchards sells apples in a large bag by weight. A sample of seven bags contained the following numbers of apples: 23, 19, 26, 17, 21, 24, 22.
  a. Compute the mean number and the median number of apples in a bag.
  b. Verify that $\sum(x - \bar{x}) = 0$

81. A sample of households that subscribe to a local phone company revealed the following number of calls received last week. Determine the mean and the median numbers of calls received.

52	43	30	38	30	42	12	46	39	37
34	46	32	18	41	5				

82. The Citizens Banking Company is studying the number of times the ATM, located in a Loblaws Super-centre at the foot of Market Street is used per day. Following are the numbers of times the machine was used over each of the last 30 days. Determine the mean number of times the machine was used per day.

83	64	84	76	84	54	75	59	70	61
63	80	84	73	68	52	65	90	52	77
95	36	78	61	59	84	95	47	87	60

83. The Canadian government wants to know the relative age of its workforce. As the "baby boom" genera-tion becomes older, the government is concerned about the availability of younger, qualified workers. To become more informed, the government hired ABC Consulting Services to survey many industries regard-ing employee ages. The mean and the median ages for two industries, communication and retail trade, are listed in the following table:

	Communication and Other Utilities		Retail Trade and Consumer Services	
	Mean	Median	Mean	Median
Managers	52.6	53	48.6	48
Professionals	50.8	50	50.0	49
Technical/Trades	51.4	52	47.1	47
Marketing/Sales	NA	NA	43.7	41
Clerical/Administrative	50.8	51	48.0	48
Production Workers	47.2	50	42.0	34

Comment on the distribution of age. Which industry appears to have older workers? Younger workers? In each industry, which job types show the greatest difference between mean age and median age?

84. Trudy Green works for the True-Green Lawn Company. Her job is to solicit lawn care business via the telephone. Listed below are the number of appointments she made in each of the last 25 hours of calling. What is the arithmetic mean number of appointments she made per hour? What is the median number of appointments per hour? Write a brief report summarizing the findings.

9	5	2	6	5	6	4	4	7	2	3	6	3
4	4	7	8	4	4	5	5	4	8	3	3	

85. The Rail & Fence Company sells three types of fence to homeowners. Grade A costs $5.00/m to install, Grade B costs $6.50/m, and Grade C, the premium quality, costs $8.00/m. Yesterday, Split-A-Rail installed 270 m of Grade A, 300 m of Grade B, and 100 m of Grade C. What was the mean cost per metre of fence installed?

86. Rolland Poust is a business student. Last semester, he took courses in statistics and accounting, three hours each, and earned an A in both. He earned a B in a five-hour history course and a B in a two-hour history of jazz course. In addition, he took a one-hour course dealing with the rules of basketball so he could get his licence to officiate high school basketball games. He got an A in this course. What was his GPA for the semester? Assume that he receives 4 points for an A, 3 for a B, and so on. What measure of central tendency did you just calculate?

87. The uncertainty in the stock market led Sam to diversify his investments. However, he still felt that stock options would earn the most, so he left the bulk of his funds in stock options. The table below lists Sam's earnings from investments last year. What is the average rate of return on his investments?

Investment Type	Performance (%)	Amount Invested ($)
Mutual Funds	4.5	15 300
GICs	3.0	10 400
Stock Options	10.2	150 600

88. Listed below are the commuting distances, in kilometres, of students attending college for their first year:

5.2	6.3	7.5	4.3	6.8	4.6	4.6	8.2	7.8	9.4	9.3	7.4	5.3	5.3	5.4

    a. What is the arithmetic mean distance travelled?
    b. What is the median distance travelled?
    c. What is the modal distance travelled?

89. The Carter Construction Company pays its summer students an hourly rate of $13 for general labour, $15.50 for landscaping, or $18 for road work. Forty students were hired for the summer, 20 for general labour, 12 for landscaping, and 8 for road work. What is the mean hourly rate paid to the 40 summer students? Calculate the variance and standard deviation.

90. A recent article suggested that if you earn $25 000 a year today and the inflation rate continues at 3% per year, you will need to make $33 598 in 10 years to have the same buying power. You would need to make $44 771 if the inflation rate jumped to 6%. Confirm that these statements are accurate by finding the geometric mean rate of increase.

91. A library has seven branches in its system. The number of volumes (in thousands) held in the branches are 83, 510, 33, 256, 401, 47, and 23.
    a. Is this a sample or a population?
    b. Compute the standard deviation.
    c. Compute the coefficient of variation. Interpret.

92. Health issues are a concern of managers, especially as they evaluate the cost of medical insurance. A recent survey of 150 executives at Elvers Industries, a large insurance and financial firm, reported the number of kilograms by which the executives were overweight. Compute the range and the standard deviation.

Number of Kilograms	Frequency
0 to under 6	14
6 to under 12	42
12 to under 18	58
18 to under 24	28
24 to under 30	8

93. A major airline wanted some information on those enrolled in its "frequent flyer" program. A sample of 48 members resulted in the following distance flown last year, in thousands of kilometres, by each participant. Develop a box plot of the data, and comment on the information.

22	29	32	38	39	41	42	43	43	43	44	44
45	45	46	46	46	47	50	51	52	54	54	55
56	57	58	59	60	61	61	63	63	64	64	67
69	70	70	70	71	71	72	73	74	76	78	88

94. The National Muffler Company claims they will change your muffler in less than 30 minutes. An investigative reporter for WTOL Channel 11 monitored 30 consecutive muffler changes at the National outlet on Liberty Street. The number of minutes to perform changes is reported below:

44	12	22	31	26	22	30	26	18	28	12
40	17	13	14	17	25	29	15	30	10	28
16	33	24	20	29	34	23	13			

    a. Develop a box plot for the time to change a muffler.
    b. Does the distribution show any outliers?
    c. Summarize your findings in a brief report.

95. The Walter Gogel Company is an industrial supplier of fasteners, tools, and springs. The amounts of its invoices vary widely, from less than $20 to over $400. During the month of January it sent out 80 invoices. Here is a box plot of these invoices. Write a brief report summarizing the amounts of its invoices. Be sure to include information on the values of the first and third quartile, the median, and whether there is any skewness. If there are any outliers, approximate the value of these invoices.

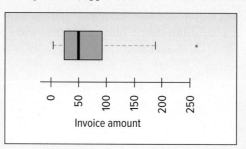

96. The following box plot shows the number of daily newspapers published. Summarize the findings. Be sure to include information on the values of the first and third quartiles, the median, and whether there is any skewness. If there are any outliers, estimate their value.

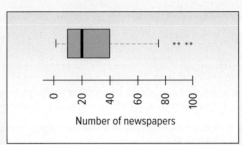

Number of newspapers

97. Bidwell Electronics Inc. recently surveyed a sample of employees to determine how far they lived from corporate headquarters. The results are shown below. Compute the mean, median, and standard deviation.

Distance (km)	Frequency
0 to under 5	4
5 to under 10	15
10 to under 15	27
15 to under 20	18
20 to under 25	6

98. On the Coast is a very popular restaurant located along the coast of Lake Erie. It serves a variety of steak and seafood dinners. During the summer beach season, it does not take reservations or accept "call ahead" seating. Management of the restaurant is concerned about the time a patron has to wait before being seated for dinner. Listed below is the wait time, in minutes, for the 25 tables seated last Saturday night:

28	39	23	67	37	28	56	40	28	50
51	45	44	65	61	27	24	61	34	44
64	25	24	27	29					

a. Explain why the wait times, in minutes, are a sample.
b. Find the mean and the median of the wait times.
c. Find the range and the standard deviation of the wait times.

99. A data distribution has a median value of 85, a first-quartile value of 80, and a third-quartile value of 100. Would the following values be considered a low outlier, a high outlier, or not an outlier: 35, 48, 52, 66, 108 and 105?

100. A recent report in *Woman's World* magazine suggested that the typical family of four with an intermediate budget spends about $106 per week on food. The following frequency distribution was included in the report. Compute the mean, median, and standard deviation. How do your results compare with those of the report?

Amount Spent ($)	Frequency
$80 to under $85	6
85 to under 90	12
90 to under 95	23
95 to under 100	35
100 to under 105	24
105 to under 110	10

101. The Apollo space program lasted from 1967 until 1972 and included 13 missions. The missions lasted from as little as 7 hours to as long as 301 hours. The duration of each flight is listed below:

9	195	241	301	216	260	7	244	192	147
10	295	142							

a. Find the mean, median, and standard deviation of the duration for the Apollo flights. Treat the data as a sample.

b. Compute the coefficient of variation and the coefficient of skewness. Comment on your findings.

c. Find the 45th and 82nd percentiles.

d. Draw a box plot, and comment on your findings.

102. A survey showed that in a class of 30 students, nine had purchased their own computers and printers. The cost of the computer systems, in dollars, is listed below:

$2235	2150	1850	1500	2025	5750	2800	2750	3300

a. Calculate the mean and median costs of the computer systems.

b. Draw a box plot and comment on your findings.

c. Would you use the mean or the median as a measure of location of your data? Explain.

For the following two questions, find the mean, median, mode, standard deviation, and interquartile range. Consider these sample data.

103.

Grade on Quiz	3	4	5	7	8	10
Number of Students	4	4	6	20	6	1

104.

Grade on Quiz	50	60	70	80	90	100
Number of Students	2	17	21	40	13	8

105. You are exploring the music contained in your iTunes library. The total play counts over the past year for the songs on your "smart playlist" are shown in the following frequency distribution:

Class	Frequency
0 to under 200	18
200 to under 400	5
400 to under 600	4
600 to under 800	4
800 to under 1000	2

Determine the mean, median, and standard deviation. Does the distribution appear to be positively or negatively skewed? Explain.

106. A social scientist is studying the use of iPods by college students. A sample of 45 students revealed that they played the following number of songs yesterday:

Class	Frequency
0 to under 2	2
2 to under 4	4
4 to under 6	5
6 to under 8	8
8 to under 10	14
10 to under 12	12

a. Determine the mean, median, and standard deviation.

b. Does the distribution appear to be positively or negatively skewed? Explain.

107. The manager of the production department for a manufacturing company is concerned about the number of units produced each week at the Calgary, Alberta, and the Vaughan, Ontario, plants. The Calgary location is a much larger facility, but the manager wants to determine if there is more variability in production units at the Vaughan location. The numbers produced at each plant over a six-week period are as follows:

	Production Units					
Location	Week 1	Week 2	Week 3	Week 4	Week 5	Week 6
Calgary	100	115	113	110	121	116
Vaughan	65	75	62	77	61	58

Compare the variability in production units at the two locations, and report your conclusion.

108. A total of 42 students wrote the first quiz in their statistics class. The following frequency distribution reports the results:

Grade (%)	Frequency
90 to 100	3
80 to under 90	12
70 to under 80	16
60 to under 70	8
50 to under 60	3

  a. Determine the mean, median, and standard deviation.
  b. Does the distribution appear to be positively or negatively skewed? Explain.

109. The ages of a sample of Canadian tourists flying from Toronto to Hong Kong were: 32, 21, 60, 47, 54, 17, 72, 55, 33, and 41.
  a. Compute the range.
  b. Compute the mean deviation.
  c. Compute the standard deviation.
  d. Using Chebyshev's theorem, at least what percentage of the observations must be within 2 standard deviations of the mean? Verify.
  e. Using the Empirical Rule, about 95% of the values would occur between what values? Verify.

110. Following are the earnings per share, in dollars, for a sample of two stocks:

			Earnings per Share ($)			
Stock A	0.09	0.13	0.55	1.20	0.89	1.05
Stock B	65.01	75.55	66.78	68.45	70.12	

Compare the variability in earnings of the two stocks. What is your conclusion?

111. The following data are the estimated market values (in millions of dollars) of 50 companies in the auto parts business:

$26.8	8.6	6.5	30.6	15.4	18.0	7.6	21.5	11.0	10.2
28.3	15.5	31.4	23.4	4.3	20.2	33.5	7.9	11.2	1.0
11.7	18.5	6.8	22.3	12.9	29.8	1.3	14.1	29.7	18.7
6.7	31.4	30.4	20.6	5.2	37.8	13.4	18.3	27.1	32.7
6.1	0.9	9.6	35.0	17.1	1.9	1.2	16.6	31.1	16.1

  a. Determine the mean and the median of the market values.
  b. Determine the standard deviation of the market values.
  c. Using the Empirical Rule, about 95% of the values would occur between what values?
  d. Determine the coefficient of variation.
  e. Determine the coefficient of skewness.
  f. Estimate the values of Q_1 and Q_3. Draw a box plot.
  g. Summarize the results.

112. The masses (in kilograms) of a sample of five boxes being sent by United Parcel Service (UPS) are: 12, 6, 7, 3, and 10.
  a. Compute the range.
  b. Compute the mean deviation.
  c. Compute the standard deviation.
  d. Using Chebyshev's theorem, at least what percentage of the observations must be within 2.5 standard deviations of the mean? Verify.
  e. Using the Empirical Rule, about 68% of the values would occur between what values? Verify.

113. The final marks for the Wednesday class in Statistics 101 are ready to be posted. The class average is 70%, with a standard deviation of 8. Use the Empirical Rule to answer the following questions.
  a. What percentage of the grades are between 62 and 78?
  b. What percentage of the grades are between 54 and 86?
  c. What percentage of the grades are between 46 and 94?
  d. What percentage of the grades are more than 86?
  e. What percentage of the grades are less than 46?
  f. What percentage of the grades are less than 46 or more than 86?

114. The final marks for the Wednesday class in Statistics 101 are ready to be posted. The class average is 72%, with a standard deviation of 9. Use the Empirical Rule to answer the following questions.
  a. What percentage of the grades are above 81?
  b. What percentage of the grades are below 54?

c. What percentage of the grades are between 54 and 90?
d. What percentage of the grades are between 54 and 81?
e. What percentage of the grades are between 54 and 99?
f. What percentage of the grades are less than 63 or more than 90?

115. Refer to the following data: 11 26 34 12 15 33 37 55 41 36 42 14 39
a. Determine the values for the first, second and third quartiles.
b. Sketch a boxplot for the data.
c. Beyond what point is a value considered an outlier?
d. Are there any outliers? If so, what is their value?
e. Determine the 20th and 60th percentiles.

116. Refer to the following data: 110 265 344 125 165 333 537 855 410 362 412 114 390 115
a. Determine the values for the first, second and third quartiles.
b. Sketch a boxplot for the data.
c. Beyond what point is a value considered an outlier?
d. Are there any outliers? If so, what is their value?
e. Are the data positively or negatively skewed? Explain.
f. Determine the 15th and 80th percentiles.

Data Set Exercises

Questions marked with ⚹ have data sets available on McGraw-Hill's online resource for *Basic Statistics.*

⚹ 117. Refer to the CREA Cities Only (Canadian Real Estate Association) data online, which reports information on average house prices nationally and in a selection of cities across Canada.
a. Select the cities for the month June 2016.
1. Find the mean, median, and standard deviation.
2. Determine the coefficient of skewness. Is the distribution positively or negatively skewed?
3. Develop a box plot. Are there any outliers? Estimate the first and third quartiles.
4. Summarize the results.
b. Select the cities for the month January 2013.
1. Find the mean, median, and standard deviation.
2. Determine the coefficient of skewness. Is the distribution positively or negatively skewed?
3. Develop a box plot. Are there any outliers? Estimate the first and third quartiles.
4. Summarize and compare the results with those of June 2016.

⚹ 118. Refer to the Real Estate Data—Orleans online, which reports information on home listings. Select the variable number of bedrooms.
1. Find the mean, median, and standard deviation.
2. Determine the coefficient of skewness. Is the distribution positively or negatively skewed?
3. Develop a box plot. Are there any outliers? Estimate the first and third quartiles.
4. Summarize the results.

⚹ 119. Refer to the Real Estate Data—Rockland Area online, which reports information on home listings.
a. Select the variable list prices.
1. Find the mean, median, and standard deviation.
2. Determine the coefficient of skewness. Is the distribution positively or negatively skewed?
3. Develop a box plot. Are there any outliers? Estimate the first and third quartiles.
4. Summarize the results.
b. Select the variable number of bedrooms.
1. Find the mean, median, and standard deviation.
2. Determine the coefficient of skewness. Is the distribution positively or negatively skewed?
3. Develop a box plot. Are there any outliers? Estimate the first and third quartiles.
4. Summarize the results.

Case

Continue with the Whitner Autoplex data and case from Chapter 2. Rob would like you to further develop tables and charts that he could review monthly and would like you to report where the selling prices tend to cluster, where the variation is in the selling prices, and to note any trends. The data are on Connect, Data Files, Whitner Autoplex.

Practice Test

Part I Objective

1. An observable characteristic of a population is called a _____.
2. A measure, such as the mean, based on sample data is called a _____.
3. The sum of the differences between each value and the mean is always equal to _____.
4. The midpoint of a set of values after they have been ordered from the minimum to the maximum is called the _____ .
5. What percentage of the values in every data set is larger than the median? _____.
6. The value of the observation that appears most frequently in a data set is called the _____ .
7. The _____ is the difference between the largest and the smallest values in a data set.
8. The _____ is the arithmetic mean of the squared deviations from the mean.
9. The square of the standard deviation is the _____.
10. The standard deviation assumes a negative value when (all the values are negative, at least half the values are negative, or never—pick one) _____.
11. Which of the following is least affected by an outlier? (mean, median, or range—pick one) _____.
12. The _____ states that for any symmetric, bell-shaped frequency distribution, approximately 68% of the observations will lie within plus and minus 1 standard deviation of the mean.
13. A _____ is a graphical display based on five statistics: the maximum and minimum values, the first and third quartiles, and the median.
14. A _____ divides a set of observations into four equal parts.
15. A _____ divides a set of observations into 100 equal parts.
16. The coefficient of _____ is a measure of the symmetry.
17. The _____ is the point below which one-fourth of the ranked values lie.
18. The _____ is the difference between the first and third quartiles.

Part II Problems

1. A sample of college students reported they owned the following number of albums:

76	64	79	80	74	66	69

   a. What is the mean number of albums owned?
   b. What is the median number of albums owned?
   c. What is the range of the number of albums owned?
   d. What is the standard deviation of the number of albums owned?

2. An investor purchased 200 shares of the Blair Company for $36 each in July of 2017, 300 shares at $40 each in September 2017, and 500 shares at $50 each in January 2017. What is the investor's weighted mean price per share?

3. After the Government of Ontario raised the taxes on cigarettes, a survey of 50 students was taken to see if the increased taxes would affect the amount that they spent on cigarettes. The estimated mean amount for the change per week was a decrease of $20.88. That indicates that the students expected to smoke less in the next year. If the standard deviation is 1.41, use the Empirical Rule to estimate the range that includes 95% of all the anticipated decreases in the amounts spent by the students on cigarettes.

4. The market capitalization at the end of the most recent fiscal year for 11 companies in the property and casualty insurance industry is (in millions of dollars):

15	17	23	26	27	35	72	88	91	98	102

   a. Determine the median.
   b. Compute the first quartile.
   c. Find the 75th percentile.
   d. Make a box plot of the data.

Computer Commands

1. **Excel** functions to find descriptive statistics are:

   a. Select **Insert Function, and** from the **Or select a category** list, select **Statistical**.

   b. In the **Select a function** list, click **AVERAGE,** and click **OK**.

   c. Enter the range in the **Number1** box. Click **OK**.
   - For the median, use **MEDIAN**.
   - For the mode, use **MODE.MULT** (the dialogue box displays all modes).
   - For the population variance, use **VAR.P**.
   - For the sample variance, use **VAR.S**.
   - For the population standard deviation, use **STDEV.P**.
   - For the sample standard deviation, use **STDEV.S**.
   - For the range, use **MAXIMUM** and **MINIMUM**.
   - For the mean deviation, use **AVEDEV**.

2. **Excel** steps to find descriptive statistics are:

   a. From McGraw-Hill's online resource, select **Data Files** and **Table 2–1: Real Estate Data—Whistler, BC**.

   b. From the menu bar select **DATA** and **Data Analysis**. Select **Descriptive Statistics**, and then click **OK**.

   c. The **Input Range** is the range of the data list prices; check that the data are grouped by **Columns**, and select **Labels in First Row**. Click **Output Range**, select

   C2 (or any cell you wish), click **Summary statistics**, then **OK**.

   d. The output will appear in cell C2.

3. **MegaStat** steps to find descriptive statistics and the box plot are:

   a. From McGraw-Hill's online resource, select **Data Sets, Real Estate Data—Whistler, BC**. or **Real Estate Data—Whistler, BC data set 2**.

   b. Click **MegaStat, Descriptive Statistics**. The **Input range** is the range of list prices. Note the checks in the first three boxes—these are the default settings. Select the descriptive statistics that you want by removing or adding the checks. Click **OK**.

   c. The output will appear in the *Output* sheet.

4. **Excel** steps to find the coefficient of skewness are:

   a. Select **Insert Function**. From the **Or select a category** list, select **Statistical**.

   b. In the **Select a function** list, select **SKEW** or **PEARSON**, and click **OK**.

   c. Enter the data range and click **OK**.

5. **MegaStat** steps to find the coefficient of skewness are:

   a. Click **MegaStat, Descriptive Statistics**. Enter the data range.

   b. Check the box **Skewness, kurtosis, CV**. Click **OK**.

   c. The output will appear in the *Output* sheet.

Answers to Self-Reviews

3–1 **1.** **(a)** $\bar{x} = \dfrac{\$267\,100}{4} = \$66\,775$

   (b) Statistic, because it is a sample value.

   (c) $66 775. The sample mean is our best estimate of the population mean.

2. **(a)** $\mu = \dfrac{498}{6} = 83$

   (b) Parameter, because it was computed using all the population values.

3–2 **(a)** $237, found by:

$$\frac{(95 \times \$400) + (126 \times \$200) + (79 \times \$100)}{95 + 126 + 79} = \$237.00$$

   (b) The profit per suit is $12, found by: $237 – $200 cost – $25 commission. The total profit for the 300 suits is $3600, found by: 300 × $12.

3–3 **1.** **(a)** $897.31

   (b) 6, 6

2. **(a)** 7, found by: $(6 + 8)/2 = 7$

   (b) 3, 3

   (c) 0

3–4 **(a)**

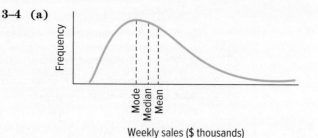

Weekly sales ($ thousands)

   (b) Positively skewed, because the mean is the largest average and the mode is the smallest.

3–5 **1.** **(a)** About 9.9%, found by: $\sqrt[4]{1.4586} - 1$

   (b) About 10.095%

   (c) Greater than, because 10.095 > 8.39

2. 8.63%, found by: $\sqrt[20]{\dfrac{120\,520}{23\,000}} - 1 = 1.0863 - 1$

3–6 **(a)** 22, found by: 112 − 90

   (b) $\bar{x} = \dfrac{824}{8} = 103$

(c)

x	$|x - \bar{x}|$	Absolute Deviation
95	$|-8|$	8
103	$|0|$	0
105	$|+2|$	2
110	$|+7|$	7
104	$|+1|$	1
105	$|+2|$	2
112	$|+9|$	9
90	$|-13|$	13
		Total 42

$$MD = \frac{42}{8} = 5.25 \text{ kg}$$

3–7 (a) $\mu = \dfrac{\$16\,900}{5} = \$3380$

(b) $\sigma^2 = \dfrac{(3356 - 3380)^2 + \cdots + (3622 - 3380)^2}{5}$

$= \dfrac{197\,454}{5} = 39\,490.8$

(c) $\sigma = \sqrt{39\,490.8} = 198.72$

(d) There is more variation in the second office because the standard deviation is larger. The mean is also larger in the second office.

3–8 (a) 2.33, found by:

$$\bar{x} = \frac{\sum x}{n} = \frac{28}{7} = 4$$

x	$x - \bar{x}$	$(x - \bar{x})^2$	x^2
4	0	0	16
2	-2	4	4
5	1	1	25
4	0	0	16
5	1	1	25
2	-2	4	4
6	2	4	36
28	0	14	126

$s^2 = \dfrac{\sum(x - \bar{x})^2}{n - 1}$

$= \dfrac{14}{7 - 1}$

$= 2.33$

or

$s^2 = \dfrac{\sum x^2 - \dfrac{(\sum x)^2}{n}}{n - 1}$

$= \dfrac{126 - \dfrac{(28)^2}{7}}{7 - 1}$

$= \dfrac{126 - 112}{6}$

$= 2.33$

$s = \sqrt{2.33} = 1.53$

3–9 (a) $k = \dfrac{1.35 - 1.2}{0.1} = 1.5$

$1 - \dfrac{1}{(1.5)^2} = 1 - 0.44 = 0.56$

$= 56\%$

(b) 1.1 to 1.3

(c) 1.0 to 1.4

3–10 CV for mechanical is 5%, found by: (10/200) (100). For finger dexterity, CV is 20%, found by: (6/30)(100). Thus, relative dispersion in finger dexterity scores is greater than relative dispersion in mechanical because 20% > 5%.

3–11 (a) $\bar{x} = \dfrac{407}{5} = 81.4$, Median = 84

$$s = \sqrt{\dfrac{34\,053 - \dfrac{(407)^2}{5}}{5 - 1}} = 15.19$$

(b) $sk = \dfrac{3(81.4 - 84.0)}{15.19} = -0.51$ using Pearson's method.

(c) The distribution is somewhat negatively skewed.

3–12 (a) 500

(b) $Q_1 = 495.5$, $Q_2 = 502.5$

3–13 The minimum value is 10 and the maximum 85; the first quartile is 25, and the third is 60. About 50% of the values are between 25 and 60. The median value is 40. The distribution is somewhat positively skewed.

3–14 (a) Frequency distribution.

(b)

f	Midpoint (x)	fx	fx^2
1	4	4	16
4	8	32	256
10	12	120	1440
3	16	48	768
2	20	40	800
20		244	3280

$\bar{x} = \dfrac{\sum fx}{N} = \dfrac{\$244}{20} = \$12.20$

(c)

Net Income ($ millions)	f	fc
$2 to under $6	1	1
6 to under 10	4	5
10 to under 14	10	15
14 to under 18	3	18
18 to under 22	2	20
Total	20	

Position of the median $= (20 + 1)/2 = 10.5$th observation

Value of the median $= 10 + \dfrac{\dfrac{20}{2} - 5}{10}(4) = 12$

(d) $s = \sqrt{\dfrac{3280 - \dfrac{(244)^2}{20}}{20 - 1}} = \$3.99$

CHAPTER 4
A Survey of Probability Concepts

© Pixtal/Superstock

It was found that 60% of the tourists to China visited the Forbidden City, the Temple of Heaven, the Great Wall, and other historical sites in or near Beijing. Forty percent visited Xi'an and its magnificent terracotta soldiers, horses, and chariots, which had been buried for over 2000 years. Thirty percent of the tourists went to both Beijing and Xi'an. What is the probability that a tourist visited at least one of these places? (Exercise 80, LO4-4)

LEARNING OBJECTIVES

When you have completed this chapter, you will be able to:

LO4-1 Define the terms *probability*, *experiment*, *event*, and *outcome*.

LO4-2 Assign probabilities using a classical, empirical, or subjective approach.

LO4-3 Determine the number of outcomes using principles of counting.

LO4-4 Calculate probabilities using the rules of addition.

LO4-5 Calculate probabilities using the rules of multiplication.

LO4-6 Compute probabilities using a contingency table.

LO4-7 Use a *tree diagram* to organize and compute probabilities.

4.1 INTRODUCTION

The emphasis in Chapters 2 and 3 was on descriptive statistics. In Chapter 2, we organized the list prices of 85 homes from Whistler, BC, into a frequency distribution. This frequency distribution showed the lowest and the highest list prices and where the largest concentration of data occurs. We then developed charts and graphs, such as a histogram, to further describe the data graphically. In Chapter 3, we used numerical measures of location and dispersion to locate a typical list price and to examine the variation in the data. We described the variation in the list prices with such measures of dispersion as the range and the standard deviation.

Descriptive statistics is concerned with summarizing data collected from past events. We now turn to the second facet of statistics, namely, *computing the chance that something will occur in the future*. This facet of statistics is called **statistical inference** or **inferential statistics**.

Seldom does a decision maker have complete information from which to make a decision. For example:

- Toys and Things, a toy and puzzle manufacturer, recently developed a new game based on sports trivia. They want to know whether sports buffs will purchase the game. "Slam Dunk" and "Home Run" are two of the names under consideration. One way to minimize the risk of making an incorrect decision is to hire a market research firm to take a sample of, say, 2000 consumers from the population and ask each respondent for a reaction to the new game and its proposed titles. Using the sample results, the company can estimate the proportion of the population that will purchase the game.

- The quality control department of a Hamilton Steel mill must assure management that the 3-millimetre (mm) wire being produced has an acceptable tensile strength. Obviously, not all the wire produced can be tested for tensile strength because testing requires the wire to be stretched until it breaks—thus, destroying it. So, a random sample of 10 pieces is selected and tested. On the basis of the test results, all the wire produced is deemed either acceptable or unacceptable.

- Other questions involving uncertainty are: Should the daytime drama *Days of Our Lives* be discontinued immediately? Will a newly developed mint-flavoured cereal be profitable if marketed? How many new television reality shows should be developed for the fall season?

Statistical inference deals with conclusions about a population based on a sample taken from that population. (The populations for the preceding illustrations are: all consumers who like sports trivia games, all the 3-mm steel wire produced, all television viewers who watch daytime drama, all who purchase breakfast cereal, and so on.)

Because there is uncertainty in decision making, it is important that all the known risks involved be scientifically evaluated. Helpful in this evaluation is *probability theory*, which has often been referred to as the *science of uncertainty*. Probability theory allows the decision maker with only limited information to analyze the risks and benefits associated with a set of decision alternatives. For example, a marketing executive who is responsible for the development of new products will use probability theory to assess the likelihood that a new product will be successful in the marketplace. A purchasing manager who is responsible for the quality of purchased materials will use probability theory to evaluate the quality standards of purchased materials and the risk of accepting an incoming shipment.

Because probability concepts are so important in the field of statistical inference (to be discussed starting with Chapter 7), this chapter introduces the basic language of probability, including such terms as *experiment*, *event*, *subjective probability*, and *addition* and *multiplication rules*.

LO4-1   4.2 WHAT IS A PROBABILITY?

No doubt you are familiar with terms such as *probability*, *chance*, and *likelihood*. They are often used interchangeably. The weather forecaster announces that there is a 70% chance of snow for the Grey Cup game. Based on a survey of consumers who tested a newly developed toothpaste with banana flavour, the probability that, if marketed, it will be a financial success is 0.03. (This means that the chance of the banana-flavoured toothpaste being accepted by the public is rather remote.) What is a **probability**? In general, it is a number that describes the chance that something will happen.

Probability A value between 0 and 1, inclusive, describing the relative possibility (chance or likelihood) an event will occur.

A probability is frequently expressed as a decimal, such as 0.70, 0.27, or 0.50. However, it may be given as a fraction such as 7/10, 27/100, or 1/2. It can assume any number from 0 to 1, inclusive. If a company has only five sales regions, and each region's name or number is written on a slip of paper and the slips put in a hat, the probability of selecting one of the five regions is 1. The probability of selecting from the hat a slip of paper that reads "Edmonton Oilers" is 0. Thus, the probability of 1 represents something that is certain to happen, and the probability of 0 represents something that cannot happen.

The closer a probability is to 0, the more improbable it is the event will happen. The closer the probability is to 1, the more certain we are that it will happen. The relationship, along with a few of our personal beliefs, is shown in the following diagram. You might, however, select a different probability for Slo Poke's chances to win the Queen's Plate or rain in Vancouver this year.

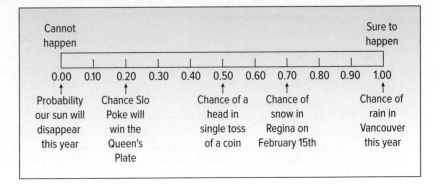

Sometimes, the likelihood of an event is expressed by using the term *odds*. For example, someone says the odds are "five to two" that an event will occur. This means that in a total of seven trials (5 + 2), the event will occur five times and not occur two times. Using odds, we can compute the probability that the event occurs as 5/(5 + 2) or 5/7.

Three key words are used in the study of probability: **experiment, outcome,** and **event**. These terms are used in our everyday language, but in statistics they have specific meanings.

The definition of experiment is more general than the one used in the physical sciences, where we picture someone manipulating test tubes or microscopes. In reference to probability, an experiment has two or more possible results, and it is uncertain which will occur.

For example, the tossing of a coin is an experiment. You may observe the toss of the coin, but you are unsure of the *outcome*—whether it will come up "heads" or "tails." If the coin is tossed, one particular outcome is a "head." The alternative outcome is a "tail." Similarly, asking 500 college students if they would travel more than 200 kilometres (km) to attend a Justin Bieber concert is an experiment. In this experiment, one possible outcome is that 273 students indicate they would travel more than 200 km to attend the concert. Another outcome is that 317 students would travel more than 200 km to attend the concert. Still another outcome is that 423 students indicate that they would travel more than 200 km to attend the concert. When one or more of the experiment's outcomes are observed, we call this an *event*.

Examples to clarify the definitions of the terms *experiment, outcome,* and *event* are presented in the following figure:

Experiment A process that leads to the occurrence of one and only one of several possible results.

Outcome A particular result of an experiment.

Event A collection of one or more outcomes of an experiment.

Experiment	Roll a die	Count the number of members of the board of directors for Fortune 500 companies who are over 60 years of age
All possible outcomes	Observe a 1 Observe a 2 Observe a 3 Observe a 4 Observe a 5 Observe a 6	None is over 60 One is over 60 Two are over 60 . . . 29 are over 60 . . . . . . 48 are over 60
Some possible events	Observe an even number Observe a number greater than 4 Observe a number 3 or less	More than 13 are over 60 Fewer than 20 are over 60

In the die-rolling experiment, there are six possible outcomes, but there are many possible events, such as an even number (2, 4, or 6), a number greater than 4 (5 or 6), and so on. When counting the number of members of the board of directors for Fortune 500 companies over 60 years of age, the number of possible outcomes can be anywhere from zero to the total number of members. There are an even larger number of possible events in this experiment.

self-review 4–1

Video Games Inc. recently developed a new video game. Its market potential is to be tested by 80 veteran game players.

(a) What is the experiment?
(b) What is one possible outcome?
(c) Suppose 65 players tried the new game and said they liked it. Is 65 a probability?
(d) The probability that the new game will be a success is computed to be −1.0. Comment.
(e) Specify one possible event.

LO4-2   4.3 APPROACHES TO ASSIGNING PROBABILITIES

In this section, we discuss three ways to assign a probability to an event: classical, empirical, and subjective. The classical and empirical methods are objective and are based on information and data. The subjective method is based on a person's belief or estimate of an event's likelihood.

Classical Probability

Classical probability is based on the assumption that the outcomes of an experiment are *equally likely*. Using the classical viewpoint, the probability of an event happening is computed by dividing the number of favourable outcomes by the number of possible outcomes:

$$\textbf{CLASSICAL PROBABILITY} \qquad \text{Probability of event happening} = \frac{\text{Number of favourable outcomes}}{\text{Number of possible outcomes}} \qquad [4\text{--}1]$$

Example	Consider an experiment of rolling a six-sided die. What is the probability of the event "an even number of spots appear face up"?
Solution	The possible outcomes are:

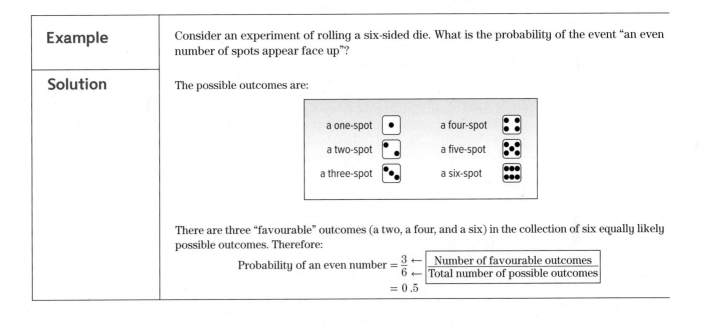

There are three "favourable" outcomes (a two, a four, and a six) in the collection of six equally likely possible outcomes. Therefore:

$$\text{Probability of an even number} = \frac{3}{6} \begin{array}{l} \leftarrow \\ \leftarrow \end{array} \boxed{\begin{array}{l} \text{Number of favourable outcomes} \\ \text{Total number of possible outcomes} \end{array}}$$

$$= 0.5$$

Mutually exclusive The occurrence of one event means that none of the other events can occur at the same time.

The **mutually exclusive** concept appeared earlier in our study of frequency distributions in Chapter 2. Recall that we create classes so that a particular event is included in only one of the classes and there is no overlap between classes. Thus, only one of several events can occur at a particular time.

The variable "gender" presents two mutually exclusive outcomes, male and female. An employee selected at random is either male or female but cannot be both. A manufactured part is defective or non-defective. The part cannot be both defective and non-defective at the same time. In a sample of manufactured parts, the event of selecting a non-defective part and the event of selecting a defective part are mutually exclusive.

If an experiment has a set of events that includes every possible outcome, such as the events "an even number" and "an odd number" in the die-tossing experiment, then the set of events is **collectively exhaustive.** For the die-tossing experiment, every outcome will be either even or odd. So, the set is collectively exhaustive.

Collectively exhaustive At least one of the events must occur when an experiment is conducted.

If the set of events is collectively exhaustive and the events are mutually exclusive, the sum of the probabilities equals 1.

Historically, the classical approach to probability was developed and applied in the seventeenth and eighteenth centuries to games of chance, such as cards and dice. It is unnecessary to do an experiment to determine the probability of an event occurring using the classical approach because the total number of outcomes is known before the experiment. The flip of a coin has two possible outcomes; the roll of a die has six possible outcomes. We can logically arrive at the probability of getting a tail on the toss of one coin or three heads on the toss of three coins.

The classical approach to probability can also be applied to lotteries. For example, in a game of "Pick 3," a person buys a lottery ticket and selects three numbers between 0 and 9. Once per week, the three numbers are randomly selected from a machine that tumbles three containers each with balls numbered 0 through 9. One way to win is to match the numbers and the order of the numbers. Then, there are 1000 possible outcomes, from 000 to 999. The probability of winning with any three-digit number is 1 in 1000 or $1/1000 = 0.001$.

Empirical Probability

Empirical probability, or relative frequency, is the second type of objective probability. It is based on the number of times an event occurs as a proportion of a known number of trials.

In terms of a formula:

$$\text{Empirical probability} = \frac{\text{Number of times the event occurs}}{\text{Total number of observations}}$$

The empirical approach to probability is based on what is called the **law of large numbers**. The key to establishing probabilities empirically is that more observations will provide a more accurate estimate of the probability.

To explain the law of large numbers, suppose we toss a fair coin. The result of each toss is either a head or a tail. With just one toss of the coin, the empirical probability for heads is either zero or one. If we toss the coin a great number of times, the probability of the outcome of heads will approach 0.5. The following table reports the results of an experiment of flipping a fair coin 1, 10, 50, 500, 1000, and 10 000 times, and then computes the relative frequency of heads. Note that as we increase the number of trials, the empirical probability of a head appearing approaches 0.5, which is its value based on the classical approach to probability.

Number of Trials	Number of Heads	Relative Frequency of Heads
1	0	0.00
10	3	0.30
50	26	0.52
100	52	0.52
500	236	0.472
1 000	494	0.494
10 000	5 027	0.5027

What have we demonstrated? On the basis of the classical definition of probability, the likelihood of obtaining a head in a single toss of a fair coin is 0.5. On the basis of the empirical or relative frequency approach to probability, the probability of the event happening approaches the same value based on the classical definition of probability.

This reasoning allows us to use the empirical or relative frequency approach to finding a probability. Here are some examples:

- Last semester, 40 students registered for Business Statistics 101. Six students earned an A. On the basis of this information and the empirical approach of assigning a probability, we estimate the likelihood a student will earn an A is 0.15 (6/40).
- Sidney Crosby of the Pittsburgh Penguins scored 36 goals from 248 shots during the 2015–16 NHL season (nhl.com). Using the empirical approach to probability, the likelihood of Sidney Crosby scoring his next goal is 14.5% ($36/248 = 0.121$).

Life insurance companies rely on past data to determine the acceptability of an applicant as well as the premium to be charged. Mortality tables list the likelihood a person of a particular age will die within the upcoming year. For example, the likelihood a 20-year old female will die within the next year is 0.00105.

Empirical probability The probability of an event happening is the fraction of the time similar events happened in the past.

law of large numbers Over a large number of trials, the empirical probability of an event will approach its true probability.

The empirical concept is illustrated with the following example:

Example	A study of 750 business administration graduates revealed that 210 of the 750 were *not* employed in their major area of study in college. For illustration, a person who majored in accounting is now the marketing manager of an e-commerce firm. What is the probability that a particular business graduate will be employed in an area other than his or her college major?
Solution	To simplify, letters or numbers may be used. P stands for probability, and in this case $P(A)$ stands for the probability a graduate is not employed in his or her major area of college study. $$\text{Probability of event happening} = \frac{\text{Number of times event occurred in past}}{\text{Total number of observations}}$$ $$P(A) = \frac{210}{750} = 0.28$$ We can use this as an estimate of probability. In other words, on the basis of past experience, the probability is 0.28, or 28%, that a new business graduate will be employed in a field other than his or her college major.

Subjective Probability

Subjective probability
The likelihood (probability) of a particular event happening that is assigned by an individual on the basis of whatever information is available.

If there is little or no experience or information on which to base a probability, it is estimated subjectively. Essentially, this means an individual evaluates the available opinions and other information and then estimates or assigns the probability. This probability is called a **subjective probability.**
Illustrations of subjective probability are:

1. Estimating the likelihood of the next federal election happening within the next year.
2. Estimating the likelihood you will be married before the age of 30.
3. Estimating the chance of the Toronto Maple Leafs winning the Stanley Cup.

The types of probability are summarized in Chart 4–1. A probability statement always assigns a likelihood to an event that has not yet occurred. There is, of course, a considerable latitude in the degree of uncertainty that surrounds this probability, based primarily on the knowledge possessed by the individual concerning the underlying process. The individual possesses a great deal of knowledge about the toss of a die and can state that the probability that a one-spot will appear face up on the toss of a true die is one-sixth. But we know very little concerning the acceptance in the marketplace of a new and untested product. For example, even though a market research director tests a newly developed product in 40 retail stores and states that there is a 70% chance that the product will have sales of more than 1 million units, she has limited knowledge of how consumers will react when it is marketed nationally. In both cases (the case of the person rolling a die and the testing of a new product), the individual is assigning a probability value to an event of interest, and a difference exists only in the predictor's confidence in the precision of the estimate. However, regardless of the viewpoint, the same laws of probability (presented in the following sections) will be applied.

CHART 4–1 Summary of Approaches to Probability

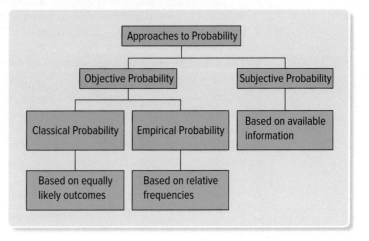

self-review 4–2

1. One card will be randomly selected from a standard 52-card deck. What is the probability the card will be a queen? Which approach to probability did you use to answer this question?
2. The Centre for Child Care reports on the parental status of 539 children. The parents of 333 children are married, 182 are divorced, and 24 are widowed. What is the probability a particular child chosen at random will have a parent who is divorced? Which approach did you use?
3. What is the probability you will save $1 million by the time you retire? Which approach to probability did you use to answer this question?

EXERCISES

1. Some people are in favour of reducing federal taxes to increase consumer spending, and others are against it. Two persons are selected, and their opinions are recorded. Assuming that no one is undecided, list the possible outcomes.

2. A quality control inspector selects a part to be tested. The part is then declared acceptable, repairable, or scrapped. Then another part is tested. List the possible outcomes of this experiment regarding two parts.

3. A survey of 34 students at a business school showed the following majors:

Accounting	10
Finance	5
E-Commerce	3
Management	6
Marketing	10

   Suppose that you select a student and observe his or her major.
   a. What is the probability he or she is a management major?
   b. Which concept of probability did you use to make this estimate?

4. A large company that must hire a new president prepares a final list of five candidates, all of whom are equally qualified. Two of these candidates are female. The company decides to select the president by lottery.
   a. What is the probability one of the female candidates is hired?
   b. Which concept of probability did you use to make this estimate?

5. In each of the following cases, indicate whether classical, empirical, or subjective probability is used.
   a. A basketball player makes 30 out of 50 free throws. The probability is 0.6 that she makes the next free throw attempted.
   b. A seven-member committee of students is formed to study environmental issues. What is the likelihood that any one of the seven is chosen as the spokesperson?
   c. You purchase one of 5 million tickets sold for LOTTO MAX. What is the likelihood you win the next jackpot?
   d. The probability of an earthquake in northern California in the next 10 years is 0.80.

6. A firm will promote two employees out of a group of six men and three women.
   a. List the outcomes of this experiment if there is particular concern about gender equity.
   b. Which concept of probability would you use to estimate these probabilities?

7. A sample of 40 executives in the oil industry were selected to answer a questionnaire. One question about environmental issues required a yes-or-no answer.
   a. What is the experiment?
   b. List one possible event.
   c. Ten of the 40 executives responded "yes." Based on these sample responses, what is the probability an executive responded "yes"?

d. What concept of probability does this illustrate?

e. Are each of the possible outcomes equally likely and mutually exclusive?

8. A sample of 2000 licensed drivers revealed the following number of speeding violations:

Number of Violations	Number of Drivers
0	1910
1	46
2	18
3	12
4	9
5 or more	5
Total	2000

a. What is the experiment?

b. List one possible event.

c. What is the probability that a particular driver had exactly two violations?

d. What concept of probability does this illustrate?

9. CIBC customers select their own four-digit personal identification number (PIN) for use at automated teller machines (ATMs).

a. Think of this as an experiment and list four possible outcomes.

b. What is the probability Mr. Jones and Mrs. Smith select the same PIN?

c. Which concept of probability did you use to answer the question above?

10. An investor buys 100 shares of AT&T stock and records its price change daily.

a. List several possible events for this experiment.

b. Estimate the probability for each event you described in (a).

c. Which concept of probability did you use in (b)?

LO4-3 4.4 PRINCIPLES OF COUNTING

If the number of possible outcomes in an experiment is small, it is relatively easy to count them. There are six possible outcomes, for example, resulting from the roll of a die, namely:

If, however, there are a large number of possible outcomes, such as the number of heads and tails for an experiment with 10 tosses, it would be tedious to count all the possibilities. They could have all heads, one head and nine tails, two heads and eight tails, and so on. To facilitate counting, three counting formulas will be examined: the **multiplication formula** (not to be confused with the multiplication *rule* described later in the chapter), the **permutation formula,** and the **combination formula.**

We begin with the multiplication formula.

> **Multiplication formula** If there are *m* ways of doing one thing and *n* ways of doing another thing, there are *m* × *n* ways of doing both.

The Multiplication Formula

In terms of a formula:

> **MULTIPLICATION FORMULA**   Total number of arrangements $= (m)(n)$ [4–2]

This can be extended to more than two events. For three events *m, n,* and *o*:

$$\text{Total number of arrangements} = (m)(n)(o)$$

Example	An automobile dealer wants to advertise that for $39 999 you can buy a convertible, a two-door sedan, or a four-door sedan, with your choice of either wire wheel covers or solid wheel covers. How many different arrangements of models and wheel covers can the dealer offer?
Solution	Of course, the dealer could determine the total number of arrangements by picturing and counting them. There are six.

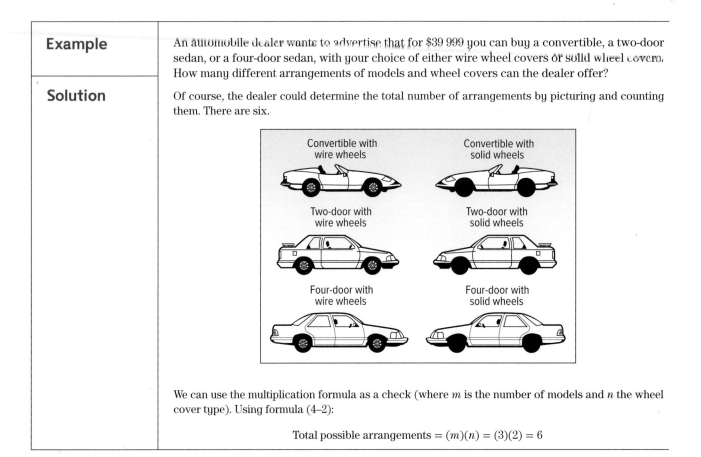

We can use the multiplication formula as a check (where m is the number of models and n the wheel cover type). Using formula (4–2):

$$\text{Total possible arrangements} = (m)(n) = (3)(2) = 6$$

It was not difficult to count all the possible model and wheel cover combinations in this example. Suppose, however, that the dealer decided to offer eight models and six types of wheel covers. It would be tedious to picture and count all the possible alternatives. Instead, the multiplication formula can be used. In this case, there are $(m)(n) = (8)(6) = 48$ possible arrangements.

Note in the preceding applications of the multiplication formula that there were *two or more groupings from which you made selections*. The automobile dealer, for example, offered a choice of models and a choice of wheel covers. If a home builder offered you four different exterior styles to choose from and three interior floor plans, the multiplication formula would be used to find how many different arrangements were possible. There are $(4 \times 3) = 12$ possibilities.

self-review 4–3

1. The Shopping Channel offers sweaters and slacks for women. The sweaters and slacks are offered in coordinating colours. If sweaters are available in five colours and the slacks are available in four colours, how many different outfits can be advertised?
2. Pioneer manufactures three models of stereo receivers, two MP3 docking stations, four speakers, and three CD carousels. When the four types of components are sold together, they form a "system." How many different systems can the electronics firm offer?

The Permutation Formula

As noted, the multiplication formula is applied to find the number of possible outcomes for two or more groups. The **permutation formula** is applied to find the possible number of arrangements when there is only *one* group of objects. Illustrations of this type of problem are:

- Three electronic parts: a transistor, an LED and a synthesizer are to be assembled into a plug-in unit for a television. The parts can be assembled in any order. In how many different ways can the three parts be assembled?

- A machine operator must make four safety checks before starting his machine. It does not matter in which order the checks are made. In how many different ways can the operator make the checks?

One order for the first illustration might be: the transistor first, the LEDs second, and the synthesizer third. This arrangement is called a **permutation.**

Note that the arrangements *a b c* and *b a c* are different permutations. The formula to count the total number of different permutations is:

Permutation Any arrangement of *r* objects selected from a single group of *n* possible objects when order is considered.

PERMUTATION FORMULA	$_nP_r = \dfrac{n!}{(n-r)!}$	[4–3]

where:

> *n* is the total number of objects.
> *r* is the number of objects selected.

Before we solve the two problems illustrated, note that permutations and combinations (to be discussed shortly) use a notation called *n factorial.* It is written *n*! and means the product $n(n-1)(n-2)(n-3)\,(1)$. For instance, $5! = 5 \cdot 4 \cdot 3 \cdot 2 \cdot 1 = 120$.

Many of your calculators have a button with $x!$ that will perform this calculation for you. It will save you a great deal of time.

The factorial notation can also be cancelled when the same number appears in both the numerator and the denominator, as shown below:

$$\frac{6!3!}{4!} = \frac{6 \cdot 5 \cdot \cancel{4} \cdot \cancel{3} \cdot \cancel{2} \cdot \cancel{1}\,(3 \cdot 2 \cdot 1)}{\cancel{4} \cdot \cancel{3} \cdot \cancel{2} \cdot \cancel{1}} = 180$$

By definition, zero factorial, written 0!, is 1. That is, $0! = 1$.

Example	Referring to the group of three electronic parts that are to be assembled in any order, in how many different ways can they be assembled?
Solution	There are three electronic parts to be assembled, so $n = 3$. Because all three are to be inserted in the plug-in unit, $r = 3$.

$$_nP_r = \frac{n!}{(n-r)!} = \frac{3!}{(3-3)!} = \frac{3!}{0!} = \frac{3!}{1} = 6$$

We can check the number of permutations arrived at using the permutation formula. We determine how many "spaces" have to be filled and the possibilities for each "space." In the problem involving three electronic parts, there are three locations in the plug-in unit for the three parts. There are three possibilities for the first place, two for the second (one has been used up), and one for the third, as follows:

$$(3)(2)(1) = 6 \text{ permutations}$$

The six ways in which the three electronic parts, lettered *A*, *B*, *C*, can be arranged are:

> ABC ACB BAC BCA CAB CBA

In the previous example, we selected and arranged all the objects, that is, $n = r$. In many cases, only some objects are selected and arranged from the *n* possible objects. We explain the details of this application in the following example:

Example	The Betts Machine Shop Inc. has eight screw machines but only three spaces available in the production area for the machines. In how many different ways can the eight machines be arranged in the three spaces available?
Solution	There are eight possibilities for the first available space in the production area, seven for the second space (one has been used up), and six for the third space. Thus:

$$(8)(7)(6) = 336$$

That is, there are a total of 336 different possible arrangements. This could also be found using formula (4–3). If $n = 8$ machines, and $r = 3$ spaces available, the formula leads to:

$$_nP_r = \frac{n!}{(n-r)!} = \frac{8!}{(8-3)!} = \frac{8!}{5!} = \frac{(8)(7)(6)5!}{5!} = 336$$

excel   Computer commands to determine the number of permutations using the Betts Machine Shop data can be found at the end of the chapter.

The Combination Formula

If the order of the selected objects is not important, any selection is called a **combination**. The formula to count the number of r object combinations from a set of n objects is:

COMBINATION FORMULA $$_nC_r = \frac{n!}{r!(n-r)!}$$ [4–4]

For example, if executives Able, Baker, and Chauncy are to be chosen as a committee to negotiate a merger, there is only one possible combination of these three; the committee of Able, Baker, and Chauncy is the same as the committee of Baker, Chauncy, and Able. Using the combination formula:

$$_nC_r = \frac{n!}{r!(n-r)!} = \frac{3 \cdot 2 \cdot 1}{3 \cdot 2 \cdot 1(1)} = 1$$

Example	The Grand 16 movie theatre uses teams of three employees to work the concession stand each evening. There are seven employees available to work each evening. How many different teams can be scheduled to staff the concession stand?
Solution	Using formula (4–4), there are 35 combinations, found by: $$_7C_3 = \frac{n!}{r!(n-r)!} = \frac{n!}{3!(7-3)!} = \frac{7!}{3!4!} = 35$$ The seven employees taken three at a time would create 35 different teams.

Example	In how many ways can three students be chosen to form a selection committee from a group of 15? How would this change if the first student selected is the president, the second student selected is the vice-president, and the third student selected is the treasurer?
Solution	If three students are chosen from a group of 15 with no regard to order, this is a combination. Using formula (4–4), there are 455 combinations, found by: $$_{15}C_3 = \frac{n!}{r!(n-r)!} = \frac{n!}{3!(15-3)!} = \frac{15!}{3!12!} = 455$$ The 15 students taken three at a time would create 455 different committees. If three students are chosen from a group of 15 where order is important, such as the first chosen is the president, the second chosen is the vice-president, and the third chosen is the treasurer, this is a permutation. Using formula (4–3), there are 2730 permutations, found by: $$_{15}P_3 = \frac{n!}{(n-r)!} = \frac{15!}{(15-3)!} = \frac{15!}{12!} = 2730$$ Therefore, 15 students taken three at a time would create 2730 permutations. Note: The number of combinations is always less than the number of permutations.

excel

When the number of permutations or combinations is large, the calculations are tedious. Calculators and computer software have "functions" to compute these numbers. Computer commands to determine the number of combinations using the Grand movie theatre example are at the end of the chapter.

self-review 4–4

1. A musician wants to write a score based on only five chords: B-flat, C, D, E, and G. However, only three chords out of the five will be used in succession, such as C, B-flat, and E. Repetitions, such as B-flat, B-flat, and E, will not be permitted.

   (a) How many permutations of the five chords, taken three at a time, are possible?
   (b) Using formula (4–3), how many permutations are possible?

2. A machine operator must make four safety checks before starting to machine a part. It does not matter in which order the checks are made. In how many different ways can the operator make the checks?

3. The 10 numbers 0 through 9 are to be used in code groups of four to identify an item of clothing. Code 1083 might identify a blue blouse, size medium; the code group 2031 might identify a pair of pants, size 18; and so on. Repetitions of numbers are not permitted. That is, the same number cannot be used twice (or more) in a total sequence. For example, 2256, 2562, or 5559 would not be permitted. How many different code groups can be designed?

4. In the preceding example involving the Grand movie theatre, we said that there are 35 possible teams of three taken from seven employees.

   (a) Use formula (4–4) to show this is true.
   (b) The manager of the theatre wants to plan for staffing the concession stand with teams of five on the weekends to serve more people. From the seven employees, how many teams of five employees are possible?

5. In a lottery game, three numbers are randomly selected from a number of balls, numbered 1 through 50.

   (a) How many permutations are possible?
   (b) How many combinations are possible?

EXERCISES

11. Solve the following:
    a. 40!/35!
    b. $_7P_4$
    c. $_5C_2$

12. Solve the following:
    a. 20!/17!
    b. $_9P_3$
    c. $_7C_2$

13. A pollster randomly selected 4 of 10 available people. How many different groups of four are possible?

14. A telephone number consists of seven digits, the first three representing the exchange. How many different telephone numbers are possible within the 537 exchange?

15. An overnight express company must include five cities on its route. How many different routes are possible, assuming that it does not matter in which order the cities are included in the routing?

16. A representative of the Ministry of the Environment wants to select samples from 10 landfills. The director has 15 landfills from which she can collect samples. How many different samples are possible?

17. A national pollster has developed 15 questions designed to rate the performance of the prime minister of Canada. The pollster will select 10 of these questions. How many different arrangements are there for the order of the 10 selected questions?

18. A company is creating three new divisions and seven managers are eligible to be appointed head of a division. How many different ways could the three new heads be appointed?

4.5 SOME RULES FOR COMPUTING PROBABILITIES

Now that we have defined probability and described the different approaches to probability, we turn our attention to combining events by applying rules of addition and multiplication.

LO4-4   Rules of Addition

There are two rules of addition, the special rule of addition and the general rule of addition. We begin with the special rule of addition.

Special Rule of Addition   When we use the **special rule of addition**, the events must be *mutually exclusive*. Recall that mutually exclusive means that when one event occurs, none of the other events can occur at the same time. An illustration of mutually exclusive events in the die-tossing experiment is the events "a number 4 or larger" and "a number 2 or smaller." If the outcome is in the first group (4, 5, and 6), then it cannot also be in the second group (1 and 2). Another example is a part coming off the assembly line. It cannot be both defective and non-defective at the same time.

If two events A and B are mutually exclusive, the special rule of addition states that the probability of occurrence of one event *or* the other equals the sum of their probabilities. This rule is expressed in the following formula:

SPECIAL RULE OF ADDITION	$P(A \text{ or } B) = P(A) + P(B)$	[4–5]

For three mutually exclusive events designated A, B, and C, the rule is written:

$$P(A \text{ or } B \text{ or } C) = P(A) + P(B) + P(C)$$

The following example will help see the details:

Example	A machine fills plastic bags with a mixture of beans, broccoli, and other vegetables. Most of the bags contain the correct weight, but because of the variation in the size of the beans and other vegetables, a package might be underweight or overweight. A check of 4000 packages filled in the past month revealed the following:

Weight	Event	Number of Packages	Probability of Occurrence	
Underweight	A	100	0.025	$\leftarrow \frac{100}{4000}$
Satisfactory	B	3600	0.900	
Overweight	C	300	0.075	
		4000	1.000	

Solution	What is the probability that a particular package will be either underweight or overweight?

The outcome "underweight" is the event A. The outcome "overweight" is the event C. Applying the special rule of addition:

$$P(A \text{ or } C) = P(A) + P(C) = 0.025 + 0.075 = 0.10$$

Note that the events are mutually exclusive, meaning that a package of mixed vegetables cannot be underweight, satisfactory, and overweight at the same time. They are also collectively exhaustive; that is, a selected package must be either underweight, satisfactory, or overweight.

English logician J. Venn (1834–1923) developed a diagram to portray graphically the outcome of an experiment. The *mutually exclusive* concept and various other rules for combining probabilities can be illustrated using this device. To construct a Venn diagram, a space is first enclosed, representing the total of all possible outcomes. This space is usually in the form of a rectangle. An event is then represented by a circular area, which is drawn inside the rectangle proportional to the probability of the event. The following Venn diagram represents the *mutually exclusive* concept. There is no overlapping of events, meaning that the events are mutually exclusive. In the following Venn diagram, assume the events A, B and C are about equally likely.

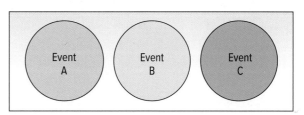

Complement Rule   The probability that a bag of mixed vegetables selected is underweight, $P(A)$, plus the probability that it is not an underweight bag, written $P(\sim A)$ and read "not A," must logically equal 1. This is written as:

$$P(A) + P(\sim A) = 1$$

This can be revised to read:

COMPLEMENT RULE	$P(\sim A) = 1 - P(A)$	[4–6]

This is the **complement rule**. It is used to determine the probability of an event occurring by subtracting the probability of the event not occurring from 1. This rule is useful because sometimes it is easier to calculate the probability of an event happening by determining the probability of it not happening and subtracting the result from 1. Note that the events A and $\sim A$ are mutually exclusive and collectively exhaustive. Therefore, the probabilities of A and $\sim A$ sum to 1. A Venn diagram illustrating the complement rule is shown as:

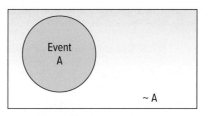

Example	Recall that the probability of a bag of mixed vegetables being underweight is 0.025 and that the probability of an overweight bag is 0.075. Use the complement rule to show the probability of a satisfactory bag is 0.900. Show the solution using a Venn diagram.
Solution	The probability the bag is unsatisfactory equals the probability the bag is overweight plus the probability it is underweight. That is, $P(A \text{ or } C) = P(A) + P(C) = 0.025 + 0.075 = 0.100$. The bag is satisfactory if it is not underweight or overweight, so $P(B) = 1 - [P(A) + P(C)] = 1 - [0.025 + 0.075] = 0.900$. The Venn diagram portraying this situation is:

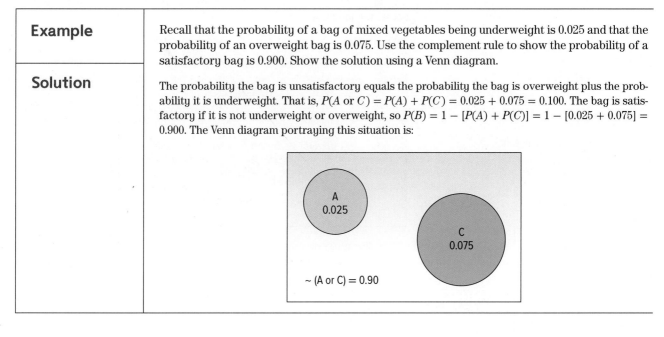

self-review 4–5

A sample of employees of Worldwide Enterprises is to be surveyed about a new pension plan. In-depth interviews are to be conducted with each employee selected in the sample. The employees are classified as follows:

Classification	Event	Number of Employees
Supervisors	A	120
Maintenance	B	50
Production	C	1460
Management	D	302
Secretarial	E	68

(a) What is the probability that the first person selected:

  (i) Is in maintenance or is a secretary?
  (ii) Is not in management?

(b) Draw a Venn diagram illustrating your answers to part (a).
(c) Are the events in part (a)(i) complementary or mutually exclusive or both?

The General Rule of Addition   The outcomes of an experiment may not be mutually exclusive. Suppose, for example, that the Caribana Festival selected a sample of 200 tourists who visited the Toronto area during the time of the festival. The survey revealed that 120 tourists visited the CN Tower and 100 went to the Toronto Islands for the festival. What is the probability that a tourist selected visited either the CN Tower or the Toronto Islands? If the special rule of addition is used, the probability of selecting a tourist who went to the CN Tower is 0.60, found by 120/200. Similarly, the probability of a tourist going to the Toronto Islands is 0.50. The sum of these probabilities is 1.10. But, we know that this probability cannot be greater than 1. So, the explanation is that some of the tourists visited both attractions and are being counted twice! A check of the survey responses reveals that 60 of the 200 sampled did visit both attractions.

To answer our question "What is the probability a selected tourist visited either the CN Tower or the Toronto Islands?", we need to add the probability that a tourist visited the CN Tower and the probability that a tourist visited the Toronto Islands and then subtract the probability of visiting both. Thus:

$$P(\text{CN Tower or Toronto Islands}) = P(\text{CN Tower}) + P(\text{Toronto Islands}) - P(\text{both})$$
$$= 0.60 + 0.50 - 0.30 = 0.80$$

Joint probability A probability that measures the likelihood two or more events will happen concurrently.

When two events both occur, the probability is called a **joint probability**. The probability that a tourist visits both attractions (0.30) is an example of a joint probability.

The following Venn diagram shows two events that are not mutually exclusive. The two events overlap to illustrate the joint event that some people have visited both attractions.

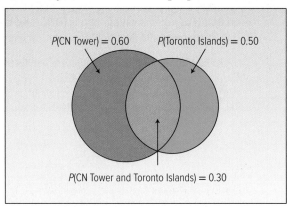

The general rule of addition to compute the probability of two events A and B that are not mutually exclusive is:

GENERAL RULE OF ADDITION $P(A \text{ or } B) = P(A) + P(B) - P(A \text{ and } B)$ [4–7]

For the expression $P(A \text{ or } B)$, the word *or* suggests that A may occur or B may occur. This also includes the possibility that A and B may occur. This use of *or* is called an **inclusive**. You could also write $P(A \text{ or } B \text{ or both})$ to emphasize that the union of the events includes the intersection of A and B.

If we compare the general and special rules of addition, the important difference is determining if the events are mutually exclusive. If the events are mutually exclusive, then the joint probability $P(A \text{ or } B)$ is 0, and we could use the special rule of addition. Otherwise, we must account for the joint probability and use the general rule of addition.

Example	What is the probability that a card chosen at random from a standard deck of cards will be either a king or a heart?
Solution	We may be inclined to add the probability of a king and the probability of a heart. But this creates a problem. If we do that, the king of hearts is counted with the kings and also with the hearts. So, if we simply add the probability of a king (there are 4 in a deck of 52 cards) to the probability of a heart (there are 13 in a deck of 52 cards) and report that 17 out of 52 cards meet the requirement, we have counted the king of hearts twice. We need to subtract 1 card from the 17 so the king of hearts is counted only once. Thus, there are 16 cards that are either hearts or kings. So, the probability is $16/52 = 0.3077$.

Card	Probability		Explanation
King	$P(A)$	$= 4/52$	4 kings in a deck of 52 cards
Heart	$P(B)$	$= 13/52$	13 hearts in a deck of 52 cards
King of hearts	$P(A \text{ and } B)$	$= 1/52$	1 king of hearts in a deck of 52 cards

Using formula (4–7):

$$P(A \text{ or } B) = P(A) + P(B) - P(A \text{ and } B)$$
$$= 4/52 + 13/52 - 1/52$$
$$= 16/52, \text{ or } 0.3077$$

A Venn diagram portrays these outcomes, which are not mutually exclusive.

P(King) = 4/52   *P*(Hearts) = 13/52

A   A and B   B

Both

P(King and Heart) = 1/52

self-review 4–6

Routine physical examinations are conducted annually as part of a health service program for General Concrete Inc. employees. It was discovered that 8% of the employees need corrective shoes, 15% need major dental work, and 3% need both corrective shoes and major dental work.

(a) What is the probability that an employee selected at random will need either corrective shoes or major dental work?
(b) Show this situation in the form of a Venn diagram.

EXERCISES

19. The events A and B are mutually exclusive. Suppose that $P(A) = 0.30$ and $P(B) = 0.20$. What is the probability of either A or B occurring? What is the probability that neither A nor B will happen?

20. The events X and Y are mutually exclusive. Suppose that $P(X) = 0.05$ and $P(Y) = 0.02$. What is the probability of either X or Y occurring? What is the probability that neither X nor Y will happen?

21. A study of 200 advertising firms revealed their incomes after taxes:

Income after Taxes	Number of Firms
Under $1 million	102
$1 million to $20 million	61
$20 million or more	37

   a. What is the probability an advertising firm selected at random has under $1 million in income after taxes?

   b. What is the probability an advertising firm selected at random has either an income between $1 million and $20 million, or an income of $20 million or more? What rule of probability was applied?

22. The chair of the board of directors says, "There is a 50% chance this company will earn a profit, a 30% chance it will break even, and a 20% chance it will lose money next quarter."

   a. Use an addition rule to find the probability the company will not lose money next quarter.

   b. Use the complement rule to find the probability the company will not lose money next quarter.

23. Suppose the probability you will get a grade of A in this class is 0.25 and the probability you will get a B is 0.50. What is the probability your grade will be above a C?

24. Two coins are tossed. If A is the event "two heads" and B is the event "two tails," are A and B mutually exclusive? Are they complements?

25. The probabilities of the events A and B are 0.20 and 0.30, respectively. The probability that both A and B occur is 0.15. What is the probability of either A or B occurring?

26. Let $P(X) = 0.55$ and $P(Y) = 0.35$. Assume the probability that they both occur is 0.20. What is the probability of either X or Y occurring?

27. Suppose the two events A and B are mutually exclusive. What is the probability of their joint occurrence?

28. A student is taking two courses, history and math. The probability the student will pass the history course is 0.60, and the probability of passing the math course is 0.70. The probability of passing both is 0.50. What is the probability of passing at least one?

29. A survey of grocery stores in Eastern Canada revealed that 40% had a pharmacy, 50% had a floral shop, and 70% had a deli. Suppose 10% of the stores have all three departments, 30% have both a pharmacy and a deli, 25% have both a floral shop and deli, and 20% have both a pharmacy and a floral shop.

   a. What is the probability of selecting a store at random and finding it has both a pharmacy and a floral shop?

   b. What is the probability of selecting a store at random and finding it has both a pharmacy and a deli?

   c. Are the events "select a store with a deli," and "select a store with a pharmacy" mutually exclusive?

   d. What is the name given to the event of "selecting a store with a pharmacy, a floral shop, and a deli"?

   e. What is the probability of selecting a store that does not have all three departments?

30. A study by the National Park Service revealed that 50% of vacationers going to the Rocky Mountain region visit Banff National Park, 40% visit Yoho National Park, and 35% visit both.

   a. What is the probability a vacationer will visit at least one of these parks?

   b. What is the probability 0.35 called?

   c. Are the events mutually exclusive? Explain.

LO4-5   Rules of Multiplication

In this section, we discuss rules for computing the likelihood that two events both happen or joint probability. For example, a marketing firm may want to estimate the likelihood that a person is 45 years old or older *and* buys a Ferrari. Venn diagrams illustrate this as the intersection of two events. To find the likelihood of two events happening we use the rules of multiplication. There are two rules of multiplication, the Special Rule and the General Rule.

Independent The occurrence of one event has no effect on the probability of the occurrence of another event.

Special Rule of Multiplication   The special rule of multiplication requires that two events, A and B, are **independent**. Two events are independent if the occurrence of one does not alter the probability of the occurrence of the other event.

One way to think about independence is to assume that events A and B occur at different times. For example, when event B occurs, does A have any effect on the likelihood that event B occurs? If the answer is no, then A and B are independent events. To illustrate independence, suppose two coins are tossed. The outcome of a coin toss (head or tail) is unaffected by the outcome of any other prior coin toss (head or tail).

For two independent events, A and B, the probability that A and B will both occur is found by multiplying the two probabilities. This is the **special rule of multiplication** and is written symbolically as:

SPECIAL RULE OF MULTIPLICATION	$P(A \text{ and } B) = P(A)P(B)$	[4–8]

For the experiment of tossing two coins, the probability of two heads, $P(H \text{ and } H) = (1/2)(1/2) = 1/4$.

For three independent events, A, B, and C, the special rule of multiplication used to determine the probability that all three events will occur is:

$$P(A \text{ and } B \text{ and } C) = P(A) \, P(B) \, P(C)$$

For the experiment of tossing three coins, the probability of three heads, $P(H \text{ and } H \text{ and } H) = (1/2)(1/2)(1/2) = 1/8$.

Example	A survey of the final grades in an advanced statistics course reveals that 60% of the students are successful. Two students are selected at random. What is the probability that both are successful in the advanced statistics course?
Solution	The probability that the first student is successful is 0.60, written as $P(S_1) = 0.60$, where S_1 refers to the fact that the first student is successful. The probability that the second student is successful is also 0.60, written as $P(S_2) = 0.60$. Since students are required to work on their own assignments and tests, S_1 and S_2 are independent. Consequently, using formula (4–8), the probability that they are both successful is 0.36, found by:

$$P(S_1 \text{ and } S_2) = P(S_1) \, P(S_2) = (0.60)(0.60) = 0.36$$

All possible outcomes can be shown as follows. S means the student is successful, and NS means the student is not successful.

Outcomes		Joint Probability
S	S	$(0.60)(0.60) = 0.36$
S	NS	$(0.60)(0.40) = 0.24$
NS	S	$(0.40)(0.60) = 0.24$
NS	NS	$(0.40)(0.40) = \underline{0.16}$
		1.00

With the probabilities and the complement rule, we can compute the joint probability of each outcome. For example, the probability that neither student is successful is 0.16. Further, the probability of the first or the second student being successful is $0.48(0.24 + 0.24)$. You can observe that the outcomes are mutually exclusive and collectively exhaustive. Therefore, the probabilities sum to 1.00.

self-review 4–7

From experience, Teton Tire knows the probability is 0.80 that their XB-70 tire will last 100 000 km before it becomes bald or fails. An adjustment is made on any tire that does not last 100 000 km. You purchase four XB-70s. What is the probability all four tires will last at least 100 000 km?

General Rule of Multiplication   If two events are not independent, they are referred to as **dependent**. To illustrate dependency, suppose there are 10 cans of cola in a cooler, 7 regular and 3 diet. A can of cola is selected from the cooler. The probability of selecting a can of diet cola is 3/10, and the probability of selecting a can of regular cola is 7/10. Then a second can is selected from the cooler, without returning the first. The probability that the second can is diet is:

> 2/9 if the first can selected is a diet cola. (Only two cans of diet cola remain in the cooler.)
> 3/9 if the can selected is a regular cola. (All three diet colas are still in the cooler.)

Conditional probability The probability of a particular event occurring, given that another event has occurred.

The fraction 2/9 (or 3/9) is aptly called a **conditional probability** because its value is conditional on (or dependent on) whether a diet or regular cola was the first selected from the cooler.

In the general rule of multiplication, the conditional probability is required to compute the *joint probability* of two events that are not independent. The conditional probability for two events, A and B, that are not independent is written $P(A|B)$. The "|" is a mathematical symbol for the expression "given that." So $P(A|B)$ is the probability of event A happening given that B has already happened. We refer to $P(A|B)$ as a conditional probability because the probability of the event A is conditional on the outcome of B. Symbolically, the general rule of multiplication for two events that are not independent is:

| **GENERAL RULE OF MULTIPLICATION** | $P(A \text{ and } B) = P(A)P(B\,|\,A)$ | [4–9] |

Example	Suppose there are 10 cans of cola in a cooler, 7 regular and 3 diet. Two cans of cola are selected from the cooler without returning the first (without replacement of the first can). What is the probability of selecting: (a) A can of diet cola first and a can of diet cola second? (b) A can of regular cola first and a can of diet cola second? (c) A can of diet cola first and a can of regular cola second? (d) A can of regular cola first and a can of regular cola second?
Solution	(a) $P(D_1 \text{ and } D_2) = P(D_1)\,P(D_2\,|\,D_1) = 0.0667$, found by: $\left(\frac{3}{10}\right)\left(\frac{2}{9}\right) = \frac{6}{90} = 0.0667$ (b) $P(R_1 \text{ and } D_1) = P(R_1)\,P(D1\,|\,R_1) = 0.2333$, found by: $\left(\frac{7}{10}\right)\left(\frac{3}{9}\right) = \frac{21}{90} = 0.2333$ (c) $P(D1 \text{ and } R1) = P(D1)\,P(R1\,|\,D1) = 0.2333$, found by: $\left(\frac{3}{10}\right)\left(\frac{7}{9}\right) = \frac{21}{90} = 0.2333$ (d) $P(R_1 \text{ and } R_2) = P(R_1)\,P(R_2\,|\,R_1) = 0.4667$, found by: $\left(\frac{7}{10}\right)\left(\frac{6}{9}\right) = \frac{42}{90} = 0.4667$ Note: all possible outcomes of selecting two cans of soda without replacement are considered. Therefore, the probabilities: $0.0667 + 0.2333 + 0.2333 + 0.4667 = 1.000$

Example	A golfer has 12 golf shirts in his closet. Suppose nine of these shirts are white and the others blue. He gets dressed in the dark, so he just grabs a shirt and puts it on. He plays golf two days in a row and does not do laundry. What is the probability both shirts selected are white? 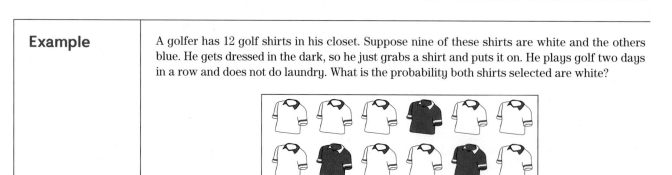

Solution

The event that the first shirt selected is white is W_1. The probability is $P(W_1) = 9/12$ because 9 of the 12 shirts are white. The event that the second shirt selected is also white is identified as W_2. The conditional probability that the second shirt selected is white, given that the first shirt selected is also white, is $P(W_2 \mid W_1) = 8/11$. Why is this so? Because after the first shirt is selected, there only 11 shirts left in the closet and 8 of these are white. To determine the probability of two white shirts being selected we use formula (4–9).

$$P(W_1 \text{ and } W_2) = P(W_1)P(W_2 \mid W_1) = \left(\frac{9}{12}\right)\left(\frac{8}{11}\right) = 0.55$$

So, the likelihood of selecting two shirts and finding them both to be white is 0.55.

It is assumed that this experiment was conducted *without replacement*. That is, the first shirt was not laundered and put back in the closet before the second shirt was selected. So, the outcome of the second event is conditional or dependent on the outcome of the first event.

We can extend the general rule of multiplication to more than two events. For three events, A, B, and C, the formula is:

$$P(A \text{ and } B \text{ and } C) = P(A)P(B \mid A) \, P(C \mid A \text{ and } B)$$

In the case of the golf shirt example, the probability of selecting three white shirts without replacement is:

$$P(W_1 \text{ and } W_2 \text{ and } W_3) = P(W_1)P(W_2 \mid W_1)P(W_3 \mid W_1 \text{ and } W_2) = \left(\frac{9}{12}\right)\left(\frac{8}{11}\right)\left(\frac{7}{10}\right) = 0.38$$

So, the likelihood of selecting three shirts without replacement and all being white is 0.38.

self-review 4–8

The board of directors of Tarbell Industries consists of eight men and four women. A four-member search committee is to be chosen at random to conduct a nationwide search for a new company president.

(a) What is the probability all four members of the search committee will be women?
(b) What is the probability all four members will be men?
(c) Does the sum of the probabilities for the events described in parts (a) and (b) equal 1? Explain.

LO4-6 4.6 CONTINGENCY TABLES

Contingency table A table used to classify sample observations according to two or more identifiable categories or classes.

Often, we tally the results of a sample into a two-way table and use the results of this tally to determine various probabilities. We refer to this two-way table as a **contingency table**.

A contingency table is a cross-tabulation that summarizes two variables of interest and their relationship. Here are some examples:

- A survey of 150 adults classified each as to gender and the number of movies attended last month. Each respondent is classified according to two criteria—the number of movies attended and gender.

Statistics in Action

In 2000, George W. Bush won the American presidency by the slimmest of margins. Many election stories resulted, some involving voting irregularities, others raising interesting election questions. In a local Michigan election,

| | Gender | | |
Movies Attended	Men	Women	Total
0	20	40	60
1	40	30	70
2 or more	10	10	20
Total	70	80	150

- The Coffee Producers Association reports the following information on age and the amount of coffee consumed in a month:

| | Coffee Consumption | | | |
Age (Years)	Low	Moderate	High	Total
Under 30	36	32	24	92
30 to under 40	18	30	27	75
40 to under 50	10	24	20	54
50 or more	26	24	29	79
Total	90	110	100	300

According to this table, each of the 300 respondents is classified according to two criteria: (1) age and (2) the amount of coffee consumed.

The following example shows how the rules of addition and multiplication are used when we employ contingency tables:

Example

A sample of executives was surveyed about loyalty to their company. One of the questions was: "If you were given an offer by another company equal to or slightly better than your present position, would you remain with the company or take the other position"? The responses of the 200 executives in the survey were cross-tabulated with their length of service with the company. (See Table 4–1.)

TABLE 4–1 Loyalty of Executives and Length of Service with Company

| | Length of Service | | | | |
Loyalty	Less than 1 Year B_1	1–5 Years B_2	6–10 Years B_3	More than 10 Years B_4	Total
Would remain, A_1	10	30	5	75	120
Would not remain, $\sim A_1$	25	15	10	30	80
	35	45	15	105	200

Solution

What is the probability of randomly selecting an executive who is loyal to the company (would remain) and has more than 10 years of service?

Note that two events occur at the same time—the executive would remain with the company, and he or she has more than 10 years of service.

1. Event A_1 happens if a randomly selected executive will remain with the company despite an equal or slightly better offer from another company. To find the probability that event A_1 will happen, refer to Table 4–1. Note there are 120 executives out of the 200 in the survey who would remain with the company, so $P(A_1) = 120/200$, or 0.60.
2. Event B_4 happens if a randomly selected executive has more than 10 years of service with the company. Thus, $P(B_4 \mid A_1)$ is the conditional probability that an executive with more than 10 years of service would remain with the company despite an equal or slightly better offer from another company. Referring to the contingency table, Table 4–1, 75 of the 120 executives who would remain have more than 10 years of service, so $P(B_4 \mid A_1) = 75/120$, or 0.625.

Solving for the probability that an executive randomly selected will be one who would remain with the company and has more than 10 years of service with the company, using the general rule of multiplication in formula (4–9):

$$P(A_1 \text{ and } B_4) = P(A_1)P(B_4 \mid A_1) = \left(\frac{120}{200}\right)\left(\frac{75}{120}\right) = \frac{75}{200} = 0.375$$

Note that the joint probability of A_1 and B_4 can be found by looking for the point of intersection of A_1 and B_4, which is 75. Divided by the total of 200, we have 75/200 = 0.375.

What is the probability of selecting an executive that would remain *or* has less than one year of service?

To find the probability of selecting an executive who would remain with the company *or* has less than one year of experience we use the general rule of addition, formula (4–7).

1. Event A_1 refers to executives .that would remain with the company. So, $P(A_1) = 120/200 = 0.60$.
2. Event B_1 refers to executives that have been with the company less than one year. The probability of B_1 is $P(B_1) = 35/200 = 0.175$.
3. The events A_1 and B_1 are not mutually exclusive. That is, an executive can both be willing to remain with the company and have less than one year of experience. We write this probability, which is called the *joint probability*, as $P(A_1 \text{ and } B_1)$. There are 10 executives who would both stay with the company and have less than one year of service, so $P(A_1 \text{ and } B_1) = 10/200 = 0.05$. These 10 people are in both groups, those who would remain with the company and those with less than one year with the company. They are actually being counted twice, so we need to subtract out this value.
4. We insert these values in formula (4–7) and the result is as follows:

$$P(A_1 \text{ or } B_1) = P(A_1) + P(B_1) - P(A_1 \text{ and } B_1)$$
$$= 0.60 + 0.175 - 0.05 = 0.725$$

So, the likelihood that a selected executive would either remain with the company or has been with the company less than one year is 0.725.

Example

A survey of 500 randomly selected adults classified each as to age and the number of movies they saw in a theatre last month.

		Age			
Movies per Month		**Less than 30 B_1**	**30 up to 60 B_2**	**60 or Older B_3**	**Total**
0	A_1	15	50	10	75
1 or 2	A_2	25	100	75	200
3, 4, or 5	A_3	55	60	60	175
6 or more	A_4	5	15	30	50
Total		100	225	175	500

Determine the probability of selecting an adult who:

1. Attended 6 or more movies last month.
2. Attended 2 or fewer movies last month.
3. Attended 6 or more movies last month or is 60 years of age or older.
4. Attended 6 or more movies last month given the person is 60 years of age or older.

Solution

1. $P(6 \text{ or more}) = P(A_4) = \frac{50}{500} = 0.10$
   This probability indicates 10% of the 500 adults attend 6 or more movies last month.
2. $P[(\text{attended } 0) \text{ or } (\text{attended } 1 \text{ or } 2)] = P(A_1) + P(A_2) = \left(\frac{75}{500} + \frac{200}{500}\right) = 0.55$
   So, 55% of the adults in the survey attended 2 or fewer movies last month.
3. $P(6 \text{ or more}) \text{ or } (60 \text{ or older}) = P(A_4) + P(B_3) - P(A_4 \text{ and } B_3) = \left(\frac{50}{500} + \frac{175}{500} + \frac{30}{500}\right) = 0.39$
   So, 39% of the adults are either 60 years or older, attended 6 or more movies last month, or both.
4. $P[(6 \text{ or more}) \text{ given } (60 \text{ or older})] = P(A_4 \mid B_3) = \frac{30}{175} = 0.17$
   So, 17% of adults who are 60 or older attended 6 or more movies last month.

self-review 4–9

Refer to Table 4–1 to find the following probabilities:

(a) What is the probability of selecting an executive with more than 10 years of service?
(b) What is the probability of selecting an executive who would not remain with the company, given that he or she has more than 10 years of service?
(c) What is the probability of selecting an executive with more than 10 years of service or one who would not remain with the company?

LO4-7 4.7 TREE DIAGRAMS

The **tree diagram** is a graph that is helpful in organizing calculations that involve several stages. Each segment in the tree is one stage of the problem. The branches of a tree diagram are weighted by probabilities. We will use the data in Table 4–1 to show the construction of a tree diagram.

Steps in constructing a tree diagram:

1. To construct a tree diagram, we begin by drawing a heavy dot on the left to represent the root of the tree (see Chart 4–2).
2. For this problem, two main branches go out from the root, the upper one representing "would remain" and the lower one "would not remain." Their probabilities are written on the branches, namely, 120/200 and 80/200. These probabilities could also be denoted $P(A_1)$ and $P(\sim A_1)$.
3. Four branches "grow" out of each of the two main branches. These branches represent the length of service—less than 1 year, 1–5 years, 6–10 years, and more than 10 years. The conditional probabilities for the upper branch of the tree, 10/120, 30/120, 5/120, and so on are written on the appropriate branches. These are $P(B_1 \mid A_1)$, $P(B_2 \mid A_1)$, $P(B_3 \mid A_1)$, and $P(B_4 \mid A_1)$, where B_1 refers to less than 1 year of service, B_2 1 to 5 years, B_3 6 to 10 years, and B_4 more than 10 years. Next, write the conditional probabilities for the lower branch.
4. Finally, joint probabilities, that the events A_1 and B_1, or the events A_2 and B_1 will occur together, are shown on the right side. For example, the joint probability of randomly selecting

CHART 4–2 Tree Diagram Showing Loyalty and Length of Service

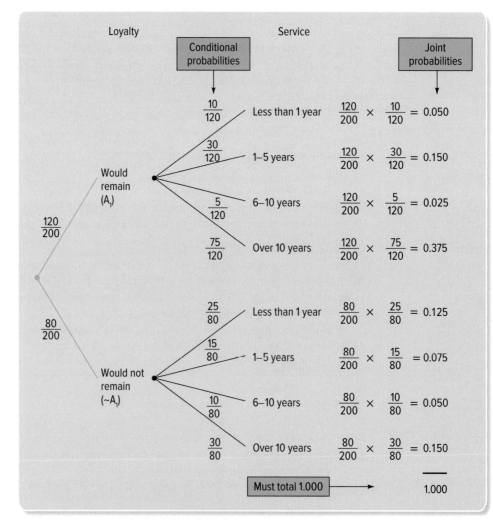

an executive who would remain with the company and who has less than one year of service, using formula (4–9), is:

$$P(A_1 \text{ and } B_1) = P(A_1)P(B_1|A_1) = \left(\frac{120}{200}\right)\left(\frac{10}{120}\right) = 0.05$$

In Chart 4–2, the joint probabilities for all possible combinations of loyalty ("would remain" and "would not remain") and service (less than 1 year, 1–5 years, 6–10 years, and over 10 years) are computed. Because all possible outcomes are listed, the sum of the joint probabilities must equal 1.00.

self-review 4–10 A random sample of the employees of the Hardware Manufacturing Company was chosen to determine their retirement plans after age 65. Those selected in the sample were divided into management and production. The results were:

Employee	Plans after Age 65		
	Retire	Not Retire	Total
Management	5	15	20
Production	30	50	80
			100

(a) What is the table called?
(b) Draw a tree diagram, and determine the joint probabilities.
(c) Do the joint probabilities total 1.00? Why?

EXERCISES

31. Suppose that the probability of a student ordering a hamburger in the cafeteria at lunch is = 0.40 and the probability that the student will also order fries given that the student has ordered a hamburger = 0.30. What is the probability the student will order a hamburger and fries?

32. Suppose that $P(X_1) = 0.75$ and $P(Y_2 | X_1) = 0.40$. What is the joint probability of X_1 and Y_2?

33. A local bank reports that 80% of its customers maintain a chequing account, 60% have a savings account, and 50% have both. If a customer is chosen at random, what is the probability the customer has either a chequing or a savings account? What is the probability the customer does not have either a chequing or a savings account?

34. All Seasons Plumbing has two service trucks which frequently break down. If the probability the first truck is available is 0.75, the probability the second truck is available is 0.50, and the probability that both trucks are available is 0.30, what is the probability neither truck is available?

35. There are 10 marbles in a bag: red, blue and green. Some are clear and some are solid. Refer to the following table:

Second Event	Colour of Marble			
	Red	Blue	Green	Total
Clear	2	1	3	6
Solid	1	2	1	4
Total	3	3	4	10

If a marble is selected:
a. Determine $P(\text{Red})$.
b. Determine $P(\text{Clear|Blue})$.
c. Determine $P(\text{Solid and Green})$.

36. Three defective electric toothbrushes were accidentally shipped to a drugstore by Cleanbrush Products along with 17 non-defective ones.
a. What is the probability the first two electric toothbrushes sold will be returned to the drugstore because they are defective?
b. What is the probability the first two electric toothbrushes sold will not be defective?

37. Each salesperson at Future Shop is rated either below average, average, or above average with respect to sales ability. Each salesperson is also rated with respect to his or her potential for advancement—either fair, good, or excellent. These traits for the 500 salespeople were cross-classified into the following table:

Sales Ability	Potential for Advancement		
	Fair	Good	Excellent
Below average	16	12	22
Average	45	60	45
Above average	93	72	135

   a. What is this table called?

   b. What is the probability a salesperson selected at random will have above average sales ability and excellent potential for advancement?

   c. Construct a tree diagram showing all the probabilities, conditional probabilities, and joint probabilities.

38. An investor owns three common stocks. Each stock, independently of the other, has equally likely chances of (1) increasing in value, (2) decreasing in value, or (3) remaining the same value. List the possible outcomes of this experiment. Estimate the probability at least two of the stocks increase in value.

39. The board of directors of a small company consists of five people. Three of those are "strong leaders." If they buy an idea, the entire board will agree. The other "weak" members have no influence. Three salespersons are scheduled, one after the other, to make sales presentations to a board member of the salesperson's choice. The salespersons are convincing but do not know who the "strong leaders" are. However, they will know who the previous salespersons spoke to. The first salesperson to find a strong leader will win the account. Do the three salespersons have the same chance of winning the account? If not, find their respective probabilities of winning.

40. If you ask three strangers on campus about their birthdays, what is the probability that (a) all were born on Wednesday? (b) all were born on different days of the week? (c) none was born on Saturday?

41. The manager of a restaurant wishes to study the relationship between the gender of a guest and whether the guest orders dessert. To investigate the relationship the manager collected the following information on 200 recent customers:

Dessert Ordered	Gender		
	Male	Female	Total
Yes	32	15	47
No	68	85	153
	100	100	200

   a. What is the level of measurement of the two variables?

   b. What is the probability that a man will order dessert?

   c. What is the probability that a woman will not order dessert?

   d. Does the evidence in the table suggest men are more likely to order dessert compared with women? Explain.

42. A corporation is evaluating a proposed merger. The board of directors surveyed 50 stockholders concerning their position on the merger. The results are reported below:

Number of Shares Held	Opinion			
	Favour	Opposed	Undecided	Total
Under 200	8	6	2	16
200 to under 1000	6	8	1	15
1000 or more	6	12	1	19
Total	20	26	4	50

   a. What is the probability that a stockholder holds 1000 or more shares?

   b. What is the probability that a stockholder holds less than 200 shares and is in favour of the merger?

   c. What is the probability that a stockholder holds between 200 to under 1000 shares or is opposed to the merger?

   d. What is the probability that a stockholder holds under 200 shares given that he or she is opposed to the merger?

43. Wendy's Old Fashioned Hamburgers offers eight different condiments (mustard, ketchup, onion, mayonnaise, pickle, lettuce, tomato, and relish) on hamburgers. A store manager collected the following information on the number of condiments ordered and the age group of the customers:

	Age			
Number of Condiments	Under 18	18 to under 40	40 to under 60	60+
0	12	18	24	52
1	21	76	50	30
2	39	52	40	12
3 or more	71	87	47	28

   a. What is the probability that a customer does not order a condiment?

   b. What is the probability that a customer is under 18 years of age?

   c. What is the probability that a customer orders two condiments and is over 60 years of age?

   d. What is the probability that a customer orders three or more condiments or is in the 18 to under 40 years age group?

   e. What is the probability that a customer orders two condiments and is in the 40 to under 60 years age group?

44. Students were surveyed on the number of visits to a Marc's Milk convenience store (often, occasional, or never) and if the store was conveniently located to their school (yes or no).

	Convenience Store		
Visits	Yes	No	Total
Often	60	20	80
Occasional	25	35	60
Never	5	50	55
Total	90	105	195

   a. What is the probability that a student never visited the store?

   b. What is the probability that a student visited the store occasionally and found the store conveniently located?

   c. What is the probability that a student visited the store often given that the student felt the store was conveniently located?

Chapter Summary

I. A probability is a value between 0 and 1 inclusive that represents the likelihood a particular event will happen.

   A. An experiment is the observation of some activity or the act of taking some measurement.

   B. An outcome is a particular result of an experiment.

   C. An event is the collection of one or more outcomes of an experiment.

II. There are three definitions of probability.

   A. The classical definition applies when there are n equally likely outcomes to an experiment.

$$\text{Probability of an event} = \frac{\text{Number of favourable outcomes}}{\text{Total number of possible outcomes}} \qquad [4\text{--}1]$$

   B. The empirical definition occurs when the number of times an event happens is divided by the number of observations.

   C. A subjective probability is based on whatever information is available.

III. Two events are mutually exclusive if by virtue of one event happening the other cannot happen.

IV. Events are independent if the occurrence of one event does not affect the occurrence of another event.

V. There are three counting rules that are useful in determining the number of outcomes in an experiment.

    A. The multiplication rule states that if there are m ways one event can happen, n ways another event can happen, and then there are mn ways the two events can happen.

$$\text{Number of outcomes} = (m)(n) \qquad\qquad [4\text{--}2]$$

    B. A permutation is an arrangement in which the order of the objects selected from a specific pool of objects is important.

$$_nP_r = \frac{n!}{(n-r)!} \qquad\qquad [4\text{--}3]$$

    C. A combination is an arrangement where the order of the objects selected from a specific pool of objects is not important.

$$_nC_r = \frac{n!}{r!(n-r)!} \qquad\qquad [4\text{--}4]$$

VI. The rules of addition refer to the probability that any of two or more events can occur.

    A. The special rule of addition is used when events are mutually exclusive.

$$P(A \text{ or } B) = P(A) + P(B) \qquad\qquad [4\text{--}5]$$

    B. The complement rule is used to determine the probability of an event happening by subtracting the probability of the event not happening from 1.

$$P(\sim A) = 1 - P(A) \qquad\qquad [4\text{--}6]$$

    C. The general rule of addition is used when the events are not mutually exclusive.

$$P(A \text{ or } B) = P(A) + P(B) - P(A \text{ and } B) \qquad\qquad [4\text{--}7]$$

VII. The rules of multiplication are applied when two or more events occur simultaneously.

    A. The special rule of multiplication refers to events that are independent.

$$P(A \text{ and } B) = P(A)P(B) \qquad\qquad [4\text{--}8]$$

    B. The general rule of multiplication refers to events that are not independent.

$$P(A \text{ and } B) = P(A)P(B|A) \qquad\qquad [4\text{--}9]$$

    C. A joint probability is the likelihood that two or more events will happen at the same time.

    D. A conditional probability is the likelihood that an event will happen, given that another event has already happened.

Chapter Exercises

45. The marketing research department at Vernors plans to survey teenagers about a newly developed soft drink. Each will be asked to compare it with his or her favourite soft drink.
    a. What is the experiment?
    b. What is one possible event?

46. The number of times a particular event occurred in the past is divided by the number of occurrences. What is this approach to probability called?

47. The probability that the cause and the cure for all cancers will be discovered before the year 2020 is 0.20. What viewpoint of probability does this statement illustrate?

48. Refer to the following picture:

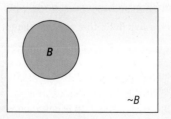

    a. What is the picture called?

    b. What rule of probability is illustrated?

    c. B represents the event of choosing a family that receives welfare payments. What does $P(B) + P(\sim B)$ equal?

49. Define each of these items:

    a. Conditional probability.

    b. Event.

    c. Joint probability.

50. How many possible outcomes are there when a coin is tossed six times?

51. A computer password consists of four characters. The characters can be one of the 26 letters of the alphabet. Each character may be used more than once. How many different passwords are possible?

52. A photographer has four pictures to arrange for a gallery showing. In how many ways can the photographer arrange the pictures?

53. How many ways are there of drawing seven cards from a deck of 52 cards? Note that the cards are not replaced.

54. In how many ways can the digits from 0 to 5 be arranged three at a time?

55. Eight-ball pool, one of the most popular pool games, has 15 coloured and striped balls, numbered from 1 to 15, and a white cue ball. In how many ways could six of the numbered balls be arranged?

56. The first card selected from a standard 52-card deck was a king.

    a. If it is returned to the deck, what is the probability that a king will be drawn on the second selection?

    b. If the king is not replaced, what is the probability that a king will be drawn on the second selection?

    c. What is the probability that a king will be selected on the first draw from the deck and another king on the second draw (assuming that the first king was not replaced)?

57. Armco, a manufacturer of traffic light systems, found that under accelerated-life tests, 95% of the newly developed systems lasted three years before failing to change signals properly.

    a. If a city purchased four of these systems, what is the probability all four systems would operate properly for at least three years?

    b. Which rule of probability does this illustrate?

    c. Using letters to represent the four systems, write an equation to show how you arrived at the answer to part (a).

58. Berdine's Chicken Factory has several retail stores. When interviewing applicants for server positions, the owner would like to include information on the amount of tip a server can expect to earn per bill. A study of 500 recent bills indicated the server earned the following tips:

Amount of Tip ($)	Number
$0 to under $5	200
5 to under 10	100
10 to under 20	75
20 to under 50	75
50 or more	50
Total	500

    a. What is the probability of a tip of $50 or more?

    b. Are the categories "$0 to under $5," "$5 to under $10," and so on considered mutually exclusive?

    c. If the probabilities associated with each outcome were totalled, what would that total be?

    d. What is the probability of a tip of up to $10?

    e. What is the probability of a tip of less than $50?

59. In a management trainee program at Claremont Enterprises, 80% of the trainees are female and 20% male. Ninety percent of the females attended college, and 78% of the males attended college.

    a. A management trainee is selected at random. What is the probability that the person selected is a female who did not attend college?

    b. Construct a tree diagram showing all the probabilities, conditional probabilities, and joint probabilities.

    c. Do the joint probabilities total 1.00? Why?

60. Assume the likelihood that any flight on Delta Airlines arrives within 15 minutes of the scheduled time is 0.90. We select four flights from yesterday for study.

    a. What is the likelihood all four of the selected flights arrived within 15 minutes of the scheduled time?

    b. What is the likelihood that none of the selected flights arrived within 15 minutes of the scheduled time?

    c. What is the likelihood at least one of the selected flights did not arrive within 15 minutes of the scheduled time?

61. There are 100 employees at Kiddie Carts International. Fifty-seven of the employees are production workers, 40 are supervisors, 2 are secretaries, and the remaining employee is the president. Suppose that an employee is selected:
  a. What is the probability the selected employee is a production worker?
  b. What is the probability the selected employee is either a production worker or a supervisor?
  c. Refer to part (b). Are these events mutually exclusive?
  d. What is the probability the selected employee is neither a production worker nor a supervisor?

62. In baseball, a batting average is the probability of the number of hits divided by the number of times at bat. A batting average over 0.300 is very good. This means that a player will get a hit 300 times for every 1000 times at bat. So, assume the probability of getting a hit is 0.359 for each time a player is at bat. In a particular game, assume the batter batted three times.
  a. This is an example of what type of probability?
  b. What is the probability of getting three hits in a particular game?
  c. What is the probability of not getting any hits in a game?
  d. What is the probability of getting at least one hit?

63. Four sports teams remain in a single-elimination playoff competition. If one team is favoured in its semi-final match by odds of 2 to 1 and another squad is favoured in its contest by odds of 3 to 1, what is the probability that:
  a. Both favoured teams win their games.
  b. Neither favoured team wins its game.
  c. At least one of the favoured teams wins its game.

64. There are three clues labelled "daily double" on the game show *Jeopardy*. If three equally matched contenders play, what is the probability that:
  a. A single contestant finds all three "daily doubles"?
  b. The returning champion gets all three of the "daily doubles"?
  c. Each of the players selects precisely one of the "daily doubles"?

65. Brooks Insurance Inc. wishes to offer life insurance to men aged 60 via the Internet. Mortality tables indicate the likelihood of a 60-year-old man surviving another year is 0.98. If the policy is offered to five men age 60:
  a. What is the probability all five men survive the year?
  b. What is the probability at least one does not survive?

66. Forty percent of the homes constructed in the Quail Creek area include a security system. Three homes are selected at random:
  a. What is the probability all three of the selected homes have a security system?
  b. What is the probability none of the three selected homes has a security system?
  c. What is the probability at least one of the selected homes has a security system?
  d. Did you assume the events to be dependent or independent?

67. Refer to Exercise 66, but assume there are 10 homes in the Quail Creek area and four of them have a security system. Three homes are selected at random:
  a. What is the probability all three of the selected homes have a security system?
  b. What is the probability none of the three selected homes has a security system?
  c. What is the probability at least one of the selected homes has a security system?
  d. Did you assume the events to be dependent or independent?

68. A juggler has a bag containing 3 green balls, 2 yellow balls, 1 red ball, and 4 blues. The juggler picks a ball at random. Then, without replacing it, he chooses a second ball. What is the probability the juggler first draws a yellow ball followed by a blue ball?

69. The board of directors of Saner Automatic Door Company consists of 12 members, 3 of whom are women. A new policy and procedures manual is to be written for the company. A committee of three is randomly selected from the board to do the writing.
  a. What is the probability that all members of the committee are men?
  b. What is the probability that at least one member of the committee is a woman?

70. A committee of 5 is selected from a group of 7 faculty and 50 students. In how many different ways can the committee be selected if it must consist of two faculty and three students?

71. A panel discussion of seven employees consists of 4 women and 3 men. In how many ways can this group be selected from 15 men and 20 women?

72. If a committee of 6 is being selected from a group of 10 men and 12 women, in how many ways can this committee be arranged if at least 3 must be women?

73. A crew of eight is required for each midnight shift at the airport. There are 50 employees to choose from, and 30 of these are men. In how many ways can the crew be selected if at least half must be men?

74. A survey of undergraduate students in the School of Business at Northern University revealed the following regarding the gender and majors of the students:

	Major			
Gender	Accounting	Marketing	Finance	Total
Male	100	150	50	300
Female	100	50	50	200
Total	200	200	100	500

a. What is the probability of selecting a female student?
b. What is the probability of selecting a finance or accounting major?
c. What is the probability of selecting a female or an accounting major? Which rule of addition did you apply?
d. What is the probability of selecting an accounting major, given that the person selected is a male?
e. Suppose two students are selected randomly to attend a lunch with the president of the university. What is the probability that both of those selected are accounting majors?

75. A recent survey reported in *BusinessWeek* concerned the salaries of chief executive officers (CEOs) at large corporations and whether company shareholders made or lost money.

	CEO Paid More than $1 Million	CEO Paid Less than $1 Million	Total
Shareholders made money	2	11	13
Shareholders lost money	4	3	7
Total	6	14	20

If a company is randomly selected from the list of 20 studied, what is the probability:
a. That the CEO made more than $1 million?
b. That the CEO made more than $1 million, or the shareholders lost money?
c. That the CEO made more than $1 million given the shareholders lost money?
d. Of selecting two CEOs and finding they both made more than $1 million?

76. A computer-supply retailer purchased a batch of 1000 CD-R disks and attempted to format them for a particular application. There were 857 perfect CDs, 112 CDs were usable but had bad sectors, and the remainder could not be used at all.
a. What is the probability a randomly chosen CD is not perfect?
b. If the disk is not perfect, what is the probability it cannot be used at all?

77. An Internet company located in Edmonton has season tickets to the Edmonton Oilers hockey games. The company president always invites one of the four vice-presidents to attend games with him and claims he selects the person to attend at random. One of the four vice-presidents has not been invited to attend any of the last five Oilers games. What is the likelihood this could be due to chance?

78. Consumers were surveyed on the number of visits to a Sears store (often, occasional, and never) and if the store was located in an enclosed mall (yes and no). The results are summarized in a contingency table:

	Enclosed Mall		
Visits	Yes	No	Total
Often	160	120	280
Occasional	125	135	260
Never	15	150	165
	300	405	705

a. Are the number of visits and enclosed mall variables independent? Why? Interpret your conclusion.
b. Draw a tree diagram and determine the joint probabilities.

79. Several years ago, Wendy's Old Fashioned Hamburgers advertised that there are 256 different ways to order your hamburger. You may choose to have, or omit, any combination of the following on your hamburger: mustard, ketchup, onion, pickle, tomato, relish, mayonnaise, and lettuce. Is the advertisement correct? Show how you arrived at your answer.

80. It was found that 60% of the tourists to China visited the Forbidden City, the Temple of Heaven, the Great Wall, and other historical sites in or near Beijing. Forty percent visited Xi'an with its magnificent terracotta soldiers, horses, and chariots, which had been buried for over 2000 years. Thirty percent of the tourists went to both Beijing and Xi'an. What is the probability that a tourist visited at least one of these places?

81. There are 20 families living in the Willbrook Farms Development. Of these families, 10 prepared their own income tax return for last year, 7 had their taxes prepared by a local professional, and the remaining 3 had their taxes prepared by H&R Block.
  a. What is the probability of selecting a family that prepared its own taxes?
  b. What is the probability of selecting two families that prepared their own taxes?
  c. What is the probability of selecting three families that prepared their own taxes?
  d. What is the probability of selecting two families that did not have their taxes prepared by H&R Block?

82. Reynolds Construction Company has agreed not to erect "look-alike" homes in a new subdivision. Five exterior designs are offered to potential home buyers. The builder has standardized three interior plans that can be incorporated in any of the five exteriors. How many different ways can the exterior and interior plans be offered to potential home buyers?

83. The marketing department has been given the assignment of designing colour codes for the 42 different lines of compact disks (CDs) sold by Goody Records. Three colours are to be used on each CD, but a combination of three colours used for one CD cannot be rearranged and used to identify a different CD. This means that if green, yellow, and violet were used to identify one line, then yellow, green, and violet (or any other combination of these three colours) cannot be used to identify another line.
  a. Would seven colours taken three at a time be adequate to colour code the 42 lines?
  b. As an alternative plan for colour coding the 42 different lines, it has been suggested that only two colours be placed on a disk. Would 10 colours be adequate to colour code the 42 different lines? (Again, a combination of two colours could be used only once).

84. a. Some Saskatchewan licence plates have three letters and three numbers. How many licence plates of this type can there be?
  b. Some Ontario licence plates have four letters and three numbers. How many licence plates of this type can there be?

85. There are four people being considered for the position of chief executive officer of Dalton Enterprises. Three of the applicants are over 60 years of age. Two are female, of which only one is over 60.
  a. What is the probability that a candidate is over 60 and female?
  b. Given that the candidate is male, what is the probability he is under 60?
  c. Given that the person is over 60, what is the probability the person is female?

86. Tim Bleckie is the owner of Bleckie Investment and Real Estate Company. The company recently purchased four tracts of land in Holly Farms Estates and six tracts in Newburg Woods. The tracts are all equally desirable and sell for about the same amount.
  a. What is the probability that the next two tracts sold will be in Newburg Woods?
  b. What is the probability that of the next four sold at least one will be in Holly Farms?
  c. Are these events independent or dependent?

87. Canadian postal codes consist of three letters and three digits, which alternate and start with a letter. For example, R2E 0M4 is a postal code from Winnipeg, Manitoba. How many postal codes can be created using this system?

88. A case of 24 cans contains one can that is contaminated. Three cans are to be chosen randomly for testing.
  a. How many different combinations of three cans could be selected?
  b. What is the probability that the contaminated can is selected for testing?

89. A study was done of the 377 vehicles parked in the college parking lot last Friday. The results were as follows:

	Red	Black	Blue	Grey	White	Total
SUVs	20	35	25	36	17	133
Sports	15	55	24	12	15	121
Compact	12	15	23	45	28	123
	47	105	72	93	60	377

  a. What is the probability of finding a white car?
  b. What is the probability of finding a red or a black car?
  c. What is the probability that the car is not an SUV?
  d. What is the probability of the car is a compact and is blue?
  e. What is the probability the car is red or black and is a sports car?
  f. What is the probability the car is black or is a sports car?

90. Two components, *A* and *B*, operate in series. Being in series means that for the system to operate, both components *A* and *B* must work. Assume the two components are independent. What is the probability the system works under these conditions? The probability *A* works is 0.90, and the probability *B* functions is also 0.90.

91. You take a trip by air that involves three independent flights. If there is an 80% chance each specific leg of the trip is done on time, what is the probability all three flights arrive on time?

92. The probability an HP network server is down is 0.05. If you have three independent servers, what is the probability that at least one of them is operational?

93. Twenty-two percent of all liquid crystal displays (LCDs) are manufactured by Samsung. What is the probability that in a collection of three independent LCD purchases, at least one is a Samsung?

94. Althoff and Roll, an investment firm, advertises extensively in the *Morning Gazette*, the newspaper serving the area where their office is located. The *Gazette* marketing staff estimates that 60% of Althoff and Roll's potential market read the newspaper. It is further estimated that 85% of those who read the *Gazette* remember the Althoff and Roll advertisement.
   a. What percentage of the investment firm's potential market sees and remembers the advertisement?
   b. What percentage of the investment firm's potential market sees but does not remember the advertisement?

95. With each purchase of a large pizza at Tony's Pizza, the customer receives a coupon that can be scratched to see if a prize will be awarded. The odds of winning a free soft drink are 1 in 10, and the odds of winning a free large pizza are 1 in 50. You plan to eat lunch tomorrow at Tony's. What is the probability:
   a. That you will win either a large pizza or a soft drink?
   b. That you will not win a prize?
   c. That you will not win a prize on three consecutive visits to Tony's?
   d. That you will win at least one prize on one of your next three visits to Tony's?

96. An investor purchased 100 shares of Bank stock and 100 shares of Cooper Electric stock. The probability the Bank stock will appreciate over a year is 0.70. The probability Cooper Electric stock will increase over the same period is 0.60.
   a. What is the probability that both stocks appreciate during the period?
   b. What is the probability that the Bank stock appreciates and the Cooper Electric stock does not?
   c. What is the probability at least one of the stocks appreciate?

97. A new chewing gum has been developed that is helpful to those who want to stop smoking. If 60% of those people chewing the gum are successful in stopping smoking, what is the probability that in a group of four smokers using the gum at least one quits smoking?

98. Winning all three "Triple Crown" races is considered the greatest feat of a pedigree racehorse. After a successful Kentucky Derby, Big Brown is a 1-to-2 favourite to win the Preakness Stakes.
   a. If he is a 1-to-2 favourite to win the Belmont Stakes as well, what is his probability of winning the Triple Crown?
   b. What do his chances for the Preakness Stakes have to be in order for him to be "even money" to earn the Triple Crown?

99. A new sports car model has defective brakes 15% of the time and a defective steering mechanism 5% of the time. Let us assume (and hope) that these problems occur independently. If one or the other of these problems is present, the car is called a "lemon." If both of these problems are present, the car is a "hazard." Your instructor purchased one of these cars yesterday. What is the probability that it is:
   a. A lemon?
   b. A hazard?

100. For a weekly lottery game in Ontario, participants select three numbers between 0 and 9. A number cannot be selected more than once, so a winning ticket could be, say, 307, but not 337. Purchasing one ticket allows you to select one set of numbers. The winning numbers are announced on TV each week.
   a. How many different outcomes (three-digit numbers) are possible?
   b. If you purchase a ticket for the game tonight, what is the likelihood you will win?
   c. Suppose you purchase three tickets for tonight's drawing and select a different number for each ticket. What is the probability that you will not win with any of the tickets?

101. A puzzle in a newspaper presents a matching problem. The names of 10 different Juno award winners are listed in one column, and their 10 winning songs are listed in random order in a second column. The puzzle asks the reader to match each winner with his or her winning song. If you make the matches randomly, how many sets of matches are possible? What is the probability that a randomly selected set of matches has all 10 winners matched correctly?

Data Set Exercises

Questions marked with ⬀ have data sets available on McGraw-Hill's online resource for *Basic Statistics*.

⬀ **102.** Refer to the Real Estate Data—Orleans online, which reports information on list prices, listing number, type, number of bathrooms, number of bedrooms, title, year built, and area.
  a. What is the probability that a dwelling is an apartment?
  b. What is the probability that a dwelling is not a rowhouse or townhouse?
  c. What is the probability that a listing has two bedrooms?
  d. What is the probability that a listing has more than two bedrooms?

⬀ **103.** Refer to the Real Estate Data—Orleans online, which reports information on list prices, listing number, type, number of bathrooms, number of bedrooms, title, year built, and area.
  a. What is the probability that a listing is less than $300 000?
  b. What is the probability that a listing is located in Nottinggate or Chapel Hill?
  c. What is the probability that a listing has more than one bathroom?
  d. What is the probability that a listing is less than $200 000 or more $400 000?

⬀ **104.** Refer to the Real Estate Data—Orleans online, which reports information on list prices, listing number, type, number of bathrooms, number of bedrooms, title, year built, and area.
  a. What is the probability that a listing is less than $200 000?
  b. What is the probability that a listing is less than $300 000 or more than $450 000?
  c. What is the probability that a listing is more than $300 000?
  d. What is the probability that a listing has exactly one bathroom?

⬀ **105.** Refer to the Real Estate Data—Orleans online, which reports information on list prices, listing number, type, number of bathrooms, number of bedrooms, title, year built, and area. Sort the data into a table by type and list price (in class widths of 100 000) and compute the following probabilities:
  1. The dwelling is an apartment.
  2. Given that the dwelling is an apartment, that it is listed from $100 000 to under $200 000.
  3. The dwelling is a rowhouse or townhouse and listed from $100 00 to under $200 000.
  4. Given that the dwelling is a house, that it is listed from $300 000 to under $400 000.

⬀ **106.** Refer to the Real Estate Data—Orleans online, which reports information on list prices, listing number, type, number of bathrooms, number of bedrooms, title, year built, and area. Sort the data into a table by list price (class widths of $100 000) and the number of bedrooms. Compute the following probabilities:
  1. The dwelling has three bedrooms.
  2. The dwelling is listed for less than $400 000.
  3. The dwelling is listed from $200 000 to under $400 000 and has two bedrooms.
  4. The dwelling has more than three bedrooms, given that the dwelling is listed for $500 000 or more.

⬀ **107.** Refer to the Real Estate Data—Saskatoon online, which reports information on list prices, type, number of full and half bathrooms, number of bedrooms, and total square feet.
  a. What is the probability that a dwelling is a house?
  b. What is the probability that a dwelling is not an apartment?
  c. What is the probability that a listing has two full baths?
  d. What is the probability that a listing has more than two full baths?

⬀ **108.** Refer to the Real Estate Data—Saskatoon online, which reports information on list prices, type, number of full and half bathrooms, number of bedrooms, and total square feet.
  a. What is the probability that a listing is less than 1000 square feet?
  b. What is the probability that a listing is between 1000 and 1500 square feet?
  c. What is the probability that a listing has one half bath?
  d. What is the probability that a listing is for more than $500 000?

⬀ **109.** Refer to the Real Estate Data—Saskatoon online, which reports information on list prices, type, number of full and half bathrooms, number of bedrooms, and total square feet.
  a. What is the probability that a listing is less than $200 000?
  b. What is the probability that a listing is less than $300 000 or more than $500 000?
  c. What is the probability that a listing is between $300 000 and $500 000?

⬀ **110.** Refer to the Real Estate Data—Saskatoon online, which reports information on list prices, type, number of full and half bathrooms, number of bedrooms, and total square feet. Sort the data into a table by type and list price (in class widths of $500 000), and compute the following probabilities:

1. The dwelling is a house.
2. Given that the dwelling is a house, that it is listed from $500 000 to under $1 000 000.
3. The dwelling is an apartment that is listed for more than $500 000.
4. Given that the dwelling is an apartment, that it is listed from $500 000 to under $1 000 000.

111. Refer to the Real Estate Data—Saskatoon online, which reports information on list prices, type, number of full and half bathrooms, number of bedrooms, and total square feet. Sort the data into a table by list price (class widths of $500 000) and the number of bedrooms. Compute the following probabilities:
1. The dwelling has three bedrooms.
2. The dwelling is listed for less than $500 000.
3. That it is a two-bedroom dwelling listed from $500 000 to under $1 000 000.
4. The dwelling has three bedrooms, given that the dwelling is listed for $500 000 or more.

112. Refer to the Real Estate Data—Saskatoon online, which reports information on list prices, type, number of full and half bathrooms, number of bedrooms, and total square feet. Sort the data into a table by list price (class widths of $500 000) and the square footage (class widths of 1000). Compute the following probabilities:
1. The dwelling has more than 1000 square feet.
2. The dwelling is listed for less than $500 000 and is from 1000 to under 2000 square feet.
3. Given that the dwelling is listed for less than $500 000 and is from 1000 to under 2000 square feet.
4. The dwelling is under 1000 square feet or is listed for less than $500 000.

Practice Test

Part I Objective

1. A _____ is a value between 0 and 1, inclusive, describing the relative chance or likelihood an event will occur.

2. An _____ is a process that leads to the occurrence of one and only one of several possible observations.

3. An _____ is a collection of one or more outcomes of an experiment.

4. Using the _____ viewpoint, the probability of an event happening is the fraction of the time similar events happened in the past.

5. Using the _____ viewpoint, an individual evaluates the available opinions and information and then estimates or assigns the probability.

6. Using the _____ viewpoint, the probability of an event happening is computed by dividing the number of favourable outcomes by the number of possible outcomes.

7. If several events are described as _____ , then the occurrence of one event means that none of the other events can occur at the same time.

8. If an experiment has a set of events that includes every possible outcome, then the set of events is described as _____ .

9. If two events *A* and *B* are _____ , the special rule of addition states that the probability of one or the other events occurring equals the sum of their probabilities.

10. The _____ is used to determine the probability of an event occurring by subtracting the probability of the event not occurring from 1.

11. A probability that measures the likelihood two or more events will happen concurrently is called a _____ .

12. The special rule of multiplication requires that two events *A* and *B* are _____ .

Part II Problems

1. Fred Friendly, CGA, has 20 tax returns to prepare before the April 30 deadline. It is late at night, so he decides to do two more before going home. In his stack of accounts, 12 are for individuals, 5 are for businesses, and 3 are for charitable organizations. If he selects the two returns at random, what is the probability that:
   a. Both are businesses?
   b. At least one is a business?

2. Fred exercises regularly. He jogs 30% of the time, rides a bike 20% of the time, and does both 12% of the time. What is the probability that on a typical day he does at least one of these two types of exercise?

3. Fred works in a tax office with four other chartered professional accountants (CPAs). There are five parking spots beside the office. If they all drive to work, how many different ways can the cars belonging to the CPAs be arranged in the five spots?

Computer Commands

1. **Excel** steps to determine the number of permutations for the Betts Machine Shop Inc. example are:

   a. Select **Insert Function**. From the **Or select a category** list, select **Statistical**.

   b. In the **Select a function** list, click **PERMUT**. Click **OK**.

   c. Enter *8* for **Number** and *3* for **Number_chosen**. The answer of *336* appears in the dialogue box.

2. **Excel** steps to determine the number of combinations for the Grand movie theatre example are:

   a. Select **Insert Function**. From the **Or select a category** list, select **Math & Trig**.

   b. In the **Select a function** list, click **COMBIN**. Click **OK**.

   c. Enter *7* for **Number** and *3* for **Number_chosen**. The answer of *35* appears in the dialogue box.

3. **MegaStat** commands to find the number of permutations for the Betts Machine Shop Inc. example are:

   a. Select **MegaStat**, **Probability**, **Counting Rules**, and select the **Permutations** tab.

   b. Enter *8* in the first box (for *n*) and *3* in the second box (for *r*).

   c. Click the **Preview** box to see the answer and/or click **OK** for the output.

4. **MegaStat** commands to find the number of combinations the Grand movie theatre example are:

   a. Select **MegaStat**, **Probability**, **Counting Rules**, and select the **Combinations** tab.

   b. Enter *7* in the first box (for *n*) and *3* in the second box (for *r*).

   c. Click the **Preview** box to see the answer, or click **OK** for the output.

Answers to Self-Reviews

4–1 (a) Testing of the new computer game.

(b) Seventy-three players liked the game. (Of course, other answers are possible.)

(c) No. Probability cannot be greater than 1. The probability that the game, if put on the market, will be successful is 65/80, or 0.8125.

(d) Cannot be less than 0. Perhaps a mistake in arithmetic.

(e) More than half of the persons testing the game liked it. (Of course, other answers are possible.)

4–2 1. $\dfrac{4 \text{ queens in deck}}{52 \text{ cards total}} = \dfrac{4}{52} = 0.0769$ Classical.

2. $\dfrac{182}{539} = 0.338$ Empirical.

3. You may be more optimistic or less optimistic that you will reach \$1 million. Subjective.

4–3 1. There are 20, found by: (5)(4)

2. There are 72, found by: (3)(2)(4)(3)

4–4 1. (a) 60, found by: (5)(4)(3)

(b) 60, found by:

$$\dfrac{5!}{(5-3)!} = \dfrac{5 \cdot 4 \cdot 3 \cdot \cancel{2 \cdot 1}}{\cancel{2 \cdot 1}}$$

2. 24, found by:

$$\dfrac{4!}{(4-4)!} = \dfrac{4!}{0!} = \dfrac{4!}{1} = \dfrac{4 \cdot 3 \cdot 2 \cdot 1}{1}$$

3. 5040, found by:

$$\dfrac{10!}{(10-4)!} = \dfrac{10 \cdot 9 \cdot 8 \cdot \cancel{7 \cdot 6 \cdot 5 \cdot 4 \cdot 3 \cdot 2 \cdot 1}}{\cancel{6 \cdot 5 \cdot 4 \cdot 3 \cdot 2 \cdot 1}}$$

4. (a) 35 is correct, found by:

$$\dfrac{7!}{3!(7-3)!} = \dfrac{7 \cdot 6 \cdot 5 \cdot \cancel{4 \cdot 3 \cdot 2 \cdot 1}}{(3 \cdot 2 \cdot 1) \cdot (\cancel{4 \cdot 3 \cdot 2 \cdot 1})}$$

(b) $\dfrac{7!}{3!(7-5)!} = \dfrac{7 \cdot 6 \cdot \cancel{5} \cdot \cancel{4} \cdot \cancel{3} \cdot 2 \cdot \cancel{1}}{(\cancel{5} \cdot \cancel{4} \cdot \cancel{3} \cdot \cancel{2} \cdot \cancel{1}) \cdot (2 \cdot 1)} = 21$

5. (a) $_nP_r = \dfrac{50!}{(50-3)!} = 117\,600$

(b) $_nC_r = \dfrac{50!}{3!(50-3)!} = 19\,600$

4–5 (a) (i) $\dfrac{(50+68)}{2000} = 0.059$

(ii) $1 - \dfrac{302}{2000} = 0.849$

(b)

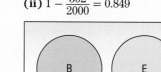

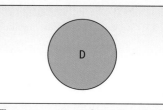

(c) They are not complementary but are mutually exclusive.

4–6 (a) Need for corrective shoes is event *A*. Need for major dental work is event *B*.

$P(A \text{ or } B) = P(A) + P(B) - P(A \text{ and } B)$

$= 0.08 + 0.15 - 0.03$

$= 0.20$

(b) One possibility is:

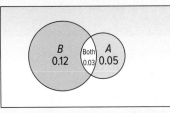

4–7 $(0.80)(0.80)(0.80)(0.80) = 0.4096.$

4–8 **(a)** 0.002, found by:

$$\left(\frac{4}{12}\right)\left(\frac{3}{11}\right)\left(\frac{2}{10}\right)\left(\frac{1}{9}\right) = \frac{24}{11880} = 0.002$$

(b) 0.14, found by:

$$\left(\frac{8}{12}\right)\left(\frac{7}{11}\right)\left(\frac{6}{10}\right)\left(\frac{5}{9}\right) = \frac{1680}{11880} = 0.1414$$

(c) No, because there are other possibilities, such as three women and one man.

4–9 **(a)** $P(B_4) = \dfrac{105}{200} = 0.525$

(b) $P(\sim A_1 | B_4) = \dfrac{30}{105} = 0.286$

(c) $P(\sim A_1 \text{ or } B_4) = \dfrac{80}{200} + \dfrac{105}{200} - \dfrac{30}{200} = \dfrac{155}{200} = 0.775$

4–10 **(a)** Contingency table.

Employee	Plans	Joint Probabilities

$\dfrac{20}{100}$ **Management**

$\dfrac{5}{20}$ **Retire** $\quad \left(\dfrac{20}{100}\right)\left(\dfrac{5}{20}\right) = \left(\dfrac{100}{2000}\right) = 0.05$

$\dfrac{15}{20}$ **Not Retire** $\quad \left(\dfrac{20}{100}\right)\left(\dfrac{15}{20}\right) = \left(\dfrac{300}{2000}\right) = 0.15$

$\dfrac{80}{100}$ **Production**

$\dfrac{30}{80}$ **Retire** $\quad \left(\dfrac{80}{100}\right)\left(\dfrac{30}{80}\right) = \left(\dfrac{2400}{8000}\right) = 0.30$

$\dfrac{50}{80}$ **Not Retire** $\quad \left(\dfrac{80}{100}\right)\left(\dfrac{50}{80}\right) = \left(\dfrac{4000}{8000}\right) = 0.50$

(b) Total $\qquad\qquad\qquad\qquad$ 1.00

(c) Yes, all possibilities are included.

CHAPTER 5
Discrete Probability Distributions

LEARNING OBJECTIVES

When you have completed this chapter, you will be able to:

LO5-1 Identify the characteristics of a *probability distribution*.

LO5-2 Distinguish between *discrete* and *continuous* random variables.

LO5-3 Compute the mean, variance, and standard deviation of a discrete probability distribution.

LO5-4 Explain the assumptions and compute probabilities of the *binomial distribution*.

LO5-5 Explain the assumptions and compute probabilities for a *hypergeometric distribution*.

LO5-6 Explain the assumptions and compute probabilities for a *Poisson distribution*.

Recent statistics suggest that 15% of those who visit a retail site on the Internet make a purchase. A retailer wished to verify this claim. To do so, she selected a sample of 16 "hits" to her site and found that four had actually made a purchase. What is the likelihood of exactly four purchases? How many purchases should she expect? What is the likelihood that four or more "hits" result in a purchase? (Exercise 55, LO5-4)

5.1 INTRODUCTION

Chapters 2 and 3 are devoted to descriptive statistics. We describe raw data by organizing it into a frequency distribution and portraying the distribution in tables, graphs, and charts. Also, we compute a measure of location—such as the arithmetic mean, median, or mode—to locate a typical value near the centre of the distribution. The range and the standard deviation are used to describe the spread in the data. These chapters focus on describing *something that has already happened*.

Starting with Chapter 4, the emphasis changes—we begin examining *something that could happen*. We note that this facet of statistics is called *statistical inference*. The objective is to make inferences (statements) about a population on the basis of a number of observations, called a *sample*, selected from the population. In Chapter 4, we state that a probability is a value between 0 and 1 inclusive, and we examine how probabilities can be combined using rules of addition and rules of multiplication.

This chapter will begin the study of **probability distributions**. A probability distribution gives the entire range of values that can occur based on an experiment. A probability distribution is similar to a relative frequency distribution. However, instead of describing the past, it describes a likely future event. For example, a drug manufacturer may claim a treatment will cause weight loss for 80% of the population. A consumer protection agency may test the treatment on a sample of six people. If the manufacturer's claim is true, it is *almost impossible* to have an outcome where no one in the sample loses weight, and it is *most likely* that five out of the six do lose weight.

In this chapter, we discuss the mean, variance, and standard deviation of a probability distribution. We also discuss three frequently occurring probability distributions: the binomial, the hypergeometric, and the Poisson.

LO5-1 5.2 WHAT IS A PROBABILITY DISTRIBUTION?

Probability distribution A listing of all the outcomes of an experiment and the probability associated with each outcome.

A **probability distribution** shows the possible outcomes of an experiment and the probability of each of these outcomes.

Below are the major characteristics of a probability distribution:

1. The probability of a particular outcome is between 0 and 1 inclusive.
2. The outcomes are mutually exclusive events.
3. The list is exhaustive. So, the sum of the probabilities of the various events is equal to 1.

How can we generate a probability distribution? The following example will explain this:

Example	Suppose that we are interested in the number of heads showing face up on three tosses of a coin. This is the experiment. The possible results are: zero heads, one head, two heads, and three heads. What is the probability distribution for the number of heads?
Solution	There are eight possible outcomes. A tail might appear face up on the first toss, another tail on the second toss, and another tail on the third toss of the coin. Or we might get tail, tail, and head. We use the multiplication formula from Chapter 4 (4–2) for counting outcomes. There are (2)(2)(2) = 8 possible outcomes. These results are listed below:

Possible Result	Coin Toss			Number of Heads
	First	Second	Third	
1	T	T	T	0
2	T	T	H	1
3	T	H	T	1
4	T	H	H	2
5	H	T	T	1
6	H	T	H	2
7	H	H	T	2
8	H	H	H	3

Note that the outcome "zero heads" occurred only once, "one head" occurred three times, "two heads" occurred three times, and the outcome "three heads" occurred only once. That is, "zero heads" happened one out of eight times. Thus, the probability of zero heads is one-eighth (1/8), the probability of one head is three-eighths (3/8), and so on. The probability distribution is shown in Table 5–1. Because one of these events must happen, the total of the probabilities of all possible events is 1. This is always true. The same information is shown in Chart 5–1.

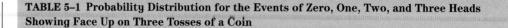

TABLE 5–1 Probability Distribution for the Events of Zero, One, Two, and Three Heads Showing Face Up on Three Tosses of a Coin

Number of Heads, x	Probability of Outcome, $P(x)$
0	$\frac{1}{8} = 0.125$
1	$\frac{3}{8} = 0.375$
2	$\frac{3}{8} = 0.375$
3	$\frac{1}{8} = 0.125$
Total	$\frac{8}{8} = 1.000$

CHART 5–1 Graphical Presentation of the Number of Heads Resulting from Three Tosses of a Coin and the Corresponding Probability

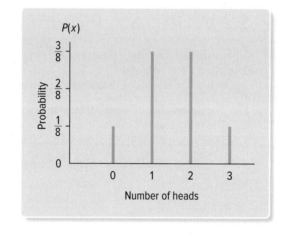

Refer to the coin-tossing example in Table 5–1. We write the probability of x as $P(x)$. So, the probability of zero heads is $P(0 \text{ heads}) = 0.125$ and the probability of one head is $P(1 \text{ head}) = 0.375$ and so forth. The sum of these mutually exclusive probabilities is 1; that is, from Table 5–1, $0.125 + 0.375 + 0.375 + 0.125 = 1.00$.

self-review 5–1

The possible outcomes of an experiment involving the roll of a six-sided die are: a one-spot, a two-spot, a three-spot, a four-spot, a five-spot, and a six-spot.

(a) Develop a probability distribution for the number of possible spots.
(b) Portray the probability distribution graphically.
(c) What is the sum of the probabilities?

5.3 RANDOM VARIABLES

In any experiment of chance, the outcomes occur randomly. So, it is often called a *random variable*. For example, rolling a single die is an experiment; any one of six possible outcomes can occur. Some experiments result in outcomes that are quantitative (e.g., dollars, weight, or number of children), and others result in qualitative outcomes (e.g., colour or soft drink preference). Each value of the random variable is associated with a probability to indicate the

Random variable A quantity resulting from an experiment that, by chance, can assume different values.

chance of a particular outcome. A few examples will further illustrate what is meant by a **random variable.**

1. If we count the number of employees absent from the day shift on Monday, the number might be 0, 1, 2, 3, ... The number absent is the random variable.
2. If we weigh four steel bars, the masses might be 24 928 kilograms (kg), 2497 kg, 2506 kg, and so on. The mass is the random variable.
3. Suppose three customers enter a restaurant. The number of these customers who purchase a dessert item after their meal could be 0, 1, 2, or 3. The number purchasing a dessert item is a random variable.
4. Other random variables might be: the number of defective light bulbs produced during the week, the heights of the members of the girls' basketball team, and the daily number of drivers charged with driving under the influence of alcohol in British Columbia.

The following diagram illustrates the terms *experiment, outcome, event,* and *random variable.* First, for the experiment where a coin is tossed three times, there are eight possible outcomes. In this experiment, we are interested in the event that one head occurs in the three tosses. The random variable is the number of heads. In terms of probability, we want to know the probability of the event that the random variable equals 1. The result is $P(1$ head in 3 tosses$) = 0.375$.

Possible *outcomes* for three coin tosses

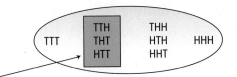

The *event* (one head) occurs and the *random variable* number of heads has the value $x = 1$.

A random variable may be either *discrete* or *continuous.*

LO5-2   Discrete Random Variable

A discrete random variable can assume only a certain number of separated values. If there are 100 employees, then the count of the number absent on Monday can only be 0, 1, 2, 3, . . . , 100. A **discrete random variable** is usually the result of counting something.

    A discrete random variable can, in some cases, assume fractional or decimal values. It may also assume a negative value. These values must be separated—that is, have distance between them. As an example, the scores awarded by judges for technical competence and artistic form in a figure skating competition may be decimal values, such as 177.2, 188.9, 169.7, and 183.4. Such values are discrete because there is distance between scores of, say, 183.4 and 183.5. A score cannot be 183.46875 or 184.52738, for example.

Discrete random variable A random variable that can assume only certain, clearly separated values.

Continuous Random Variable

A random variable can also be continuous. If we measure something, such as the width of a room, the height of a person, or the pressure in an automobile tire, the variable is a *continuous random variable.* It can assume one of an infinitely large number of values, within certain limitations. Examples are as follows:

- The times of commercial flights between Toronto and Ottawa are 1 hour, 1.1 hours, and so on. The random variable is the time in hours.
- Tire pressures, measured in pounds per square inch (psi), for a new Chevy TrailBlazer may be 32 psi, 31 psi, 33 psi, and so on. In other words, any values between 28 and 35 could reasonably occur. The random variable is the tire pressure.
- The waiting time for customers to receive their order at a Starbucks is recorded to the nearest hundredth of a minute. The random variable is the time, which may be reported as 2.17 minutes, 3.86 minutes, and so on.

As with discrete random variables, the likelihood of a continuous random variable can be summarized with a **probability distribution**. So, what is the difference between a probability distribution and a random variable? A random variable reports the particular outcome of an experiment. A probability distribution reports all the possible outcomes as well as the corresponding probability.

The tools used, as well as the probability interpretations, are different for discrete and continuous probability distributions. This chapter is limited to the discussion and interpretation of discrete distributions. In the next chapter, we discuss continuous distributions. How do you tell the difference between the two types of distributions? Usually, a discrete distribution is the result of counting something such as:

- The number of heads appearing when a coin is tossed three times.
- The number of students earning an A in this class.
- The number of production employees absent from the second shift today.
- The number of 30-second commercials during the Super Bowl on Sunday.

Continuous distributions are usually the result of some type of measurement such as:

- The length of each song on the latest Drake album.
- The height of each student in the class.
- The temperature outside while you are reading this book.
- The age of Facebook employees.

LO5-3   5.4 THE MEAN, VARIANCE, AND STANDARD DEVIATION OF A PROBABILITY DISTRIBUTION

In Chapter 3, we discussed measures of location and variation for a frequency distribution. The mean reports the central location of the data, and the variance describes the spread in the data. In a similar fashion, a probability distribution is summarized by its mean and variance. We identify the mean of a probability distribution by the lowercase Greek letter mu (μ) and the standard deviation by the lowercase Greek letter sigma (σ).

Mean

The mean is a typical value used to represent the central location of a probability distribution. It also is the long-run average value of the random variable. The mean of a probability distribution is also referred to as its **expected value**. It is a weighted average, where the possible values of a random variable are weighted by their corresponding probabilities of occurrence.

The mean of a discrete probability distribution is computed by the formula:

MEAN OF A DISCRETE PROBABILITY DISTRIBUTION	$\mu = \Sigma[xP(x)]$	[5–1]

where $P(x)$ is the probability of a particular value x. In other words, to find the mean, multiply each x value by its probability of occurrence, and then add these products.

Variance and Standard Deviation

The mean is a typical value used to summarize a discrete probability distribution. However, it does not describe the amount of spread (variation) in a distribution. The variance does this. The formula for the variance of a probability distribution is:

VARIANCE OF A DISCRETE PROBABILITY DISTRIBUTION	$\sigma^2 = \Sigma[(x - \mu)^2 P(x)]$	[5–2]

The computational steps are as follows:

1. Subtract the mean from each value of the random variable, and square this difference.
2. Multiply each squared difference by its probability.
3. Sum the resulting products to arrive at the variance.

The standard deviation, σ, is found by taking the square root of σ^2; that is, $\sigma = \sqrt{\sigma^2}$.

The following example will help explain the details of the calculation and interpretation of the mean and standard deviation of a probability distribution.

Example	John Ragsdale sells developed new cars for Pelican Ford. John usually sells the largest number of cars on Saturday. He has the following probability distribution for the number of cars he expects to sell on a particular Saturday:

Number of Cars Sold, x	Probability, P(x)
0	0.1
1	0.2
2	0.3
3	0.3
4	0.1
	Total 1.0

1. What type of distribution is this?
2. On a typical Saturday, how many cars does John expect to sell?
3. What is the variance of the distribution?

Solution

1. This is a discrete probability distribution for the random variable called "number of cars sold." Note that John expects to sell only within a certain range of cars; he does not expect to sell five cars, 50 cars, or –2 cars. Further, he cannot sell half a car. He can sell only 0, 1, 2, 3, or 4 cars. Also, the outcomes are mutually exclusive—he cannot sell a total of both 3 and 4 cars on the same Saturday. The sum of all possible outcomes totals 1. Hence, these circumstances qualify as a probability distribution.

2. The mean number of cars sold is computed by weighting the number of cars sold by the probability of selling that number and adding or summing the products using formula (5–1):

$$\mu = \sum[xP(x)]$$
$$= 0(.1) + 1(.2) + 2(.3) + 3(.3) + 4(.1)$$
$$= 2.1$$

These calculations are summarized in the following table:

Number of Cars Sold, x	Probability, P(x)	x · P(x)
0	0.1	0.0
1	0.2	0.2
2	0.3	0.6
3	0.3	0.9
4	0.1	0.4
	Total 1.0	$\mu = 2.1$

How do we interpret a mean of 2.1? This value indicates that over a large number of Saturdays, John Ragsdale expects to sell a mean of 2.1 cars a day. Of course, it is not possible for him to sell *exactly* 2.1 cars on any particular Saturday. However, the expected value can be used to predict the arithmetic mean number of cars sold on Saturdays in the long run. For example, if John works 50 Saturdays during a year, he can expect to sell (50) (2.1) = 105 cars on Saturdays during the 50 weeks. Thus, the mean is sometimes called the *expected value*.

The following table illustrates the steps to calculate using formula (5–2). The first two columns show the probability distribution. The third column shows that the mean is subtracted from each value of the random variable x. The fourth column shows that each difference in column three is squared. In the last column, each value in column four is multiplied by the corresponding probability in column two. The variance is the sum of the values in the last column.

Number of Cars Sold, x	Probability, $P(x)$	$(x - \mu)$	$(x - \mu)^2$	$(x - \mu)^2 P(x)$
0	0.1	0.0 − 2.1	4.41	0.441
1	0.2	1.0 − 2.1	1.21	0.242
2	0.3	2.0 − 2.1	0.01	0.003
3	0.3	3.0 − 2.1	0.81	0.243
4	0.1	4.0 − 2.1	3.61	0.361
				$\sigma^2 = 1.29$

Recall that the standard deviation, σ, is the positive square root of the variance. In this example, $\sqrt{\sigma^2} = \sqrt{1.29} = 1.136$ cars. How do we interpret a standard deviation of 1.136 cars? If salesperson Rita Kirsch also sold a mean of 2.1 cars on Saturdays, and the standard deviation in her sales was 1.91 cars, we would conclude that there is more variability in the Saturday sales of Ms. Kirsch than in those of Mr. Ragsdale (because 1.91 > 1.136).

---

self-review 5–2

The Pizza Palace offers three sizes of cola—small, medium, and large—to go with its pizza. The colas are sold for $0.80, $0.90, and $1.20, respectively. Thirty percent of the orders are for small, 50% are for medium, and 20% are for the large sizes. Organize the size of the colas and the probability of a sale into a probability distribution.

(a) Is this a discrete probability distribution? Indicate why or why not.
(b) Compute the mean amount charged for a cola.
(c) What is the variance in the amount charged for a cola? The standard deviation?

EXERCISES

1. Sam Simone is the manager of a family-run pet store. He is deciding whether to open an hour later on Sundays. From past sales on Sundays he has determined that the probability of zero sales during this hour is 20%, one sale is 40%, two sales is 30%, and three sales is 10%. The results are summarized in the following table in the form of a discrete probability distribution.

x	$P(x)$
0	0.2
1	0.4
2	0.3
3	0.1

Compute the mean (the expected number) and the standard deviation of sales for Sam so he can use this information to make an informed decision.

2. Compute the mean and variance of the following discrete probability distribution:

x	$P(x)$
2	0.5
8	0.3
10	0.2

3. Three tables listed below show random variables and their probabilities. However, only one of these is actually a probability distribution.

x	$P(x)$		x	$P(x)$		x	$P(x)$
5	0.3		5	0.1		5	0.5
10	0.3		10	0.2		10	0.3
15	0.2		15	0.3		15	−0.2
20	0.4		20	0.4		20	0.4

    a. Which of the above tables is a probability distribution?

    b. Using the correct probability distribution, find the probability that x is:

        (1) Exactly 15.

        (2) No more than 10.

        (3) More than 5.

    c. Compute the mean, variance, and standard deviation of this distribution.

4. Which of these variables are discrete variables, and which are continuous random variables?

    a. The number of new accounts established by a salesperson in a year.

    b. The time between customer arrivals to a bank automatic teller machine (ATM).

    c. The number of customers in Big Nick's barber shop.

    d. The amount of fuel in your car's gas tank last week.

    e. The outside temperature today.

5. The information below is the number of daily emergency assists made to skiers by the volunteer ski team at Alpine Ski Lodge for the last 50 days. To explain, there were 22 days on which there were 2 emergency assists, and 9 days on which there were 3 emergency assists.

Number of Calls	Frequency
0	8
1	10
2	22
3	9
4	1
	Total 50

    a. Convert this information on the number of calls to a probability distribution.

    b. Is this an example of a discrete or a continuous probability distribution?

    c. What is the mean number of emergency assists per day?

    d. What is the standard deviation of the number of assists made daily?

6. The director of admissions at Kinzua University in Nova Scotia estimated the distribution of student admissions for the fall semester on the basis of past experience. What is the expected number of admissions for the fall semester? Compute the variance and the standard deviation.

Admissions	Probability
1000	0.60
1200	0.30
1500	0.10

7. The following table lists the probability distribution for cash prizes in a lottery conducted at Lawson's Department Store:

Prize ($)	Probability
$0	0.45
10	0.30
100	0.20
500	0.05

If you buy a single ticket, what is the probability that you will win:

    a. Exactly $100?

    b. At least $10?

    c. No more than $100?

    d. Compute the mean, variance, and standard deviation of this distribution.

156
Chapter 5

8. You are asked to match three songs with the performers who made those songs famous. If you guess, the probability distribution for the number of correct matches is:

Probability	0.333	0.500	0.000	0.167
Number correct	0	1	2	3

What is the probability you will get:

a. Exactly one correct?

b. At least one correct?

c. Exactly two correct?

d. Compute the mean, variance, and standard deviation of this distribution.

9. Belk Department Store is having a special sale this weekend. Customers charging purchases of more than $50 to their Belk credit card will be given a special Belk Lottery card. The customer will scratch off the card, which will indicate the amount to be taken off the total amount of the purchase. Listed below are the amount of the prize and the percentage of the time that amount will be deducted from the total amount of the purchase:

Prize Amount	Probability
$10	0.50
25	0.40
50	0.08
100	0.02

a. What is the mean amount deducted from the total purchase amount?

b. What is the standard deviation of the amount deducted from the total purchase?

10. The parking authority in downtown Halifax reported the following information for a sample of 250 customers on the number of hours cars are parked and the amount they are charged:

Number of Hours	Frequency	Amount Charged
1	20	$3
2	38	6
3	53	9
4	45	12
5	40	14
6	13	16
7	5	18
8	36	20

a. Convert the information on the number of hours parked to a probability distribution. Is this a discrete or a continuous probability distribution?

b. Find the mean and the standard deviation of the number of hours parked. How would you answer the question, how long is a typical customer parked?

c. Find the mean and standard deviation of the amount charged.

LO5-4 5.5 BINOMIAL PROBABILITY DISTRIBUTION

The **binomial probability distribution** is a widely occurring discrete probability distribution. To describe experimental outcomes with a binomial distribution, there are four requirements. The first requirement is there are only two possible outcomes on a particular trial of an experiment. For example, on a test, a true/false question is either true or false. The outcomes are *mutually exclusive*, meaning that the answer to a true/false question must be either true or false but cannot be true and false at the same time. Another example is the outcome of a sales call. Either a customer purchases the product or does not purchase the product, but the sale cannot result in both outcomes. Frequently, we classify the two possible outcomes as "success" and "failure." However, this distinction does *not* imply that one outcome is good and the other is bad, only that there are two mutually exclusive outcomes.

The second requirement is that the random variable is the number of successes for a fixed and known number of trials. For example, we flip a coin five times and count the number of times a head appears in the five flips, or we decide to randomly select 10 workers and count the number who are older than 50 years of age, or we randomly select 20 boxes of Kellogg's Raisin Bran and count the number of boxes that weigh more than the amount indicated on the package. In each example, we count the number of successes from the fixed number of trials.

A third requirement is that we know the probability of a success and it is the same for each trial. Three examples are:

- If past experience revealed that the swing bridge near Little Current, Ontario, was raised 1 out of every 20 times you approach it, then the probability is one-twentieth the following time, and so on.
- In a recent poll, 18% of adults said that a Skor bar was their favourite chocolate bar. We select a sample of 15 adults and ask each for his or her favourite chocolate bar. The likelihood a Skor bar is the answer for each adult is 0.18.

The final requirement of a binomial probability distribution is that each trial is *independent* of any other trial. Independent means that there is no pattern to the trials. The outcome of a particular trial does not affect the outcome of any other trial. Two examples are:

- A young family has two children, both boys. The probability of a third birth being a boy is still 0.50. That is, the gender of the third child is independent of the other two.
- Suppose 20% of the customers served in the Marché restaurant pay in cash for their meal. If the second customer served on the afternoon shift today paid in cash, that does not affect the probability the third, the tenth, or any of the other customers will or will not pay in cash.

In summary, a binomial distribution has these characteristics:

Binomial Probability Experiment

1. An outcome on each trial of an experiment is classified into one of two mutually exclusive categories—a success or a failure.
2. The random variable counts the number of successes in a fixed number of trials.
3. The probability of success is the same for each trial.
4. The trials are independent, meaning that the outcome of one trial does not affect the outcome of any other trial.

How Is a Binomial Probability Distribution Computed?

To construct a particular binomial probability distribution, we use (1) the number of trials and (2) the probability of success on each trial. For example, if an examination consists of 20 multiple-choice questions, the number of trials is 20. If each question has five choices and only one choice is correct, the probability of success for a person with no knowledge of the subject on each trial is $1/5 = 0.20$. Thus, the probability is 0.20 that a person with no knowledge of the subject matter will guess the answer to a question correctly. So, the conditions of the binomial distribution just noted are met.

The binomial probability distribution is computed by the formula:

BINOMIAL PROBABILITY DISTRIBUTION	$P(x) = {}_nC_x p^x (1-p)^{n-x}$	[5–3]

where:

> C denotes a combination.
> n is the number of trials.
> x is the number of successes.
> p is the probability of a success on each trial.

Example	Toss a coin three times. What is the probability of getting exactly two heads?
Solution	We can use the probability rules from Chapter 4 to solve the above problem. We will start with tossing the coin three times.

Outcomes	$P(x)$
HHH	$\frac{1}{8}$
HHT	$\frac{1}{8}$
HTH	$\frac{1}{8}$
HTT	$\frac{1}{8}$
THH	$\frac{1}{8}$
THT	$\frac{1}{8}$
TTH	$\frac{1}{8}$
TTT	$\frac{1}{8}$
	1.0

We can count the occurrences of two heads as: HHT, HTH, and THH. The probability of two heads is then 3/8 = 0.375. Or, we could use formula (5–3) to solve the problem, where $X = 2$, $n = 3$, $p = 0.5$, and $(1 - p) = 0.5$. (*Note:* $p = 0.5$ is the probability of a head on a single toss of the coin.)

$$P(2) = {}_nC_x p^x (1-p)^{n-x}$$
$$P(2) = {}_3C_2 (0.5)^2 (1 - 0.5)^{3-2}$$
$$P(2) = (3)(0.25)(0.5) = 0.375$$

Example	There are five daily morning flights from Edmonton to Calgary. Suppose the probability that any flight arrives late is 0.20. What is the probability that none of the flights is late today? What is the probability that exactly one of the flights is late today?
Solution	We can use formula (5–3). The probability that a particular flight is late is 0.20, so let $p = 0.20$. There are five flights, so $n = 5$, and x refers to the number of successes. In this case a "success" is a plane that arrives late. Because there are no late arrivals, $x = 0$.

$$P(0) = {}_nC_x p^x (1-p)^{n-x}$$
$$= {}_5C_0 (0.20)^0 (1 - 0.20)^{5-0} = (1)(1)(0.3277) = 0.3277$$

The probability that exactly one of the five flights will arrive late today is 0.4096 found by:

$$P(1) = {}_nC_x p^x (1-p)^{n-x}$$
$$= {}_5C_1 (0.20)^1 (1 - 0.20)^{5-1} = (5)(0.20)(0.4096) = 0.4096$$

The entire probability distribution is shown in Table 5–2.

TABLE 5–2 Binomial Probability Distribution for the Number of Late Flights

Number of Late Flights	Probability
0	0.3277
1	0.4096
2	0.2048
3	0.0512
4	0.0064
5	0.0003
	Total 1.0000

The random variable in Table 5–2 is plotted in Chart 5–2. Note that the distribution of late arriving flights is positively skewed.

CHART 5–2 Binomial Probability Distribution for the Number of Late Flights

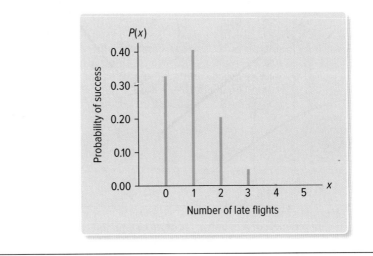

The mean (μ) and the variance (σ^2) of a binomial distribution are computed in a "shortcut" fashion by:

MEAN OF A BINOMIAL DISTRIBUTION	$\mu = np$	[5–4]

VARIANCE OF A BINOMIAL DISTRIBUTION	$\sigma^2 = np(1-p)$	[5–5]

For the example regarding the number of late flights, $p = 0.20$ and $n = 5$. Hence:

$$\mu = np = (5)(0.20) = 1.0$$
$$\sigma^2 = np(1-p) = 5(0.20)(1-0.20) = 0.80$$

The mean of 1.0 and the variance of 0.80 can be verified from formulas (5–1) and (5–2). The probability distribution from Table 5–2 and detailed calculations are shown below:

Number of Late Flights x	$P(x)$	$xP(x)$	$x - \mu$	$(x-\mu)^2$	$(x-\mu)^2 P(x)$
0	0.3277	0.0000	−1	1	0.3277
1	0.4096	0.4096	0	0	0.0000
2	0.2048	0.4096	1	1	0.2048
3	0.0512	0.1536	2	4	0.2048
4	0.0064	0.0256	3	9	0.0576
5	0.0003	0.0015	4	16	0.0048
		$\mu = 1.0000$			$\sigma^2 = 0.7997$

Binomial Probability Tables

Formula (5–3) can be used to build a binomial probability distribution for any value of n and p. However, for larger n, the calculations take more time. For convenience, the tables in Appendix B.3 show the result of using the formula for various values of n and p. Table 5–3 shows part of Appendix B.3 for $n = 6$ and various values of probability. We can use the results in this table for the following example:

TABLE 5–3 Binomial Probabilities for $n = 6$ and Selected Values of p

						$n = 6$ Probability						
x	0.05	0.10	0.20	0.30	0.40	0.50	0.60	0.70	0.80	0.90	0.95
0	0.735	0.531	0.262	0.118	0.047	0.016	0.004	0.001	0.000	0.000	0.000
1	0.232	0.354	0.393	0.303	0.187	0.094	0.037	0.010	0.002	0.000	0.000
2	0.031	0.098	0.246	0.324	0.311	0.234	0.138	0.060	0.015	0.001	0.000
3	0.002	0.015	0.082	0.185	0.276	0.313	0.276	0.185	0.082	0.015	0.002
4	0.000	0.001	0.015	0.060	0.138	0.234	0.311	0.324	0.246	0.098	0.031
5	0.000	0.000	0.002	0.010	0.037	0.094	0.187	0.303	0.393	0.354	0.232
6	0.000	0.000	0.000	0.001	0.004	0.016	0.047	0.118	0.262	0.531	0.735

Example

In a region of a country, 5% of all cell phone calls are dropped. What is the probability that out of six randomly selected calls, none was dropped? Exactly one? Exactly two? Exactly three? Exactly four? Exactly five? Exactly six out of six?

Solution

The binomial conditions are met: (a) there are only two possible outcomes (a call is either dropped or not dropped), (b) there is a fixed number of trials (6), (c) there is a constant probability of success (0.05), and (d) the trials are independent.

Refer to Table 5–3 for the probability of exactly zero dropped calls. Go down the left margin to an x of 0. Now, move horizontally to the column headed by a p of 0.05 to find the probability. It is 0.735.

The probability of exactly one defective dropped call in a sample of six calls is 0.232. The complete binomial probability distribution for $n = 6$ and $p = 0.05$ is:

Number of Dropped Calls, x	Probability of Occurrence, $P(x)$
0	0.735
1	0.232
2	0.031
3	0.002
4	0.000
5	0.000
6	0.000

Of course, there is a slight chance of getting exactly five dropped calls out of six random selections. It is 0.00000178, found by inserting the appropriate values in formula (5–3) for the binomial probability distribution.

$$P(5) = {}_6C_5(0.05)^5(0.95)^1 = (6)(0.05)^5(0.95) = 0.00000178$$

For six out of the six, the exact probability is 0.000000016. Thus, the probability is very small that five or six dropped calls will occur in a sample of six.

We can compute the mean or expected value of the distribution of the number of dropped calls.

$$\mu = np = (6)(0.05) = 0.30$$

$$\sigma^2 = np(1 - p) = 6(0.05)(0.95) = 0.285$$

Computer commands for this example can be found at the end of the chapter.

self-review 5–3	Ninety-five percent of the employees at the General Mills plant have their bimonthly cheques sent directly to their bank by electronic funds transfer. This is also called *direct deposit*. Suppose that we select a random sample of seven recipients.

(a) Does this situation fit the assumptions of the binomial distribution?
(b) What is the probability that all seven employees use direct deposit?
(c) Use formula (5–3) to determine the exact probability that four of the seven sampled employees use direct deposit.

Appendix B.3 is limited. It gives probabilities for n values from 1 to 15 and p values of 0.05, 0.10, . . . , 0.90, and 0.95. A software program can generate the probabilities for a specified number of successes, given n and p. The *following* **Excel** output shows the probability when $n = 40$ and $p = 0.09$. Note that the number of successes stops at 15 because the probabilities for 16 to 40 are very close to 0.

	A	B
1	**Success**	**Probability**
2	0	0.0230
3	1	0.0910
4	2	0.1754
5	3	0.2198
6	4	0.2011
7	5	0.1432
8	6	0.0826
9	7	0.0397
10	8	0.0162
11	9	0.0057
12	10	0.0017
13	11	0.0005
14	12	0.0001
15	13	0.0000
16	14	0.0000
17	15	0.0000

Several additional points should be made regarding the binomial probability distribution.

1. If n remains the same but p increases from 0.05 to 0.95, the shape of the distribution changes. Look at Table 5–4 and Chart 5–3. The probabilities for a p of 0.05 are positively skewed. As p approaches 0.50, the distribution becomes symmetrical. As p goes beyond 0.50 and moves toward 0.95, the probability distribution becomes negatively skewed. Table 5–4 highlights

TABLE 5–4 Probability of 0, 1, 2, . . . Successes for a p of 0.05, 0.10, 0.20, 0.50, and 0.70 and an n of 10

x	0.05	0.10	0.20	0.30	0.40	0.50	0.60	0.70	0.80	0.90	0.95
0	0.599	0.349	0.107	0.028	0.006	0.001	0.000	0.000	0.000	0.000	0.000
1	0.315	0.387	0.268	0.121	0.040	0.010	0.002	0.000	0.000	0.000	0.000
2	0.075	0.194	0.302	0.233	0.121	0.044	0.011	0.001	0.000	0.000	0.000
3	0.010	0.057	0.201	0.267	0.215	0.117	0.042	0.009	0.001	0.000	0.000
4	0.001	0.011	0.088	0.200	0.251	0.205	0.111	0.037	0.006	0.000	0.000
5	0.000	0.001	0.026	0.103	0.201	0.246	0.201	0.103	0.026	0.001	0.000
6	0.000	0.000	0.006	0.037	0.111	0.205	0.251	0.200	0.088	0.011	0.001
7	0.000	0.000	0.001	0.009	0.042	0.117	0.215	0.267	0.201	0.057	0.010
8	0.000	0.000	0.000	0.001	0.011	0.044	0.121	0.233	0.302	0.194	0.075
9	0.000	0.000	0.000	0.000	0.002	0.010	0.040	0.121	0.268	0.387	0.315
10	0.000	0.000	0.000	0.000	0.000	0.001	0.006	0.028	0.107	0.349	0.599

probabilities for $n = 10$ and p values of 0.05, 0.10, 0.20, 0.50, and 0.70. The graphs of these probability distributions are shown in Chart 5–3.

CHART 5–3 Graphing the Binomial Probability Distribution for a p of 0.05, 0.10, 0.20, 0.50, and 0.70 and an n of 10

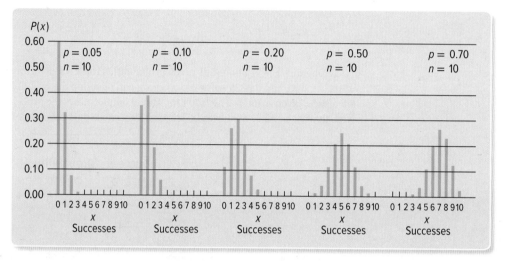

2. If p, the probability of success, remains the same but n becomes larger, the shape of the binomial distribution becomes more symmetrical. Chart 5–4 shows a situation where p remains constant at 0.10 but n increases from 7 to 40.

CHART 5–4 Chart Representing the Binomial Probability Distribution for a p of 0.10 and an n of 7, 12, 20, and 40

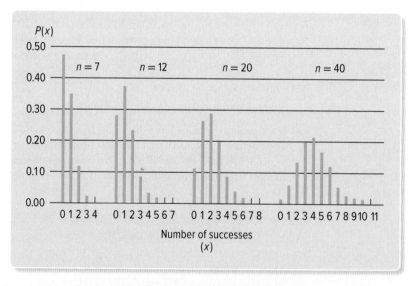

EXERCISES

11. The likelihood that a student will go to the cafeteria during a class break is 0.25. In a sample of 4 students, determine the probabilities of the following events:

   a. $x = 2$

   b. $x = 3$

   c. $x \geq 2$

   d. $x < 3$

12. The likelihood that an adult attending a weekday afternoon theatre performance is a senior is 0.40. In a sample of 5 adults, determine the probabilities of the following events:

    a. $x = 1$

    b. $x = 2$

    c. $x > 2$

    d. $x \leq 4$

13. A recent survey found that the probability of a household having a pet was 0.60. If 3 households are selected:

    a. Refer to Appendix B.3, and list the probabilities for values of x from 0 to 3.

    b. Determine the mean and standard deviation of the distribution from the general definitions given in formulas (5–1) and (5–2).

14. Assume a binomial distribution where $n = 5$ and $p = 0.30$.

    a. Refer to Appendix B.3, and list the probabilities for values of x from 0 to 5.

    b. Determine the mean and standard deviation of the distribution from the general definitions given in formulas (5–1) and (5–2).

15. An investment firm's survey found 30% of individual investors have used a discount broker. In a random sample of nine individuals, what is the probability that:

    a. Exactly two of the sampled individuals have used a discount broker?

    b. Exactly four of them have used a discount broker?

    c. None of them has used a discount broker?

16. A local courier service reports that 95% of bulk parcels within the same city are delivered within two days. Six parcels are randomly sent to different locations.

    a. What is the probability that all six arrive within two days?

    b. What is the probability that exactly five arrive within two days?

    c. Find the mean number of parcels that will arrive within two days.

    d. Compute the variance and standard deviation of the number that will arrive within two days.

17. Industry standards suggest that 10% of new vehicles require warranty service within the first year. Jones Nissan, sold 12 Nissans yesterday.

    a. What is the probability that none of these vehicles requires warranty service?

    b. What is the probability exactly one of these vehicles requires warranty service?

    c. Determine the probability that exactly two of these vehicles require warranty service.

    d. What is the probability that less than three of these vehicles require warranty service?

    e. Compute the mean and standard deviation of this probability distribution.

18. A telemarketer makes six phone calls per hour and is able to make a sale on 30% of these contacts. During the next two hours, find:

    a. The probability of making exactly four sales.

    b. The probability of making no sales.

    c. The probability of making exactly two sales.

    d. The mean number of sales in the two-hour period.

19. A recent survey of first-year college students found that 23% choose accounting as their major. Suppose that we select a sample of 15 first-year students.

    a. What is the probability that two chose accounting?

    b. What is the probability that five chose accounting?

    c. How many of the 15 would you expect to choose accounting?

20. It is reported that 16% of American households use a cell phone exclusively for their telephone service. In a sample of eight households, find the probability that:

    a. None uses a cell phone as the exclusive service.

    b. At least one uses the cell phone exclusively.

    c. At least five use the cell phone.

Cumulative Binomial Probability Distributions

We may wish to know the probability of correctly guessing the answers to six *or more* true/false questions out of 10. Or we may be interested in the probability of *selecting less than two* defectives at random from production during the previous hour. In these cases, we need cumulative frequency distributions similar to the ones developed in Chapter 2. The following example will illustrate.

Example	A recent study revealed that 76.2% of front seat occupants used seat belts. That means that both occupants of the front seat were using their seat belts. Suppose that we decide to compare that information with current usage. We select a sample of 12 vehicles.
	1. What is the probability the front seat occupants in exactly 7 of the 12 vehicles selected are wearing seat belts?
	2. What is the probability the front seat occupants in at least 7 of the 12 vehicles selected are wearing seat belts?
Solution	This situation meets the binomial requirements as follows:
	• In a particular vehicle both the front seat occupants are either wearing seat belts or they are not. There are only two possible outcomes.
	• There is a fixed number of trials—12 in this case because 12 vehicles are checked.
	• The probability of "success" (occupants wearing seat belts) is the same from one vehicle to the next: 76.2%.
	• The trials are independent. If the fourth vehicle selected in the sample has all the occupants wearing their seat belts, this does not have any effect on the results for the fifth or tenth vehicle.
	To find the likelihood the occupants of *exactly* 7 of the sampled vehicles are wearing seat belts, we use formula (5–3). In this case, $n = 12$ and $p = 0.762$.
	$$P(x = 7 \mid n = 12 \text{ and } p = 0.762)$$
	$$P(x) = {_n}C_x \, p^x (1-p)^{n-x} = {_{12}}C_7 (0.762)^7 (1 - 0.762)^{12-7} = 792(0.149171)(0.000764) = 0.0902$$
	So, we conclude that the likelihood that the occupants of exactly 7 of the 12 sampled vehicles will be wearing their seat belts is about 9%. We often use, as we did in this question, a bar "|" to mean "given that." So, in this equation, we want to know the probability that $x = 7$ "given that the number of trials is 12 and the probability of a success is 0.762."
	To find the probability that the occupants in 7 or more of the vehicles will be wearing seat belts, we use formula (5–3) from this chapter as well as the special rule of addition, formula (4–5), from Chapter 4. Because the events are mutually exclusive (i.e., a particular sample of 12 vehicles cannot have both a total of 7 and a total of 8 vehicles where the occupants are wearing seat belts), we find the probability of 7 vehicles where the occupants are wearing seat belts, the probability of 8, and so on up to the probability that occupants of all 12 sample vehicles are wearing seat belts. The probability of each of these outcomes is then totalled.
	$$P(x \geq 7 \mid n = 12 \text{ and } p = 0.762)$$ $$= P(x = 7) + P(x = 8) + P(x = 9) + P(x = 10) + P(x = 11) + P(x = 12)$$ $$= 0.0902 + 0.1805 + 0.2569 + 0.2467 + 0.1436 + 0.0383$$ $$= 0.9562$$
	So, the probability of selecting 12 cars and finding 7 or more of the occupants wearing seat belts is 0.9562.

self-review 5–4

A recent study of college students found that 60% had part-time jobs. If 4 students are randomly selected, find the probability that:

(a) Exactly 2 had part-time jobs.
(b) Less than 3 had part-time jobs.
(c) More than 2 had part-time jobs.

EXERCISES

21. In a binomial distribution, $n = 8$ and $p = 0.30$. Find the probabilities of the following events:

a. $x = 2$.

b. $x \leq 2$ (the probability that x is equal to or less than 2).

c. $x \geq 3$ (the probability that x is equal to or greater than 3).

22. A recent survey found that 60% of college students had part-time jobs. If 12 students are selected, find the following probabilities:

a. $x = 5$.

b. $x \leq 5$.

c. $x \geq 6$.

23. In a recent study, 90% of homes in Canada were found to have large-screen TVs. In a sample of nine homes, what is the probability that:

a. All nine have large-screen TVs?

b. Less than five have large-screen TVs?

c. More than five have large-screen TVs?

d. At least seven homes have large-screen TVs?

24. A manufacturer of window frames knows from long experience that 5% of the production will have some type of minor defect that will require an adjustment. What is the probability that in a sample of 20 window frames:

a. None will need adjustment?

b. At least one will need adjustment?

c. More than two will need adjustment?

25. The speed with which utility companies can resolve problems is very important. The Georgetown Telephone Company (GTC), reports that it can resolve customer problems the same day they are reported in 70% of the cases. Suppose that the 15 cases reported today are representative of all complaints.

a. How many of the problems would you expect to be resolved today? What is the standard deviation?

b. What is the probability 10 of the problems can be resolved today?

c. What is the probability 10 or 11 of the problems can be resolved today?

d. What is the probability more than 10 of the problems can be resolved today?

26. Steele Electronics Inc. sells expensive brands of stereo equipment in several shopping malls. The marketing research department of Steele reports that 30% of the customers entering the store that indicate they are browsing will, in the end, make a purchase. Let the last 20 customers who enter the store be a sample.

a. How many of these customers would you expect to make a purchase?

b. What is the probability that exactly five of these customers make a purchase?

c. What is the probability 10 or more make a purchase?

d. Does it seem likely at least one will make a purchase?

LO5-5   5.6 HYPERGEOMETRIC PROBABILITY DISTRIBUTION

For the binomial distribution to be applied, the probability of a success must stay the same for each trial. For example, the probability of guessing the correct answer to a true/false question is 0.50. This probability remains the same for each question on an examination. Likewise, suppose that 40% of the registered voters in a district are Liberals. If 27 registered voters are to be selected at random, the probability of choosing a Liberal on the first selection is 0.40. The chance of choosing a Liberal on the next selection is also 0.40, assuming that the sampling is done *with replacement*, meaning that the person selected is put back in the population before the next person is selected.

Most sampling, however, is done *without replacement*. Thus, if the population is small, the probability of a success will change for each observation. For example, if the population consists of 20 items, the probability of selecting a particular item from that population is 1/20. If the sampling is done without replacement, after the first selection there are only 19 items remaining; the probability of selecting a particular item on the second selection is only 1/19. For the third selection, the probability is 1/18, and so on. This assumes that the population is **finite**—that is, the number in the population is known and relatively small in number. Examples of a finite population are: 37 public schools in the Superior School District, 18 Jeeps currently in stock at Northend Chrysler and 40 students registered in a statistics class.

Recall that one of the criteria for the binomial distribution is that the probability of success remains the same from trial to trial. Since the probability of success does not remain the same from trial to trial when sampling is from a relatively small population without replacement, the binomial distribution should not be used. Instead, the **hypergeometric distribution** should be applied. Therefore, (1) if a sample is selected from a finite population without replacement and (2) if the size of the sample n is more than 5% of the population N, then the hypergeometric distribution is used to determine the probability of a specified number of successes or failures. It is especially appropriate when the size of the population is small.

The formula for the hypergeometric distribution is:

HYPERGEOMETRIC DISTRIBUTION $$P(x) = \frac{(_sC_x)(_{N-s}C_{n-x})}{_NC_n}$$ [5–6]

---

where:

> N is the size of the population.
> S is the number of successes in the population.
> x is the number of successes in the sample. It may be 0, 1, 2, 3, ...
> n is the size of the sample or the number of trials.
> C is the symbol for a combination.

In summary, a hypergeometric probability distribution has these characteristics:

Hypergeometric Probability Experiment

1. An outcome on each trial of an experiment is classified into one of two mutually exclusive categories—a success or a failure.
2. The random variable is the number of successes in a fixed number of trials.
3. The trials are *not independent.*
4. We assume that we sample from a finite population without replacement and $n/N > 0.05$. So, the probability of a success *changes* for each trial.

The following example illustrates the details of determining a probability using the hypergeometric distribution.

Example	PlayTime Toys Inc. employs 50 people in the Assembly Department. Forty of the employees belong to a union, and 10 do not. Five employees are selected at random to form a committee to meet with management regarding shift starting times. What is the probability that four of the five selected for the committee belong to a union?
	The population in this case is the 50 Assembly Department employees. An employee can be selected for the committee only once. Hence, the sampling is without replacement. Thus, the probability of selecting a union employee, for example, changes from one trial to the next. The hypergeometric distribution is appropriate for determining the probability. In this problem:
	N is 50, the number of employees. S is 40, the number of union employees. x is 4, the number of union employees selected. n is 5, the number of employees selected.
Solution	We wish to find the probability 4 of the 5 committee members belong to a union. Inserting these values into formula (5–6):

$$P(4) = \frac{(_{40}C_4)(_{50-40}C_{5-4})}{_{50}C_5} = \frac{\left(\frac{40!}{4!36!}\right)\left(\frac{10!}{1!9!}\right)}{\frac{50!}{5!45!}} = \frac{(91\,390)(10)}{2\,118\,760} = 0.431$$

Thus, the probability of selecting 5 assembly workers at random from the 50 workers and finding 4 of the 5 are union members is 0.431.

Table 5–5 shows the hypergeometric probabilities of finding 0, 1, 2, 3, 4, and 5 union members on the committee.

TABLE 5–5 Hypergeometric Probabilities ($n = 5, N = 50$, and $S = 40$) for the Number of Union Members on the Committee

Union Members	Probability
0	0.000
1	0.004
2	0.044
3	0.210
4	0.431
5	0.311
	1.000

To help you compare the two probability distributions, Table 5–6 shows the hypergeometric and binomial probabilities for the PlayTime Toys Inc. example. Because 40 of the 50 Assembly Department employees belong to the union, we let $p = 0.80$ for the binomial distribution. The binomial probabilities for Table 5–6 come from the binomial table in Appendix B.3, with $n = 5$ and $p = 0.80$.

TABLE 5–6 Hypergeometric and Binomial Probabilities for PlayTime Toys Inc. Assembly Department

Number of Union Members on Committee	Hypergeometric Probability, $P(x)$	Binomial Probability ($n = 5$ and $p = 0.80$)
0	0.000	0.000
1	0.004	0.006
2	0.044	0.051
3	0.210	0.205
4	0.431	0.410
5	0.311	0.328
	1.000	1.000

When the binomial requirement of a constant probability of success cannot be met, the hypergeometric distribution should be used. However, as Table 5–6 shows, under many conditions the results of the binomial distribution approximate those of the hypergeometric. This leads to a rule of thumb:

- If the selected items are not returned to the population, the binomial distribution can be used to closely approximate the hypergeometric distribution when $n < 0.05N$. In words, the binomial will suffice if the sample is less than 5% of the population.

excel

Computer commands to find the hypergeometric distribution can be found at the end of the chapter.

self-review 5–5

Horwege Discount Brokers plans to hire five new financial analysts this year. There is a pool of 12 approved applicants, and George Horwege, the owner, decides to randomly select those who will be hired. There are eight men and four women among the approved applicants. What is the probability that three of the five hired are men?

EXERCISES

27. A CD contains 10 songs: 6 are classical and 4 are rock. In a sample of three songs, what is the probability that exactly two are classical?

28. A population consists of 15 items, 10 of which are acceptable. In a sample of four items, what is the probability that exactly three are acceptable? Assume the samples are drawn without replacement.

29. Kolzak Appliance Outlet just received a shipment of 10 TV sets. Shortly after they were received, the manufacturer called to report that he had inadvertently shipped three defective sets. Ms. Kolzak, the owner of the outlet, decided to test two of the 10 sets she received. What is the probability that neither of the two sets tested is defective?

30. The computer systems department has eight faculty members, six of whom are tenured. Dr. Vonder, the chairman, wants to establish a committee of three department faculty members to review the curriculum. If she selects the committee at random:

   a. What is the probability all members of the committee are tenured?

   b. What is the probability that at least one member is not tenured? (*Hint:* for this question, use the complement rule.)

31. Keith's Florists has 15 delivery trucks used mainly to deliver flowers and flower arrangements. Of these 15 trucks, six have brake problems. A sample of five trucks is randomly selected. What is the probability that two of those tested have defective brakes?

32. Professor Jon Hammer has a pool of 15 multiple-choice questions regarding probability distributions. Four of these questions involve the hypergeometric distribution. What is the probability at least one of these hypergeometric questions will appear on the five-question quiz on Monday?

LO5-6 5.7 POISSON PROBABILITY DISTRIBUTION

The **Poisson probability distribution** describes the number of times some event occurs during a specified interval. The interval may be time, distance, area, or volume.

The distribution is based on two assumptions. The first assumption is that the probability is proportional to the length of the interval. The second assumption is that the intervals are independent. To put it another way, the longer the interval, the larger the probability, and the number of occurrences in one interval does not affect the other intervals. This distribution is also a limiting form of the binomial distribution when the probability of a success is very small and n is large. It is often referred to as the "law of improbable events," meaning that the probability, p, of a particular event happening is quite small. The Poisson distribution is a discrete probability distribution because it is formed by counting.

In summary, a Poisson probability distribution has these characteristics:

Poisson Probability Experiment

1. The random variable is the number of times some event occurs during a defined interval.
2. The probability of the event is proportional to the size of the interval.
3. The intervals do not overlap and are independent.

This probability distribution has many applications. It is used as a model to describe the distribution of errors in data entry, the number of scratches and other imperfections in newly painted car panels, the number of defective parts in outgoing shipments, the number of customers waiting to be served at a restaurant or waiting to get into an attraction at the Canadian National Exhibition (CNE), and the number of accidents on the Trans-Canada Highway during a three-month period.

The Poisson distribution can be described mathematically by the formula:

| **POISSON DISTRIBUTION** | $$P(x) = \frac{\mu^x e^{-\mu}}{x!}$$ | [5–7] |

where:

   μ (mu) is the mean number of occurrences (successes) in a particular interval.
   e is the constant 2.71828 (base of the Napierian logarithmic system).
   x is the number of occurrences (successes).
   $P(x)$ is the probability for a specified value of x.

The mean number of successes, $\bar{\mu}$, can be determined by np, where n is the total number of trials and p the probability of success.

| **MEAN OF A POISSON DISTRIBUTION** | $\mu = np$ | [5–8] |

The variance of the Poisson distribution is equal to its mean. If, for example, the probability that a cheque cashed by a bank will bounce is 0.0003, and 10 000 cheques are cashed, the mean and the variance for the number of bad cheques is 3.0, found by the formula $\mu = np = 10\ 000\ (0.0003) = 3.0$.

Recall that for a binomial distribution there is a fixed number of trials. For example, for a four-question, multiple-choice test there can only be 0, 1, 2, 3, or 4 successes (correct answers). The random variable, x, for a Poisson distribution, however, can assume an *infinite number of values*—that is, 0, 1, 2, 3, 4, 5, ... However, *the probabilities become very small after the first few occurrences* (successes).

To illustrate the Poisson probability computation, assume that baggage is rarely lost by Northwest Airlines. Most flights do not experience any mishandled bags; some have one bag lost; a few have two bags lost; rarely, a flight may have three bags lost; and so on. Suppose a random sample of 1000 flights shows a total of 300 bags were lost. Thus, the arithmetic mean number of lost bags per flight is 0.3, found by 300/1000. If the number of lost bags per flight follows a Poisson distribution with ī = 0.3, we can compute the various probabilities by the formula (5–7):

$$P(x) = \frac{\mu^x e^{-\mu}}{x!}$$

For example, the probability of not losing any bags is:

$$P(0) = \frac{(0.3)^0 (e^{-0.3})}{0!} = 0.7408$$

In other words, 74% of the flights will have no lost baggage. The probability of exactly one lost bag is:

$$P(1) = \frac{(0.3)^1 (e^{-0.3})}{1!} = 0.2222$$

Thus, we would expect to find exactly one lost bag on 22% of the flights.

Poisson probabilities can also be found in the table in Appendix B.4.

Example	Recall from the previous illustration that the number of lost bags follows a Poisson distribution with a mean of 0.3. Use Appendix B.4 to find the probability that no bags will be lost on a particular flight. What is the probability exactly one bag will be lost on a particular flight? When should the supervisor become suspicious that a flight is having too many lost bags?
Solution	Part of Appendix B.4 is repeated as Table 5–7. To find the probability of no lost bags, locate the column headed "0.3" and read down that column to the row labelled "0." The probability is 0.7408. That is the probability of no lost bags. The probability of one lost bag is 0.2222, which is in the next row of the table, in the same column. The probability of two lost bags is 0.0333, in the row below; for three lost bags it is 0.0033; and for four lost bags it is 0.0003. Thus, a supervisor should not be surprised to find one lost bag but should expect to see more than one lost bag infrequently.

TABLE 5–7 Poisson Table for Various Values of μ (from Appendix B.4)

					μ				
x	0.1	0.2	0.3	0.4	0.5	0.6	0.7	0.8	0.9
0	0.9048	0.8187	0.7408	0.6703	0.6065	0.5488	0.4966	0.4493	0.4066
1	0.0905	0.1637	0.2222	0.2681	0.3033	0.3293	0.3476	0.3595	0.3659
2	0.0045	0.0164	0.0333	0.0536	0.0758	0.0988	0.1217	0.1438	0.1647
3	0.0002	0.0011	0.0033	0.0072	0.0126	0.0198	0.0284	0.0383	0.0494
4	0.0000	0.0001	0.0003	0.0007	0.0016	0.0030	0.0050	0.0077	0.0111
5	0.0000	0.0000	0.0000	0.0001	0.0002	0.0004	0.0007	0.0012	0.0020
6	0.0000	0.0000	0.0000	0.0000	0.0000	0.0000	0.0001	0.0002	0.0003
7	0.0000	0.0000	0.0000	0.0000	0.0000	0.0000	0.0000	0.0000	0.0000

excel These probabilities can also be found using **Excel**. Computer commands to find the probabilities for the Poisson distribution can be found at the end of the chapter.

Earlier in this section, we mentioned that the Poisson probability distribution is a limiting form of the binomial. That is, we could estimate a binomial probability using the Poisson. The Poisson probability distribution is characterized by the number of times an event happens during some interval or continuum. Examples include:

- The number of misspelled words per page in a newspaper.
- The number of calls per hour received by the Dyson Vacuum Cleaner Company.
- The number of vehicles sold per day at Team Chrysler.
- The number of goals scored in a National Hockey League (NHL) game.

In each of these examples, there is some type of continuum—misspelled words per page, calls per hour, vehicles per day, or goals per game.

In the previous example, we investigated the number of bags lost per flight, so the continuum was a "flight." We knew the mean number of bags of luggage lost per flight, but we did not know the number of passengers or the probability of a bag being lost. We suspected the number of passengers was fairly large and the probability of a passenger losing his or her bag of luggage was small. In the following example, we use the Poisson distribution to estimate a binomial probability when n, the number of trials, is large, and p, the probability of a success, is small:

Example	Coastal Insurance Company underwrites insurance for beachfront properties along the Eastern Coast Line. It uses the estimate that the probability of a named Category III hurricane (sustained winds of 178 to 208 km per hour) striking a particular region of the coast in any one year is 0.05. If a homeowner takes a 30-year mortgage on a recently purchased property in the coastal area, what is the likelihood that the owner will experience at least one hurricane during the mortgage period?
Solution	To use the Poisson probability distribution, we begin by determining the mean or expected number of storms meeting the criterion hitting the coastal area during the 30-year period. That is:

$$\mu = np = 30(0.05) = 1.5$$

where:

- n is the number of years, 30 in this case.
- p is the probability a hurricane meeting the strength criteria comes ashore.
- μ is the mean or expected number of storms in a 30-year period.

To find the probability of at least one storm hitting the coastal area, we first find the probability of no storms hitting the coast and subtract that value from 1.

$$P(x \geq 1) = 1 - P(x = 0) = 1 - \frac{\mu^0 e^{-1.5}}{0!} = 1 - 0.2231 = 0.7769$$

We conclude that the likelihood a hurricane meeting the strength criteria will strike the beachfront property in the coastal area during the 30-year period when the mortgage is in effect is 0.7769. To put it another way, the probability the coastal area will be hit by a Category III or higher hurricane during the 30-year period is a little more than 75%.

We should emphasize that the continuum, as previously described, still exists. That is, there are expected to be 1.5 storms hitting the coast per 30-year period. The continuum is the 30-year period.

In the preceding case, we are actually using the Poisson distribution as an estimate of the binomial. Note that we have met the binomial conditions outlined previously.

- There are only two possible outcomes: a hurricane hits the coastal area, or it does not.
- There is a fixed number of trials, in this case 30 years.

- There is a constant probability of success; that is, the probability of a hurricane hitting the area is 0.05 each year.
- The years are independent. That means if a named storm strikes in the fifth year, it has no effect on any other year.

To find the probability of at least one storm striking the area in a 30-year period using the binomial distribution:

$$P(x \geq 1) = 1 - P(x = 0) = 1 - {}_{30}C_0(0.05)^0(0.95)^{30} = 1 - (1)(1)(0.2146) = 0.7854$$

The probability of at least one hurricane hitting the coastal area during the 30-year period using the binomial distribution is 0.7854.

Which answer is correct? Why should we look at the problem both ways? The binomial is the more "technically correct" solution. The Poisson can be thought of as an approximation for the binomial, when n, the number of trials, is large, and p, the probability of a success, is small. We look at the problem using both distributions to emphasize the convergence of the two discrete distributions. In some instances, using the Poisson may be the quicker solution, and, as you can see, there is little practical difference in the answers. In fact, as n gets larger and p smaller, the difference between the two distributions gets smaller.

The Poisson probability distribution is always positively skewed, and the random variable has no specific upper limit. The Poisson distribution for the lost bags illustration, where $\bar{\imath} = 0.3$, is highly skewed. As $\bar{\imath}$ becomes larger, the Poisson distribution becomes more symmetric. For example, Chart 5–5 shows the distributions of the number of transmission services, muffler replacements, and oil changes per day at Avellino's Auto Shop. They follow Poisson distributions with means of 0.7, 2.0, and 6.0, respectively. Observe that the distributions are more symmetrical as μ increases.

CHART 5–5 Poisson Probability Distributions for Means of 0.7, 2.0, and 6.0

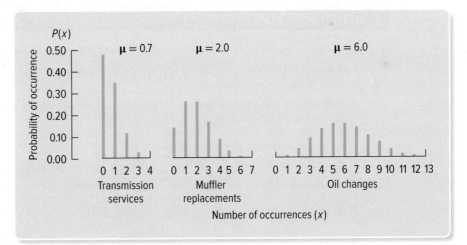

In summary, the Poisson distribution is actually a family of discrete distributions. **All that is needed to construct a Poisson probability distribution is the mean number of defects, errors, and so on—designated as μ.**

self-review 5–6

From actuary tables, an insurance company determined the likelihood that a man aged 25 will die within the next year is 0.0002. If the company sells 4000 policies to 25-year-old men this year, what is the probability it will pay on exactly one policy?

EXERCISES

33. In a Poisson distribution, $\mu = 0.4$.
  a. What is the probability that $x = 0$?
  b. What is the probability that $x > 0$?

34. Professor Hunking finds an average of 4 grammatical errors (x) per case study submitted by his Business Policy class. The distribution of errors approximates a Poisson distribution.
  a. What is the probability that $x = 2$?
  b. What is the probability that $x \leq 2$?
  c. What is the probability that $x > 2$?

35. Ms. Bergen is a loan officer at a trust company. On the basis of her years of experience, she estimates that the probability is 0.025 that an applicant will not be able to repay his or her installment loan. Last month she made 40 loans.
  a. What is the probability that three loans will be defaulted?
  b. What is the probability that at least three loans will be defaulted?

36. Automobiles frequently arrive at the Bronte exit of the Queen Elizabeth Way at the rate of two per minute. The distribution of arrivals approximates a Poisson distribution.
  a. What is the probability that no automobiles arrive in a particular minute?
  b. What is the probability that at least one automobile arrives during a particular minute?

37. It is estimated that 0.5% of the callers to the billing department of a local telephone company will receive a busy signal. What is the probability that of today's 1200 callers at least five received a busy signal?

38. Textbook authors and publishers work very hard to minimize the number of errors in a text. However, some errors are unavoidable. Ms. Kimberley Veevers, statistics editor, reports that the mean number of errors per chapter is 0.8. What is the probability that there are less than two errors in a particular chapter?

Chapter Summary

I. A random variable is a numerical value determined by the outcome of an experiment.

II. A probability distribution is a listing of all possible outcomes of an experiment and the probability associated with each outcome.

  A. A discrete probability distribution can assume only certain values. The main features are as follows:
    1. The sum of the probabilities is 1.00.
    2. The probability of a particular outcome is between 0.00 and 1.00.
    3. The outcomes are mutually exclusive.

  B. A continuous distribution can assume an infinite number of values within a specific range.

III. The mean and variance of a discrete probability distribution are computed as follows:

  A. The mean is equal to:

$$\mu = \sum[xP(x)] \tag{5–1}$$

  B. The variance is equal to:

$$\sigma^2 = \sum[(x - \mu)^2 P(x)] \tag{5–2}$$

IV. The binomial distribution has the following characteristics:

  A. Each outcome is classified into one of two mutually exclusive categories.

  B. The distribution results from a count of the number of successes in a fixed number of trails.

  C. The probability of a success remains the same from trial to trial.

  D. Each trial is independent.

  E. A binomial probability is determined as follows:

$$P(x) = {}_nC_x p^x (1 - p)^{n-x} \tag{5–3}$$

F. The mean is computed as:

$$\mu = np \qquad\qquad [5\text{–}4]$$

G. The variance is:

$$\sigma^2 = np(1 - \mathrm{p}) \qquad\qquad [5\text{–}5]$$

V. The hypergeometric distribution has the following characteristics:

   A. There are only two possible outcomes.

   B. The probability of a success is not the same on each trial.

   C. The distribution results from a count of the number of successes in a fixed number of trials.

   D. It is used when sampling without replacement from a finite population.

   E. A hypergeometric probability is computed from the following equation:

$$P(x) = \frac{(_SC_x)(_{N-S}C_{n-x})}{(_NC_n)} \qquad\qquad [5\text{–}6]$$

VI. The Poisson distribution has the following characteristics:

   A. It describes the number of times some event occurs during a specified interval.

   B. The probability of a "success" is proportional to the length of the interval.

   C. Non-overlapping intervals are independent.

   D. It is a limiting form of the binomial distribution when n is large and p is small.

   E. A Poisson probability is determined from the following equation:

$$P(x) = \frac{\mu^x e^{-\mu}}{x!} \qquad\qquad [5\text{–}7]$$

   F. The mean and the variance are:

$$\mu = np$$
$$\sigma^2 = np$$

Chapter Exercises

39. What is the difference between a random variable and a probability distribution?

40. For each of the following, indicate whether the random variable is discrete or continuous.
   a. The length of time to get a haircut.
   b. The number of cars a jogger passes each morning while running.
   c. The number of hits for a team in a high school girls' softball game.
   d. The number of patients treated at the South Strand Medical Centre between 6 p.m. and 10 p.m. each night.
   e. The distance your car travelled on the last fill-up.
   f. The number of customers who used the drive-through facility at the Oak Street Wendy's.
   g. The distance between Toronto, Ontario, and all Ontario cities with a population of at least 50 000.

41. What are the requirements for the binomial distribution?

42. Under what conditions will the binomial and the Poisson distributions give roughly the same results?

43. Samson Apartments has a large number of units available to rent each month. A concern of management is the number of vacant apartments each month. A recent study revealed the percentage of the time that a given number of apartments are vacant. Compute the mean and the standard deviation of the number of vacant apartments.

Number of Vacant Units	Probability
0	0.10
1	0.20
2	0.30
3	0.40

44. An investment will be worth $1000, $2000, or $5000 at the end of the year. The probabilities of these values are 0.25, 0.60, and 0.15, respectively. Determine the mean and the variance of the worth of the investment.

45. The vice-president of human resources at Lowes Inc. is studying the number of on-the-job accidents over a period of one month. He developed the following probability distribution. Compute the mean, variance, and standard deviation of the number of accidents in a month.

Number of Accidents	Probability
0	0.40
1	0.20
2	0.20
3	0.10
4	0.10

46. In the past, schools in northern Manitoba have closed an average of three days each year due to weather conditions. What is the probability that schools in that area will close for four days next year?

47. Croissant Bakery Inc. offers specially decorated cakes for birthdays, weddings, and other occasions. It also has regular cakes available in its display case. The following table gives the total number of cakes sold per day and the corresponding probability. Compute the mean, variance, and standard deviation of the number of cakes sold per day.

Number of Cakes Sold in a Day	Probability
12	0.25
13	0.40
14	0.25
15	0.10

48. In a recent survey, 35% indicated chocolate was their favourite flavour of ice cream. Suppose that we select a sample of 10 people and ask them to name their favourite flavour of ice cream.
  a. How many of those in the sample would you expect to name chocolate?
  b. What is the probability exactly four of those in the sample name chocolate?
  c. What is the probability four or more name chocolate?

49. Which of these variables are discrete and which are continuous random variables?
  a. The number of new sales associates hired for the Christmas season.
  b. The time between buses from the airport to downtown.
  c. The number of students registered in second year accounting.
  d. The number of cups of coffee consumed by the average student in a year.
  e. The median age of college-age students.

50. Three tables listed below show random variables and their probabilities. However, only one of these is actually a probability distribution.

x	$P(x)$		x	$P(x)$		x	$P(x)$
25	0.1		25	−0.6		25	0.5
50	0.7		50	0.2		50	0.3
75	0.2		75	0.1		75	0.1
100	0.4		100	0.1		100	0.1

  a. Which of the above tables is a probability distribution?
  b. Using the correct probability distribution, find the probability that x is:
    1. Exactly 75.
    2. No more than 50.
    3. More than 25.
  c. Compute the mean, variance, and standard deviation of this distribution.

51. An auditor for an insurance company in Alberta reports 40% of the policyholders 55 years or older submit a claim during the year. Fifteen policyholders are randomly selected for company records.
  a. How many of the policyholders would you expect to have filed a claim within the last year?
  b. What is the probability that 10 of the selected policyholders submitted a claim last year?
  c. What is the probability that 10 or more of the selected policyholders submitted a claim last year?
  d. What is the probability that less than six of the selected policyholders submitted a claim last year?

52. Take one card from a deck of 52. Do not put the card back in the deck. Take a second, third, and fourth card from the deck without replacement. What is the probability that two of the four cards are spades?

53. A study reported that 7.5% of the workforce has a drug problem. A drug enforcement official wished to investigate this statement. In his sample of 20 employed workers:
  a. How many would you expect to have a drug problem? What is the standard deviation?
  b. What is the likelihood that *none* of the workers sampled has a drug problem?
  c. What is the likelihood *at least one* has a drug problem?

54. The Bank of Hudson Bay reports that 7% of its credit card holders will default at some time in their life. The Moose Factory branch just mailed out 12 new cards today.
  a. How many of these new cardholders would you expect to default? What is the standard deviation?
  b. What is the likelihood that *none* of the cardholders will default?
  c. What is the likelihood *at least one* will default?

55. Recent statistics suggest that 15% of those who visit a retail site on the World Wide Web make a purchase. A retailer wished to verify this claim. To do so, she selected a sample of 16 "hits" to her site and found that four had actually made a purchase.
  a. What is the likelihood of exactly four purchases?
  b. How many purchases should she expect?
  c. What is the likelihood that four or more "hits" result in a purchase?

56. Dr. Richmond, a psychologist, is studying the daytime television viewing habits of college students. She believes 45% of college students watch soap operas during the afternoon. To further investigate, she randomly selects a sample of 10.
  a. Develop a probability distribution for the number of students in the sample who watch soap operas.
  b. Find the mean and the standard deviation of this distribution.
  c. What is the probability of finding exactly four who watch soap operas?
  d. What is the probability less than half of the students selected watch soap operas?

57. A recent study conducted by Penn, Shone, and Borland, on behalf of LastMinute.com, revealed that 52% of business travellers plan their trips less than two weeks before departure. The study is to be replicated in the London area with a sample of 12 frequent business travellers.
  a. Develop a probability distribution for the number of travellers who plan their trips within two weeks of departure.
  b. Find the mean and standard deviation of this distribution.
  c. What is the probability exactly five of the 12 selected business travellers plan their trips within two weeks of departure?
  d. What is the probability five or fewer of the 12 selected business travellers plan their trips within two weeks of departure?

58. A manufacturer of computer chips claims that the probability of a defective chip is 0.002. The manufacturer sells chips in batches of 1000 to major computer companies.
  a. How many defective chips would you expect in a batch?
  b. What is the probability that none of the chips are defective in a batch?
  c. What is the probability at least one chip is defective in a batch?

59. The sales of Lexus automobiles in the Calgary area follow a Poisson distribution with a mean of three per day.
  a. What is the probability that no Lexus is sold on a particular day?
  b. What is the probability that for five consecutive days at least one Lexus is sold?

60. Suppose 1.5% of the antennas on new Nokia cell phones are defective. For a random sample of 200 antennas, find the probability that:
  a. None of the antennas is defective.
  b. Three or more of the antennas are defective.

61. A study of the checkout lines at the Safeway Supermarket revealed that between 4 p.m. and 7 p.m. on weekdays, there is an average of four customers waiting in line. What is the probability that you visit Safeway today during this period and find:
  a. No customers are waiting?
  b. Four customers are waiting?
  c. Four or fewer are waiting?
  d. Four or more are waiting?

62. An internal study at Lahey Electronics, a large software development company, revealed the mean time for an internal email message to arrive at its destination was two seconds. Further, the distribution of the arrival times followed a Poisson distribution.

 a. What is the probability a message takes exactly one second to arrive at its destination?
 b. What is the probability it takes more than four seconds to arrive at its destination?
 c. What is the probability it takes virtually no time, that is, "zero" seconds?

63. Recent crime reports indicate that 18.4 motor vehicle thefts occur every hour in Canada. Assume that the distribution of thefts per hour can be approximated by a Poisson probability distribution.
 a. Calculate the probability exactly *four* thefts occur in an hour.
 b. What is the probability there are *no* thefts in an hour?
 c. What is the probability there are *at least* 20 thefts in an hour?

64. New Process Inc., a large mail-order supplier of women's fashions, advertises same-day service on every order. Recently, the movement of orders has not gone as planned, and there were a large number of complaints. Bud Owens, director of customer service, has completely redone the method of order handling. The goal is to have fewer than five unfilled orders on hand at the end of 95% of the working days. Frequent checks of the unfilled orders at the end of the day revealed that the distribution of the unfilled orders follows a Poisson distribution with a mean of two orders.
 a. Has New Process Inc. lived up to its internal goal? Cite evidence.
 b. Draw a histogram representing the Poisson probability distribution of unfilled orders.

65. The National Aeronautics and Space Administration (NASA) has experienced two disasters. The *Challenger* exploded over the Atlantic Ocean in 1986, and the *Columbia* exploded over east Texas in 2003. There have been a total of 123 space missions. Assume that failures continue to occur at the same rate. For the next 23 missions, what is the probability of exactly two failures? What is the probability of no failures?

66. The law firm of Hagel and Hagel is located in downtown Winnipeg. There are 10 partners in the firm: 7 live in Osborne Village and 3 live in St Boniface. Wendy Hagel, the managing partner, wants to appoint a committee of 3 partners to look into relocating the firm to larger office space with more parking available for customers. If the committee is selected at random from the 10 partners, what is the probability that:
 a. One member of the committee lives in St Boniface and the others live in Osborne Village?
 b. At least one member of the committee lives in St Boniface?

67. According to the "January theory," if the stock market is up for the month of January, it will be up for the year. If it is down in January, it will be down for the year. According to an article in *The Wall Street Journal*, this theory has held for 29 out of the last 34 years. Suppose there is no truth to this theory; that is, the probability it is either up or down is 0.50. What is the probability that this could occur by chance?

68.

Number of Big-Screen TVs Sold x	Number of Days
0	4
1	15
2	5
3	3
4	2
5	1
Total	30

 a. Construct a probability distribution for x = number of big-screen TVs sold.
 b. What is the expected number of big-screen TVs sold per month? Interpret this value.
 c. The price of a big-screen TV is on average is on average $3575 per TV. If the salesperson's commission on a big screen TV is 15% of sales, what is his or her expected monthly commission on the big screen TVs?

69. A recent study revealed that 40% of women in the St. John's area who work full-time also volunteer in the community. Suppose we randomly select eight women in the St. John's area.
 a. What is the probability that exactly three of the women volunteer in the community?
 b. What is the probability that at least one of the women volunteers in the community?

70. Simone has a quiz in class today. The quiz will consist of 10 multiple-choice questions, each with four possible answers. Simone has not had time to review the material or to do the practice questions and figures that she will have to guess the correct answers. What is the probability that Simone will:
 a. Guess all of the answers correctly?
 b. Guess none of the answers correctly?
 c. Guess the first five questions correctly and the last five questions incorrectly?
 d. Pass the quiz with a grade of 50% or more?

71. It is asserted that 80% of the cars approaching an exit point on the 407 ETR (Express Toll Route) are equipped with an ETR transponder. Find the probability that in a sample of six cars:

  a. All six will have the transponder.
  b. At least three will have the transponder.
  c. None will have a transponder.

72. In the game of heads or tails, if two coins are tossed, you win $0.75 if you throw two heads, win $0.50 if you throw a head and a tail, and lose $1.00 if you throw two tails. What are the expected winnings of this game?

73. Acceptance sampling is a statistical method used to monitor the quality of purchased parts and components. To ensure the quality of incoming parts, a purchaser or manufacturer normally samples 20 parts and allows one defect.
  a. What is the likelihood of accepting a lot that is 1% defective?
  b. If the quality of the incoming lot was actually 2%, what is the likelihood of accepting it?
  c. If the quality of the incoming lot was actually 5%, what is the likelihood of accepting it?

74. Unilever Inc. recently developed a new body wash with a scent of ginger. Their research indicates that 30% of men like the new scent. To further investigate, Unilever's marketing research group randomly selected 15 people and asked them whether they liked the scent. What is the probability that six or more people like the ginger scent in the body wash?

75. Recent difficult economic times have caused an increase in the foreclosure rate of home mortgages. Statistics from the Penn Bank and Trust Company show their monthly foreclosure rate is now one loan out of every 136 loans. Last month the bank approved 300 loans.
  a. How many foreclosures would you expect the bank to have last month?
  b. What is the probability of exactly two foreclosures?
  c. What is the probability of at least one foreclosure?

76. Suppose the National Hurricane Centre forecasts that hurricanes will hit the strike area with a 0.95 probability.
  a. What is the probability that 10 hurricanes reach landfall in the strike area?
  b. What is the probability at least one of 10 hurricanes reaches land outside the strike area?

77. A recent CBS News survey reported that 67% of adults felt the U.S. Treasury should continue making pennies. Suppose that we select a sample of 15 adults.
  a. How many of the 15 would we expect to indicate that the Treasury should continue making pennies? What is the standard deviation?
  b. What is the likelihood that exactly eight adults would indicate the Treasury should continue making pennies?
  c. What is the likelihood at least eight adults would indicate the Treasury should continue making pennies?

78. Tire and Auto Supply is considering a 2-for-1 stock split. Before the transaction is finalized, at least two-thirds of the 1200 company stockholders must approve the proposal. To evaluate the likelihood the proposal will be approved, the director of finance randomly selected a sample of 18 stockholders. He contacted each and found that 14 approved of the proposed split. What is the likelihood of this event, assuming two-thirds of the stockholders approve?

79. During the second round of the 1989 U.S. Open golf tournament, four golfers scored a hole-in-one on the sixth hole. The odds of a professional golfer making a hole-in-one are estimated to be 3708 to 1, so the probability is 1/3709. There were 155 golfers participating in the second round that day. Estimate the probability that four golfers would score a hole-in-one on the sixth hole.

80. The payouts for the U.S. Powerball lottery and their corresponding odds and probabilities of occurrence are shown below. The price of a ticket is $1.00. Find the mean and standard deviation of the payout. (*Hint:* be sure to include the cost of the ticket and its corresponding probability.)

Divisions	Payout	Odds	Probability
Five plus Powerball	$50 000 000	146 107 962	0.000000006844
Match 5	200 000	3 563 609	0.000000280614
Four plus Powerball	10 000	584 432	0.000001711060
Match 4	100	14 255	0.000070145903
Three plus Powerball	100	11 927	0.000083836351
Match 3	7	291	0.003424657534
Two plus Powerball	7	745	0.001340482574
One plus Powerball	4	127	0.007812500000
Zero plus Powerball	3	69	0.014285714286

Data Set Exercises

> Questions marked with ⚡ have data sets available on McGraw-Hill's online resource for *Basic Statistics*.

⚡ **81.** Refer to the Real Estate Data—Orleans online, which reports information on home listings.
   a. Create a probability distribution for the number of bedrooms. Compute the mean and standard deviation of this distribution.
   b. Create a probability distribution for the number of bathrooms. Compute the mean and standard deviation of this distribution.

⚡ **82.** Refer to the Real Estate Data—Saskatoon online, which reports information on home listings.
   a. Create a probability distribution for the number of full bathrooms. Compute the mean and standard deviation of this distribution.
   b. Create a probability distribution for the number of bedrooms. Compute the mean and the standard deviation of this distribution.

Practice Test

Part I Objective

1. A listing of the possible outcomes of an experiment and the probability associated with each outcome is called a _____ .

2. The essential difference between a discrete random variable and a discrete probability distribution is a discrete probability distribution includes the _____ .

3. In a discrete probability distribution, the sum of the possible probabilities is always equal to _____ .

4. The expected value of a probability distribution is also called the _____ .

5. How many outcomes are there in a particular binomial trial? _____ .

6. Under what conditions will the probability of a success change from trial to trial in a binomial experiment? _____ .

7. In a Poisson experiment, the mean and the variance are _____ .

8. The Poisson distribution is a limiting case of the _____ probability distribution when n is large and π is small.

9. Suppose that 5% of patients who take a certain drug suffer undesirable side effects. If we select 10 patients currently taking the drug, what is the probability that exactly two suffer undesirable side effects? _____

10. The mean number of work-related accidents per month in a manufacturing plant is 1.70. What is the probability that there will be no work-related accidents in a particular month? _____

Part II Problems

1. An auditor suggests that 15% of tax returns where the gross income is more than $1 000 000 will be subject to computer audit. For a particular year a certified general accountant (CGA) completed 16 returns where the adjusted gross income was more than $1 000 000.
   a. Which probability model does this situation follow?
   b. What is the probability exactly one of these returns is audited?
   c. What is the probability at least one of these returns is audited?

2. Under certain conditions, the Canada Revenue Agency (CRA) will compute the amount of refund that is due to a taxpayer. Suppose that the Vancouver office of the CRA completes an average of three of this type of return per hour.
   a. Which probability distribution applies to this situation?
   b. What is the probability the CRA completes exactly three of this type of return in a particular hour?
   c. What is the probability the CRA does not complete any of this type of return in an hour?
   d. What is the probability the CRA completes at least one of these returns in a particular hour?

3. A data entry clerk studied the number of errors found on expense forms. The data are summarized in the following table:

Errors Found	Percentage
1	20
2	50
3	20
4	10

a. What is the mean number of errors found?

b. What is the variance of the number of errors found?

Computer Commands

1. MegaStat steps to create the binomial probability distribution for the worm gears example are as follows:

a. Select **MegaStat**, **Probability**, and **Discrete Probability Distributions**.

b. Select the **Binomial** tab. Enter *6* for **n_number of trials** and *0.05* for **p_probability of occurrence**. To display a graph, select **display graph**. Click **OK**. See the Output sheet for the probabilities.

2. Excel steps to create the binomial probability distribution for the number of dropped calls example are as follows:

a. In a blank **Excel** worksheet, enter the word *Number of Dropped Calls* in cell *A1* and the word *Probability* in *B1*. In cells *A2* through *A8*, enter the integers *0* to *6*. Click *B2* as the active cell.

b. Select **Insert Function**. From the **Or select a category** list, select **Statistical**.

c. In the **Select a function** list, double-click **BINOM.DIST**.

d. Enter *0* for **Number_s**, *6* for **Trials**, *0.05* for **Probability_s** of a success, and *0* for **Cumulative**. Click **OK**. **Excel** will compute the probability of 0 successes in 6 trials, with a 0.05 probability of success. The result, 0.735 is stored in cell *B2*.

e. To complete the probability distribution for successes of 1 through 6, double-click the cell *B2*. The binomial function should appear. Replace the **0** to the right of the open parentheses with the cell reference *A2*. The contents of cell *B2* should now be: =BINOM.DIST(A2,6,0.05,0).

f. Copy cell *B2* to cells *B3:B8*. The probability of a success for the various values of the random variable will be in cells *B2:B8*.

3. Excel steps to create the hypergeometric probability distribution for the PlayTime Toys example are as follows:

a. On a blank **Excel** worksheet enter the word *Success* in cell *A1* and the word *Probability* in *B1*. In cells *A2:A7*, enter the integers *0* to *5*. Click *B2* as the active cell.

b. Select **Insert Function**. From the **Or select a category** list, select **Statistical**.

c. In the **Select a function list**, double-click **HYPGEOM.DIST**.

d. Enter *0* for **Sample_s**, *5* for **Number_sample**, *40* for **Population_s**, and *50* for **Number_pop** box, and *0* for

Cumulative. Click **OK**. The result, *0.0001189* is stored in cell *B2*.

e. To copy, double-click on cell *B2*. The hypergeometric function will. Replace the **0** to the right of the open parentheses with the cell reference *A2*. The contents of cell *B2* should now be: =HYPGEOM.DIST(A2,5,40,50,0).

f. Copy cell *B2* to cells *B3:B7*.

4. MegaStat steps to create the hypergeometric probability distribution for the PlayTime Toys example are as follows:

a. Select **MegaStat, Probability,** and **Discrete Probability Distributions**.

b. Select the **Hypergeometric** tab. Enter *50* for **N, population size**, *40* for **S, number of possible occurrences**, and *5* for **n, sample size**. To add a graph, select **display graph**. Click **OK**. See the *Output* sheet for the results.

5. Excel steps to create the Poisson probability distribution for the lost luggage example are as follows:

a. On a blank **Excel** worksheet enter the word *Success* in cell A1 and the word *Probability* in B1. In cells A2 through A7, enter the integers *0* to *5* (for 0 to 5 lost bags). Click *B2* as the active cell.

b. Select **Insert Function**. From the **Or select a category** list, select **Statistical**.

c. In the **Select a function list**, double-click **POISSON.DIST**.

d. Enter *0* for **X**, *0.3* for **Mean**, and *0* for **Cumulative**. Click **OK**. The result, *0.7408* is stored in cell *B2*.

e. To copy, double-click cell *B2*. The Poisson function should appear. Replace the *0* to the right of the open parentheses with the cell reference *A2*. The contents of cell *B2* should now be: =POISSON.DIST(A2,0.3,0).

f. Copy cell *B2* to cells *B3:B7*.

6. MegaStat steps to create the Poisson probability distribution for the lost luggage example are as follows:

a. Select **MegaStat, Probability,** and **Discrete Probability Distributions**.

b. Select the **Poisson** tab. Enter *0.3* for **mu, mean rate of occurrence**. Leave **maximum x value (optional)** blank. To add a graph, select **display graph**. Click **OK**. See the *Output* sheet for the probabilities.

Answers to Self-Reviews

5–1 **(a)**

Number of Spots	Probability
1	$\frac{1}{6}$
2	$\frac{1}{6}$
3	$\frac{1}{6}$
4	$\frac{1}{6}$
5	$\frac{1}{6}$
6	$\frac{1}{6}$
Total	$\frac{6}{6} = 1.00$

(b)

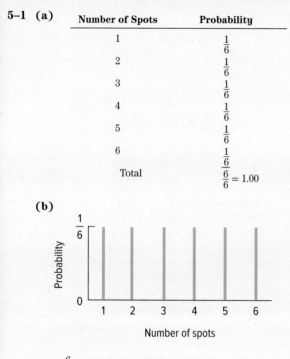

(c) $\frac{6}{6}$, or 1.

5–2 **(a)** It is discrete, because the values 0.80, 0.90, and 1.20 are clearly separated from each other, the sum of the probabilities is 1.00, and the outcomes are mutually exclusive.

(b)

x	$P(x)$	$xP(x)$
0.80	0.30	0.24
0.90	0.50	0.45
1.20	0.20	0.24
		0.93

The mean is $0.93.

(c)

x	$P(x)$	$(x-\mu)$	$(x-\mu)^2\,P(x)$
$0.80	0.30	−0.13	0.00507
0.90	0.50	−0.03	0.00045
1.20	0.20	0.27	0.01458
			0.02010

The variance is 0.02010, and the standard deviation is $0.14.

5–3 **(a)** It is reasonable because each employee either uses direct deposit or does not, the employees are independent, the probability of using direct deposit is 95% for all, and we count the number using the service out of 7.

(b) $P(7) = (0.95)^7 = 0.6983$

(c) $P(4) = {_7C_4}(0.95)^4(0.05)^3 = 0.0036$

5–4 $n = 4, p = 0.60$

(a) $P(x = 2) = 0.3456$

(b) $P(x < 3) = 0.5248$

(c) $P(x > 2) = 1 - 0.526 = 0.4752$

5–5 $P(3) = \dfrac{{_8C_3}\,{_4C_2}}{{_{12}C_5}} = \dfrac{\left(\frac{8!}{3!5!}\right)\left(\frac{4!}{2!2!}\right)}{\left(\frac{12!}{5!7!}\right)}$

$= \dfrac{(56)(6)}{792} = 0.424$

5–6 $\mu = 4000(0.0002) = 0.8$

$P(1) = \dfrac{0.8^1 e^{-0.8}}{1!} = 0.3595$

CHAPTER 6
Continuous Probability Distributions

© Ilene MacDonald/Alamy RF

CRUISE SHIPS of the Royal Viking line report that 80% of their rooms are occupied during September. For a cruise ship having 800 rooms, what is the probability that 665 or more are occupied in September? (See Exercise 66 and LO6-5)

LEARNING OBJECTIVES

When you have completed this chapter, you will be able to:

LO6-1 Describe the uniform probability distribution and use it to calculate probabilities.

LO6-2 List the characteristics of a normal probability distribution.

LO6-3 Describe the standard normal distribution and use it to calculate probabilities.

LO6-4 Determine the value of a normally distributed random variable for a given probability.

LO6-5 Approximate the binomial probability distribution using the standard normal probability distribution to calculate probabilities.

6.1 INTRODUCTION

Chapter 5 began our study of probability distributions. We considered three discrete probability distributions: the binomial, hypergeometric, and the Poisson. These distributions are based on discrete random variables, which can assume only clearly separated values. For example, the number of correct answers on a 10-question examination can only be 0, 1, 2, 3, ..., 10. There cannot be a negative number of correct answers, such as -7, nor can there be $7\frac{1}{4}$ or 15 correct answers. In this example, only certain outcomes are possible, and these outcomes are represented by clearly separated values. In addition, the result is usually found by counting the number of successes. We count the number of questions answered correctly.

We continue our study of probability distributions by examining *continuous* probability distributions. A continuous probability distribution usually results from measuring something, such as the distance from the residence to the classroom, the weight of an individual, or the amount of bonus earned by chief financial officers (CFOs). For example, suppose that we select five students per day for the duration of the semester and find the distance, in kilometres (km), that they travel to attend class. The distribution of the distance has a mean of 18 km and a standard deviation of 5.2 km per day. This distribution is continuous because the distance is measured per day and there is an infinite number of values within a particular range. So, for a continuous random variable, the probability is for a range of values. The probability for a specific value of a continuous random variable is 0.

This chapter shows how to use two continuous probability distributions: the **uniform probability distribution** and the **normal probability distribution**.

LO6-1 6.2 THE FAMILY OF UNIFORM PROBABILITY DISTRIBUTIONS

The uniform probability distribution is perhaps the simplest distribution for a continuous random variable. This distribution is rectangular in shape and is defined by minimum and maximum values. Here are some examples that follow a uniform distribution:

- The time to fly via a commercial airliner from Orlando, Florida, to Toronto, Ontario, on a non-stop flight is uniformly distributed and ranges from 150 minutes to 210 minutes. The random variable is the flight time within this interval. The variable of interest, flight time in minutes, is continuous in the interval from 150 minutes to 210 minutes.
- The local transit provides bus service to and from college campuses. The buses run every 20 minutes. Students arrive at the bus stop at random times to catch the next bus. The time spent waiting at the bus stop follows a uniform distribution over the interval between 0 and 20 minutes. The random variable is the number of minutes a student waits for the next bus, and it can assume any value between 0 and 20.

A uniform distribution is shown in Chart 6–1. The distribution's shape is rectangular and has a minimum value of a and a maximum of b. Also, note in Chart 6–1 that the height of the distribution is constant or uniform for all values between a and b.

CHART 6–1 A Continuous Uniform Distribution

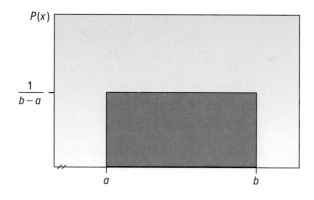

The mean of a uniform distribution is located in the middle of the interval between the minimum and maximum values. It is computed as:

MEAN OF THE UNIFORM DISTRIBUTION $\mu = \dfrac{a + b}{2}$ [6–1]

The standard deviation describes the dispersion of a distribution. In the uniform distribution, the standard deviation is also related to the interval between the maximum and minimum values.

STANDARD DEVIATION OF THE UNIFORM DISTRIBUTION $\sigma = \sqrt{\dfrac{(b - a)^2}{12}}$ [6–2]

The equation for the uniform probability distribution is:

UNIFORM DISTRIBUTION $P(x) = \dfrac{1}{b - a}$ if $a \le x \le b$ and 0 elsewhere   [6–3]

As described in Chapter 5, probability distributions are useful for making probability statements concerning the values of a random variable. For distributions describing a continuous random variable, areas within the distribution represent probabilities. In the uniform distribution, its rectangular shape allows us to apply the area formula for a rectangle. We find the area of a rectangle by multiplying its length by its height. For the uniform distribution the height of the rectangle is $P(x)$, which is $1/(b - a)$. The length or base of the distribution is $b - a$. So, if we multiply the height of the distribution by its entire range to find the area, the result is always 1.00. To put it another way, the total area within a continuous probability distribution is equal to 1.00. In general:

$$\text{Area} = (\text{height})(\text{base}) = \frac{1}{b - a}(b - a) = 1.00$$

If a uniform distribution ranges from 10 to 15, the height is 0.20, found by: $1/(15 - 10)$. The base is 5, found by: $15 - 10$. The total area is:

$$\text{Area} = (\text{height})(\text{base}) = \frac{1}{15 - 10}(15 - 10) = 1.00$$

The following example will illustrate the features of a uniform distribution and how to calculate probabilities using it.

Example	A college provides bus service to students while they are on campus. A bus arrives at the North Main Street and College Drive stop every 30 minutes between 6 a.m. and 11 p.m. during weekdays. Students arrive at the bus stop at random times. The time that a student waits is uniformly distributed from 0 to 30 minutes. 1. Draw a graph of this distribution. 2. Show that the area of this uniform distribution is 1.00. 3. How long will a student "typically" have to wait for a bus? In other words, what is the mean waiting time? What is the standard deviation of the waiting times? 4. What is the probability a student will wait more than 25 minutes? 5. What is the probability a student will wait between 10 and 20 minutes?
Solution	In this case, the random variable is the length of time a student must wait. Time is measured on a continuous scale, and the wait times range from 0 minutes up to 30 minutes. 1. The graph of the uniform distribution is shown in Chart 6–2. The horizontal line is drawn at a height of 0.0333, found by: $1/(30 - 0)$. The range of this distribution is 30 minutes.

CHART 6–2 Uniform Probability Distribution of Student Waiting Times

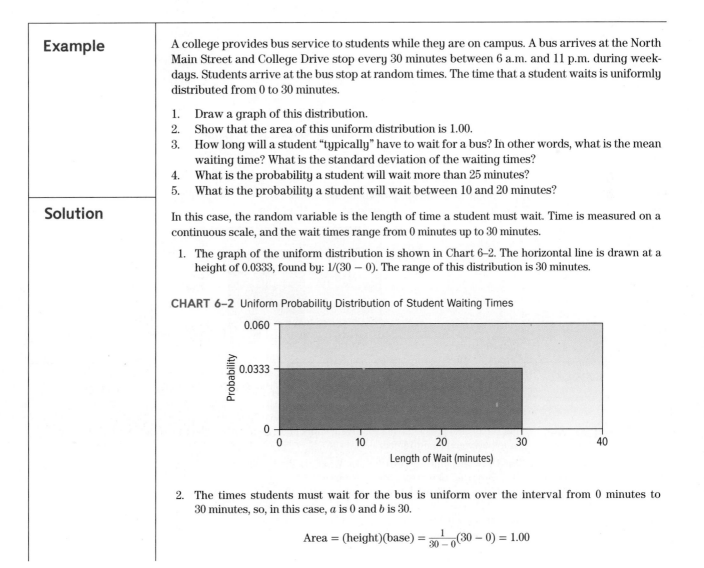

2. The times students must wait for the bus is uniform over the interval from 0 minutes to 30 minutes, so, in this case, a is 0 and b is 30.

$$\text{Area} = (\text{height})(\text{base}) = \frac{1}{30 - 0}(30 - 0) = 1.00$$

3. To find the mean, we use formula (6–1).

$$\mu = \frac{a + b}{2} = \frac{0 + 30}{2} = 15$$

The mean of the distribution is 15 minutes, so the typical wait time for bus service is 15 minutes. To find the standard deviation of the wait times, we use formula (6–2).

$$\sigma = \sqrt{\frac{(b - a)^2}{12}} = \sqrt{\frac{(30 - 0)^2}{12}} = 8.66$$

The standard deviation of the distribution is 8.66 minutes. This measures the variation in the student wait times.

4. The area within the distribution for the interval 25 to 30 represents this particular probability. From the area formula:

$$P(25 < \text{wait time} < 30) = (\text{height})(\text{base}) = \frac{1}{30 - 0}(5) = 0.1667$$

So, the probability a student waits between 25 and 30 minutes is 0.1667. This conclusion is illustrated by the graph below:

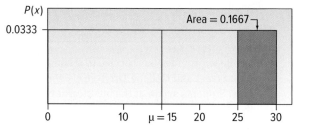

5. The area within the distribution for the interval 10 to 20 represents the probability.

$$P(10 < \text{wait time} < 20) = (\text{height})(\text{base}) = \frac{1}{30 - 0}(10) = 0.3333$$

We can illustrate this probability as follows:

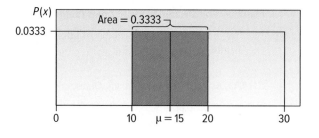

self-review 6–1

Australian sheepdogs have a relatively short life. The length of their life follows a uniform distribution between 8 and 14 years.

(a) Draw this uniform distribution. What are the height and base values?
(b) Show the total area under the curve is 1.00.
(c) Calculate the mean and the standard deviation of this distribution.
(d) What is the probability a particular dog lives between 10 and 14 years?
(e) What is the probability a dog will live less than 9 years?

EXERCISES

1. It takes Sandip between 6 and 10 minutes to drive to work each day, depending on the weather and traffic. His travel time is uniformly distributed between these times.
   a. What are the values for a and b?
   b. What is the mean of this uniform distribution?
   c. What is the standard deviation?
   d. Show that the total area is 1.00.
   e. Find the probability of a value more than 7.
   f. Find the probability of a value between 7 and 9.

2. It takes between 2 and 5 minutes to go from the 6th floor of the college to the cafeteria, depending on the wait times of the elevator and the number of people in the hallways. The time is uniformly distributed over the interval from 2 to 5 minutes.
   a. What are the values for a and b?
   b. What is the mean of this uniform distribution?
   c. What is the standard deviation?
   d. Show that the total area is 1.00.
   e. Find the probability of a value more than 2.6.
   f. Find the probability of a value between 2.9 and 3.7.

3. The closing price of Schnur Sporting Goods, Inc., common stock is uniformly distributed between $20 and $30 per share. What is the probability that the stock price will be:
   a. More than $27?
   b. Less than or equal to $24?

4. According to an insurance survey, a family of four spends between $400 and $3800 per year on all types of insurance. Suppose the money spent is uniformly distributed between these amounts.
   a. What is the mean amount spent on insurance?
   b. What is the standard deviation of the amount spent?
   c. If we select a family at random, what is the probability they spend less than $2000 per year on insurance?
   d. What is the probability a family spends more than $3000 per year?

5. The waiting time, in minutes, for service at the Tim Hortons at the front entrance of the college follows a uniform distribution between 0.5 and 8.0 minutes.
   a. What are the values for a and b?
   b. What is the mean amount of waiting time in minutes? What is the standard deviation?
   c. What is the probability of waiting less than 2 minutes?
   d. What is the probability of waiting *exactly* 3.0 minutes?
   e. What is the probability of waiting more than 5.0 minutes?

6. Customers experiencing technical difficulty with their Internet cable hookup may call an 800 number for technical support. It takes the technician between 30 seconds to 10 minutes to resolve the problem. The distribution of this support time follows the uniform distribution.
   a. What are the values for a and b in minutes?
   b. What is the mean time to resolve the problem? What is the standard deviation of the time?
   c. What fraction of the problems takes more than 5 minutes to resolve?
   d. Suppose we wish to find the middle 50% of the problem solving times. What are the endpoints of these two times?

LO6-2 6.3 THE FAMILY OF NORMAL PROBABILITY DISTRIBUTIONS

Next, we consider the normal probability distribution. The normal probability distribution has the following major characteristics:

1. It is **bell-shaped** and has a single peak in the centre of the distribution. The arithmetic mean, median, and mode are equal and located in the centre of the distribution. The total area

under the curve is 1.00. Half the area under the curve is to the right of this centre point, and the other half is to the left of it.

2. It is **symmetric** about the mean. If we cut the normal curve vertically at the central value, the two halves will be mirror images.

3. It falls off smoothly in either direction from the central value. Also, the distribution is **asymptotic,** meaning that the curve gets closer and closer to the X-axis but never actually touches it. To put it another way, the tails of the curve extend indefinitely in both directions.

4. The location of a normal distribution is determined by the mean, μ. The dispersion or spread of the distribution is determined by the standard deviation, σ.

These characteristics are shown graphically in Chart 6–3.

CHART 6–3 Characteristics of a Normal Distribution

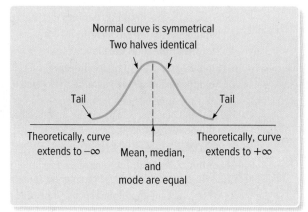

There is not just one normal probability distribution but, rather, a "family" of them. For example, in Chart 6–4, the probability distributions of length of employee service in three different plants can be compared. In the Camden plant, the mean is 20 years, and the standard deviation is 3.1 years. There is another normal probability distribution for the length of service in the Dunkirk plant, where $\mu = 20$ years and $\sigma = 3.9$ years. In the Elmira plant, $\mu = 20$ years, and $\sigma = 5.0$. Note that the means are the same but the standard deviations are different. As the standard deviation gets smaller, the distribution becomes more narrow and "peaked."

CHART 6–4 Normal Probability Distributions with Equal Means but Different Standard Deviations

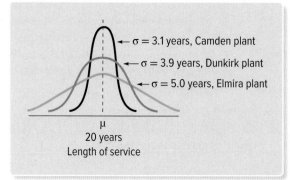

Chart 6–5 shows the distribution of box masses of three different cereals. The masses follow a normally distribution with different means but identical standard deviations.

CHART 6–5 Normal Probability Distributions Having Different Means but Equal Standard Deviations

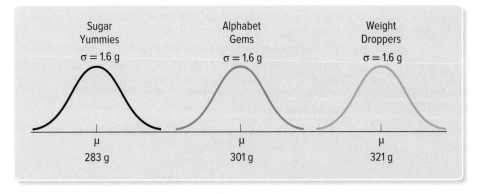

Finally, Chart 6–6 shows three normal distributions having different means and standard deviations. They show the distribution of tensile strengths, measured in kilograms per square metre (kg/m^2), for three types of cables.

CHART 6–6 Normal Probability Distributions with Different Means and Standard Deviations

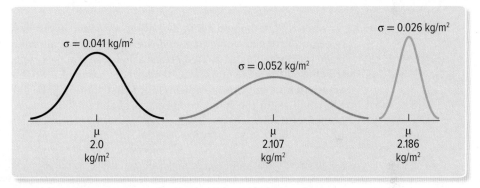

In Chapter 5, recall that discrete probability distributions show the specific likelihood a discrete value will occur. For example, the binomial distribution is used to calculate the probability that none of five flights arriving at the Calgary Airport would be late.

With a continuous probability distribution, areas below the curve define probabilities. The total area under the normal curve is 1.0. This accounts for all possible outcomes. Since a normal probability distribution is symmetric, the area under the curve to the left of the mean is 0.5, and the area under the curve to the right of the mean is 0.5. Apply this to the distribution of Sugar Yummies in Chart 6–5. It is normally distributed with a mean of 283 grams (g). Therefore, the probability of filling a box with more than 283 g is 0.5, and the probability of filling a box with less than 283 g is 0.5. We can also determine the probability that the mass of a box is between 280 and 286 g. However, to determine this probability we need to know about the standard normal probability distribution.

LO6-3   6.4 THE STANDARD NORMAL PROBABILITY DISTRIBUTION

The number of normal distributions is unlimited, each having a different mean (μ), standard deviation (σ), or both. While it is possible to provide probability tables for discrete distributions, such as the binomial and the Poisson, providing tables for the infinite number of normal distributions is impractical. Fortunately, one member of the family can be used to determine the probabilities for all normal probability distributions. It is called the **standard normal probability distribution**, and it is unique because it has a mean of 0 and a standard deviation of 1.

Any normal probability distribution can be converted into a *standard normal distribution* by subtracting the mean from each observation and dividing this difference by the standard deviation. The results are called **z-values** or **z-scores.**

So, a z-value is the distance from the mean, measured in units of the standard deviation. There is only one standard normal distribution. It has a mean of 0 and a standard deviation of 1.

In terms of a formula:

STANDARD NORMAL VALUE	$z = \dfrac{x - \mu}{\sigma}$	[6–4]

where:

    x is the value of any particular observation or measurement.
    μ is the mean of the distribution.
    σ is the standard deviation of the distribution.

As noted in the preceding definition, a z-value expresses the distance or difference between a particular value of x and the arithmetic mean in units of the standard deviation. Once the normally distributed observations are standardized, the z-values are normally distributed with a mean of 0 and a standard deviation of 1. So the z distribution has all the characteristics of any normal probability distribution. The table in Appendix B.1 lists the probabilities for the standard normal probability distribution. See Table 6-1 for a small portion of this table.

Table 6–1 Areas under the Normal Curve

Z	0.00	0.01	0.02	0.03	0.04	0.05	...
1.3	0.4032	0.4049	0.4066	0.4082	0.4099	0.4115	
1.4	0.4192	0.4207	0.4222	0.4236	0.4251	0.4265	
1.5	0.4332	0.4345	0.4357	0.4370	0.4382	0.4394	
1.6	0.4452	0.4463	0.4474	0.4484	0.4495	0.4505	
1.7	0.4554	0.4564	0.4573	0.4582	0.4591	0.4599	
1.8	0.4641	0.4649	0.4656	0.4664	0.4671	0.4678	
1.9	0.4713	0.4719	0.4726	0.4732	0.4738	0.4744	

To explain, suppose that we wish to compute the probability that boxes of Sugar Yummies have a weight between 283 g and 285.4 g. From Chart 6–5, we know that the box weight of Sugar Yummies follows the normal distribution with a mean of 283 g and a standard deviation of 1.6 g. We want to know the probability or area under the curve between the mean, 283 g, and 285.4 g. We can also express this problem using probability notation, similar to the style used in the previous chapter: $P(283 < \text{mass} < 285.4)$. To find the probability, it is necessary to convert both 283 g and 285.4 g to z-values using formula (6–4). The z-value corresponding to 283 is 0, found by: $(283 − 283)/1.6$. The z-value corresponding to 285.4 is 1.50 found by: $(285.4 − 283)/1.6$. Next, we go to the table in Appendix B.1. A portion of the table is repeated as Table 6–1. Go down the column of the table headed by the letter z to 1.5. Then move horizontally to the right and read the probability under the column headed 0.00. It is 0.4332. This means the area under the curve between 0.00 and 1.50 is 0.4332. This is the probability that a randomly selected box of Sugar Yummies will have a weight between 283 g and 285.4 g. This is illustrated in the following graph:

z-value The signed distance between a selected value, designated X, and the mean, μ, divided by the standard deviation, σ.

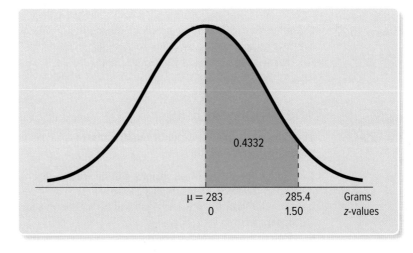

Note that we show both grams and z-values on the horizontal scale. The values of 285.4 g and a z-score of 1.50 are the same distance from $\mu = 283$ and $z = 0$, respectively.

You can use the **Excel** function **NORM.S.DIST** to find the area under the normal curve if you have a z value. Enter z = 1.50 and 1 for **z** and **1** (cumulative). The result is 0.9332, which represents the cumulative area under the normal curve to **z** = 1.50. To find the area from the mean to a z-value of 1.5, subtract 0.5000 (0.9332 − 0.5000) = 0.4332.

Applications of the Standard Normal Distribution

The standard normal distribution is very useful for determining probabilities for any normally distributed random variable. The basic procedure is to find the z value for a particular value of the random variable based on the mean and the standard deviation of its distribution. Then using the z value, we can use the standard normal distribution to find various probabilities. So, what is the area under the curve between the mean and x for the following z-values? Check your answers against those given. You will need to use Appendix B.1.

Computed z-Value	Area under Curve
2.84	0.4977
1.00	0.3413
0.49	0.1879

Now, we will compute the z-value given the population mean, μ, the population standard deviation, σ, and a selected x in the following example.

Example	The weekly incomes of shift supervisors in the glass industry are normally distributed with a mean of $1000 and a standard deviation of $100. What is the z value for the income x of a supervisor who earns $1100 per week? For a supervisor who earns $900 per week?
Solution	Using formula (6–4), the z-values for the two x values ($1100 and $900) are:

$$\text{For } x = \$1100:\qquad \text{For } x = \$900:$$
$$z = \frac{x - \mu}{\sigma}\qquad\qquad z = \frac{x - \mu}{\sigma}$$
$$= \frac{\$1100 - \$1000}{\$100}\qquad = \frac{\$900 - \$1000}{\$100}$$
$$= 1.00\qquad\qquad\quad = -1.00$$

The z of 1.00 indicates that a weekly income of $1100 is 1 standard deviation above the mean, and a z of −1.00 shows that a $900 income is 1 standard deviation below the mean. Note that both incomes ($1100 and $900) are the same distance ($100) from the mean.

self-review 6–2   Using the information in the preceding example ($\mu = \$1000$, $\sigma = \$100$), convert:

(a)   The weekly income of $1225 to a z-value.
(b)   The weekly income of $775 to a z-value.

The Empirical Rule

The Empirical Rule is introduced in in Chapter 3. To review, it states that if a random variable is normally distributed, then:

1.   About 68% of the observations will lie within plus and minus one standard deviation of the mean. This can be written as $\mu \pm 1\sigma$.
2.   About 95% of the observations will lie within plus and minus two standard deviations of the mean, written as $\mu \pm 2\sigma$.
3.   Practically all, or 99.7% of the observations, will lie within plus or minus three standard deviations of the mean, written as $\mu \pm 3\sigma$.

Now, knowing how to apply the standard normal probability distribution, we can verify the Empirical Rule. For example, one standard deviation from the mean is the same as a z value of 1.00. When we refer to the standard normal probability table, a z value of 1.00 corresponds to a probability of 0.3413. Multiply $0.3413(2) = 0.6826 = 68.26\%$, which is approximately 68% of the observations that are within plus and minus one standard deviation of the mean.

The Empirical Rule is summarized in the following graph:

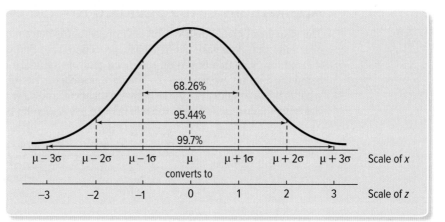

Transforming measurements to z-values changes the scale. The conversions are also shown in the graph. For example, $\mu + 1\sigma$ is converted to a z-value of $+1.00$. Likewise, $\mu - 2\sigma$ is transformed to a z-value of -2.00. Note that the centre of the z distribution is zero, indicating no deviation from the mean, μ.

Statistics in Action

An individual's skills depend on a combination of many hereditary and environmental factors, each having about the same amount of weight or influence on the skills. Thus, much like a binomial distribution with a large number of trials, many skills and attributes follow the normal distribution. For example, scores on the Scholastic Aptitude Test (SAT) are normally distributed with a mean of 1000 and a standard deviation of 140.

Example

As part of its quality control program, the Autolite Battery Company conducts tests on battery life. For a particular D cell alkaline battery, the mean life is 19 hours. The useful life of the battery follows a normal distribution with a standard deviation of 1.2 hours. Answer the following questions:

1.   About 68% of the batteries failed between what two values?
2.   About 95% of the batteries failed between what two values?
3.   Nearly all of the batteries failed between what two values?

Solution

We can use the Empirical Rule to answer these questions.

1.   About 68% of the batteries will fail between 17.8 and 20.2 hours, found by: $19.0 \pm 1(1.2)$ hours.
2.   About 95% of the batteries will fail between 16.6 and 21.4 hours, found by: $19.0 \pm 2(1.2)$ hours.
3.   Nearly all failed between 15.4 and 22.6 hours, found by: $19.0 \pm 3(1.2)$ hours.

This information is summarized on the following chart:

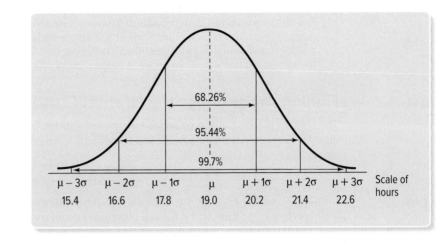

self-review 6–3

The distribution of the annual incomes of a group of middle-management employees at Compton Plastics approximates a normal distribution with a mean of $47 200 and a standard deviation of $800.

(a) About 68% of the incomes lie between what two amounts?
(b) About 95% of the incomes lie between what two amounts?
(c) Nearly all of the incomes lie between what two amounts?
(d) What are the median and the modal incomes?
(e) Is the distribution of incomes symmetrical?

EXERCISES

7. Explain what is meant by this statement: "There is not just one normal probability distribution but a 'family' of them."

8. List the major characteristics of a normal probability distribution.

9. The mean of a normal probability distribution is 500; the standard deviation is 10.
   a. About 68% of the observations lie between what two values?
   b. About 95% of the observations lie between what two values?
   c. Nearly all of the observations lie between what two values?

10. The amount spent per month by employees for parking at a municipal lot is normally distributed with a mean of $60 and a standard deviation of $5.
    a. About what percentage of the observations lie between $55 and $65?
    b. About what percentage of the observations lie between $50 and $70?
    c. About what percentage of the observations lie between $45 and $75?

11. The number of customers entering the StopOne variety store per day is normally distributed with a mean of 100 and a standard deviation of 15.
    a. About what percentage of the observations lie between 85 and 115?
    b. About what percentage of the observations lie between 70 and 130?
    c. About what percentage of the observations lie between 55 and 145?

12. The mean of a normal probability distribution is 350; the standard deviation is 75.
    a. $\mu \pm 1\sigma$ of the observations lie between what two values?
    b. $\mu \pm 2\sigma$ of the observations lie between what two values?
    c. $\mu \pm 3\sigma$ of the observations lie between what two values?

13. The Kamp family has twins, Rob and Rachel. Both Rob and Rachel graduated from college two years ago, and each is now earning $50 000 per year. Rachel works in the retail industry, where the mean salary for executives with less than five years' experience is $35 000, with a standard deviation of $8000. Rob is an engineer. The mean salary for engineers with less than five years'

experience is $60 000, with a standard deviation of $5000. Compute the z values for both Rob and Rachel, and comment on your findings.

14. A recent article in the Collingwood *Sun Times* reported that the mean labour cost to repair a heat pump is $90, with a standard deviation of $22. Dawson's Heating Repairs and Services completed repairs on two heat pumps this morning. The labour cost for the first was $75, and it was $100 for the second. Compute z-values for each, and comment on your findings.

Finding Areas under the Normal Curve

The next application of the standard normal distribution involves finding the area in a normal distribution between the mean and a selected value, which we identify as x. The following example will illustrate the details:

Example

Recall in an earlier example we reported that the mean weekly income of a shift supervisor in the glass industry followed the normal distribution with a mean of $1000 and a standard deviation of $100. That is, $\mu = \$1000$ and $\sigma = \$100$. What is the likelihood of selecting a supervisor whose weekly income is between $1000 and $1100? We write this question in probability notation as: $P(\$1000 < \text{weekly income} < \$1100)$.

Solution

We have already converted $1100 to a z-value of 1.00 using formula (6–4). To repeat:

$$z = \frac{x - \mu}{\sigma} = \frac{\$1100 - \$1000}{\$100} = 1.00$$

The probability associated with a z of 1.00 is available in Appendix B.1. A portion of Appendix B.1 follows. To locate the probability, go down the left column to 1.0, and then move horizontally to the column headed 0.00. The value is 0.3413.

z	0.00	0.01	0.02
⋮	⋮	⋮	⋮
0.7	0.2580	0.2611	0.2642
0.8	0.2881	0.2910	0.2939
0.9	0.3159	0.3186	0.3212
1.0	0.3413	0.3438	0.3461
1.1	0.3643	0.3665	0.3686

The area under the normal curve between $1000 and $1100 is 0.3413. We could also say 34.13% of the shift supervisors in the glass industry earn between $1000 and $1100 weekly, or the likelihood of selecting a supervisor and finding his or her income is between $1000 and $1100 is 0.3413.

This information is summarized in the following diagram:

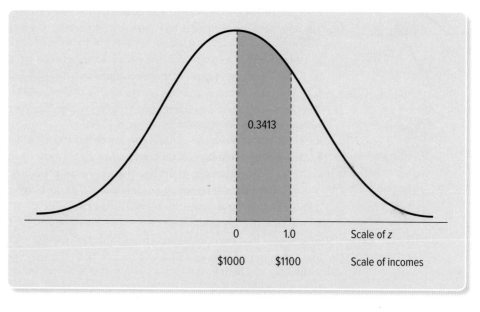

Statistics in Action

Many processes, such as filling soft drink bottles and canning fruit, are normally distributed. Manufacturers must guard against both over- and underfilling. If they put too much in the can or bottle, they are giving away their products. If they put too little in, the customer may feel cheated, and the government may question the label description. "Control charts," with limits drawn three standard deviations above and below the mean, are routinely used to monitor this type of production process.

In the example just completed, we are interested in the probability between the mean and a given value. Let us change the question. Instead of wanting to know the probability of selecting a supervisor at random who earned between $1000 and $1100, suppose that we wanted the probability of selecting a supervisor who earned less than $1100. In probability notation, we write this statement as P(weekly income < $1100). The method of solution is the same. We find the probability of selecting a supervisor who earns between $1000, the mean, and $1100. This probability is 0.3413. Next, recall that half the area, or probability, is above the mean and half is below. So, the probability of selecting a supervisor earning less than $1000 is 0.5000. Finally, we add the two probabilities, so $0.3413 + 0.5000 = 0.8413$. So, 84.13% of the supervisors in the glass industry earn less than $1100 per month.

excel

Computer commands to find the probability for the weekly incomes of shift supervisors example can be found at the end of the chapter.

Example	Refer to the information regarding the weekly income of shift supervisors in the glass industry. The distribution of weekly incomes follows the normal distribution, with a mean of $1000 and a standard deviation of $100. What is the probability of selecting a shift supervisor in the glass industry whose income is:

1. Between $790 an$1000?
2. Less than $790?

Solution

We begin by finding the z-value corresponding to a weekly income of $790. From formula (6–4):

$$z = \frac{x - \mu}{\sigma} = \frac{\$790 - \$1000}{\$100} = -2.10$$

See Appendix B.1. Move down the left margin to the row 2.1 and across that row to the column headed 0.00. The value is 0.4821. So the area under the standard normal curve corresponding to a z-value of 2.10 is 0.4821. However, because the normal distribution is symmetric, the area between 0 and a negative z is the same as that between 0 and z. The likelihood of finding a supervisor earning between $790 and $1000 is 0.4821. In probability notation we write $P(\$790 <$ weekly income $< \$1000) = 0.4821$.

z	0.00	0.01	0.02
...	...	...	...
2.0	0.4772	0.4778	0.4783
2.1	0.4821	0.4826	0.4830
2.2	0.4861	0.4864	0.4868
2.3	0.4893	0.4896	0.4898
⋮	⋮	⋮	⋮

The mean divides the normal curve into identical halves. The area under the half to the left of the mean is 0.5000, and the area to the right is also 0.5000. Because the area under the curve between $790 and $1000 is 0.4821, the area below $790 is 0.0179, found by $0.5000 - 0.4821$. In probability notation, we write P(weekly income < $790) = 0.0179.

We conclude that 48.21% of the supervisors have weekly incomes between $790 and $1000. Further, we can anticipate that 1.79% earn less than $790 per week. This information is summarized in the following diagram:

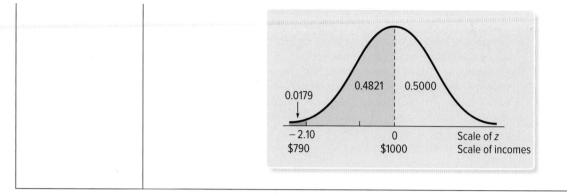

excel   Computer commands to find the probabilities for the last example are at the end of the chapter.

self-review 6–4   The employees of Cartwright Manufacturing are awarded efficiency ratings. The distribution of the ratings follows a normal distribution. The mean is 400, the standard deviation 50.

(a) What is the area under the normal curve between 400 and 482?
(b) What is the area under the normal curve for ratings greater than 482?

EXERCISES

15. Given the following z-values, find the areas under the normal curve to the left and right of the z-value.

   a. $z = 1.0$ **c.** $z = 2.83$
   b. $z = -1.25$ **d.** $z = -2.35$

16. Given the following pairs of z-values, find the area under the normal curve between each pair of z-values.

   a. $z = 1.0$ and $z = -1.0$ **c.** $z = 2.83$ and $z = 1.75$
   b. $z = -1.25$ and $z = -2.0$ **d.** $z = -2.35$ and $z = 1.5$

17. The average grade in a quiz was 20.0, with a standard deviation of 4.0. The grades follow the normal distribution.

   a. Compute the z-value for a grade of 25.0.
   b. What proportion of students achieved a grade between 20.0 and 25.0?
   c. What proportion of students achieved a grade less than 18.0?

18. The average time it takes to walk to the shopping mall from campus is normally distributed, with a mean of 12.2 minutes and a standard deviation of 2.5 minutes.

   a. Compute the z-value associated with 14.3 minutes.
   b. What proportion of the population takes between 12.2 and 14.3 minutes to walk to the mall?
   c. What proportion of the population takes less than 10.0 minutes to walk to the mall?

19. A recent study of the hourly wages of maintenance crews for major airlines showed that the mean hourly salary was $16.50, with a standard deviation of $3.50. If we select a crew member at random, what is the probability the crew member earns:

   a. Between $16.50 and $20.00 per hour?
   b. More than $20.00 per hour?
   c. Less than $15.00 per hour?

20. The mean of a normal distribution is 400 kg. The standard deviation is 10 kg.

   a. What is the area between 415 kg and the mean of 400 kg?
   b. What is the area between the mean and 395 kg?
   c. What is the probability of selecting a value at random and discovering that it has a value of less than 395 kg?

Another application of the normal distribution involves combining two areas, or probabilities. One of the areas is to the right of the mean and the other to the left. The following example will illustrate this:

Example	Continuing with the example using the weekly incomes of shift supervisors in the glass industry, weekly income follows the normal distribution, with a mean of $1000 and a standard deviation of $100. What is the area under this normal curve between $840 and $1200?
Solution	The problem can be divided into two parts. For the area between $840 and the mean of $1000:

$$z = \frac{\$840 - \$1000}{\$100} = \frac{-\$160}{\$100} = -1.60$$

For the area between the mean of $1000 and $1200:

$$z = \frac{\$1200 - \$1000}{\$100} = \frac{\$200}{\$100} = 2.00$$

The area under the curve for a z of -1.60 is 0.4452 (from Appendix B.1). The area under the curve for a z of 2.00 is 0.4772. Adding the two areas: $0.4452 + 0.4772 = 0.9224$. Thus, the probability of selecting an income between $840 and $1200 is 0.9224. In probability notation, we write $P(\$840 < \text{weekly income} < \$1200) = 0.4452 + 0.4772 = 0.9224$. To summarize, 92.24% of the supervisors have weekly incomes between $840 and $1200. This is shown in the following diagram:

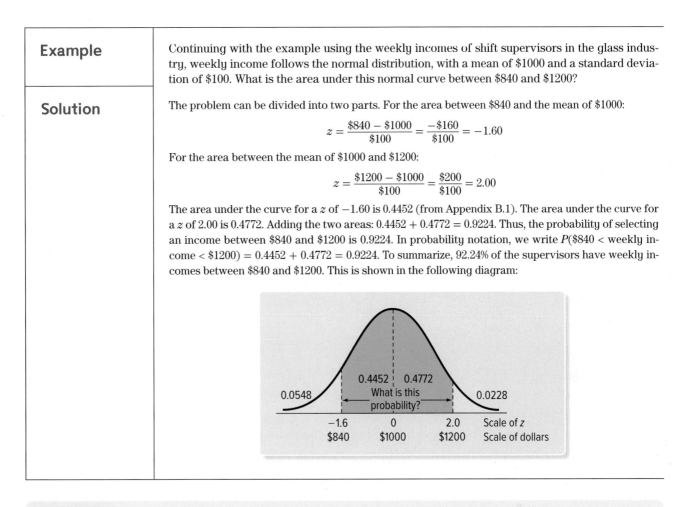

---

excel   Computer commands to find probabilities of the last example can be found at the end of the chapter.

Another application of the normal distribution involves determining the area between values on the *same* side of the mean.

Example	Returning to the weekly income distribution of shift supervisors in the glass industry ($\mu = \$1000$, $\sigma = \$100$), what is the area under the normal curve between $1150 and $1250?
Solution	The situation is again separated into two parts, and formula (6–4) is used. First, we find the z-value associated with a weekly salary of $1250:

$$z = \frac{\$1250 - \$1000}{\$100} = 2.50$$

Next, we find the z-value for a weekly salary of $1150:

$$z = \frac{\$1150 - \$1000}{\$100} = 1.50$$

From Appendix B.1, the area associated with a z-value of 2.50 is 0.4938. So, the probability of a weekly salary between $1000 and $1250 is 0.4938. Similarly, the area associated with a z-value of 1.50 is 0.4332, so the probability of a weekly salary between $1000 and $1150 is 0.4332. We find the probability of a weekly salary between $1150 and $1250 is found by subtracting the area associated with a z-value of 1.50 (0.4332) from that associated with a z of 2.50 (0.4938). Thus, the probability of a weekly salary between $1150 and $1250 is 0.0606. In probability notation, we write $P(\$1150 < \text{weekly income} < \$1250) = 0.4938 - 0.4332 = 0.0606$. This information is summarized in the following diagram:

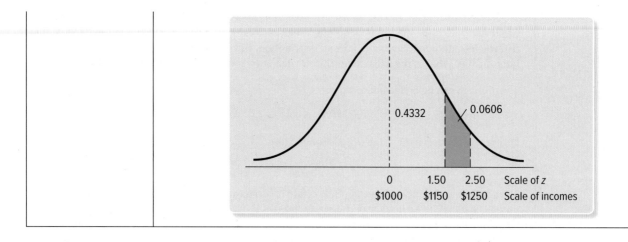

Computer commands to find the probability of the last example can be found at the end of the chapter.

excel

In review, there are four situations for finding the area under the standard normal distribution.

1.   To find the area between 0 and z (or $-z$), look up the probability directly in the table.
2.   To find the area beyond z or $(-z)$, locate the probability of z in the table, and subtract that probability from 0.5000.
3.   To find the area between two points on different sides of the mean, determine the z-values and add the corresponding probabilities.
4.   To find the area between two points on the same side of the mean, determine the z-values and subtract the smaller probability from the larger.

Example

The average list price of 90 homes in a city in Canada is \$320 000, with a standard deviation of \$99 500. What is the probability that:

1.   A house is listed for more than \$500 000?
2.   A house is listed between \$270 995 and \$442 500?
3.   A house is listed between \$186 000 and \$242 250?

Solution

1.   We begin by finding the z-value corresponding to a list price of \$320 000. From formula (6–4):

$$z = \frac{x - \mu}{\sigma} = \frac{500\,000 - 320\,000}{99\,500} = 1.81$$

See Appendix B.1. Move down the left margin to the row 1.8 and across that row to the column headed 0.01. The value is 0.4649. However, the required area is to the right of \$500 000, so we subtract 0.4649 from 0.5. Then, 0.5 − 0.4649 = 0.0351. The probability that a house is listed for more than \$500 000 is 3.51%.

2.   We will require two z-values corresponding to list prices of \$270 995 and \$442 500. Note that the values are on different sides of the mean. From formula (6–4):

$$z = \frac{x - \mu}{\sigma} = \frac{270\,995 - 320\,000}{99\,500} \quad \text{and} \quad z = \frac{x - \mu}{\sigma} = \frac{442\,500 - 320\,000}{99\,500}$$

$$= -0.49 \qquad\qquad\qquad\qquad\qquad = 1.23$$

See Appendix B.1. Move down the left margin to the row 0.4 and across that row to the column headed 0.09. The value is 0.1879. Then, move down the left margin to the row 1.2 and across that row to the column headed 0.03. The value is 0.3907. But, the required area is between $270 995 and $442 500, so we must add the two areas: 0.1879 + 0.3907 = 0.5786. The probability that a house is listed for between $270 995 and $442 500 is 57.86%.

3. Again, we will require two z-values corresponding to list prices of $186 000 and $242 250. Note that the values are on the same side of the mean. From formula (6–4):

$$z = \frac{x - \mu}{\sigma} = \frac{186\,000 - 320\,000}{99\,500} \quad \text{and} \quad z = \frac{x - \mu}{\sigma} = \frac{242\,250 - 320\,000}{99\,500}$$
$$= -1.35 \qquad\qquad\qquad\qquad\qquad = -0.78$$

See Appendix B.1. Move down the left margin to the row 1.3 and across that row to the column headed 0.05. The value is 0.4115. Then, move down the left margin to the row 0.7 and across that row to the column headed 0.08. The value is 0.2823. But, the required area is between $186 000 and $242 250, so we must subtract the two areas: 0.4115 − 0.2823 = 0.1292. The probability that a house is listed for between $186 000 and $242 250 is 12.92%.

self-review 6–5

Refer to the previous example, where the distribution of weekly incomes follows the normal distribution with a mean of $1000 and the standard deviation is $100.

(a) What percentage of the shift supervisors earn a weekly income between $750 and $1225? Draw a normal curve, and shade the desired area on your diagram.

(b) What percentage of the shift supervisors earn a weekly income between $1100 and $1225? Draw a normal curve, and shade the desired area on your diagram.

EXERCISES

21. StopOne stock follows a normal distribution with a mean price of $50 and a standard deviation of $4.
    a. Compute the probability the stock will range between $44 and $55 during the month of May?
    b. Compute the probability the stock will rise above $55?
    c. Compute the probability the stock will range between $52 and $55 after an announcement concerning new management?

22. The average life of a battery is advertised as 80 hours. A quality control check found that the mean life was normally distributed at 80 hours with a standard deviation of 14 hours.
    a. Compute the probability of a mean life between 75 and 90 hours.
    b. Compute the probability of a mean life less than 75 hours.
    c. Compute the probability of a mean life between 55 and 70 hours.

23. A cola-dispensing machine is set to dispense on average 225 millilitres (mL) of cola per cup. The standard deviation is 10 mL. The distribution amounts dispensed follows a normal distribution.
    a. What is the probability that the machine will dispense between 235 mL and 250 mL of cola?
    b. What is the probability that the machine will dispense 250 mL of cola or more?
    c. What is the probability that the machine will dispense between 205 mL and 250 mL of cola?

24. The amounts of money requested on home loan applications at Down River Federal Savings follow the normal distribution, with a mean of $70 000 and a standard deviation of $20 000. A loan application is received this morning. What is the probability that:
    a. The amount requested is $80 000 or more?
    b. The amount requested is between $65 000 and $80 000?
    c. The amount requested is $65 000 or more?

25. CNAE, an all-news AM station, finds that the distribution of the lengths of time listeners are tuned to the station follows the normal distribution. The mean of the distribution is 15.0 minutes and the standard deviation is 3.5 minutes. What is the probability that a particular listener will tune in:

    a. More than 20 minutes?

    b. For 20 minutes or less?

    c. Between 10 and 12 minutes?

26. A survey reported that the mean starting salary for college graduates after a three-year program was $33 176. Assume that the distribution of starting salaries follows the normal distribution with a standard deviation of $3500. What percentage of the graduates have starting salaries:

    a. Between $30 000 and $38 000?

    b. More than $42 000?

    c. Between $38 000 and $42 000?

LO6-4   Previous examples require finding the percentage of the observations located between two observations or the percentage of the observations above, or below, a particular observation x. A further application of the normal distribution involves finding the value of the observation x when the percentage above or below the observation is given. The example following will illustrate this type of problem.

Example	The Layton Tire and Rubber Company wishes to set a minimum distance guarantee on its new MX100 tire. Tests reveal the mean number of kilometres is 109 000 with a standard deviation of 3300 km and that the distribution of kilometres follows the normal distribution. Layton wants to set the minimum guaranteed number of kilometres so that no more than 4% of the tires will have to be replaced. What minimum guaranteed kilometres should Layton announce?
Solution	The details of this problem are shown in the following diagram, where x represents the minimum guaranteed number of kilometres:

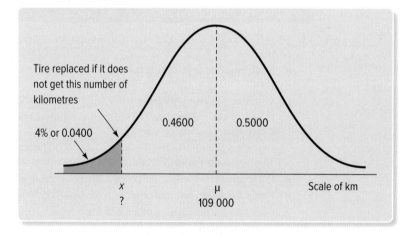

Inserting the mean and the standard deviation in formula (6–4) for z:

$$z = \frac{x - \mu}{\sigma} = \frac{x - 109\ 000}{3300}$$

Note that there are two unknowns, z and x. To find x, we first find z, and then solve for x. Note the area under the normal curve to the left of μ is 0.5000. The area between μ and x is 0.4600, found by: $0.5000 - 0.0400$. Now, refer to Appendix B.1. Search the body of the table for the area closest to 0.4600. The closest area is 0.4599. Move to the margins from this value and read the z-value of 1.75. Because the value is to the left of the mean, it is actually -1.75. These steps are illustrated in Table 6–2.

Table 6–2 Selected Areas under the Normal Curve

Z	0.03	0.04	0.05	0.06
...				
1.5	0.4370	0.4382	0.4394	0.4406
1.6	0.4484	0.4495	0.4505	0.4515
1.7	0.4582	0.4591	0.4599	0.4608
1.8	0.4664	0.4671	0.4678	0.4686

Knowing that the distance between μ and x is -1.75σ or $z = -1.75$, we can now solve for x (the minimum guaranteed kilometres):

$$z = \frac{x - 109\,000}{3300}$$

$$-1.75 = \frac{x - 109\,000}{3300}$$

$$-1.75(3300) = x - 109\,000$$

$$x = 109\,000 - 1.75(3300) = 103\,225$$

So, Layton can advertise that it will replace for free any tire that wears out before it reaches 103 225 km, and the company will know that only 4% of the tires will be replaced under this plan.

Note: the **Excel** function **NORM.S.INV** will return a z value given a probability. In the above example, entering 0.04 for the probability as: NORM.S.INV(0.04) will return a z-value of 1.7507.

Computer commands to find the number of kilometres for the last example can be found at the end of the chapter.

self-review 6–6

An analysis of the final test scores for Introduction to Business reveals the scores follow the normal distribution. The mean of the distribution is 75, and the standard deviation is 8. The professor wants to award an A to students whose scores are in the highest 10%. What is the dividing point for those students who earn an A and those earning a B?

EXERCISES

27. StopOne stock follows a normal distribution, with a mean price of $50 and a standard deviation of $4. Determine the value below which 95% of the observations will occur.

28. The average life of a battery is advertised at 80 hours. A quality control check found that the mean life was normally distributed at 80 hours, with a standard deviation of 14 hours. Determine the value above which 80% of the values will occur.

29. The amounts dispensed by a cola machine follow the normal distribution with a mean of 200 mL and a standard deviation of 0.3 mL per cup. How much cola is dispensed in the largest 1% of the cups?

30. Refer to Exercise 24, where the amount requested for home loans followed the normal distribution with a mean of $70 000 and a standard deviation of $20 000.

   a. What is the minimum amount requested on the largest 3% of loans?

   b. What is the maximum amount requested on the smallest 10% of loans?

31. Assume that the mean hourly cost to operate a commercial airplane follows the normal distribution with a mean $2100 per hour and a standard deviation of $250. What is the maximum operating cost for the lowest 3% of the airplanes?

32. The monthly sales of mufflers follow the normal distribution with a mean of 1200 and a standard deviation of 225. The manufacturer would like to establish inventory levels such that there is only a 5% chance of running out of stock. Where should the manufacturer set the inventory levels?

33. The newsstand at the corner of Bloor and Yonge finds that the number of papers sold each day follows a normal probability distribution with a mean of 900 copies and a standard deviation of 150 copies. How many copies should the owner of the newsstand order so that he only runs out of papers on 20% of the days?

34. The manufacturer of a laser printer reports the mean number of pages a cartridge will print before it needs replacing is 12 200. The distribution of pages printed per cartridge closely follows the normal probability distribution and the standard deviation is 820 pages. The manufacturer wants to provide guidelines to potential customers as to how long they can expect a cartridge to last. How many pages should the manufacturer advertise for each cartridge if it wants to be correct 99% of the time?

LO6-5   6.5 THE NORMAL APPROXIMATION TO THE BINOMIAL

Chapter 5 describes the binomial probability distribution, which is a discrete distribution. The table of binomial probabilities in Appendix B.1 goes successively from an n of 1 to an n of 15. If a problem involved taking a sample of 60, generating a binomial distribution for that large a number would be very time consuming. A more efficient approach is to apply the *normal approximation to the binomial*.

We can use the normal distribution (a continuous distribution) as a substitute for a binomial distribution (a discrete distribution) for large values of n because as n increases, a binomial distribution gets closer and closer to a normal distribution. Chart 6–7 shows the change in the shape of a binomial distribution with $p = 0.50$ from an n of 1, to an n of 3, to an n of 20. Notice how the case where $n = 20$ approximates the shape of the normal distribution. That is, compare the case where $n = 20$ to the normal curve in Chart 6–3.

CHART 6–7 Binomial Distributions for an n of 1, 3, and 20, Where $p = 0.50$

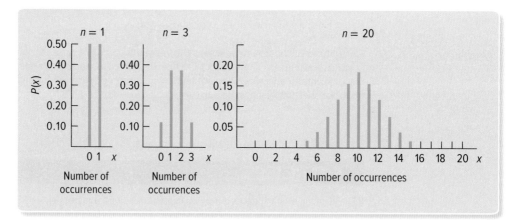

When can we use the normal approximation to the binomial? The normal probability distribution is a good approximation to the binomial probability distribution when np and $n(1 - p)$ are both at least 5. However, before we apply the normal approximation, we must make sure that our distribution of interest is in fact a binomial distribution. Recall from Chapter 5 that four criteria must be met:

1. There are only two mutually exclusive outcomes to an experiment: a "success" and a "failure."
2. The distribution results from counting the number of successes in a fixed number of trials.
3. The probability, p, remains the same from trial to trial.
4. Each trial is independent.

Continuity Correction Factor

To show the application of the normal approximation to the binomial and the need for a correction factor, suppose that the management of the Santoni Pizza Restaurant found that 70% of its new customers return for another meal. For a week in which 80 new (first-time) customers dined at Santoni's, what is the probability that 60 or more will return for another meal?

Note that the binomial conditions are met: (1) There are only two possible outcomes—a customer either returns for another meal or does not return. (2) We can count the number of successes; for example, 57 of the 80 customers return. (3) The probability of a customer returning remains at 0.70 for all 80 customers. (4) The trials are independent, that is, if the 34th person returns for a second meal, that does not affect whether the 58th person returns.

Therefore, we could use the binomial formula (5–3).

$$P(x) = {}_nC_x(p)^x(1 - p)^{n-x}$$

To find the probability 60 or more customers return for another pizza, we need to first find the probability exactly 60 customers return. That is:

$$P(x = 60) = {}_{80}C_{60}(0.70)^{60}(1 - 0.70)^{20} = 0.063$$

Next, we find the probability that exactly 61 customers return. It is:

$$P(x = 61) = {}_{80}C_{61}(0.70)^{61}(1 - 0.70)^{19} = 0.048$$

We continue this process until we have the probability all 80 customers return. Finally, we add the probabilities from 60 to 80. Solving the above problem in this manner is tedious. We can also use a computer software package such as **MegaStat** or **Excel** to find the various probabilities. Listed below are the binomial probabilities for $n = 80$, $p = 0.70$, and x, the number of customers returning, ranging from 43 to 68. The probability of any number of customers less than 43 or more than 68 returning is less than 0.001.

Number Returning	Probability	Number Returning	Probability
43	0.001	56	0.097
44	0.002	57	0.095
45	0.003	58	0.088
46	0.006	59	0.077
47	0.009	60	0.063
48	0.015	61	0.048
49	0.023	62	0.034
50	0.033	63	0.023
51	0.045	64	0.014
52	0.059	65	0.008
53	0.072	66	0.004
54	0.084	67	0.002
55	0.093	68	0.001

We can find the probability of 60 or more returning by summing $0.063 + 0.048 + \ldots + 0.001$, which is 0.197. However, a look at the plot below shows the similarity of this distribution to a normal distribution. All we need do is "smooth out" the discrete probabilities into a continuous distribution. Furthermore, working with a normal distribution will involve far fewer calculations than working with the binomial.

The trick is to let the discrete probability for 56 customers be represented by an area under the continuous curve between 55.5 and 56.5. Then, let the probability for 57 customers be represented by an area between 56.5 and 57.5 and so on. This is just the opposite of rounding off the numbers to a whole number.

Statistics in Action

Many variables are approximately, normally distributed, such as IQ (intelligence quotient) scores, life expectancies, and adult height. This implies that nearly all observations occur within 3 standard deviations of the mean. However, observations that occur beyond 3 standard deviations from the mean are extremely rare. For example, the mean adult male height is 68.2 inches (about 5 feet 8 inches), with a standard deviation of 2.74. This means that almost all males are between 60.0 inches (5 feet) and 76.4 inches (6 feet 4 inches). Shaquille O'Neal, a retired professional basketball player, is 86 inches, or 7 feet 2 inches, which is clearly beyond 3 standard deviations from the mean. The height of a standard doorway is 6 feet 8 inches and should be high enough for almost all adult males, except for a rare person like Shaquille O'Neal.

As another example, the driver's seat in most vehicles is set to comfortably fit a person who is at least 159 centimetres (cm) (62.5 inches) tall. The distribution of heights of adult women is approximately a normal distribution, with a mean of 161.5 cm and a standard deviation of 6.3 cm. Thus, about 35% of women will not fit comfortably in the driver's seat.

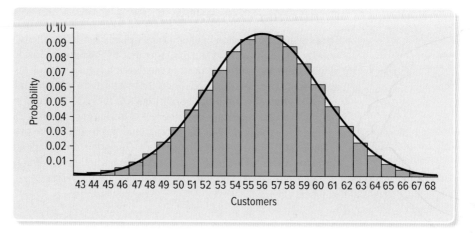

Because we use the normal distribution to determine the binomial probability of 60 or more successes, we must subtract, in this case, 0.5 from 60. The value 0.5 is called the **continuity correction factor**. This small adjustment must be made because a continuous distribution (the normal distribution) is being used to approximate a discrete distribution (the binomial distribution). Subtracting, $60.0 - 0.5 = 59.5$.

How to Apply the Correction Factor

Only four cases may arise. These cases are:

1. For the probability that *at least* x occur, use the area *above* $(x - 0.5)$.
2. For the probability that *more than* x occur, use the area *above* $(x + 0.5)$.
3. For the probability that x *or fewer* occur, use the area *below* $(x + 0.5)$.
4. For the probability that *fewer than* x occur, use the area *below* $(x - 0.5)$.

A helpful hint is that the shaded area should always contain the x value.

To use the normal distribution to approximate the probability that 60 or more first-time Santoni customers out of 80 will return, follow the procedure shown below:

Step 1. Find the z corresponding to an x of 59.5 using formula (6–4), and formulas (5–4) and (5–5) for the mean and the variance of a binomial distribution:

$$\mu = np = 80(0.70) = 56$$
$$\sigma^2 = np(1 - p) = 80(0.70)(1 - 0.70) = 16.8$$
$$\sigma = \sqrt{16.8} = 4.10$$
$$z = \frac{x - \mu}{\sigma} = 59.5 - 56/4.10 = 0.85$$

Step 2. Determine the area under the normal curve between a μ of 56 and an x of 59.5. From step 1, we know that the z-value corresponding to 59.5 is 0.85. So, we go to Appendix B.1 and read down the left margin to 0.8, and then we go horizontally to the area under the column headed by 0.05. That area is 0.3023.

Step 3. Calculate the area beyond 59.5 by subtracting 0.3023 from 0.5000, that is, $0.5000 - 0.3023 = 0.1977$. Thus, 0.1977 is the probability that 60 or more first-time Santoni customers out of 80 will return for another meal. In probability notation, $P(\text{customers} > 59.5) = 0.5000 - 0.3023 = 0.1977$. The details of this problem are shown graphically:

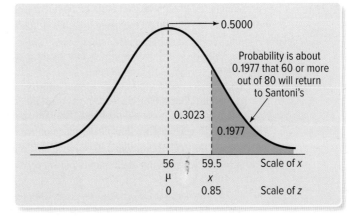

No doubt you will agree that using the normal approximation to the binomial is a more efficient method of estimating the probability of 60 or more first-time customers returning. The result compares favourably with that computed previously using the binomial distribution. The probability using the binomial distribution is 0.197, whereas the probability using the normal approximation is 0.1977.

---

self-review 6–7

A study by Great Southern Home Insurance revealed that none of the stolen goods was recovered by homeowners in 80% of reported thefts.

(a) During a period in which 200 thefts occurred, what is the probability that no stolen goods were recovered in 170 or more of the robberies?

(b) During a period in which 200 thefts occurred, what is the probability that no stolen goods were recovered in 150 or more robberies?

EXERCISES

35. Assume a binomial probability distribution with $n = 50$ and $p = 0.25$. Compute the following:
  a. The mean and standard deviation of the random variable.
  b. The probability that x is 15 or more.
  c. The probability that x is 10 or less.

36. Assume a binomial probability distribution with $n = 40$ and $p = 0.55$. Compute the following:
  a. The mean and standard deviation of the random variable.
  b. The probability that x is 25 or greater.
  c. The probability that x is 15 or less.
  d. The probability that x is between 15 and 25 inclusive.

37. Dottie's Tax Service specializes in tax returns for professional clients, such as physicians, dentists, accountants, and lawyers. A recent audit of the returns she prepared indicated that an error was made on 5% of the returns she prepared last year. Use the normal approximation to the binomial distribution to answer all parts of this question. Assuming this rate continues into this year and she prepares 60 returns, what is the probability that she makes errors on:
  a. More than six returns?
  b. At least six returns?
  c. Exactly six returns?

38. Shorty's Muffler advertises that it can install a new muffler in 30 minutes or less. However, the work standards department at corporate headquarters recently conducted a study and found that 20% of the mufflers were not installed in 30 minutes or less. The Maumee branch installed 50 mufflers last month. If the corporate report is correct:
  a. How many of the installations at the Maumee branch would you expect to take more than 30 minutes?
  b. What is the likelihood that fewer than eight installations took more than 30 minutes?

    c. What is the likelihood that eight or fewer installations took more than 30 minutes?

    d. What is the likelihood that exactly eight of the 50 installations took more than 30 minutes?

39. A study conducted by the nationally known Taurus Health Club revealed that 30% of its new members are significantly overweight. A membership drive in a metropolitan area resulted in 500 new members.

    a. It has been suggested that the normal approximation to the binomial be used to determine the probability that 175 or more of the new members are significantly overweight. Does this problem qualify as a binomial problem? Explain.

    b. What is the probability that 175 or more of the new members are significantly overweight?

    c. What is the probability that 140 or more new members are significantly overweight?

40. Research on new juvenile delinquents put on probation revealed that 38% of them committed another crime.

    a. What is the probability that of the last 100 new juvenile delinquents put on probation, 30 or more will commit another crime?

    b. What is the probability that 40 or fewer of the delinquents will commit another crime?

    c. What is the probability that from 30 to 40 of the delinquents will commit another crime?

Chapter Summary

I. The uniform distribution is a continuous probability distribution with the following characteristics:

  A. It is rectangular in shape.

  B. The mean and median are equal.

  C. It is completely described by its minimum value a and its maximum value b.

  D. It is also described by the following equation for the region from a to b:

$$P(x) = \frac{1}{b-a} \qquad \text{[6–3]}$$

  E. The mean and standard deviation of a uniform distribution are computed as follows:

$$\mu = \frac{a+b}{2} \qquad \text{[6–1]}$$

$$\sigma = \sqrt{\frac{(b-a)^2}{12}} \qquad \text{[6–2]}$$

II. The normal probability distribution is a continuous probability distribution with the following characteristics:

  A. It is bell-shaped and has a single peak at the centre of the distribution.

  B. The distribution is symmetric.

  C. It is asymptotic, meaning the curve approaches but never touches the X-axis.

  D. It is completely described by the mean and standard deviation.

  E. There is a family of normal distributions.

    1. Another normal probability distribution is created when either the mean or the standard deviation changes.

    2. The area under a normal curve expresses the probability of an outcome.

III. The standard normal probability distribution is a particular normal distribution.

  A. It has a mean of 0 and a standard deviation of 1.

  B. Any normal distribution can be converted to the standard normal distribution by the following formula:

$$z = \frac{x - \mu}{\sigma} \qquad \text{[6–4]}$$

  C. By standardizing a normal distribution, we can report the distance from the mean in units of the standard deviation.

IV. The normal distribution can approximate a binomial distribution under certain conditions.

  A. np and $n(1-p)$ must both be at least 5.

    1. n is the number of observations.

    2. p is the probability of a success.

B. The four conditions for a binomial distribution are as follows:
1. There are only two possible outcomes.
2. p remains the same from trial to trial.
3. The trials are independent.
4. The distribution results from a count of the number of successes in a fixed number of trials.

C. The mean and variance of a binomial distribution are computed as follows:

$$\mu = np$$
$$\sigma^2 = np(1 - p)$$

D. The continuity correction factor of 0.5 is used to extend the continuous value of x one-half unit in either direction. This correction compensates for estimating a discrete distribution by a continuous distribution.

Chapter Exercises

41. The amount of cola in a 12-ounce can is uniformly distributed between 11.96 ounces and 12.05 ounces.
   a. What is the mean amount per can?
   b. What is the standard deviation amount per can?
   c. What is the probability of selecting a can of cola and finding it has less than 12 ounces?
   d. What is the probability of selecting a can of cola and finding it has more than 11.98 ounces?
   e. What is the probability of selecting a can of cola and finding it has more than 11.00 ounces?

42. A tube of Listerine Tartar Control toothpaste contains 4.2 ounces. As people use the toothpaste, the amount remaining in any tube is random. Assume the amount of toothpaste left in the tube follows a uniform distribution. From this information, we can determine the following information about the amount remaining in a toothpaste tube without invading anyone's privacy.
   a. How much toothpaste would you expect to be remaining in the tube?
   b. What is the standard deviation of the amount remaining in the tube?
   c. What is the likelihood there is less than 3.0 ounces remaining in the tube?
   d. What is the probability there is more than 1.5 ounces remaining in the tube?

43. Many retail stores offer their own credit cards. At the time of the credit application, the customer is given a 10% discount on the purchase. The time required for the credit application process follows a uniform distribution with the times ranging from 4 minutes to 10 minutes.
   a. What is the mean time for the application process?
   b. What is the standard deviation for the process time?
   c. What is the likelihood a particular application will take less than 6 minutes?
   d. What is the likelihood an application will take more than 5 minutes?

44. The time patrons at the Grande Dunes Hotel in the Bahamas spend waiting for an elevator follows a uniform distribution between 0 and 3.5 minutes.
   a. Show that the area under the curve is 1.00.
   b. How long does the typical patron wait for elevator service?
   c. What is the standard deviation of the waiting time?
   d. What fraction of the patrons wait for less than a minute?
   e. What fraction of the patrons wait more than two minutes?

45. Given the following z-values, find the areas under the normal curve to the left and right of the z-value:
   a. $z = 1.56$ **c.** $z = -0.78$
   b. $z = 1.83$ **d.** $z = -2.45$

46. Given the following pairs of z-values, find the area under the normal curve between each pair of z-values:
   a. $z = -1.5$ and $z = 1.75$ **c.** $z = -2.58$ and $z = -1.05$
   b. $z = 1.23$ and $z = 2.71$ **d.** $z = -2.45$ and $z = -0.79$

47. The mean of a normal probability distribution is 25 with a standard deviation of 8.
   a. $\mu \pm 1\sigma$ of the observations lie between what two values?
   b. $\mu \pm 2\sigma$ of the observations lie between what two values?
   c. $\mu \pm 3\sigma$ of the observations lie between what two values?
   d. What percentage of the values will lie between $\mu - 1\sigma$ and $\mu + 2\sigma$?
   e. What percentage of the values will lie less than $\mu - 2\sigma$ or more than $\mu + 1\sigma$?

48. The average salary of merchandisers is $45 000 per year with a standard deviation of $6000.
   a. What is the probability that a merchandiser earns more than $55 000 per year?
   b. What is the probability that a merchandiser earns less than $32 000 per year?

   c. What is the probability that a merchandiser earns between $40 000 and $50 000 per year?
   d. What is the probability that a merchandiser will earn between $30 000 and $54 000 per year?
   e. What is the average salary below which 20% of the merchandisers earn?
   f. What is the average salary above which the top 10% of the merchandisers earn?

49. The net sales and the number of employees for aluminum fabricators with similar characteristics are organized into frequency distributions. Both are normally distributed. For the net sales, the mean is $180 million and the standard deviation is $25 million. For the number of employees, the mean is 1500 and the standard deviation is 120. Clarion Fabricators had sales of $170 million and 1850 employees.
   a. Convert Clarion's sales and number of employees to z-values.
   b. Locate the two z-values.
   c. Compare Clarion's sales and number of employees with those of the other fabricators.

50. The accounting department at Weston Materials Inc., a national manufacturer of unattached garages, reports that it takes two construction workers a mean of 32 hours and a standard deviation of 2 hours to erect the Red Barn model. Assume the assembly times follow the normal distribution.
   a. Determine the z-values for 29 and 34 hours. What percentage of the garages take between 32 hours and 34 hours to erect?
   b. What percentage of the garages take between 29 hours and 34 hours to erect?
   c. What percentage of the garages take 28.7 hours or less to erect?
   d. Of the garages, 5% take how many hours or more to erect?

51. A recent report indicated a typical family of four spends $490 per month on food. Assume the distribution of food expenditures for a family of four follows the normal distribution, with a mean of $490 and a standard deviation of $90.
   a. What percentage of the families spend more than $30 but less than $490 per month on food?
   b. What percentage of the families spend less than $430 per month on food?
   c. What percentage of the families spend between $430 and $600 per month on food?
   d. What percentage of the families spend between $500 and $600 per month on food?

52. A study of long distance phone calls made from the corporate offices of the Pepsi Bottling Group Inc. showed the calls follow the normal distribution. The mean length of time per call was 4.2 minutes and the standard deviation was 0.60 minutes.
   a. What is the probability the calls lasted between 4.2 and 5 minutes?
   b. What is the probability the calls lasted more than 5 minutes?
   c. What is the probability the calls lasted between 5 and 6 minutes?
   d. What is the probability the calls lasted between 4 and 6 minutes?
   e. As part of her report to the president, the director of communications would like to report the minimum length of the longest (in duration) 4% of the calls. What is this time?

53. Shaver Manufacturing Inc. offers dental insurance to its employees. A recent study by the human resource director shows the annual cost per employee per year followed the normal distribution, with a mean of $1280 and a standard deviation of $420 per year.
   a. What is the probability that the employees' dental expenses will be more than $1500 per year?
   b. What is the probability that the employees' dental expenses will be between $1500 and $2000 per year?
   c. Estimate the percentage that did not have any dental expense.
   d. What was the minimum cost for the 10% of employees that incurred the highest dental expense?

54. The annual commissions earned by sales representatives of Machine Products Inc., a manufacturer of light machinery, follow the normal distribution. The mean yearly amount earned is $40 000 and the standard deviation is $5000.
   a. What percentage of the sales representatives earn more than $42 000 per year?
   b. What percentage of the sales representatives earn between $32 000 and $42 000?
   c. What percentage of the sales representatives earn between $32 000 and $35 000?
   d. The sales manager wants to award the sales representatives who earn the largest commissions a bonus of $1000. He can award a bonus to 20% of the representatives. What is the cutoff point between those who earn a bonus and those who do not?

55. According to a recent survey, the mean number of hours of TV viewing per week is higher among adult women than among men. A recent study showed women spent an average of 34 hours per week watching TV and men 29 hours per week. Assume that the distribution of hours watched follows the normal distribution for both groups, and that the standard deviation among women is 4.5 hours and is 5.1 hours for men.

    a. What percentage of the women watch TV less than 40 hours per week?

    b. What percentage of the men watch TV more than 25 hours per week?

    c. How many hours of TV do the 1% of women who watch the most TV per week watch? Find the comparable value for men.

56. According to a government study among adults in the 25- to 34-year age group, the mean amount spent per year on reading and entertainment is $1994. Assume that the distribution of the amounts spent follows the normal distribution with a standard deviation of $450.

    a. What percentage of the adults spend more than $2500 per year on reading and entertainment?

    b. What percentage of the adults spend between $2500 and $3000 per year on reading and entertainment?

    c. What percentage of the adults spend less than $1000 per year on reading and entertainment?

57. Management at Gordon Electronics is considering adopting a bonus system to increase production. One suggestion is to pay a bonus on the highest 5% of production on the basis of past experience. Past records indicate weekly production follows the normal distribution. The mean of this distribution is 4000 units per week, and the standard deviation is 60 units per week. If the bonus is paid on the upper 5% of production, the bonus will be paid on how many units or more?

58. Fast Service Truck Lines uses the Ford Super 1310 exclusively. Management made a study of the maintenance costs and determined the number of kilometres travelled during the year followed the normal distribution. The mean of the distribution was 96 600 km and the standard deviation 3200 km.

    a. What percentage of the Ford Super 1310s logged 104 970 km or more?

    b. What percentage of the trucks logged more than 95 500 but less than 96 000 km?

    c. What percentage of the Fords travelled 99 800 or less during the year?

    d. Is it reasonable to conclude that any of the trucks were driven more than 112 700 km? Explain.

59. Best Electronics offers a "no hassle" returns policy. The number of items returned per day follows the normal distribution. The mean number of customer returns is 10.3 per day and the standard deviation is 2.25 per day.

    a. In what percentage of the days eight or fewer customers are returning items?

    b. In what percentage of the days between 12 and 14 customers are returning items?

    c. Is there any chance of a day with no returns?

60. A recent study shows that 20% of all employees prefer their vacation time during March break. If a company employs 50 people, what is the probability that:

    a. Fewer than five employees want their vacation during March break?

    b. More than five employees want their vacation during March break?

    c. Exactly five employees want their vacation during March break?

    d. More than 5 but fewer than 15 employees want their vacation during March break?

61. The average grade on a quiz was 39.5/50 (79%). Assume that the distribution of grades is normally distributed, with a standard deviation of 1.5.

    a. What is the probability that the average grade is more than 37.0?

    b. What is the probability that the average grade is less than 41.5?

    c. What is the probability that the average grade is between 36.0 and 37.0?

    d. What is the probability that the average grade is less than 36.0 or more than 37.0?

62. The funds dispensed at the automatic teller machine (ATM) at the Queensway site of the Trillium Hospital follows a normal distribution with a mean of $4200 per day and a standard deviation of $720 per day. The machine is programmed to notify the bank if the amount dispensed is very low, less than $2500, or very high, more than $6000.

    a. What percentage of the time will the bank be notified because the amount dispensed is very low?

    b. What percentage of the time will the bank be notified because the amount dispensed is very high?

    c. What percentage of the time will the bank not be notified regarding the amount of funds dispensed?

63. A recent survey reported that 64% of men over the age of 18 consider nutrition a top priority in their lives. Suppose we select a sample of 60 men. What is the likelihood that:

    a. 32 or more consider nutrition important?

    b. 44 or more consider nutrition important?

    c. More than 32 but fewer than 43 consider nutrition important?

    d. Exactly 44 consider nutrition important?

64. It is estimated that 10% of those taking the quantitative methods portion of the certified public accountant (CPA) examination fail that section. Sixty students are taking the examination this Saturday.

   a. How many would you expect to fail? What is the standard deviation?
   b. What is the probability that exactly two students will fail?
   c. What is the probability at least two students will fail?

65. The Georgetown Traffic Division reported 40% of the high-speed chases involving automobiles result in a minor or major accident. During a month in which 50 high-speed chases occur, what is the probability that 25 or more will result in a minor or major accident?

66. Cruise ships of the Royal Viking line report that 80% of their rooms are occupied during September. For a cruise ship having 800 rooms, what is the probability that 665 or more are occupied in September?

67. The goal at U.S. airports handling international flights is to clear these flights within 45 minutes. Let us interpret this to mean that 95% of the flights are cleared in 45 minutes, so 5% of the flights take longer to clear. Let us also assume that the distribution is approximately normal.

   a. If the standard deviation of the time to clear an international flight is five minutes, what is the mean time to clear a flight?
   b. Suppose the standard deviation is 10 minutes, not the 5 minutes suggested in part (a). What is the new mean?
   c. A customer has 30 minutes from the time her flight landed to catch her limousine. Assuming a standard deviation of 10 minutes, what is the likelihood that she will be cleared in time?

68. The registrar at Elmwood University (EU) studied the grade point averages (GPAs) of students over many years. Assume the GPA distribution follows a normal distribution with a mean of 3.10 and a standard deviation of 0.30.

   a. What is the probability that a randomly selected Elmwood student has a GPA between 2.00 and 3.00?
   b. What is the percentage of students who are on probation, that is, have a GPA less than 2.00?
   c. The student population at EU is 10 000. How many students are on the dean's list, that is, have GPAs of 3.70 or higher?
   d. To qualify for a Bell scholarship, a student must be in the top 10%. What minimum GPA must a student attain to qualify for a Bell scholarship?

69. According to media research, the average person listened to 195 hours of music in the last year. This is down from 290 hours four years earlier. Dick Trythall is a big country and western music fan. He listens to music while working around the house, reading, and riding in his truck. Assume the number of hours spent listening to music follows a normal probability distribution with a standard deviation of 8.5 hours.

   a. If Dick is in the top 1% in terms of listening time, how many hours does he listen per year?
   b. Assume that the distribution of times four years earlier also follows the normal probability distribution with a standard deviation of 8.5 hours. How many hours did the 1% who listen to the *least* music actually listen?

70. For the most recent year available, the mean annual cost to attend a private college was $25 000. Assume that the distribution of annual costs follows the normal probability distribution and the standard deviation is $4500.

   a. What percentage of students attending a private college pay between $20 000 and $30 000?
   b. Ninety-five percent of all students at private colleges pay less than what amount?

71. Many three-year automobile leases allow up to 100 000 km. If the lease goes beyond this amount, a penalty per kilometre is added to the lease cost. Suppose the distribution of kilometres driven on three-year leases follows the normal distribution. The mean is 85 000 km and the standard deviation is 8000 km.

   a. What percentage of the leases will yield a penalty because of excess distance travelled?
   b. If the automobile company wanted to change the terms of the lease so that 25% of the leases went over the limit, where should the new upper limit be set?
   c. One definition of a low-mileage car is one that is three years old and has been driven less than 72 000 km. What is the percentage of cars returned that are considered low-mileage?

72. The price of shares of the Continental Bank at the end of trading each day for the last year followed the normal distribution. Assume there were 240 trading days in the year. The mean price was $42.00 per share and the standard deviation was $2.25 per share.

   a. What percentage of the days was the price over $45.00? How many days would you estimate?
   b. What percentage of the days was the price between $38.00 and $40.00?
   c. What was the minimum price of the stock on the *highest* 15 days of the year?

73. The distribution of the number of viewers for the *American Idol* television broadcasts follows the normal distribution with a mean of 29 million and a standard deviation of 5 million. What is the probability that next week's show will:
    a. Have between 30 and 34 million viewers?
    b. Have at least 23 million viewers?
    c. Exceed 40 million viewers?

74. In establishing warranties on high-definition TV (HDTV) sets, the manufacturer wants to set the limits so that few will need repair at manufacturer expense. However, the warranty period must be long enough to make the purchase attractive to the buyer. For a new HDTV, the mean number of months until repairs are needed is 36.84, with a standard deviation of 3.34 months. Where should the warranty limits be set so that only 10% of the large-screen TVs need repairs at the manufacturer's expense?

75. DeKorte Tele-Marketing Inc. is considering purchasing a machine that randomly selects and automatically dials telephone numbers. DeKorte Tele-Marketing makes most of its calls during the evening, so calls to business phones are wasted. The manufacturer of the machine claims that its programming reduces the calling to business phones to 15% of all calls. To test this claim, the director of purchasing at DeKorte programmed the machine to select a sample of 150 phone numbers. What is the likelihood that more than 30 of the phone numbers selected are that of a business, assuming the manufacturer's claim is correct?

76. A recent survey reported that the average person consumes six glasses of water per day (250 mL per glass). Assume the standard deviation of water consumption is 378.5 mL per day and the consumption rate follows a normal probability distribution. What is the z-value for a person who drinks 1900 mL of water per day? On the basis of the z-value, how does this person compare to the average reported in the survey?

77. The number of cupcakes sold per week at the Coffee Bean Cafe follows the normal probability distribution, with a mean of 150 cupcakes. The standard deviation of this distribution is 5 cupcakes.
    a. What is the probability that the number sold is between 150 and 154 cupcakes?
    b. What is the probability that the number sold is more than 164 cupcakes?
    c. What is the probability that the number sold is between 146 and 156 cupcakes?
    d. What is the probability that the number sold is more than 156 but less than 162 cupcakes?

78. According to the Show Box Office at the Smythe Production Company, the mean cost to run a performance is $3000. Assume that the standard deviation is $410 and that the performance cost follows a normal probability distribution.
    a. What percentage of the performances cost more than $3100 to run?
    b. What percentage of the performances cost more than $3100 but less than $3500 to run?
    c. What percentage of the performances cost more than $2250 but less than $3500 to run?

79. The annual sales of romance novels follow the normal distribution. However, the mean and standard deviation are unknown. Forty percent of the time sales are more than 470 000, and 10% of the time sales are more than 500 000. What are the mean and the standard deviation?

80. Among cities with a population of more than 250 000, the mean one-way commute time to work is 24.3 minutes, providing there are no accidents or inclement weather along the way. A city with a population of 1 million has a mean commute time to work of 38.3 minutes. Assume that the distribution of travel times for this city follows the normal probability distribution and the standard deviation is 7.5 minutes.
    a. What percentage of the commute times is less than 30 minutes?
    b. What percentage of the commute times is between 30 and 35 minutes?
    c. What percentage of the commute times is between 30 and 40 minutes?
    d. What percentage of the commute times will be more than 1 hour?

81. A normal population has a mean of 50 and a standard deviation of 7.
    a. Compute the z-value associated with 45.
    b. What percentage of the population is between 45 and 63?
    c. What percentage of the population is less than 55?
    d. What percentage of the population is more than 40?
    e. What percentage of the population is less than 40 or more than 55?
    f. Below what value do 80% of the observations lie?

82. The SAT Reasoning Test is perhaps the most widely used standardized test for college admissions in the United States. Scores are based on a normal distribution with a mean of 1500 and a standard deviation of 300. Clinton College would like to offer an honours scholarship to

students who score in the top 10% of this test. What is the minimum score that qualifies for the scholarship?

83. The weights of canned hams processed at the Henline Ham Company follow the normal distribution, with a mean of 3.1 kg and a standard deviation of 0.125 kg. The label weight is given as 3 kg.
   a. What proportion of the hams actually weigh less than the amount claimed on the label?
   b. The owner, Glen Henline, is considering two proposals to reduce the proportion of hams below label weight. He can increase the mean weight to 3.15 kg and leave the standard deviation the same, or he can leave the mean weight at 3.1 kg and reduce the standard deviation from 0.125 kg to 0.10 kg. Which change would you recommend?

84. The *Gravenhurst Enquirer* reported that the mean number of hours worked per week by those employed full-time is 43.9. The article further indicated that about one-third of those employed full-time work less than 40 hours per week.
   a. Given this information and assuming that number of hours worked follows the normal distribution, what is the standard deviation of the number of hours worked?
   b. The article also indicated that 20% of those working full-time work more than 49 hours per week. Determine the standard deviation with this information. Are the two estimates of the standard deviation similar? What would you conclude?

85. In economic theory, a "hurdle rate" is the minimum return that a person requires before they will make an investment. A research report says that annual returns from a specific class of common equities are distributed according to a normal distribution with a mean of 12% and a standard deviation of 18%. A stock screener would like to identify a hurdle rate such that only 1 in 20 equities is above that value. Where should the hurdle rate be set?

Data Set Exercises

Questions marked with ⤴ have data sets available on McGraw-Hill's online resource for Basic Statistics.

86. Refer to the Real Estate Data—Halifax Area online, which reports information on home listings. The mean list price (in $ thousands) of the homes was computed earlier. Use the normal distribution to estimate the percentage of homes listed for more than $475 000. Compare this to the actual results. Does the normal distribution yield a good approximation of the actual results?

87. Refer to the Real Estate Data—Saskatoon online, which reports information on home listings. The mean list price (in $ thousands) of the homes was computed earlier. Use the normal distribution to estimate the percent of homes listed for more than $350 000. Compare this to the actual results. Does the normal distribution yield a good approximation of the actual results?

88. Refer to the CREA (Canadian Real Estate Association) Cities Only data online, which reports information on average house prices nationally and in a selection of cities across Canada.
   a. Calculate the mean and the standard deviation for June 2016. Consider the data a population. Use the normal distribution to estimate the average house prices less than $400 000. Compare the estimate to the actual results. Does the normal distribution yield a good approximation of the actual results?
   b. Calculate the mean and the standard deviation for January 2011. Consider the data a population. Use the normal distribution to estimate the average house prices more than $400 000. Compare the estimate to the actual results. Does the normal distribution yield a good approximation of the actual results?

Practice Test

Part I Objective

1. For a continuous probability distribution, the total area under the curve is equal to _____.

2. For a uniform distribution that ranges from 10 to 20, how many values can be in that range? (1, 10, 100, infinite—pick one) _____.

3. Which of the following is *NOT* a characteristic of the normal distribution? (bell-shaped, symmetric, discrete, asymptotic) _____.

4. For a normal distribution, the mean and the median are _____ (always equal, mean is twice the median, equal to the standard deviation, none of these is true).

5. How many normal distributions are there? (1, 10, 30, infinite) _____.

6. How many standard normal distributions are there? (1, 10, 30, infinite) _____.

7. The signed difference between a selected value and the mean divided by the standard deviation is called a _____. (z-score, z-value, standardized value, any of these)

8. What is the probability of a z-value between 0 and −0.76? _____.

9. What is the probability of a z-value between −2.03 and 1.76? _____.

10. What is the probability of a z-value between −1.86 and −1.43? _____.

Part II Problems

1. In a memo to all those involved in tax preparation, the Canada Revenue Agency (CRA) indicated the mean amount of refund was $1600. The distribution of tax returns follows a normal distribution with a standard deviation of $850.
   a. What percentage of the returns is between $1600 and $2000?
   b. What percentage of the returns is between $900 and $2000?
   c. What percentage of the returns is between $1800 and $2000?
   d. Ninety-five percent of the returns are for less than what amount?

Computer Commands

1. **Excel** steps to find a probability when you have the z-value follows:
   a. Select **Insert Function**. From the **Or select a category** list, select **Statistical**. In the **Select a function** list, click **NORM.S.DIST**. Click **OK**.
   b. For z = 1, enter 1 for **z** and **1** for cumulative. The result is 0.8413 which represents the cumulative area under the normal curve to **z** = 1.

2. **Excel** steps to find the probability for the weekly incomes of shift supervisors that are less than $1100 are as follows:
   a. Select **Insert Function**. From the **Or select a category** list, select **Statistical**. In the **Select a function** list, click **NORM.DIST**. Click **OK**.
   b. Enter *1100* for X, *1000* for the **Mean**, *100* for the **Standard_dev**, *1* for **Cumulative** and click **OK**.
   c. The result will be in your spreadsheet.

3. **MegaStat** steps to find the probability for the weekly incomes of shift supervisors that are less than $1100 are as follows:
   a. Select **MegaStat**, **Probability**, and **Continuous Probability Distributions**.
   b. Enter *1000* for the **mean**. You will notice that the screen changes to add an extra box for the *x*-value. Enter *100* for the **standard deviation**, and *1100* in the *x* box. Click the **Preview** box to see the answer.

Function Arguments		? X
NORM.DIST		
X	1100	= 1100
Mean	1000	= 1000
Standard_dev	100	= 100
Cumulative	1	= TRUE
		= 0.841344746

Returns the normal distribution for the specified mean and standard deviation.

Cumulative is a logical value: for the cumulative distribution function, use TRUE; for the probability density function, use FALSE.

Formula result = 0.841344746

Help on this function   OK   Cancel

Continuous Probability Distributions   X

| normal distribution | t-distribution | F-distribution | chi-square distribution |

z   1.00   X   1100   —   ⦿ calculate P given X   OK

○ calculate X given P   Clear

Cancel

mean   1000   —   Help

standard deviation   100   —

P(lower)   P(upper)
.8413   .1587   [Preview]   ☐ round to match tables

---

c. Click **OK** for the output to appear on the **Output** sheet as follows:

normal distribution

P(lower)	P(upper)	Z	X	mean	std. dev
0.8413	0.1587	1.00	1100	1000	100

4. **Excel** steps to find the probability for the weekly incomes of shift supervisors that are between $1000 and $1100 are as follows:

a. Select **Insert Function**. From the **Or select a category** list, select **Statistical**. In the **Select a function** list, click **NORM.DIST**. Click **OK**.

b. Enter *1100* for **X**, *1000* for the **Mean**, *100* for the **Standard_dev**, *1* for **Cumulative** and click **OK**.

c. The result will be in your spreadsheet.

The answer is 0.8413. Since **NORM.DIST** is a cumulative function, it measures the total area to the left of $1100 (the area in the lower tail). To find the area under the curve between $1000 (the mean) and $1100 ($x$), subtract the area to the left of the mean (0.5). This gives 0.8413 − 0.5 = 0.3413.

5. **MegaStat** steps to find the probability for the weekly incomes of shift supervisors that are between $1000 and $1100 are as follows:

a. Select **MegaStat, Probability,** and **Continuous Probability Distributions.**

b. Enter *1000* for the **mean**. You will notice that the screen changes to add an extra box for the *x*-value. Enter *100* for the **standard deviation**, and *1100* in the *x* box. Click **the Preview** box to see the answer.

MegaStat computes the result as a cumulative function. It measures the total area to the left of $1100 (the area in the lower tail). To find the area under the curve between $1000 (the mean) and $1100 ($x$), subtract the area to the left of the mean (0.5). This gives 0.8413 − 0.5 = 0.3413.

6. **Excel** steps to find the area less than $790 are as follows:

a. Follow the **Excel** steps in #1 above, entering 790 for x.

b. The answer is 0.0179, which is the area in the left tail (less-than) $790.

7. **MegaStat** steps to find the area less than $790 are as follows:

a. Follow the **MegaStat** steps in #2 above, entering 790 for x.

b. The answer is 0.0179, which is the area in the left tail (less-than) $790.

8. The steps (**Excel** and **MegaStat**) to find the area between $790 and $1000 are as follows:

a. Use the result 0.0179 in the lower tail from #5 or #6.

b. Recall that the total area to the left of the mean is 0.5. To find the area between $790 and $1000, subtract the area that is not needed, which is the area less than $790 (0.0179) from 0.5. The result is 0.5 − 0.0179 = 0.4821.

9. **Excel** and **MegaStat** steps to find the area between $840 and $1200 are as follows:

a. Use #1 or #2 above to find the areas under the curve for the values of $840 and $1200.

The output from **MegaStat** (**Excel** is similar) for the values of $840 and $1200 follow. Note that the area in the two tails of the above example are calculated as 0.5 − 0.4452 = 0.0548 in the lower tail and 0.5 − 0.4772 = 0.0228 in the upper tail.

p(lower)	p(upper)	Z	X	mean	std. dev.
0.0548	0.9452	−1.60	840	1000	100

p(lower)	p(upper)	Z	X	mean	std. dev.
0.9772	0.0228	2.00	1200	1000	100

The output from **MegaStat** for the value of $840 is 0.0548 in the lower tail and 0.9452 in the upper tail. The output for the value of $1200 is 0.9772 in the lower tail and 0.0228 in the upper tail. To obtain the required result, take the total area and subtract the areas that you do not need. (This is using the complement rule). The required result is computed as 1.000 − 0.0548 − 0.0228 = 0.9224.

10. **Excel** and **MegaStat** steps to find the area between $1150 and $1250 are as follows:

a. Use #1 or #2 above to find the areas under the curve for the values of $1150 and $1250.

The output from **MegaStat** (**Excel** is similar) for the value of $1150 is 0.9332 in the lower tail and 0.0668 in the upper tail.

p(lower)	p(upper)	Z	X	mean	std. dev.
0.9332	0.0668	1.50	1150	1000	100

p(lower)	p(upper)	Z	X	mean	std. dev.
0.9938	0.0062	2.50	1250	1000	100

The output for the value of $1250 is 0.9938 in the lower tail and 0.0062 in the upper tail. Use the complement rule and subtract the areas that are not needed. The required result is $1.000 - 0.9332 - 0.0062 = 0.0606$.

11. **Excel** steps to find the number of kilometres in the Layton Tire and Rubber example are as follows:

a. Select **Insert Function.** From the **Or select a category** list, select **Statistical.** In the **Select a function** list, click **NORM.INV.** Click **OK.**

b. Enter *0.04* for **Probability,** *109000* for the **Mean** and *3300* for the **Standard_dev.** Click **OK.**

Note: The result may be slightly different from a calculator answer due to rounding.

MegaStat steps to find the number of kilometres in the Layton Tire and Rubber example are as follows:

12. a. Select **MegaStat, Probability,** and **Continuous Probability Distributions.**

b. Click the dial in front of the box **calculate z given P.**

c. Enter *0.96* for **P,** *109000* for the **mean** and *3300* for the **standard deviation**.

Note: **MegaStat** steps require that **P** be the value in the upper tail.

The result may be slightly different from a calculator answer due to rounding.

Answers to Self-Reviews

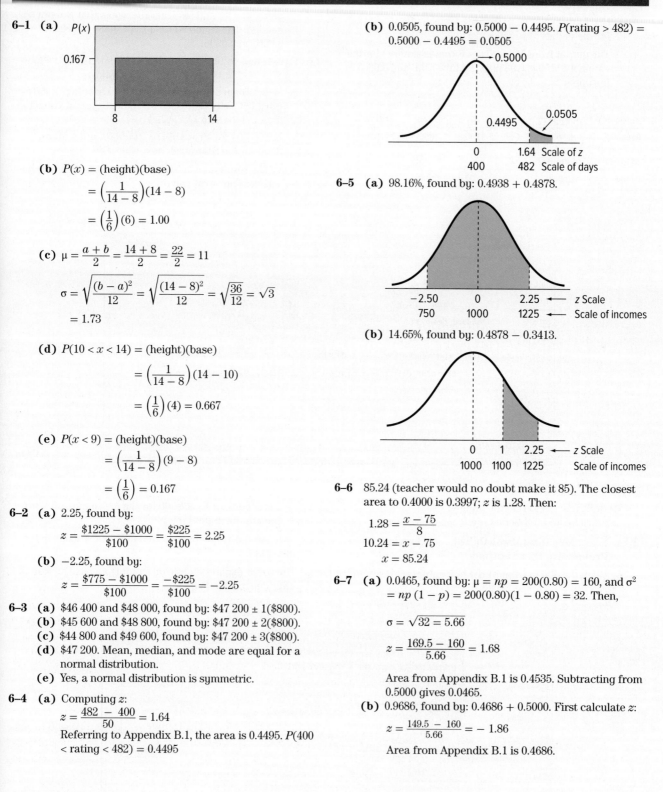

6–1 (a)

(b) $P(x) = $ (height)(base)

$$= \left(\frac{1}{14-8}\right)(14-8)$$

$$= \left(\frac{1}{6}\right)(6) = 1.00$$

(c) $\mu = \dfrac{a+b}{2} = \dfrac{14+8}{2} = \dfrac{22}{2} = 11$

$$\sigma = \sqrt{\frac{(b-a)^2}{12}} = \sqrt{\frac{(14-8)^2}{12}} = \sqrt{\frac{36}{12}} = \sqrt{3}$$

$$= 1.73$$

(d) $P(10 < x < 14) = $ (height)(base)

$$= \left(\frac{1}{14-8}\right)(14-10)$$

$$= \left(\frac{1}{6}\right)(4) = 0.667$$

(e) $P(x < 9) = $ (height)(base)

$$= \left(\frac{1}{14-8}\right)(9-8)$$

$$= \left(\frac{1}{6}\right) = 0.167$$

6–2 (a) 2.25, found by:

$$z = \frac{\$1225 - \$1000}{\$100} = \frac{\$225}{\$100} = 2.25$$

(b) −2.25, found by:

$$z = \frac{\$775 - \$1000}{\$100} = \frac{-\$225}{\$100} = -2.25$$

6–3 (a) \$46 400 and \$48 000, found by: \$47 200 ± 1(\$800).
(b) \$45 600 and \$48 800, found by: \$47 200 ± 2(\$800).
(c) \$44 800 and \$49 600, found by: \$47 200 ± 3(\$800).
(d) \$47 200. Mean, median, and mode are equal for a normal distribution.
(e) Yes, a normal distribution is symmetric.

6–4 (a) Computing z:

$$z = \frac{482 - 400}{50} = 1.64$$

Referring to Appendix B.1, the area is 0.4495. $P(400 < \text{rating} < 482) = 0.4495$

(b) 0.0505, found by: $0.5000 - 0.4495$. $P(\text{rating} > 482) = 0.5000 - 0.4495 = 0.0505$

6–5 (a) 98.16%, found by: $0.4938 + 0.4878$.

(b) 14.65%, found by: $0.4878 - 0.3413$.

6–6 85.24 (teacher would no doubt make it 85). The closest area to 0.4000 is 0.3997; z is 1.28. Then:

$$1.28 = \frac{x - 75}{8}$$
$$10.24 = x - 75$$
$$x = 85.24$$

6–7 (a) 0.0465, found by: $\mu = np = 200(0.80) = 160$, and $\sigma^2 = np(1-p) = 200(0.80)(1 - 0.80) = 32$. Then,

$$\sigma = \sqrt{32} = 5.66$$

$$z = \frac{169.5 - 160}{5.66} = 1.68$$

Area from Appendix B.1 is 0.4535. Subtracting from 0.5000 gives 0.0465.

(b) 0.9686, found by: $0.4686 + 0.5000$. First calculate z:

$$z = \frac{149.5 - 160}{5.66} = -1.86$$

Area from Appendix B.1 is 0.4686.

CHAPTER 7
Sampling Methods and the Central Limit Theorem

© Maridav / Getty Images

The Nike annual report states that the average customer buys 6.5 pairs of sports shoes per year. Suppose that the population standard deviation is 2.1 and that a sample of 81 customers will be examined next year. What is the standard error of the mean in this experiment? (Exercise 54, LO7-4)

7.1 INTRODUCTION

Chapters 1 through 3 emphasize techniques to describe data. To illustrate these techniques, we organize the real estate listings of 85 homes in Whistler, BC, into a frequency distribution and compute various measures of location and dispersion. Such measures as mean and standard deviation describe the typical list price and the spread in the list prices. In these chapters, the emphasis is on describing the condition of the data. That is, we describe something that has already happened.

Chapter 4 starts to lay the foundation for statistical inference with the study of probability. Recall that in statistical inference our goal is to determine something about a *population* based only on the *sample*. The population is the entire group of individuals or objects under consideration, and the sample is a part or subset of that population. Chapter 5 extends the probability concepts by describing three discrete probability distributions: the binomial, the hypergeometric, and the Poisson. Chapter 6 describes the uniform probability distribution and the normal probability distribution. Both are continuous distributions. Probability distributions encompass all possible outcomes of an experiment and the probability associated with each outcome. We use probability distributions to evaluate something that might occur in the future.

This chapter begins our study of sampling. Sampling is a process of selecting items from a population so that we can use this information to make judgments or inferences about the population. We begin this chapter by discussing methods of selecting a sample from a population. Next, we construct a distribution of the sample mean to understand how the sample means tend to cluster around the population mean. Finally, we show that for any population, the shape of this sampling distribution tends to follow the normal probability distribution.

LO7-1 7.2 SAMPLING METHODS

In Chapter 1, we said the purpose of inferential statistics is to find something about a population based on a sample. A sample is a portion or part of the population of interest. In many cases, sampling is more feasible than studying the entire population. In this section, we show major reasons for sampling, and then several methods for selecting a sample.

Reasons to Sample

When studying characteristics of a population, there are many practical reasons why we prefer to select portions or samples of a population to observe and measure. Here are some of the reasons for sampling:

1. **To contact the whole population would be time consuming.** A candidate for public office may wish to determine her chances for election. A sample poll using the regular staff and field interviews of a professional polling firm would take only one or two days. Using the same staff and interviewers and working seven days a week, it could take years to contact all the voting population! Even if a large staff of interviewers could be assembled, the benefit of contacting all of the voters would probably not be worth the time.

2. **The cost of studying all the items in a population may be prohibitive.** Public opinion polls and consumer testing organizations, such as Gallup Polls, usually contact only a small portion of the population. One consumer panel-type organization charges about $40 000 to mail samples and tabulate responses in order to test a product (e.g., breakfast cereal, cat food, or perfume). The same product test using all population families would cost a great deal more.

3. **The physical impossibility of checking all items in the population.** Some populations are infinite. It would be impossible to check all the water in Okanagan Lake for bacterial levels, so we select samples at various locations. The populations of fish, birds, snakes, mosquitoes, and the like are large and are constantly moving, being born, and dying. Instead of even attempting to count all the ducks in Canada or all the fish in Rainbow Lake, we make estimates using various techniques—such as counting all the ducks on a pond picked at random, tracking fish catches, or netting fish at predetermined places in the lake.

4. **The destructive nature of some tests.** If the wine tasters in Niagara-on-the-Lake drank all the wine to evaluate the vintage, they would consume the entire crop, and none would be available for sale. In the area of industrial production, steel plates, wires, and similar products must have a specific minimum tensile strength. To ensure that the product meets the minimum standard, samples are selected from the current production. Each piece is stretched until it breaks, and the breaking strength recorded. Obviously, if all the wire or all the plates were tested for tensile strength, none would be available for sale or use. For the same reason, only a few seeds are tested for germination by Burpee Seeds Inc. prior to the planting season.

5. **The sample results are adequate.** Even if funds are available, it is doubtful the additional accuracy of a 100% sample—that is, studying the entire population—is essential in most problems. For example, the federal government uses a sample of grocery stores scattered throughout Canada to determine the monthly index of food prices. The prices of bread, beans, milk, and other major food items are included in the index. It is unlikely that the inclusion of all grocery stores in Canada would significantly affect the index, since the prices of milk, bread, and other major foods usually do not vary by more than a few cents from one chain store to another.

Simple Random Sampling

The most widely used type of sample is a **simple random sample.**

To illustrate simple random sampling and selection, suppose the population of interest consists of 845 employees of Nitra Industries. A sample of 52 employees is to be selected from that population. One way of ensuring that every employee in the population has the same chance of being chosen is to first write the name of each one on a small slip of paper and deposit all of the slips in a box. After the slips of paper have been thoroughly mixed, the first selection is made by

Statistics in Action

With the significant role played by inferential statistics in all branches of science, the availability of large sources of random numbers has become a necessity. The first book of random numbers, containing 41 600 random digits generated by L. Tippett, was published in 1927. In 1938, R. A. Fisher and F. Yates published 15 000 random digits generated using two decks of cards. In 1955, RAND Corporation published a million random digits, generated by the random frequency pulses of an electronic roulette wheel. By 1970, applications of sampling required billions of random numbers. Methods have since been developed for generating digits, using a computer, that are "almost" random and hence are called *pseudo-random*. The question of whether a computer program can be used to generate numbers that are truly random remains a debatable issue.

Simple random sample A sample is selected so that each item or person in the population has the same chance of being included.

drawing a slip out of the box without looking at it. The slip of paper is not returned to the box. This process is repeated until the sample size of 52 is chosen.

The process of writing all names on a slip of paper is very time-consuming. A more convenient method of selecting a random sample is to use the identification number of each employee and a **table of random numbers** such as the one in Appendix B.5. As the name implies, these numbers have been generated by a random process (in this case, by a computer). For each digit of a number, the probability of 0, 1, 2, . . . , 9 is the same. Thus, the probability that employee number 011 will be selected is the same as for employee 722 or employee 382. Using random numbers to select employees removes any bias from the selection process.

A portion of a table of random numbers is shown in the following illustration:

50525	57454	28455	68226	34656	38884	39018
72507	53380	53827	42486	54465	71819	91199
34986	74297	00144	38676	89967	98869	39744
68851	27305	037 59	447 23	96108	784 89	189 10
06738	62879	03910	17350	49169	03850	18910
11448	10734	05837	24397	10420	16712	94496

| | Starting point | Second employee | Third employee | Fourth employee |

The following example shows how to select random numbers using a portion of a random number table. First, we choose a starting point in the table. Any starting point will do. Suppose the time is 3:04. You might look at the third column and then move down to the fourth set of numbers. The number is 03759. Since there are only 845 employees, we will use the first three digits of a five-digit random number. Thus, 037 is the number of the first employee to be a member of the sample. Another way of selecting the starting point is to close your eyes and point at a number in the table. To continue selecting employees, you could move in any direction. Suppose you move right. The first three digits of the number to the right of 03759 are 447—the number of the employee selected to be the second member of the sample. The next three-digit number to the right is 961. You skip 961 because there are only 845 employees. You continue to the right and select employee 784, then 189, and so on.

Most statistical software packages have functions that will select a simple random sample. The following example uses **Excel** to select a random sample.

Example	Jane and Joe Miley operate a bed-and-breakfast (B&B) place called the Foxtrot Inn. There are eight rooms available for rent at this B&B. Listed below are the dates in June and the number of rooms rented each night. Use **Excel** to select a sample of five of the nights during the month.

June	Rentals	June	Rentals	June	Rentals
1	0	11	3	21	3
2	2	12	4	22	2
3	3	13	4	23	3
4	2	14	4	24	6
5	3	15	7	25	0
6	4	16	0	26	4
7	2	17	5	27	1
8	3	18	3	28	1
9	4	19	6	29	3
10	7	20	2	30	3

Solution	**Excel** will select the random sample and report the results. The information is listed in column D of the following **Excel** spreadsheet. On the first sampled date, four of the eight rooms were rented. On the second sampled date, seven of the eight rooms were rented, and so on. **Excel** performs the sampling with replacement, so it is possible for the same day to appear more than once in a sample. The results will vary each time the random sample is selected.

excel   Computer commands to find a random sample can be found at the end of
the chapter.

Num 1 one sample

	A	B	C	D	E
1	June	Rentals		Sample	
2	1	0		4	
3	2	2		7	
4	3	3		4	
5	4	2		3	
6	5	3		1	
7	6	4			
8	7	2			
9	8	3			
10	9	4			
11	10	7			
12	11	3			
13	12	4			
14	13	4			
15	14	4			

self-review 7–1   The following class roster lists the students enrolling in an introductory course in business
statistics:

```
                 CSPM 264 01 BUSINESS & ECONOMIC STAT
                  8:00 AM  9:40 AM  MW  ST 118  LIND D
```

RANDOM NUMBER	NAME	CLASS RANK	RANDOM NUMBER	NAME	CLASS RANK
00	ANDERSON, RAYMOND	SO	23	MEDLEY, CHERYL ANN	SO
01	ANGER, CHERYL RENEE	SO	24	MITCHELL, GREG R	FR
02	BALL, CLAIRE JEANETTE	FR	25	MOLTER, KRISTI MARIE	SO
03	BERRY, CHRISTOPHER G	FR	26	MULCAHY, STEPHEN ROBERT	SO
04	BOBAK, JAMES PATRICK	SO	27	NICHOLAS, ROBERT CHARLES	JR
05	BRIGHT, M. STARR	JR	28	NICKENS, VIRGINIA	SO
06	CHONTOS, PAUL JOSEPH	SO	29	PENNYWITT, SEAN PATRICK	SO
07	DETLEY, BRIAN HANS	JR	30	POTEAU, KRIS E	JR
08	DUDAS, VIOLA	SO	31	PRICE, MARY LYNETTE	SO
09	DULBS, RICHARD ZALFA	JR	32	RISTAS, JAMES	SR
10	EDINGER, SUSAN KEE	SR	33	SAGER, ANNE MARIE	SO
11	FINK, FRANK JAMES	SR	34	SMILLIE, HEATHER MICHELLE	SO
12	FRANCIS, JAMES P	JR	35	SNYDER, LEISHA KAY	SR
13	GAGHEN, PAMELA LYNN	JR	36	STAHL, MARIA TASHERY	SO
14	GOULD, ROBYN KAY	SO	37	ST. JOHN, AMY J	SO
15	GROSENBACHER, SCOTT ALAN	SO	38	STURDEVANT, RICHARD K	SO
16	HEETFIELD, DIANE MARIE	SO	39	SWETYE, LYNN MICHELE	SO
17	KABAT, JAMES DAVID	JR	40	WALASINSKI, MICHAEL	SO
18	KEMP, LISA ADRIANE	FR	41	WALKER, DIANE ELAINE	SO
19	KILLION, MICHELLE A	SO	42	WARNOCK, JENNIFER MARY	SO
20	KOPERSKI, MARY ELLEN	SO	43	WILLIAMS, WENDY A	SO
21	KOPP, BRIDGETTE ANN	SO	44	YAP, HOCK BAN	SO
22	LEHMANN, KRISTINA MARIE	JR	45	YODER, ARLAN JAY	JR

Three students are to be randomly selected and asked various questions regarding course content and method of instruction.

(a) The numbers 00 through 45 are handwritten on slips of paper and placed in a bowl. The three numbers selected are 31, 07, and 25. Which students would be included in the sample?

(b) Now use the table of random digits, Appendix B.5, to select your own sample.

(c) What would you do if you encountered the number 59 in the table of random digits?

Systematic Random Sampling

The simple random sampling procedure is awkward in some research situations. For example, suppose the sales division of Computer Printers Unlimited needs to quickly estimate the mean dollar revenue per sale during the past month. It finds that 2000 sales invoices were recorded and stored in file drawers, and decides to select 100 invoices to estimate the mean dollar revenue. Simple random sampling requires the numbering of each invoice before using the random number table to select the 100 invoices. The numbering process would be a very time consuming task. Instead, we can select a representative sample using **systematic random sampling.**

First, k is calculated as the population size divided by the sample size. For Computer Printers Unlimited, we would select every 20th (2000/100) invoice from the file drawers until we reach our goal of 100 invoices. In so doing, the numbering process is avoided. Note: if k is not a whole number, we would round down.

Random sampling is used in the selection of the first invoice. For example, a number from a random number table between 1 and k, or 20, would be selected. Say, the random number was 18. Then, starting with the 18th invoice, every 20th invoice (18, 38, 58, etc.) would be selected as the sample.

Before using systematic random sampling, we should carefully observe the physical order of the population. When the physical order is related to the population characteristic, then systematic random sampling should not be used. For example, if the invoices in the example were filed in order of increasing sales, systematic random sampling would not guarantee a random sample. Other sampling methods should be used.

Stratified Random Sampling

When a population can be clearly divided into groups based on some characteristic, we may use a **stratified random sample.** It guarantees that each group is represented in the sample. The groups are called **strata**. For example, college students can be grouped as full-time or part-time; male or female; or as certificate, diploma, or degree students. Usually the strata are formed based on members' shared attributes or characteristics. Once the strata are defined, a random sample is taken from each stratum in a number proportional to the stratum's size when compared to the population. We use simple random sampling within each group or stratum to collect the sample.

For instance, we might study the advertising expenditures for the 200 largest companies in Canada. Suppose that the objective of the study is to determine whether firms with high returns on equity (a measure of profitability) spent more on advertising than firms with low returns on equity. To make sure that the sample is a fair representation of the 200 companies, the companies are grouped on percentage return on equity. Table 7–1 shows the strata and the relative frequencies. If simple random sampling is used, observe that firms in the third and fourth strata have a high chance of selection (probability of 0.87), but firms in the other strata have a low chance of selection (probability of 0.13). We might not select any firms in stratum 1 or 5 *simply by chance*. However, stratified random sampling will guarantee that at least one firm in strata 1 and one firm in strata 5 is represented in the sample. Let us say that 50 firms are selected for intensive study. Then, one (0.02 × 50) firm from stratum 1 would be randomly selected, 5 (0.10 × 50) firms from stratum 2 would be randomly selected, and so on. In this case, the number of firms sampled from each stratum is proportional to the stratum's relative frequency in the population. Stratified sampling has the advantage, in some cases, of more accurately reflecting the characteristics of the population compared with simple random or systematic random sampling.

TABLE 7–1 Number Selected for a Proportional Stratified Random Sample

Stratum	Profitability (return on equity)	Number of Firms	Relative Frequency	Number Sampled
1	30% and over	4	0.02	1*
2	20 up to 30%	20	0.10	5*
3	10 up to 20%	108	0.54	27
4	0 up to 10%	66	0.33	16
5	Deficit	2	0.01	1
Total		200	1.00	50

*0.02 of 50 = 1; 0.10 of 50 = 5, etc.

Cluster Sampling

Cluster sample A population is divided into clusters using naturally occurring geographic or other boundaries. Then, clusters are randomly selected and a sample is collected by randomly selecting from each cluster.

Another common type of sample is a **cluster sample.** It is often employed to reduce the cost of sampling a population scattered over a large geographic area.

Suppose that you want to determine the views of residents in a province about provincial and federal environmental protection policies. Selecting a random sample of residents in the province and personally contacting each one would be time consuming and very expensive. Instead, you could employ cluster sampling by subdividing the province into small units—either counties or regions. These are often called *primary units*.

Suppose that you divided the province into 12 primary units, then selected at random four regions—2, 7, 4, and 12—and concentrated your efforts in these primary units. You could take a random sample of the residents in each of these regions and interview them. (Note that this is a combination of cluster sampling and simple random sampling.)

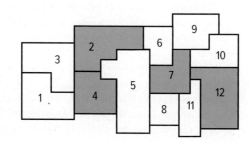

The discussion of sampling methods in the preceding sections did not include all the sampling methods available to a researcher. Should you become involved in a major research project in marketing, finance, accounting, or other areas, you would need to consult books devoted solely to sample theory and sample design.

---

self-review 7–2

Refer to self-review 7–1 and the class roster. Suppose a systematic random sample will select every ninth student enrolled in the class. Initially, the fourth student on the list was selected at random. That student is numbered 03. Remembering that the random numbers start with 00, which students will be chosen to be members of the sample?

EXERCISES

1. The following is a list of Marco's Pizza stores in Lucas County. Also noted is whether the store is corporate-owned (C) or manager-owned (M). A sample of four locations is to be selected and inspected for customer convenience, safety, cleanliness, and other features.

ID No.	Address	Type	ID No.	Address	Type
00	2607 Starr Av	C	12	2040 Ottawa River Rd	C
01	309 W Alexis Rd	C	13	2116 N Reynolds Rd	C
02	2652 W Central Av	C	14	3678 Rugby Dr	C
03	630 Dixie Hwy	M	15	1419 South Av	C
04	3510 Dorr St	C	16	1234 W Sylvania Av	C
05	5055 Glendale Av	C	17	4624 Woodville Rd	M
06	3382 Lagrange St	M	18	5155 S Main	M
07	2525 W Laskey Rd	C	19	106 E Airport Hwy	C
08	303 Louisiana Av	C	20	6725 W Central	M
09	149 Main St	C	21	4252 Monroe	C
10	835 S McCord Rd	M	22	2036 Woodville Rd	C
11	3501 Monroe St	M	23	1316 Michigan Av	M

a. The random numbers selected are 08, 18, 11, 54, 02, 41, and 54. Which stores are selected?

b. Use the table of random numbers to select your own sample of locations.

c. A sample is to consist of every seventh location. The number 03 is the starting point. Which locations will be included in the sample?

d. Suppose a sample is to consist of three locations, of which two are corporate owned, and one is manager owned. Select a sample accordingly.

Classify the situations in questions 2 to 4 as stratified random sampling, systematic random sampling, or cluster sampling.

A college decided to survey its students to see how they felt about using a computer in all classes, and how much extra tuition they would be willing to pay for the service.

2. The college made a list of all of the classes registered in the semester and then randomly selected 25 classes. All students in the selected 25 classes were surveyed.

3. The college determined that of its 10 000 students, 500 surveys would be sufficient to achieve satisfactory results. The students attending in that semester were sorted according to their student number, and every 20th student on the list was selected for the survey.

4. The college decided to survey the students according to their programs of study. A random sample was selected from each program.

LO7-2 7.3 SAMPLING "ERROR"

The previous section discussed sampling methods that are used to select a sample that is a fair or unbiased representation of the population. In each method, the selection of every possible sample of a specified size from a population has a known chance or probability. This is another way to describe an unbiased sampling method.

Samples are used to estimate population characteristics. For example, the mean of a sample is used to estimate the population mean. However, since the sample is a part or portion of the population, it is unlikely that the sample mean would be *exactly equal* to the population mean. Similarly, it is unlikely that the sample standard deviation would be *exactly equal* to the population standard deviation. We can therefore expect a difference between a *sample statistic* and its corresponding *population parameter*. This difference is called **sampling error.**

The following example clarifies the idea of sampling error:

Sampling error The difference between a sample statistic and its corresponding population parameter.

Example	Refer to the previous example of Jane and Joe Miley, who operate a B&B called the Foxtrot Inn. The population is the number of rooms rented each of the 30 nights in June. Find the mean of the population. Use **Excel** or other means to select three random samples of five nights. Calculate the mean of each sample and compare it to the population mean. What is the sampling error in each case?
Solution	During the month of June there were 94 rentals. So, the mean number of units rented per night is 3.13. This is the population mean. Hence, we designate this value with the Greek letter μ.

$$\mu = \frac{\Sigma x}{N} = \frac{0 + 2 + 3 + \cdots + 3}{30} = \frac{94}{30} = 3.13$$

The first random sample of five nights resulted in the following number of rooms rented: 4, 7, 4, 3, and 1. The mean of this sample is 3.8 rooms, which we designate $\bar{x}_1$. The bar over the x reminds us that it is a sample mean and the subscript 1 indicates that it is the mean of the first sample. The mean is calculated by:

$$\bar{x}_1 = \frac{\Sigma x}{n} = \frac{4 + 7 + 4 + 3 + 1}{5} = \frac{19}{5} = 3.8$$

The sampling error for the first sample is the difference between the population mean (3.13) and the first sample mean (3.8). So, the sampling error is $(3.8 - 3.13) = 0.67$. The second random sample of five nights resulted in the following number of rooms rented: 3, 3, 2, 3, and 6. The mean of this sample is 3.4 rooms, found by:

$$\bar{x}_2 = \frac{\Sigma x}{n} = \frac{3 + 3 + 2 + 3 + 6}{5} = \frac{17}{5} = 3.4$$

The sampling error is: $(3.4 - 3.13) = 0.27$.

In the third random sample, the sampling error was found to be -1.33.

Each of these differences, 0.67, 0.27, and -1.33, is the sampling error made in estimating the population mean. Sometimes, these errors are positive values, indicating that the sample mean overestimated the population mean. Other times, the errors are negative values, indicating the sample mean was less than the population mean.

Random Samples

	A	B	C	D	E	F	G	H
1	June	Rentals			Sample 1	Sample 2	Sample 3	
2	1	0			4	3	0	
3	2	2			7	3	0	
4	3	3			4	2	3	
5	4	2			3	3	3	
6	5	3			1	6	3	
7	6	4		Totals	19	17	9	
8	7	2		Sample means	3.8	3.4	1.8	
9	8	3						
10	9	4						
11	10	7						
12	11	3						
13	12	4						
14	13	4						
15	14	4						
16	15	7						

In this case, where we have a population of 30 values, and a sample size of 5 values, there is a very large number of possible samples—142 506, to be exact! To find this value, use the combination formula (4–4) from Chapter 4, with $n = 30$, and $r = 5$. Each of the 142 506 different samples has the same chance of being selected. Each sample may have a different sample mean and, therefore, a different sampling error. The value of the sampling error is based on the particular one of the 142 506 different possible samples selected. Therefore, the sampling errors are random and occur by chance. If you were to determine the sum of these sampling errors over a large number of samples, the result would be very close to zero. This is true because the **sample mean** is an *unbiased estimator* of the population mean. And, if all possible samples were chosen and the sampling errors determined, their sum would be exactly zero.

LO7-3 7.4 SAMPLING DISTRIBUTION OF THE SAMPLE MEAN

In the previous section, we defined sampling error and presented the results when a sample statistic such as the sample mean was compared to the population mean. So, when we use the sample mean to estimate the population mean, how can we determine how accurate the estimate is? How does:

- A quality-control department in a mass-production firm release a shipment of microchips based only on a sample of 10 chips?
- A polling organization make an accurate prediction about a federal or provincial election based on a sample of 2000 registered voters out of a voting population of millions?

Sampling distribution of the sample mean A probability distribution of all possible sample means of a given sample size.

To answer these questions, we first develop a *sampling distribution of the sample mean*.

The sample means in the B&B example varied from one sample to the next. The mean of the first sample of five nights was 3.8 rooms, and the second sample was 3.4 rooms. The population mean was 3.13 rooms. If we organize the means of all possible samples of five days into a probability distribution, the result is called the **sampling distribution of the sample mean**.

The following example illustrates the construction of a sampling distribution of the sample mean:

Example	Schauer Industries has seven production employees (considered the population). The hourly earnings of each employee are given in Table 7–2.

Table 7–2 Hourly Earnings of the Production Employees of Schauer Industries

Employee	Hourly Earnings ($)
Joe	$19
Sam	19
Haley	18
Matt	18
Monida	18
Colton	17
Tom	13

1. What is the population mean?
2. What is the sampling distribution of the sample mean for samples of size 2?
3. What is the mean of the sampling distribution?
4. What observations can be made about the population and the sampling distribution?

Solution

1. The population mean is $17.43, found by:

$$\mu = \frac{\$19 + \$19 + \$18 + \$18 + \$18 + \$17 + \$13}{7} = \$17.43$$

We identify the population mean with the Greek letter μ.

2. To arrive at the sampling distribution of the sample mean, we need to select all possible samples of 2 without replacement from the population, then compute the mean of each sample. There are 21 possible samples, found by using formula (4–4).

$$_nC_r = \frac{n!}{r!(n-r)!} = \frac{7!}{2!(7-2)!} = 21$$

where $n = 7$ is the number of items in the population and $r = 2$ is the number of items in the sample.

The 21 sample means from all possible samples of 2 that can be drawn from the population are shown in Table 7–3. These 21 sample means are used to construct a probability distribution. This is the sampling distribution of the sample mean, and it is summarized in Table 7–4.

TABLE 7–3 Sample Means for All Possible Samples of Two Employees

Sample	Employees	Hourly Earnings ($)	Sum ($)	Mean ($)	Sample	Employees	Hourly Earnings ($)	Sum ($)	Mean ($)
1	Joe, Sam	$19, $19	$38	$19.00	12	Haley, Matt	18, 18	36	18.00
2	Joe, Haley	19, 18	37	18.50	13	Haley, Monida	18, 18	36	18.00
3	Joe, Matt	19, 18	37	18.50	14	Haley, Colton	18, 17	35	17.50
4	Joe, Monida	19, 18	37	18.50	15	Haley, Tom	18, 13	31	15.50
5	Joe, Colton	19, 17	36	18.00	16	Matt, Monida	18, 18	36	18.00
6	Joe, Tom	19, 13	32	16.00	17	Matt, Colton	18, 17	35	17.50
7	Sam, Haley	19, 18	37	18.50	18	Matt, Tom	18, 13	31	15.50
8	Sam, Matt	19, 18	37	18.50	19	Monida, Colton	18, 17	35	17.50
9	Sam, Monida	19, 18	37	18.50	20	Monida, Tom	18, 13	31	15.50
10	Sam, Colton	19, 17	36	18.00	21	Colton, Tom	17, 13	30	15.00
11	Sam, Tom	19, 13	32	16.00					

TABLE 7–4 Sampling Distribution of the Sample Mean for r = 2

Sample Mean ($)	Number of Means	Probability
$19.00	1	0.0476
18.50	6	0.2857
18.00	5	0.2381
17.50	3	0.1429
16.00	2	0.0952
15.50	3	0.1429
15.00	1	0.0476
	21	1.0000

3. The mean of the sampling distribution of the sample mean is obtained by summing all sample means and dividing the sum by the number of samples. The mean of all the sample means is usually written $\mu_{\bar{x}}$. The μ reminds us that it is a population value because we have considered all possible samples. The subscript $\bar{x}$ indicates that it is the sampling distribution of the sample mean.

$$\mu_{\bar{x}} = \frac{Sum \ of \ all \ sample \ means}{Total \ number \ of \ samples} = \frac{\$19 + \$18.50 + \$18 \cdots + \$15}{21}$$

$$= \frac{\$366}{21} = \$17.43$$

The population mean is equal to the mean of the sample means.

4. Refer to Chart 7–1, which shows both the population distribution and the distribution of the sample mean. The following observations can be made:

    a. The mean of the distribution of the sample mean ($17.43) is equal to the mean of the population: $\mu = \mu_{\bar{x}}$

    b. The spread in the distribution of the sample mean is less than the spread in the population values. The sample mean ranges from $15.00 to $19.00, but the population values vary from $13.00 up to $19.00. Note that as we increase the size of the sample, the spread of the distribution of the sample mean becomes smaller.

    c. The shape of the sampling distribution of the sample mean and the shape of the frequency distribution of the population values are different. The distribution of the sample mean tends to be more bell shaped and to approximate the normal probability distribution.

CHART 7–1 Distributions of Population Values and Sample Means

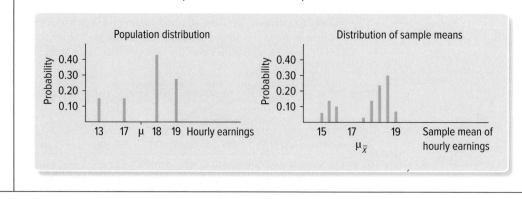

In summary, we took all possible random samples from a population and for each sample calculated a sample statistic (the mean amount earned). This example illustrates important relationships between the population distribution and the sampling distribution of the sample mean:

1. The mean of the sample means is exactly equal to the population mean.
2. The dispersion of the sampling distribution of sample means is narrower than the population distribution.

3. The sampling distribution of the sample means tends to become bell shaped and to approximate the normal probability distribution. This approximation improves with larger samples.

Given a bell-shaped or normal probability distribution, we will be able to apply concepts from Chapter 6 to determine the probability of selecting a sample with a specified sample mean. In the next section, we will show the importance of sample size as it relates to the sampling distribution of sample means.

---

self-review 7–3

The lengths of service of all the executives employed by Standard Chemicals are as follows:

Name	Years
Mr. Snow	20
Ms. Tolson	22
Mr. Kraft	26
Ms. Irwin	24
Mr. Jones	28

(a) Using the combination formula, how many samples of size 2 are possible?
(b) List all possible samples of two executives from the population, and compute their means.
(c) Organize the means into a sampling distribution.
(d) Compare the population mean and the mean of the sample means.
(e) Compare the dispersion in the population with that in the distribution of the sample mean.
(f) A chart portraying the population values follows. Is the distribution of population values normally distributed (bell shaped)?

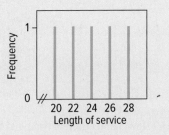

(g) Is the distribution of the sample mean computed in part (c) starting to show some tendency toward being bell shaped?

EXERCISES

5. A population consists of the following four values: 12, 12, 14, and 16.
   a. List all samples of size 2, and compute the mean of each sample.
   b. Compute the mean of the distribution of the sample mean and the population mean. Compare the two values.
   c. Compare the dispersion in the population with that of the sample mean.

6. A population consists of the following five values: 2, 2, 4, 4, and 8.
   a. List all samples of size 2, and compute the mean of each sample.
   b. Compute the mean of the distribution of the sample mean and the population mean. Compare the two values.
   c. Compare the dispersion in the population with that of the sample means.

7. A population consists of the following five values: 12, 12, 14, 15, and 20.
    a. List all samples of size 3, and compute the mean of each sample.
    b. Compute the mean of the distribution of the sample mean and the population mean. Compare the two values.
    c. Compare the dispersion in the population with that of the sample means.

8. A population consists of the following five values: 0, 0, 1, 3, and 6.
    a. List all samples of size 3, and compute the mean of each sample.
    b. Compute the mean of the distribution of the sample mean and the population mean. Compare the two values.
    c. Compare the dispersion in the population with that of the sample means.

9. In the law firm Tybo and Associates, there are six partners. Listed below is the number of cases each associate actually tried in court last month:

Associate	Number of Cases
Ruud	3
Austin	6
Sass	3
Palmer	3
Wilhelms	0
Schueller	1

    a. How many different samples of size 3 are possible?
    b. List all possible samples of size 3, and compute the mean number of cases in each sample.
    c. Compare the mean of the distribution of the sample mean to the population mean.
    d. On a chart similar to Chart 7–1, compare the dispersion in the population with that of the sample means.

10. There are five sales representatives at Mid-Motors Ford. The five representatives and the number of cars they sold last week are as follows:

Sales Representative	Cars Sold
Peter Hankish	8
Connie Stallter	6
Ron Eaton	4
Ted Barnes	10
Peggy Harmon	6

    a. How many different samples of size 2 are possible?
    b. List all possible samples of size 2, and compute the mean of each sample.
    c. Compare the mean of the sampling distribution of the sample mean with that of the population.
    d. On a chart similar to Chart 7–1, compare the dispersion in the sample mean with that of the population.

LO7-4   The Central Limit Theorem

Central limit theorem If all samples of a particular size are selected from any population, the sampling distribution of the sample mean is approximately a normal distribution. This approximation improves with larger samples.

In this section, we examine the **central limit theorem**. Its application to the sampling distribution of the sample mean, introduced in the previous section, allows us to use the normal probability distribution to create confidence intervals for the population mean (described in Chapter 8) and perform tests of hypothesis (described in Chapter 9). The central limit theorem states that for large random samples, the shape of the sampling distribution of the sample mean is close to the normal probability distribution. The approximation is more accurate for large samples than for small samples. This is one of the most useful conclusions in statistics. We can reason about the distribution of the sample mean with absolutely no information about the shape of the population distribution from which the sample is taken. In other words, the central limit theorem is true for all distributions.

If the population follows a normal probability distribution, then for any sample size the sampling distribution of the sample mean will also be normal. If the population distribution is symmetric (but not normal), you will see the normal shape of the distribution of the sample mean emerge with samples as small as 10. However, if you start with a distribution that is skewed or has thick tails, it may require samples of 30 or more to observe the normality feature. This concept is summarized in Chart 7–2 for various population shapes. Observe the convergence to a normal distribution regardless of the shape of the population distribution.

CHART 7–2 Results of the Central Limit Theorem for Several Populations

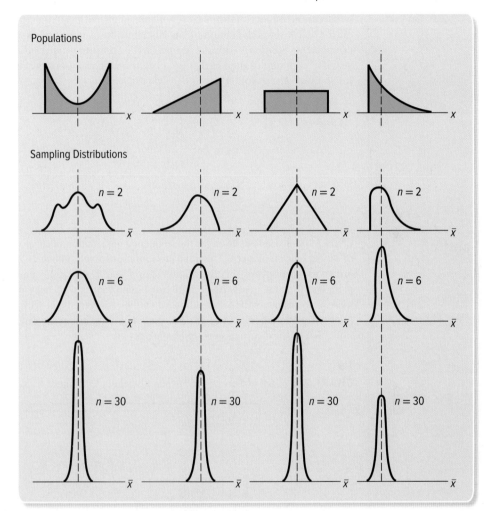

The idea that the distribution of the sample means from a population that is not normal will converge to normality is also illustrated in Charts 7–3, 7–4, and 7–5. We will discuss this example in more detail shortly, but Chart 7–3 is a graph of a frequency distribution that is positively skewed. There are many possible samples of 5 that might be selected from this population. Suppose that we randomly select 25 samples of 5 each and compute the mean of each sample. These results are shown in Chart 7–4. Note that the shape of the distribution of the sample means has changed from the shape of the original population, even though we selected only 25 of the many possible samples. To put it another way, we selected 25 random samples of 5 each from a population that is positively skewed and found the distribution of the sample mean has changed from the shape of the population. As we take larger samples, that is, $n = 20$ instead of $n = 5$, we will find the distribution of the sample mean will approach the normal distribution. Chart 7–5 shows the results of 25 random samples of 20 observations each from the same population. Observe the clear trend toward the normal probability distribution. This is the point of the central limit theorem. Any sampling distribution of the sample mean will move toward a normal distribution as we increase the sample size. The following example will demonstrate this condition:

Example

Ed Spence began his sprocket business 20 years ago. The business has grown over the years and now employs 40 people. Spence Sprockets Inc. faces some major decisions regarding health care for these employees. Before making a final decision on which health care plan to purchase, Ed decides to form a committee of five representative employees. The committee will be asked to study the health care issue carefully and make a recommendation as to what plan best fits the employees' needs. Ed feels the views of newer employees toward health care may differ from those of more experienced employees. If Ed randomly selects this committee, what can he expect in terms of the mean years with Spence Sprockets for those on the committee? How does the shape of the distribution of years of experience of all employees (the population) compare with the shape of the sampling distribution of the mean? The years of service (rounded to the nearest year) of the 40 employees currently on the Spence Sprockets Inc. payroll are as follows:

11	4	18	2	1	2	0	2	2	4
3	4	1	2	2	3	3	19	8	3
7	1	0	2	7	0	4	5	1	14
16	8	9	1	1	2	5	10	2	3

Solution

Chart 7–3 shows a histogram for the frequency distribution of the years of service for the population of 40 current employees. This distribution is positively skewed. Why? Because the business has grown in recent years, the distribution shows that 29 of the 40 employees have been with the company less than six years. Also, there are 11 employees who have worked at Spence Sprockets for more than six years, In particular, four employees have been with the company 12 years or more (count the frequencies above 12). So, there is a long tail in the distribution of service years to the right; that is, the distribution is positively skewed.

CHART 7–3 Years of Service for Spence Sprockets Employees

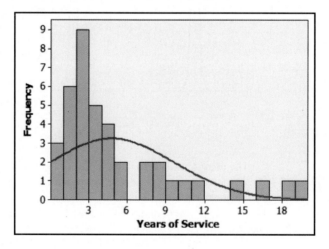

Let's consider the first of Ed Spence's problems. He would like to form a committee of five employees to look into the health care question and suggest what type of health care coverage would be most appropriate for the majority of workers. How should he select the committee? If he selects the committee randomly, what might he expect in terms of mean years of service for those on the committee?

To begin, Ed writes the years of service for each of the 40 employees on pieces of paper and puts them into an old baseball hat. Next, he shuffles the pieces of paper around and randomly selects five slips of paper. The years of service for these five employees are 1, 9, 0, 19, and 14 years. Thus, the mean years of service for these five sampled employees is 8.60 years. How does that compare with the population mean? At this point Ed does not know the population mean, but the number of employees in the population is only 40, so he decides to calculate the mean years of service for *all* his employees. It is 4.8 years, found by adding the lengths of service for *all* the employees and dividing the total by 40.

$$\mu = \frac{11 + 4 + 18 + \cdots + 2 + 3}{40} = 4.80$$

The difference between the sample mean ($\bar{x}$) and the population mean (μ) is called *sampling error*. In other words, the difference of 3.80 years between the population mean of 4.80 and the sample mean of 8.60 is the sampling error. It is due to chance. Thus, if Ed selected these five employees to constitute the committee, their mean years of service would be larger than the population mean.

What would happen if Ed put the five pieces of paper back into the baseball hat and selected another sample? Would you expect the mean of this second sample to be exactly the same as the previous one? Suppose that he selects another sample of five employees and finds the years of service in this sample to be 7, 4, 4, 1, and 3. This sample mean is 3.80 years. The result of selecting 25 samples of five employees each is shown in Table 7–5 and Chart 7–4. There are actually 658 008 possible samples of 5 from the population of 40 employees, found by the combination formula (4–4) for 40 things taken 5 at a time. Note the difference in the shape of the population and the distribution of these sample means. The population of the years of service for employees (see Chart 7–3) is positively skewed, but the distribution of these 25 sample means does not reflect the same positive skew. There is also a difference in the range of the sample means versus the range of the population. The population ranged from 0 to 19 years, whereas the sample means range from 1.6 to 8.6 years.

TABLE 7–5 Twenty-Five Random Samples of Five Employees

Sample I.D.	Sample Data					Sample Mean
A	1	9	0	19	14	8.6
B	7	4	4	1	3	3.8
C	8	19	8	2	1	7.6
D	4	18	2	0	11	7.0
E	4	2	4	7	18	7.0
F	1	2	0	3	2	1.6
G	2	3	2	0	2	1.8
H	11	2	9	2	4	5.6
I	9	0	4	2	7	4.4
J	1	1	1	11	1	3.0
K	2	0	0	10	2	2.8
L	0	2	3	2	16	4.6
M	2	3	1	1	1	1.6
N	3	7	3	4	3	4.0
O	1	2	3	1	4	2.2
P	19	0	1	3	8	6.2
Q	5	1	7	14	9	7.2
R	5	4	2	3	4	3.6
S	14	5	2	2	5	5.6
T	2	1	1	4	7	3.0
U	3	7	1	2	1	2.8
V	0	1	5	1	2	1.8
W	0	3	19	4	2	5.6
X	4	2	3	4	0	2.6
Y	1	1	2	3	2	1.8

CHART 7–4 Histogram of Mean Years of Service for 25 Samples of Five Employees

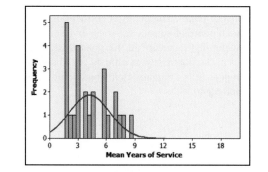

Now let us change the example by increasing the size of each sample from 5 emloyees to 20. Table 7–6 reports the result of selecting 25 samples of 20 employees each and computing their sample means. These sample means are shown graphically in Chart 7–5. Compare the shape of this distribution to the population (see Chart 7–3) and to the distribution of sample means where the sample is $n = 5$ (see Chart 7–4). You should observe two important features:

1. The shape of the distribution of the sample mean is different from that of the population. In Chart 7–3, the distribution of all employees is positively skewed. However, as we select random samples from this population, the shape of the distribution of the sample mean changes. As we increase the size of the sample, the distribution of the sample mean approaches the normal probability distribution. This illustrates the central limit theorem.

TABLE 7–6 Twenty-Five Random Samples of 20 Employees

Sample I.D.								Sample Data (Years of Service)														Mean
A	3	8	3	0	2	1	2	3	11	5	1	3	4	2	7	1	1	2	4	16	3.95
B	2	3	8	2	1	5	2	0	3	1	0	7	1	4	3	11	4	4	3	1	3.25
C	14	5	0	3	2	14	11	9	2	2	1	2	19	1	0	1	4	2	19	8	5.95
D	9	2	1	1	4	10	0	8	4	3	2	1	0	8	1	14	5	10	1	3	4.35
E	18	1	2	2	4	3	2	8	2	1	0	19	4	19	0	1	4	0	3	14	5.35
F	10	4	4	18	3	3	1	0	0	2	2	4	7	10	2	0	3	4	2	1	4.00
G	5	7	11	8	11	18	1	1	16	2	2	16	2	3	2	16	2	2	2	4	6.55
H	3	0	2	0	5	4	5	3	8	3	2	5	1	1	2	9	8	3	16	5	4.25
I	0	0	18	2	1	7	4	1	3	0	3	2	11	7	2	8	5	1	2	3	4.00
J	2	7	2	4	1	3	3	2	5	10	0	1	1	2	9	3	2	19	3	2	4.05
K	7	4	5	3	3	0	18	2	0	4	2	7	2	7	4	2	10	1	1	2	4.20
L	0	3	10	5	9	2	1	4	1	2	1	8	18	1	4	3	3	2	0	4	4.05
M	4	1	2	1	7	3	9	14	8	19	4	4	1	2	0	3	1	2	1	2	4.40
N	3	16	1	2	4	4	4	2	1	5	2	3	5	3	4	7	16	1	11	1	4.75
O	2	19	2	0	2	2	16	2	3	11	9	2	8	0	8	2	7	3	2	2	5.10
P	2	18	16	5	2	2	19	0	1	2	11	4	2	2	1	4	2	0	4	3	5.00
Q	3	2	3	11	10	1	1	5	19	16	7	10	3	1	1	1	2	2	3	1	5.10
R	2	3	1	2	7	4	3	19	9	2	2	1	1	2	2	2	1	8	0	2	3.65
S	2	14	19	1	19	2	8	4	2	2	14	2	8	16	4	7	2	9	0	7	7.10
T	0	1	3	3	2	2	3	1	1	0	3	2	3	5	2	10	14	4	2	0	3.05
U	1	0	1	2	16	1	1	2	5	1	4	1	2	2	2	2	8	9	3	3.25
V	1	9	4	4	2	8	7	1	14	18	1	5	10	11	19	0	3	7	2	11	6.85
W	8	1	9	19	3	19	0	5	2	1	5	3	3	4	1	5	3	1	8	7	5.35
X	4	2	0	3	1	16	1	11	3	3	2	18	2	0	1	5	0	7	2	5	4.30
Y	1	2	1	2	0	2	7	2	4	8	19	2	5	3	3	0	19	2	1	18	5.05

CHART 7–5 Histogram of Mean Years of Service for 25 Samples of 20 Employees

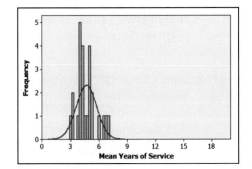

2. There is less dispersion in the sampling distribution of sample mean than in the population distribution. In the population, the years of service ranged from 0 to 19 years. When we selected samples of 5, the sample means ranged from 1.6 to 8.6 years, and when we selected samples of 20, the means ranged from 3.05 to 7.10 years.

We use the symbol $\mu_{\bar{x}}$ to identify the mean of the distribution of the sample mean. The subscript reminds us that the distribution is of the sample mean. It is read "mu sub x bar." We observe that the mean of the sample means, 4.676 years, is very close to the population mean of 4.80.

We can also compare the mean of the sample means to the population mean. The mean of the 25 samples reported in Table 7–6 is 4.676 years.

$$\mu_{\bar{x}} = \frac{3.95 + 3.25 + \cdots + 4.30 + 5.05}{25} = 4.676$$

What should we conclude from this example? The central limit theorem indicates that regardless of the shape of the population distribution, the sampling distribution of the sample mean will move toward the normal probability distribution. The larger the number of observations in each sample, the stronger is the convergence. The Spence Sprockets Inc. example shows how the central limit theorem works. We began with a positively skewed population (see Chart 7–3). Next, we selected 25 random samples of 5 observations, computed the mean of each sample, and finally organized these 25 sample means into a graph (see Chart 7–4). We observe a change in the shape of the sampling distribution of sample mean from that of the population. The movement is from a positively skewed distribution to a distribution that has the shape of the normal probability distribution.

To further illustrate the effects of the central limit theorem, we increased the number of observations in each sample from 5 to 20. We selected 25 samples of 20 observations each and calculated the mean of each sample. Finally, we organized these sample means into a graph (see Chart 7–5). The shape of the histogram in Chart 7–5 is clearly moving toward the normal probability distribution.

If you go back to Chart 5–4 in Chapter 5, which shows several binomial distributions with a "success" proportion of 0.10, you can see yet another demonstration of the central limit theorem. Observe as n increases from 7 through 12 and 20 up to 40 that the profile of the probability distributions moves closer and closer to a normal probability distribution. Chart 7–5 also shows the convergence to normality as n increases. This again reinforces the fact that, as more observations are sampled from any population distribution, the shape of the sampling distribution of the sample mean will get closer to a normal distribution.

The central limit theorem itself does not say anything about the dispersion of the sampling distribution of sample mean or about the comparison of the mean of the sampling distribution of sample mean to the mean of the population. However, in our Spence Sprockets example, we did observe that there was less dispersion in the distribution of the sample mean than in the population distribution by noting the difference in the range in the population and the range of the sample means. We observe that the mean of the sample means is close to the mean of the population. It can be demonstrated that the mean of the sampling distribution is the population mean, $\mu_{\bar{x}} = \mu$, and if the standard deviation in the population is σ, the standard deviation of the sample means is $\sigma/\sqrt{n}$, where n is the number of observations in each sample. We refer to $\sigma/\sqrt{n}$ as the **standard error of the mean.** Its longer name is actually the *standard deviation of the sampling distribution of the sample mean.*

STANDARD ERROR OF THE MEAN $\sigma_{\bar{x}} = \dfrac{\sigma}{\sqrt{n}}$ [7–1]

In this section, we also came to other important conclusions.

1. The mean of the distribution of the sample mean will be *exactly* equal to the population mean if we are able to select all possible samples of a particular size from a given population. That is:

$$\mu = \mu_{\bar{x}}$$

Even if we do not select all samples, we can expect the mean of the distribution of the sample mean to be close to the population mean.

2. There will be less dispersion in the sampling distribution of the sample mean than in the population. If the standard deviation of the population is σ, the standard deviation of the distribution of the sample mean is $\sigma/\sqrt{n}$. Note that when we increase the size of the sample, the standard error of the mean decreases.

self-review 7–4

Refer to the Spence Sprockets Inc. data. Select 10 random samples of five employees each. Use the methods described earlier in the chapter and the Table of Random Numbers (see Appendix B.5) to find the employees to include in the sample. Compute the mean of each sample and plot the sample means on a chart similar to Chart 7–3. What is the mean of your 10 sample means?

EXERCISES

11. Appendix B.5 is a table of random numbers. Hence, each digit from 0 to 9 has the same likelihood of occurrence.
    a. Draw a graph showing the population distribution. What is the population mean?
    b. Following are the first 10 rows of five digits from Appendix B.5. Assume that these are 10 random samples of five values each. Determine the mean of each sample and plot the means on a chart similar to Chart 7–3. Compare the mean of the sampling distribution of the sample mean with the population mean.

0	2	7	1	1
9	4	8	7	3
5	4	9	2	1
7	7	6	4	0
6	1	5	4	5
1	7	1	4	7
1	3	7	4	8
8	7	4	5	5
0	8	9	9	9
7	8	8	0	4

12. The Scrapper Elevator Company has 20 sales representatives who sell the company's product throughout the United States and Canada. The number of units sold by each representative is listed below. Assume these sales figures to be the population values.

2	3	2	3	3	4	2	4	3	2	2	7	3	4	5	3	3	3	3	5

    a. Draw a graph showing the population distribution.
    b. Compute the mean of the population.
    c. Select five random samples of five each. Compute the mean of each sample. Use the methods described in this chapter and Appendix B.5 to determine the items to be included in the sample.

    d. Compare the mean of the sampling distribution of the sample mean to the population mean. Would you expect the two values to be about the same?

    e. Draw a histogram of the sample means. Do you notice a difference in the shape of the distribution of sample means compared with the population distribution?

13. Consider all of the coins (nickels, quarters, loonies, etc.) in your pocket or purse as a population. Make a frequency table beginning with the current year and counting backward to record the ages (in years) of the coins. For example, if the current year is 2017, then a coin with 2015 on it is two years old.

    a. Draw a histogram or other graph showing the population distribution.

    b. Randomly select five coins, and record the mean age of the sampled coins. Repeat this sampling process 20 times. Now draw a histogram or other graph showing the distribution of the sample means.

    c. Compare the shapes of the two distributions.

14. Consider the digits in the phone numbers on a randomly selected page of your local phone book a population. Make a frequency table of the last four digits of 30 random phone numbers. For example, if a phone number is 555-9704, record 9704.

    a. Draw a histogram or other graph of this population distribution.

    b. Record the sample mean of the final four digits (9704 has a mean of 5). Draw a histogram or other graph showing the distribution of the sample means.

    c. Compare the shapes of the two distributions.

LO7-5 7.5 USING THE SAMPLING DISTRIBUTION OF THE SAMPLE MEAN

The previous discussion is important because most business decisions are made on the basis of sampling results. Here are some examples:

1. Arm and Hammer Company wants to ensure that its laundry detergent actually contains 2.95 litres (L), as indicated on the label. Historical summaries from the filling process indicate the mean amount per container is 2.95 L and the standard deviation is 0.025 L. The quality control technician checked 40 containers in her routine morning sample test and found the mean amount per container to be 2.930 L. Should the technician shut down the filling operation, or is the sampling error reasonable?

2. A. C. Nielsen Company provides information to organizations advertising on television. Prior research indicates that adult Americans watch an average of 6.0 hours per day of television. The standard deviation is 1.5 hours. For a sample of 50 adults, would it be likely that we could randomly select a sample and find that they watch an average of 6.5 hours of television per day? Advertisers are especially interested in these viewing habits.

3. Haughton Elevator Company wishes to develop specifications for the number of people who can ride in a new oversized elevator. Suppose the mean weight for an adult is 73 kilograms (kg) and the standard deviation is 7 kg. However, the distribution of weights does not follow a normal probability distribution. It is positively skewed. What is the likelihood that for a sample of 30 adults their mean weight is 77 kg or more? Safety inspectors and insurance companies would be especially interested in these results.

We can answer the questions in each of these situations using the ideas discussed in the previous section. In each case, we have a population with information about its mean and standard deviation. Using this information and sample size, we can determine the distribution of sample means and compute the probability that a sample mean will fall within a certain range. The sampling distribution will be normally distributed under two conditions:

1. When the samples are taken from populations known to follow the normal distribution. In this case, the size of the sample is not a factor.

2. When the shape of the population distribution is not known or the shape is known to be nonnormal, sample size is important. In general, the sampling distribution will be normally distributed as the sample size approaches infinity. In practice, a sampling distribution will be close to a normal distribution with samples of at least 30 observations. We should point out that the number 30 is a guideline that has evolved over the years. In this case, the central limit theorem guarantees the sampling distribution of the mean follows a normal distribution.

We use formula (6–4), from the previous chapter to convert any normal distribution to the standard normal distribution. Using formula (6-4) to compute z-values, we can use the standard normal table, Appendix B.1, to find the probability that an observation is within a specific range. The formula for finding a z-value is:

$$z = \frac{x - \mu}{\sigma}$$

In this formula, x is the value of the *random variable*, μ is the population mean, and σ is the population standard deviation.

However, most business decisions refer to a sample—not just one observation. So, we are interested in the distribution of $\bar{x}$, the sample mean, instead of x, the value of one observation. That is the first change we make in formula (6–4). The second is that we use the standard error of the mean of n observations instead of the population standard deviation. That is, we use $\sigma/\sqrt{n}$ in the denominator rather than σ. Therefore, to find the likelihood of a sample mean with a specified range, we first use the following formula to find the corresponding z-value. Then, we use Appendix B.1 or statistical software to locate the probability.

| FINDING THE z-VALUE OF $\bar{x}$ WHEN THE POPULATION STANDARD DEVIATION IS KNOWN | $z = \dfrac{\bar{x} - \mu}{\sigma/\sqrt{n}}$ | [7–2] |

The following example will show the application:

Example	The quality control department for Cola Inc. maintains records regarding the amount of cola in its "Jumbo" bottle. The actual amount of cola in each bottle is critical but varies a small amount from one bottle to the next. Cola Inc. does not wish to underfill the bottles because it will have a problem with truth in labelling. However, it cannot overfill each bottle because it would be giving cola away, hence reducing its profits. Its records indicate that the amount of cola follows a normal probability distribution. The mean amount per bottle is 1 L and the population standard deviation is 12.8 millilitres (mL). At 8 a.m. today, the quality control technician randomly selected 16 bottles from the filling line. The mean amount of cola contained in the bottles is 1.006 L. Is this an unlikely result? Is it likely the process is putting too much cola in the bottles?
Solution	We can use the results of the previous section to find the likelihood that we could select a sample of 16 (n) bottles from a normal population with a mean of 1 L (μ) and a population standard deviation of 12.8 mL (σ) and find the sample mean to be 1.006 L ($\bar{x}$). We use formula 7–2 to find the value of z.

$$z = \frac{\bar{x} - \mu}{\sigma/\sqrt{n}} = \frac{1006 - 1000}{12.8/\sqrt{16}} = 1.875$$

The numerator of this equation, $\bar{x} - \mu = 1006 - 1000 = 6$ mL, is the sampling error. The denominator, $\sigma/\sqrt{n} = 12.8/\sqrt{16} = 3.2$ mL is the standard error of the sampling distribution of the sample mean. So, the z-values express the sampling error in standard units, that is, the standard error.

Next, we compute the likelihood of a z-value greater than 1.88. In Appendix B.1, locate the probability corresponding to a z-value of 1.88. It is 0.4699. The likelihood of a z-value greater than 1.88 is 0.0301, found by $0.5 - 0.4699 = 0.0301$.

What do we conclude? It is unlikely, about a 3% chance, we would select a sample of 16 observations from a normal population with a mean of 1 L and a population standard deviation of 12.8 mL and find the sample mean equal to or greater than 1.006 L. We conclude that the process is putting too much cola in the bottles. The quality control technician should contact the production supervisor about reducing the amount of cola in each bottle. This information is summarized in Chart 7–6.

CHART 7–6 Sampling Distribution of the Mean Amount of Cola in a Jumbo Bottle

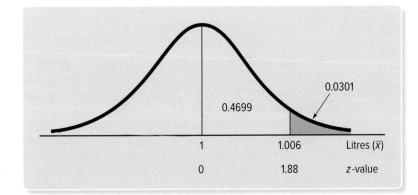

---

self-review 7–5

Refer to the Cola Inc. information. Suppose the quality technician selected a sample of 16 Jumbo Cola bottles that averaged 0.996 L. What can you conclude about the filling process?

EXERCISES

15. A normal population has a mean of 60 and a standard deviation of 12. You select a random sample of 9. Compute the probability the sample mean is:
  a. Greater than 63.
  b. Less than 56.
  c. Between 56 and 63.

16. A normal population has a mean of 75 and a standard deviation of 5. You select a sample of 40. Compute the probability that the sample mean is:
  a. Less than 74.
  b. Between 74 and 76.
  c. Between 76 and 77.
  d. Greater than 77.

17. The mean rent for a one-bedroom apartment in Southern Ontario is $1200 per month, with a standard deviation of $250. The distribution of the monthly costs does not follow the normal distribution. In fact, it is positively skewed. What is the probability of selecting a sample of 50 one-bedroom apartments and finding the mean to be at least $950 per month?

18. According to a study, it takes an average of 330 minutes for taxpayers to prepare, copy, and electronically file an income tax return. The distribution of times follows the normal distribution and the standard deviation is 80 minutes. A random sample of 40 taxpayers is picked.
  a. What is the standard error of the mean in this example?
  b. What is the likelihood the sample mean is greater than 320 minutes?
  c. What is the likelihood the sample mean is between 320 and 350 minutes?
  d. What is the likelihood the sample mean is greater than 350 minutes?
  e. What assumption or assumptions do you need to make about the shape of the population?

LO7-6 7.6 SAMPLING DISTRIBUTION OF THE PROPORTION

The material presented so far in this chapter uses the ratio scale of measurement. That is, we use such variables as incomes, weights, distances, and ages. We now want to consider some situations, such as the following:

- A company representative claims that 45% of Burger King sales are made at the drive-through window.
- A survey of homes in the Windsor area indicated that 85% of the new construction had central air conditioning.

- A recent survey of married men between the ages of 35 and 50 found that 03% felt that both partners should earn a living.

- The career services manager in the local college reports that 80% of its graduates enter the job market in a position related to their field of study.

These examples illustrate the nominal scale of measurement when the outcome is limited to two values. In these cases, an observation is classified into one of two or more mutually exclusive groups. For example, a particular Burger King customer either made a purchase at the drive-through window or did not make a purchase at the drive-through window. A graduate from the local college either entered the job market in a position related to his or her field of study or did not. We can talk about the groups in terms of proportions.

Proportion The fraction, ratio, or percent indicating the part of the sample or the population having a particular trait of interest.

As an example of a **proportion,** a recent survey indicated that 92 out of 100 people favoured the continued use of daylight savings time in the summer. The sample proportion is 92/100, or 0.92, or 92%. If we let $\bar{p}$ represent the sample proportion, x the number of successes, and n the number of items sampled, we can determine a sample proportion as follows:

SAMPLE PROPORTION	$\bar{p} = \dfrac{x}{n}$	[7–3]

The population proportion is identified by p. Therefore, p refers to the percent of successes in the population. Recall from Chapter 5 that p is the proportion of successes in a binomial distribution. Ordinarily, we use Greek letters to identify population parameters and Roman letters to identify sample statistics, but in this case, we use $\bar{p}$ and p, to avoid confusion with the number $\pi = 3.14159\ldots$.

There are many instances when we may be interested only in the proportion of successes in the population, such as the following:

- The proportion of voters who will vote Liberal in the next federal election
- The percentage of customers who preferred the taste of Coke to Pepsi in the recent taste test
- The fraction of students who travel more than 40 km one way to class each day

In each case, we can take a sample and find the sample proportion, $\bar{p}$, which can be used as an estimate for the population, p. If the sample size is large enough, where np and $n(1 - p)$ are greater than 5, then the distribution of all possible sample proportions will be approximately normally distributed.

Sampling distribution of the sampling proportion A probability distribution of all possible sample proportions of a given sample size.

When np and $n(1 - p) > 5$, the **sampling distribution of the sampling proportion** will be approximately normally distributed with a mean of $\mu_p = p$, and the standard error of the proportion, σ_p.

STANDARD ERROR OF THE PROPORTION	$\sigma_P = \sqrt{\dfrac{p(1 - p)}{n}}$	[7–4]

and

FINDING THE z-VALUE OF $\bar{p}$ WHEN THE POPULATION PROPORTION IS KNOWN	$z = \dfrac{\bar{p} - p}{\sqrt{\dfrac{p(1 - p)}{n}}}$	[7–5]

Using the Sampling Distribution of a Proportion

Example	Alpha Corporation receives a shipment of flour every morning from its supplier. The flour is in 40-kg bags, and Alpha will reject any shipment that is more than 5% underweight. The supervisor samples 50 bags with each shipment, and if the bags average more than 5% underweight, the whole shipment is returned to the supplier. What is the probability that in a sample of 150 bags, the supervisor will find that less than 3% are underweight?

Solution	$p = 0.05$ and $n = 150$, so $\sigma_p = \sqrt{\dfrac{0.05\,(1 - 0.05)}{150}} = 0.0178$
	and $z = \dfrac{0.03 - 0.05}{0.0178} = -1.12$

We want to know the probability that the supervisor will find less than 3% underweight, so we are looking for the area to the left of $z = -1.12$. Using the value from Appendix B.1, we find the probability is $(0.5 - 0.3686) = 0.1314$.

---

self-review 7–6   Refer to the Alpha Corporation information. Compute the probability that in a sample of 200, the supervisor will find more than 4% of the bags underweight.

EXERCISES

19. Given $p = 0.45$ and $n = 200$, compute the standard error of the proportion.

20. Given $p = 0.09$ and $n = 50$, compute the standard error of the proportion.

21. Dawson's Repair Service orders parts from an electronic company, which advertises its parts to be no more than 2% defective. What is the probability that Bill Dawson finds three or more parts out of a sample of 50 to be defective?

22. The college cafeteria finds that 30% of students will buy a dessert if it is properly advertised. The cafeteria manager is thinking of hiring an arts student to create a poster of a new apple and ice cream dessert, which could then be displayed at the front entrance to the cafeteria during the lunch hours. Normally, 650 students use the cafeteria during lunch time. What is the probability that more than 35% of the students will buy the apple and ice cream dessert?

23. Ms. Angelina Marie is considering running for mayor of her town for the second time. The first time, she received 75% of the popular vote. What is the probability that in a sample of 300 town residents, at least 240 would vote in favour of her for town mayor for the second time?

24. It has been estimated that 25% of all university students switch majors within their first two years of starting classes. If a random sample of 500 third-year students is taken at a city university, what is an estimate of the probability that 20% or less had switched majors within their first two years?

Chapter Summary

I. There are many reasons for sampling a population.

   A. The results of a sample may adequately estimate the value of the population parameter, thus saving time and money.

   B. It may be too time consuming to contact all members of the population.

   C. It may be impossible to check or locate all the members of the population.

   D. The cost of studying all the items in the population may be prohibitive.

   E. Often, as testing destroys the sampled item, it cannot be returned to the population.

II. In an unbiased or probability sample, all members of the population have a chance of being selected for the sample. There are several probability sampling methods.

   A. In a simple random sample, all members of the population have the same chance of being selected for the sample.

   B. In a systematic sample, a random starting point is selected, and then every kth item thereafter is selected for the sample.

   C. In a stratified sample, the population is divided into several groups, called *strata*, and then a random sample is selected from each stratum.

   D. In cluster sampling, the population is divided into primary units, then samples are drawn from the primary units.

III. The sampling error is the difference between a population parameter and a sample statistic.

IV. The sampling distribution of the sample mean is a probability distribution of all possible sample means of the same sample size.

    A. For a given sample size, the mean of all possible sample means selected from a population is equal to the population mean.

    B. There is less variation in the distribution of the sample mean than in the population distribution.

    C. The standard error of the mean measures the variation in the sampling distribution of the sample mean. The standard error is found by:

$$\sigma_{\bar{x}} = \frac{\sigma}{\sqrt{n}} \qquad\qquad [7\text{--}1]$$

    D. If the population follows a normal distribution, the sampling distribution of the sample mean will also follow a normal distribution for samples of any size. If the population is not normally distributed, the sampling distribution of the sample mean will approach a normal distribution when the sample size is at least 30. Assume the population standard deviation is known. To determine the probability that a sample mean falls in a particular region, use the following formula:

$$z = \frac{\bar{x} - \mu}{\sigma/\sqrt{n}} \qquad\qquad [7\text{--}2]$$

V. A proportion is a ratio, fraction, or percentage that indicates the part of the sample or population that has a particular characteristic.

    1. A sample proportion is found by $\bar{p}$, the number of successes, divided by n, the number of observations.

$$\bar{p} = \frac{x}{n} \qquad\qquad [7\text{--}3]$$

    2. The sampling distribution of the proportion follows a normal distribution if np and $n(1 - p) > 5$.

    3. To determine the probability that a sample proportion falls in a particular region, use the following formula:

$$z = \frac{\bar{p} - p}{\sqrt{\dfrac{p(1 - p)}{n}}} \qquad\qquad [7\text{--}5]$$

Chapter Exercises

25. The retail stores located in the North Towne Square Mall are as follows:

00	GAP	09	M Studios	18	County Seat
01	Montgomery Ward	10	Bootleggers	19	Kid Mart
02	Deb Shop	11	Formal Man	20	Eddie Bauer
03	Frederick's of Hollywood	12	Leather Ltd.	21	Coach House Gifts
04	Petries	13	B Dalton Bookseller	22	Spence Gifts
05	Easy Dreams	14	Pat's Hallmark	23	CPI Photo Finish
06	Summit Stationers	15	Things Remembered	24	Regis Hairstylists
07	E. B. Brown Opticians	16	Pearle Vision Express		
08	Kay-Bee Toy & Hobby	17	Dollar Tree		

    a. If the following random numbers are selected, which retail stores should be contacted for a survey? 11, 65, 86, 62, 06, 10, 12, 77, and 04.

    b. Select a random sample of four retail stores. Use Appendix B.5.

    c. A systematic sampling procedure is to be used. The first store is to be contacted and then every third store. Which stores will be contacted?

26. Canada's Wonderland theme park would like to do a survey to find out how often families visit in a season and how long they stay on each visit. How would you suggest taking this sample? What type of sampling have you described?

27. What is sampling error? Could the value of the sampling error be zero? If it were zero, what would this mean?

28. List the reasons for sampling. Give an example of each reason for sampling.

29. Answer the following questions in one or two well-constructed sentences:
    a. What happens to the standard error of the mean when the sample size is increased?
    b. What happens to the distribution of the sample means when the sample size in increased?
    c. When using the distribution of sample means to estimate the population mean, what is the benefit of using larger sample sizes?

30. A population consists of the following three values: 1, 2, and 3.
    a. List all possible samples of size 2 (including possible repeats), and compute the mean of every sample.
    b. Find the means of the distribution of the sample mean and the population mean. Compare the two values.
    c. Compare the dispersion of the population with that of the sample mean.
    d. Describe the shapes of the two distributions.

31. The commercial banks in the financial district are to be surveyed. Some of them are very large, with assets of more than $500 million; others are medium-sized, with assets between $100 million and $500 million; and the remaining banks have assets of less than $100 million. Explain how you would select a sample of these banks.

32. Plastic Products is concerned about the inside diameter of the plastic PVC pipe it produces. A machine extrudes the pipe, which is then cut into three-metre lengths. About 720 pipes are produced per machine during a two-hour period. How would you go about taking a sample from the two-hour production period?

33. A study of motel facilities in Rock Hill showed there are 25 facilities. The city's convention and visitors bureau is studying the number of rooms at each facility. The results are as follows:

90	72	75	60	75	72	84	72	88	74	105	115	68
74	80	64	104	82	48	58	60	80	48	58	100	0

   a. Using a table of random numbers (see Appendix B.5), select a random sample of five motels from this population.
   b. Obtain a systematic sample by selecting a random starting point among the first five motels and then select every fifth motel.
   c. Suppose the last five motels are "cut-rate" motels. Describe how you would select a random sample of three regular motels and two cut-rate motels.

34. As a part of its customer-service program, WestJet randomly selected 10 passengers from today's 9 A.M. Edmonton–Calgary flight. Each sampled passenger is to be interviewed in depth regarding airport facilities, service, food, and so on. To identify the sample, each passenger was given a number as he or she boarded the aircraft. The numbers started with 001 and ended with 250.
    a. Select 10 usable numbers at random using Appendix B.5.
    b. The sample of 10 could have been chosen using a systematic sample. Choose the first number using Appendix B.5, and then list the numbers to be interviewed.
    c. Evaluate the two methods by giving the advantages and possible disadvantages.
    d. In what other way could a random sample be selected from the 250 passengers?

35. Suppose that your statistics instructor gave six examinations during the semester. You received the following grades (percentage correct): 79, 64, 84, 82, 92, and 77. Instead of averaging the six scores, the instructor indicated he would randomly select two grades and report that grade to the student records office.
    a. How many different samples of two test grades are possible?
    b. List all possible samples of size 2, and compute the mean of each.
    c. Compute the mean of the sample means, and compare it with the population mean.
    d. If you were a student, would you like this arrangement? Would the result be different from dropping the lowest score? Explain.

36. At the downtown office of First National Bank, there are five tellers. Last week, the tellers made the following numbers of errors: 2, 3, 5, 3, and 5.
    a. How many different samples of two tellers are possible?
    b. List all possible samples of size 2, and compute the mean of each.
    c. Compute the mean of the sample means, and compare it with the population mean.

37. The quality control department employs five technicians during the day shift. Listed below are the numbers of times the technicians instructed the production supervisor to shut down the manufacturing process last week:

Technician	Shutdowns
Taylor	4
Hurley	3
Fowler	5
Rousche	3
Telatko	2

a. How many different samples of two technicians are possible from this population?

b. List all possible samples of two observations each, and compute the mean of each sample.

c. Compare the mean of the sample means with the population mean.

d. Compare the shape of the population distribution with the shape of the distribution of the sample means.

38. The Appliance Centre has six sales representatives at its store. Listed below are the numbers of refrigerators sold by the representatives last month:

Sales Representative	Number Sold
Zina Craft	54
Woon Junge	50
Ernie DeBrul	52
Jan Niles	48
Molly Camp	50
Rachel Myak	52

a. How many samples of size 2 are possible?

b. Select all possible samples of two, and compute the mean number sold.

c. Organize the sample means into a frequency distribution.

d. What is the mean of the population? What is the mean of the sample means?

e. What is the shape of the population distribution?

f. What is the shape of the distribution of the sample mean?

39. Power+, produces AA batteries used in remote-controlled toy cars. The mean life of these batteries follows the normal probability distribution with a mean of 35.0 hours and a standard deviation of 5.5 hours. As a part of its testing program, Power+ tests samples of 25 batteries.

a. What can you say about the shape of the distribution of sample mean?

b. What is the standard error of the distribution of the sample mean?

c. What proportion of the samples will have a mean useful life of more than 36 hours?

d. What proportion of the sample will have a mean useful life greater than 34.5 hours?

e. What proportion of the sample will have a mean useful life between 34.5 and 36.0 hours?

40. CRA CDs Inc. wants the mean lengths of the "cuts" on a CD to be 135 seconds (2 minutes and 15 seconds). This will allow the disk jockeys to have plenty of time for commercials within each 10-minute segment. Assume the distribution of the length of the cuts follows a normal distribution with a standard deviation of eight seconds. Suppose that we select a sample of 16 cuts from various CDs sold by CRA CDs Inc.

a. What can we say about the shape of the distribution of the sample mean?

b. What is the standard error of the mean?

c. What percentage of the sample means will be greater than 140 minutes?

d. What percentage of the sample means will be greater than 128 minutes?

e. What percentage of the sample means will be greater than 128 but less than 140 minutes?

41. Recent studies indicate that the typical 50-year-old woman spends $350 per year for personal care products, with a population standard deviation of $45. The distribution of the amounts spent is positively skewed. We select a random sample of 40 women. The mean amount spent for those sampled is $335. What is the likelihood of finding a sample mean this large or larger from the specified population?

42. The mean amount of life insurance per household is $110 000. This distribution is positively skewed. The standard deviation of the population is $40 000.

a. A random sample of 50 households revealed a mean of $112 000. What is the standard error of the mean?

b. Suppose that you selected 50 samples of households. What is the expected shape of the distribution of the sample mean?

   c. What is the likelihood of selecting a sample with a mean of at least $112 000?

   d. What is the likelihood of selecting a sample with a mean of more than $100 000?

   e. Find the likelihood of selecting a sample with a mean of more than $100 000 but less than $112 000.

43. The mean age at which men in Canada marry for the first time is 30.6 years. The standard deviation of the population distribution is 2.5 years. For a random sample of 60 men, what is the likelihood that the age at which they were married for the first time is less than 31.5 years?

44. A recent study by the Island Resort Taxi Drivers Association showed that the mean fare charged for service from the beach to the airport is $21.00 and the standard deviation is $3.50. We select a sample of 15 fares.

   a. What is the likelihood that the sample mean is between $20.00 and $23.00?

   b. What must you assume to make the above calculation?

45. The Crossett Trucking Company claims that the mean mass of its delivery trucks when they are fully loaded is 2700 kg and the standard deviation is 68 kg. Assume that the population follows the normal distribution. Forty trucks are randomly selected and their masses measured. Within what limits will 95% of the sample means occur?

46. The mean amount purchased by each customer at Churchill's Grocery Store is $23.50, with a standard deviation of $5.00. The population is positively skewed. For a sample of 50 customers, answer the following questions:

   a. What is the likelihood the sample mean is at least $25.00?

   b. What is the likelihood the sample mean is greater than $22.50 but less than $25.00?

   c. Within what limits will 90% of the sample means occur?

47. The mean SAT score for Division I student-athletes is 947, with a standard deviation of 205. If you select a random sample of 60 of these students, what is the probability the mean is below 900?

48. Suppose that we roll a fair die two times.

   a. How many different samples are there?

   b. List each of the possible samples, and compute the mean.

   c. On a chart similar to Chart 7–1, compare the distribution of sample means with the distribution of the population.

   d. Compute the mean and standard deviation of each distribution, and compare them.

49. The average grade in a statistics course has been 69, with a standard deviation of 12.5. If a random sample of 50 is selected from this population, what is the probability that the average grade is more than 73?

50. A preliminary survey shows that 35% of college students smoke. In a class of 42 students, what is the probability that more than half the students smoke?

51. A convenience store estimates that 25% of its customers come in to buy milk. What is the probability that out of the next 200 customers, 60 or fewer will buy milk?

52. A manufacturing process produces 5% defective items. What is the probability that in a sample of 50 items:

   a. 10% or more will be defective?

   b. Less than 1% will be defective?

   c. More than 10% or less than 1% will be defective?

53. A retailer claims that 90% of its customers are pleased or very pleased with the customer service. In a survey of 300 customers taken last week, what is the probability that:

   a. 85% or more will be pleased or very pleased with the service?

   b. 92% or more will be pleased or very pleased with the service?

   c. Between 85% and 92% will be pleased or very pleased with the service?

54. Nike's annual report says that the average customer buys 6.5 pairs of sports shoes per year. Suppose that the population standard deviation is 2.1 and that a sample of 81 customers will be examined next year.

   a. What is the standard error of the mean in this experiment?

   b. What is the probability that the sample mean is between 6 and 7 pairs of sports shoes?

   c. What is the probability that the difference between the sample mean and the population mean is less than 0.25 pairs?

   d. What is the likelihood the sample mean is greater than 7 pairs?

55. The owner of the Coffee Bean Cafe states that she sells 500 cupcakes per day. Along with staple flavours, such as double chocolate and vanilla bean, which are always available, each day of the week has its own special—such as lemon—which is only baked on Tuesday. Therefore, cupcake sales are fairly consistent from day to day, and the number sold follows a normal probability distribution, with a standard deviation of 20 cupcakes. A random sample is taken over 36 days.

a. What is the standard error of the mean?

b. What is the probability that the average number of cupcakes sold is between 490 and 510 cupcakes?

c. What is the probability that the average number of cupcakes sold is more than 490 cupcakes?

56. A recent survey reported that the average person consumes 6 glasses of water per day (250 mL per glass). Assume the standard deviation of water consumption is 1.5 glasses per day and the consumption rate follows a normal probability distribution. A sample of 100 students is taken.

a. What is the standard error of the mean?

b. What is the probability that the average student drinks between 6 and 6.25 glasses of water per day?

c. What is the probability that the average student drinks less than 5.8 glasses of water per day?

57. A recent report indicated a typical family of five spends $650 per month on food. Assume the distribution of food expenditures for a family of five follows a normal distribution, with a mean of $650 and a standard deviation of $120. A sample of 64 is taken.

a. What percentage of the families spends more than $675 per month on food?

b. What percentage of the families spends less than $660 per month on food?

c. What percentage spends between $660 and $670 per month on food?

d. What percentage spends less than $650 or more than $675 per month on food?

58. Human Resource Consulting (HRC) surveyed a random sample of 60 construction companies to find information on the costs of their health care plans. One of the items being tracked is the annual deductible that employees must pay. The BayShore Construction Company reports that historically the mean deductible amount per employee is $502, with a standard deviation of $100.

a. Compute the standard error of the sample mean for HRC.

b. What is the chance HRC finds a sample mean between $477 and $527?

c. Calculate the likelihood that the sample mean is between $492 and $512.

d. What is the probability the sample mean is greater than $550?

59. An economist uses the price of milk as a measure of inflation. She finds that the average price is $3.50 per four litres, and the population standard deviation is $0.33. You decide to sample 40 stores, collect their price for four litres of milk, and compute the mean price for the sample.

a. What is the standard error of the mean in this experiment?

b. What is the probability that the sample mean is between $3.46 and $3.54?

c. What is the probability that the difference between the sample mean and the population mean is less than 0.01?

d. What is the likelihood the sample mean is greater than $3.60?

60. Over the past decade, the mean number of members of the Information Systems Security Association who have experienced a denial-of-service attack each year is 510, with a standard deviation of 14.28 attacks. Suppose that nothing in this environment changes.

a. What is the likelihood this group will suffer an average of more than 600 attacks in the next 10 years?

b. Compute the probability that the mean number of attacks over the next 10 years is between 500 and 600.

c. What is the possibility that they will experience an average of less than 500 attacks over the next 10 years?

61. A marketing survey was conducted to estimate the proportion of homemakers who would recognize the brand name of a cleanser based on the shape and the colour of the container. Of the 1400 homemakers sampled, 420 were able to identify the brand by name.

a. Estimate the value of the population proportion.

b. Estimate the value of the standard error of proportions.

c. What is the probability that less than 390 homemakers would recognize the brand name of a cleanser based on the shape and the colour of the container?

62. A total of 2000 college and university students responded to a provincial survey concerning the number of paid hours they worked during the week while registered in classes. Of particular interest was the number of students who held at least two part-time jobs at the same time while attending school. The results follow:

Number of Jobs	Number of Students Responding Yes
1	925
2	600
2+	150

    a. Estimate the value of the population proportion of the number of students who held at least two part-time jobs while attending school.

    b. Estimate the value of the standard error of proportions for part (a).

    c. What is the probability that the number of students holding at least two part-time jobs while attending school is between 700 and 725 students.

63. The Canadian operation of the Customer Care Department of a global pharmaceutical company receives between 600 and 700 calls per day. The department's objective is that no more than 5% of the calls are transferred to voice mail. In a random sample of 45 days:

    a. What is the probability that less than 2% go to voice mail?

    b. What is the probability that more than 10% of the calls go to voice mail?

    c. What is the probability that no calls go to voice mail?

64. The Tea Delish Company claims that 40% of its customers are between 35 to 45 years of age. In a random sample of 250 customers:

    a. What is the probability that between 100 and 115 customers were in the 35 to 45 years age range?

    b. What is the probability that more than 120 customers were in the 35 to 45 years age range?

    c. What is the probability that fewer than 90 or more than 120 customers were in the 35 to 45 years age range?

Data Set Exercises

Questions marked with 🏹 have data sets available on McGraw-Hill's online resource for *Basic Statistics*.

65. Refer to the Real Estate Data—Halifax Area online, which reports information on home listings.

    a. Compute the mean and standard deviation of the distribution of the list prices for the homes. Assume this to be the population. Develop a histogram of the data. Would it seem reasonable from this histogram to conclude that the population of list prices follows a normal distribution?

    b. Select a sample of 35 homes. Compute the mean of the sample. Determine the likelihood of finding a sample mean that is this large or larger from the population.

66. Refer to the Real Estate Data—Saskatoon online, which reports information on home listings.

    a. Compute the mean and standard deviation of the distribution of the list prices for the homes. Assume this to be the population. Develop a histogram of the data. Would it seem reasonable from this histogram to conclude that the population of list prices follows a normal distribution?

    b. Select a sample of 32 homes. Compute the mean of the sample. Determine the likelihood of finding a sample mean that is this large or larger from the population.

Case

Refer to the Whitner Autoplex data on Connect, which include information on the selling prices of vehicles sold at Rob Whitner's dealership.

1.   Calculate the mean and standard deviation for the selling prices. Assume this to be the population. Develop a histogram of the data. Would it seem reasonable from this histogram to conclude that the population of selling prices follows a normal distribution?

2.   Select a sample of 35 selling prices. Calculate the mean of the sample. Determine the likelihood of finding a sample mean that is this large or larger from the population.

Practice Test

Part I Objective

1. In a _____, each item in the population has the same chance of being included in the sample.

2. A sample should have at least how many observations? (10, 30, 100, 1000, no size restriction) _____

3. When a population is divided into groups based on some characteristic, such as a region of the country, the groups are called _____.

4. The difference between a sample mean and the population mean is the _____.

5. A probability distribution of all possible samples means for a particular sample size is the _____.

6. Suppose a population consisted of 10 items and we wished to list all possible samples of size 3. How many samples are there? _____

7. What is the name given to the standard deviation of the distribution of sample means? _____

8. The mean of all possible sample means is _____ the population mean. (always larger than, always smaller than, always equal to, or not a constant relationship with)

9. If we increase the sample size from 10 to 20, the standard error of the mean will _____. (increase, decrease, stay the same, or the result is not predictable)

10. If a population follows the normal distribution, what will be the shape of the distribution of sample means? _____

Part II Problems

1. Suppose that an adult spends an average (mean) of 12.2 minutes (per day) in the shower. The distribution of times follows the normal distribution with a population standard deviation of 2.3 minutes. What is the likelihood that the mean time in the shower per day for a sample of 12 adults is 11 minutes or less?

Computer Commands

1. **Excel** commands to select a simple random sample for the B&B example are as follows:

   a. Select **Data, Data Analysis, Sampling,** and click **OK.**

   b. For **Input Range** insert *B1:B31.* Check the **Labels** box. Select **Random,** and enter the sample size for the

   Number of Samples, in this case 5. Click the **Output Range,** and indicate the place in the spreadsheet you want the sample information. Note that your sample results will differ from those in the text. Also, recall that **Excel** samples with replacement, so it is possible for the same day to appear more than once in the sample.

Answers to Self-Reviews

7–1 **(a)** Students selected are Price, Detley, and Molter.
   (b) Answers will vary.
   (c) Skip it, and move to the next random number.

7–2 The students selected are Berry, Francis, Kopp, Poteau, and Swetye.

7–3 **(a)** 10, found by:

$$_5C_2 = \frac{5!}{2!(5-2)!}$$

(b)

	Service	Sample Mean
Snow, Tolson	20, 22	21
Snow, Kraft	20, 26	23
Snow, Irwin	20, 24	22
Snow, Jones	20, 28	24
Tolson, Kraft	22, 26	24
Tolson, Irwin	22, 24	23
Tolson, Jones	22, 28	25
Kraft, Irwin	26, 24	25
Kraft, Jones	26, 28	27
Irwin, Jones	24, 28	26

(c)

Mean	Number	Probability
21	1	0.10
22	1	0.10
23	2	0.20
24	2	0.20
25	2	0.20
26	1	0.10
27	1	0.10
	10	1.00

(d) Identical: population mean, μ, is 24, and mean of sample means $\mu_{\bar{x}}$ is also 24.

(e) Sample means range from 21 to 27. Population values go from 20 to 28.

(f) Non-normal.

(g) Yes.

7–4 The answers will vary. Here is one solution:

Sample Number

	1	2	3	4	5	6	7	8	9	10	
	8	2	2	19	3	4	0	4	1	2	
	19	1	14	9	2	5	8	2	14	4	
	8	3	4	2	4	4	1	14	4	1	
	0	3	2	3	1	2	16	1	2	3	
	2	1	7	2	19	18	18	16	3	7	
Total	37	10	29	35	29	33	43	37	24	17	mean
$\bar{x}$	7.4	2	5.8	7.0	5.8	6.6	8.6	7.4	4.8	3.4	= 5.88

7–5 $z = \dfrac{996 - 1000}{12.8/\sqrt{6}} = -1.25$

The probability that z is greater than -1.25 is: $0.3944 + 0.5 = 0.8944$. There is more than an 89% chance that the filling operation will produce bottles with at least 0.996 L.

7–6 $p = 0.05$ and $n = 200$, so, $\sigma_p = \sqrt{\dfrac{0.05(1 - 0.05)}{200}} = 0.154$

and $z = \dfrac{0.04 - 0.05}{0.0154} = -0.65$.

The probability is: 0.7422 ($0.5 + 0.2422$).

Tanya Constantine / age fotostock

A restaurant group collected information on the number of meals eaten outside the home per week by young married couples. A survey of 60 couples showed that the sample mean number of meals eaten outside the home was 2.76 meals per week, with a standard deviation of 0.75 meals per week. Construct a 97% confidence interval for the population mean. (Exercise 44, LO8-3)

LEARNING OBJECTIVES

When you have completed this chapter, you will be able to:

LO8-1 Compute and interpret a point estimate of a population mean.

LO8-2 Compute and interpret a confidence interval for a population mean when the population standard deviation is known.

LO8-3 Compute and interpret a confidence interval for a population mean when the population standard deviation is unknown.

LO8-4 Compute and interpret a confidence interval for a population proportion.

LO8-5 Calculate the required sample size to estimate a a population mean or population proportion.

LO8-6 Adjust a confidence interval for a finite population.

8.1 INTRODUCTION

The previous chapter began our discussion of statistical inference. It introduced both the reasons for and the methods of sampling. The reasons for sampling were:

- Contacting the entire population is too time consuming.
- Studying all the items in the population is often too expensive.
- The sample results are usually adequate.
- Certain tests are destructive.
- Checking all items is physically impossible.

There are several methods of sampling. Simple random sampling is the most widely used method. With this type of sampling, each member of the population has the same chance of being selected to be a part of the sample. Other methods of sampling include systematic sampling, stratified sampling, and cluster sampling.

Chapter 7 assumes that information about the population, such as the mean, the standard deviation, or the shape of the population, is known. In most business situations, such information is not available. In fact, the purpose of sampling may be to estimate some of these values. For example, you select a sample from a population and use the mean of the sample to estimate the mean of the population.

This chapter considers several important aspects of sampling. We begin by studying **point estimates**. A point estimate is a single value (point) derived from a sample and used to estimate a population value. For example, suppose that we select a sample of 50 junior executives and asked how many hours they worked last week. Then we compute the mean of this sample of 50 and use the value of the sample mean as a point estimate of the unknown population mean. But a point estimate is a single value. A more informative estimate is to present a range of values in which we expect the population parameter to occur. Such a range of values is called a **confidence interval**.

Frequently in business we need to determine the size of a sample. How many voters should a polling organization contact to forecast the election outcome? How many products do we need to examine to ensure our quality level? This chapter also develops a strategy for determining the appropriate number of observations in the sample.

LO8-1 8.2 POINT ESTIMATE FOR A POPULATION MEAN

Point estimate The statistic, computed from sample information, that is used to estimate the population parameter.

A **point estimate** is a single statistic used to estimate a population parameter. Suppose Best Buy Inc. wants to estimate the mean age of people who purchase LCD HDTVs. They select a random sample of 50 recent purchases, determine the age of each buyer, and compute the mean age of the buyers in the sample. The mean of this sample is a point estimate of the population mean.

The following examples illustrate point estimates of population means:

1. Tourism is a major source of income for many Caribbean countries, such as Barbados. Suppose that the Bureau of Tourism for Barbados wants an estimate of the mean amount spent by tourists visiting the country. It would not be feasible to contact each tourist. Therefore, 500 tourists are randomly selected as they depart the country and asked in detail about their spending while visiting the island. The mean amount spent by the sample of 500 tourists, is an estimate of the unknown population parameter. That is, we let the sample mean serve as an estimate of the population mean.
2. Centex Home Builders Inc. builds quality homes. One of the major concerns of new buyers is the date on which the home will be completed. In recent times, Centex has been telling customers, "Your home will be completed 45 working days from the date we begin installing drywall." The customer relations department at Centex wishes to compare this pledge with recent experience. A sample of 50 homes completed this year revealed the mean number of working days from the start of drywall to the completion of the home was 46.7 days. Is it reasonable to conclude that the population mean is still 45 days and that the difference between the sample mean (46.7 days) and the proposed population mean is sampling error? In other words, is the sample mean significantly different from the population mean?
3. Recent medical studies indicate that exercise is an important part of a person's overall health. The director of human resources at OCF, a large glass manufacturer, wants an estimate of the number of hours per week employees spend exercising. A sample of 70 employees reveals the mean number of hours of exercise last week is 3.3. This value is a point estimate of the unknown population mean.

The sample mean, $\bar{x}$, is not the only point estimate of a population parameter. For example, $\bar{p}$, a sample proportion, is a point estimate of p, the population proportion; and s, the sample standard deviation, is a point estimate of σ, the population standard deviation.

8.3 CONFIDENCE INTERVALS FOR A POPULATION MEAN

Confidence interval A range of values constructed from sample data so that the population parameter is likely to occur within that range at a specified probability. The specified probability is called the *level of confidence*.

A point estimate, however, tells only part of the story. While we expect the point estimate to be close to the population parameter, we would like to measure how close it really is. A **confidence interval** serves this purpose.

For example, we estimate the mean yearly income for construction workers to be $65 000. The range of this estimate might be from $61 000 to $69 000. We can describe how confident we are that the population parameter is in the interval by making a probability statement. We might say, for instance, that we are 90% sure that the mean yearly income of construction workers is between $61 000 and $69 000.

To compute a confidence interval for a population mean, we will consider two situations:

- We use sample data to estimate μ with $\bar{x}$, and the population standard deviation (σ) is known.
- We use sample data to estimate μ with $\bar{x}$, and the population standard deviation is unknown. In this case, we substitute the sample standard deviation (s) for the population standard deviation (σ).

There are important distinctions in the assumptions between these two situations. We first consider the case where σ is known.

LO8-2 Population Standard Deviation (σ) Known

A confidence interval is computed using two statistics: the sample mean, $\bar{x}$, and the standard deviation. From previous chapters, you know that the standard deviation is an important statistic because it measures the dispersion, or variation, of a population or sample distribution. In computing a confidence interval, the standard deviation is used to compute the limits of the confidence interval.

To demonstrate the idea of a confidence interval, we start with one simplifying assumption. That assumption is that we know the value of the population standard deviation, σ. Typically, we know the population standard deviation in situations where we have a long history of collected data. Examples are data from monitoring processes that fill pop bottles or cereal boxes, and the results of SAT tests (Scholastic Aptitude Test; used in some college and university admissions). Knowing σ allows us to simplify the development of a confidence interval because we can use the standard normal distribution from Chapter 7.

Recall that the sampling distribution of the sample mean is the distribution of all sample means, $\bar{x}$, of sample size n from a population. The population standard deviation, σ, is known. From this information, and the central limit theorem, we know that the sampling distribution follows the normal probability distribution with a mean of μ and a standard deviation $\sigma/\sqrt{n}$. Also recall that this value is called the standard error.

The results of the central limit theorem allow us to make the following general confidence interval statements using z-statistics:

1. Ninety-five percent of all confidence intervals computed from random samples selected from a population will contain the population mean. These intervals are computed using a z-statistic equal to 1.96.
2. Ninety-nine percent of all confidence intervals computed from random samples selected from a population will contain the population mean. These intervals are computed using a z-statistic equal to 2.58.

These confidence interval statements provide examples of *levels of confidence* and are called **95% confidence interval** and **99% confidence interval**. The *95%* and *99%* are the levels of confidence and refer to the percentage of similarly constructed intervals that would include the parameter being estimated—in this case, μ, the population mean. The *95%*, for example, refers to the middle 95% of the observations. Therefore, the remaining 5% is equally divided between the two tails.

How are the values of 1.96 and 2.58 obtained? First, let us look for the z-value for a 95% confidence interval. The following diagram and table will help explain this. The table is a partial reproduction of Appendix B.1, the standard normal table. Several rows and columns have been eliminated to allow us to better focus on the rows and columns we need for this example:

1. First, we divide the confidence level in half, so $0.9500/2 = 0.4750$.
2. Next, we find the value 0.4750 in the body of the table. Note that 0.4750 is located in the table at the intersection of a row and a column.
3. Locate the corresponding row value in the left margin, which is 1.9, and the column value in the top margin, which is 0.06. Adding the row and column values gives us a z-value of 1.96.
4. Thus, the probability of finding a z-value between 0 and 1.96 is 0.4750.

Z	0.00	0.01	0.02	0.03	0.04	0.05	0.06	0.07	0.08	0.09
0.0	0.0000	0.0040	0.0080	0.0120	0.0160	0.0199	0.0239	0.0279	0.0319	0.0359
0.1	0.0398	0.0438	0.0478	0.0517	0.0557	0.0596	0.0636	0.0675	0.0714	0.0753
0.2	0.0793	0.0832	0.0871	0.0910	0.0948	0.0987	0.1026	0.1064	0.1103	0.1141
0.3	0.1179	0.1217	0.1255	0.1293	0.1331	0.1368	0.1406	0.1443	0.1480	0.1517
0.4	0.1554	0.1591	0.1628	0.1664	0.1700	0.1736	0.1772	0.1808	0.1844	0.1879
0.5	0.1915	0.1950	0.1985	0.2019	0.2054	0.2088	0.2123	0.2157	0.2190	0.2224
0.6	0.2257	0.2291	0.2324	0.2357	0.2389	0.2422	0.2454	0.2486	0.2517	0.2549
0.7	0.2580	0.2611	0.2642	0.2673	0.2704	0.2734	0.2764	0.2794	0.2823	0.2852
0.8	0.2881	0.2910	0.2939	0.2967	0.2995	0.3023	0.3051	0.3078	0.3106	0.3133
0.9	0.3159	0.3186	0.3212	0.3238	0.3264	0.3289	0.3315	0.3340	0.3365	0.3389
1.0	0.3413	0.3438	0.3461	0.3485	0.3508	0.3531	0.3554	0.3577	0.3599	0.3621
1.1	0.3643	0.3665	0.3686	0.3708	0.3729	0.3749	0.3770	0.3790	0.3810	0.3830
1.2	0.3849	0.3869	0.3888	0.3907	0.3925	0.3944	0.3962	0.3980	0.3997	0.4015
1.3	0.4032	0.4049	0.4066	0.4082	0.4099	0.4115	0.4131	0.4147	0.4162	0.4177
1.4	0.4192	0.4207	0.4222	0.4236	0.4251	0.4265	0.4279	0.4292	0.4306	0.4319
1.5	0.4332	0.4345	0.4357	0.4370	0.4382	0.4394	0.4406	0.4418	0.4429	0.4441
1.6	0.4452	0.4463	0.4474	0.4484	0.4495	0.4505	0.4515	0.4525	0.4535	0.4545
1.7	0.4554	0.4564	0.4573	0.4582	0.4591	0.4599	0.4608	0.4616	0.4625	0.4633
1.8	0.4641	0.4649	0.4656	0.4664	0.4671	0.4678	0.4686	0.4693	0.4699	0.4706
1.9	0.4713	0.4719	0.4726	0.4732	0.4738	0.4744	0.4750	0.4756	0.4761	0.4767
2.0	0.4772	0.4778	0.4783	0.4788	0.4793	0.4798	0.4803	0.4808	0.4812	0.4817
2.1	0.4821	0.4826	0.4830	0.4834	0.4838	0.4842	0.4846	0.4850	0.4854	0.4857
2.2	0.4861	0.4864	0.4868	0.4871	0.4875	0.4878	0.4881	0.4884	0.4887	0.4890
2.3	0.4893	0.4896	0.4898	0.4901	0.4904	0.4906	0.4909	0.4911	0.4913	0.4916
2.4	0.4918	0.4920	0.4922	0.4925	0.4927	0.4929	0.4931	0.4932	0.4934	0.4936

5. Likewise, because the normal distribution is symmetric, the probability of finding a z-value between -1.96 and 0 is also 0.4750.
6. When we add these two probabilities, the probability that a z-value is between -1.96 and 1.96 is 0.9500.

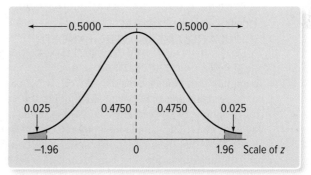

For the 99% level of confidence, we follow the same steps. First, one-half of the desired confidence interval is 0.4950. A search of Appendix B.1 does not reveal this exact value. However, it is between two values, 0.4949 and 0.4951. As in step three, we locate each value in the table. The first, 0.4949, corresponds to a z-value of 2.57 and the second, 0.4951, corresponds to a z-value of 2.58. To be conservative, we will select the larger of the two z-values, 2.58.

How do we determine a 95% confidence interval? The width of the interval is determined by two factors: (1) the level of confidence as described in the previous section, and (2) the size of the standard error of the mean. To find the standard error of the mean, recall from Chapter 7 that the standard error of the mean reports the variation in the distribution of sample means. It is really the standard deviation of sample means. The formula is repeated below:

$$\sigma_{\bar{x}} = \frac{\sigma}{\sqrt{n}}$$

where:

$\sigma_{\bar{x}}$ is the symbol for the standard error of the mean. We use a Greek letter because it is a population value, and the subscript $\bar{x}$ reminds us that it refers to a sampling distribution of the sample means.

σ is the population standard deviation.

n is the number of observations in the sample.

The size of the standard error is affected by two values. The first is the standard deviation of the population. The larger the population standard deviation (σ), the larger is ($\sigma/\sqrt{n}$). If the population is homogeneous, resulting in a small population standard deviation, the standard error will also be small. However, the standard error is also affected by the number of observations in the sample. A large number of observations in the sample will result in a small standard error of estimate, indicating that there is less variability in the sample means.

We can summarize the calculation for a 95% confidence interval using the following formula:

$$\bar{x} \pm 1.96\left(\frac{\sigma}{\sqrt{n}}\right)$$

Similarly a 99% confidence interval is computed as follows:

$$\bar{x} \pm 2.58\left(\frac{\sigma}{\sqrt{n}}\right)$$

The values 1.96 and 2.58 are the z-values corresponding to the 95% and the 99% confidence intervals, respectively. However, we are not restricted to these values. We can select any confidence level between 0% and 100% and find the corresponding value for z. In general, a confidence interval for the population mean when the population follows the normal distribution and the population standard deviation is known is computed by:

CONFIDENCE INTERVAL FOR THE POPULATION MEAN WITH σ KNOWN	$\bar{x} \pm z\dfrac{\sigma}{\sqrt{n}}$	[8–1]

To explain these ideas, consider the following example. Assume that your research involves the annual starting salary of business school graduates. You compute the sample mean to be $45 000 from a sample of 25 graduates. Of course, some graduates will earn less than $45 000, and some will earn more. The sample mean of $45 000 is the point estimate of the population mean. Let us also assume that the population standard deviation is known to be $2000 and follows the normal probability distribution. The confidence interval is the point estimate plus or minus the error of estimation. The standard error is then $400, found by $\sigma/\sqrt{n} = \left(2000/\sqrt{25}\right) = \$400$. The 95% confidence interval is between $44 216 and $45 784, found by:

$$\$45\,000 \pm 1.96(400)$$

The 95% confidence interval estimates that the population mean is between $44 216 and $45 784. Another survey states that the actual population mean is $45 500. In this case, we observe that the population mean of $45 500 is in the 95% confidence interval. But that will not always be the case. Theoretically, if we selected 100 samples of 25 graduates from the population, calculated the sample mean, and developed a confidence interval based on each sample mean, we would expect to find the population mean in about 95 of the 100 intervals. Or, in contrast, about 5 of the intervals would not contain the population mean. From Chapter 7, this is called *sampling error*.

Common *z*-values

Confidence Level	Nearest Probability	z-Value
80%	0.3997	1.28
94%	0.4699	1.88
96%	0.4798	2.05

excel　　　Computer commands to find the *z*-value can be found at the end of the chapter.

The following example details repeated sampling from a population:

Example	A marketing company wishes to have information on the mean income of store managers in the retail industry. A random sample of 256 managers reveals a sample mean of $55 420. The standard deviation of this population is $2150. The company would like answers to the following questions: 1. What is the population mean? 2. What is a reasonable range of values for the population mean? 3. How do we interpret these results?
Solution	Generally, distributions of salary and income are positively skewed because a few individuals earn considerably more than others, thus skewing the distribution in the positive direction. Fortunately, the central limit theorem stipulates the sampling distribution of the mean becomes a normal distribution as the sample sizes increases. In this instance, a sample of 256 middle managers is large enough that the sampling distribution will follow the normal distribution. Now, to answer the questions posed in the example.

1. **What is the population mean?** In this case, we do not know. We do know the sample mean is $55 420. Hence, our best estimate of the unknown population value is the corresponding sample statistic. Thus, the sample mean of $55 420 is a *point estimate* of the unknown population mean.
2. **What is a reasonable range of values for the population mean?** The company decides to use the 95% level of confidence. To determine the corresponding confidence interval, we use formula (8–1).

$$\bar{x} \pm z\frac{\sigma}{\sqrt{n}} = 55\ 420 \pm 1.96\frac{2150}{\sqrt{256}} = 55\ 420 \pm 263$$

The confidence interval limits are $55 157 and $55 683 (the usual practice is to round the endpoints). The ±$263 is called the *margin of error*.
3. **How do we interpret these results?** Suppose that we select many samples of 256 managers, perhaps several hundred. For each sample, we compute the mean and then construct a 95% confidence interval, as we did in the previous section. We could expect about 95% of these confidence intervals to contain the *population* mean. About 5% of the intervals would not contain the population mean annual income μ. However, a particular confidence interval either contains the population parameter or it does not. The following diagram shows the results of selecting samples from the population of store managers in the retail industry, computing the mean of each, and then, using formula (8–1), determining a 95% confidence interval for the population mean. Note that not all intervals include the population mean. Both the endpoints of the fifth sample are less than the population mean. We attribute this to sampling error, and it is the risk we assume when we select the level of confidence.

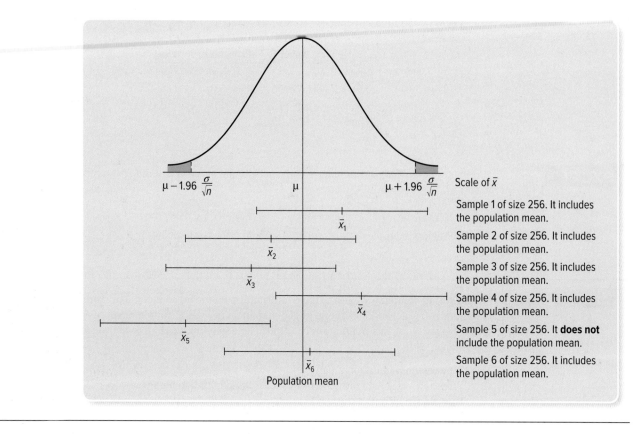

Computer commands to find the confidence interval for the above example can be found at the end of the chapter.

self-review 8–1

The mean daily sales are $2000 for a sample of 40 days at a fast-food restaurant. The standard deviation of the population is $300.

(a) What is the population mean?
(b) What is the best estimate of the population mean? What is this value called?
(c) Develop a 99% confidence interval for the population mean.
(d) Interpret the confidence interval.

EXERCISES

1. A sample of 49 marketing sales representatives was taken from a normal population to determine the amount of their salary after five years. The sample mean was $55 000, with a known population standard deviation of $10 000. Determine the 99% confidence interval for the population mean salary.

2. A sample of 81 adults attending a country fair determined that the mean age was 40. Given that the population standard deviation is known to be 5, determine the 95% confidence interval for the population mean age.

3. A sample of 10 observations is selected from a normal population for which the population standard deviation is known to be 5. The sample mean is 20.

   a. Determine the standard error of the mean.

   b. Explain why we can use formula (8–1) to determine the 95% confidence interval, even though the sample size is less than 30.

   c. Determine the 95% confidence interval for the population mean.

4. In a sample of 40 days taken at Town Talk Bakery, it was found that an average of 75 cakes per day were sold. From past surveys, the population standard deviation was found to be 25 cakes per day.

   a. Determine the standard error of the mean number of cakes sold per day.

   b. Determine the 90% confidence interval for the population mean number of cakes sold per day.

   c. If you wanted a wider interval, would you increase or decrease the confidence level?

5. A sample of 25 observations is selected from a normal population where the population standard deviation is 4.75. The sample mean is 16.85.

   a. Determine the standard error of the mean.

   b. Determine the 98% confidence interval for the population mean.

   c. If you wanted a narrower interval, would you increase or decrease the confidence level?

6. Suppose that you know σ and you want an 85% confidence level. What value would you use to multiply the standard error of the mean?

7. A research firm conducted a survey to determine the mean amount steady smokers spend on cigarettes during a week. They found the distribution of amounts spent per week followed the normal distribution with a standard deviation of $5. A sample of 49 steady smokers revealed that $\bar{x} = 20$.

   a. What is the point estimate of the population mean? Explain what it indicates.

   b. Using the 95% level of confidence, determine the confidence interval for μ. Explain what it indicates.

8. Refer to the previous exercise. Suppose that 64 smokers (instead of 49) were sampled. Assume that the sample mean remained the same.

   a. What is the 95% confidence interval estimate of μ?

   b. Explain why this confidence interval is narrower than the one determined in the previous exercise.

9. Bob Nale is the owner of Nale's Texaco Gas Town. Bob would like to estimate the mean number of litres (L) of gasoline sold to his customers. Assume that the number of litres sold follows the normal distribution with a standard deviation of 10 L. From his records, he selects a random sample of 60 sales and finds the mean number of litres sold is 40.

   a. What is the point estimate of the population mean?

   b. Develop a 99% confidence interval for the population mean.

   c. Interpret the meaning of part (b).

10. Dr. Patton is a professor of English. Recently, she counted the number of misspelled words in a group of student essays. She noted the distribution of misspelled words per essay followed the normal distribution with a standard deviation of 2.44 words per essay. For her Tuesday class of 40 students, the mean number of misspelled words per essay was 6.05. Construct a 95% confidence interval for the mean number of misspelled words in the population of student essays.

LO8-3 Population Standard Deviation (σ) Unknown

In the previous section, we assumed the population standard deviation was known. In these cases, there would likely be a history of data. Therefore, it is reasonable to assume the standard deviation of the population is available. However, in most sampling situations the population standard deviation (σ) is not known. Here are some examples where we want to estimate the population means, and it is unlikely we would know the population standard deviations. Suppose each of these surveys involves students at your college or university.

- The Dean of the Faculty of Business wants to estimate the mean number of hours full-time students work at paying jobs each week. She selects a sample of 35 students, contacts each student and asks them how many hours they worked last week. From the sample information she can calculate the sample mean, but it is not likely she would know or be able to find the *population* (σ) standard deviation required in formula (8–1). She could calculate the standard deviation of the sample and use that as an estimate of the population standard deviation, but she would not likely know the population standard deviation.

- The Dean of Student Affairs wants to estimate the distance the typical commuter student travels to class. He selects a sample of 40 commuter students, contacts each, and determines the one-way distance from each student's home to the centre of campus. From the sample data, he calculates the mean travel distance—that is, $\bar{x}$. It is unlikely the standard deviation of the population would be known or available, again making formula (8–1) unusable.

- The Manager of Student Loans wants to know the mean amount owed on student loans at the time of his or her graduation. The director selects a sample of 20 graduating students

and contacts each to find the information. From the sample information he can estimate the mean amount. However, to develop a confidence interval using formula (8–1), the population standard deviation is necessary. It is not likely this information is available.

Fortunately, we can use the sample standard deviation to estimate the population standard deviation. That is, we use s, the sample standard deviation, to estimate σ, the population standard deviation. But in doing so, we can no longer use formula (8–1). Because we do not know σ, we cannot use the z distribution. However, there is a remedy. We use the sample standard deviation and replace the z distribution with the t distribution.

The t distribution is a continuous probability distribution, with many similar characteristics to the z distribution. William Gosset, an English brewmaster, was the first to study the t distribution. He was particularly concerned with the exact behaviour of the distribution of the following statistic:

$$t = \frac{\bar{x} - \mu}{s/\sqrt{n}}$$

where s is an estimate of σ. He was especially worried about the discrepancy between s and σ when s was calculated from a very small sample. The t distribution and the standard normal distribution are shown graphically in Chart 8–1. Note that the t distribution is flatter, more spread out, than the standard normal distribution. This is because the standard deviation of the t distribution is larger than that of the standard normal distribution.

CHART 8–1 The Standard Normal Distribution and Student's t Distribution

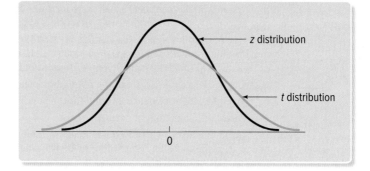

The following characteristics of the t distribution are based on the assumption that the population of interest follows the normal distribution:

1. It is, like the z distribution, a continuous distribution.
2. It is, like the z distribution, bell-shaped and symmetric.
3. There is not one t distribution, but rather a "family" of t distributions. All t distributions have a mean of 0, but their standard deviations differ according to the sample size, n. There is a t distribution for a sample size of 20, another for a sample size of 22, and so on. The standard deviation for a t distribution with 5 observations is larger than for a t distribution with 20 observations.
4. The t distribution is more spread out and flatter at the centre than is the standard normal distribution (see Chart 8–1). As the sample size increases, however, the t distribution approaches the standard normal distribution because the errors in using s to estimate σ decrease with larger samples.

Because Student's t distribution has a greater spread than the z distribution, the value of t for a given level of confidence is larger in magnitude than the corresponding z-value. Chart 8–2 shows the values of z and of t for a 95% level of confidence when the sample size is $n = 5$. How we obtained the actual value of t will be explained shortly. For now, observe that for the same level of confidence the t distribution is more spread out than the standard normal distribution.

To develop a confidence interval for the population mean using the t distribution, we adjust formula (8–1) as follows.

| **CONFIDENCE INTERVAL FOR THE POPULATION MEAN WITH σ UNKNOWN** | $\bar{x} \pm t\dfrac{s}{\sqrt{n}}$ | [8–2] |

CHART 8–2 Values of *z* and *t* for the 95% Level of Confidence

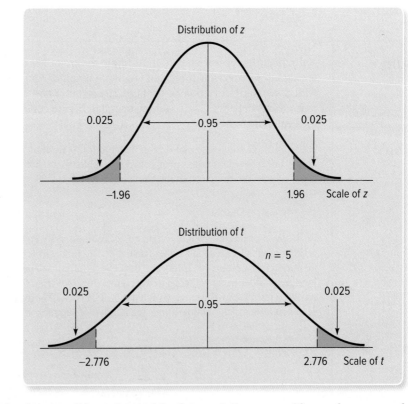

To develop a confidence interval for the population mean with an unknown population standard deviation (σ), we:

1. Assume the sampled population is either normal or approximately normal.
2. Estimate the population standard deviation (σ) with the sample standard deviation (*s*).
3. Use the *t* distribution rather than the *z* distribution.

We should be clear at this point. We based the decision on whether to use *t* or *z* on whether or not we know σ, the population standard deviation. If we know the population standard deviation, then we use *z*. If we do not know the population standard deviation, then we use *t*. Chart 8–3 summarizes the decision-making process.

CHART 8–3 Determining When to Use the *z* Distribution or the *t* Distribution

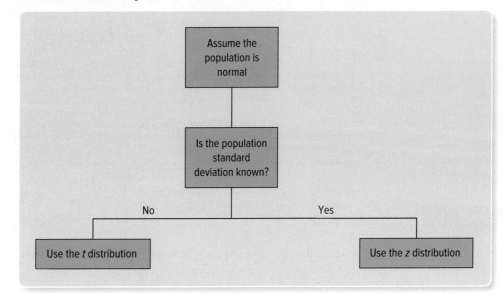

The following example will illustrate a confidence interval for a population mean when the population standard deviation is unknown and how to find the appropriate value of t in a table.

Example	A tire manufacturer wishes to investigate the tread life of its tires. A sample of 10 tires driven 80 000 kilometres (km) revealed a sample mean of 0.81 centimetres (cm) of tread remaining with a standard deviation of 0.23 cm. Construct a 95% confidence interval for the population mean. Would it be reasonable for the manufacturer to conclude that after 80 000 km the population mean amount of tread remaining is 0.76 cm?
Solution	To begin, we assume the population distribution is normal. In this case, we do not have a lot of evidence, but the assumption is probably reasonable. We do not know the population standard deviation, but we know the sample standard deviation, which is 0.23 cm. We use formula (8–2):

$$\bar{x} \pm t\frac{s}{\sqrt{n}}$$

From the information given, $\bar{x} = 0.81$, $s = 0.23$, and $n = 10$. To find the value of t, we use Appendix B.2, a portion of which is reproduced as Table 8–1. The first step for locating t is to move across the columns identified for "Confidence Intervals" to the level of confidence required. In this case, we want the 95% level of confidence, so we move to the column headed "95%." The column on the left margin is identified as "df." This refers to the number of degrees of freedom. The number of degrees of freedom is the number of observations in the sample minus the number of samples, written $n - 1$.* In this case it is $10 - 1 = 9$.

TABLE 8–1 A Portion of the t Distribution

	Confidence Intervals				
	80%	90%	95%	98%	99%
	Level of Significance for One-Tailed Test				
df	0.100	0.050	0.025	0.010	0.005
	Level of Significance for Two-Tailed Test				
	0.20	0.10	0.05	0.02	0.01
1	3.078	6.314	12.706	31.821	63.657
2	1.886	2.920	4.303	6.965	9.925
3	1.638	2.353	3.182	4.541	5.841
4	1.533	2.132	2.776	3.747	4.604
5	1.476	2.015	2.571	3.365	4.032
6	1.440	1.943	2.447	3.143	3.707
7	1.415	1.895	2.365	2.998	3.499
8	1.397	1.860	2.306	2.896	3.355
9	1.383	1.833	2.262	2.821	3.250
10	1.372	1.812	2.228	2.764	3.169

---

* Why did we decide there were 9 degrees of freedom? When sample statistics are being used, it is necessary to determine the number of values that are *free to vary*. To illustrate: assume that the mean of four numbers is known to be 5. The four numbers are 7, 4, 1, and 8. The deviations of these numbers from the mean must total 0. The deviations of $+2$, -1, -4, and $+3$ do total 0. If the deviations of $+2$, -1, and -4 are known, then the value of $+3$ is fixed (restricted) in order to satisfy the condition that the sum of the deviations must equal 0. Thus, 1 degree of freedom is lost in a sampling problem involving the standard deviation of the sample because one number (the arithmetic mean) is known. For a 95% level of confidence and 9 degrees of freedom, we select the row with 9 degrees of freedom. The value of t is 2.262.

excel   Computer commands to find the t-value can be found at the end of the chapter.

To determine the confidence interval, we substitute the values in formula (8–2).

$$\bar{x} \pm t\frac{s}{\sqrt{n}} = 0.81 \pm 2.262\frac{0.23}{\sqrt{10}} = 0.81 \pm 0.165$$

The endpoints of the confidence interval are 0.645 and 0.975. How do we interpret this result? If we repeated this study 200 times, calculating the 95% confidence interval with each sample's mean and the standard deviation, 190 (95% × 200) of the intervals would include the population mean. Ten (5% × 200) of the intervals would not include the population mean. This is the effect of sampling error. A further interpretation is to conclude that the population mean is in this interval. The manufacturer can be reasonably sure (95% confident) that the mean remaining tread depth is between 0.645 and 0.975 cm. Because the value of 0.76 is in this interval, it is possible that the mean of the population is 0.76.

Here is another example to clarify the use of confidence intervals: Suppose that an article in your local newspaper reported that the mean time to sell a residential property in the area is 60 days. You select a random sample of 20 homes sold in the last year and find the mean selling time is 65 days. On the basis of the sample data, you develop a 95% confidence interval for the population mean. You find that the endpoints of the confidence interval are 62 days and 68 days. How do you interpret this result? You can be reasonably confident the population mean is within this range. The value proposed for the population mean, that is, 60 days, is not included in the interval. Therefore, it is not likely that the population mean is 60 days. The evidence indicates the statement in the local newspaper may not be correct. To put it another way, it seems unreasonable to obtain the sample you did from a population with a mean selling time of 60 days.

The following example will show additional details for determining and interpreting a confidence interval:

Example	The manager of the Inlet Square Mall wants to estimate the mean amount spent per shopping visit by customers. A sample of 20 customers reveals the following amounts spent in dollars:

$48.16	42.22	46.82	51.45	23.78	41.86	54.86
37.92	52.64	48.59	50.82	46.94	61.83	61.69
49.17	61.46	51.35	52.68	58.84	43.88	

What is the best estimate of the population mean? Determine a 95% confidence interval. Interpret the result. Would it be reasonable to conclude that the population mean is $50? What about $60?

Solution

The mall manager assumes that the population of the amounts spent follows a normal distribution. This is a reasonable assumption in this case. Additionally, the confidence interval technique is quite powerful and tends to commit any errors on the conservative side if the population is not normal. We should not make the normality assumption when the population is severely skewed.

The population standard deviation is not known, so it is appropriate to use the t distribution and formula (8–2) to find the confidence interval. We used **Excel** to find the mean, the standard deviation, and the skewness of this sample. The sample mean is $49.35, the sample standard deviation is $9.01, and the coefficient of skewness is −0.9961.

We should not make the normality assumption when the population is severely skewed. However, in this case, the coefficient of skewness is −0.9961, so the normality assumption is reasonable.

The mall manager does not know the population mean. The sample mean is the best estimate of that value. The sample mean is $49.35, which is the best estimate, the *point estimate*, of the unknown population mean.

We use formula (8–2) to find the confidence interval. The value of t is available from Appendix B.2. There are $n - 1 = 20 - 1 = 19$ degrees of freedom. We move across the row with 19 degrees of freedom to the column for the 95% confidence level. The value at this intersection is 2.093. We substitute these values into formula (8–2) to find the confidence interval.

$$\bar{x} \pm t\frac{s}{\sqrt{n}} = \$49.35 \pm 2.093\frac{\$9.01}{\sqrt{20}} = \$49.35 \pm \$4.22$$

The endpoints of the confidence interval are $45.13 and $53.57. It is reasonable to conclude that the population mean is in that interval.

The manager of Inlet Square wondered whether the population mean could have been $50 or $60. The value of $50 is within the confidence interval. It is reasonable that the population mean could be $50. The value of $60 is not in the confidence interval. Hence, we conclude that the population mean is unlikely to be $60.

Note: The t table does not show all degrees of freedom. If you want a value that is not shown, then use the smaller value for the degrees of freedom that is shown. For example, if the degrees of freedom is 110, then use $df = 100$.

excel

Computer commands to find the confidence interval for this example can be found at the end of the chapter.

self-review 8–2

Dottie Kleman is the "Cookie Lady." She bakes and sells cookies at 50 different locations. Ms. Kleman is concerned about absenteeism among her workers. The information below reports the number of days absent for a sample of 10 workers during the last two-week pay period.

4	1	2	2	1	2	2	1	0	3

(a) Determine the mean and standard deviation of the sample.
(b) What is the population mean? What is the best estimate of that value?
(c) Develop a 95% confidence interval for the population mean. Assume that the population distribution is normal.
(d) Explain why the t distribution is used as a part of the confidence interval.
(e) Is it reasonable to conclude that the typical worker does not miss any days during a pay period?

EXERCISES

11. Use Appendix B.2, **Excel**, or another software package to locate the value of t under the following conditions:
    a. The sample size is 12, and the level of confidence is 95%.
    b. The sample size is 20, and the level of confidence is 90%.
    c. The sample size is 8, and the level of confidence is 99%.

12. Use Appendix B.2, **Excel**, or another software package to locate the value of t under the following conditions:
    a. The sample size is 15, and the level of confidence is 95%.
    b. The sample size is 24, and the level of confidence is 98%.
    c. The sample size is 12, and the level of confidence is 90%.

13. A sample of 20 observations is selected from a normal population. The sample standard deviation is 26.25, and the sample mean is 75.
    a. Determine the standard error of the mean.
    b. Determine the 90% confidence interval for the population mean.
    c. If you wanted a wider interval, would you increase or decrease the confidence level?

14. In a class of 25 students the average grade on a quiz is 16.85, with a standard deviation is 4.75. The grades are known to be normally distributed.
    a. Determine the standard error of the mean.
    b. Determine the 98% confidence interval for the class grades.
    c. If you wanted a narrower interval, would you increase or decrease the confidence level?

15. The owner of Britten's Egg Farm wants to estimate the mean number of eggs laid per chicken. A sample of 20 chickens shows they laid an average of 20 eggs per month with a standard deviation of 2 eggs per month.

 a. What is the value of the population mean? What is the best estimate of this value?

 b. Explain why we need to use the t distribution. What assumption do you need to make?

 c. For a 95% confidence interval, what is the value of t?

 d. Develop the 95% confidence interval for the population mean.

 e. Would it be reasonable to conclude that the population mean is 21 eggs? What about 25 eggs?

16. The Sugar Producers Association wants to estimate the mean yearly sugar consumption. A sample of 16 people reveals the mean yearly consumption to be 27 kilograms (kg) with a standard deviation of 9 kg. Assume a normal population.

 a. What is the value of the population mean? What is the best estimate of this value?

 b. Explain why we need to use the t distribution. What assumption do you need to make?

 c. For a 90% confidence interval, what is the value of t?

 d. Develop the 90% confidence interval for the population mean.

 e. Would it be reasonable to conclude that the population mean is 28 kg?

17. Taylor Industries and Caldwell Securities are considering jointly offering child care for their employees. As a part of the feasibility study, they wish to estimate the mean weekly child care cost of their employees. A sample of 10 employees who use child care reveals the following amounts, in dollars, spent last week:

| $107 | 92 | 97 | 95 | 105 | 101 | 91 | 99 | 95 | 104 |

 Develop a 90% confidence interval for the population mean. Interpret the result.

18. An automobile insurance company wants to estimate the mean time workers who are employed in the downtown office spend getting to work. A sample of 15 workers reveals the following number of minutes travelled:

| 29 | 38 | 38 | 33 | 38 | 21 | 45 | 34 |
| 40 | 37 | 37 | 42 | 30 | 29 | 35 | |

 Develop a 98% confidence interval for the population mean. Interpret the result.

LO8-4 8.4 A CONFIDENCE INTERVAL FOR A PROPORTION

Statistics in Action

Many survey results reported in newspapers, in news magazines, and on TV use confidence intervals. For example, a recent survey of 800 TV viewers found 44% watched the evening news on the local CBC affiliate. The article went on to indicate the margin of error was 3.4%. The margin of error is actually the amount that is added and subtracted from the point estimate to find the end-points of a confidence interval. Using formula (8–5) and the 95% level of confidence:

$$z\sqrt{\frac{\bar{p}(1-\bar{p})}{n}}$$

$$= 1.96\sqrt{\frac{0.44(1-0.44)}{800}}$$

$$= 0.034$$

We introduced proportions in Chapter 7. Recall that a proportion is the fraction, ratio, or percentage indicating the part of the sample or the population having a particular trait of interest. So, an observation is classified into one of two or more mutually exclusive groups. For example, a recent survey indicated that 92 out of 100 people surveyed supported the continued use of daylight savings time in the summer. There are only two possibilities, and the outcome must be classified into one of two groups—supports the continuation of daylight savings time or does not. The sample proportion ($\bar{p}$) is 92/100 or 0.92 or 92%. We can determine a sample proportion using the following formula:

| **SAMPLE PROPORTION** | $\bar{p} = \dfrac{x}{n}$ | [7–3] |

To develop a confidence interval for a proportion, we need to meet the following assumptions.

1. The binomial conditions, discussed in Chapter 5, have been met. Briefly, these conditions are:

 (a) The sample data are the number of successes in n trials.

 (b) There are only two possible outcomes. (We usually label one of the outcomes a "success" and the other a "failure.")

 (c) The probability of a success remains the same from one trial to the next.

 (d) The trials are independent. This means the outcome on one trial does not affect the outcome of another.

2. The values np and $n(1-p)$ should both be greater than or equal to 5. This condition allows us to use the central limit theorem and employ the standard normal distribution, that is, z, as a part of the confidence interval.

Developing a point estimate for a population proportion and a confidence interval for a population proportion is similar to doing so for a mean. To illustrate, a candidate is running for the office of mayor of Calgary. From a random sample of 100 voters in the city, 60 indicate they plan to vote for the candidate in the upcoming election. The sample proportion is 0.60, but the population proportion is unknown. That is, we do not know what proportion of voters in the *population* will vote for the candidate. The sample value, 0.60, is the best estimate we have of the unknown population parameter. So, we let $\bar{p}$, which is 0.60, be an estimate of p, which is not known.

To develop a confidence interval for a population proportion, we change formula (8–1) to:

CONFIDENCE INTERVAL FOR A POPULATION PROPORTION	$\bar{p} \pm z\sigma_p$, where $\sigma_p = \sqrt{\dfrac{p(1-p)}{n}}$	[8–3]

The term σ_p is the "standard error" of the proportion. It measures the variability in the sampling distribution of the population proportion. For sample data:

STANDARD ERROR OF THE SAMPLE PROPORTION	$s_p = \sqrt{\dfrac{\bar{p}(1-\bar{p})}{n}}$	[8–4]

We can then construct a confidence interval for a population proportion from the following formula:

CONFIDENCE INTERVAL FOR A SAMPLE PROPORTION	$\bar{p} \pm z\sqrt{\dfrac{\bar{p}(1-\bar{p})}{n}}$	[8–5]

The following example will help explain the details of determining a confidence interval and interpreting the result:

Example	The union representing the Bottle Blowers Association (BBA) is considering a proposal to merge with the Teamsters Union. According to BBA union bylaws, at least three-fourths of the union membership must approve any merger. A random sample of 2000 current BBA members reveals 1600 plan to vote for the merger proposal. What is the estimate of the population proportion? Develop a 95% confidence interval for the population proportion. Basing your decision on this sample information, can you conclude that the necessary proportion of BBA members favours the merger?
Solution	First, calculate the sample proportion from formula (8–3). It is 0.8, found by: $$\bar{p} = \frac{x}{n} = \frac{1600}{2000} = 0.8$$ Thus, we estimate that 80% of the population favours the merger proposal. We determine the 95% confidence interval using formula (8–5). The z-value corresponding to the 95% level of confidence is 1.96. $$\bar{p} \pm z\sqrt{\frac{\bar{p}(1-\bar{p})}{n}} = 0.8 \pm 1.96\sqrt{\frac{0.8(1-0.8)}{2000}} = 0.8 \pm 0.018$$ The endpoints of the confidence interval are 0.782 and 0.818. The lower endpoint is greater than 0.75. Hence, we conclude that the merger proposal will pass because the interval estimate includes values greater than 75% of the union membership.

excel

Computer commands to find the confidence interval for the above example can be found at the end of the chapter.

To review the interpretation of the confidence interval: If the poll was conducted 100 times with 100 different samples, the confidence intervals constructed from 95 of the samples would contain the true population proportion. So, the interpretation of a confidence interval can be very useful in decision making and play a very important role on election night. For example, Cliff Obermeyer is running in the federal member of Parliament (MP) election in the riding of Fundy Royal. Suppose that 500 voters are contacted upon leaving the polls, and that 275 indicated they voted for Mr. Obermeyer. We will assume that the exit poll of 500 voters is a random sample of those voting in the riding. That means that 55% of those in the sample voted for Mr. Obermeyer, calculated as follows:

$$\bar{p} = \frac{x}{n} = \frac{275}{500} = 0.55$$

Now, to be assured of winning the election, he must earn more than 50% of the votes in the population of those voting. At this point, we know a point estimate, which is 0.55 of the population of voters that will vote for him, but we do not know the percentage in the population that will vote for him. So, the question is, could we take a sample of 500 voters from a population where 50% or less of the voters support Mr. Obermeyer and find that 55% of the sample support him? To put it another way, could the sampling error, which is $\bar{p} - p = (0.55 - 0.50)$ be due to chance, or is the population of voters who support Mr. Obermeyer greater than 0.50? If we develop a confidence interval for the sample proportion and find that 0.50 is not in the interval, then we conclude that the proportion of voters supporting Mr. Obermeyer is greater than 0.50. What does that mean? Well, it means he should be elected! What if 0.50 is in the interval? Then, we conclude that it is possible that 50% or less of the voters support his candidacy, and we cannot conclude that he will be elected on the basis of the sample information. In this case, using the 95% significance level and formula (8–5):

$$\bar{p} \pm z \sqrt{\frac{\bar{p}(1-\bar{p})}{n}} = 0.55 \pm 1.96 \sqrt{\frac{0.55(1-0.55)}{500}} = 0.55 \pm 0.044$$

So, the endpoints of the confidence interval are: $0.55 - 0.044 = 0.506$ and $0.55 + 0.044 = 0.594$. The value of 0.50 is not in this interval, so we conclude that probably more than 50% of the voters support Mr. Obermeyer and that is enough to get him elected. Is this procedure ever used? Yes! It is exactly the procedure used by television networks, news magazines, and polling organizations on election night.

self-review 8–3

A market survey was conducted to estimate the proportion of homemakers who would recognize the brand name of a cleanser based on the shape and the colour of the container. Of the 1400 homemakers sampled, 420 were able to identify the brand by name.

(a) Estimate the value of the population proportion.
(b) Develop a 99% confidence interval for the population proportion.
(c) Interpret your findings.

EXERCISES

19. Out of a sample of 200 students, 75 indicated that they preferred chocolate ice cream to vanilla ice cream.

    a. Estimate the value of the population proportion of those who preferred chocolate ice cream.

    b. Compute the standard error of the proportion.

    c. Determine a 90% confidence interval for the population proportion of those who preferred chocolate ice cream.

    d. Interpret your findings.

20. Seventy-three percent of the 500 students surveyed voted in favour of the new breakfast menu in the college cafeteria

    a. Estimate the value of the population proportion of those college students who would prefer the new menu.

    b. Compute the standard error of the proportion.

    c. Determine a 95% confidence interval for the population proportion of those college students who would prefer the new menu.

    d. Interpret your findings.

21. The owner of the West End Kwick Fill Gas Station wished to determine the proportion of customers who use his pay-at-the-pump feature. This feature allows customers to use a credit card at the pump and never enter the station. He surveyed 100 customers and found that 80 paid at the pump.

    a. Estimate the value of the population proportion.

    b. Compute the standard error of the proportion.

    c. Develop a 95% confidence interval for the population proportion.

    d. Interpret your findings.

22. Ms. Maria Wilson is considering running for mayor of her town. Before completing her nomination papers, she decides to conduct a survey of voters. A sample of 400 voters reveals that 300 would support her in the November election.

    a. Estimate the value of the population proportion.

    b. Compute the standard error of the proportion.

    c. Develop a 99% confidence interval for the population proportion.

    d. Interpret your findings.

23. The Fox TV network is considering replacing one of its prime-time crime investigation shows with a new family-oriented comedy show. Before a final decision is made, network executives commission a sample of 400 viewers. After viewing the comedy, 250 indicated they would watch the new show and suggested it replace the crime investigation show.

    a. Estimate the value of the population proportion.

    b. Compute the standard error of the proportion.

    c. Develop a 99% confidence interval for the population proportion.

    d. Interpret your findings.

24. Schadek Silkscreen Printing Inc. purchases plastic cups on which to print logos for sporting events, proms, birthdays, and other special occasions. Zack Schadek, the owner, received a large shipment this morning. To ensure the quality of the shipment, he selected a random sample of 300 cups. He found 15 to be defective.

    a. What is the estimated proportion that was defective in the population?

    b. Develop a 95% confidence interval for the proportion that was defective.

    c. Zack has an agreement with his supplier that he is to return lots that are 10% or more defective. Should he return this lot? Explain your decision.

LO8-6   8.5 FINITE-POPULATION CORRECTION FACTOR

The populations we have sampled so far have been very large or infinite. What if the sampled population is not very large? We need to make some adjustments in the way we compute the standard error of the sample means and the standard error of the sample proportions.

A population that has a fixed upper bound is *finite*. For example, there are 17 376 students enrolled at a college, there are 40 employees at Spence Sprockets, or there were 65 surgical patients at St. Paul's Memorial Hospital yesterday. A finite population can be rather small; it could be all the students registered for this class. It can also be very large, such as all senior citizens living in Victoria, British Columbia.

For a finite population, where the total number of objects or individuals is N and the number of objects or individuals in the sample is n, we need to adjust the standard errors in the confidence interval formulas. To put it another way, to find the confidence interval for the mean we adjust the standard error of the mean. If we are determining the confidence interval for a proportion, then we need to adjust the standard error of the proportion.

This adjustment is called the **finite-population correction factor**. It is often shortened to *FPC* and is:

$$FPC = \sqrt{\frac{N - n}{N - 1}}$$

Why is it necessary to apply a factor, and what is its effect? Logically, if the sample is a substantial percentage of the population, the estimate is more precise. Note the effect of the term $(N - n)/(N - 1)$. Suppose that the population is 1000 and the sample is 100. Then, this ratio is: $(1000 - 100)/(1000 - 1)$, or 900/999. Taking the square root gives the correction factor, 0.9492. Multiplying this correction factor by the standard error *reduces* the standard error by about 5% $(1 - 0.9492 = 0.0508)$. This reduction in the size of the standard error yields a smaller range of values in estimating the population mean or the population proportion. If the sample is 200, the correction factor is 0.8949; that is, the standard error has been reduced by more than 10%. Table 8–2 shows the effects of various sample sizes. Note that when the sample is less than about 5% of the population, the impact of the correction factor is quite small. The usual rule is if the ratio of n/N is less than 0.05, the correction factor is ignored.

Table 8–2 Finite-Population Correction Factor for Selected Sample Sizes When the Population Is 1000

Sample Size	Fraction of Population	Correction Factor
10	0.010	0.9955
25	0.025	0.9879
50	0.050	0.9752
100	0.100	0.9492
200	0.200	0.8949
500	0.500	0.7075

So, if we wish to develop a confidence interval for the mean or proportion from a finite population, we would adjust the standard error of the mean or proportion as follows:

STANDARD ERROR OF THE SAMPLE MEAN, USING A CORRECTION FACTOR (KNOWN σ) $\sigma_{\bar{x}} = \dfrac{\sigma}{\sqrt{n}} \sqrt{\dfrac{N - n}{N - 1}}$ [8–6]

STANDARD ERROR OF THE SAMPLE MEAN, USING A CORRECTION FACTOR (UNKNOWN σ) $s_{\bar{x}} = \dfrac{s}{\sqrt{n}} \sqrt{\dfrac{N - n}{N - 1}}$ [8–7]

STANDARD ERROR OF THE SAMPLE PROPORTION, USING A CORRECTION FACTOR $s_p = \sqrt{\dfrac{\bar{p}(1 - \bar{p})}{n}} \sqrt{\dfrac{N - n}{N - 1}}$ [8–8]

The following example summarizes the steps to find a confidence interval for the mean:

Example

There are 250 families in a small Alberta town. A random sample of 40 families reveals the mean annual church contribution is $450, with a standard deviation of $75. Could the population mean be $445 or $425?

1. What is the population mean? What is the best estimate of the population mean?
2. Discuss why the finite-population correction factor should be used.
3. Develop a 90% confidence interval for the population mean. What are the endpoints of the confidence interval?
4. Interpret the confidence interval.

Solution

First, note that the population is finite. That is, there is a limit to the number of people in this Alberta town, in this case 250.

1. We do not know the population mean. This is the value we wish to estimate. The best estimate we have of the population mean is the sample mean, which is $450.
2. The sample size is 16% of the population size, found by $n/N = 40/250 = 0.16$. Because the sample size is more than 5% of the population size, we should use the FPC to adjust the standard error in determining the confidence interval.
3. The formula to find the confidence interval for a population mean follows:

$$\bar{x} \pm t\frac{s}{\sqrt{n}}\left(\sqrt{\frac{N-n}{N-1}}\right)$$

In this case, we know $\bar{x} = 450$, $s = 75$, $N = 250$, and $n = 40$. We do not know the population standard deviation, so we use the t distribution. To find the appropriate value of t, we use Appendix B.2 and move across the top row to the column headed 90%. The degrees of freedom is: $(n-1) = (40-1) = 39$, so we move to the cell where the df row of 39 intersects with the column headed 90%. The value is 1.685. Inserting these values in the formula:

$$\bar{x} \pm t\frac{s}{\sqrt{n}}\left(\sqrt{\frac{N-n}{N-1}}\right) = \$450 \pm 1.685\frac{75}{\sqrt{40}}\left(\sqrt{\frac{250-40}{250-1}}\right) = \$450 \pm 18.35$$

The endpoints of the confidence interval are $431.65 and $468.35.

4. It is likely that the population mean is more than $431.65 but less than $468.35. To put it another way, could the population mean be $445? Yes, but it is not likely that it is $425. Why is this so? Because the value $445 is within the confidence interval and $425 is not within the confidence interval.

---

self-review 8–4

The same study of church contributions revealed that 15 of the 40 families sampled attend church regularly. Construct the 95% confidence interval for the proportion of families attending church regularly. Should the finite-population correction factor be used? Why or why not?

EXERCISES

25. Thirty-six items are randomly selected from a population of 300 items. The sample mean is 35, and the sample standard deviation is 5. Develop a 95% confidence interval for the population mean.

26. A gift shop advertises that they stock 500 items that are priced under $50. A sample of 49 items are randomly selected and the sample mean price is $40, with a sample standard deviation of 9. Develop a 99% confidence interval for the population mean price. Is the gift shop advertisement true?

27. The attendance at the Foresters Falls baseball game last night was 400. A random sample of 50 of those in attendance revealed that the mean number of soft drinks consumed per person was 1.86, with a standard deviation of 0.50. Develop a 99% confidence interval for the mean number of soft drinks consumed per person.

28. Sixty items are randomly selected from a population of 900. The number of defective items is found to be 12. Develop a 95% confidence interval for the population proportion of defective items.

29. A shipment of 500 dolls is received by Panda Importers. The quality control manager selects a random sample of 75 to test. Five are found to be defective. Construct a 90% confidence interval for the population proportion of defective dolls in the shipment. Would it be reasonable to find 10 defective dolls?

30. There are 300 welders employed at the Weller Shipyards Corporation. A sample of 30 welders revealed that 18 had graduated from a registered welding course. Construct the 95% confidence interval for the proportion of all welders who graduated from a registered welding course.

LO8-5 8.6 CHOOSING AN APPROPRIATE SAMPLE SIZE

When working with confidence intervals, one important variable is sample size. However, in practice, sample size is not a variable. It is a decision we make so that our estimate of a population parameter is a good one. Our decision is based on three variables:

1. The margin of error the researcher will tolerate
2. The level of confidence desired, for example, 95%
3. The variation or dispersion of the population being studied

The first variable is the *margin of error*. It is designated as E and is the amount that is added and subtracted to the sample mean (or sample proportion) to determine the endpoints of the confidence interval. For example, in a study of wages, we may decide that we want to estimate the mean wage of the population with a margin of error of plus or minus $1000. Or in an opinion poll, we may decide that we want to estimate the population proportion with a margin of error of plus or minus 3.5%. The margin of error is the amount of error we are willing to tolerate in estimating a population parameter. You may wonder why we do not choose small margins of error. There is a trade-off between the margin of error and sample size. A small margin of error will require a larger sample and more money and time to collect the sample. A larger margin of error will permit a smaller sample and result in a wider confidence interval.

The second factor is the *level of confidence*. In working with confidence intervals, we logically choose relatively high levels of confidence such as 95% and 99%. To compute the sample size, we need the z-statistic that corresponds to the chosen level of confidence. The 95% level of confidence corresponds to a z-value of 1.96, and a 90% level of confidence corresponds to a z-value of 1.645 (using the t table). Note that larger sample sizes (and more time and money to collect the sample) correspond with higher levels of confidence. Also, note that we use a z-statistic.

The third factor to determine the sample size is the *population standard deviation*. If the population is widely dispersed, a large sample is required. However, if the population is concentrated (homogeneous), the required sample size will be smaller. Often, we do not know the population standard deviation. Here are three suggestions for finding a value that will estimate it:

1. **Use a comparable study**. Use this approach when there is an estimate of the standard deviation from another study. Suppose that we want to estimate the number of hours worked per week by refuse workers. Information from certain provincial or federal agencies who regularly sample the workforce might be useful to provide an estimate of the standard deviation.
2. **Use a range-based approach**. To use this approach we need to know or have an estimate of the largest and smallest values in the population. Recall from Chapter 3, where we described the Empirical Rule, that virtually all the observations could be expected to be within plus or minus 3 standard deviations of the mean, assuming that the distribution follows the normal distribution. Thus, the distance between the largest and the smallest values is 6 standard deviations. So, we could estimate the standard deviation as one-sixth of the range. For example, suppose the director of operations at University Bank on campus wants an estimate of the number of cheques written per month by college students. She believes that the distribution of the number of cheques written follows the normal distribution. The minimum number written per month is 2 and 50 is the most. The range of the number of cheques written per month is 48, found by: $(50 - 2)$. The estimate of the standard deviation then would be 8 cheques per month, 48/6.
3. **Conduct a pilot study**. This is the most common method. Suppose that we want an estimate of the number of hours per week worked by students enrolled in Seneca College. To test the validity of our questionnaire, we use it on a small sample of students. From this small sample, we compute the standard deviation of the number of hours worked and use this value as the population standard deviation.

Sample Size to Estimate a Population Mean

To estimate a population mean, we can express the interaction among these three factors and the sample size in the following formula. Note that this formula is the margin of error used to calculate the endpoints of confidence intervals to estimate a population mean!

$$E = z\frac{\sigma}{\sqrt{n}}$$

Solving this equation for n yields the following result:

SAMPLE SIZE FOR ESTIMATING THE POPULATION MEAN	$n = \left(\frac{z\sigma}{E}\right)^2$	[8–9]

where:

n is the size of the sample.
z is the standard normal value corresponding to the desired level of confidence.
σ is the population standard deviation.
E is the maximum allowable error.

The result of this calculation is not always a whole number. When the outcome is not a whole number, the usual practice is to round up *any* fractional result. For example, 201.22 would be rounded up to 202.

Example	A student in business administration wants to determine the mean amount members of city councils in large cities earn per month as remuneration for being a council member. The error in estimating the mean is to be less than \$100, with a 95% level of confidence. The student found a report by the Department of Labour that estimated the standard deviation to be \$1000. What is the required sample size?
Solution	The maximum allowable error, E, is \$100. The value of z for a 95% level of confidence is 1.96, and the estimate of the standard deviation is \$1000. Substituting these values into formula (8–9), gives the required sample size as:

$$n = \left(\frac{z\sigma}{E}\right)^2 = \left(\frac{(1.96)\,(1000)}{\$100}\right)^2 = 384.16$$

The computed value of 384.16 is rounded up to 385. A sample of 385 is required to meet the specifications. If the student wants to increase the level of confidence, for example, to 99%, this will require a larger sample. The z-value corresponding to the 99% level of confidence is 2.58.

$$n = \left(\frac{z\sigma}{E}\right)^2 = \left(\frac{(2.58)\,(1000)}{\$100}\right)^2 = 665.64$$

We recommend a sample of 666. Observe how much the change in the confidence level changed the size of the sample. An increase from the 95% to the 99% level of confidence resulted in an increase of 281 observations. This could greatly increase the cost of the study, both in terms of time and money. Hence, the level of confidence should be considered carefully.

Computer commands to find the sample size for the above example can be found at the end of the chapter.

Sample Size to Estimate a Population Proportion

To determine the sample size for a proportion, the same three variables need to be specified:

1. The margin of error
2. The desired level of confidence
3. The variation or dispersion of the population being studied

The formula to determine the sample size for a proportion is:

SAMPLE SIZE FOR THE POPULATION PROPORTION	$n = p(1-p)\left(\dfrac{z}{E}\right)^2$	[8–10]

where:

> n is the size of the sample.
> z is the standard normal value corresponding to the desired level of confidence.
> p is the population proportion.
> E is the maximum allowable error.

The choices for the z-statistic and the margin of error, E, are the same as the choices for estimating the population mean. However, in this case the population standard deviation for a proportion is represented by $p(1-p)$. To find a value of the population proportion, we would find a comparable study or conduct a pilot study. If a reliable value cannot be found, then a value of 0.50 should be used for p. Note that $p(1-p)$ has the largest value using 0.50 and, therefore, without a good estimate of the population proportion, overstates the sample size. This difference will not hurt the estimate of the population proportion.

Example	The study in the previous example also estimates the proportion of cities that have private refuse collectors. The student wants the estimate to be within 0.10 of the population proportion, the desired level of confidence is 90%, and no estimate is available for the population proportion. What is the required sample size?
Solution	The estimate of the population proportion is to be within 0.10, so $E = 0.10$. The desired level of confidence is 0.90, which corresponds to a z-value of 1.645. Because no estimate of the population proportion is available, we use 0.50. The suggested number of observations is: $$n = (0.5)(1 - 0.5)\left(\frac{1.645}{0.10}\right)^2 = 67.65$$ The student needs a random sample of 68 cities.

excel   Computer commands to find the sample size for the above example can be found at the end of the chapter.

self-review 8–5   Will you assist the college registrar in determining how many transcripts need to be studied? The registrar wants to estimate the arithmetic mean grade point average (GPA) of all graduating seniors during the past 10 years. GPAs range between 2.0 and 4.0. The mean GPA is to be estimated within plus or minus 0.05 of the population mean. The standard deviation is estimated to be 0.279. Use the 99% level of confidence. How many transcripts should the registrar study?

31. The Pear Tree would like to estimate the mean amount spent by their customers at their weekend brunch during the summer. The population estimate of the standard deviation is 30 and they want the mean estimate to be within $8, using a 95% level of confidence. How large a sample is required?

32. We want to estimate the population mean within 5, with a 99% level of confidence. The population standard deviation is estimated to be 15. How large a sample is required?

33. Previous surveys estimated that 15% of students use the college gym. The manager would like to verify this estimate within plus or minus 0.05. At a 95% level of confidence, how large a sample is required?

34. The estimate of the population proportion is to be within plus or minus 0.10, with a 99% level of confidence. The best estimate of the population proportion is 0.45. How large a sample is required?

35. A survey is being planned to determine the mean amount of time corporation executives watch television. A pilot survey indicated that the mean time per week is 12 hours, with a standard deviation of 3 hours. It is desired to estimate the mean viewing time within one-quarter hour. The 95% level of confidence is to be used. How many executives should be surveyed?

36. A processor of carrots cuts the green top off each carrot, washes the carrots, and inserts six to a package. Twenty packages are inserted in a box for shipment. To test the mass of the boxes, a few were checked. The mean mass was 9.3 kg, and the standard deviation was 0.23 kg. How many boxes must the processor sample to be 95% confident that the sample mean does not differ from the population mean by more than 0.09 kg?

37. Suppose that the prime minister wants an estimate of the proportion of the population that supports his current policy on health care. The prime minister wants the estimate to be within 0.04 of the true proportion. Assume a 95% level of confidence. The prime minister's political advisors estimated the proportion supporting the current policy to be 0.60.

    a. How large a sample is required?

    b. How large a sample would be necessary if no estimate were available for the proportion that supports current policy?

38. Past surveys reveal that 30% of tourists going to Las Vegas to gamble during a weekend spend more than $1000. Management wants to update this percentage.

    a. The new study is to use the 90% confidence level. The estimate is to be within 1% of the population proportion. What is the necessary sample size?

    b. Management said that the sample size determined above is too large. What can be done to reduce the sample? Recalculate the sample size, on the basis of your suggestion.

Chapter Summary

I. A point estimate is a single value (statistic) used to estimate a population value (parameter).

II. A confidence interval is a range of values within which the population parameter is expected to occur.

    A. The factors that determine the width of a confidence interval for a mean are:
       1. The number of observations in the sample, n.
       2. The variability in the population, usually estimated by the sample standard deviation, s.
       3. The level of confidence.

       a. To determine the confidence limits when the population standard deviation is known, we use the z distribution. The formula is:

$$\bar{x} \pm z \frac{\sigma}{\sqrt{n}} \qquad \text{[8–1]}$$

       b. To determine the confidence limits when the population standard deviation is unknown, we use the t distribution. The formula is:

$$\bar{x} \pm t \frac{s}{\sqrt{n}} \qquad \text{[8–2]}$$

III. The major characteristics of the t distribution are as follows:

    A. It is a continuous distribution.

    B. It is mound shaped and symmetric.

C. It is flatter, or more spread out, than the standard normal distribution.

D. There is a family of t distributions, depending on the number of degrees of freedom.

IV. A proportion is a ratio, fraction, or percentage that indicates the part of the sample or population that has the particular characteristic.

   A. A sample proportion is found by x, the number of successes, divided by n, the number of observations.

   B. The standard error of the sample proportion reports the variability in the distribution of sample proportions. It is found by:

$$s_p = \sqrt{\frac{\bar{p}(1-\bar{p})}{n}}$$ [8–4]

   C. We construct a confidence interval for a population proportion from the following formula:

$$\bar{p} \pm z\sqrt{\frac{\bar{p}(1-\bar{p})}{n}}$$ [8–5]

V. For the finite population, the standard error is adjusted by the factor:

$$\sqrt{\frac{N-n}{N-1}}$$

VI. We can determine an appropriate sample size for estimating both means and proportions.

   A. There are three factors that determine the sample size when we wish to estimate the population mean:

   1. The margin of error, E.

   2. The desired level of confidence.

   3. The variation in the population.

   The formula to determine the sample size for the mean is:

$$n = \left(\frac{z\sigma}{E}\right)^2$$ [8–9]

   B. There are three factors that determine the sample size when we wish to estimate a population proportion:

   1. The margin of error, E.

   2. The desired level of confidence.

   3. A value for p to calculate the variation in the population. If no estimate is available, use 0.50.

   The formula to determine the sample size for a proportion is:

$$n = p(1-p)\left(\frac{z}{E}\right)^2$$ [8–10]

Chapter Exercises

39. A random sample of 85 group leaders, supervisors, and similar personnel at General Motors revealed that, on the average, they spent 6.5 years on the job before being promoted. The standard deviation of the sample was 1.7 years. Construct a 95% confidence interval.

40. A meat inspector has been given the assignment of estimating the mean net mass of packages of ground chuck labelled "1.4 kg." Of course, he realizes that the masses cannot be precisely 1.4 kg. A sample of 36 packages reveals the mean mass to be 1.401 kg, with a standard deviation of 0.01 kg.

   a. What is the estimated population mean?

   b. Determine a 95% confidence interval for the population mean.

41. A recent study of 50 self-service gasoline stations in a metropolitan area revealed that the mean price of unleaded gas was $1.30 per litre. The sample standard deviation was $0.07 per litre.

   a. Determine a 99% confidence interval for the population mean price.

   b. Would it be reasonable to conclude that the population mean was $1.40? Why, or why not?

42. A recent survey of 50 executives who were laid off from their previous position revealed it took an average of 26 weeks for them to find another position. The standard deviation of the sample was 6.2 weeks. Construct a 95% confidence interval for the population mean. Is it reasonable that the population mean is 28 weeks? Justify your answer.

43. The Badik Construction Company limits its business to constructing decks. The mean time to construct one of its standard decks is 8 hours for a two-person construction crew. The information is based on a sample of 40 decks recently constructed. The standard deviation of the sample was 3 hours.

   a. Determine a 90% confidence interval for the population mean.

   b. Would it be reasonable to conclude that the population mean is actually 9 hours? Justify your answer.

44. A restaurant group collected information on the number of meals eaten outside the home per week by young married couples who lived in large cities. A survey of 60 couples showed the sample mean number of meals eaten outside the home was 2.76 meals per week, with a standard deviation of 0.75 meals per week. Construct a 97% confidence interval for the population mean.

45. The manager of Apache Burger felt that an average of 70 customers made purchases daily between the hours of 3 p.m. and 5 p.m. A random sample over 50 days showed the sample mean to be 68.6 customers with a standard deviation of 8.2 hours.

   a. Using the sample data, construct a 99% confidence interval for the population mean.

   b. Does the 99% confidence interval include the value suggested by the manager? Interpret this result.

   c. Suppose you decided to switch from a 99% confidence interval to a 95% confidence interval. Without performing any calculations, will the interval increase, decrease, or stay the same? Which of the values in the formula will change?

46. The employees of Electronics Inc. would like to have a dental plan as part of their benefits package. The question is: how much does a typical employee and his or her family spend per year on dental expenses? A sample of 45 employees reveals the mean amount spent last year was $1820, with a standard deviation of $660.

   a. Construct a 95% confidence interval for the population mean.

   b. The information from part (a) was given to the president of Electronics Inc. He indicated he could afford $1700 of dental expenses per employee. Is it possible that the population mean could be $1700? Justify your answer.

47. A student conducted a study and reported that the 95% confidence interval for the mean ranged from 46 to 54. He was sure that the mean of the sample was 50, that the standard deviation of the sample was 16, and that the sample was at least 30 but could not remember the exact number. Can you help him out?

48. A recent study by an automobile dealer revealed the mean amount of profit per car sold for a sample of 20 salespeople was $290, with a standard deviation of $125. Develop a 95% confidence interval for the population mean.

49. A study of 25 graduates of colleges revealed the mean amount owed by a student was $14 381. The standard deviation of the sample was $1892. Construct a 90% confidence interval for the population mean. Is it reasonable to conclude that the mean of the population is actually $15 000? Explain why or why not.

50. An important factor in selling a residential property is the number of people who look through the home. A sample of 15 homes recently sold in the Halifax, Nova Scotia, area revealed the mean number looking through each home was 24 and the standard deviation of the sample was 5 people. Develop a 98% confidence interval for the population mean.

51. The Simcoe County Food Emporium claims that "the typical customer spends $60 per visit." A sample of 12 customers revealed the following purchases, in dollars, spent last visit:

      $64   66   64   66   59   62   67   61   64   58   54   66

   a. What is the point estimate of the population mean?

   b. Develop a 90% confidence interval for the population mean.

   c. Is the restaurant's claim that the "typical customer" spends $60 per visit reasonable? Justify your answer.

52. The manufacturer of a new line of ink jet printers would like to include as part of its advertising the number of pages a user can expect from a print cartridge. A sample of 10 cartridges revealed the following number of pages printed:

      2698   2028   2474   2395   2372   2475   1927   3006   2334   2379

   a. What is the point estimate of the population mean?

   b. Develop a 95% confidence interval for the population mean.

53. Dr. Susan Benner is an industrial psychologist. She is currently studying stress among executives of Internet companies. She has developed a questionnaire that she believes measures stress. A score above 80 indicates stress at a dangerous level. A random sample of 15 executives revealed the following stress level scores:

      94   78   83   90   78   99   97   90   97   90   93   94   100   75   84

   a. Find the mean stress level for this sample. What is the point estimate of the population mean?

   b. Construct a 95% confidence level for the population mean.

   c. Is it reasonable to conclude that Internet executives have a mean stress level in the dangerous level, according to Dr. Benner's test?

54. Furniture Land surveyed 600 consumers and found that 414 were enthusiastic about a new home dècor it plans to show in its store in High Point. Construct the 99% confidence interval for the population proportion.

55. There are 20 000 eligible voters in York County. A random sample of 500 York County voters revealed 350 plan to vote to re-elect their current member of parliament. Construct a 99% confidence interval for the proportion of voters in the county who plan to re-elect the returning member. From this sample information, can you confirm the re-election?

56. In a poll to estimate the prime minister's popularity, each person in a random sample of 1000 voters was asked to agree with one of the following statements:

1. The prime minister is doing a good job.

2. The prime minister is doing a poor job.

3. I have no opinion.

A total of 560 respondents selected the first statement, indicating they thought the prime minister was doing a good job.

a. Construct a 95% confidence interval for the proportion of respondents who feel the prime minister is doing a good job.

b. On the basis of your interval in part (a), is it reasonable to conclude that a majority (more than half) of the population believes the prime minister is doing a good job?

57. Brampton's traffic patrol reports 500 traffic citations were issued last month. A sample of 35 of these citations showed the mean amount of the fine was $54, with a standard deviation of $4.50. Construct a 95% confidence interval for the mean amount of a citation in Brampton.

58. The bank in Cobden, Ontario, has 650 chequing account customers. A recent sample of 50 of these customers showed 26 to have a Visa card with the bank. Construct the 99% confidence interval for the proportion of chequing account customers who have a Visa card with the bank.

59. It is claimed that 60% of households now subscribe to cable TV. You would like to verify this statement for your class in mass communications. If you want your estimate to be within 5 percentage points, with a 95% level of confidence, how large of a sample is required?

60. You need to estimate the mean number of travel days per year for outside salespeople. The mean of a small pilot study was 150 days, with a standard deviation of 14 days. If you must estimate the population mean within 2 days, how many outside salespeople should you sample? Use the 90% confidence level.

61. You are to conduct a sample survey to determine the mean family income in a rural area. The question is, how many families should be sampled? In a pilot sample of 10 families, the standard deviation of the sample was $500. The sponsor of the survey wants you to use the 95% confidence level. The estimate is to be within $100. How many families should be interviewed?

62. You plan to conduct a survey to find what proportion of the workforce has two or more jobs. You decide on the 95% confidence level and state that the estimated proportion must be within 2% of the population proportion. A pilot survey reveals that 5 of the 50 sampled hold two or more jobs. How many in the workforce should be interviewed to meet your requirements?

63. An employment agency wants to update an estimate of the proportion of accountants who have changed companies within the last three years, to be estimated within 3%. A 95% level of confidence is to be used. A study conducted several years ago revealed that the percentage of accountants changing companies within 3 years was 21.

a. To update this study, the files of how many accountants should be studied?

b. How many accountants should be contacted if no previous estimates of the population proportion are available?

64. The National Bank, like most other large banks, found that using automatic teller machines (ATMs) reduces the cost of routine bank transactions. National installed an ATM in the corporate offices of the Fun Toy Company. The ATM is for the exclusive use of Fun's 605 employees. After several months of operation, a sample of 100 employees revealed the following use of the ATM machine by Fun employees in a month:

Number of Times ATM Used	Frequency
0	25
1	30
2	20
3	10
4	10
5	5

a. What is the estimate of the proportion of employees who do not use the ATM in a month?

b. Develop a 95% confidence interval for this estimate. Can National be sure that at least 40% of the employees of Fun Toy Company will use the ATM?

c. How many transactions does the average Fun employee make per month?

d. Develop a 95% confidence interval for the mean number of transactions per month.

e. Is it possible that the population mean is 0? Explain.

65. In a recent poll of 1000 adults nationwide, 613 said they believe other forms of life exist elsewhere in the universe. Construct the 99% confidence interval for the population proportion of those believing life exists elsewhere in the universe. Does your result imply that the majority of Canadians believe life exists outside of Earth?

66. As part of an annual review of its accounts, a discount brokerage selects a random sample of 36 customers. Their accounts are reviewed for total account valuation, which showed a mean of $32 000, with a sample standard deviation of $8200. What is a 90% confidence interval for the mean account valuation of the population of customers?

67. A sample of 352 subscribers to *Wired* magazine shows the mean time spent using the Internet is 13.4 hours per week, with a sample standard deviation of 6.8 hours. Find the 95% confidence interval for the mean time *Wired* subscribers spend on the Internet.

68. The Manitoba Tourism Board plans to sample information centre visitors entering the province to learn the fraction of visitors who plan to camp in the province. Current estimates are that 35% of visitors are campers. How large a sample would you take to estimate at a 95% confidence level the population proportion with an allowable error of 2%?

69. A survey of 36 randomly selected "iPhone" owners showed that the purchase price has a mean of $416, with a sample standard deviation of $180.
   a. Compute the standard error of the sample mean.
   b. Compute the 95% confidence interval for the mean.
   c. How large a sample is needed to estimate the population mean within $10 at a 95% degree of confidence?

70. Passenger comfort is influenced by the amount of pressurization in an airline cabin. Higher pressurization allows a closer-to-normal environment and a more relaxed flight. A study by an airline user group recorded the corresponding air pressure on 30 randomly chosen flights. The study revealed a mean equivalent pressure of 8000 feet, with a standard deviation of 300 feet.
   a. Develop a 99% confidence interval for the population mean equivalent pressure.
   b. How large a sample is needed to find the population mean within 25 feet at 95% confidence?

71. As part of their business promotional package, the Costa Rica Chamber of Commerce would like an estimate of the mean cost per day to lease a one-bedroom apartment. A random sample of 40 apartments currently available for lease showed the mean cost per day was $323. The standard deviation of the sample was $25.
   a. Develop a 98% confidence interval for the population mean.
   b. Would it be reasonable to conclude that the population mean is $350 per day?

72. Marty Rowatti recently assumed the position of director of the YMCA. He would like some current data on how long current members of the YMCA have been members. To investigate, suppose he selects a random sample of 40 current members. The mean length of membership of those included in the sample is 8.32 years and the standard deviation is 3.07 years.
   a. What is the mean of the population?
   b. Develop a 90% confidence interval for the population mean.
   c. The previous director, in the summary report she prepared as she retired, indicated the mean length of membership was now "almost 10 years." Does the sample information substantiate this claim? Explain your reasoning.

73. The National Collegiate Athletic Association (NCAA) reported that the mean number of hours spent per week on coaching and recruiting by college football assistant coaches during the season was 70. A random sample of 50 assistant coaches showed the sample mean to be 68.6 hours, with a standard deviation of 8.2 hours.
   a. Using the sample data, construct a 99% confidence interval for the population mean.
   b. Does the 99% confidence interval include the value suggested by the NCAA? Interpret this result.
   c. Suppose you decided to switch from a 99% to a 95% confidence interval. Without performing any calculations, will the interval increase, decrease, or stay the same? Which of the values in the formula will change?

74. A random sample of 25 people who purchased tickets to the Limelight Theatre on a regular basis stated they paid an average of $65.00 per ticket. The sample standard deviation was $6.25 per ticket.
   a. What is the population mean? What is the best estimate of the population mean?
   b. Develop a 99% confidence interval for the population mean ticket price for these theatregoers.
   c. How large a sample is needed to assess the population mean with an allowable error of $1.00 at 95% confidence?

75. A film alliance used a random sample of 50 U.S. citizens to estimate that the typical American spent 78 hours watching videos and DVDs last year. The standard deviation of this sample was 9 hours.
   a. Develop a 95% confidence interval for the population mean number of hours spent watching videos and DVDs last year.
   b. How large a sample should be used to be 90% confident the sample mean is within 1.0 hour of the population mean?

76. Fashion Industries randomly tests its employees throughout the year. Last year, in the 400 random tests conducted, 14 employees failed the test. Develop a 99% confidence interval for the proportion of applicants that fail the test. Would it be reasonable to conclude that less than 5% of the employees are not able to pass the random drug test? Explain your reasoning.

77. As a condition of acceptance into a Business Program, the local college requires that applicants must pass a mathematics basic skills test. Of the last 220 applicants, 14 failed the test. Develop a 99% confidence interval for the proportion of applicants that fail the test. Would it be reasonable to conclude that more than 10% of the applicants are now failing the test?

78. During a provincial debate on changes to health care, a cable news service performs an opinion poll of 500 small-business owners. It shows that 65% of small-business owners do not approve of the changes. Develop a 95% confidence interval for the proportion opposing health care changes. Comment on the result.

79. *Families USA*, a monthly magazine that discusses issues related to health and health costs, surveyed 20 of its subscribers. It found that the annual health insurance premiums for a family with coverage through an employer averaged $10 979. The standard deviation of the sample was $1000.

   a. On the basis of this sample information, develop a 90% confidence interval for the population mean yearly premium.

   b. How large a sample is needed to find the population mean within $250 at 99% confidence?

80. The proportion of public accountants who have changed companies within the last three years is to be estimated within 3%. The 95% level of confidence is to be used. A study conducted several years ago revealed that the percentage of public accountants changing companies within three years was 21.

   a. To update this study, the files of how many public accountants should be studied?

   b. How many public accountants should be contacted if no previous estimates of the population proportion are available?

Data Set Exercises

Questions marked with ⚡ have data sets available on McGraw-Hill's online resource for *Basic Statistics*.

⚡ 81. Refer to the Real Estate Data—Halifax Area online, which reports information on home listings. Consider this a population, and take a sample of 40 listings.

   a. Develop a 95% confidence interval for the mean list price of the homes. Does the true population mean fall in the confidence interval?

   b. Develop a 95% confidence interval for the mean number of square feet per home. Does the true population mean fall in the confidence interval?

   c. Develop a 95% confidence interval for the proportion of homes that have three or more bedrooms. Does the true population proportion fall in the confidence interval?

⚡ 82. Refer to the CREA Cities Only (Canadian Real Estate Association) data online, which reports information on average house prices nationally and in a selection of cities across Canada.

   a. Develop a 97% confidence interval for the mean list price for all cities for January 2014.

   b. Is it possible that the population mean is $400 000? Explain.

⚡ 83. Refer to the CREA Cities Only data online, which reports information on average house prices nationally and in a selection of cities across Canada.

   a. Develop an 80% confidence interval for the mean list price for all cities for June 2016. Select all cities.

   b. Is it possible that the population mean is $300 000? Explain.

⚡ 84. Refer to the Real Estate Data—Saskatoon online, which reports information on home listings. Consider this a population, and take a sample of 20 listings.

   a. Develop a 90% confidence interval for the mean list price of the homes. Does the true population mean fall in the confidence interval?

   b. Develop a 90% confidence interval for the mean number of square feet per home. Does the true population mean fall in the confidence interval?

   c. Develop a 90% confidence interval for the proportion of homes that have less than two bedrooms. Does the true population proportion fall in the confidence interval?

Practice Test

Part I Objective

1. A _____ is a single value computed from sample information used to estimate a population parameter.

2. A _____ is a range of values within which the population parameter is likely to occur.

3. Assuming the same sample size and the same standard deviation, a 90% confidence interval will be _____ than a 05% confidence interval. (equal to, wider, narrower, cannot tell)

4. A _____ shows the fraction of a sample that has a particular characteristic.

5. For a 95% confidence interval, approximately % of the similarly constructed intervals will include the population parameter being estimated.

6. To construct a confidence interval for a mean, the z distribution is used only when the population is _____ known.

7. To develop a confidence interval for a proportion, the four conditions of the _____ must be met.

8. The finite population correction factor is used when the sample is more than _____ % of the population. (5, 20, 50, 100)

9. The _____ has no effect on the size of the sample. (level of confidence, margin of error, size of the population, variability in the population)

10. To locate the appropriate t value, which is not necessary? (degrees of freedom, level of confidence, population mean) _____

Part II Problems

1. A recent study of 26 Cobden, Ontario, residents revealed they had lived at their current address for a mean of 9.3 years, with a sample standard deviation of 2 years.
   a. What is the population mean?
   b. What is the best estimate of the population mean?
   c. What is the standard error of the mean?
   d. Develop a 90% confidence interval for the population mean.

2. A recent federal report indicated 27% of children ages 2 to 5 ate vegetables at least five times a week. How large a sample is necessary to estimate the true population proportion within 2% with a 98% level of confidence?

3. The City Transport Authority wants to estimate the proportion of central city workers that use public transportation to get to work. A sample of 100 workers revealed 64 used public transportation. Develop a 95% confidence interval.

Computer Commands

1. The **Excel** function to find the z-value is **NORM.S.INV**. To find the z-value for a 95% confidence level, we would enter "=NORM.S.INV(97.5%)" into a cell. Note that the function is cumulative, and so 97.5% includes the 95% confidence level plus the area in the lower tail (5%/2 = 2.5%).

2. **MegaStat** steps to find the confidence interval for the store manager's example are as follows:

   a. Select **MegaStat, Confidence Intervals/Sample Size,** and click the **Confidence interval – mean** tab.

   b. Enter *55420* for the **Mean,** *2150* for the **Std. Dev.** and *256* for **n.**

   c. Select z.

   d. Select 95% as the **Confidence Level.** Click the **Preview** box to see the answer, and click **OK.** *Note:* the answer may be slightly different from the calculator answer due to rounding.

Confidence Intervals / Sample Size — Mean 55420, Std. Dev. 2150, n 256, Confidence Level 95%, z, lower 55156.630, upper 55683.370

3. The **Excel** function to find the *t*-value is **T.INV.2T.** For the tire tread example, we would enter "=T.INV.2T(5%,9)" into a cell. The 5% is from 100% − 95% = 5%. The number of degrees of freedom is 10 − 1 = 9.

4. **MegaStat** steps to find the confidence interval for the tire tread example are as follows:

   a. Select **MegaStat, Confidence Intervals/Sample Size,** and click the **Confidence interval − mean** tab.

   b. Enter *.81* for the **Mean,** *.23* for the **Std. Dev.** and *10* for **n.**

   c. Select *t.*

   d. Select 95% as the **Confidence Level,** and click the **Preview** box to see the answer. *Note:* the answer may be slightly different due to rounding.

5. **MegaStat** steps to find the confidence interval for the Bottle Blowers of America example are as follows:

   a. Select **MegaStat, Confidence Intervals/Sample Size,** and click the **Confidence interval − p** tab.

   b. Enter *.8* for **p** and *2000* for **n.**

   c. Select 95% as the **Confidence Level,** and click the **Preview** box to see the answer. *Note:* the answer may be slightly different due to rounding.

6. **MegaStat** steps to find the sample size for the business administration example are as follows:

   a. Select **MegaStat, Confidence Intervals/Sample Size,** and select the **Sample size – mean** tab.

   b. Enter *100* for **E** and *1000* for the **Std. Dev.**

   c. Select 95% as the **Confidence Level,** and click the Preview box to see the answer. *Note:* two answers will appear: **N** and **N rounded up.** The answers may be slightly different from the answers obtained by using formulas due to rounding.

Confidence Intervals / Sample Size

Confidence interval - mean	
Confidence interval - p	`100` E
Sample size - mean	`1000` Std. Dev.
Sample size - (alpha, beta)	
Sample size - p	Confidence Level `95%`

OK Clear Cancel Help

N	N rounded up
Preview 384.146	385

7. **MegaStat** steps to find the sample size for the private refuse collectors example are as follows:

   a. Select **MegaStat, Confidence Intervals/Sample Size,** and select the **Sample size – p** tab.

   b. Enter *.10* for **E** and *.5* for **p.**

   c. Select 90% as the **Confidence Level,** and click the **Preview** box to see the answer. *Note:* two answers will appear: **N** and **N rounded up.** The answers may be slightly different from the answers obtained by using formulas due to rounding.

Confidence Intervals / Sample Size

Confidence interval - mean	
Confidence interval - p	`.10` E
Sample size - mean	`.5` p
Sample size - (alpha, beta)	
Sample size - p	Confidence Level `90%`

OK Clear Cancel Help

N	N rounded up
Preview 67.639	68

Answers to Self-Reviews

8–1 (a) Unknown. This is the value we want to estimate.

(b) $2000. This is called the *point estimate.*

(c) $2000 \pm 2.58 \dfrac{\$300}{\sqrt{40}} = \$2000 \pm 122.$

(d) The endpoints of the confidence interval are $1878 and $2122. About 99% of the intervals similarly constructed would include the population mean.

8–2 **(a)** $\bar{x} = \dfrac{18}{10} = 1.8$; $s = \sqrt{\dfrac{44 - \dfrac{(18)^2}{10}}{10 - 1}} = 1.1353$

(b) The population mean is not known. The best estimate is the sample mean, 1.8 days.

(c) $1.80 \pm 2.262 \dfrac{1.1353}{\sqrt{10}} = 1.80 \pm 0.81 = 0.99$ to 2.61

(d) t is used because the standard deviation of the population is unknown, but the population is assumed to be normally distributed.

(e) The value of 0 is not in the interval. It is unreasonable to conclude that the mean number of days of work missed is 0 per employee.

8–3 **(a)** $p = \dfrac{420}{1400} = 0.30.$

(b) $0.30 \pm 2.58(0.0122) = 0.30 \pm 0.03.$

(c) The interval is between 0.27 and 0.33. About 99% of the similarly constructed intervals would include the population mean.

8–4 $0.375 \pm 1.96 \sqrt{\dfrac{0.375(1 - 0.375)}{40}} \left(\sqrt{\dfrac{250 - 40}{250 - 1}} \right)$

$= 0.375 \pm 1.96(0.0765)(0.9184)$

$= 0.375 \pm 0.138$

$= 0.237$ to 0.513

The correction factor should be applied because $40/240 > 0.05$.

8–5 $n = \left(\dfrac{2.58(0.279)}{0.05} \right)^2 = 207.26.$

The sample should be rounded to 208.

CHAPTER 9
One-Sample Tests of Hypothesis

Noppawat Tom Charoensinphon/Getty Images

Dole Pineapple, Inc., is concerned that the 450 millilitre (mL) can of sliced pineapple is being overfilled. Assume that the standard deviation of the process is 0.85 mL. The quality control department took a random sample of 50 cans and found that the arithmetic mean volume was 451.4 mL. At the 5% level of significance, can we conclude that the mean volume is greater than 450 mL? Determine the p-value. (Exercise 32, LO9-6 & LO9-7)

LEARNING OBJECTIVES

When you have completed this chapter, you will be able to:

LO9-1 Define a hypothesis.

LO9-2 Explain the process of testing a hypothesis.

LO9-3 Apply the five-step procedure for testing a hypothesis.

LO9-4 Define Type I and Type II errors.

LO9-5 Distinguish between a one-tailed and a two-tailed test of hypothesis.

LO9-6 Conduct a test of hypothesis about a population mean.

LO9-7 Compute and interpret a p-value.

LO9-8 Use a t statistic to test a hypothesis.

LO9-9 Conduct a test of hypothesis about a population proportion.

9.1 INTRODUCTION

Chapter 7 began our study of statistical inference. We described how we could select a random sample to estimate the value of a population parameter. For example, we selected a sample of five employees at Spence Sprockets, found the number of years of service for each sampled employee, computed the mean years of service, and used the sample mean to estimate the mean years of service for all employees. In other words, we estimated a population parameter from a sample statistic.

Chapter 8 continued the study of statistical inference by developing a confidence interval. A confidence interval is a range of values within which we expect the population parameter to occur. In this chapter, rather than develop a range of values within which we expect the population parameter to occur, we develop a procedure to test the validity of a statement about a population parameter. Some examples of statements we can test are as follows:

- The mean number of kilometres (km) driven by those leasing a Chevy TrailBlazer for three years is 51 500 km.
- The mean time a Canadian family lives in a particular single-family dwelling is 11.8 years.
- The mean starting salary for graduates of business schools is $3500 per month.
- Eighty percent of those who play the lotteries regularly never win more than $100 in any one play.

This chapter and several of the following chapters describe statistical hypothesis testing. We begin by defining what we mean by a statistical hypothesis and statistical hypothesis testing. Next, we outline the steps in statistical hypothesis testing. Then we conduct tests of hypothesis

Hypothesis A statement about a population parameter subject to verification.

for means and proportions. In the last section of the chapter, we describe possible errors due to sampling in hypothesis testing.

LO9-1 ## 9.2 WHAT IS A HYPOTHESIS?

A **hypothesis** is a statement about a population. Data are then used to check the reasonableness of the statement. To begin, we need to define the word *hypothesis*. In the Canadian legal system, a person is presumed innocent until proven guilty. A jury hypothesizes that a person charged with a crime is innocent and reviews the evidence to assess if it is enough to support the claim that the person is guilty as charged. In a similar sense, a patient goes to a physician and reports various symptoms. The physician will order certain diagnostic tests and, on the basis of the symptoms and the test results, determine the treatment to be provided.

In statistical analysis, we make a claim, that is, state a hypothesis, collect data, and then use the data to test the claim.

In most cases, the population is so large that it is not feasible to study all the items, objects, or persons in the population. For example, it would not be possible to contact every business analyst in Canada to find out what his or her monthly income is. Likewise, the quality control department at Cooper Tire cannot check each tire produced to determine whether it will last more than 100 000 km.

As noted in Chapter 7, an alternative to measuring or interviewing the entire population is to take a sample from the population. We can, therefore, test a statement to determine whether the sample does or does not support the statement concerning the population.

Statistics in Action

LASIK (laser-assisted in situ keratomileusis) is a 15-minute surgical procedure that uses laser to reshape the cornea in the eye with the goal of improving eyesight. Research shows that about 5% of all surgeries involve complications, such as glare, corneal haze, overcorrection or undercorrection of vision, and loss of vision. In a statistical sense, the research tests a null hypothesis that the surgery will not improve eyesight with the alternative hypothesis that the surgery will improve eyesight. The sample data of LASIK surgery shows that 5% of all cases result in complications. The 5% represents a Type I error rate. When a person decides to have the surgery, he or she expects to reject the null hypothesis. In 5% of future cases, this expectation will not be met.
Source: Adapted from the American Academy of Ophthalmology, San Francisco.

Hypothesis testing A procedure based on sample evidence and probability theory to determine whether the hypothesis is a reasonable statement.

LO9-2 ## 9.3 WHAT IS HYPOTHESIS TESTING?

The terms *hypothesis testing* and *testing a hypothesis* are used interchangeably. **Hypothesis testing** starts with a statement, a claim, or an assumption about a population parameter—such as the population mean. This statement is referred to as a *hypothesis*. A hypothesis might be that the mean monthly commission of sales associates in retail electronic stores, such as Best Buy, is $3500. We cannot contact all these sales associates to ascertain that the mean is, in fact, $3500. The cost of locating and interviewing every sales associate would be exorbitant. To test the validity of the assumption ($\mu = \$3500$), we select a sample from the population of all electronics sales associates, calculate sample statistics and, on the basis of specific decision rules, reject or not reject the hypothesis. A sample mean of $1500 for the electronic sales associate would certainly cause rejection of the hypothesis. However, suppose that the sample mean is $3350. Is that close enough to $3500 for us to accept the assumption that the population mean is $3500? Can we attribute the difference of $150 between the two means to sampling error, or is that difference statistically significant?

LO9-3 ## 9.4 FIVE-STEP PROCEDURE FOR TESTING A HYPOTHESIS

There is a five-step procedure that systematizes hypothesis testing; when we get to step 5, we are ready to reject or not reject the hypothesis. However, hypothesis testing as used by statisticians does not provide proof that something is true in the manner in which a mathematician "proves" a statement. It does provide a kind of "proof beyond a reasonable doubt" in the manner of the court system. Hence, specific rules of evidence, or procedures, are followed. The steps are shown in the following diagram. We will discuss in detail each of the steps.

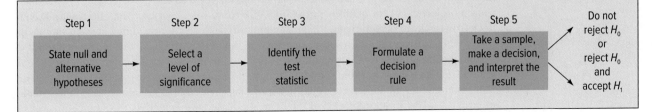

Step 1: State the Null Hypothesis (H_0) and the Alternative Hypothesis (H_1)

Null hypothesis A statement about the value of a population parameter developed for the purpose of testing numerical evidence.

The first step is to state the hypothesis being tested. It is called the **null hypothesis**, designated H_0, and read "*H sub zero.*" The capital letter *H* stands for hypothesis, and the subscript zero implies "no difference." There is usually a "not" or a "no" term in the null hypothesis; that is, there is "no change." For example, the null hypothesis is that the mean number of kilometres driven on the steel-belted tire is not different from 100 000. The null hypothesis would be written as: H_0: $\mu =$ 100 000 km. Generally, the null hypothesis is developed for the purpose of testing. We either reject or do not reject the null hypothesis. The null hypothesis is a statement that is not rejected unless the sample data provide convincing evidence that it is false.

We should emphasize that if the null hypothesis is not rejected on the basis of the sample data, we cannot say that the null hypothesis is true. To put it another way, the null hypothesis not being rejected does not prove that H_0 is true; it means that we have *failed to disprove H_0*. To prove without any doubt the null hypothesis is true, the population parameter would have to be known. To actually determine it, we would have to test, survey, or count every item in the population. This is usually not feasible. The alternative is to take a sample from the population.

It should be noted that we often begin the null hypothesis by stating, "There is no *significant* difference between . . . ," or "The mean impact strength of the glass is not *significantly* different from. . . ." When we select a sample from a population, the sample statistic is usually numerically different from the hypothesized population parameter. As an illustration, suppose the hypothesized impact strength of a glass plate is 500 kilopascals (kPa), and the mean impact strength of a sample of 12 glass plates is 495 kPa. We must make a decision about the difference of 5 kPa. Is it a true difference, that is, a significant difference, or is the difference between the sample statistic (495) and the hypothesized population parameter (500) due to chance (sampling)? To answer this question, we conduct a test of significance, commonly referred to as a test of hypothesis.

Alternative hypothesis A statement that is accepted if the sample data provide sufficient evidence that the null hypothesis is false.

The term **alternative hypothesis** describes what you will conclude if you reject the null hypothesis. It is written H_1 and is read "*H sub one.*" It is also referred to as the *research hypothesis*. The alternative hypothesis is accepted if the sample data provide us with enough statistical evidence that the null hypothesis is false.

The following example will help clarify what is meant by the null hypothesis and the alternative hypothesis: A recent article indicated that the mean age of U.S. commercial aircraft is 15 years. To conduct a statistical test regarding this statement, the first step is to determine the null and the alternative hypotheses. The null hypothesis represents the current or reported condition. It is written as: H_0: $\mu = 15$. The alternative hypothesis is that the statement is not true, written as: H_1: $\mu \neq 15$. It is important to remember that no matter how the problem is stated, *the null hypothesis will always contain the equal sign*. The equal sign ($=$) will never appear in the alternative hypothesis. Why? Because the null hypothesis is the statement being tested, and we need a specific value to include in our calculations. We turn to the alternative hypothesis only if the data suggest that the null hypothesis is not true.

Step 2: Select a Level of Significance

After setting up the null hypothesis and alternative hypothesis, the next step is to state the **level of significance**.

Level of significance The probability of rejecting the null hypothesis when it is true.

The level of significance is designated α, the Greek letter alpha. It is also sometimes called the level of risk. This may be a more appropriate term because it is the risk you take of rejecting the null hypothesis when it is really true.

There is no one level of significance that is applied to all tests. The 0.05 level (often stated as the 5% level), the 0.01 level, and the 0.10 level are the most common levels of significance, but any value between 0 and 1 can be used. Traditionally, the 0.05 level is selected for consumer research projects, 0.01 for quality control, and 0.10 for political polling. You, the researcher, must decide on the level of significance *before* formulating a decision rule and collecting sample data.

To illustrate how it is possible to reject a true hypothesis, suppose that a firm manufacturing personal computers uses a large number of printed circuit boards. Suppliers bid on the boards, and the one with the lowest bid is awarded a sizable contract. Suppose that the contract specifies that the computer manufacturer's quality control department will sample all incoming shipments of circuit boards. If more than 6% of the boards sampled are defective, the shipment is rejected.

LO9-4

Type I error Rejecting the null hypothesis, H_0, when it is true.

Type II error Not rejecting the null hypothesis when it is false.

The null hypothesis is that the incoming shipment of boards contains 6% or less defective boards. The alternative hypothesis is that more than 6% of the boards are defective.

A shipment of 4000 circuit boards was received from Allied Electronics and a random sample of 50 circuit boards was selected for testing. Of the 50 circuit boards sampled, 4 boards, or 8%, were defective. The shipment was rejected because it exceeded the maximum of 6% defective circuit boards. If the shipment actually failed to meet the criteria for acceptance, then the decision to return the boards to the supplier was correct. However, suppose that the 4 defective circuit boards selected in the sample of 50 were the only ones in the shipment of 4000 boards. Then only 1/10 of 1% were defective (4/4000 = 0.001). In that case, less than 6% of the entire shipment was defective, and rejecting the shipment was an error. In terms of hypothesis testing, we rejected the null hypothesis when we should not have rejected the null hypothesis. By rejecting a true null hypothesis, we committed a **Type I error**. The probability of committing a Type I error is α.

The probability of committing another type of error, called a **Type II error**, is designated by the Greek letter beta (β).

The firm manufacturing personal computers would commit a Type II error if, unknown to the manufacturer, an incoming shipment of circuit boards from Allied Electronics contained 15% defective boards, yet the shipment was not rejected. How could this happen? Suppose 2 of the 50 boards in the sample (4%) tested were defective, and 48 of the 50 were good boards. According to the stated procedure, because the sample contained less than 6% defective boards, the shipment was accepted. It could be that *by chance* the 48 good boards selected in the sample were the only acceptable ones in the entire shipment of thousands of boards!

In retrospect, the researcher cannot study every item or individual in the population. Thus, there is a possibility of two types of error—a Type I error, wherein the null hypothesis is rejected when it should not have been rejected, and a Type II error, wherein the null hypothesis is not rejected when it should have been rejected.

We often refer to the probability of these two possible types of errors as *alpha*, α, and *beta*, β. Alpha (α) is the probability of making a Type I error, and beta (β) is the probability of making a Type II error. The following table summarizes the decisions the researcher could make and the possible consequences:

	Researcher	
Null Hypothesis	**Not Rejecting H_0**	**Rejects H_0**
H_0 is true.	Correct decision	Type I error
H_0 is false.	Type II error	Correct decision

Step 3: Select the Test Statistic

Test statistic A value, determined from sample information, used to determine whether to reject the null hypothesis.

There are many **test statistics**. In this chapter, we use both z and t as the test statistic. In other chapters, we will use such test statistics as F and χ^2, called *chi-square*.

In hypothesis testing for the mean (μ) when σ is known, the test statistic z is computed by:

z TEST STATISTIC	$z = \dfrac{\overline{x} - \mu}{\sigma/\sqrt{n}}$	[9–1]

The z value is based on the sampling distribution of $\overline{x}$, which follows the normal distribution with a mean ($\mu_{\overline{x}}$) equal to μ, and a standard deviation $\sigma_{\overline{x}}$, which is equal to $\sigma/\sqrt{n}$. We can thus determine whether the difference between $\overline{x}$ and μ is statistically significant by finding the number of standard deviations $\overline{x}$ is from μ using formula (9–1).

Step 4: Formulate the Decision Rule

A decision rule is a statement of the specific conditions for which the null hypothesis is rejected and of the conditions under which it is not rejected. The region or area of rejection defines the location of all those values that are so large or so small that the probability of their occurrence for a true null hypothesis is rather remote.

Statistics in Action

During World War II, allied military planners needed estimates of the number of German tanks. The information provided by traditional spying methods was not reliable, but statistical methods proved to be valuable. For example, espionage and reconnaissance led analysts to estimate that 1550 tanks were produced during June of 1941. However, using the serial numbers of captured tanks and statistical analysis, military planners estimated the number to be 244. The actual number of tanks produced, as determined from German production records, was 271. The estimate using statistical analysis turned out to be much more accurate. A similar type of analysis was used to estimate the number of Iraqi tanks destroyed during the Desert Storm operation more recently.

Critical value The dividing point between the region where the null hypothesis is rejected and the region where it is not rejected.

Chart 9–1 portrays the rejection region for a test of significance that will be conducted later in the chapter.

CHART 9–1 Sampling Distribution of the Statistic z, a Right-Tailed Test, 0.05 Level of Significance

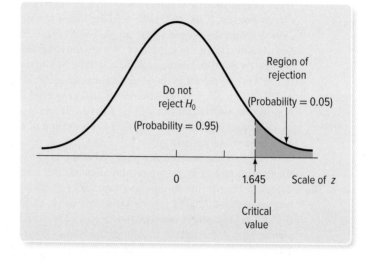

Note in the chart that:

1. The area where the null hypothesis is not rejected is equal to or to the left of 1.645. We will explain how to get the 1.645 value shortly.
2. The area of rejection is to the right of 1.645.
3. A one-tailed test is being applied. (This will also be explained later.)
4. The 0.05 level of significance was chosen.
5. The sampling distribution of the statistic z follows the normal probability distribution.
6. The value 1.645 separates the regions where the null hypothesis is rejected and where it is not rejected.
7. The value 1.645 is the **critical value**.

Step 5: Make a Decision and Interpret the Result

The fifth and final step in hypothesis testing is to compute the test statistic, compare it with the critical value, make a decision to reject or not reject the null hypothesis, and interpret the results. Referring to Chart 9–1, if, based on sample information, the test statistic z is computed to be 2.34, the null hypothesis is rejected at the 0.05 level of significance. The decision to reject H_0 was made because 2.34 falls in the region of rejection, that is, beyond 1.645. We would reject the null hypothesis, reasoning that it is highly improbable that a computed z-value this large is due to sampling error (chance).

Had the computed value been 1.645 or less, say, 0.71, the null hypothesis is not rejected. It is reasoned that such a small computed value could be attributed to chance, that is, sampling error. As noted, only one of two decisions is possible in hypothesis testing—either reject or do not reject the null hypothesis. If the null hypothesis is not rejected, some researchers prefer to phrase the decision as: "Do not reject H_0," "We fail to reject H_0," or "There is not enough evidence to reject H_0."

However, because the decision is based on a sample, it is always possible to make either of two decision errors. A Type I error is when the null hypothesis is rejected when it should not be rejected. Or, it is also possible to make a Type II error when the null hypothesis is not rejected and it should have been rejected. So, be cautious with your interpretation because by not rejecting the null hypothesis, you did not prove it to be true, simply that the difference between the sample mean and hypothesized population mean was not large enough to reject the null hypothesis.

Summary of the Steps in Hypothesis Testing

1. Establish the null hypothesis (H_0) and the alternative hypothesis (H_1).
2. Select the level of significance, that is, α.
3. Select an appropriate test statistic.

4. Formulate a decision rule based on steps 1, 2, and 3 above.
5. Make a decision regarding the null hypothesis based on the sample information. Interpret the results of the test.

Before actually conducting a test of hypothesis, we describe the difference between a one-tailed test of significance and a two-tailed test.

LO9-5 9.5 ONE-TAILED AND TWO-TAILED TESTS OF SIGNIFICANCE

Refer to Chart 9–1. It shows a one-tailed test. It is called a one-tailed test because the rejection region is only in one tail. In this case, it is in the right, or upper tail, of the curve. To illustrate, suppose that the packaging department at General Foods Corporation is concerned that some boxes of the Grape Nuts cereal are significantly overweight. The cereal is packaged in 453-gram (g) boxes, so the null hypothesis is: H_0: $\mu \leq 453$. This is read as: "the population mean (μ) is equal to or less than 453." The alternative hypothesis, therefore, is: H_1: $\mu > 453$. This is read as: "μ is greater than 453." Note that the inequality sign in the alternative hypothesis ($>$) points to the region of rejection in the upper tail. (See Chart 9–1.) Also note that the null hypothesis includes the equal sign. That is, H_0: $\mu \leq 453$. The equality condition always appears in H_0 but never in H_1.

Chart 9–2 portrays a situation where the rejection region is in the left (lower) tail of the standard normal distribution. As an illustration, consider the problem of automobile manufacturers, large automobile leasing companies, and other organizations that purchase large quantities of tires. They want the tires to average, say, 100 000 km of wear under normal usage. They will, therefore, reject a shipment of tires if tests reveal that the mean life of the tires is significantly below 100 000 km. They gladly accept a shipment if the mean life is greater than 100 000 km! They are not concerned about this possibility, however. They are concerned only if they have sample evidence to conclude that the tires will average less than 100 000 km of useful life. Thus, the test is set up to satisfy the concern of the automobile manufacturers that *the mean life of the tires is not less than 100 000 km.* This statement appears in the alternative hypothesis. The null and alternative hypotheses in this case are written as: H_0: $\mu \geq 100\ 000$ and H_1: $\mu < 100\ 000$.

CHART 9–2 Sampling Distribution for the Statistic z, Left-Tailed Test, 0.05 Level of Significance

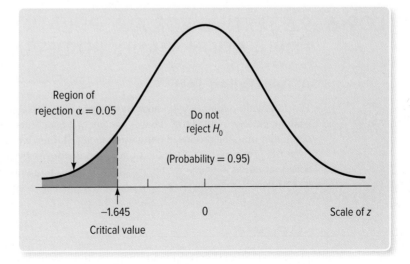

One way to determine the location of the rejection region is to look at the direction in which the inequality sign in the alternative hypothesis is pointing (either $<$ or $>$). In the tire wear problem, it is pointing to the left, and the rejection region is therefore in the left tail.

In summary, a test is *one-tailed* when the alternative hypothesis, H_1, states a direction, such as:

H_0: The mean income of female stockbrokers is less than or equal to $85 000 per year.
H_1: The mean income of female stockbrokers is *greater* than $85 000 per year.

If no direction is specified in the alternative hypothesis, we use a *two-tailed* test. Changing the previous problem to illustrate the following:

H_0: The mean income of female stockbrokers is $85 000 per year.
H_1: The mean income of female stockbrokers is *not equal to* $85 000 per year.

If the null hypothesis is rejected and H_1 is not rejected in the two-tailed case, the mean income could be significantly greater than $85 000 per year, or it could be significantly less than $85 000 per year. To accommodate these two possibilities, the 5% area of rejection is divided equally into the two tails of the sampling distribution (2.5% each). Chart 9–3 shows the two areas and the critical values. Note that the total area in the normal distribution is 1.0000, found by 0.9500 + 0.0250 + 0.0250.

Chart 9–3 Regions of Nonrejection and Rejection for a Two-Tailed Test, 0.05 Level of Significance

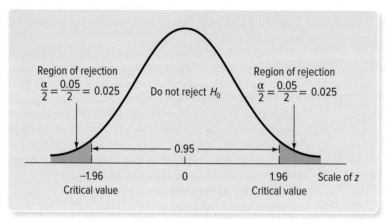

LO9-6   9.6 TESTING FOR A POPULATION MEAN: KNOWN POPULATION STANDARD DEVIATION

A Two-Tailed Test

The following example will show the details of the five-step hypothesis testing procedure. We wish to use a two-tailed test. That is, we are *not* concerned whether the sample results are larger or smaller than the proposed population mean. Rather, we are interested in whether it is *different from* the proposed value for the population mean. We begin, as we did in the previous chapter, with a situation in which we have historical information about the population and, in fact, know its standard deviation.

Example

Jamestown Steel Company manufactures and assembles desks and other office equipment at several plants. The weekly production of the Model A325 desk follows a normal probability distribution, with a mean of 200 and a standard deviation of 16. Recently, due to market expansion, new production methods have been introduced and new employees hired. The vice-president of manufacturing would like to investigate whether there has been a change in the weekly production of the Model A325 desk. Is the mean number of desks produced different from 200? Test using the 0.01 significance level.

Solution

In this example, we know two important pieces of information: (1) the population of weekly production follows the normal distribution, and (2) the standard deviation of this normal distribution is 16 desks per week. So, it is appropriate to use the z statistic for this problem. We use the statistical hypothesis testing procedure to investigate whether the production rate has changed from 200 per week.

Step 1: **State the null hypothesis and the alternative hypothesis.** The null hypothesis is: "The population mean is 200." The alternative hypothesis is: "The mean is different from 200" or "The mean is not 200." These two hypotheses are written as:

$$H_0: \mu = 200$$
$$H_1: \mu \neq 200$$

This is a *two-tailed test* because the alternative hypothesis does not state a direction. In other words, it does not state whether the mean production is greater than 200 or less than 200. The vice-president only wants to find out whether the production rate is different from 200.

Before moving to Step 2 of the hypothesis-testing procedure, we emphasize two points.

- The null hypothesis has the equal sign. Why? Because the value we are testing is always in the null hypothesis. Logically, the alternative hypothesis never contains the equal sign.
- Both the null hypothesis and the alternative hypothesis contain Greek letters—in this case μ, which is the symbol for the population mean. Tests of hypothesis **always** refer to population parameters, never sample statistics. To put it another way, you will never see the symbol $\bar{x}$ as part of the null hypothesis or the alternative hypothesis.

Step 2: **Select the level of significance.** In the example description, the significance level selected is 0.01. This is α, the probability of committing a Type I error, and it is the probability of rejecting a true null hypothesis.

Step 3: **Select the test statistic.** The test statistic is z when the population standard deviation is known. Transforming the production data to standard units (z-values) permits their use not only in this problem but also in other hypothesis-testing problems. Formula (9–1) for z is repeated below with the various letters identified.

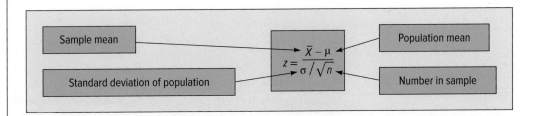

Step 4: **Formulate the decision rule.** We formulate the decision rule by first determining the critical values of z. Since this is a two-tailed test, half of 0.01, or 0.005, is placed in each tail. The area where H_0 is not rejected, located between the two tails, is therefore 0.99. Using Student's t distribution in Appendix B.2, move to the top of the margin called "Level of Significance for Two-Tailed Tests, α," select the column with $\alpha = 0.01$, and move to the last row, which is labelled ∞, or infinite degrees of freedom. The z-value in this cell is 2.576, which is rounded to 2.58.

The details of this problem are shown in Chart 9–4.

CHART 9–4 Decision Rule for the 0.01 Significance Level

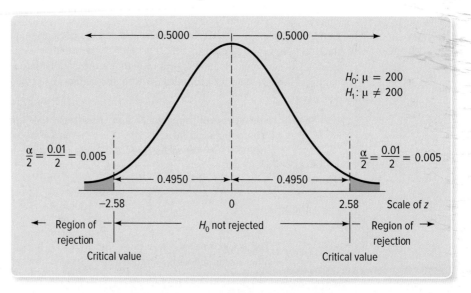

The decision rule is: if the computed value of z is not between -2.58 and 2.58, reject the null hypothesis. If z falls between -2.58 and 2.58, do not reject the null hypothesis.

Step 5: Make a decision and interpret the results. Take a sample from the population (weekly production), compute z, apply the decision rule, and arrive at a decision to reject H_0 or not reject H_0. The mean number of desks produced last year (50 weeks, because the plant was shut down two weeks for vacation) is 203.5. The standard deviation of the population is 16 desks per week. Computing the z-value from formula (9–1):

$$z = \frac{\bar{x} - \mu}{\sigma/\sqrt{n}} = \frac{203.5 - 200}{16/\sqrt{50}} = 1.55$$

Because 1.55 does not fall in the rejection region, H_0 is not rejected. We were not able to demonstrate that the population mean has changed from 200 per week. Therefore, we conclude that the population mean is *not* different from 200. To put it another way, the difference between the population mean of 200 per week and the sample mean of 203.5 could simply be due to chance.

What should we report to the vice-president of manufacturing? That the sample information did not indicate that the new production methods result in a change in the weekly production rate. The difference of 3.5 units per week between the past weekly production rate and that last year can reasonably be attributed to sampling error. Therefore, there was not enough evidence to reject the null hypothesis. This information is summarized in the following chart:

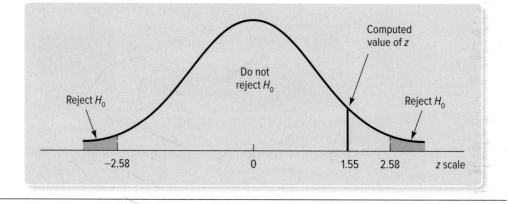

excel   Computer commands for hypothesis testing for the above example can be found at the end of the chapter.

Did we prove that the assembly rate is still 200 per week? Not really. What we did, technically, was *fail to disprove the null hypothesis*. Failing to disprove the hypothesis that the population mean is 200 is not the same thing as proving it to be true. As we suggested in the chapter introduction, the conclusion is analogous to the Canadian judicial system. To explain, suppose that a person is accused of a crime but is acquitted by a jury. If a person is acquitted of a crime, the conclusion is that there was not enough evidence to prove the person guilty. The trial did not prove that the individual was innocent but only that there was not enough evidence to prove the defendant was guilty. That is what we do in statistical hypothesis testing when we do not reject the null hypothesis. The correct interpretation is that we have failed to disprove the null hypothesis.

We selected the significance level, 0.01 in this case, before setting up the decision rule and sampling the population. This is the appropriate strategy. The significance level should be set by the investigator, but it should be determined *before* gathering the sample evidence and not changed on the basis of the sample evidence.

How does the hypothesis testing procedure just described compare with that of confidence intervals discussed in the previous chapter? When we conducted the test of hypothesis regarding the production of desks, we changed the units from desks per week to a z-value. Then, we compared the computed value of the test statistic (1.55) to that of the critical values (-2.58 and 2.58). Because the computed value was in the region where the null hypothesis was not rejected, we concluded that the population mean could be 200. To use the confidence interval approach, however, we would develop a confidence interval, on the basis of formula (8–1). The interval would be from 197.66 to 209.34, found by $203.5 \pm 2.58 \ (16/\sqrt{50})$. Note that the hypothesized population parameter, 200, is within this interval. Hence, we would conclude that the population mean could reasonably be 200.

In general, H_0 is rejected if the confidence interval does not include the hypothesized value. If the confidence interval includes the hypothesized value, then H_0 is not rejected. So, the "do not reject" region for a test of hypothesis is equivalent to the proposed population value occurring in the confidence interval.

---

self-review 9–1

The mean annual turnover rate of the 200-count bottle of Bayer Aspirin is 6.0 with a standard deviation of 0.50. (This indicates that the stock of Bayer Aspirin turns over on the pharmacy shelves an average of six times per year.) It is suspected that the mean turnover has changed and is not 6.0. Use the 0.05 significance level.

(a) State the null hypothesis and the alternative hypothesis.
(b) What is the probability of a Type I error?
(c) Give the formula for the test statistic.
(d) State the decision rule.
(e) A random sample of 64 bottles of the 200-count size Bayer Aspirin showed a mean of 5.84. Should we reject the hypothesis that the population mean is 6.0? State your conclusion.

A One-Tailed Test

In the previous example, we emphasized that we were only concerned with reporting to the vice-president whether there had been a change in the mean number of desks assembled. We were not concerned with whether the change was an increase or a decrease in the production.

To illustrate a one-tailed test, let us change the problem. Suppose the vice-president wants to know whether there has been an *increase* in the number of units assembled. Can we conclude, because of the improved production methods, that the mean number of desks assembled in the last 50 weeks was more than 200? Look at the difference in the way the problem is formulated. In the first case, we wanted to know whether there was a *difference* in the mean number assembled, but now we want to know whether there has been an *increase*. Because we are investigating different questions, we will set our hypotheses differently. The biggest difference occurs in the

alternative hypothesis. Before, we stated the alternative hypothesis as "different from"; now we want to state it as "greater than." In symbols:

A two-tailed test:	A one-tailed test:
$H_0: \mu = 200$	$H_0: \mu \leq 200$
$H_1: \mu \neq 200$	$H_1: \mu > 200$

The critical values for a one-tailed test are different from a two-tailed test at the same significance level. In the previous example, we split the significance level in half and put half in the lower tail and half in the upper tail. In a one-tailed test, we put all the rejection region in one tail. See Chart 9–5.

CHART 9–5 Rejection Regions for Two-Tailed and One-Tailed Tests, $\alpha = 0.01$

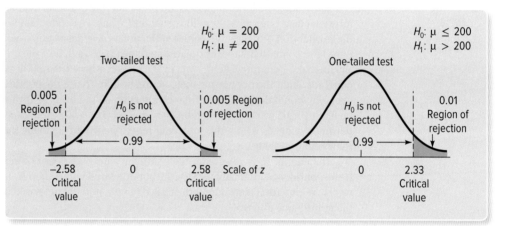

For the one-tailed test, the critical value is 2.33. Refer to the Student's t Distribution table in Appendix B.2, move to the top heading called "level of Significance for One-Tailed Tests, α", select the column with $\alpha = 0.01$, and move to the last row, which is labelled ∞, or infinite degrees of freedom. The value in this cell is 2.326, rounded to 2.33.

The following table summarizes common z-values used in hypothesis testing:

Significance Level	Two-tailed Test	One-tailed Test
0.01	2.58	2.33
0.02	2.33	2.05
0.05	1.96	1.645
0.10	1.645	1.28

LO9-7   9.7 p-VALUE IN HYPOTHESIS TESTING

In testing a hypothesis, we compared the test statistic to a critical value. A decision is made to either reject the null hypothesis or not reject it. So, for example, if the critical value is 1.96 and the computed value of the test statistic is 2.19, the decision is to reject the null hypothesis.

In recent years, spurred by the availability of computer software, additional information is often reported on the strength of the rejection. That is, how confident are we in rejecting the null hypothesis? This approach reports the probability (assuming that the null hypothesis is true) of getting a value of the test statistic at least as extreme as the value actually obtained. This process compares the probability, called the **p-value**, with the significance level. If the p-value is smaller than the significance level, H_0 is rejected. If it is larger than the significance level, H_0 is not rejected.

p-value The probability of
observing a sample value
as extreme as, or more
extreme than, the value
observed, when the null
hypothesis is true.

Determining the p-value not only results in a decision regarding H_0, but it gives us additional insight into the strength of the decision. On the one hand, a very small p-value, such as 0.0001, indicates that there is little likelihood the H_0 is true. On the other hand, a p-value of 0.2033 means that H_0 is not rejected, and there is little likelihood that it is false.

How do we find the p-value? To calculate p-values, we will use the z table (Appendix B.1) and round z to two decimal places. To illustrate how to compute the p-value, we use the example in which we tested the null hypothesis that the mean number of desks produced per week was 200. We did not reject the null hypothesis because the value of 1.55 fell in the region between −2.58 and 2.58. We agreed not to reject the null hypothesis if the computed value of z fell in this region. Using the z table, the probability of finding a z-value of 1.55 or more is 0.0606, found by $0.5000 − 0.4394$. To put it another way, the probability of obtaining an $\bar{x}$ greater than 203.5 if $\mu = 200$ is 0.0606. To compute the p-value, we need to be concerned with the region less than −1.55 as well as the values greater than 1.55 (because the rejection region is in both tails). The two-tailed p-value is 0.1212, found by 2(0.0606). The p-value of 0.1212 is greater than the significance level of 0.01 decided upon initially, so H_0 is not rejected. The details are shown in the following graph. In general, the area is doubled in a two-sided test. Then the p-value can be easily compared with the significance level. The same decision rule is used as in the one-sided test.

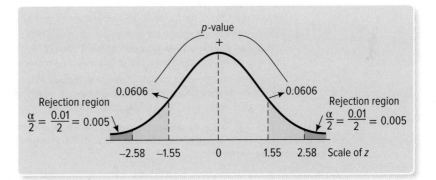

A p-value is a way to express the likelihood that H_0 is false. But how do we interpret a p-value? We have already said that if the p-value is less than the significance level, then we reject H_0; if it is greater than the significance level, then we do not reject H_0. Also, if the p-value is very large, then it is likely that H_0 is true. If the p-value is small, then it is likely that H_0 is not true. The following will help to interpret p-values:

Interpreting the Weight of Evidence Against H_0

If the p-value is less than:

(a) 0.10, we have *some evidence* that H_0 is not true.
(b) 0.05, we have *strong evidence* that H_0 is not true.
(c) 0.01, we have *very strong evidence* that H_0 is not true.
(d) 0.001, we have *extremely strong evidence* that H_0 is not true.

self-review 9–2

Refer to self-review 9–1.

(a) Suppose that the situation was changed to read as follows: Does this evidence suggest that the mean annual turnover rate is less than 6.0? State the null hypothesis and the alternative hypothesis under these conditions.
(b) What is the decision rule under the new conditions stated in part (a)? Show the decision rule graphically. Show the rejection region and indicate the critical value.
(c) What is the p-value? What is your decision regarding the null hypothesis based on the p-value?

EXERCISES

1. For each of the following, state the null hypothesis and the alternative hypothesis:

   a. A new cash register has been installed at the Stop One Convenience Store. The manager wants to see if the new register has made a difference in the average amount of time a customer takes to be served. The previous mean time for a customer to be served was two minutes.

   b. The shipping dock receives 40-kilogram (kg) bags of flour to use in the production of the baked goods produced by Little Cakes Inc. A sample of 25 bags is taken from each shipment and weighed to ensure that the average weight is at least 40 kg. If not, the shipment is returned to the supplier.

   c. An insurance company states that its average claim is $1750. However, the company auditor feels that the average amount is actually higher than $1750 and takes a sample of 60 recent claims to test his theory.

   d. The college cafeteria claims that the average amount spent by a student per visit is $3.25. A random sample of 200 students is taken to see if this claim can be verified.

2. For each of the following, state the null hypothesis and the alternative hypothesis:

   a. The publisher of *Celebrity Living* claims that the mean sales of personality magazines featuring such celebrities as Angelina Jolie or Kim Kardashian is at least 1.5 million per week. A sample of 10 comparable titles shows that the mean weekly sales last week was 1.3 million. The publisher's claim is to be verified.

   b. The manager of Little Cakes Inc. states that an average of 1500 muffins is sold each week in the retail store. One of the bakers feels that the average is less than 1500 and decides to test this claim.

   c. For the past three years, an insurance company has stated that its average claim amount is $2000. The manager feels that this amount should be updated and takes a sample of 55 claims to see if there is a difference in the average claim amount.

   d. A machine on a production line is set to automatically fill each bottle with 500 mL of water. The quality control manager regularly takes random samples of the bottles from the production line to ensure that the machine is filling the bottles correctly. If not, the machine will need adjusting.

For Exercises 3–6, answer the questions: (a) Is this a one- or two-tailed test? (b) What is the decision rule? (c) What is the value of the test statistic? (d) What is your decision regarding H_0? (e) Determine the p-value and interpret it.

3. A sample of 36 observations is selected from a normal population. The sample mean is 49, and the population standard deviation is 5. Conduct the following test of hypothesis using the 0.05 significance level:

$$H_0: \mu = 50$$
$$H_1: \mu \neq 50$$

4. An online retailer ships products from overseas with an advertised delivery date within 10 days. To test whether or not deliveries are made within the advertised time, a random sample of 36 orders is selected from a normal population. The sample mean delivery time is 12 days, and the known population standard deviation is 3 days. Conduct the following test of hypothesis using the 0.01 significance level:

$$H_0: \mu \leq 10$$
$$H_1: \mu > 10$$

5. Made Fresh pasta averages a wait time of 20 minutes for customers to pick up their take-out orders. Periodically, the manager will take a sample of the orders to see if the wait times have increased. A sample of 36 orders is selected from a Friday afternoon. The sample mean wait time is 21 minutes. The population is known to be normally distributed with a standard deviation of 5 minutes. Conduct the following test of hypothesis using the 0.05 significance level:

$$H_0: \mu \leq 20$$
$$H_1: \mu > 20$$

6. A sample of 64 observations is selected from a normal population. The sample mean is 215, and the population standard deviation is 15. Conduct the following test of hypothesis using the 0.03 significance level:

$$H_0: \mu \geq 220$$
$$H_1: \mu < 220$$

For Exercises 7–10: (a) State the null hypothesis and the alternative hypothesis. (b) State the decision rule. (c) Compute the value of the test statistic. (d) What is your decision regarding H_0? (e) What is the p-value? Interpret it.

7. The manufacturer of the X-15 steel-belted radial truck tire claims that the mean mileage the tire can be driven before the tread wears out is 96 600 km. The population standard deviation of the mileage is 8050 km. The Crosset Truck Company bought 48 tires and found that the mean mileage for its trucks is 95 795 km. Is Crosset's experience different from that claimed by the manufacturer at the 0.05 level of significance

8. The waiting time for customers at MacBurger Restaurants follows a normal distribution with a population standard deviation of 1 minute. At the Warren Road MacBurger, the quality assurance department sampled 50 customers and found that the mean waiting time was 2.75 minutes. At the 0.05 significance level, can we conclude that the mean waiting time is less than 3 minutes?

9. A recent national survey found that high school students watched an average (mean) of 6.8 DVDs per month, with a population standard deviation of 0.5 DVDs per month. The distribution of the number of DVDs watched follows the normal distribution. A random sample of 36 college students revealed that the mean number of DVDs watched last month was 6.2. At the 0.05 significance level, can we conclude that college students watch fewer DVDs a month than high school students?

10. At the time she was hired as a server at the Grumney Family Restaurant, Beth Brigden was told, "You can average more than $80 a day in tips." Assume that the population of daily tips is normally distributed, with a standard deviation of $3.24. Over the first 35 days she was employed at the restaurant, the mean daily amount of her tips was $84.65. At the 0.01 significance level, can Ms. Brigden conclude that her daily tips average more than $80?

LO9-8 9.8 TESTING FOR A POPULATION MEAN: POPULATION STANDARD DEVIATION (σ) UNKNOWN

In the preceding example, we knew σ, the population standard deviation, and that the population followed the normal distribution. In most cases, however, the population standard deviation is unknown. Thus, σ must be based on prior studies or estimated by the sample standard deviation, s. The population standard deviation in the following example is not known, so the sample standard deviation is used to estimate σ.

To find the value of the test statistic, we use the t distribution and revise formula (9–1) as follows:

PTESTING A MEAN, σ UNKNOWN	$$t = \frac{\overline{x} - \mu}{s/\sqrt{n}}$$	[9–2]

with $n - 1$ degrees of freedom, where

$\overline{x}$ is the sample mean.
μ is the hypothesized population mean.
s is the sample standard deviation.
n is the number of observations in the sample.

We encountered this same situation when constructing confidence intervals in Chapter 8. We summarized this problem in Chart 8–3. Under these conditions, the correct statistical procedure is to replace the standard normal distribution with the t distribution. To review, the major characteristics of the t distribution are as follows:

1. It is a continuous distribution.
2. It is bell shaped and symmetric.
3. There is a family of t distributions. Each time the degrees of freedom change, a new distribution is created.
4. As the number of degrees of freedom increases, the shape of the t distribution approaches that of the standard normal distribution.
5. The t distribution is more spread out than the standard normal distribution.

The following example shows the details:

Example	The McFarland Insurance Company Claims Department reports that the mean cost to process a claim is $60. An industry comparison showed this amount to be larger than most other insurance companies, so the company instituted cost-cutting measures. To evaluate the effect of the cost-cutting measures, McFarland selected a random sample of 26 claims processed last month and determined the cost to process these selected claims. The sample information is reported below:

$45	49	62	40	43	61
48	53	67	63	78	64
48	54	51	56	63	69
58	51	58	59	56	57
38	76				

At the 0.01 significance level, is it reasonable to conclude that the mean cost to produce a claim is now less than $60?

Solution	We will use the five-step hypothesis testing procedure.

Step 1: **State the null hypothesis and the alternative hypothesis.** The null hypothesis is that the population mean is at least $60. The alternative hypothesis is that the population mean is less than $60. We can express the null and alternative hypotheses as follows:

$$H_0: \mu \geq \$60$$

$$H_0: \mu < \$60$$

The test is *one*-tailed because we want to determine if there has been a *reduction* in the cost. The inequality in the alternative hypothesis points to the region of rejection in the left tail of the distribution.

Step 2: **Select the level of significance.** We decided on the 0.01 significance level.

Step 3: **Select the test statistic.** The test statistic in this situation is the t distribution. Why? First, it is reasonable to conclude that the distribution of the cost per claim follows the normal distribution. We can confirm this from the following histogram and from the normal curve superimposed on the chart:

Summary of Cost
Normal

Mean 56.42
Std. dev. 10.04
N 26

the same for each trial; and (4) the trials are independent, meaning the outcome of one trial does not affect the outcome of any other trial. **The test we will conduct is appropriate when both n_p and $n(1-p)$ are at least 5,** where n is the sample size, and p is the population proportion. It uses the fact that a binomial distribution can be approximated by a normal distribution.

Example	Suppose that prior elections in a northern riding of the province indicate that it is necessary for a candidate to receive at least 80% of the vote to be elected. The incumbent Member of Parliament (MP) is interested in assessing his chances of returning to office and plans to conduct a survey of 2000 registered voters in the northern riding of the province. Using the hypothesis testing procedure, assess the incumbent's chances of re-election.
Solution	This situation meets binomial conditions following:

- There are only two possible outcomes. That is, a sampled voter will either vote or not vote for the MP.
- The probability of success is the same for each trial. In this case, the likelihood a particular sampled voter will support re-election is 0.80.
- The trials are independent. This means, for example, the likelihood the 23rd voter sampled will support re-election is not affected by what the 22nd or 55th voter does.
- The sampled data is the result of counts. We are going to count the number of voters who support re-election in the sample of 2000.

We can use the normal approximation to the binomial distribution when both np and $n(1-p)$ exceed 5. In this case, $n = 2000$ and $p = 0.80$ (p is the proportion of the vote in the riding, or 80% needed to be elected). Thus, $np = 2000(0.80) = 1600$ and $n(1-p) = 2000(1-0.80) = 400$. Both 1600 and 400 are greater than 5.

Step 1: **State the null hypothesis and the alternative hypothesis.** The null hypothesis, H_0, is that the population proportion, p, is 0.80 or larger. The alternative hypothesis, H_1, is that the proportion is less than 0.80. From a practical standpoint, the incumbent feels concerned only when the proportion is less than 0.80. If it is equal to or greater than 0.80, he will have no problem; that is, the sample data would indicate he will probably be re-elected. These hypotheses are written symbolically as:

$$H_0: p \geq 80$$
$$H_1: p < 80$$

H_1 states a direction. Thus, as noted previously, the test is one-tailed with the inequality sign pointing to the tail of the distribution containing the region of rejection.

Step 2: **Select the level of significance.** The level of significance is 0.05. This is the likelihood that a true hypothesis will be rejected.

Step 3: **Select the test statistic.** z is the appropriate statistic, found by:

TEST OF HYPOTHESIS, ONE PROPORTION	$z = \dfrac{\bar{p} - p}{\sigma_p}$	[9–3]

where:

- p is the hypothesized population proportion parameter.
- $\bar{p}$ is the sample proportion.
- n is the sample size.
- σ_p is the standard error of the population proportion. It is computed by $\sqrt{p(1-p)/n}$, so the formula for z becomes:

TEST OF HYPOTHESIS, ONE PROPORTION	$z = \dfrac{\bar{p} - p}{\sqrt{\dfrac{p(1-p)}{n}}}$	[9–4]

Step 4: **Formulate the decision rule.** The critical value or values of z form the dividing point or points between the regions where H_0 is rejected and where it is not rejected. Since the alternative hypothesis states a direction, this is a one-tailed test. The sign of the inequality points to the left, so only the left side of the curve is used. See Chart 9–8. The significance level was given as 0.05 in step 2. This probability is in the left tail and determines the region of rejection. The area between zero and the critical value is 0.4500, found by: $0.5000 - 0.0500$. Referring to Appendix B.1 and searching for 0.4500, we find the critical value of z is 1.645 (or use the table of common z-values). The decision rule is, therefore: reject the null hypothesis if the computed value of z falls to the left of -1.645; otherwise, do not reject H_0.

CHART 9–8 Rejection Region for the 0.05 Level of Significance, One-Tailed Test

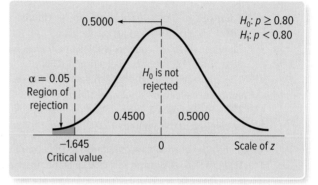

Step 5: **Make a decision and interpret the result.** Select a sample and make a decision about H_0. A sample survey of 2000 potential voters in the northern riding revealed that 1550 planned to vote for the incumbent. Is the sample proportion of 0.775 (found by: 1550/2000) close enough to 0.80 to conclude that the difference is due to chance? In this case:

$\bar{p}$ is 0.775, the proportion in the sample who plan to vote for the incumbent.
n is 2000, the number of voters surveyed.
p is 0.80, the hypothesized population proportion.
z is a normally distributed test statistic when the hypothesis is true and the other assumptions are true.

Using formula (9–4) and computing z:

$$z = \frac{\bar{p} - p}{\sqrt{\dfrac{p(1-p)}{n}}} = \frac{\dfrac{1550}{2000} - 0.80}{\sqrt{\dfrac{0.80(1-0.80)}{2000}}} = \frac{0.775 - 0.80}{\sqrt{0.00008}} = -2.80$$

The computed value of z (-2.80) is in the rejection region, so the null hypothesis is rejected at the 0.05 level. The difference of 2.5 percentage points between the sample percentage (77.5%) and the hypothesized population percentage in the northern riding necessary to carry the province (80%) is statistically significant. It is probably not due to sampling variation. To put it another way, the evidence at this point does not support the claim that the incumbent will return to office.

The p-value is the probability of finding a z-value less than -2.80. From Appendix B.1, the probability of a z-value between 0 and -2.80 is 0.4974. So the p-value is 0.0026, found by: $0.5000 - 0.4974$. The incumbent cannot be confident of re-election, as the p-value is less than the significance level.

Computer commands for hypothesis testing for the above example can be found at the end of the chapter.

Note that the p-value is 0.0026, which is smaller than our significance level of 0.05, and is also smaller than a significance level of 0.01. This tells us that we have enough evidence to reject the null hypothesis, so we conclude that the proportion of the vote for the incumbent in the northern section of the province will be less than 80%.

self-review 9–5

A recent insurance industry report indicated that 40% of those persons involved in minor traffic accidents this year have been involved in at least one other traffic accident in the last five years. An advisory group decided to investigate this claim, believing it was too large. A sample of 200 traffic accidents this year showed 74 persons were also involved in another accident within the last five years. Use the 0.01 significance level.

(a) Can we use z as the test statistic? Explain why or why not.
(b) State the null hypothesis and the alternative hypothesis.
(c) Show the decision rule graphically.
(d) Compute the value of z and state your decision regarding the null hypothesis.
(e) Determine and interpret the p-value.

EXERCISES

23. The following hypotheses are given:

$$H_0: p \le 0.70$$
$$H_1: p > 0.70$$

A sample of 100 observations revealed that $\bar{p} = 0.75$. At the 0.05 significance level, can the null hypothesis be rejected?

a. State the decision rule.
b. Compute the value of the test statistic.
c. What is your decision regarding the null hypothesis?

24. The manager of Tea for Us has been ordering stock based on the assumption that 40% of her customers prefer black teas. The following hypotheses are given:

$$H_0: p = 0.40$$
$$H_1: p \ne 0.40$$

She sampled 120 of her customers and found that only 30% of those preferred black teas. At the 0.05 significance level, can the null hypothesis be rejected?

a. State the decision rule.
b. Compute the value of the test statistic.
c. What is your decision regarding the null hypothesis?

Note: it is recommended that you use the five-step hypothesis testing procedure in solving the following problems:

25. An Ontario safety council reported that 52% of highway drivers are men. A sample of 300 cars travelling southbound on Highway 400 yesterday revealed that 170 were driven by men. Can we conclude that a larger proportion of men were driving on Highway 400 than the provincial figures indicate? Use a significance level of 0.01.

26. A recent article in a magazine reported that a job awaits only one in three new college graduates. The major reasons given were an overabundance of college graduates and a weak economy. A survey of 200 recent graduates revealed that 80 students had jobs. At the 0.02 significance level, can we conclude that a larger proportion of students have jobs?

27. Chicken Delight claims that 90% of its orders are delivered within 10 minutes of the time the order is placed. A sample of 100 orders revealed that 82 were delivered within the promised time. At the 0.01 significance level, can we conclude that less than 90% of the orders are delivered in less than 10 minutes?

28. Research at a university indicates that 50% of the students change their major area of study after their first year in a program. A random sample of 100 students in business revealed that 48 had changed their major area of study after their first year of the program. Has there been a significant decrease in the proportion of students who change their major after the first year in this program? Choose an appropriate level of significance.

Chapter Summary

I. The objective of hypothesis testing is to check the validity of a statement about a population parameter.

II. The steps to conduct a test of hypothesis are:

   A. State the null hypothesis (H_0) and the alternative hypothesis (H_1).

   B. Select the level of significance.
   1. The level of significance is the likelihood of rejecting a true null hypothesis.
   2. The most frequently used significance levels are 0.01, 0.05, and 0.10, but any value between 0 and 1.00 is possible.

   C. Select the test statistic.
   1. A test statistic is a value calculated from sample information used to determine whether to reject the null hypothesis.
   2. Two test statistics were considered in this chapter.
      a. The standard normal distribution (the z distribution) is used when the population follows a normal distribution and the population standard deviation is known.
      b. The t distribution is used when the population follows a normal distribution and the population standard deviation is unknown.
      c. The z distribution is used in a test of proportions when both np and $n(1 - p)$ are greater than 5.

   D. State the decision rule.
   1. The decision rule indicates the condition or conditions when the null hypothesis is rejected.
   2. In a two-tailed test, the rejection region is evenly split between the upper and lower tails.
   3. In a one-tailed test, all of the rejection region is in either the upper tail or the lower tail.

   E. Select a sample, compute the value of the test statistic, make a decision regarding the null hypothesis, and interpret the results.

III. A p-value is the probability that the value of the test statistic is as extreme as the value computed, when the null hypothesis is true.

IV. Testing a hypothesis about a population mean:

   A. If the population standard deviation, σ, is known, the test statistic is the standard normal distribution and is determined from:

$$z = \frac{\overline{x} - \mu}{\sigma/\sqrt{n}}$$

[9–1]

   B. If the population standard deviation is not known, s is substituted for σ. The test statistic is the t distribution, and its value is determined from:

$$t = \frac{\overline{x} - \mu}{s/\sqrt{n}}$$

[9–2]

   The major characteristics of the t distribution are:
   1. It is a continuous distribution.
   2. It is mound shaped and symmetric.
   3. It is flatter, or more spread out, than the standard normal distribution.
   4. There is a family of t distributions, depending on the number of degrees of freedom.

V. Testing about a population proportion.

   A. The binomial conditions must be met.

   B. Both np and $n(1 - p) \geq 5$.

   C. The test statistic is:

$$z = \frac{\overline{p} - p}{\sqrt{\dfrac{p(1 - p)}{n}}}$$

[9–4]

Chapter Exercises

29. According to the local union president, the mean gross income of plumbers is normally distributed, with a mean of $60 000 and a standard deviation of $6000. An investigative reporter for the local television station recently found, for a sample of 120 plumbers, the mean gross income was $62 500. At the 0.10 significance level, is it reasonable to conclude that the mean income is not equal to $60 000? Determine the p-value and the 90% confidence interval. Use this information to support your decision.

30. The Rutter Nursery Company packages its mulch in 50-kg bags. From a long history, the shipping department reports that the distribution of the bag masses follows the normal distribution and the standard deviation of this process is 3 kg per bag. At the end of each day, Jeff Rutter, the shipping manager, selects 10 bags and computes the mean mass of the sample. Below are the masses of 10 bags from today's production:

> 45.6   47.7   47.6   46.3   46.2   47.4   49.2   55.8   47.5   48.5

   a. Can Mr. Rutter conclude that the mean mass of the bags is less than 50 kg? Use the 0.01 significance level.
   b. In a brief report, tell why Mr. Rutter can use the z distribution as the test statistic.
   c. Compute the p-value.

31. A new weight-watching company, Weight Reducers International, advertises that those who join will lose, on the average, 10 pounds the first two weeks. The population standard deviation is 2.8 pounds. A random sample of 50 people who joined the new weight reduction program revealed the mean loss to be 9 pounds. At the 0.05 level of significance, can we conclude that those joining Weight Reducers will lose, on average, less than 10 pounds? Determine the p-value.

32. Dole Pineapple Inc. is concerned that the 450 mL can of sliced pineapple is being overfilled. The population standard deviation is 0.85 mL. The quality control department took a random sample of 50 cans and found that the arithmetic mean volume was 451.4 mL. At the 5% level of significance, can we conclude that the mean volume is greater than 450 mL? Determine the p-value.

33. A recent survey states that the typical adult gets a mean of seven hours sleep per night. A random sample of 50 university students found that the mean number of hours slept the previous night was 6 hours and 48 minutes (6.8 hours). The standard deviation of the sample was 0.9 hours. Is it reasonable to conclude that university students sleep less than the typical adult? Compute the p-value and use the information in your answer.

34. A real estate sales agency specializes in selling vacation property. Its records indicate that the mean selling time of vacation property is 90 days. However, it believes that because of the recent hurricanes, the mean selling time is now greater than 90 days. A survey of 100 properties sold recently revealed that the mean selling time was 94 days, with a standard deviation of 22 days. At the 0.10 significance level, has there been an increase in selling time?

35. Global TV news, in a segment on the price of gasoline, reported last evening that the mean price nationwide is $1.25 per litre for self-serve regular unleaded. A random sample of 35 stations in Edmonton revealed that the mean price was $1.27 per litre and that the standard deviation was $0.05 per litre. At the 0.05 significance level, can we conclude that the price of gasoline is higher in this city? Determine the p-value.

36. A recent article in *Vitality* magazine reported that the mean amount of leisure time per week for men is 40.0 hours. You believe this figure is too large and decide to conduct your own test. In a random sample of 60 men, you find that the mean is 37.8 hours of leisure per week and that the standard deviation of the sample is 12.2 hours. Can you conclude that the information in the article is untrue? Use the 0.05 significance level. Determine the p-value, and explain its meaning.

37. In recent years, interest rates on home mortgages have been lowered to less than 6.0%. However, a recent study shows that the rate charged on credit card debt is more than 14%. A sample of 10 credit cards showed that the mean rate charged is 15.64%, with a standard deviation of 1.561%. Is it reasonable to conclude the mean rate charged is greater than 14%? Use the 0.01 significance level.

38. The 30-year mortgage rate is now less than 6.0%. A sample of eight financial institutions in Canada showed the mean mortgage rate to be 5.6375%, with a standard deviation of 0.6346%. At the 0.01 significance level, can we conclude that the 30-year mortgage rate is less than 6.0%? Determine or estimate the p-value. Interpret the p-value.

39. It is estimated that a typical college student drinks about 23 L of bottled water per year, or 1.92 L per month. A sample of 12 college students revealed the following amounts of water consumed last month:

$$1.75 \quad 1.96 \quad 1.57 \quad 1.82 \quad 1.85 \quad 1.82 \quad 2.43 \quad 2.65 \quad 2.60 \quad 2.24 \quad 1.69 \quad 2.66$$

At the 0.05 significance level, is there a significant difference between the average amount consumed at the college surveyed and the national average? Construct a 95% confidence interval. Use the results of the confidence interval to support your decision.

40. The post-anesthesia care area (recovery room) at St. Luke's Hospital was recently enlarged. The hope was that with the enlargement the mean number of patients per day would be more than 25. A random sample of 15 days revealed the following numbers of patients:

$$25 \quad 27 \quad 25 \quad 26 \quad 25 \quad 28 \quad 28 \quad 27 \quad 24 \quad 26 \quad 25 \quad 29 \quad 25 \quad 27 \quad 24$$

At the 0.01 significance level, can we conclude that the mean number of patients per day is more than 25? Estimate the p-value, and interpret it.

41. The site www.golfsmith.com receives an average of 6.5 returns per day from online shoppers. For a sample of 12 days, it received the following number of returns:

$$0 \quad 4 \quad 3 \quad 4 \quad 9 \quad 4 \quad 5 \quad 9 \quad 1 \quad 6 \quad 7 \quad 10$$

At the 0.01 significance level, can we conclude the mean number of returns is less than 6.5?

42. During the recent seasons, Major League Baseball has been criticized for the length of games. A report indicated that the average game lasts 3 hours and 30 minutes. A sample of 17 games revealed the following times to completion. (Note that the minutes have been changed to fractions of hours, so that a game that lasted 2 hours and 24 minutes is reported at 2.40 hours.)

$$2.98 \quad 2.40 \quad 2.70 \quad 2.25 \quad 3.23 \quad 3.17 \quad 2.93 \quad 3.18 \quad 2.80$$
$$2.38 \quad 3.75 \quad 3.20 \quad 3.27 \quad 2.52 \quad 2.58 \quad 4.45 \quad 2.45$$

Can we conclude that the mean time for a game is less than 3.50 hours? Use the 0.05 significance level.

43. The Watch Corporation of Switzerland claims that its watches on average will neither gain nor lose time during a week. A sample of 18 watches provided the following gains (+) or losses (−) in seconds per week.

$$-0.38 \quad -0.20 \quad -0.38 \quad -0.32 \quad +0.32 \quad -0.23 \quad +0.30 \quad +0.25 \quad -0.10$$
$$-0.37 \quad -0.61 \quad -0.48 \quad -0.47 \quad -0.64 \quad -0.04 \quad -0.20 \quad -0.68 \quad +0.05$$

Is it reasonable to conclude that the mean gain or loss in time for the watches is 0? Use the 0.05 significance level. Determine or estimate the p-value. Interpret the p-value.

44. Listed below is the rate of return for one year (reported in percentage) for a sample of 12 mutual funds that are classified as taxable money market funds:

$$4.63 \quad 4.15 \quad 4.76 \quad 4.70 \quad 4.65 \quad 4.52 \quad 4.70 \quad 5.06 \quad 4.42 \quad 4.51 \quad 4.24 \quad 4.52$$

Using the 0.05 significance level, is it reasonable to conclude that the mean rate of return is more than 4.50%?

45. Many grocery stores and large retailers such as Loblaws and Wal-Mart have installed self-checkout systems so shoppers can scan their own items and cash out themselves. How do customers like this service, and how often do they use it? The results of a sample of the numbers of customers using the self-checkout system over a period of 15 days are listed below:

$$120 \quad 108 \quad 120 \quad 114 \quad 118 \quad 91 \quad 118 \quad 92$$
$$112 \quad 97 \quad 118 \quad 108 \quad 117 \quad 104 \quad 104$$

Is it reasonable to conclude that the mean number of customers using the self-checkout system is more than 100 per day? Use the 0.05 significance level.

46. The campus bookstore reported that students paid an average of $267 per semester for textbooks. To verify this statement, the student union decided to select a random sample of students and found the following amounts, in dollars, spent for textbooks:

$321 286 290 330 310 250 270 280 299 265 291 275 281

At the 0.01 significance level, can we conclude that the average amount spent on textbooks per semester has increased? What is the p-value?

47. Tina Dennis is the comptroller for Meek Industries. She believes that the current cash-flow problem at Meek is due to the slow collection of accounts receivable. She believes that more than 60% of the accounts are in arrears more than three months. A random sample of 200 accounts showed that 140 were more than three months old. At the 0.01 significance level, can she conclude that more than 60% of the accounts are in arrears for more than three months?

48. The policy of the Suburban Transit Authority is to add a bus route if more than 55% of the potential commuters indicate they would use the particular route. A sample of 70 commuters revealed that 42 would use a proposed route from Bowman Park to the downtown area. Does the Bowman-to-downtown route meet the STA criterion? Use the 0.05 significance level.

49. Past experience at the Crowder Travel Agency indicated that 44% of those persons who wanted the agency to plan a vacation for them wanted to go to Europe. During the most recent busy season, a sampling of 1000 plans was selected at random from the files. It was found that 480 persons wanted to go to Europe on vacation. Has there been a significant shift upward in the percentage of persons who want to go to Europe? Test at the 0.05 significance level.

50. From past experience a television manufacturer found that 10% or less of its sets needed any type of repair in the first two years of operation. In a sample of 50 sets manufactured two years ago, 9 needed repair. At the 0.05 significance level, has the percentage of sets needing repair increased? Determine the p-value.

51. An urban planner claims that, nationally, 20% of all families renting condominiums move during a given year. A random sample of 200 families renting condominiums in Vancouver revealed that 56 had moved during the past year. At the 0.01 significance level, does this evidence suggest that a larger proportion of condominium owners moved in the Vancouver area? Determine the p-value.

52. The cost of a wedding has skyrocketed in recent years. As a result, many couples are opting to have their weddings in the Caribbean. A Caribbean vacation resort recently advertised that the cost of a Caribbean wedding was less than $10 000. Listed below is the total cost (in $ thousands) for a sample of eight Caribbean weddings:

$9.7 9.4 11.7 9.0 9.1 10.5 9.1 9.8

At the 0.05 significance level, is it reasonable to conclude the mean wedding cost is less than $10 000 as advertised?

53. The Myers Summer Casual Furniture Store tells customers that a special order will take six weeks (42 days). During recent months, the owner has received several complaints that the special orders are taking longer than 42 days. A sample of 12 special orders delivered in the last month showed that the mean waiting time was 51 days, with a standard deviation of 8 days. At the 0.05 significance level, are customers waiting an average of more than 42 days? Estimate the p-value.

54. A fast food restaurant chain claims that lunch will be served within nine minutes of placing your order, or it is free. A sample of eight customers revealed the following waiting times in minutes:

10.1 9.3 9.2 10.2 9.3 9.6 9.4 8.8

At the 0.01 significance level, can we conclude that the waiting time for lunch exceeds nine minutes? Estimate the p-value.

55. A national grocer's magazine reports the typical shopper spends eight minutes in line waiting to check out. A sample of 24 shoppers at the local No Frills showed a mean of 7.5 minutes, with a standard deviation of 3.2 minutes. Is the waiting time at the local No Frills less than that reported in the national magazine? Use the 0.05 significance level.

56. A shopping centre wants to examine the amount of space required for parking. Studies indicated that 50% of staff and shoppers use public transportation. A survey of 1002 was taken, and 483 responded that they used public transportation. Is it reasonable to conclude that the survey results indicate a change? Use the 0.05 significance level.

57. A government "think tank" estimates that the typical teenager sends 50 text messages per day. To verify this statement, you call a sample of teenagers and ask them how many text messages they sent the previous day. Their responses were as follows:

| 51 | 175 | 47 | 49 | 44 | 54 | 145 | 203 | 21 | 59 | 42 | 100 |

At the 0.05 level, can you conclude that the mean number is greater than 50? Estimate the p-value, and describe what it tells you.

58. During the 1990s, the mortality rate for lung cancer was 80 per 100 000 people. At the turn of the twenty-first century, following the establishment of newer treatments and improvements in public health advertising, a random sample of 10 000 people showed only 6 deaths from lung cancer per 100 000 people. Test at the 0.05 significance level whether these data are proof of a reduced mortality rate for lung cancer.

59. The publisher of *Celebrity Living* claims that the mean sales of personality magazines that feature such celebrities as Angelina Jolie or Kim Kardashian are 1.5 million copies per week. A sample of 10 comparable titles shows a mean weekly sales last week of 1.3 million copies, with a standard deviation of 0.9 million copies. Do these data contradict the publisher's claim? Use the 0.01 significance level.

60. Research in the gaming industry showed that 10% of all slot machines stop working each year. Short's Game Arcade has 60 slot machines and only 3 failed last year. Use the five-step hypothesis-testing procedure at the 0.05 significance level to test whether these data contradict the research report.
a. Why can you employ z as the test statistic?
b. State the null and alternative hypotheses.
c. Evaluate the test statistic and make the decision.
d. Determine the p-value. What does this imply?

61. According to a recent news survey, 40% of adults do not eat breakfast. A sample of 30 college students found 16 had skipped breakfast that day. Use the 0.01 significance level to check whether college students are more likely to skip breakfast.

62. The 2011 census reports that the average number of residents per private household in Canada is 2.5. A sample of 28 households in Swift Current, Saskatchewan, showed the mean number of residents per household was 2.86 residents. The standard deviation of this sample was 1.20 residents. At the 0.05 significance level, is it reasonable to conclude the mean number of residents in Swift Current is more than 2.5 persons?

63. For a recent year, the mean fare to fly from Halifax, Nova Scotia, to Corner Brook, Newfoundland, on a discount ticket was $370. A random sample of round-trip discount fares on this route last month gives the following:

| $421 | $386 | $390 | $430 | $410 | $350 | $370 | $380 | $399 | $365 | $391 | $375 | $381 |

At the 0.01 significance level, can we conclude that the mean fare has increased? Determine and interpret the p-value.

64. According to an article appearing in *The Canadian Veterinary Journal*, 56% of Canadian households have at least one dog or a cat. To test the validity of the article, a random sample of 300 households showed that 180 owned pets. Do these data disagree with *The Canadian Veterinary Journal* data? Use a 0.05 level of significance.

65. After a losing season, there is a great uproar to fire the head basketball coach. In a random sample of 200 college students, 80 favour keeping the coach. Test at the 0.05 level of significance whether the proportion of students who support the coach is less than 50%.

66. A coin toss is used to decide which team gets the ball first in most sports. It involves little effort and is believed to give each side the same chance. In 45 Super Bowl games, the National Football Conference has won the coin flip 31 times. Meanwhile, the American Football Conference has won only 14 times. Use the five-step hypothesis-testing procedure at the 0.01 significance level to test whether this data suggest a fair coin flip.
a. Why can you employ z as the test statistic?
b. State the null and alternative hypotheses.
c. Make a diagram of the decision rule.
d. Evaluate the test statistic and make the decision.
e. Determine the p-value. What does this imply?

Data Set Exercises

Questions marked with 📶 have data sets available on McGraw-Hill's online resource for *Basic Statistics*.

📶 **67.** Refer to the CREA (Canadian Real Estate Association) Cities Only data online, which reports information on average house prices nationally and in a selection of cities across Canada.

    a. Develop a 95% confidence interval for the mean list price for all cities for January 2014.

    b. Is it possible that the population mean is $450 000? Test at the 0.02 significance level.

    c. Is it possible that the population mean is $275 000? Use the results in part (a) to test at the 0.05 significance level.

    d. What is the p-value for part (c)? Use the p-value to support your answer in part (c).

📶 **68.** Refer to the Real Estate Data—Halifax Area online, which reports information on home listings.

    a. A recent article indicated that the mean list price of the homes is more than $600 000. Can we conclude that the mean list price is more than $600 000? Use the 0.01 significance level. What is the p-value? Interpret the p-value.

    b. The same article reported the mean size was more than 2100 square feet. Can we conclude that the mean size of homes listed is more than 2100 square feet? Use the 0.01 significance level. What is the p-value? Interpret the p-value.

    c. Determine the proportion of homes that are apartments. At the 0.05 significance level, can we conclude that more than 60% of the homes listed are apartments? What is the p-value? Interpret the p-value.

    d. Determine the proportion of homes with more than two bedrooms. At the 0.05 significance level, can we conclude that more than 60% of the homes listed have more than two bathrooms? What is the p-value? Interpret the p-value.

📶 **69.** Refer to the Real Estate Data—Saskatoon online, which reports information on home listings.

    a. A recent article indicated that the mean list price of the homes is less than $600 000. Can we conclude that the mean list price is $350 000? Use the 0.01 significance level. Confirm your answer with the 99% confidence interval. What is the p-value? Interpret the p-value.

    b. The same article reported the mean size was 1500 square feet. Can we conclude that the mean size of homes listed is 1500 square feet? Use the 0.05 significance level. Confirm your answer with the 95% confidence interval. What is the p-value? Interpret the p-value.

    c. Determine the proportion of listings that are houses. At the 0.05 significance level, can we conclude that more than 50% of the listings are houses? What is the p-value? Interpret the p-value.

    d. Determine the proportion of homes with more than two bathrooms. At the 0.05 significance level, can we conclude that more than 50% of the homes listed have more than two bedrooms? What is the p-value? Interpret the p-value.

📶 **70.** Refer to the CREA (Canadian Real Estate Association) Cities Only data online, which reports information on average house prices nationally and in a selection of cities across Canada.

    a. Develop a 98% confidence interval for the mean list price for all cities for January 2014.

    b. Is it possible that the population mean is $300 000? Test at the 0.05 significance level. What is the p-value? Use this result in your answer.

    c. Is it possible that the population mean is $400 000? Use the results in part (a) to test at the 0.02 significance level. What is the p-value? Use this result to support your answer.

Practice Test

Part I Objective

1. The _____ is a statement about the value of a population parameter.

2. We commit a Type II error when we _____ the null hypothesis when it is actually false.

3. The probability of committing a Type I error is equal to the _____.

4. The _____ , based on sample information, is used to determine whether to reject the null hypothesis.

5. The _____ value separates the region where the null hypothesis is rejected from the region where it is not rejected.

6. In a _____ -tailed test, the significance level is divided equally between the two tails. (one, two, neither)

7. When conducting a test of hypothesis for means (assuming a normal population), we use the standard normal distribution when the population _____ is known.

8. The _____ is the probability of finding a value of the test statistic at least as extreme as the one observed, given that the null hypothesis is true.

9. The _____ conditions are necessary to conduct a test of hypothesis about a proportion.

10. To conduct a test of proportions, the value of np and $n(1 - p)$ must be at least _____. (1, 5, 30, 1000)

Part II Problems

For each of these problems, use the five-step hypothesis-testing procedure:

1. The Park Manager at Fort Fisher State Park believes the typical park visitor spends at least 90 minutes in the park during the summer months. A sample of 18 visitors during the summer months of 2017 revealed the mean time in the park was 96 minutes with a standard deviation of 12 minutes. At the 0.01 significance level, is it reasonable to conclude that the mean time in the park is greater than 90 minutes?

2. The weights of full boxes of Frosted Flakes breakfast cereal follow the normal probability distribution with a mean of 485 g and a standard deviation of 13.43 g. A sample of 25 boxes packed this morning showed the mean to be 489.97 g. Can we conclude that the mean weight is more than 485 g per box? Test at a significance level of 0.05.

3. A recent newspaper article reported that 67% of young married couples consulted with and sought the approval of their spouse on any purchase of more than $500. A sample of 300 young married couples revealed 180 consulted with their spouse on their most recent purchase of more than $500. At the 0.05 significance level, can we conclude that less than 67% of those sampled sought the approval of their spouse?

Computer Commands

1. **MegaStat** steps for hypothesis testing for the Jamestown Steel Company example are:

   a. In an **Excel** spreadsheet, enter *Jamestown Steel Company* in cell A3, *203.5* in cell A4, *16* in cell A5 and *50* in cell A6. This is the **summary input**.

   b. Select **MegaStat, Hypothesis Tests** and **Mean vs. Hypothesized Value**.

   c. Select **summary input**. Enter *A3:A6* as the **Input Range**.

   d. Enter *200* as the **Hypothesized mean**, select *not equal* for the **Alternative:** and **z-test**.

   e. Select **Display** 99% **confidence interval**. Click **OK**. *Note:* the z-value and confidence limits may be slightly different due to rounding.

	A	B	C
1			
2			
3	**Jamestown Steel Company**		
4	203.5		
5	16		
6	50		
7			
8			

Hypothesis Test: Mean vs. Hypothesized Value

○ data input   ● summary input

Sheet1!$A$3:$A$6 ▭ Input Range

Select range with label, mean, s.d., n

200 ▭ Hypothesized mean

Alternative: [not equal ▾]

○ t-test ● z-test   ☑ Display [99% ▾] confidence interval

OK | Clear | Cancel | Help

2. **MegaStat** steps for hypothesis testing for the McFarland Insurance Company example are as follows:

   a. In an **Excel** spreadsheet, enter *McFarland Insurance Company* in cell A3 and the data in cells A4 to A29. This is the **data input.**

   b. Select **MegaStat, Hypothesis Tests,** and **Mean vs. Hypothesized Value.**

   c. Select **data input.** Enter the data range in the **Input Range** box.

   d. Enter *60* as the **Hypothesized mean**, select *less than* for the **Alternative:** and **t-test.**

   e. Click **OK.** The *p*-value (0.0407) is part of the output. *Note:* values may be slightly different due to rounding.

Hypothesis Test: Mean vs. Hypothesized Value

⦿ data input   ○ summary input

Sheet1!$A$3:$A$29   Input Range

60   Hypothesized mean

Alternative: less than

⦿ t-test   ○ z-test   ☐ Display 95% confidence interval

OK
Clear
Cancel
Help

---

3. **MegaStat** steps for hypothesis testing for the mean time customers are parked in the public parking lot example are as follows:

   a. In an **Excel** spreadsheet, enter *Parking Time* in cell A3 and the data in cells *A4: A15* This is the **data input.**

   b. Select **MegaStat, Hypothesis Tests** and **Mean vs. Hypothesized Value.**

   c. Select data input. Enter the data range in the Input Range box.

   d. Enter *43* as the **Hypothesized mean**, select *not equal* for the **Alternative:** and **t-test.**

   e. Select **Display** 98% **confidence interval.** Click **OK.** The *p*-value (0.0141) is part of the output. *Note:* values may be slightly different due to rounding.

Hypothesis Test: Mean vs. Hypothesized Value

⦿ data input   ○ summary input

Sheet1!$A$3:$A$15   Input Range

43   Hypothesized mean

Alternative: not equal

⦿ t-test   ○ z-test   ☑ Display 98% confidence interval

OK
Clear
Cancel
Help

---

4. **MegaStat** steps for hypothesis testing for the proportion example are as follows:

   a. Select **MegaStat, Hypothesis Tests** and **Proportion vs. Hypothesized Value.**

   b. In the **Observed** column, enter *1550* for **X** and *2000* as **n.** In the **Hypothesized** column, enter *.8* for **p.** Select *less than* for the **Alternative.**

   c. Click **OK.** The *p*-value (0.0026) is part of the output. *Note:* values may be slightly different due to rounding.

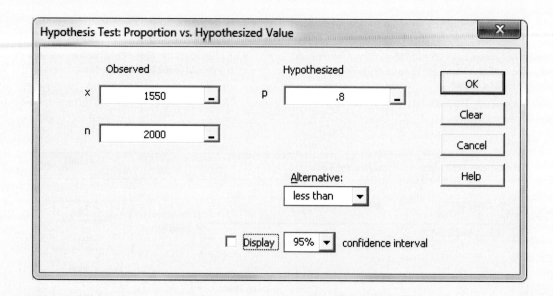

Hypothesis Test: Proportion vs. Hypothesized Value

Observed		Hypothesized	
x	1550	p	.8
n	2000		

OK
Clear
Cancel
Help

Alternative:
less than ▼

☐ Display 95% ▼ confidence interval

Answers to Self-Reviews

9–1 (a) H_0: $\mu = 6.0$; H_1: $\mu \neq 6.0$.

(b) 0.05.

(c) $z = \dfrac{\bar{x} - \mu}{\sigma/\sqrt{n}}$

(d) Do not reject the null hypothesis if the computed z-value falls between -1.96 and $+1.96$.

(e) Yes. Computed $z = -2.56$, found by:

$$z = \frac{5.84 - 6.0}{0.5/\sqrt{64}} = \frac{-0.16}{0.0625} = -2.56.$$

Reject H_0 at the 0.05 level of significance and conclude that the mean turnover rate is not equal to 6.0.

9–2 (a) H_0: $\mu \geq 6.0$;
H_1: $\mu < 6.0$.
Note that the inequality sign ($<$) in the alternative hypothesis points in the direction of the region of rejection.

(b) To determine the critical value: $0.5000 - 0.05 = 0.4500$. The z-value from Appendix A.1 is about -1.645.

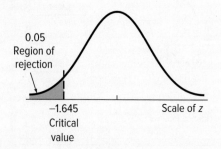

0.05
Region of
rejection

-1.645
Critical
value

Scale of z

(c) Using Appendix A.1, the p-value is $(0.5 - 0.4948) = 0.0052$. The p-value is less than the significance level of 0.05, so we reject H_0 and conclude that the mean is less than 6.0.

9–3 (a) H_0: $\mu \leq 305$; H_1: $\mu > 305$.

(b) $df = n - 1 = 20 - 1 = 19$.

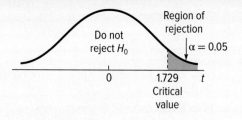

Region of
rejection

Do not
reject H_0

$\alpha = 0.05$

0   1.729 t
Critical
value

(c) $t = \dfrac{\bar{x} - \mu}{s/\sqrt{n}} = \dfrac{311 - 305}{12/\sqrt{20}} = 2.236.$

Reject H_0 because $2.236 > 1.729$. The modification increased the mean battery life to more than 305 days.

(d) The p-value is between 0.01 and 0.025 (0.0188 using a computer), which is less than the significance level of 0.05, so we reject H_0 and conclude that mean battery life has increased.

9–4 (a) H_0: $\mu \geq 9.0$; H_1: $\mu < 9.0$.

(b) 7, found by: $n - 1 = 8 - 1 = 7$.

(c) Reject H_0 if $t < -2.998$.

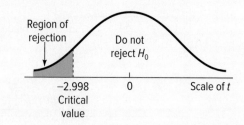

Region of
rejection

Do not
reject H_0

-2.998 0   Scale of t
Critical
value

(d) $t = -2.494$, found by:

$$s = \sqrt{\frac{619.88 - \dfrac{(70.4)^2}{8}}{8 - 1}} = 0.2268.$$

$$\bar{x} = \frac{70.4}{8} = 8.8.$$

Then:

$$t = \frac{8.8 - 9.0}{0.2268/\sqrt{8}} = -2.494.$$

Since -2.494 lies to the right of -2.998, H_0 is not rejected. We have not shown that the mean is less than 9.0.

(e) The p-value is 0.0207, which is greater than the significance level of 0.01, so there is not enough evidence to reject H_0. We conclude that the mean is at least 9.0.

9–5 (a) Yes, because both np and $n(1 - p)$ exceed 5:
$np = 200(0.40) = 80$, and $n(1 - p) = 200(0.60) = 120$.

(b) H_0: $p \geq 0.40$.

(c) H_1: $p < 0.40$.

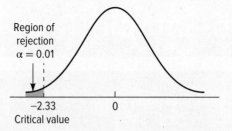

(d) $z = -0.87$, found by:

$$z = \frac{0.37 - 0.40}{\sqrt{\dfrac{0.40(1 - 0.40)}{200}}} = \frac{0.03}{\sqrt{0.0012}} = -0.87$$

Do not reject H_0.

(e) The p-value is 0.1922, found by $0.5000 - 0.3078$. The p-value is greater than the significance level of 0.01, so we do not have enough evidence to reject H_0 and conclude that the population proportion is at least 0.40.

CHAPTER 10
Two-Sample Tests of Hypothesis

The Damon family owns a large grape vineyard in the Niagara Peninsula. The grapevines must be sprayed at the beginning of the growing season to protect them against various insects and diseases. Two new insecticides have just been marketed, Pernod 5 and Action. To test their effectiveness, six long rows were selected. Three rows were sprayed with Pernod 5, and three were sprayed with Action. When the grapes ripened, 400 of the vines treated with Pernod 5 were checked for infestation, and 400 of the vines treated with Action were checked. At the 0.05 significance level, can we conclude that there is a difference in the proportion of vines infested using Pernod 5 as opposed to Action? (Exercise 19, LO10-5)

LEARNING OBJECTIVES

When you have completed this chapter, you will be able to:

LO10-1 Test a hypothesis that two independent population means are equal, assuming that the population standard deviations are known and equal.

LO10-2 Test of a hypothesis that two independent population means are equal, assuming equal but unknown population standard deviations.

LO10-3 Test a hypothesis about the mean population difference between paired or dependent observations.

LO10-4 Explain the difference between dependent and independent samples.

LO10-5 Test a hypothesis that two population proportions are equal.

10.1 INTRODUCTION

Chapter 9 began our study of hypothesis testing. We described the nature of hypothesis testing and conducted tests of a hypothesis in which we compared the results of a single sample to a population value. That is, we selected a random sample from a population and conducted a test of whether the proposed population value was reasonable. Recall in Chapter 9 that we selected a sample of the number of desks assembled per week at the Jamestown Steel Company to determine whether there was a change in the production rate. Similarly, we sampled voters in one area of a particular riding to determine whether the population proportion that would support the incumbent for re-election was less than 0.80. In both these cases, we compared the results of a *single* sample statistic to a population parameter.

In this chapter, we expand the idea of hypothesis testing to two populations. That is, we select random samples from two different populations to determine whether the population means or proportions are equal. Some questions we might want to test are:

1. Is there a difference in the mean value of residential real estate sold by male agents and female agents in Halifax?
2. Were more calls for technical assistance received during the afternoon shift than the morning shift at the company's help desk?
3. In the fast-food industry, is the mean number of days absent for workers under 21 years of age difference from the mean number of days absent for workers more than 60 years of age?

4. Is there a difference in the proportion of University of Calgary graduates and University of British Columbia graduates who pass the Chartered Professional Accountant (CPA) examinations on their first attempt?

5. Is there an increase in the production rate if music is piped into the production area?

We begin this chapter with the case in which we select random samples from two independent populations and wish to investigate whether these populations have the same mean.

Statistics in Action

LO10-1 10.2 TWO-SAMPLE TESTS OF HYPOTHESIS: INDEPENDENT SAMPLES

A city planner in Winnipeg wishes to know whether there is a difference in the mean hourly wage rate of plumbers and electricians in the city. A financial accountant wishes to know whether the mean rate of return for high-yield mutual funds is different from the mean rate of return on global mutual funds. In each of these cases, there are two independent populations. In the first case, the plumbers represent one population and the electricians the other. In the second case, high-yield mutual funds are one population and global mutual funds the other.

In each of these cases, to investigate the question, we would select a random sample from each population and compute the mean of the two samples. If the two population means are the same, that is, the mean hourly rate is the same for the plumbers and the electricians, we would expect the *difference* between the two sample means to be zero. But what if our sample results yield a difference other than zero? Is that difference due to chance or is it because there is a real difference in the hourly earnings? A two-sample test of means will help to answer this question.

We do need to return to the results of Chapter 7. Recall that we showed that a distribution of sample means would tend to approximate the normal distribution. We need to again assume that a distribution of sample means will follow the normal distribution. It can be shown mathematically that the distribution of the differences between sample means for two normal distributions is also normal.

We can illustrate this theory in terms of the city planner in Winnipeg. To begin, let us assume some information that is not usually available. Suppose that the population of wages of plumbers has a mean of $30.00 per hour and a standard deviation of $5.00 per hour. The population of wages of electricians has a mean of $29.00 and a standard deviation of $4.50. Now, from this information it is clear that the two population means are not the same. The plumbers actually earn $1.00 per hour more than the electricians. But, we cannot expect to uncover this difference each time we sample the two populations.

Suppose that we select a random sample of 40 plumbers and a random sample of 35 electricians and compute the mean of each sample. Then, we determine the difference between the sample means. It is this difference between the sample means that holds our interest. If the populations have the same mean, then we would expect the difference between the two sample means to be zero. If there is a difference between the population means, then we expect to find a difference between the sample means.

To understand the theory, we need to take several pairs of samples, compute the mean of each, determine the difference between the sample means, and study the distribution of the differences in the sample means. Because of our study of the distribution of sample means in Chapter 7, we know that the distribution of the sample means follows the normal distribution. If the two distributions of sample means follow the normal distribution, then we can reason the distribution of their differences will also follow the normal distribution. This is the first hurdle.

The second hurdle involves the mean of this distribution of differences. On the one hand, if we find that the mean of this distribution is zero, it implies that there is no difference in the two populations. On the other hand, if the mean of the distribution of differences is equal to some value other than zero, either positive or negative, then we conclude that the two populations do not have the same mean.

To report some concrete results, let us return to the city planner in Winnipeg. Table 10–1 shows the result of selecting 20 samples of 40 plumbers and 35 electricians, computing the mean of each sample, and finding the difference between the two sample means. In the first case, the sample of 40 plumbers has a mean of $29.80, and for the 35 electricians the mean is $28.76. The difference between the sample means is $1.04. This process was repeated 19 more times. Observe that in 17 of the 20 cases the mean of the plumbers is larger than the mean of the electricians.

TABLE 10–1 The Mean Wages of Random Samples of Plumbers and Electricians

Sample	Plumbers	Electricians	Difference
1	$29.80	$28.76	$1.04
2	30.32	29.40	0.92
3	30.57	29.94	0.63
4	30.04	28.93	1.11
5	30.09	29.78	0.31
6	30.02	28.66	1.36
7	29.60	29.13	0.47
8	29.63	29.42	0.21
9	30.17	29.29	0.88
10	30.81	29.75	1.06
11	30.09	28.05	2.04
12	29.35	29.07	0.28
13	29.42	28.79	0.63
14	29.78	29.54	0.24
15	29.60	29.60	0.00
16	30.60	30.19	0.41
17	30.79	28.65	2.14
18	29.14	29.95	−0.81
19	29.91	28.75	1.16
20	28.74	29.21	−0.47

Our final hurdle is that we need to know something about the *variability* of the distribution of differences. To put it another way, what is the standard deviation of this distribution of differences? Statistical theory shows that when we have independent populations, such as the case here, the distribution of the differences has a variance (standard deviation squared) equal to the sum of the two individual variances. This means that we can add the variances of the two sampling distributions. To put it another way, the variance of the difference in sample means $(\bar{x}_1 - \bar{x}_2)$ is equal to the sum of the variance for the plumbers and the variance of the electricians.

VARIANCE OF THE DISTRIBUTION OF DIFFERENCES IN MEANS
$$\sigma^2_{\bar{x}_1 - \bar{x}_2} = \frac{\sigma^2_1}{n_1} + \frac{\sigma^2_2}{n_2}$$
[10–1]

The term $\sigma^2_{\bar{x}_1 - \bar{x}_2}$ looks complex but need not be difficult to interpret. The σ^2 portion reminds us that it is a population variance, and the subscript $\bar{x}_1 - \bar{x}_2$ that it is a distribution of differences in the sample means.

We can put this equation in more usable form by taking the square root, so that we have the standard deviation of the distribution or "standard error" of the differences. Finally, we standardize the distribution of the differences. The result is the following equation:

TWO-SAMPLE TEST OF MEANS—KNOWN σ
$$z = \frac{\bar{x}_1 - \bar{x}_2 - (\mu_1 - \mu_2)}{\sqrt{\dfrac{\sigma^2_1}{n_1} + \dfrac{\sigma^2_2}{n_2}}}$$
[10–2]

Before we present an example, let us review the assumptions necessary for using formula (10–2).

1. The two populations follow normal distributions.
2. The two samples must be unrelated, that is, independent.
3. The standard deviations for both populations are known.

The following example shows the details of the test of hypothesis for two population means:

Example

Customers at FoodTown Supermarkets have a choice when paying for their groceries. They may check out and pay using the standard cashier-assisted checkout, or they may use the new Fast Lane procedure. In the standard procedure, a FoodTown employee scans each item, puts it on a short conveyor where another employee puts it in a bag and then into the grocery cart. In the Fast Lane procedure, customers scan each item, bag it, and place the bags in the cart themselves. The Fast Lane procedure is designed to reduce the time a customer spends in the checkout line.

The Fast Lane facility was recently installed at the Lyons Road FoodTown location. The store manager would like to know if the mean checkout time using the standard checkout method is longer than using the Fast Lane. She gathered the following sample information. The time is measured from when the customer enters the line until their bags are in the cart. Hence, the time includes both waiting in line and checking out. What is the *p*-value?

Customer Type	Sample Mean	Population Standard Deviation	Sample Size
Standard	5.50 minutes	0.40 minutes	50
Fast Lane	5.30 minutes	0.30 minutes	100

Solution

Statistics in Action

Do you live to work or work to live? A recent poll of 802 workers revealed that among those who considered their work a career, the mean number of hours worked per day was 8.7. Among those who considered their work a job, the mean number of hours worked per day was 7.6.

We use the five-step hypothesis testing procedure to investigate the question.

Step 1: State the null hypothesis and the alternative hypothesis. The null hypothesis is that the mean standard checkout time is less than or equal to the Fast Lane checkout time. In other words, the difference of 0.20 minutes between the mean checkout time for the standard method and the mean checkout time for Fast Lane is due to chance. The alternative hypothesis is that the mean checkout time is longer for those using the standard method. We will let μ_1 refer to the mean checkout time for the population of standard customers and μ_2 the mean checkout time for the Fast Lane customers. The null and alternative hypotheses are:

$$H_0: \mu_1 - \mu_2 \leq 0$$
$$H_1: \mu_1 - \mu_2 > 0$$

Step 2: Select the level of significance. The significance level is the probability that we reject the null hypothesis when it is actually true. This likelihood is determined prior to selecting the sample or performing any calculations. The 0.05 and 0.01 significance levels are the most common, but other values, such as 0.02 and 0.10, are also used. In theory, we may select any value between 0 and 1 for the significance level. In this case, we selected the 0.01 significance level.

Step 3: Determine the test statistic. In Chapter 9, we used the standard normal distribution (i.e., *z*) and *t* as test statistics. In this case, we use the *z* distribution as the test statistic because the standard deviations of both populations are known.

Step 4: Formulate a decision rule. The decision rule is based on the null and the alternative hypotheses (i.e., one-tailed or two-tailed test), the level of significance, and the test statistic used. We selected the 0.01 significance level, the *z* distribution as the test statistic, and we wish to determine whether the mean checkout time is longer using the standard method. We set the alternative hypothesis to indicate that the mean checkout time is longer for those using the standard method than the Fast Lane method. Hence, the rejection region is in the upper tail of the standard normal distribution (a one-tailed test). To find the critical value, go to the Student's *t* distribution (see Appendix B.2). In the table headings, find the row labelled "**Level of Significance for One-Tailed Test, α**" and select the column for an alpha of 0.01. Go to the bottom row with infinite degrees of freedom. The *z* critical value is 2.326. Round this value to 2.33. So, our decision rule is to reject H_0 if the value computed from the test statistic exceeds 2.33. Chart 10–1 depicts the decision rule.

Step 5: Make the decision regarding H_0 and interpret the result. We use formula (10–2) to compute the value of the test statistic.

$$z = \frac{\bar{x}_1 - \bar{x}_2 - (\mu_1 - \mu_2)}{\sqrt{\dfrac{\sigma_1^2}{n_1} + \dfrac{\sigma_2^2}{n_2}}} = \frac{5.5 - 5.3 - 0}{\sqrt{\dfrac{0.40^2}{50} + \dfrac{0.30^2}{100}}} = \frac{0.2}{0.064} = 3.13$$

CHART 10–1 Decision Rule for One-Tailed Test at 0.01 Significance Level

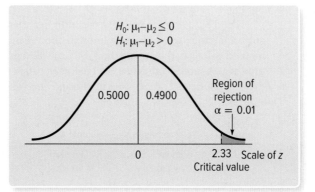

The computed value of 3.13 is larger than the critical value of 2.33. Our decision is to reject the null hypothesis and accept the alternative hypothesis. The difference of 0.20 minutes between the mean checkout times, found by using the standard method, is too large to have occurred by chance. To put it another way, we conclude that the Fast Lane method is faster.

What is the p-value for the test statistic? Recall that the p-value is the probability of finding a value of the test statistic this extreme when the null hypothesis is true. To calculate the p-value, we need the probability of a z-value larger than 3.13. From Appendix B.1, we cannot find the probability associated with 3.13. The largest value available is 3.09. The area corresponding to 3.09 is 0.4990. In this case we can report that the p-value is less than 0.0010, found by: 0.5000 − 0.4990. We conclude that there is very little likelihood that the null hypothesis is true! Also, note that the p-value is less than the significance level, $\alpha = 0.01$, so the test statistic lies in the rejection region.

excel   Computer commands for hypothesis testing for the above example can be found at the end of the chapter.

In summary, the criteria for using formula (10–2) are as follows:

1. *The samples are from independent populations.* This means that the checkout time for the Fast Lane customers is unrelated to the checkout time for the other customers. For example, Mr. Smith's checkout time does not affect any other customer's checkout time.
2. *Both populations follow the normal distribution.* In the FoodTown example, this means the population of times in both the standard checkout line and the Fast Lane follow the normal distribution.
3. *Both population standard deviations are known.* In the FoodTown example, the population standard deviation of the Fast Lane times was 0.30 minutes. The standard deviation of the standard checkout times was 0.40 minutes.

self-review 10–1   Tom Sevits is the owner of the Appliance Patch. Recently, Tom observed a difference in the dollar value of sales between the men and women he employs as sales associates. A sample of 40 days revealed the men sold a mean of $1400 worth of appliances per day. For a sample of 50 days, the women sold a mean of $1500 worth of appliances per day. Assume that the population standard deviation for men is $200 and for women it is $250. At the 0.05 significance level, can Mr. Sevits conclude that the mean amount sold per day is larger for the women?

(a) State the null hypothesis and the alternative hypothesis.
(b) What is the decision rule?
(c) What is the value of the test statistic?
(d) What is your decision regarding the null hypothesis?
(e) What is the p-value?
(f) Interpret the result.

EXERCISES

1. A sample of 40 observations is selected from one population with a population standard deviation of 5. The sample mean is 102. A sample of 50 observations is selected from a second population with a population standard deviation of 6. The sample mean is 99. Conduct the following test of hypothesis using the 0.04 significance level:

$$H_0: \mu_1 - \mu_2 = 0$$
$$H_1: \mu_1 - \mu_2 \neq 0$$

   a. Is this a one-tailed or a two-tailed test?
   b. State the decision rule.
   c. Compute the value of the test statistic.
   d. What is your decision regarding H_0?
   e. What is the p-value? Interpret the p-value.

2. A sample of 65 observations is selected from one population with a population standard deviation of 0.75. The sample mean is 2.67. A sample of 50 observations is selected from a second population with a population standard deviation of 0.66. The sample mean is 2.59. Conduct the following test of hypothesis using the 0.08 significance level:

$$H_0: \mu_1 - \mu_2 \leq 0$$
$$H_1: \mu_1 - \mu_2 > 0$$

   a. Is this a one-tailed or a two-tailed test?
   b. State the decision rule.
   c. Compute the value of the test statistic.
   d. What is your decision regarding H_0?
   e. What is the p-value? Interpret the p-value.

Note: Use the five-step hypothesis testing procedure to solve the following exercises:

3. The Gibbs Baby Food Company wishes to compare the weight gain of infants using its brand versus its competitor's. A sample of 40 babies using the Gibbs products revealed a mean weight gain of 3.5 kilograms (kg) in the first three months after birth. For the Gibbs brand, the standard deviation of the population is 1.05 kg. A sample of 55 babies using the competitor's brand revealed a mean increase in weight of 3.7 kg, with a standard deviation of 1.3 kg. Can we conclude that babies using the Gibbs brand gained less weight? Choose an appropriate significance level. Compute the p-value, and interpret it.

4. As part of a study of corporate employees, the director of human resources for PNC Inc. wants to compare the distance travelled to work by employees at its downtown and midtown offices. A sample of 35 downtown employees showed they travel a mean of 595 kilometres (km) per month. A sample of 40 midtown employees showed they travel a mean of 610 km per month. The population standard deviations for the downtown and midtown offices are 48 km and 42 km, respectively. Is there a difference in the mean distance travelled per month between downtown and midtown employees? Use the five-step hypothesis testing procedure. Choose an appropriate significance level.

5. A financial analyst wants to compare the turnover rates, in percentages, for shares of oil-related stocks versus other stocks, such as General Electric (GE) and IBM. She selected 32 oil-related

stocks and 49 other stocks. The mean turnover rate of oil-related stocks is 31.4% and the population standard deviation is 5.1%. For the other stocks, the mean rate was computed to be 34.9% and the population standard deviation is 6.7%. Is there a significant difference in the turnover rates of the two types of stock? Use the 0.01 significance level. Compute the p-value, and interpret it.

6. Mary Jo Fitzpatrick is the vice president for nursing services at St. Luke's Memorial Hospital. Recently, she noticed that in the job postings for nurses, unionized jobs seemed to offer higher wages. She decided to investigate this and gathered the following sample information:

Group	Mean Wage	Population Standard Deviation	Sample Size
Unionized	$20.75	$2.25	40
Nonunionized	$19.80	$1.90	45

Would it be reasonable for her to conclude that unionized nurses earn more? Use the 0.02 significance level. What is the p-value? What conclusions can you make given the p-value?

LO10-2 10.3 COMPARING POPULATION MEANS WITH UNKNOWN POPULATION STANDARD DEVIATIONS

In the previous section, we used the standard normal distribution and z as the test statistic to test a hypothesis that two population means from independent populations were equal. The hypothesis tests presumed that the populations were normally distributed and that we knew the population standard deviations. However, in most cases, we do not know the population standard deviation. We can overcome this problem, as we did in the one sample case in the previous chapter, by substituting the sample standard deviation (s) for the population standard deviation (σ). See formula (9–2).

In this section, we describe another method for comparing the sample means of two independent populations to determine if the sampled populations could reasonably have the same mean. The method described does *not* require that we know the standard deviations of the populations. This gives us a great deal more flexibility when investigating the difference in sample means. There are two major differences in this test and the previous test described earlier in this chapter.

1. We assume that the sampled populations have equal but unknown standard deviations. Because of this assumption, we combine or "pool" the sample standard deviations.
2. We use the t distribution as the test statistic.

The formula for computing the test statistic t is similar to formula (10–2), but an additional calculation is necessary. The two sample standard deviations are pooled to form a single estimate of the unknown population standard deviation. In essence, we compute a weighted mean of the two sample standard deviations and use this value as an estimate of the unknown population standard deviation. The weights are the degrees of freedom that each sample provides. Why do we need to pool the standard deviations? Because we assume that the two populations have equal standard deviations, the best estimate we can make of that value is to combine or pool all the sample information we have about the value of the population standard deviation.

The following formula is used to pool the sample variances. Note that two factors are involved: the number of observations in each sample and the sample standard deviations themselves.

POOLED SAMPLE VARIANCE	$s_p^2 = \dfrac{(n_1 - 1)s_1^2 + (n_2 - 1)s_2^2}{n_1 + n_2 - 2}$	[10–3]

where:

s_1^2 is the variance (standard deviation squared) of the first sample.

s_2^2 is the variance of the second sample.

The value of t is computed from the following equation:

TWO-SAMPLE TEST OF MEANS—UNKNOWN σ	$t = \dfrac{\bar{x}_1 - \bar{x}_2 - (\mu_1 - \mu_2)}{\sqrt{s_p^2\left(\dfrac{1}{n_1} + \dfrac{1}{n_2}\right)}}$	[10–4]

where:

$\bar{x}_1$ is the mean of the first sample.

$\bar{x}_2$ is the mean of the second sample.

n_1 is the number of observations in the first sample.

n_2 is the number of observations in the second sample.

s_p^2 is the pooled estimate of the population variance.

The number of degrees of freedom in the test is the total number of items sampled minus the total number of samples. Because there are two samples, there are $n_1 + n_2 - 2$ degrees of freedom. To summarize, there are three requirements or assumptions for the test:

1. The sampled populations follow the normal distribution.
2. The sampled populations are independent.
3. The standard deviations of the two populations are equal.

The following example explains the details of the test:

Example	Owens Lawn Care Inc. manufactures and assembles lawnmowers that are shipped to dealers throughout the United States and Canada. Two different procedures have been proposed for mounting the engine on the frame of the lawnmower. The question is: is there a difference in the mean time to mount the engines on the frames of the lawnmowers? The first procedure was developed by longtime Owens employee Herb Welles (designated as Procedure 1), and the other procedure was developed by Owens vice president of engineering William Atkins (designated as Procedure 2). To evaluate the two methods, it was decided to conduct a time and motion study. A sample of five employees was timed using the Welles method and six using the Atkins method. The results, in minutes, are shown below. Is there a difference in the mean mounting times? Use the 0.10 significance level.

Welles (minutes)	Atkins (minutes)
2	3
4	7
9	5
3	8
2	4
	3

Solution	Following the five steps to test a hypothesis, the null hypothesis states that there is no difference in mean mounting times between the two procedures. The alternative hypothesis indicates that there is a difference.

$$H_0: \mu_1 - \mu_2 = 0$$
$$H_1: \mu_1 - \mu_2 \neq 0$$

The required assumptions are as follows:

1. The observations in the Welles sample are *independent* of the observations in the Atkins sample.
2. The two populations follow a normal distribution.
3. The two populations have equal standard deviations.

Is there a difference between the mean assembly times using the Welles and the Atkins methods? The degrees of freedom are equal to the total number of items sampled minus the number of samples. In this case, that is $n_1 + n_2 - 2$. Five assemblers used the Welles method and six the Atkins method. Thus, there are 9 degrees of freedom, found by: $5 + 6 - 2$. The critical values of t, from Appendix B.2 for $df = 9$, a two-tailed test, and the 0.10 significance level, are -1.833 and 1.833. The decision rule is portrayed graphically in Chart 10–2. We do not reject the null hypothesis if the computed value of t falls between -1.833 and 1.833.

CHART 10–2 Regions of Rejection, Two-Tailed Test, $df = 9$, and 0.10 Significance Level

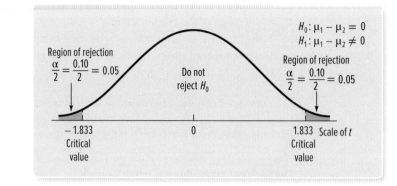

We use three steps to compute the value of t.

Step 1:   Calculate **the sample standard deviations.** Use **Excel**, **MegaStat**, or formulas (see the details below).

Welles Method		Atkins Method	
x_1	x_1^2	x_2	x_2^2
2	4	3	9
4	16	7	49
9	81	5	25
3	9	8	64
2	4	4	16
20	114	3	9
		30	172

$$s_1 = \sqrt{\dfrac{\sum x_1^2 - \dfrac{(\sum x_1)^2}{n_1}}{n_1 - 1}}$$

$$= \sqrt{\dfrac{114 - \dfrac{(20)^2}{5}}{5 - 1}} = 2.9155$$

$$s_2 = \sqrt{\dfrac{\sum x_2^2 - \dfrac{(\sum x_2)^2}{n_2}}{n_2 - 1}}$$

$$= \sqrt{\dfrac{172 - \dfrac{(30)^2}{6}}{6 - 1}} = 2.0976$$

Step 2:   **Pool the sample variances.** We use formula (10–3) to pool the sample variances (standard deviations squared).

$$s_p^2 = \dfrac{(n_1 - 1)s_1^2 + (n_2 - 1)s_2^2}{n_1 + n_2 - 2} = \dfrac{(5 - 1)(2.9155)^2 + (6 - 1)(2.0976)^2}{5 + 6 - 2} = 6.2222$$

Step 3:   **Determine the value of t.** The mean mounting time for procedure 1 is 4.00 minutes, found by $\bar{x}_1 = 20/5$. The mean mounting time for procedure 2 is 5.00 minutes, found by $\bar{x}_2 = 30/6$. We use formula (10–4) to calculate the value of t.

$$t = \dfrac{\bar{x}_1 - \bar{x}_2 - (\mu_1 - \mu_2)}{\sqrt{s_p^2\left(\dfrac{1}{n_1} + \dfrac{1}{n_2}\right)}} = \dfrac{4.00 - 5.00 - 0}{\sqrt{6.2222\left(\dfrac{1}{5} + \dfrac{1}{6}\right)}} = -0.662$$

The decision is not to reject the null hypothesis, because -0.662 falls in the region between -1.833 and 1.833. We conclude that there is no difference in the mean times to mount the engine on the frame using the two methods.

We can also estimate the p-value by using Appendix B.2. Locate the row with 9 degrees of freedom, and use the two-tailed test column. Find the t-value, without regard to the sign, which is closest to our computed value of -0.662. It is 1.383, corresponding to a significance level of 0.20. Thus, even had we used the 20% significance level, we would not have rejected the null hypothesis of equal means. We can report that the p-value is greater than 0.20.

excel Computer commands for hypothesis testing for the above example can be found at the end of the chapter.

---

self-review 10–2 The production manager at Bellevue Steel, a manufacturer of wheelchairs, wants to compare the number of defective wheelchairs produced on the day shift with the number on the afternoon shift. A sample of the production from six day shifts and eight afternoon shifts revealed the following number of defects:

Day	5	8	7	6	9	7		
Afternoon	8	10	7	11	9	12	14	9

Is there a difference in the mean number of defects per shift? Choose an appropriate significance level.

(a) State the null hypothesis and the alternative hypothesis.
(b) What is the decision rule?
(c) What is the value of the test statistic?
(d) What is your decision regarding the null hypothesis?
(e) What is the p-value?
(f) Interpret the result.
(g) What assumptions are necessary for this test?

EXERCISES

For Exercises 7 and 8: (a) state the decision rule, (b) compute the pooled estimate of the population variance, (c) compute the test statistic, (d) state your decision about the null hypothesis, and (e) estimate the p-value.

7. The null and alternative hypotheses are:

$$H_0: \mu_1 - \mu_2 = 0$$
$$H_1: \mu_1 - \mu_2 \neq 0$$

A random sample of 10 observations from one population revealed a sample mean of 23 and a sample deviation of 4. A random sample of 8 observations from another population revealed a sample mean of 26 and a sample standard deviation of 5. At the 0.05 significance level, is there a difference between the population means?

8. The null and alternative hypotheses are:

$$H_0: \mu_1 - \mu_2 = 0$$
$$H_1: \mu_1 - \mu_2 \neq 0$$

A random sample of 15 observations from the first population revealed a sample mean of 350 and a sample standard deviation of 12. A random sample of 17 observations from the second population revealed a sample mean of 342 and a sample standard deviation of 15. At the 0.10 significance level, is there a difference in the population means?

Note: Use the five-step hypothesis testing procedure for the following exercises:

9. A sample of scores on an examination given in Statistics 201 is as follows:

Men	72	69	98	66	85	76	79	80	77
Women	81	67	90	78	81	80	76		

At the 0.01 significance level, is the mean grade of the women higher than that of the men? Calculate and interpret the p-value.

10. A recent study compared the time spent together by single- and dual-earner couples. According to the records kept by the wives during the study, the mean amount of time spent together watching television among the single-earner couples was 61 minutes per day, with a standard deviation of 15.5 minutes. For the dual-earner couples, the mean number of minutes spent watching television was 48.4 minutes, with a standard deviation of 18.1 minutes. At the 0.01 significance level, can we conclude that the single-earner couples on average spend more time watching television together? There were 15 single-earner and 12 dual-earner couples studied. Estimate and interpret the p-value.

11. Ms. Lisa Monnin is the budget director for the New Process Company. She would like to compare the daily travel expenses for the sales staff and the audit staff. She collected the following sample information:

Sales ($)	131	135	146	165	136	142	
Audit ($)	130	102	129	143	149	120	139

At the 0.10 significance level, can she conclude that the mean daily expenses are greater for the sales staff than the audit staff? What is the *p*-value? Interpret the *p*-value.

12. The Milton Area Chamber of Commerce wanted to know whether the mean weekly salary of nurses was larger than that of school teachers. To investigate, it collected the following information on the amounts earned last week by a sample of school teachers and nurses:

School teachers ($)	845	826	827	875	784	809	802	820	829	830	842	832
Nurses ($)	841	890	821	771	850	859	825	829				

Is it reasonable to conclude that the mean weekly salary of nurses is higher? Use the 0.01 significance level. What is the *p*-value? Interpret the *p*-value.

LO10-3 10.4 TWO-SAMPLE TESTS OF HYPOTHESIS: DEPENDENT SAMPLES

Previously in this chapter, we tested the difference between the means from two independent samples. We compared the mean time required to mount an engine using the Welles method to the time to mount the engine using the Atkins method. The samples were *independent*; that is, the sample of assembly times using the Welles method was in no way related to the sample of assembly times using the Atkins method.

There are situations, however, in which the samples are not independent. To put it another way, the samples are *dependent* or *related*. As an example, Nickel Savings and Loan employs two firms, Schadek Appraisals and Bowyer Real Estate, to appraise the value of the real estate properties on which it makes loans. It is important that these two firms be similar in their appraisal values. To review the consistency of the two appraisal firms, Nickel Savings randomly selects 10 homes and has both Schadek Appraisals and Bowyer Real Estate appraise the value of the selected homes. For each home, there will be a pair of appraisal values. That is, for each home there will be an appraised value from both Schadek Appraisals and Bowyer Real Estate. The appraised values depend on, or are related to, the home selected. This is also referred to as a **paired sample**.

For hypothesis testing, we are interested in the distribution of the *differences* in the appraised value of each home. Hence, there is only one sample. To put it more formally, we are investigating whether the mean of the distribution of differences in the appraised values is 0. The sample is made up of the *differences* between the appraised values determined by Schadek Appraisals and the values from Bowyer Real Estate. If the two appraisal firms are reporting similar estimates, then sometimes Schadek Appraisals will be the higher value, and sometimes Bowyer Real Estate will have the higher value. However, the mean of the distribution of differences will be 0. On the other hand, if one of the firms consistently reports the larger appraisal values, then the mean of the distribution of the differences will not be 0.

We will use the symbol μd to indicate the population mean of the distribution of differences. We assume the distribution of the population of differences follows the normal distribution. The test statistic follows the *t* distribution, and we calculate its value from the following formula:

PAIRED *t* TEST	$$t = \frac{\bar{d} - \mu_d}{s_d/\sqrt{n}}$$	[10–5]

There are $n - 1$ degrees of freedom and:

$\bar{d}$ is the mean of the difference between the paired or related observations.

s_d is the sample standard deviation of the differences between the paired or related observations.

n is the number of paired observations.

The standard deviation of the differences is computed by the direct formula for the standard deviation, except d is substituted for x. The formula is:

$$s_d = \sqrt{\frac{\sum d^2 - \frac{(\sum d)^2}{n}}{n-1}}$$

The following example illustrates this test:

Example	Recall that Nickel Savings and Loan wishes to compare the two companies it uses to appraise the value of residential homes. Nickel Savings selected a sample of 10 residential properties and scheduled both firms for an appraisal. The results, reported in thousands of dollars ($000), are as follows:

Home	Schadek ($ thousands)	Bowyer ($ thousands)
1	$235	$228
2	210	205
3	231	219
4	242	240
5	205	198
6	230	223
7	231	227
8	210	215
9	225	222
10	249	245

At the 0.05 significance level, can we conclude there is a difference in the mean appraised values of the homes?

Solution	The first step is to state the null and the alternative hypotheses. In this case, a two-tailed alternative is appropriate because we are interested in determining whether there is a *difference* in the appraised values. We are not interested in showing whether one particular firm appraises property at a higher value than the other. The question is whether the sample differences in the appraised values could have come from a population with a mean of 0. If the population mean of the differences is 0, then we conclude that there is no difference in the appraised values. The null and alternative hypotheses are:

$$H_0: \mu_d = 0$$
$$H_1: \mu_d \neq 0$$

There are 10 homes appraised by both firms, so $n = 10$, and $df = n - 1 = 10 - 1 = 9$. We have a two-tailed test, and the significance level is 0.05. To determine the critical value, go to Appendix B.2, and move across the row with 9 degrees of freedom to the column for a two-tailed test and the 0.05 significance level. The value at the intersection is 2.262. This value appears in the box in Table 10–2. The decision rule is to reject the null hypothesis if the computed value of t is less than -2.262 or greater than 2.262. Here are the computational details:

Home	Schadek ($ thousands)	Bowyer ($ thousands)	Difference, d	Difference Squared, d^2
1	$235	$228	7	49
2	210	205	5	25
3	231	219	12	144
4	242	240	2	4
5	205	198	7	49
6	230	223	7	49
7	231	227	4	16
8	210	215	−5	25
9	225	222	3	9
10	249	245	4	16
			46	386

$$\bar{d} = \frac{\Sigma d}{n} = \frac{46}{10} = 4.60$$

$$s_d = \sqrt{\frac{\Sigma d^2 - \frac{(\Sigma d)^2}{n}}{n - 1}} = \sqrt{\frac{386 - \frac{(46)^2}{10}}{10 - 1}} 4.402$$

Using formula (10–5), the value of the test statistic is 3.305, found by:

$$t = \frac{\bar{d} - \mu_d}{s_d/\sqrt{n}} = \frac{4.6 - 0}{4.402/\sqrt{10}} = 3.305$$

Because the computed t falls in the rejection region, the null hypothesis is rejected. The population distribution of differences does not have a mean of 0. We conclude that there is a difference in the mean appraised values of the homes. The largest difference of \$12 000 is for Home 3. Perhaps that would be an appropriate place to begin a more detailed review.

To find the p-value, we use Appendix B.2 and the section for a two-tailed test. Move along the row with 9 degrees of freedom, and find the values of t that are closest to our calculated value. For a 0.01 significance level, the value of t is 3.250. The computed value is larger than this value, but smaller than the value of 4.781 corresponding to the 0.001 significance level. Hence, the p-value is less than 0.01. Therefore, there is very little likelihood that the null hypothesis is true. Also, as the p-value is less than the level of significance $\alpha = 0.01$, the test statistic lies in the rejection region. This information is highlighted in Table 10–2.

TABLE 10–2 A Portion of the t Distribution Table from Appendix B.2

			Confidence Intervals			
	80%	90%	95%	98%	99%	99.9%
	Level of Significance for One-Tailed Test					
df	0.100	0.050	0.025	0.010	0.005	0.0005
	Level of Significance for Two-Tailed Test					
	0.20	0.10	0.05	0.02	0.01	0.001
1	3.078	6.314	12.706	31.821	63.657	636.619
2	1.886	2.920	4.303	6.965	9.925	31.599
3	1.638	2.353	3.182	4.541	5.841	12.924
4	1.533	2.132	2.776	3.747	4.604	8.610
5	1.476	2.015	2.571	3.365	4.032	6.869
6	1.440	1.943	2.447	3.143	3.707	5.959
7	1.415	1.895	2.365	2.998	3.499	5.408
8	1.397	1.860	2.306	2.896	3.355	5.041
9	1.383	1.833	2.262	2.821	3.250	4.781
10	1.372	1.812	2.228	2.764	3.169	4.587

excel Computer commands for hypothesis testing for the above example can be found at the end of the chapter.

LO10-4 ## 10.5 COMPARING DEPENDENT AND INDEPENDENT SAMPLES

Students are often confused by the difference between tests for independent samples (formula 10–4) and tests for dependent samples (formula 10–5). How do we tell the difference between dependent and independent samples? There are two types of dependent samples: (1) those characterized by a measurement, an intervention of some type, and then another measurement; and (2) a matching or pairing of the observations. To explain further:

1. The first type of dependent sample is characterized by a measurement followed by an intervention of some kind and then another measurement. This could be called a "before-and-after" study. Two examples will help to clarify. Suppose we want to show that by placing speakers in the production area and playing soothing music, we are able to increase production. We begin by selecting a sample of workers and measuring their output under the current conditions. The speakers are then installed in the production area, and we again measure the output of the same workers. There are two measurements, before placing the speakers in the production area, and after. The intervention is placing speakers in the production area.

    A second example involves an educational firm that offers courses designed to increase test scores and reading ability. Suppose the firm wants to offer a course that will help high school students increase their SAT (Scholastic Aptitude Test) scores. To begin, each student takes the SAT in the second year of high school. During the summer between the second and third years, they participate in the course that gives them tips on taking tests. Finally, during the fall of their third year of high school, they retake the SAT. Again, the procedure is characterized by a measurement (taking the SAT as a second-year student), an intervention (the summer workshops), and another measurement (taking the SAT as third-year students).

2. The second type of dependent sample is characterized by matching or pairing observations. Nickel Savings, in the previous example, illustrates dependent samples. A property is selected and both firms appraise the same property. As a second example, suppose an industrial psychologist wishes to study the intellectual similarities of newly married couples. She selects a sample of newlyweds. Next, she administers a standard intelligence test to both the man and the woman to determine the difference in the scores. Note the matching that occurred: comparing the scores that are paired or matched by marriage.

Why do we prefer dependent samples to independent samples? By using dependent samples, we are able to reduce the variation in the sampling distribution. To illustrate, we will use the Nickel Savings and Loan example just completed. Suppose that we assume that we have two independent samples of real estate property for appraisal and conduct the following test of hypothesis, using formula (10–4). The null and alternative hypotheses are:

$$H_0: \mu_1 - \mu_2 = 0$$
$$H_1: \mu_1 - \mu_2 \neq 0$$

There are now two independent samples of 10 each. So, the number of degrees of freedom is $10 + 10 - 2 = 18$. From Appendix B.2, using the 0.05 significance level, H_0 is rejected if t is less than -2.101 or greater than -2.101.

The mean of the appraised value of the 10 properties by Schadek is \$226 800, and the standard deviation is \$14 450. For Bowyer Real Estate, the mean appraised value is \$222 200, and the standard deviation is \$14 290. To make the calculations easier, we use \$000 (thousands of dollars) instead of dollars. The value of the pooled estimate of the variance from formula (10–3) is:

$$s_p^2 = \frac{(n_1 - 1)s_1^2 + (n_2 - 1)s_2^2}{n_1 + n_2 - 2} = \frac{(10 - 1)(14.45)^2 + (10 - 1)(14.29)^2}{10 + 10 - 2} = 206.50$$

Using formula (10–4), t is 0.716.

$$t = \frac{\overline{x}_1 - \overline{x}_2 - (\mu_1 - \mu_2)}{\sqrt{s_p^2 \left(\frac{1}{n_1} + \frac{1}{n_2}\right)}} = \frac{226.8 - 222.2 - 0}{\sqrt{206.50\left(\frac{1}{10} + \frac{1}{10}\right)}} = \frac{4.6}{6.4265} = 0.716$$

We computed that t (0.716) is less than 2.101, so the null hypothesis is not rejected. We cannot show that there is a difference in the mean appraisal value. That is not the same conclusion that we got before! Why does this happen? The numerator is the same in the paired observations test (4.6). However, the denominator is smaller. In the paired test, the denominator is 1.3920. In the case of the independent samples, the denominator is 6.4265. There is more variation or uncertainty. This accounts for the difference in the t-values and the difference in the statistical decisions. The denominator measures the standard error of the statistic. When the samples are *not* paired, two kinds of variation are present: differences between the two appraisal firms and the difference in the value of the real estate. Properties numbered 4 and 10 have relatively high values, whereas number 5 is relatively low. These data show how different the values of the property are, but we are really interested in the difference between the two appraisal firms.

When we can pair or match observations that measure differences for a common variable, a hypothesis test based on dependent samples is more sensitive to detecting a significance difference than a hypothesis test based on independent samples. In the case of comparing the property valuations by Schadek Appraisals and Bowyer Real Estate, the hypothesis test based on dependent samples eliminates the variation between the values of the properties and focuses only on the comparisons in the two appraisals for each property. There is a bit of bad news here. In the paired observations test, the degrees of freedom are half of what they are if the samples are not paired. For the real estate example, the degrees of freedom drop from 18 to 9 when the observations are paired. However, in most cases, this is a small price to pay for a better test.

self-review 10–3

Advertisements by Sylph Fitness Centre claim that completing its course will result in losing weight. A random sample of eight recent participants showed the following weights before and after completing the course. At the 0.01 significance level, can we conclude the students lost weight?

Name	Before	After
Hunter	155	154
Cashman	228	207
Mervine	141	147
Massa	162	157
Creola	211	196
Perterson	164	150
Redding	184	170
Poust	172	165

(a) State the null hypothesis and the alternative hypothesis.
(b) What is the critical value of t?
(c) What is the computed value of t?
(d) Interpret the result. What is the p-value?
(e) What assumption needs to be made about the distribution of the differences?

EXERCISES

13. The null and alternative hypotheses are:

$$H_0: \mu_d \leq 0$$
$$H_1: \mu_d > 0$$

The following sample information shows the number of defective units produced on the day shift and the afternoon shift for a sample of four days last month:

	Day			
	1	2	3	4
Day shift	10	12	15	11
Afternoon shift	8	9	12	15

At the 0.05 significance level, can we conclude there are more defects produced on the afternoon shift?

14. The null and alternative hypotheses are:

$$H_0: \mu_d = 0$$
$$H_1: \mu_d \neq 0$$

The following paired observations show the number of traffic citations given for speeding by Officer Dhondt and Officer Meredith of the Ontario Provincial Police (OPP) for the last five months:

	May	June	July	August	September
Officer Dhondt	30	22	25	19	26
Officer Meredith	26	19	20	15	19

At the 0.05 significance level, is there a difference in the mean number of citations given by the two officers?

Note: Use the five-step hypothesis testing procedure to solve the following exercises:

15. The management of Discount Furniture designed an incentive plan for salespeople. To evaluate this innovative plan, 12 salespeople were selected at random, and their weekly incomes before and after the plan were recorded.

Salesperson	Before	After
Sid Mahone	$320	$340
Carol Quick	290	285
Tom Jackson	421	475
Andy Jones	510	510
Jean Sloan	210	210
Jack Walker	402	500
Peg Mancuso	625	631
Anita Loma	560	560
John Cuso	360	365
Carl Utz	431	431
A. S. Kushner	506	525
Fern Lawton	505	619

Was there a significant increase in the typical salesperson's weekly income due to the innovative incentive plan? Use the 0.05 significance level. Estimate the p-value, and interpret it.

16. The federal government recently granted funds for a special program designed to reduce crime in high-crime areas. A study of the results of the program in eight high-crime areas yielded the following results:

	Number of Crimes by Area							
	A	**B**	**C**	**D**	**E**	**F**	**G**	**H**
Before	14	7	4	5	17	12	8	9
After	2	7	3	6	8	13	3	5

Has there been a decrease in the number of crimes since the inauguration of the program? Use the 0.01 significance level. Estimate the p-value.

LO10-5   10.6 TWO-SAMPLE TESTS ABOUT PROPORTIONS

In the previous section, we considered a test involving population means. However, we are often as well interested in whether two sample proportions come from populations that are equal. Here are several examples:

- The vice-president of human resources wishes to know whether there is a difference in the proportion of hourly employees who miss more than five days of work per year at the Sudbury and the Hamilton plants.
- General Motors (GM) is considering a new design for the Chevy Malibu. The design is shown to a group of potential buyers under 30 years of age and to another group over 60 years of age. GM wishes to know whether there is a difference in the proportion of the two groups who like the new design.
- A consultant in the airline industry is investigating the fear of flying among adults. Specifically, the company wishes to know whether there is a difference in the proportion of men versus women who are fearful of flying.

In the above cases, each sampled item or individual can be classified as a "success" or a "failure." That is, in the Chevy Malibu example, each potential buyer is classified as "liking the new design" or "not liking the new design." We then compare the proportion in the under-30 group with the proportion in the over-60 group who indicated they liked the new design. Can we conclude that the differences are due to chance? In this study, there is no measurement obtained, only classifying the individuals or objects.

To conduct the test, we assume that each sample is large enough that the normal distribution will serve as a good approximation of the binomial distribution. The test statistic follows the standard normal distribution. We compute the value of z with the following formula:

TWO-SAMPLE TEST OF PROPORTIONS

$$z = \frac{\bar{p}_1 - \bar{p}_2 - (p_1 - p_2)}{\sqrt{\dfrac{p_c(1 - p_c)}{n_1} + \dfrac{p_c(1 - p_c)}{n_2}}} \qquad [10\text{–}6]$$

Formula (10–6) is formula (10–2) with the respective sample proportions replacing the sample means and $p_c(1 - p_c)$ replacing the two variances. In addition:

n_1 is the number of observations in the first sample.

n_2 is the number of observations in the second sample.

$\bar{p}_1$ is the proportion in the first sample possessing the trait.

$\bar{p}_2$ is the proportion in the second sample possessing the trait.

p_c is the pooled proportion possessing the trait in the combined samples. It is called the *pooled estimate of the population* proportion and is computed with the following formula:

POOLED PROPORTION

$$p_c = \frac{x_1 + x_2}{n_1 + n_2} \qquad [10\text{–}7]$$

where:

x_1 is the number possessing the trait in the first sample.

x_2 is the number possessing the trait in the second sample.

The following example will illustrate the two-sample test of proportions:

Example	The Manelli Perfume Company recently developed a new fragrance that it plans to market under the name Heavenly. A number of market studies indicate that Heavenly has very good market potential. The sales department at Manelli is particularly interested in whether there is a difference in the proportions of younger and older women who would purchase Heavenly if it were marketed. There are two independent populations—a population consisting of the younger women and a population consisting of the older women. Each sampled woman will be asked to smell Heavenly and indicate whether she likes the fragrance well enough to purchase a bottle.
Solution	We will use the usual five-step hypothesis testing procedure.

> **Step 1:** **State H_0 and H_1.** In this case, the null hypothesis is: "There is no difference in the proportion of young women and older women who prefer Heavenly." We designate p_1 as the proportion of young women who would purchase Heavenly and p_2 as the proportion of older women who would purchase it. The alternative hypothesis is that the two proportions are not equal.
>
> $$H_0: p_1 - p_2 = 0$$
> $$H_1: p_1 - p_2 \neq 0$$
>
> **Step 2:** **Select the level of significance.** We choose the 0.05 significance level in this example.
>
> **Step 3:** **Determine the test statistic.** The test statistic follows the standard normal distribution. The value of the test statistic can be computed from formula (10–6).
>
> **Step 4:** **Formulate the decision rule.** Recall that the alternative hypothesis from **Step 1** does not state a direction, so this is a two-tailed test. To find the critical value, go to the Student's *t distribution* table in Appendix B.2. In the table headings, find the row labelled "Level of Significance for Two-Tailed Test" and select the column for an alpha of 0.05. Go to the bottom row with infinite degrees of freedom. The z critical value is 1.960, so the critical values are -1.96 and $+1.96$. As before, if the computed z-value falls in the region between $+1.96$ and -1.96, the null hypothesis is not rejected. If that does occur, it is assumed that any difference between the two sample proportions is due to chance variation. This information is summarized in Chart 10–3.

$$\bar{p}_1 = \frac{x_1}{n_1} = \frac{19}{100} = 0.19 \qquad \bar{p}_2 = \frac{x_2}{n_2} = \frac{62}{200} = 0.31$$

The research question is whether the difference of 0.12 in the two sample proportions is due to chance or whether there is a difference in the proportion of younger and older women who like the Heavenly fragrance.

CHART 10–3 Decision Rules for Heavenly Fragrance Test, 0.05 Significance Level

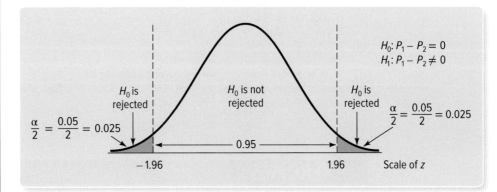

Step 5: **Select a sample and make a decision.** A random sample of 100 young women revealed 19 liked the Heavenly fragrance well enough to purchase it. Similarly, a sample of 200 older women revealed 62 liked the fragrance well enough to make a purchase. We let $\bar{p}_1$ refer to the young women and p_2 to the older women.

Next, we combine or pool the sample proportions. We use formula (10–7).

$$p_c = \frac{x_1 + x_2}{n_1 + n_2} = \frac{19 + 62}{100 + 200} = \frac{81}{300} = 0.27$$

Note that the pooled proportion is closer to 0.31 than to 0.19 because more older women than younger women were sampled.

We use formula (10–6) to find the value of the test statistic.

$$z = \frac{\bar{p}_1 - \bar{p}_2 - (p_1 - p_2)}{\sqrt{\frac{p_c(1 - p_c)}{n_1} + \frac{p_c(1 - p_c)}{n_2}}} = \frac{0.19 - 0.31 - 0}{\sqrt{\frac{0.27(1 - 0.27)}{100} + \frac{0.27(1 - 0.27)}{200}}} = -2.21$$

The computed value of -2.21 is in the area of rejection; that is, it is to the left of -1.96. Therefore, the null hypothesis is rejected at the 0.05 significance level. To put it another way, we reject the null hypothesis that the proportion of young women who would purchase Heavenly is equal to the proportion of older women who would purchase Heavenly. It is unlikely that the difference between the two sample proportions is due to chance. To find the p-value, we go to Appendix B.1 and look for the likelihood of finding a z-value less than -2.21 or greater than 2.21. The z-value corresponding to 2.21 is 0.4864, so the likelihood of finding the value of the test statistic to be less than -2.21 or greater than 2.21 is:

$$p\text{-value} = 2(0.5000 - 0.4864) = 0.0272$$

The p-value of 0.0272 is less than the significance level of 0.05, so our decision is to reject the null hypothesis. Again, we conclude that there is a difference in the proportion of younger and older women who would purchase the fragrance Heavenly.

Computer commands for hypothesis testing for the above example can be found at the end of the chapter.

self-review 10–4   Of 150 adults who tried a new peach-flavoured peppermint patty, 87 rated it excellent. Of 200 children sampled, 123 rated it excellent. Using the 0.10 level of significance, can we conclude that there is a significant difference in the proportion of adults and the proportion of children who rate the new flavour excellent?

(a) State the null hypothesis and the alternative hypothesis.
(b) What is the probability of a Type I error?
(c) Is this a one-tailed or a two-tailed test?
(d) What is the decision rule?
(e) What is the value of the test statistic?
(f) What is your decision regarding the null hypothesis?
(g) What is the p-value? Explain what it means in terms of this problem.

EXERCISES

17. The null and alternative hypotheses are:

$$H_0: p_1 - p_2 \le 0$$
$$H_1: p_1 - p_2 > 0$$

A sample of 100 observations from the first population indicated that x_1 is 70. A sample of 150 observations from the second population revealed x_2 to be 90. Use the 0.05 significance level to test the hypothesis.

a. State the decision rule.
b. Compute the pooled proportion.
c. Compute the value of the test statistic.
d. What is your decision regarding the null hypothesis?
e. Determine and interpret the p-value.

18. The null and alternative hypotheses are:

$$H_0: p_1 - p_2 = 0$$
$$H_1: p_1 - p_2 \ne 0$$

A sample of 200 observations from the first population indicated that x_1 is 170. A sample of 150 observations from the second population revealed x_2 to be 110. Use the 0.05 significance level to test the hypothesis.

a. State the decision rule.
b. Compute the pooled proportion.
c. Compute the value of the test statistic.
d. What is your decision regarding the null hypothesis?
e. Determine and interpret the p-value.

Note: Use the five-step hypothesis testing procedure in solving the following exercises.

19. The Damon family owns a large grape vineyard in the Niagara Peninsula. The grapevines must be sprayed at the beginning of the growing season to protect them against various insects and diseases. Two new insecticides have just been marketed: Pernod 5 and Action. To test their effectiveness, six long rows were selected. Three rows were sprayed with Pernod 5 and three were sprayed with Action. When the grapes ripened, 400 of the vines treated with Pernod 5 were checked for infestation. Likewise, a sample of 400 vines sprayed with Action was checked. The results are:

Insecticide	Number of Vines Checked (sample size)	Number of Infested Vines
Pernod 5	400	24
Action	400	40

Can we conclude that there is a difference in the proportion of vines infested using Pernod 5 as opposed to Action? Test at the 0.05 significance level. Determine and interpret the p-value.

20. The GfK Custom Research Organization conducted identical surveys five years apart. One question asked women: "Are most men basically kind, gentle, and thoughtful"? The earlier survey revealed that, of the 3000 women surveyed, 2010 said that they were. In the later survey, 1530 of the 3000 women surveyed thought that men were kind, gentle, and thoughtful. Can we conclude that women think men are less kind, gentle, and thoughtful in the later survey compared with the earlier one? Choose an appropriate significance level. Calculate and interpret the p-value.

21. A nationwide sample of influential Liberals and Conservatives was asked as a part of a comprehensive survey whether they favoured lowering environmental standards so that high-sulphur coal could be burned in coal-fired power plants. The results were:

	Liberals	Conservatives
Number sampled	1000	800
Number in favour	200	168

At the 0.02 level of significance, can we conclude that there is a larger proportion of Conservatives in favour of lowering the standards? Calculate and interpret the p-value.

22. The research department at the home office of Superior Insurance conducts ongoing research on the causes of automobile accidents, the characteristics of the drivers, and so on. A random sample of 400 policies written on single persons revealed 120 had at least one accident in the previous three-year period. Similarly, a sample of 600 policies written on married persons revealed that 150 had been in at least one accident. At the 0.05 significance level, is there a significant difference in the proportions of single and married persons having an accident during a three-year period? Determine and interpret the p-value.

Chapter Summary

I. In comparing two population means, we wish to know whether they could be equal.

A. We are investigating whether the distribution of the difference between the means could have a mean of 0.

B. The test statistic follows the standard normal distribution if the population standard deviations are known.
1. The two populations follow normal distributions.
2. The samples are from independent populations.
3. The formula to compute the value of z is:

$$z = \frac{\bar{x}_1 - \bar{x}_2 - (\mu_1 - \mu_2)}{\sqrt{\dfrac{\sigma_1^2}{n_1} + \dfrac{\sigma_2^2}{n_2}}} \qquad [10\text{--}2]$$

II. We can also test whether two samples came from populations with an equal proportion of successes.

A. The two sample proportions are pooled using the following formula:

$$p_c = \frac{x_1 + x_2}{n_1 + n_2} \qquad [10\text{--}7]$$

B. We compute the value of the test statistic from the following formula:

$$z = \frac{\bar{p}_1 - \bar{p}_2 - (p_1 - p_2)}{\sqrt{\dfrac{p_c(1 - p_c)}{n_1} + \dfrac{p_c(1 - p_c)}{n_2}}} \qquad [10\text{--}6]$$

III. The test statistic to compare two means is the t distribution if the population standard deviations are not known.

A. Both populations must follow the normal distribution.

B. The populations must have equal standard deviations.

C. The samples are independent.

D. Finding the value of t requires two steps.

1. The first step is to pool the sample standard deviations according to the following formula:

$$s_p^2 = \frac{(n_1 - 1)s_1^2 + (n_2 - 1)s_2^2}{n_1 + n_2 - 2}$$ [10–3]

2. The value of t is computed from the following formula:

$$t = \frac{\bar{x}_1 - \bar{x}_2 - (\mu_1 - \mu_2)}{\sqrt{s_p^2 \left(\frac{1}{n_1} + \frac{1}{n_2}\right)}}$$ [10–4]

3. The degrees of freedom for the test are $n_1 + n_2 - 2$.

IV. For dependent samples, we assume the distribution of the paired differences between the populations has a mean of 0.

A. We first compute the mean and the standard deviation of the sample differences.

B. The value of the test statistic is computed from the following formula:

$$t = \frac{\bar{d} - \mu_d}{s_d / \sqrt{n}}$$ [10–5]

Chapter Exercises

23. A recent study focused on the number of times men and women who live alone buy takeout dinners in a month. The information is summarized below:

Number of Dinners per Month

Statistic	Men	Women
Mean	24.51	22.69
Population standard deviation	4.48	3.86
Sample size	35.00	40.00

At the 0.01 significance level, is there a difference in the mean number of times men and women order takeout dinners in a month? Calculate and interpret the p-value.

24. A coffee manufacturer is interested in whether the mean daily consumption of regular-coffee drinkers is less than that of decaffeinated-coffee drinkers. Assume the population standard deviation for those drinking regular coffee is 1.20 cups per day and for those drinking decaffeinated coffee is 1.36 cups per day. A random sample of 50 regular-coffee drinkers showed a mean of 4.35 cups per day. A sample of 40 decaffeinated-coffee drinkers showed a mean of 5.84 cups per day. Use the 0.01 significance level. Compute and interpret the p-value.

25. An official of the Ministry of Transport wants to compare the useful life, in months, of two brands of paint used for striping roads. The mean number of months Cooper Paint lasted was 36.2. The official reviewed 35 road stripes. For King Paint, the mean number of months was 37.0. The official reviewed 40 road stripes. The population standard deviation for the Cooper Paint is 1.14 months and for the King Paint, 1.3 months. At the 0.01 significance level, is there a difference in the useful life of the two paints? Compute and interpret the p-value.

26. Clark Heter is an industrial engineer at Lyons Products. He would like to determine whether there are more units produced on the afternoon shift than on the day shift. A sample of 54 day-shift workers showed that the mean number of units produced was 345. A sample of 60 afternoon-shift workers showed that the mean number of units produced was 351. Assume that the population standard deviation for the number of units produced on the day shift is 21 and on the afternoon shift is 28. At the 0.05 significance level, is the number of units produced on the afternoon shift larger?

27. Fry Brothers Heating and Air Conditioning Inc. employs Larry Clark and George Murnen to make service calls to repair furnaces and air-conditioning units in homes. Tom Fry, the owner, would like to know whether there is a difference in the mean number of service calls they make per day. A random sample of 40 days last year showed that Larry Clark made an average of 4.77 calls per day. For a sample of 50 days, George Murnen made an average of 5.02 calls per day. The population standard deviation for Larry Clark

is 1.05 calls per day, and for George Murnen, it is 1.23 calls per day. At the 0.05 significance level, is there a difference in the mean number of calls per day between the two employees? Compute and interpret the p-value.

28. The Simone Company is considering a new computer program to speed up the processing of its inventory. Two programs are being considered: Program A and Program B. To test the programs, 50 employees were divided into two groups of 25. The mean processing time of Program A was 30 seconds, with a standard deviation of 5 seconds. The mean processing time of Program B was 28 seconds, with a standard deviation of 3 seconds. Is there a difference in the speed of the two programs? Choose an appropriate significance level. Calculate and interpret the p-value.

29. Fairfield Homes is developing two parcels of land near White Pigeon. To test different advertising approaches, it uses different media to reach potential buyers. The mean annual family income for 15 people making inquiries at the first development is $150 000, with a standard deviation of $40 000. A corresponding sample of 25 people at the second development had a mean income of $180 000, with a standard deviation of $30 000. At the 0.05 significance level, can Fairfield conclude that the population means are different?

30. The following data on annual rates of return were collected from five stocks listed on the New York Stock Exchange (NYSE, or the "Big Board") and five stocks listed on NASDAQ. At the 0.10 significance level, can we conclude that the annual rates of return are higher on the Big Board?

NYSE	NASDAQ
17.16	15.80
17.08	16.28
15.51	16.21
8.43	17.97
25.15	7.77

31. Suppose the manufacturer of ibuprofen, a common headache remedy, recently developed a new formulation of the drug that is claimed to be more effective. To evaluate the new drug, a sample of 200 current users is asked to try it. After a one-month trial, 180 indicated the new drug was more effective in relieving a headache. At the same time, a sample of 300 current ibuprofen users is given the current drug but told it is the new formulation. From this group, 261 said it was an improvement. At the 0.05 significance level can we conclude that the new drug is more effective?

32. Each month the National Association of Purchasing Managers (NAPM) publishes the NAPM index. One of the questions asked on the survey to purchasing agents is: do you think the economy is expanding? Last month, of the 300 responses, 160 answered "yes" to the question. This month, 170 of the 290 responses indicated they felt the economy was expanding. At the 0.05 significance level, can we conclude that a larger proportion of the agents believe the economy is expanding this month?

33. Century Business Products tested 180 whiteboard markers that they had in stock and found that 13 failed to perform adequately and had to be replaced immediately. The same test was applied to a sample of 67 whiteboard markers from a new supplier and found that 7 of those failed. Use the 0.05 significance level to test if it is reasonable to conclude that the whiteboard markers from the new supplier are not performing as well as those in stock.

34. A financial services company has 39 female top executives (presidents or vice presidents) among its 388 senior managers in its Banking Services division, while there are only 11 female top executives among its 307 senior managers in its Investment Services division. Test at the 0.05 significance level if this reveals the Banking Services division has significantly more female top executives in higher levels of management.

35. In a poll recently conducted at a downtown college, 68 out of 98 male students and 45 out of 85 female students expressed "at least some support" for implementing regulations to limit greenhouse gases. Test, at the 0.05 significance level, if the population proportions are equal.

36. A study was conducted to determine if there was a difference in the humour content in British and Canadian trade magazine advertisements. In an independent random sample of 270 Canadian trade magazine advertisements, 56 were humorous. An independent random sample of 203 British trade magazines contained 52 humorous ads. Do these data provide evidence, at the 0.05 significance level, that there is a difference in the proportion of humorous ads in British versus Canadian trade magazines?

37. As part of a recent survey among dual-wage-earner couples, an industrial psychologist found that 990 men out of the 1500 surveyed believed the division of household duties was fair. A sample of 1600 women found 970 believed the division of household duties was fair. At the 0.01 significance level, is it reasonable to conclude that the proportion of men who believe the division of household duties is fair is larger? Calculate and interpret the p-value.

38. Two major cell phone providers want to investigate whether there is a difference in the proportion of times a call is successful. During a one-week period, 500 calls were placed at random times throughout the day and night to the first provider, and 450 calls were successful. A similar one-week study with the second provider showed that 352 of 400 calls were successful. At the 0.01 significance level, is there a difference in the percentage of time that cell phone connections are successful? Calculate and interpret the p-value.

39. The owner of Bun 'N' Run Hamburger wishes to compare the sales per day at two locations. The mean number sold for 10 randomly selected days at the Northside site was 83.55, and the standard deviation was 10.50. For a random sample of 12 days at the Southside location, the mean number sold was 78.80 and the standard deviation was 14.25. At the 0.05 significance level, is there a difference in the mean number of hamburgers sold at the two locations? Calculate and interpret the p-value.

40. The Grand Strand Family Medical Centre is specifically set up to treat minor medical emergencies for visitors. There are two facilities, one in the Little River Area and the other in Murrells Inlet. The quality control department wishes to compare the mean waiting time for patients at the two locations. Samples of the waiting times, reported in minutes, are as follows:

Location	Waiting Time										
Little River	31.73	28.77	29.53	22.08	29.47	18.60	32.94	25.18	29.82	26.49	
Murrells Inlet	22.93	23.92	26.92	27.20	26.44	25.62	30.61	29.44	23.09	23.10	26.69	22.31

At the 0.05 significance level, is there a difference in the mean waiting time?

41. The Commercial Bank and Trust Company is studying the use of its automatic teller machines (ATMs). Of particular interest is whether young adults (under 25 years old) use the machines more than senior citizens. To investigate further, samples of customers under 25 years of age and customers over 60 years of age were selected. The number of ATM transactions last month was determined for each selected individual, and the results are shown below. At the 0.01 significance level, can bank management conclude that younger customers use the ATMs more?

Under 25	10	10	11	15	7	11	10	9		
Over 60	4	8	7	7	4	5	1	7	4	10	5

42. Two horses, Rocky and Duke, are competing in the Coliseum Grand Prize horse race next month. To decide which is faster, they race over a part of the course several times. Below are the sample times in minutes. At the 0.05 significance level, can we conclude that there is a difference in their mean times?

Horse	Times (minutes)											
Rocky	12.9	12.5	11.0	13.3	11.2	11.4	11.6	12.3	14.2	11.3		
Duke	14.1	14.1	14.2	17.4	15.8	16.7	16.1	13.3	13.4	13.6	10.8	19.0

43. The manufacturer of an MP3 player wanted to know whether a 10% reduction in price is enough to increase the sales of its product. To investigate, the owner randomly selected eight outlets and sold the MP3 player at the reduced price. At seven randomly selected outlets, the MP3 player was sold at the regular price. Reported below is the number of units sold last month at the sampled outlets. At the 0.01 significance level, can the manufacturer conclude that the price reduction resulted in an increase in sales?

Regular price	138	121	88	115	141	125	96	
Reduced price	128	134	152	135	114	106	112	120

44. A number of minor automobile accidents occur at various high-risk intersections despite traffic lights. The traffic department claims that a modification in the type of light will reduce these accidents. The traffic commissioners have agreed to a proposed experiment. Eight intersections were chosen at random, and the lights at those intersections were modified. The numbers of minor accidents during a six-month period before and after the modifications were as follows:

	Number of Accidents							
	A	**B**	**C**	**D**	**E**	**F**	**G**	**H**
Before modification	5	7	6	4	8	9	8	10
After modification	3	7	7	0	4	6	8	2

At the 0.01 significance level, is it reasonable to conclude that the modification reduced the number of traffic accidents?

45. An investigation of the effectiveness of a training program to improve customer relationships included a pre-training and post-training customer survey. To compare the differences, they computed (post-training survey score—pre-training survey score). Seven customers were randomly selected and completed both surveys. The results are as follows:

Customer	Pre-training Survey	Post-training Survey
A	6	8
B	5	5
C	10	10
D	7	10
E	6	8
F	5	6
G	2	8

Do the results of the survey show that the training program has improved customer service? Test at the 0.10 level of significance.

46. The president of an insurance company wants to compare the yearly costs of auto insurance offered by two leading competitors. He selects a sample of 15 families, some with only a single insured driver, others with several teenage drivers, and pays each family a stipend to contact the two competitors and ask for a price quote. To make the data comparable, certain features, such as the amount deductible and limits of liability, are standardized. The sample information is reported below. At the 0.10 significance level, can we conclude that there is a difference in the amounts quoted?

Family	Competitor A	Competitor B
Becker	$2090	$1610
Berry	1683	1247
Cobb	1402	2327
Debuck	1830	1367
DuBrul	930	1461
Eckroate	697	1789
German	1741	1621
Glasson	1129	1914
King	1018	1956
Kucic	1881	1772
Meredith	1571	1375
Obeid	874	1527
Price	1579	1767
Phillips	1577	1636
Tresize	860	1188

47. A cell phone company offers two plans to its subscribers. At the time new subscribers sign up, they are asked to provide some demographic information. The mean yearly income for a sample of 40 subscribers to Plan A is $57 000, with a standard deviation of $9200. For a sample of 30 subscribers to Plan B, the mean income is $61 000, with a standard deviation of $7100. At the 0.05 significance level, is it reasonable to conclude the mean income of those selecting Plan B is larger? What is the p-value?

48. The following data resulted from a taste test of two different chocolate bars. The first number is a rating of the taste, which could range from 0 to 5, with a 5 indicating the person liked the taste. The second number indicates whether a "secret ingredient" was present. If the ingredient was present, a code of "1" was used and, if not, a "0" was used. At the 0.05 significance level, do these data show a difference in the taste ratings?

Rating	"With/Without"	Rating	"With/Without"
3	1	1	1
1	1	4	0
0	0	4	0
2	1	2	1
3	1	3	0
1	1	4	0

49. An investigation of the effectiveness of an antibacterial soap in reducing operating room contamination resulted in the following table. The new soap was tested in a sample of eight operating rooms in the Cambridge area during the last year.

	Operating Room							
	A	**B**	**C**	**D**	**E**	**F**	**G**	**H**
Before	6.6	6.5	9.0	10.3	11.2	8.1	6.3	11.6
After	6.8	2.4	7.4	8.5	8.1	6.1	3.4	2.0

50. A computer manufacturer offers a help line that purchasers can call for help 24 hours a day, 7 days a week. Clearing these calls for help in a timely fashion is important to the company's image. After telling the caller that resolution of the problem is important, the caller is asked whether the issue is "software" or "hardware" related. The mean time it takes a technician to resolve a software issue is 18 minutes, with a standard deviation of 4.2 minutes. This information was obtained from a sample of 35 monitored calls. For a study of 45 hardware issues, the mean time for the technician to resolve the problem was 15.5 minutes, with a standard deviation of 3.9 minutes. This information was also obtained from monitored calls. At the 0.05 significance level, is it reasonable to conclude that it takes longer to resolve software issues? Calculate and interpret the p-value.

51. The AP-Petside.com poll contacted 300 married women and 200 married men. All owned pets. One hundred of the women and 36 of the men replied that their pets are better listeners than their spouses. At the 0.05 significance level, is there a difference between the responses of women and men?

52. Ten randomly selected statistics questions were given 15 multiple-choice questions and 15 open-ended questions, all on the same material. The professor was interested in determining if students scored higher on the open-ended questions. Each mark is out of 15. The results are as follows:

Student	A	B	C	D	E	F	G	H	I	J
Multiple Choice	10	11	8	7	5	12	8	11	8	9
Open-Ended	9	11	9	6	8	10	12	6	10	9

Did students score higher on the open-ended questions? Test at the 0.05 level of significance.

53. Lester Hollar is vice-president for human resources for a large manufacturing company. In recent years, he has noticed an increase in absenteeism, which he thinks is related to the general health of the employees. Four years ago, in an attempt to improve the situation, he began a fitness program in which employees exercise during their lunch hour. To evaluate the program, he selected a random sample of eight participants and found the number of days each was absent in the six months before the exercise program began and in the last six months. Below are the results. At the 0.05 significance level, can he conclude that the number of absences has declined? Estimate the p-value.

Employee	Before	After
1	6	5
2	6	2
3	7	1
4	7	3
5	4	3
6	3	6
7	5	3
8	6	7

54. To compare the effect of weather on soft drink sales, a distributor surveyed people in Vancouver to ask if they purchased soft drinks in the months of January and June. The following are the results:

	January	June
Sample size	1000	1000
Number who purchased	400	450

Given the survey results, can the distributor conclude there are significantly fewer sales in the month of January? Test at the 0.05 level of significance.

	Region A	Region B
Sample size	1000	1500
Number who purchased	400	500

55. A company is researching the effectiveness of a new design to decrease the time to access a website. Ten website users were randomly selected—five accessed websites using the old web design, and the other five accessed websites using the new web design, and their times (in seconds) to access the website with the old and new designs were recorded. The results are as follows:

User	Old Website Design	New Website Design
A	30	15
B	45	20
C	25	10
D	32	25
E	28	20

Can the company conclude that the new web design allows users to access websites faster than with the old design? Test at the 0.05 level.

56. Personnel in a consumer testing laboratory are evaluating the absorbency of paper towels. They wish to compare a set of store brand towels to a similar group of name brand ones. For each brand they dip a ply of the paper into a tub of fluid, allow the paper to drain back into the vat for two minutes, and then evaluate the amount of liquid the paper has taken up from the vat. A random sample of 9 store-brand paper towels absorbed the following amounts of liquid in millilitres:

$$8 \quad 8 \quad 3 \quad 1 \quad 9 \quad 7 \quad 5 \quad 5 \quad 12$$

An independent random sample of 10 name brand towels absorbed the following amounts of liquid in millilitres:

$$12 \quad 11 \quad 10 \quad 6 \quad 8 \quad 9 \quad 9 \quad 10 \quad 11 \quad 9$$

Use the 0.10 significance level and test if there is a difference in the mean amount of liquid absorbed by the two types of paper towels. Assume equal population variances.

57. The Index of Consumer Confidence, published by the Conference Board of Canada, is survey of Canadian households that has been ongoing since 1980. It measures consumers' levels of optimism regarding current economic conditions and is based on a typical sample of 2000 households. Last month, the index was 88.5 (2002 = 100), an indication that conditions were "good." In the prior month, the index was only 85.7. Use the five-step hypothesis-testing method at the 0.05 level of significance to see whether you can determine if there is an increase in the opinion that conditions are "good." Find the p-value, and explain what it means.

58. The city of Laguna Beach operates two public parking lots. The one on Ocean Drive can accommodate up to 125 cars and the one on Rio Rancho can accommodate up to 130 cars. City planners are considering both increasing the size of the lots and changing the fee structure. To begin, the Planning Office would like some information on the number of cars in the lots at various times of the day. A junior planner officer is assigned the task of visiting the two lots at random times of the day and evening and counting the number of cars in the lots. In both studies, assume that the population standard deviations are equal.

a) The first study was conducted over a period of 10 days. The results are given below. Is it reasonable to conclude that there is a difference in the mean number of cars in the two lots? Use the 0.05 significance level.

Ocean Drive

93	51	75	109	125	115	79	54

Rio Ranch

110	125	82	45	71	73	117	80	93

b) The second study lasted over a period of one month. The results follow. Is it reasonable to conclude that there is a difference in the mean number of cars in the two lots? Use the 0.05 significance level.

Ocean Drive

89	115	93	79	113	77	51	75	118	105	106	91	54
63	121	53	81	115	67	53	69	95	121	88	64	

Rio Ranch

128	110	81	126	82	114	93	40	94	45	84	71	74
92	66	69	100	114	113	107	62	77	80	107	90	129
105	124											

59. A goal of financial literacy for children is to learn how to manage money wisely. One question is: how much money do children have? A recent study by Schnur Educational Research Associates revealed the following sample information regarding the monthly allowance that children receive. Is it reasonable to conclude that the mean allowance received by children between 11 and 14 years is more than the allowance received by children between 8 and 10 years? Use the 0.01 significance level. What is the p-value?

| 8–10 Years | 6 | 13 | 10 | 6 | 14 | 6 | 7 | 7 | 10 | 6 | 5 | 7 | 9 | 14 | 12 | | | |
| 11–14 Years | 10 | 14 | 12 | 0 | 9 | 11 | 9 | 8 | 8 | 11 | 8 | 14 | 9 | 20 | 19 | 11 | 12 | 20 |

60. The amount of income spent on housing is an important component of the cost of living. The total costs of housing for homeowners might include mortgage payments, property taxes, and utility costs (water, heat, electricity). An economist selected a sample of 20 homeowners in Regina and then calculated these total housing costs as a percentage of monthly income, five years ago and now. The resulting information is given below. Is it reasonable to conclude the percentage is less now than five years ago?

Homeowner	Five Years Ago	Now
1	17%	10%
2	20	39
3	29	37
4	43	27
5	36	12
6	43	41
7	45	24
8	19	26
9	49	28
10	49	26
11	35	32
12	16	32
13	23	21
14	33	12
15	44	40
16	44	42
17	28	22
18	29	19
19	39	35
20	22	12

Data Set Exercises

Questions marked with 📈 have data sets available on McGraw-Hill's online resource for *Basic Statistics*.

📈 **61.** Refer to the Real Estate Data—Halifax Area online, which reports information on home listings.

   a. At the 0.05 significance level, can we conclude that there is a difference in the mean list price of homes with up to and including 2000 square feet compared with those with more than 2000 square feet? Compute and interpret the p-value.

   b. At the 0.01 significance level, can we conclude that there is a difference in the mean list price of homes with more than two bedrooms? Compute and interpret the p-value.

📈 **62.** Refer to the CREA (Canadian Real Estate Association) Cities Only data online, which reports information on average house prices nationally and in a selection of cities across Canada.

   a. At the 0.01 significance level, can we conclude that the mean list price for all cities for January 2014 is more than January 2013?

   b. What is the p-value? Use this result to support your answer.

📈 **63.** Refer to the Average retail prices for gasoline and fuel oil, by urban centre, computed annual average (cents per litre) data, online, found in the file Gasoline Prices.

   a. Using the data from November 2012 to November 2016, compare the gasoline prices for Winnipeg and Calgary. At the 0.05 significance level, can we conclude that there is a difference in the average gasoline price? Compute and interpret the p-value.

   b. Using the data from November 2012 to November 2016, compare the gasoline prices for Halifax, Nova Scotia, and Saint John, New Brunswick. At the 0.01 significance level, can we conclude that there is a difference in the average gasoline price? Compute and interpret the p-value.

   c. Using the data from November 2010 to November 2016, compare the gasoline prices for Toronto and Montreal. At the 0.05 significance level, can we conclude that the gasoline prices in Toronto are less than the gasoline prices in Montreal? Compute and interpret the p-value.

    d. Using the data from November 2012 to November 2016, compare the gasoline prices for St. John's and Edmonton. At the 0.02 significance level, can we conclude that the gasoline prices in Edmonton are less than the gasoline prices in St. John's? Compute and interpret the *p*-value.

64. Refer to the Real Estate Data—Saskatoon online, which reports information on home listings.

    a. At the 0.05 significance level, can we conclude that there is a difference in the mean list price of homes with up to and including 1000 square feet compared with those with more than 1000 square feet? Compute and interpret the *p*-value.

    b. At the 0.01 significance level, can we conclude that there is a difference in the mean list price of homes with a half bath? Compute and interpret the *p*-value.

Practice Test

Part I Objective

1. The hypothesized difference between two population means is _____.

2. If the population standard deviations are known for a test of differences for two independent populations, the test statistic is _____.

3. When sampled items from two populations are classified as "success" or "failure," the hypothesis test is for differences in population _____.

4. For two independent populations, sample standard deviations are pooled to compute a single estimate of the _____. (population mean, population standard deviation, population proportion, *z*-value.)

5. A hypothesis test of differences between two dependent populations is based on a single population of mean _____. (differences, populations, standard deviations, *t*-values)

6. The test statistic for a hypothesis test of differences between two dependent populations follows the _____.

7. Degrees of freedom are calculated as the total number of observations less the number of _____.

8. For dependent samples, observations are matched or _____.

9. For independent samples, the two samples are different or _____.

10. In a statistics class, for each student, the percentage correct on Exam 2 is subtracted from the percentage correct on Exam 1. This is an example of _____ samples.

Part II Problems

For each of these problems, use the five-step hypothesis testing procedure:

1. Is there a difference in the mean kilometres travelled per week by each of the two taxi cab companies operating in the Grand Strand area? The *Sun News*, the local newspaper, is investigating and obtained the following sample information. At the 0.05 significance level, is there a difference in the mean number of kilometres travelled?

Variable	Yellow Cab	Diamond Cab
Mean kilometres travelled	837	797
Standard deviation	30	40
Sample size	14	12

2. Dial Soap Company developed a new soap for men that it wants to test in two cities. The sample information is reported below:

City	Liked New Soap	Number Sampled
Regina	128	300
Collingwood	149	400

At the 0.05 significance level, can we conclude there is a difference in the proportion in the two cities that liked the new soap?

Computer Commands

1. **MegaStat** steps for hypothesis testing for the FoodTown Supermarkets example are as follows:

   a. In an **Excel** spreadsheet, enter Standard in cell *A3*, and Fast Lane in cell *B3*. Enter *5.50* in cell *A4*, *5.30* in cell *B4*, *0.40* in cell *A5* *0.30* in cell *B5*, *50* in cell *A6* and *100* in cell *B6*. This is the **summary input.**

	A	B	C
1			
2			
3	Standard	Fast Lane	
4	5.50	5.30	
5	0.40	0.30	
6	50	100	
7			
8			
9			

   b. Select **MegaStat, Hypothesis Tests,** and **Compare Two Independent Groups.**

   c. Select **summary input.** Select *A3:A6* as the input range for **Group 1** and *B3:B6* as the input range for **Group 2.**

   d. Enter *0* as the **Hypothesized difference,** select *greater than* for the **Alternative:** and select **z-test.**

2. **MegaStat** steps for hypothesis testing for the Owens Lawn Care example are as follows:

	A	B
1		
2		
3	**Welles**	**Atkins**
4	2	3
5	4	7
6	9	5
7	3	8
8	2	4
9		3
10		

   a. In an **Excel** spreadsheet, enter Welles in cell *A3*, and Atkins in cell *B3*. Then enter the data for Welles starting in cell *A4* and the data for Atkins starting in cell *B4*. This is the **data input.**

   b. Select **MegaStat, Hypothesis Tests,** and **Compare Two Independent Groups.**

   c. Select **data input.** Select *A3:A8* as the input range for **Group 1** and *B3:B9* as the input range for **Group 2.**

Hypothesis Test: Compare Two Independent Groups

- ○ data input ● summary input

  Sheet1!$A$3:$A$6   Group 1

  Sheet1!$B$3:$B$6   Group 2

  For each group select ranges with label, mean, s.d., n

  0   Hypothesized difference   Alternative: greater than ▼

  ○ t-test (pooled variance)
  ○ t-test (unequal variance)   □ Display 95% ▼ confidence interval
  ● z-test   □ Test for equality of variances

  [OK] [Clear] [Cancel] [Help]

---

e. Click **OK.** The *p*-value (0.0009) is part of the output. *Note:* values may be slightly different due to rounding.

d. Enter *0* as the **Hypothesized difference,** select *not equal* for the **Alternative,** and select **t-test (pooled variance).**

e. Click **OK.** The *p*-value (0.5245) is part of the output. *Note:* values may be slightly different due to rounding.

3. **Excel** steps for hypothesis testing for the Owens Lawn Care example are as follows:

   a. In an **Excel** spreadsheet, enter Welles in cell *A3*, and Atkins in cell *B3*. Then enter the data for Welles starting in cell *A4* and the data for Atkins starting in cell *B4*. This is the **data input.**

   b. Select **Data Analysis** and **t-Test: Two-Sample Assuming Equal Variances.** Click **OK.**

c. For **Input** select *A3:A8* as the input range for **Variable 1 Range** and *B3:B9* as the input range for **Variable 2 Range.**

d. Enter *0* as the **Hypothesized Mean Difference**, check the **Labels** box, enter *0.1* for **Alpha** and *D3* for the **Output Range.**

e. Click **OK.** The *p*-value (0.5245) is part of the output. *Note:* values may be slightly different due to rounding.

For the Nickel Savings and Loan example, enter the data as shown:

	A	B	C
1			
2			
3	**Home**	**Schadek**	**Bowyer**
4	1	235	228
5	2	210	205
6	3	231	219
7	4	242	240
8	5	205	198
9	6	230	223
10	7	231	227
11	8	210	215
12	9	225	222
13	10	249	245
14			

4. **MegaStat** steps for hypothesis testing for the Nickel Savings and Loan example are as follows:

   a. In an **Excel** spreadsheet, enter Home in cell *A3*, Schadek in cell *B3* and Bowyer in cell *C3*. Then enter the data for the home number starting in cell *A4*, the data for Schadek starting in cell *B4* and the data for Bowyer starting in cell *C4*. This is the **data input.**

   b. Select **MegaStat**, **Hypothesis Tests,** and **Paired Observations.**

   c. Select **data input.** Select *B3:B13* as the input range for **Group 1** and *C3:C13* as the input range for **Group 2.**

   d. Enter *0* as the **Hypothesized difference**, select *not equal* for the **Alternative,** and select **t-test.**

   e. Click **OK.** The *p*-value (0.0092) is part of the output. *Note:* values may be slightly different due to rounding. Because the *p*-value is less than 0.05, we reject the hypothesis that the mean of the distribution of the differences between the appraised values is zero.

In fact, this *p*-value is less than 1.0%. There is very little likelihood that the null hypothesis is true.

5. **Excel** steps for hypothesis testing for the Nickel Savings and Loan example are as follows:

   a. In an **Excel** spreadsheet, enter Home in cell *A3*, Schadek in cell *B3* and Bowyer in cell *C3*. Then, enter the data for the home number starting in cell *A4*, the data for Schadek starting in cell *B4* and the data for Bowyer starting in cell *C4*. This is the **data input.**

   b. Select **Data Analysis** and **t-Test: Paired Two-Sample for Means.** Click **OK.**

   c. For **Input** select *B3:B13* as the input range for **Variable 1 Range** and *C3:C13* as the input range for **Variable 2 Range.**

   d. Enter *0* as the **Hypothesized Mean Difference**, check the **Labels** box, enter *0.05* for **Alpha** and **New Worksheet Ply** for the **Output option.**

   e. Click **OK.** The computed value of *t* is 3.3045, and the two-tailed *p*-value is 0.00916. Because the *p*-value is less than 0.05, we reject the hypothesis that the mean of the distribution of the differences between the appraised values is zero. In fact, this *p*-value is less than 1.0%. There is very little likelihood that the null hypothesis is true. *Note:* values may be slightly different due to rounding.

6. **MegaStat** steps for hypothesis testing for the Manelli Perfume Company example are as follows:

   a. Select **MegaStat, Hypothesis Tests,** and **Compare Two Independent Proportions.**

   b. In the **Group 1** column, enter *19* for **X** and *100* for **n.**

   In the **Group 2** column, enter *62* for **X** and *200* for **n.**

c. Enter *0* as the **Hypothesized difference,** select *not equal* for the **Alternative.** Select **Display** *95%* **confidence interval.**

d. Click **OK.** To interpret the MegaStat output, we see a *p*-value of 0.0273. The slight difference in the value is due to rounding. Also, note the 95% confidence

level, which ranges from −0.2201 to −0.0199. As the confidence interval does not contain the hypothesized value of zero, the null hypothesis is rejected.

For the Owens Lawn Care example, enter the data into a spreadsheet as follows:

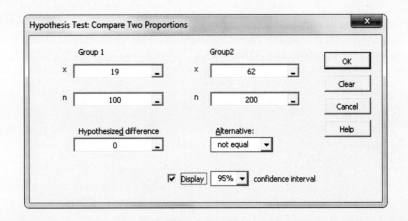

Answers to Self-Reviews

10–1 **(a)** H_0: $\mu_1 - \mu_2 \le 0$.

H_1: $\mu_1 - \mu_2 > 0$.

The subscript 1 refers to the women and 2 to the men.

(b) Reject H_0 if $z > 1.645$.

(c) $z = \dfrac{\$1500 - \$1400 - 0}{\sqrt{\dfrac{(\$250)^2}{50} + \dfrac{(\$200)^2}{40}}} = 2.11.$

(d) Reject the null hypothesis.

(e) *p*-value = $0.5000 - 0.4826 = 0.0174$.

(f) The *p*-value is less than the significance level, $\alpha = 0.05$, so the test statistic lies in the rejection region. We conclude that the mean amount sold per day is larger for women.

10–2 **(a)** H_0: $\mu_1 - \mu_2 = 0$

H_1: $\mu_1 - \mu_2 \ne 0$

(b) $df = 6 + 8 - 2 = 12$.

An appropriate significance level is $\alpha = 0.05$. Reject H_0 if *t* is less than −2.179 or *t* is greater than 2.179.

(c)

$\bar{x}_1 = \dfrac{42}{6} = 7.00. \; s_1 \sqrt{\dfrac{304 - \dfrac{42^2}{6}}{6 - 1}} = 1.4142$

$\bar{x}_2 = \dfrac{80}{6} = 10.00. \; s_2 \sqrt{\dfrac{836 - \dfrac{80^2}{8}}{8 - 1}} = 2.2678$

$= 3.8333.$

$t = \dfrac{7.00 - 10.00 - 0}{\sqrt{3.8333\left(\dfrac{1}{6} + \dfrac{1}{8}\right)}} = -2.837.$

(d) Reject H_0 because −2.837 is less than the critical value.

(e) The *p*-value is less than 0.02.

(f) The *p*-value is less than the significance level, so the test statistic lies in the rejection region. Reject H_0, and conclude that the mean number of defects is not the same on the two shifts.

(g) Independent populations; populations follow the normal distribution; populations have equal standard deviations.

10–3 **(a)** H_0: $\mu_d \le 0, H_1$: $\mu_d > 0$.

(b) Reject H_0 if $t > 2.998$.

(c)

Name	Before	After	d	d^2
Hunter	155	154	1	1
Cashman	228	207	21	441
Mervine	141	147	−6	36
Massa	162	157	5	25
Creola	211	196	15	225
Peterson	164	150	14	196
Redding	184	170	14	196
Poust	172	165	7	49
			71	1169

$\bar{d} = \dfrac{71}{8} = 8.875.$

$s_d = \sqrt{\dfrac{1169 - \dfrac{(71)^2}{8}}{8 - 1}} = 8.774.$

$t = \dfrac{8.875}{8.774/\sqrt{8}} = 2.86$

(d) Do not reject H_0. We cannot conclude that the students lost weight. The p-value is greater than the significance level of 0.01.

(e) The distribution of the differences must follow a normal distribution.

10–4 (a) H_0: $p_1 - p_2 = 0$

H_1: $p_1 - p_2 \neq 0$

(b) 0.10.

(c) Two-tailed.

(d) Reject H_0 if z is less than -1.645 or greater than 1.645.

(e) $p_c = \dfrac{87 + 123}{150 + 200} = \dfrac{210}{350} = 0.60.$

$\bar{p}_1 = \dfrac{87}{150} = 0.58 \quad \bar{p}_2 = \dfrac{123}{200} = 0.615.$

$z = \dfrac{0.58 - 0.615 - 0}{\sqrt{\dfrac{0.60(0.40)}{150} + \dfrac{0.60(0.40)}{200}}} = -0.66.$

(f) Do not reject H_0.

(g) p-value $= 2(0.5000 - 0.2454) = 0.5092$. The p-value is greater than the significance level, $\alpha = 0.10$, so the test statistic lies in the acceptance region. There is not enough evidence to reject H_0 and so we conclude that there is no difference in the proportion of adults and children that liked the proposed flavour.

Analysis of Variance

A software design company is creating a new, faster search engine. The search engine is clearly faster, but initial tests indicate there is more variation in the time to perform a search. A sample of 16 different searches showed that the standard deviation of the search time was 22 hundredths of a second for the new search engine and 12 hundredths of a second for the current search engine. At the 0.05 significance level, can we conclude that there is more variation in the search time of the new search engine? (Exercise 16, LO11-1)

LEARNING OBJECTIVES

When you have completed this chapter, you will be able to:

LO11-1 Apply the F distribution to test a hypothesis that two population variances are equal.

LO11-2 Use ANOVA to test a hypothesis that three or more population means are equal.

LO11-3 Develop and use confidence intervals to test and interpret differences between pairs of population means.

11.1 INTRODUCTION

In this chapter, we continue our discussion of hypothesis testing. Recall that in Chapters 9 and 10 we examined the general theory of hypothesis testing. We described the case where a sample was selected from the population. We used the z distribution (the standard normal distribution) or the t distribution to determine whether it was reasonable to conclude that the population mean was equal to a specified value. We tested whether two population means are the same. We also conducted both one- and two-sample tests for population proportions, using the standard normal distribution as the distribution of the test statistic. In this chapter, we expand our idea of hypothesis tests. We describe a test for variances and then a test that simultaneously compares several means to determine if they came from equal populations.

11.2 THE F DISTRIBUTION

The probability distribution used in this chapter is the F distribution. It was named to honour Sir Ronald Fisher, one of the founders of modern-day statistics. The test statistic for several situations follows this probability distribution. It is used to test whether two samples are from populations having equal variances, and it is also applied when we want to compare several population means simultaneously. The simultaneous comparison of several population means is called

analysis of variance (ANOVA). In both these situations, the populations must follow a normal distribution, and the data must be at least interval-scale.

What are the characteristics of the F distribution?

1. **There is a "family" of F distributions.** A particular member of the family is determined by two parameters: (1) the degrees of freedom in the numerator and (2) the degrees of freedom in the denominator. The shape of the distribution is illustrated by the following graph. There is one F distribution for the combination of 29 degrees of freedom in the numerator (df) and 28 degrees of freedom in the denominator. There is another F distribution for 19 degrees of freedom in the numerator and 6 degrees of freedom in the denominator. The final distribution shown has 6 degrees of freedom in the numerator and 6 degrees of freedom in the denominator. We will describe the concept of degrees of freedom later in the chapter. Note that the shapes of the curves change as the degrees of freedom change.

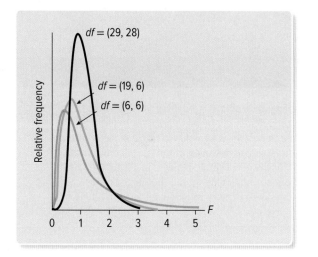

2. **The F distribution is continuous.** This means that it can assume an infinite number of values between 0 and positive infinity.
3. **The F distribution cannot be negative.** The smallest value F can assume is 0.
4. **It is positively skewed.** The long tail of the distribution is to the right-hand side. As the number of degrees of freedom increases in both the numerator and denominator, the distribution approaches a normal distribution.
5. **It is asymptotic.** As the values of x increase, the F distribution approaches the x-axis but never touches it. This is similar to the behaviour of the normal probability distribution, described in Chapter 6.

LO11-1   11.3 COMPARING TWO POPULATION VARIANCES

The first application of the F-test that we describe occurs when we test the hypothesis that the variance of one normal population equals the variance of another normal population. The following examples will show the use of the test:

- An assisted-living corporation manages two homes in Manitoba. In each home, the mean waiting time for a response once an emergency signal is received is one minute. The administrator of the corporation believes that the home in Portage la Prairie has more variation in emergency response time than the home in Thompson.
- The mean rate of return on two types of common stock may be the same, but there may be more variation in the rate of return in one than the other. A sample of 10 technology stocks

and 10 utility stocks shows the same mean rate of return, but there is likely more variation in the technology stocks.

- A study by the marketing department for a large newspaper found that men and women spent about the same amount of time per day surfing the Net. However, the same report indicated there was nearly twice as much variation in time spent per day among the men than the women.

The F distribution is also used to test assumptions for some statistical tests. Recall that in the previous chapter, we used the t distribution to investigate whether the means of two independent populations differed. To conduct that test, we assume that the variances of two normal populations are the same. The F distribution is used to test that the variances of two normal populations are equal.

Regardless of whether we want to determine if one population has more variation than another population or validate an assumption for a statistical test, we first state the null hypothesis. The null hypothesis is that the variance of one normal population, σ_1^2, equals the variance of the other normal population, σ_2^2. The alternative hypothesis could be that the variances differ. In this instance, the null hypothesis and the alternative hypothesis are:

$$H_0: \sigma_1^2 - \sigma_2^2 = 0$$
$$H_1: \sigma_1^2 - \sigma_2^2 \neq 0$$

To conduct the test, we select a random sample of n_1 observations from one population, and a random sample of n_2 observations from the second population. The test statistic is defined as follows:

TEST STATISTIC FOR COMPARING TWO VARIANCES	$F = \dfrac{s_1^2}{s_2^2}, s_1^2 > s_2^2$ [11–1]

The terms s_1^2 and s_2^2 are the respective sample variances. If the null hypothesis is true, the test statistic follows the F distribution with $n_1 - 1$ and $n_2 - 1$ degrees of freedom. To reduce the size of the table of critical values, the *larger* sample variance is placed in the numerator; hence, the tabled F ratio is always larger than 1.00. Thus, the right-tail critical value is the only one required. The critical value of F for a two-tailed test is found by dividing the significance level in half ($\alpha/2$) and then referring to the appropriate degrees of freedom in Appendix B.7. The following example will illustrate this:

Example

Luxury Limos offers limousine service from the city hall in downtown Toronto, Ontario, to the Toronto Pearson International Airport. Sean Lammers, president of the company, is considering two routes. One is via Highway 427 and the other via Avenue Road. He wants to study the time it takes to drive to the airport using each route and then compare the results. He collected the following sample data, which is reported in minutes. Using the 0.10 significance level, is there a difference in the variation in the driving times using the two routes?

Avenue Road	Highway 427
52	59
67	60
56	61
45	51
70	56
54	63
64	57
	65

Solution

The mean driving times along the two routes are nearly the same. The mean time is 58.29 minutes for the Avenue Road route and 59.0 minutes along the Highway 427 route. However, in evaluating travel times, Mr. Lammers is also concerned about the variation in the travel times. The first step is to compute the two sample variances. We will use formula (3–12) to compute the sample standard deviations. To obtain the sample variances, we can compute the variances directly or square the standard deviations.

Avenue Road:

$$\bar{x} = \frac{\sum x}{n} = \frac{408}{7} = 58.29 \quad s = \sqrt{\frac{\sum x^2 - \frac{(\sum x)^2}{n}}{n-1}} = \sqrt{\frac{24\,266 - \frac{(408)^2}{7}}{7-1}} = 8.9947$$

Highway 427:

$$\bar{x} = \frac{\sum x}{n} = \frac{472}{8} = 59.00 \quad s = \sqrt{\frac{\sum x^2 - \frac{(\sum x)^2}{n}}{n-1}} = \sqrt{\frac{27\,982 - \frac{(472)^2}{8}}{8-1}} = 4.3753$$

There is more variation, as measured by the standard deviation, in the Avenue Road route than in the Highway 427 route. This is somewhat consistent with his knowledge of the two routes; the Avenue Road route contains more traffic lights, whereas Highway 427 is a limited-access highway. However, Highway 427 route is several kilometres longer. It is important that the service offered be both timely and consistent, so he decides to conduct a statistical test to determine whether there really is a difference in the variation of the two routes.

The usual five-step hypothesis testing procedure will be employed.

Step 1: We begin by stating the null hypothesis and the alternative hypothesis. The test is two-tailed because we are looking for a difference in the variation of the two routes. We are *not* trying to show that one route has more variation than the other.

$$H_0 : \sigma_1^2 - \sigma_2^2 = 0$$
$$H_1 : \sigma_1^2 - \sigma_2^2 \neq 0$$

Step 2: We selected the 0.10 significance level.

Step 3: The appropriate test statistic follows the F distribution.

Step 4: The critical value is obtained from Appendix B.7, a portion of which is reproduced as Table 11–1. Because we are conducting a two-tailed test, the tabled significance level is 0.05, found by: $\alpha/2 = 0.10/2 = 0.05$. There are $n_1 - 1 = 7 - 1 = 6$ degrees of freedom in the numerator, and $n_2 - 1 = 8 - 1 = 7$ degrees of freedom in the denominator. To find the critical value, move horizontally across the top portion of the F table (Table 11–1 or Appendix B.7) for the 0.05 significance level to 6 degrees of freedom in the numerator. Then move down that column to the critical value opposite 7 degrees of freedom in the denominator. The critical value is 3.87. Thus, the decision rule is: reject the null hypothesis if the ratio of the sample variances exceeds 3.87.

Step 5: The final step is to take the ratio of the two sample variances, determine the value of the test statistic, and make a decision regarding the null hypothesis. Note that formula (11–1) refers to the sample *variances* but we calculated the sample *standard deviations*. We need to square the standard deviations to determine the variances.

$$F = \frac{s_1^2}{s_2^2} = \frac{(8.9947)^2}{(4.3753)^2} = 4.23$$

The decision is to reject the null hypothesis, because the computed F-value (4.23) is larger than the critical value (3.87). We conclude that there is a difference in the variation of the travel times along the two routes.

From the computer output, the p-value $= 0.081$. Since the significance level is 0.10, the decision is to reject the null hypothesis.

TABLE 11–1 Critical Values of the F Distribution, $\alpha = 0.05$

Degrees of Freedom for Denominator	Degrees of Freedom for Numerator			
	5	6	7	8
1	230	234	237	239
2	19.3	19.3	19.4	19.4
3	9.01	8.94	8.89	8.85
4	6.26	6.16	6.09	6.04
5	5.05	4.95	4.88	4.82
6	4.39	4.28	4.21	4.15
7	3.97	3.87	3.79	3.73
8	3.69	3.58	3.50	3.44
9	3.48	3.37	3.29	3.23
10	3.33	3.22	3.14	3.07

excel

Computer commands for the above example can be found at the end of the chapter.

As noted, the usual practice is to determine the F ratio by putting the larger of the two sample variances in the numerator. Therefore, the F ratio will be larger than 1.00, so we can use the right tail of the F distribution thus avoiding the need for more extensive F tables.

A logical question arises: is it possible to conduct one-tailed tests? For example, suppose that in the previous example, we suspected that the variance of the times using the Avenue Road route was *larger* than the variance of the times along the Highway 427 route. We would state the null and alternative hypotheses as:

$$H_0\text{: } \sigma_1^2 - \sigma_2^2 \leq 0$$
$$H_1\text{: } \sigma_1^2 - \sigma_2^2 > 0$$

The test statistic is computed as s_1^2/s_2^2. Note that we labelled the population with the suspected larger variance as population 1. So, s_1^2 appears in the numerator. The F ratio will be larger than 1.00, so we can use the upper tail of the F distribution. Under these conditions, it is not necessary to divide the significance level in half. Because Appendix B.7 gives us only the 0.05 and 0.01 significance levels, we are restricted to these levels for one-tailed tests and 0.10 and 0.02 for two-tailed tests, unless we consult a more complete table or use statistical software to compute the F-statistic.

self-review 11–1

Steele Electric Products Inc. assembles electrical components for stereo equipment. For the last 10 days, Mark Nagy has averaged nine rejects, with a standard deviation of two rejects per day. Debbie Richmond averaged 8.5 rejects, with a standard deviation of 1.5 rejects, over the same period. At the 0.05 significance level, can we conclude that there is more variation in the number of rejects per day attributed to Mark?

EXERCISES

1. What is the critical F-value for a sample of six observations in the numerator and four in the denominator? Use a two-tailed test and the 0.10 significance level.
2. What is the critical F-value for a sample of four observations in the numerator and seven in the denominator? Use a one-tailed test and the 0.01 significance level.
3. The following hypotheses are given:

$$H_0\text{: } \sigma_1^2 - \sigma_2^2 = 0$$
$$H_1\text{: } \sigma_1^2 - \sigma_2^2 \neq 0$$

A random sample of eight observations from the first population resulted in a standard deviation of 10. A random sample of six observations from the second population resulted in a standard deviation of 7. At the 0.02 significance level, is there a difference in the variation of the two populations?

4. The following hypotheses are given:

$$H_0: \sigma_1^2 - \sigma_2^2 \le 0$$
$$H_1: \sigma_1^2 - \sigma_2^2 > 0$$

A random sample of five observations from the first population resulted in a standard deviation of 12. A random sample of seven observations from the second population showed a standard deviation of 7. At the 0.01 significance level, is there more variation in the first population?

5. Arbitron Media Research Inc. conducted a study of the iPod listening habits of men and women. One facet of the study involved the mean listening time. It was discovered that the mean listening time for men was 35 minutes per day. The standard deviation of the sample of the 10 men studied was 10 minutes per day. The mean listening time for the 12 women studied was also 35 minutes, but the standard deviation of the sample was 12 minutes. At the 0.10 significance level, can we conclude that there is a difference in the variation in the listening times for men and women?

6. A stockbroker at Critical Securities reported that the mean rate of return on a sample of 10 oil stocks was 12.6%, with a standard deviation of 3.9%. The mean rate of return on a sample of eight utility stocks was 10.9%, with a standard deviation of 3.5%. At the 0.05 significance level, can we conclude that there is more variation in the oil stocks?

11.4 ANOVA ASSUMPTIONS

The F distribution is used to perform a wide variety of tests. For example, when we want to test whether three or more population means could be equal, the Analysis of Variance (ANOVA) technique is used and the F distribution is used as the test statistic.

The ANOVA to test the equality of more than two population means requires that three assumptions are true:

1. The populations follow the normal distribution.
2. The populations have equal standard deviations (σ).
3. The populations are independent.

When these conditions are met, F is used as the distribution of the test statistic.

Why do we need to study ANOVA? Why can't we just use the test of differences in population means discussed in the previous chapter? We could compare the means two at a time. **The major reason is the unsatisfactory buildup of Type I error.** To explain further, suppose we have four different methods (A, B, C, and D) of training new recruits to be firefighters. We randomly assign each of the 40 recruits in this year's class to one of the four methods. At the end of the training program, we administer to the four groups a common test to measure understanding of firefighting techniques. The question is: is there a difference in the mean test scores among the four groups? An answer to this question will allow us to compare the four training methods.

Using the t distribution to compare the four population means, we would have to conduct six different t tests. That is, we would need to compare the mean scores for the four methods as follows: A versus B, A versus C, A versus D, B versus C, B versus D, and C versus D. For each t-test, suppose that we choose an $\alpha = 0.05$. Therefore, the probability of a Type I error, rejecting the null when it is true, is 0.05. The complement is the probability of 0.95 that we do not reject the null when it is true. Because we conduct six separate (independent) tests, the probability that all six decisions are correct is:

$$P \text{ (All correct)} = (0.95)(0.95)(0.95)(0.95)(0.95)(0.95) = 0.735$$

To find the probability of a least one error due to sampling, we subtract this result from 1. Thus, the probability of at least one incorrect decision due to sampling is: $1 - 0.735 = 0.265$. To summarize, if we conduct six independent tests using the t distribution, the likelihood of rejecting a true null hypothesis because of sampling error is increased from 0.05 to an unsatisfactory level of 0.265. ANOVA will allow us to compare the treatment means simultaneously and avoid the buildup of Type I error.

ANOVA was first developed for applications in agriculture, and many of the terms related to that context remain. In particular, the term *treatment* is used to identify the different populations being examined. For example, treatment refers to how a plot of ground was treated with a particular type of fertilizer. The following illustration will clarify the term *treatment* and demonstrate an application of ANOVA.

Example

Joyce Kuhlman manages a regional financial centre. She wishes to compare the productivity, as measured by the number of customers served, among three employees. Four days are randomly selected and the number of customers served by each employee is recorded. The results are as follows:

Wolfe	White	Korosa
55	66	47
54	76	51
59	67	46
56	71	48

Solution

Is there a difference in the mean number of customers served? Chart 11–1 illustrates how the populations would appear if there was a difference in the treatment means. Note that the populations follow the normal distribution and the variation in each population is the same, but the means are *not* the same.

CHART 11–1 Case Where Treatment Means Are Different

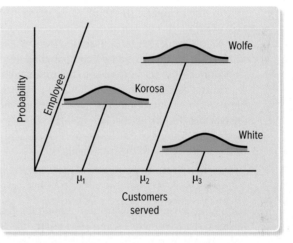

Suppose the populations are the same. That is, there is no difference in the (treatment) means. This is shown in Chart 11–2. This would indicate that the population means are the same. Note, again, that the populations follow the normal distribution and the variation in each of the populations is the same.

CHART 11–2 Case Where Treatment Means Are the Same

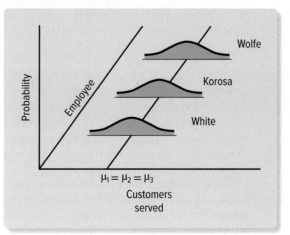

LO11-2   11.5 THE ANOVA TEST

How does the ANOVA test work? Recall that we want to determine whether the various sample means came from a single population or populations with different means. We actually compare these sample means through their variances. To explain, recall that we listed the assumptions required for ANOVA. One of those assumptions was that the standard deviations of the various normal populations had to be the same. We take advantage of this requirement in the ANOVA test. The underlying strategy is to estimate the population variance (standard deviation squared) two ways and then find the ratio of these two estimates. If this ratio is about 1, then logically the two estimates are the same, and we conclude that the population means are the same. If the ratio is quite different from 1, then we conclude that the population means are not the same. The F distribution serves as a referee by indicating when the ratio of the sample variances is too much greater than 1 to have occurred by chance.

Refer to the example/solution in the previous section. The manager wants to determine whether there is a difference in the mean number of customers served. To begin, find the overall mean of the 12 observations. It is 58, found by: $(55 + 54 + \cdots + 48)/12$. Next, for each of the 12 observations, find the difference between the particular value and the overall mean. Each of these differences is squared and these squares summed. This term is called the **total variation**.

Total variation The sum of the squared differences between each observation and the overall mean.

In our example, the total variation is 1082, found by: $(55 - 58)^2 + (54 - 58)^2 + \cdots + (48 - 58)^2$.

Next, break this total variation into two components: **treatment variation** and **random variation**. To find these two components, determine the mean of each of the treatments. The first source of variation is due to the treatments.

Treatment variation The sum of the squared differences between each treatment mean and the grand or overall mean.

In the example, the variation due to the treatments is the sum of the squared differences between the mean number of customers served by each employee and the overall mean. This term is 992. To calculate it, we first find the mean of each of the three treatments. The mean for Wolfe is 56, found by: $(55 + 54 + 59 + 56)/4$. The other means are 70 and 48, respectively. The sum of the squares due to the treatments is:

$$(56 - 58)^2 + (56 - 58)^2 + \cdots + (48 - 58)^2 = 4(56 - 58)^2 + 4(70 - 58)^2 + 4(48 - 58)^2$$
$$= 992$$

If there is considerable variation among the treatment means, it is logical that this term will be large. If the treatment means are similar, this term will be a small value. The smallest possible value would be zero. This would occur when all the treatment means are the same.

Random component The sum of the squared differences between each observation and its treatment mean.

The other source of variation is referred to as the **random component**, or the *error component*.

In the example, this term is the sum of the squared differences between each value and the mean for that particular employee. The error variation is 90.

$$(55 - 56)^2 + (54 - 56)^2 + \cdots + (48 - 48)^2 = 90$$

We determine the test statistic, which is the ratio of the two estimates of the population variance, from the following equation:

$$F = \frac{\text{Estimate of the population variance based on the differences among the sample means}}{\text{Estimate of the population variance based on the variation within the samples}}$$

Our first estimate of the population variance is based on the treatments, that is, the difference *between* the means. It is 992/2. Why did we divide by 2? Recall from Chapter 3 that to find a sample variance (see formula 3–10), we divide by the number of observations minus 1. In this case, there are three treatments, so we divide by: $(3 - 1) = 2$. Our first estimate of the population variance is 992/2.

The variance estimate *within* the treatments is the random variation divided by the total number of observations less the number of treatments. That is, $90/(12 - 3)$. Hence, our second estimate of the population variance is 90/9. This is actually a generalization of formula (10–3), where we pooled the sample variances from two populations.

The last step is to take the ratio of these two estimates.

$$F = \frac{992/2}{90/9} = 49.6$$

Because this ratio is quite different from 1, we can conclude that the population means are not the same. There is a difference in the mean number of customers served by the three employees.

Here is another example, which deals with samples of different sizes:

Example

Recently, airlines have cut services, such as meals and snacks during flights, and started charging for baggage. A group of four carriers (the names have been changed for confidentiality) recently hired Muir Marketing Research Inc. to survey passengers regarding their level of satisfaction with a recent flight. The survey included questions on ticketing, boarding, in-flight service, baggage handling, pilot communication, and so forth. Twenty-five questions offered a range of possible answers: excellent, good, fair, or poor. A response of excellent was given a rating of 4, good a 3, fair a 2, and poor a 1. These responses were then totalled, so the total score was an indication of the satisfaction with the flight. The greater the score, the higher the level of satisfaction with the service. The highest possible score was 100.

Marilyn Muir randomly selected and surveyed passengers from the four airlines. Below is the sample information. Is there a difference in the mean satisfaction level among the four airlines? *Note:* the airlines are labelled AirWaves, Belle Air, Cirrus Airlines, and Debonair. Use the 0.05 significance level.

Mean Satisfaction Level			
AirWaves	**Belle Air**	**Cirrus Airlines**	**Debonair**
94	75	70	68
90	68	73	70
85	77	76	72
80	83	78	65
	88	80	74
		68	65
		65	

Solution

We will use the five-step hypothesis testing procedure.

Step 1: State the null hypothesis and the alternative hypothesis. The null hypothesis is that the mean scores are the same for the four airlines. We can write this symbolically as:

$$H_0: \mu_1 = \mu_2 = \mu_3 = \mu_4$$

The alternative hypothesis is that the mean scores are not all the same for the four airlines.

$$H_1: \text{The mean scores are not all equal.}$$

We can also think of the alternative hypothesis as "at least two mean scores are not equal."

If the null hypothesis is not rejected, we conclude that there is no difference in the mean ratings for the four airlines. If H_0 is rejected, we conclude that there is a difference in at least one pair of mean scores, but at this point we do not know which pair or how many pairs differ.

Step 2: Select the level of significance. We selected the 0.05 significance level.

Step 3: Determine the test statistic. The test statistic follows the F distribution.

Step 4: **Formulate the decision rule.** To determine the decision rule, we need the critical value. The critical value for the F statistic is found in Appendix B.7. The critical values for both the 0.05 significance level and the 0.01 significance level are given in Appendix B.7. To use this table, we need to know the degrees of freedom in the numerator and the denominator. The degrees of freedom in the numerator equal the number of treatments, designated as k, minus 1. The degrees of freedom in the denominator are the total number of observations, n, minus the number of treatments. For this problem, there are four treatments and a total of 22 observations.

$$\text{Degrees of freedom in the numerator} = k - 1 = 4 - 1 = 3$$
$$\text{Degrees of freedom in the denominator} = n - k = 22 - 4 = 18$$

Refer to Appendix B.7 and the 0.05 significance level. Move horizontally across the top of the table to 3 degrees of freedom in the numerator. Then, move down that column to the row with 18 degrees of freedom. The value at this intersection is 3.16. So, the decision rule is to reject H_0 if the computed value of F exceeds 3.16.

Step 5: **Select the sample, perform the calculations, and make a decision.** It is convenient to summarize the calculations of the F-statistic in an **ANOVA table**. The format for an ANOVA table is as follows. Statistical software packages also use this format.

ANOVA Table				
Source of Variation	**Sum of Squares**	**Degrees of Freedom**	**Mean Square**	**F**
Treatments	SST	$k - 1$	MST = SST/$(k - 1)$	MST/MSE
Error	SSE	$n - k$	MSE = SSE/$(n - k)$	
Total	SS total	$n - 1$		

There are three values, or sum of squares, used to compute the test statistic, F. You can determine these values by finding SS total and SSE, then finding SST by subtraction. The SS total term is the total variation, SST is the variation due to the treatments, and SSE is the variation within the treatments, or the random error.

We usually start the process by finding SS total. This is the sum of the squared differences between each observation and the overall mean. The formula for finding SS total is:

$$\text{SS total} = \sum (x - \bar{x}_G)^2 \qquad [11\text{--}2]$$

where:

x is each sample observation.

$\bar{x}_G$ is the overall or grand mean.

Next, determine SSE or the sum of the squared errors. This is the sum of the squared differences between each observation and its respective treatment mean. The formula for finding SSE is:

$$\text{SSE} = \sum (x - \bar{x}_c)^2 \qquad [11\text{--}3]$$

where:

$\bar{x}_c$ is the sample mean for treatment c. The subscript c refers to the particular column.

The detailed calculations of SS total and SSE for this example follow. To determine the values of SS total and SSE, we start by calculating the overall or grand mean. There are 22 observations and the total is 1664, so the grand mean is 75.64.

$$\bar{x}_G = \frac{1664}{22} = 75.64$$

	AirWaves	Belle Air	Cirrus Airlines	Debonair	Total
	94	75	70	68	
	90	68	73	70	
	85	77	76	72	
	80	83	78	65	
		88	80	74	
			68	65	
			65		
Column Total	349	391	510	414	1664
n	4	5	7	6	22
Mean	87.25	78.20	72.86	69.00	75.64

Next, we find the deviation of each observation from the grand mean, square those deviations, and sum this result for all 22 observations. For example, the first sampled passenger had a score of 94 and the overall or grand mean is 75.64. So, $(x - \overline{x}_G) = 94 - 75.64 = 18.36$. For the last passenger, $65 - 75.64 = -10.64$. The calculations for all other passengers are as follows:

AirWaves	Belle Air	Cirrus Airlines	Debonair
18.36	−0.64	−5.64	−7.64
14.36	−7.64	−2.64	−5.64
9.36	1.36	0.36	−3.64
4.36	7.36	2.36	−10.64
	12.36	4.36	−1.64
		−7.64	−10.64
		−10.64	

Then, square each of these differences and sum the values. Thus, for the first passenger:

$$(x - \overline{x}_G)^2 = (94 - 75.64)^2 = (18.36)^2 = 337.09$$

Finally, sum all the squared differences as formula (11–2) directs. Our SS total value is 1485.10.

	AirWaves	Belle Air	Cirrus Airlines	Debonair	Total
	337.09	0.41	31.81	58.37	
	206.21	58.37	6.97	31.81	
	87.61	1.85	0.13	13.25	
	19.01	54.17	5.57	113.21	
		152.77	19.01	2.69	
			58.37	113.21	
			113.21		
Total	649.92	267.57	235.07	332.54	1485.10

To compute the term SSE, find the deviation between each observation and its treatment mean. In the example, the mean of the first treatment (i.e., the passenger ratings for AirWaves) is 87.25, found by: $\overline{x}_{AW} = 349/4$.

The subscript AW refers to the first airline.

The first passenger rated AirWaves at 94, so, $(x - \overline{x}_{AW}) = (94 - 87.25) = 6.75$.

The first passenger in Belle Air's group responded with a rating of 75, so, $(x - \overline{x}_{BA}) = (75 - 78.20) = -3.20$.

The details of each of these calculations are as follows.

AirWaves	Belle Air	Cirrus Airlines	Debonair
6.75	−3.2	−2.86	−1
2.75	−10.2	0.14	1
−2.25	−1.2	3.14	3
−7.25	4.8	5.14	−4
	9.8	−7.14	5
		−4.86	−4
		−4.86	

Each of these values is squared and then summed for all 22 observations. The values are shown in the following table:

	AirWaves	Belle Air	Cirrus Airlines	Debonair	Total
	45.5625	10.24	8.18	1	
	7.5625	104.04	0.02	1	
	5.0625	1.44	9.86	9	
	52.5625	23.04	26.42	16	
		96.04	50.98	25	
			23.62	16	
			61.78		
Total	110.7500	234.80	180.86	68	594.41

So, the SSE value is 594.41. That is, $\sum (x - \bar{x}_c)^2 = 594.41$.

Finally, we determine SST, the sum of the squares due to the treatments, by subtraction:

$$SST = SS \text{ total} - SSE \qquad [11–4]$$

For this example:

$$SST = SS \text{ total} - SSE = 1485.09 - 594.41 = 890.68$$

To find the computed value of F, work your way across the ANOVA table. The degrees of freedom for the numerator and the denominator are the same as in **Step 4** above when we were finding the critical value of F. The term **mean square** is another expression for an estimate of the variance. The mean square for treatments is SST divided by its degrees of freedom. The result is the **mean square for treatments** and is written MST. Compute the **mean square error** in a similar fashion. To be precise, divide SSE by its degrees of freedom. To complete the process and find F, divide MST by MSE.

Insert the particular values of F into an ANOVA table and compute the value of F as follows:

Source of Variation	Sum of Squares	Degrees of Freedom	Mean Square	F
Treatments	890.68	3	296.89	8.99
Error	594.41	18	33.02	
Total	1485.09	21		

The computed value of F is 8.99, which is greater than the critical value of 3.16, so the null hypothesis is rejected. We conclude the population means are not all equal. The mean scores are not the same for the four airlines. It is likely that the passenger scores are related to the particular airline. At this point, we can only conclude there is a difference in the treatment means. We cannot determine which treatment groups differ or how many treatment groups differ.

excel	Computer commands for the above example can be found at the end of the chapter.

self-review 11–2

Citrus Clean is a new all-purpose cleaner being test marketed by placing displays in three different locations within various supermarkets. The number of 950-millilitre (mL) bottles sold from each location within the supermarket is given below:

Near bread	18	14	19	17
Near water	12	18	10	16
Other cleaners	26	28	30	32

At the 0.05 significance level, is there a difference in the mean number of bottles sold at the three locations?

(a) State the null hypothesis and the alternative hypothesis.
(b) What is the decision rule?
(c) Compute the values of SS total, SST, and SSE.
(d) Develop an ANOVA table.
(e) What is your decision regarding the null hypothesis?

EXERCISES

7. The following is sample information. Test the hypothesis that the treatment means are equal. Use the 0.05 significance level.

Treatment 1	Treatment 2	Treatment 3
$8	$3	$3
6	2	4
10	4	5
9	3	4

a. State the null hypothesis and the alternative hypothesis.
b. What is the decision rule?
c. Compute SST, SSE, and SS total.
d. Complete an ANOVA table.
e. State your decision regarding the null hypothesis.

8. The following is sample information. Test the hypothesis at the 0.05 significance level that the treatment means are equal.

Servers	Waiters	Head Waiters
$9	$13	$10
7	20	9
11	14	15
9	13	14
12		15
10		

a. State the null hypothesis and the alternative hypothesis.
b. What is the decision rule?
c. Compute SST, SSE, and SS total.
d. Complete an ANOVA table.
e. State your decision regarding the null hypothesis.

9. A real estate developer is considering investing in a shopping mall. Three parcels of land are being evaluated. Of particular importance is the income in the area surrounding the proposed mall. A random sample of four families is selected near each proposed mall. Following are the sample results. At the 0.05 significance level, can the developer conclude there is a difference in the mean income? Use the usual five-step hypothesis testing procedure.

Area 1 ($000)	Area 2 ($000)	Area 3 ($000)
$64	$74	$75
68	71	80
70	69	76
60	70	78

10. The manager of a computer software company wishes to study the number of hours top executives spend at their computer terminals by type of industry. The manager selected a sample of five executives from each of three industries. At the 0.05 significance level, can she conclude there is a difference in the mean number of hours spent at a terminal per week by industry?

Banking	Retail	Insurance
12	8	10
10	8	8
10	6	6
12	8	8
10	10	10

LO11-3   11.6 INFERENCES ABOUT PAIRS OF TREATMENT MEANS

Suppose that we carry out the ANOVA procedure and make the decision to reject the null hypothesis. This allows us to conclude that the treatment means are not the same. Sometimes, we may be satisfied with this conclusion, but in other instances, we may want to know which treatment means differ. This section provides the details for such a test.

Recall that in the example regarding airline passenger ratings there was a difference in the treatment means. That is, the null hypothesis was rejected and the alternative hypothesis accepted. If the passenger ratings do differ, the question is: between which groups do the treatment means differ?

Several procedures are available to answer this question. The simplest is through the use of confidence intervals, that is, formula (8–2). From the computer output of the previous example, note that the sample mean score for those passengers rating AirWaves is 87.25, and for those rating Debonair's service the sample mean is 69.00. Is there enough disparity to justify the conclusion that there is a significant difference in the mean satisfaction scores of the two airlines?

The t distribution, described in Chapters 8, 9, and 10, is used as the basis for this test. Recall that one of the assumptions of ANOVA is that the population variances are the same for all treatments. This common population value is the **mean square error**, or MSE, and is determined by: $SSE/(n - k)$. A confidence interval for the difference between two populations is found by:

CONFIDENCE INTERVAL FOR THE DIFFERENCE IN TREATMENT MEANS	$(\bar{x}_1 - \bar{x}_2) \pm t \sqrt{MSE\left(\dfrac{1}{n_1} + \dfrac{1}{n_2}\right)}$	[11–5]

where:
$\bar{x}_1$ is the mean of the first sample.
$\bar{x}_2$ is the mean of the second sample.
t is obtained from Appendix B.2. The degrees of freedom are equal to $n - k$.
MSE is the mean square error term obtained from the ANOVA table [SSE $/(n - k)$].
n_1 is the number of observations in the first sample.
n_2 is the number of observations in the second sample.

How do we decide whether there is a difference in the treatment means? If the confidence interval includes zero, there is *no* difference between the treatment means. For example, if the left endpoint of the confidence interval has a negative sign and the right endpoint has a positive sign, the interval includes zero, and the two means do not differ. So, if we develop a confidence interval from formula (11–5) and find the difference in the sample means was 5.00, the confidence interval would range from −7.00 up to 17, that is, if:

$$(\bar{x}_1 - \bar{x}_2) = 5 \text{ and } t\sqrt{\text{MSE}\left(\frac{1}{n_1} + \frac{1}{n_2}\right)} = 12$$

To put it in symbols:

$$(\bar{x}_1 - \bar{x}_2) \pm t\sqrt{\text{MSE}\left(\frac{1}{n_1} + \frac{1}{n_2}\right)} = 5.00 \pm 12.00 = -7.00 \text{ up to } 17.00$$

Note that zero is included in this interval. Therefore, we conclude that there is no significant difference in the selected treatment means.

However, if the endpoints of the confidence interval have the same sign, this indicates that the treatment means differ. For example, the confidence interval would range from −0.60 up to −0.10, if:

$$(\bar{x}_1 - \bar{x}_2) = -0.35 \text{ and } t\sqrt{\text{MSE}\left(\frac{1}{n_1} + \frac{1}{n_2}\right)} = 0.25$$

Because −0.60 and −0.10 have the same sign, both negative, zero is not in the interval, and we conclude that these treatment means differ.

Using the previous airline example, let us compute the confidence interval for the difference between the mean scores of passengers on AirWaves and Debonair airlines. With a 95% level of confidence, the endpoints of the confidence interval are 10.46 and 26.04.

$$(\bar{x}_1 - \bar{x}_4) \pm t\sqrt{\text{MSE}\left(\frac{1}{n_1} + \frac{1}{n_4}\right)} = \left(87.25 - 69.00\right) \pm 2.101\sqrt{33.0\left(\frac{1}{4} + \frac{1}{6}\right)}$$
$$= 18.25 \pm 7.79$$

where:

   $\bar{x}_1$ is 87.25.
   $\bar{x}_4$ is 69.00.
   t is 2.101: from Appendix B.2 with $(n - k) = 22 - 4 = 18$ degrees of freedom.
   MSE is 33.0: from the ANOVA table with SSE $/(n - k) = 594.4/18$.
   n_1 is 4.
   n_4 is 6.

The 95% confidence interval ranges from 10.46 up to 26.04. Both endpoints are positive; hence, we can conclude these treatment means differ significantly. That is, passengers on AirWaves rated service significantly different from those on Debonair. Approximate results can also be obtained directly by using a computer statistical software package. Results from MINITAB output are as follows:

```
         Individual 95% CIs For Mean Based on Pooled St Dev

Level        N    Mean   StDev    +---------+---------+---------+---------
AirWaves     4  87.250   6.076                           (------*-------)
Belle Air    5  78.200   7.662                  (------*-----)
Cirrus       7  72.857   5.490             (-----*-----)
Debonair     4  69.000   3.688      (-----*-----)
                                    +---------+---------+---------+---------
                                  64.0      72.0      80.0      88.0
```

Pooled StDev = 5.747

On the left side are the name of the airline, number of observations, the mean, and the standard deviation for each treatment. On the right side are the confidence intervals for each treatment mean. We can get an idea of where the treatment means differ by examining the confidence intervals. The asterisk (*) indicates the location of the treatment mean and the open and close parentheses are the endpoints of the confidence intervals. Where the intervals overlap, the treatment means may not differ. If there is no common area in the confidence intervals, that pair of means likely differs.

The endpoints of the 95% confidence interval for the mean passenger scores for Cirrus Airlines are about 69 and 77. For Debonair the endpoints of the 95% confidence interval for the mean passenger score are about 64 and 73. There is a common area between these points, so we can conclude that this pair probably does not differ. In other words, there is no significant difference between the mean passenger ratings for Cirrus Airlines and Debonair. The differences in the mean scores are due to chance.

There appear to be two pairs of means that differ. The mean score of passengers on Air-Waves is significantly higher than the mean scores of passengers on Cirrus Airlines, and the mean scores of passengers on Debonair. There is no common area between these two pairs of confidence intervals.

We should emphasize that this investigation is a step-by-step process. The initial step is to conduct the ANOVA test. Only if the null hypothesis that the treatment means are equal is rejected should any analysis of the individual treatment means be attempted.

self-review 11–3

The following data are the tuition charges in thousands of dollars for a sample of private high schools in various regions of Canada. At the 0.05 significance level, can we conclude there is a difference in the mean tuition rates for the various regions?

East ($000)	Central ($000)	West ($000)
$10	$8	$7
11	9	8
12	10	6
10	8	7
12		6

(a) State the null and the alternative hypotheses.
(b) What is the decision rule?
(c) Develop an ANOVA table. What is the value of the test statistic?
(d) What is your decision regarding the null hypothesis?
(e) Could there be a significant difference between the mean tuition in the East and that of the West? If so, develop a 95% confidence interval for that difference.

EXERCISES

11. Given the following sample information, test the hypothesis that the treatment means are equal at the 0.05 significance level:

Treatment 1	Treatment 2	Treatment 3
8	3	3
11	2	4
10	1	5
	3	4
	2	

a. State the null hypothesis and the alternative hypothesis.
b. What is the decision rule?
c. Compute SST, SSE, and SS total.
d. Complete an ANOVA table.

   e. State your decision regarding the null hypothesis.

   f. If H_0 is rejected, can we conclude that treatment 1 and treatment 2 differ? Use the 95% level of confidence.

12. Given the following sample information, test the hypothesis that the treatment means are equal at the 0.05 significance level:

Treatment 1	Treatment 2	Treatment 3
3	9	6
2	6	3
5	5	5
1	6	5
3	8	5
1	5	4
	4	1
	7	5
	6	
	4	

   a. State the null hypothesis and the alternative hypothesis.

   b. What is the decision rule?

   c. Compute SST, SSE, and SS total.

   d. Complete an ANOVA table.

   e. State your decision regarding the null hypothesis.

   f. If H_0 is rejected, can we conclude that treatment 2 and treatment 3 differ? Use the 95% level of confidence.

13. A senior accounting major has job offers from four CGA (certified general accountant) firms. To explore the offers further, she asked a sample of recent trainees how many months each worked for the firm before receiving a raise in salary. The sample information is as follows:

		Analysis of Variance			
Source	**DF**	**SS**	**MS**	**F**	**P**
Factor	3	32.33	10.78	2.36	0.133
Error	10	45.67	4.57		
Total	13	78.00			

At the 0.05 level of significance, is there a difference in the mean number of months before a raise was granted among the four CGA firms?

14. A stock analyst wants to determine whether there is a difference in the mean rate of return for three types of stock: utility, retail, and banking stocks. The following output is obtained:

		Analysis of Variance			
Source	**DF**	**SS**	**MS**	**F**	**P**
Factor	2	86.49	43.25	13.09	0.001
Error	13	42.95	3.30		
Total	15	129.44			

   a. Using the 0.05 level of significance, is there a difference in the mean rate of return among the three types of stock?

   b. Suppose the null hypothesis is rejected. Can the analyst conclude there is a difference between the mean rates of return for the utility and the retail stocks? Explain.

Chapter Summary

I. The characteristics of the F distribution are as follows:

  A. It is continuous.

  B. Its values cannot be negative.

  C. It is positively skewed.

  D. There is a family of F distributions. Each time the degrees of freedom in the numerator or the denominator changes, a new distribution is created.

II. The F distribution is used to test whether two population variances are the same.

  A. The sampled populations must follow the normal distribution.

  B. The larger of the two sample variances is placed in the numerator, forcing the ratio to be at least 1.00.

  C. The value of F is computed using the following equation:

$$F = \frac{s_1^2}{s_2^2}, s_1^2 > s_2^2 \tag{11–1}$$

III. A one-way ANOVA is used to compare several treatment means.

  A. A treatment is a source of variation.

  B. The assumptions underlying ANOVA are as follows:
    1. The samples are from populations that follow the normal distribution.
    2. The populations have equal standard deviations.
    3. The populations are independent.

  C. The information for finding the value of F is summarized in an ANOVA table.
    1. The formula for SS total, the sum of squares total, is:

$$\text{SS total} = \sum (x - \bar{x}_G)^2 \tag{11–2}$$

    2. The formula for SSE, the sum of squares error, is:

$$\text{SSE} = \sum (x - \bar{x}_c)^2 \tag{11–3}$$

    3. The formula for the SST, the sum of squares treatment, is:

$$\text{SST} = \text{SS total} - \text{SSE} \tag{11–4}$$

    4. This information is summarized in the following table and the value of F determined:

Source of Variation	Sum of Squares	Degrees of Freedom	Mean Square	F
Treatments	SST	$k - 1$	$\text{MST} = \text{SST}/(k - 1)$	MST/MSE
Error	SSE	$n - k$	$\text{MSE} = \text{SSE}/(n - k)$	
Total	SS total	$n - 1$		

IV. If a null hypothesis of equal treatment means is rejected, we can identify the pairs that differ from the following confidence interval:

$$(\bar{x}_1 - \bar{x}_2) \pm t \sqrt{\text{MSE}\left(\frac{1}{n_1} + \frac{1}{n_2}\right)} \tag{11–5}$$

Chapter Exercises

15. A real estate agent in Northern Ontario wants to compare the variation in the selling price of homes on waterfronts with those one to three blocks from the water. A sample of 21 waterfront homes sold within the last year revealed the standard deviation of the selling prices was $45 600. A sample of 18 homes, also sold within the last year, that were one to three blocks from the water, revealed that the standard deviation was $21 330. At the 0.01 significance level, can we conclude that there is more variation in the selling prices of the waterfront homes?

16. A software design company is creating a new, faster search engine. The search engine is clearly faster, but initial tests indicate there is more variation in the time to perform a search. A sample of 16 different searches showed that the standard deviation of the search time was 22 hundredths of a second for the new search engine and 12 hundredths of a second for the current search engine. At the 0.05 significance level, can we conclude that there is more variation in the search time of the new search engine?

17. There are two Chevrolet dealers in Jamestown. The mean weekly sales at Sharkey Chevy and Dave White Chevrolet are about the same. However, Tom Sharkey, the owner of Sharkey Chevy, believes his sales are more consistent. Below is the number of new cars sold at Sharkey in the last seven months and for the last eight months at Dave White. Do you agree with Mr. Sharkey? Use the 0.01 significance level.

Sharkey	98	78	54	57	68	64	70	
Dave White	75	81	81	30	82	46	58	101

18. Random samples of five were selected from each of three populations. The sum of squares total was 100. The sum of squares due to the treatments was 40.
a. Set up the null hypothesis and the alternative hypothesis.
b. What is the decision rule? Use the 0.05 significance level.
c. Complete the ANOVA table. What is the value of F?
d. What is your decision regarding the null hypothesis?

19. In an ANOVA table, MSE was equal to 10. Random samples of six were selected from each of four populations, where the sum of squares total was 250.
a. Set up the null hypothesis and the alternative hypothesis.
b. What is the decision rule? Use the 0.05 significance level.
c. Complete the ANOVA table. What is the value of F?
d. What is your decision regarding the null hypothesis?

20. The following is a partial ANOVA table:

Source	SS	Df	MS	F
Treatment		2		
Error			20	
Total	500	11		

Complete the table, and answer the following questions. Use the 0.05 significance level.
a. How many treatments are there?
b. What is the total sample size?
c. What is the critical value of F?
d. Write out the null and alternative hypotheses.
e. What is your conclusion regarding the null hypothesis?

21. A consumer organization wants to know whether there is a difference in the price of a particular toy at three different types of stores. The price of the toy was checked in a sample of five discount stores, five variety stores, and five department stores. The results are shown below. Use the 0.05 significance level.

Discount	Variety	Department
$12	$15	$19
13	17	17
14	14	16
12	18	20
15	17	19

22. A physician who specializes in weight control has three different diets she recommends. As an experiment, she randomly selected 15 patients and then assigned 5 to each diet. After three months the following weight losses, in kilograms, were noted. At the 0.05 significance level, can she conclude that there is a difference in the mean amount of weight loss among the three diets?

Plan A	Plan B	Plan C
5	6	7
7	7	8
4	7	9
5	5	8
4	6	9

23. The City of Maumee comprises four districts. Chief of Police Andy North wants to determine whether there is a difference in the mean number of crimes committed among the four districts. He recorded the number of crimes reported in each district for a sample of six days. At the 0.05 significance level, can the chief of police conclude there is a difference in the mean number of crimes?

Number of Crimes			
Rec Centre	**Key Street**	**Monclova**	**Whitehouse**
13	21	12	16
15	13	14	17
14	18	15	18
15	19	13	15
14	18	12	20
15	19	15	18

24. A study of the effect of television commercials on 12-year-old children measured their attention span, in seconds. The commercials were for clothes, food, and toys. At the 0.05 significance level, is there a difference in the mean attention span of the children for the various commercials? Are there significant differences between pairs of means?

Clothes	Food	Toys
26	45	60
21	48	51
43	43	43
35	53	54
28	47	63
31	42	53
17	34	48
31	43	58
20	57	47
	47	51
	44	51
	54	

a. At the 0.05 level, can it be concluded that there is a difference in the three mean scores?
b. Would you recommend dropping one of the three commercial types?

25. When only two treatments are involved, ANOVA and the Student t-Test (Chapter 10) result in the same conclusions. Also, $t^2 = F$. As an example, suppose that 14 randomly selected college students were divided into two groups, one consisting of six students and the other of eight. One group was taught using a combination of lecture and programmed instruction, the other using a combination of lecture and television. At the end of the course, each group was given a 50-item test. The following is a list of the number correct for each of the two groups:

Lecture and Programmed Instruction	Lecture and Television
19	32
17	28
23	31
22	26
17	23
16	24
	27
	25

a. Using analysis of variance techniques, test H_0 that the two mean test scores are equal; $\alpha = 0.05$.
b. Using the t-test from Chapter 10, compute t.
c. Interpret the results.

26. Jack Wolicki is a production supervisor in an industrial manufacturing company. He would like to determine whether there is more variation in the number of units produced on the afternoon shift than on the day shift. A sample of 15 day-shift workers showed that the mean number of units produced was 200 with a standard deviation of 19.6. A sample of 10 afternoon-shift workers showed that the mean number of units produced was 205 with a standard deviation of 23.8. At the 0.05 significance level, is there more variation in the number of units produced on the afternoon shift?

27. There are four auto body shops in Shell River, Manitoba, all of which claim to serve customers promptly. To check if there is any difference in service, customers are randomly selected from each repair shop and their waiting times in days are recorded. The output from a statistical software package is as follows:

Summary				
Groups	**Count**	**Sum**	**Average**	**Variance**
Body Shop A	3	15.4	5.133333	0.323333
Body Shop B	4	32	8	1.433333
Body Shop C	5	25.2	5.04	0.748
Body Shop D	4	25.9	6.475	0.595833

ANOVA					
Source	**SS**	**DF**	**MS**	**F**	**p-Value**
Between groups	23.37321	3	7.791069	9.612506	0.001632
Within groups	9.726167	12	0.810514		
Total	33.09938	15			

Is there evidence to suggest a difference in the mean waiting times at the four body shops? Use the 0.05 significance level.

28. The fuel efficiencies for a sample of 27 compact, midsize, and large cars are entered into a statistical software package. To test whether there is a difference among the mean fuel efficiencies for the three car types, an analysis of variance is computed. What do you conclude? Use the 0.01 significance level.

Summary

Groups	Count	Sum	Average	Variance
Compact	12	268.3	22.35833	9.388106
Midsize	9	172.4	19.15556	7.315278
Large	6	100.5	16.75	7.303

ANOVA

Source	SS	DF	MS	F	p-Value
Between groups	136.4803	2	68.24014	8.258752	0.001866
Within groups	198.3064	24	8.262766		
Total	334.7867	26			

29. The Simone Company is considering a new computer program to speed up the processing of its inventory. Two programs are being considered: Program A and Program B. To test the programs, 23 employees were divided into two groups of 12 and 11. The mean processing time of the 12 employees for Program A was 35 seconds, with a standard deviation of 8 seconds. The mean processing time of the 11 employees for Program B was 34 seconds, with a standard deviation of 12 seconds. Is there a difference in the variation of the two programs? Test at the 0.10 significance level.

30. There are four McBurger restaurants on and within 30 kilometres of the college campus. The numbers of burgers sold at the respective restaurants for each of the last six weeks are shown below. At the 0.05 significance level, is there a difference in the mean number sold among the four locations?

Food Court	Downtown	Bus Depot	Library
124	160	320	190
234	220	340	230
430	290	290	240
105	245	310	170
240	205	280	180
310	260	270	205

31. Listed below are the masses (in grams) of a sample of M&M's plain candies, classified according to colour. Determine whether there is a difference in the mean masses of candies of different colours. Use the 0.05 significance level.

Red	Orange	Yellow	Brown	Tan	Green
0.946	0.902	0.929	0.896	0.845	0.935
1.107	0.943	0.960	0.888	0.909	0.903
0.913	0.916	0.938	0.906	0.873	0.865
0.904	0.910	0.933	0.941	0.902	0.822
0.926	0.903	0.932	0.838	0.956	0.871
0.926	0.901	0.899	0.892	0.959	0.905
1.006	0.919	0.907	0.905	0.916	0.905
0.914	0.901	0.906	0.824	0.822	0.852
0.922	0.930	0.930	0.908		0.965
1.052	0.883	0.952	0.833		0.898
0.903		0.939			
0.895		0.940			
		0.882			
		0.906			

32. There are four radio stations in Midland. The stations have different formats (hard rock, classical, country and western, and easy listening), but each is concerned with the number of minutes of music played per hour. From a sample of 10 hours from each station, the following sample means were offered:

$$\bar{x}_1 = 51.43 \quad \bar{x}_2 = 44.64 \quad \bar{x}_3 = 47.2 \quad \bar{x}_4 = 50.85$$
$$\text{SS total} = 650.75$$

a. Determine SST.
b. Determine SSE.
c. Complete an ANOVA table.
d. At the 0.05 significance level, is there a difference in the treatment means?
e. Is there a difference in the mean amount of music time between station 1 and station 4? Use the 0.05 significance level.

33. Jacob Lee is a frequent traveller between Regina and Saskatoon. For the past month, he wrote down the flight times on three different airlines. The results are as follows:

Airline A	Airline B	Airline C
51	50	52
51	53	55
52	52	60
42	62	64
51	53	61
57	49	49
47	50	49
47	49	
50	58	
60	54	
54	51	
49	49	
48	49	
48	50	

a. Use the 0.05 significance level and the five-step hypothesis-testing process to check if there is a difference in the mean flight times among the three airlines.
b. Develop a 95% confidence interval for the difference in the means between Airline B and Airline C.

34. The postal service handles different types of mail, such as registered mail, letters, parcels, pre-paid mail, and so on. Over a period of three weeks, one item of each kind was sent from a particular postal code administrative office. The total time in transit was recorded. The results are as follows:

Source	DF	SS	MS	F	p-Value
Factor	3	13.82	4.61	2.72	0.051
Error	68	115.17	1.69		
Total	71	128.99			

S = 1.301
R-Sq = 10.71%
R-Sq(adj) = 6.77%

			Individual 95% CIs for Mean Based on Pooled St Dev
Level N	Mean	Standard Deviation	------ + --------- + --------- + --------- + ---
Registered 18	1.444	1.097	(--------*--------)
Letters 18	1.667	1.455	(--------*--------)
Parcels 18	2.444	1.617	(--------*--------)
Pre-paid 18	2.389	0.916	(--------*--------)
			--------- + -------- + -------- + -------- + ------
			1.20 1.80 2.40 3.00

Use the 0.05 significance level to test if this evidence suggests a difference in the means for the different types of mail.

35. For your email, you use a filter to block spam from your inbox. The number of items recorded by the day of the week is recorded. The results are as follows.

Source	DF	SS	MS	F	P
Factor	6	1367.8	228.0	5.72	0.000
Error	48	1913.2	39.9		
Total	54	3281.0			

S = 6.313
R-Sq = 41.69%
R-Sq(adj) = 34.40%

Individual 95% CIs for Mean Based on Pooled St Dev

Level	N	Mean	Standard Deviation	---- + --------- + --------- +--------- + -----
Monday	10	74.000	6.164	(-----*-----)
Tuesday	9	66.111	7.288	(-----*-----)
Wednesday	7	74.143	2.268	(------*-------)
Thursday	8	62.375	5.041	(-----*-----)
Friday	8	75.125	4.454	(-----*-----)
Saturday	5	63.200	7.259	(------*--------)
Sunday	8	72.375	9.164	(-----*-----)

```
          --------- +--------- +--------- +--------- +----------
                 60.0      66.0      72.0      78.0
```

Use the 0.05 significance level to test if this evidence suggests a difference in the means for the different days of the week.

36. Investors can now make stock trades online for as little as $7 per trade. Some suggest that this will motivate investors to increase the percentage of stocks in their portfolios. Further, stocks as a percentage of an investor's portfolio may be related to age. To investigate, Dr. Merenick, professor of finance, selected a sample of 64 investors and determined the percentage of stocks in their portfolios. The sample data is classified by the investors' age and reported below:

20 up to 35	35 up to 50	50 up to 65	65 or older
39.2	10.6	29.0	58.9
32.4	64.5	88.2	35.6
50.8	80.0	29.2	26.1
73.6	59.2	81.5	64.8
46.3	65.8	61.4	30.4
40.0	69.5	79.3	71.0
44.8	72.3	73.9	46.1
69.3	78.4	40.8	70.1
45.3	68.6	57.5	91.8
38.8	67.9	55.2	67.2
33.5	40.1	46.9	63.2
34.0	46.7	62.8	59.6
42.7	66.4	62.8	50.2
68.0	71.7	62.5	49.0
42.1	60.1	26.1	
54.4	44.9		
60.2	59.9		
	71.3		

At the 0.05 significance level, can we conclude that there is a difference in the mean percentage of stocks owned between the various age groups?

37. Three assembly lines are used to produce a certain component for an airliner. To examine the production rate, a random sample of six-hourly periods is chosen for each assembly line, and the number of components produced during these periods for each line is recorded. The output from a statistical software package is as follows:

Summary

Groups	Count	Sum	Average	Variance
Line A	6	250	41.66667	0.266667
Line B	6	260	43.33333	0.666667
Line C	6	249	41.5	0.7

ANOVA

Source	SS	DF	MS	F	p-Value
Between groups	12.33333	2	6.166667	11.32653	0.001005
Within groups	8.166667	15	0.544444		
Total	20.5	17			

a. Use a 0.01 level of significance to test if there is a difference in the mean production of the three assembly lines.

b. Develop a 99% confidence interval for the difference in the means between Line B and Line C.

38. One reads that a business school graduate with a college diploma or an undergraduate degree earns more than a high school graduate with no additional education and that a person with a master's degree or a doctorate earns even more. To test this, a random sample of 25 executives from companies with assets over $1 million was selected. Their incomes, classified by highest level of education, are as follows:

Income ($ thousands)

High School or Less	College Diploma or Undergraduate Degree	Master's Degree or More
$45	$49	$51
47	57	73
53	85	82
62	73	59
39	81	94
43	84	89
54	89	89
	92	95
	62	73

Test at the 0.05 level of significance that there is no difference in the arithmetic mean salaries of the three groups. If the null hypothesis is rejected, conduct further tests to determine which groups differ.

39. Chapin Manufacturing Company operates 24 hours a day, five days a week. The workers rotate shifts each week. Management is interested in whether there is a difference in the number of units produced on each of the three shifts. A sample of five days is selected and the output on each shift is recorded. The results are as follows:

Day	Afternoon	Night
31	25	35
33	26	33
28	24	30
30	29	28
28	26	27

At the 0.05 significance level, can we conclude there is a difference in the mean production rate by shift or by employee?

40. A grocery store wants to monitor the amount of withdrawals that its customers make from automatic teller machines (ATMs) located within its stores. It samples 10 withdrawals from each location and the output from a statistical software package is as follows:

Summary

Groups	Count	Sum	Average	Variance
Location X	10	825	82.5	1808.056
Location Y	10	540	54	921.1111
Location Z	10	382	38.2	1703.733

ANOVA

Source	SS	DF	MS	F	p-Value
Between Groups	10081.27	2	5040.633	3.411288	0.047766
Within Groups	39896.1	27	1477.633		
Total	49977.37	29			

a. Use a 0.01 level of significance to test if there is a difference in the mean amount of money withdrawn.

b. Develop a 90% confidence interval for the difference in the means between Location X and Location Z.

41. Shank's Inc., a nationwide advertising firm, wants to know whether the colour of an advertisement makes a difference in the response of magazine readers. A random sample of readers is shown ads of four different colours. Each reader is asked to give the colour a rating between 1 and 10 (10 is the highest rating). Assume that the ratings follow the normal distribution. The ratings are shown in the following table:

Red	Blue	Orange	Green
2	9	3	8
3	8	6	7
6	9	8	8

a. Is there a difference in the effectiveness of an advertisement by colour? Use the 0.05 level of significance.

b. On the basis of your results in part (a), determine where the differences between the means exist, if any.

42. Three superstore chains claim to have the lowest overall prices. As part of a class project, a group of students conducted an investigative study on superstore advertising. A random sample of nine items was selected, and the price of each selected item was checked at each of the three superstore chains on the same day.

Super$	Ralph's	LowName
$24.99	$29.99	$28.99
14.50	18.00	17.99
11.72	18.25	20.25
12.12	13.45	13.55
13.66	17.99	19.99
14.04	19.99	20.99
10.00	17.99	18.99
13.85	19.99	19.99
15.52	21.00	19.99

a. At the 0.05 significance level, is there a difference in the mean prices at the super stores?

b. On the basis of your results in part (a), determine where the differences between the means exist, if any.

Data Set Exercises

Questions marked with ⤴ have data sets available on McGraw-Hill's online resource for *Basic Statistics*.

43. Refer to the Real Estate Data—Halifax Area online, which reports information on home listings.
   a. At the 0.05 significance level, is there a difference in the variability of the mean list prices of the homes that are townhouses, apartments, or houses?
   b. At the 0.05 significance level, is there a difference in the variability of the mean list prices of the homes with 1 and 2, 3, or more than three bedrooms?
   c. At the 0.05 significance level, is there a difference in the variability of list price of the homes with less than 1500 square feet?

44. Refer to the CREA (Canadian Real Estate Association) Cities Only data online, which reports information on average house prices nationally and in a selection of cities across Canada. At the 0.05 significance level, is there a difference in the variation in the list prices of all cities between January 2014 and January 2011?

45. Refer to the data in the file Gasoline Prices online.
   a. Using the data from November 2012 to November 2016, compare the gasoline prices for Winnipeg, Calgary, and Saskatoon. At the 0.05 significance level, can we conclude that there is a difference in the average gasoline prices?
   b. Using the data from November 2012 to November 2016, compare the gasoline prices for Halifax, Calgary, and Saint John. At the 0.05 significance level, can we conclude that there is a difference in the average gasoline prices?
   c. Using the data from November 2012 to November 2016, compare the gasoline prices for Toronto, Vancouver, and Montreal. At the 0.10 significance level, can we conclude that average gasoline prices are different in the three cities?

46. Refer to the Real Estate Data—Saskatoon online, which reports information on home listings.
   a. At the 0.05 significance level, is there a difference in the variability of the mean list prices of the homes that are townhouses, apartments, or houses?
   b. At the 0.05 significance level, is there a difference in the variability of the mean list prices of the homes with 1 and 2, 3, or more than three bedrooms?
   c. At the 0.05 significance level, is there a difference in the variability of list price of the homes with less than 1500 square feet?

Practice Test

Part I Objective

1. The test statistic for comparing two population variances follows the _____.

2. The shape of the F distribution is _____. (symmetrical, positively skewed, negatively skewed, uniform)

3. The F-statistic is computed as the ratio of two_____.

4. Analysis of Variance (ANOVA) is used to compare two or more _____. (means, proportions, samples sizes, z-values)

5. The ANOVA test assumes equal _____. (population means, population standard deviations, sample sizes, z-values)

6. One-way ANOVA partitions total variation into two parts. One is the treatment variation, and the other is the _____.

7. In one-way ANOVA, the null hypothesis is that the population means are _____.

8. A mean square is computed as a sum of squares divided by the _____.

9. In one-way ANOVA, differences between treatment means are tested with _____. (confidence intervals, z-values, significance levels, variances)

10. For a one-way ANOVA, the treatments must be _____.

Part II Problems

1. Is the variance of the distance travelled per week by two taxi cab companies operating in the Grand Strand area different? The *Sun News*, the local newspaper, is investigating and obtained the following sample information:

Variable	Yellow Cab	Diamond Cab
Mean kilometres travelled	837	797
Standard deviation	30	40
Sample size	14	12

Using the 0.10 significance level, is there a difference in the variance of the number of kilometres travelled?

2. The results of a one-way ANOVA are reported below:

ANOVA

Source of Variation	SS	Df	MS	F
Between Groups	6.90	2	3.45	5.15
Within Groups	12.04	18	0.67	
Total	19.34	20		

   a. How many treatments are in the study?
   b. What is the total sample size?
   c. What is the critical value of F using a significance level of 0.05?
   d. Write out the null hypothesis and the alternate hypothesis.
   e. What is your decision regarding the null hypothesis?
   f. Can we conclude any of the treatment means differ?

Computer Commands

1. **Excel** steps for the test of variances for the Luxury Limos example are as follows:

   a. In an **Excel** spreadsheet, enter the data as shown in the example. This is the **data input.**

   b. Select **Data Analysis, F-Test: Two-Sample for Variances,** and click **OK.**

   c. For Input select the input range for **Variable 1 Range** and the input range for **Variable 2 Range.**

   d. Check the **Labels** box if included in the input range, enter *0.05* for **Alpha** and any empty cell for the **Output Range.**

   e. Click **OK.** The *p*-value is part of the output. *Note:* values may be slightly different due to rounding.

Note: **Excel's F.TEST** function will return a *p*-value for a two-tailed test.

Since the *p*-value (0.081) < than the significance level (0.10), the decision is to reject the null hypothesis.

2. **Excel** steps for the airline example one-way ANOVA are as follows:

   a. Enter the data into a spreadsheet as shown in the example.

   b. Select **Data Analysis** and **ANOVA: Single Factor;** click **OK.**

   c. In the dialog box enter the **Input Range** as *A1:D8*, check **Grouped by Columns,** check **Labels in first row,** enter *0.05* in the **Alpha** box, and select the **Output Range** as any empty cell; click **OK.**

Note: The **Excel** output uses the term "Between Groups" for "Treatments", and "Within Groups" for "Error." However, they have the same meanings. The *p*-value is 0.0007. This is the probability of finding a value of the test statistic this large or larger when the null hypothesis is true. To put it another way, it is the likelihood of calculating an *F*-value larger than 8.99 with 3 degrees of freedom in the numerator and 18 degrees of freedom in the denominator. So, when we reject the null hypothesis in this instance, there is a very small likelihood of committing a Type I error!

3. **MegaStat** steps for the airline example one-way ANOVA are as follows:

   a. Enter the data into a spreadsheet as shown above.

   b. Select **MegaStat**, **Analysis of Variance**, and **One-Factor Anova.**

   c. Enter the **Input range.** Click **OK.**

The *p*-value (0.0007) is shown in the output. Because the *p*-value is less than 0.05, we reject the hypothesis that the mean of the distribution of the differences between the appraised values is zero. In fact, this *p*-value is less than 0.01. There is very little likelihood that the null hypothesis is true.

Answers to Self-Reviews

11–1 Let Mark's assemblies be population 1, then $H_0 : \sigma_1^2 \leq \sigma_2^2$; $H_1: \sigma_1^2 > \sigma_2^2$; $df_1 = 10 - 1 = 9$; and df_2 also equals 9. H_0 is rejected if $F > 3.18$.

$$F = \frac{(2.0)^2}{(1.5)^2} = 1.78.$$

H_0 is not rejected. The variation is the same for both employees.

11–2 **(a)** $H_0: \mu_1 = \mu_2 = \mu_3$.

    H_1: At least one treatment mean is different.

(b) Reject H_0 if $F > 4.26$.

(c) $\bar{x} = \dfrac{240}{12} = 20$

    SS total $= (18 - 20)^2 + \cdots + (32 - 20)^2 = 578$

    SSE $= (18 - 17)^2 + (14 - 17)^2 + \cdots + (32 - 29)^2 = 74$

    SST $= 578 - 74 = 504$

(d)

Source	Sum of Squares	Degrees of Freedom	Mean Squares	F
Treatment	504	2	252	30.65
Error	74	9	8.22	
Total	578	11		

(e) H_0 is rejected. There is a difference in the mean number of bottles sold at the various locations.

11–3 **(a)** $H_0: \mu_1 = \mu_2 = \mu_3$.

    H_1: Not all means are equal.

(b) H_0 is rejected if $F > 3.98$.

(c) $\bar{x}_G = 8.86, \bar{x}_1 = 11, \bar{x}_2 = 8.75, \bar{x}_3 = 6.8$

    SS total $= 53.71$

    SST $= 44.16$; SSE $= 9.55$

Source	Sum of Squares	Df	Mean Square	F
Treatment	44.16	2	22.08	25.43
Error	9.55	11	0.8682	
Total	53.71	13		

(d) H_0 is rejected. The treatment means differ.

(e) $(11.0 - 6.8) \pm 2.201 \sqrt{0.8682\left(\dfrac{1}{5} + \dfrac{1}{5}\right)}$

    $= 4.2 \pm 1.30 = 2.90$ and 5.50

These treatment means differ because both endpoints of the confidence interval are of the same sign—positive in this problem.

NASA Photo/Tony Landis

An air travel service samples domestic airline flights to explore the relationship between airfare and distance. The service would like to know if there is a correlation between airfare and flight distance. If there is a correlation, what percentage of the variation in airfare is accounted for by distance? How much does each additional mile add to the fare? (See Exercise 65 and LO12–1, and LO12–4.)

LEARNING OBJECTIVES

When you have completed this chapter, you will be able to:

LO12-1 Apply regression analysis to estimate the linear relationship between two variables.

LO12-2 Evaluate a regression equation to predict the dependent variable.

LO12-3 Calculate and interpret confidence and prediction intervals.

LO12-4 Calculate and interpret the correlation coefficient and the coefficient of determination.

LO12-5 Test and interpret the relationship between two variables using the correlation coefficient.

12.1 INTRODUCTION

Chapters 2 and 3 presented *descriptive statistics*. We organized raw data into a frequency distribution and computed several measures of location and measures of dispersion to describe the major characteristics of the data. In Chapters 4 through 6, we described probability, and from probability statements, we created probability distributions. In Chapter 7, we began the study of *statistical inference*, where we collected a sample to estimate a population parameter, such as the population mean or population proportion. In addition, we used the sample data to test a hypothesis about a population mean or a population proportion, the difference between two population means, or the equality of several population means. Each of these tests involved just *one* interval-level or ratio-level variable, such as the profit made on a car sale, the mean cost to process a claim, or the difference in checkout time between customers using standard checkouts or a self-checkout system.

In this chapter, we shift the emphasis to the study of relationships between two interval-level or ratio-level variables. In all business fields, identifying and studying relationships between variables can provide information on ways to increase profits, methods to decrease costs, or variables to predict demand. In marketing products, many firms use price reductions through coupons and discount pricing to increase sales. In this example, we are interested in the relationship between two variables: price reductions and sales. To collect the data, a company can test-market a variety of price reduction methods and observe sales. We hope to confirm a relationship that decreasing price leads to increased sales. In economics, you will find many relationships between two variables that are the basis of economics, such as supply and demand and demand and price.

Other examples of relationships between two variables are:

- Does the amount a company spends per month on training its customer care representatives affect its monthly statistics?
- Is the number of square feet in a home related to the cost to heat the home in January?
- Is there a relationship between the kilometres per litre achieved by large pickup trucks and the size of the engine?
- Does the number of hours that students study for an exam influence the exam score?

In this chapter, we carry this idea further. That is, we develop numerical measures to express the relationship between two variables. Is the relationship strong or weak? This will allow us to estimate one variable on the basis of another.

To begin our study of the relationship between two variables, we start by examining a chart, called a **scatter diagram**, which is designed to portray the relationship between the two variables. We continue our study by developing a mathematical equation that will allow us to estimate the value of one variable based on the value of another. This is called **regression analysis**. We will (1) determine the equation of the line that best fits the data, (2) use the equation to estimate the value of one variable based on another, (3) measure the error in our estimate, and (4) establish confidence and prediction intervals for our estimate. Then, we examine the meaning and purpose of **correlation analysis**.

> **Scatter diagram** A chart that portrays the relationship between two variables.
>
> **Correlation analysis** A group of techniques to measure the strength of the association between two variables.

Describing the Relationship between Two Variables

There are situations where we wish to study and visually portray the relationship between two variables. When we study the relationship between two variables we refer to the data as **bivariate.** A scatter diagram is a graphical technique we will use to show this relationship between the two variables.

To draw a scatter diagram we scale one variable along the horizontal axis (*X*-axis) of a graph and the other variable along the vertical (*Y*-axis). Usually, one variable depends to some degree on the other. In our first example, it is very likely that the monthly sales of a company depend on advertising. So, we scale the amount spent on advertising on the horizontal axis and that of sales on the vertical axis.

Three scatter diagrams are given in Chart 12–1. The one on the left shows a rather strong positive relationship between the age in years and the maintenance cost last year for a sample of 10 buses owned by the city of Miramichi. Note that as the age of the bus increases, the yearly maintenance cost also increases. The example in the centre, for a sample of 20 vehicles, shows a rather strong indirect (inverse) relationship between the odometer reading and the selling price of the car. That is, as the number of kilometres driven increases, generally, the selling price decreases. The example on the right depicts the relationship between the height and yearly salary for a sample of 15 shift supervisors. This graph indicates there is little relationship between their height and yearly salary.

CHART 12–1 Three Examples of Scatter Diagrams

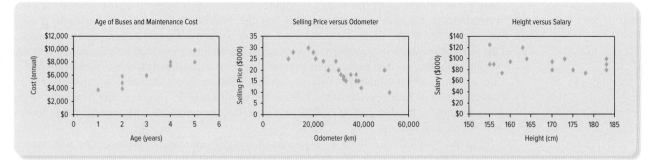

The following example will show how a scatter diagram is used.

| **Example** | Copier Sales Inc. sells copiers to businesses of all sizes. Ms. Marcy Bancer was recently promoted to the position of national sales manager. At the upcoming sales meeting, the sales representatives from all over the country will be in attendance. She would like to impress on them the importance of making that extra sales call each day. She decides to gather some information on the relationship between the number of sales calls and the number of copiers sold. She selects a |

random sample of 10 sales representatives and determines the number of sales calls they made last month and the number of copiers they sold. The sample information is reported in Table 12–1. What observations can you make about the relationship between the number of sales calls and the number of copiers sold? Develop a scatter diagram to display the information.

TABLE 12–1 Sales Calls and Copiers Sold for 10 Sales Representatives

Sales Representative	Number of Sales Calls	Number of Copiers Sold
Tom Keller	20	30
Jeff Hall	40	60
Brian Virost	20	40
Greg Fish	30	60
Susan Welch	10	30
Carlos Ramirez	10	40
Rich Niles	20	40
Mike Kiel	20	50
Mark Reynolds	20	30
Soni Jones	30	70

Solution

Independent variable A variable that provides the basis for estimation. It is the predictor variable.

Dependent variable The variable that is being predicted or estimated.

On the basis of the information in Table 12–1, Ms. Bancer suspects there is a relationship between the number of sales calls made in a month and the number of copiers sold. Soni Jones sold the most copiers last month, and she was one of three representatives making 30 or more sales calls. Susan Welch and Carlos Ramirez, however, made only 10 sales calls last month. Ms. Welch was tied with two other individuals for the lowest number of copiers sold among the sampled representatives.

The implication is that the number of copiers sold is related to the number of sales calls made. As the number of sales calls increases, the number of copiers sold also increases. We refer to number of sales calls as the **independent variable** and number of copiers sold as the **dependent variable**.

We will scale the dependent variable (copiers sold) on the vertical or Y-axis and the independent variable (number of sales calls) on the horizontal or X-axis. To develop the scatter diagram of the Copier Sales Inc. sales information, we begin with the first sales representative, Tom Keller. Tom made 20 sales calls last month and sold 30 copiers, so $x = 20$ and $y = 30$. To plot this point, move along the horizontal axis to $x = 20$, then go vertically to $y = 30$, and place a dot at the intersection. This process is continued until all the paired data are plotted, as shown in Chart 12–2. *Note:* only eight data points show on the graph as two sets of data are the same.

CHART 12–2 Scatter Diagram Showing Sales Calls and Copiers Sold

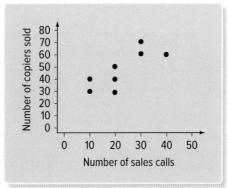

The scatter diagram shows graphically that the sales representatives who make more calls tend to sell more copiers. It is reasonable for Ms. Bancer, the national sales manager at Copier Sales Inc., to tell her sales representatives that the more sales calls they make, the more copiers they can expect to sell. Note that while there appears to be a positive relationship between the two variables, all the points do not fall on a line. In the following section, you will develop an equation to express the relationship between two variables.

Reliable Furniture is a family business that has been selling to retail customers in the Oakville area for many years. It advertises extensively on radio and TV, emphasizing its low prices and easy credit terms. The owner would like to review the relationship between sales and the amount spent on advertising. Below is information on sales and advertising expense for the last four months:

Month	Advertising Expense ($ thousands)	Sales Revenue ($ thousands)
July	$2	$7
August	1	3
September	3	8
October	4	10

(a) The owner wants to forecast sales based on advertising expense. Which variable is the dependent variable? Which variable is the independent variable?

(b) Draw a scatter diagram.

LO12-1   ## 12.2 REGRESSION ANALYSIS

Regression analysis provides information about the relationship between two variables by expressing the relationship in the form of an equation. Using this equation, we will be able to estimate the value of the dependent variable y based on a selected value of the independent variable x. The technique used to develop the equation and provide estimates is called **regression analysis**. We start by using a scatter diagram to visually position the line that best represents the relationship between the two variables.

The scatter diagram in Chart 12–2 is reproduced in Chart 12–3, with a line drawn with a ruler through the dots to illustrate that a straight line would probably fit the data. However, the line drawn using a straight edge has one disadvantage: its position is based, in part, on the judgment of the person drawing the line. The hand-drawn lines in Chart 12–4 represent the judgments of four people. All the lines except line A seem to be reasonable. However, each would result in a different estimate of units sold for a particular number of sales calls.

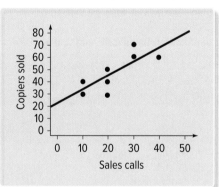

CHART 12–3 Sales Calls and Copiers Sold for 10 Sales Representatives

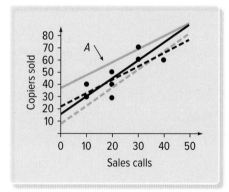

CHART 12–4 Four Lines Superimposed on the Scatter Diagram

Least Squares Principle

Least squares principle A mathematical procedure that uses data to position a line with the objective of minimizing the sum of the squares of the vertical distances between the actual values and the predicted values of Y.

However, we would prefer a method that results in a simple, best regression line. This method is called the **least squares principle**. It gives what is commonly referred to as the "**best-fitting**" line.

To illustrate this concept, the same data are plotted in Chart 12–5, Chart 12–6, and Chart 12–7. The dots are the actual values of y, and the asterisks are the predicted values of y for a given value of x. The regression line in Chart 12–5 was determined using the least squares method. It is the best-fitting line because the sum of the squares of the vertical deviations about it is at a minimum. The first plotted point ($x = 3$, $y = 8$) deviates by 2 from the line, found by: $10 - 8$. The deviation squared is 4. The squared deviation for the point $x = 4$,

CHART 12–5 The Least Squares Line

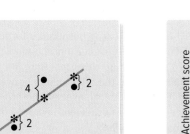

CHART 12–6 Line Drawn with a Straight Edge

CHART 12–7 Different Line Drawn with a Straight Edge

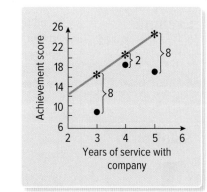

$y = 18$ is 16. The squared deviation for the point $x = 5$, $y = 16$ is 4. The sum of the squared deviations is 24, found by: $4 + 16 + 4$.

Assume that the lines in Charts 12–6 and 12–7 were drawn using a straight edge. The sum of the squared vertical deviations in Chart 12–6 is 44. For Chart 12–7, it is 132. Both sums are greater than the sum for the line in Chart 12–5, found using the least squares method.

The equation of a line has the following form:

GENERAL FORM OF LINEAR REGRESSION EQUATION $\quad y' = a + bx \quad$ [12–1]

where:

y' read y prime, is the predicted value of the y variable for a selected x value.

a is the y-intercept. It is the estimated value of y when $x = 0$. Another way to put it is: a is the estimated value of y where the regression line crosses the y-axis when x is zero.

b is the slope of the line, or the average change in y' for each change of one unit (either increase or decrease) in the independent variable, x.

x is any value of the independent variable that is selected.

The general form of the linear **regression equation** is exactly the same form as the equation of any line; a is the y intercept and b is the slope. The purpose of regression analysis is to calculate the values of a and b to develop a linear equation that best fits the data.

The formulas for b and a are:

SLOPE OF THE REGRESSION LINE $\quad b = \dfrac{n(\sum xy) - (\sum x)(\sum y)}{n(\sum x^2) - (\sum x)^2} \quad$ [12–2]

Y-INTERCEPT $\quad a = \dfrac{\sum y}{n} - b\dfrac{\sum x}{n} \quad$ [12–3]

where:

Σx is the sum of the values of the independent variable.
Σy is the sum of the values of the dependent variable.
n is the number of items in the sample.
Σxy is the sum of the products of the two variables.
Σx^2 is the sum of the squares of the independent variable.

The following example will illustrate this.

Example

Solution

Statistics in Action

In finance, investors are interested in the trade-off between returns and risk. One technique to quantify risk is a regression analysis of a company's stock price (dependent variable) and an average measure of the stock market (independent variable). Often, the Standard and Poor's (S&P) 500 Index is used to estimate the market. The regression coefficient, called "beta" in finance, shows the change in a company's stock price for a one-unit change in the S&P Index. For example, if a stock has a beta of 1.5, when the S&P Index increases by 1%, the stock price will increase by 1.5%. The opposite is also true. If the S&P decreases by 1%, the stock price will decrease by 1.5%. If the beta is 1.0, then a 1% change in the index should show a 1% change in a stock price. If the beta is less than 1.0, then a 1% change in the index shows less than a 1% change in the stock price.

Recall the example involving Copier Sales Inc. The sales manager gathered information on the number of sales calls made and the number of copiers sold for a random sample of 10 sales representatives. As a part of her presentation at the upcoming sales meeting, Ms. Bancer, the sales manager, would like to offer specific information about the relationship between the number of sales calls and the number of copiers sold. Use the least squares method to determine a linear equation to express the relationship between the two variables. What is the expected number of copiers sold by a representative who makes 20 calls?

Table 12–2 repeats the sample information from Table 12–1. It also includes the sums needed in formulas (12–2) and (12–3) to calculate the regression equation.

TABLE 12–2 Calculations Needed for Determining the Least Squares Regression Equation

Sales Representative	Sales Calls (x)	Copiers Sold (y)	x^2	y^2	xy
Tom Keller	20	30	400	900	600
Jeff Hall	40	60	1600	3600	2400
Brian Virost	20	40	400	1600	800
Greg Fish	30	60	900	3600	1800
Susan Welch	10	30	100	900	300
Carlos Ramirez	10	40	100	1600	400
Rich Niles	20	40	400	1600	800
Mike Kiel	20	50	400	2500	1000
Mark Reynolds	20	30	400	900	600
Soni Jones	30	70	900	4900	2100
Total	220	450	5600	22 100	10 800

The first step in determining the regression equation is to find the slope of the least squares regression line. That is, we need to find the value of b using formula (12–2). Then, we need to find the value of a. To do this we use the value for b that we calculated first and use formula (12–3). The results are as follows:

$$b = \frac{n(\sum xy) - (\sum x)(\sum y)}{n\sum x^2 - (\sum x)^2} = \frac{10(10\,800) - (220)(450)}{10(5600) - (220)^2} = 1.1842$$

$$a = \frac{\sum y}{n} - b\frac{\sum x}{n} = \frac{450}{10} - (1.1842)\frac{220}{10} = 18.9476$$

Thus, the regression equation is $y' = 18.9476 + 1.1842x$. So, if a sales representative makes 20 calls, he or she can expect to sell 42.6316 copiers, found by: $y' = 18.9476 + 1.1842x = 18.9476 + 1.1842(20)$. The b value of 1.1842 indicates that for each additional sales call made the sales representative can expect to increase the number of copiers sold by about 1.2. To put it another way, five additional sales calls in a month will result in about six more copiers being sold $1.1842(5) = 5.921$.

The a value of 18.9476 is the point where the equation crosses the Y-axis. A literal interpretation is that if no sales calls are made, that is, $x = 0$, 18.9476 copiers will be sold. Note that $x = 0$ is outside the range of values included in the sample and, therefore, should not be used to estimate the number of copiers sold. The sales calls ranged from 10 to 40, so estimates should be limited to that range.

Computer commands for the above example can be found at the end of the chapter.

Drawing the Regression Line

The least squares equation, $y' = 18.9476 + 1.1842x$, can be drawn on the scatter diagram. The first sales representative in the sample is Tom Keller. He made 20 calls. His estimated number of copiers sold is $y' = 18.9476 + 1.1842(20) = 42.6316$. The point $x = 20$ and $y' = 42.6316$ is located by moving to 20 on the x-axis and then going vertically to 42.6316. The other points on the regression equation can be determined by substituting the particular value of x into the regression equation.

Sales Representative	Sales Calls (x)	Estimated Sales (y')	Sales Representative	Sales Calls (x)	Estimated Sales (y')
Tom Keller	20	42.6316	Carlos Ramirez	10	30.7896
Jeff Hall	40	66.3156	Rich Niles	20	42.6316
Brian Virost	20	42.6316	Mike Kiel	20	42.6316
Greg Fish	30	54.4736	Mark Reynolds	20	42.6316
Susan Welch	10	30.7896	Soni Jones	30	54.4736

All the points are connected to draw the line. See Chart 12–8.

CHART 12–8 The Line of Regression Drawn on the Scatter Diagram

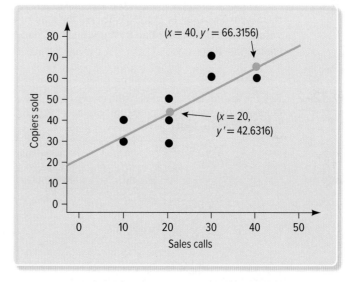

The least squares regression line has some interesting and unique features. First, it will always pass through the point $(\overline{x}, \overline{y})$. To show this is true, we can use the mean number of sales calls to predict the number of copiers sold. In this example, the mean number of sales calls is 22.0, found by: $\overline{x} = \sum x/10 = 220/10 = 22.0$. The mean number of copiers sold is 45.0, found by: $\overline{y} = \sum y/10 = 450/10 = 45.0$. If we let $x = 22$ and then use the regression equation to find the estimated value for y', the result is:

$$y' = 18.9476 + (1.1842 \times 22) = 45$$

The estimated number of copiers sold is exactly equal to the mean number of copiers sold. This simple example shows the regression line will pass through the point represented by the two means. In this case, the regression equation will pass through the point $x = 22$ and $y = 45$.

Second, as we discussed earlier in this section, there is no other line through the data where the sum of the squared deviations is smaller. To put it another way, the term $\Sigma(y - y')^2$ is smaller for the least squares regression equation than for any other equation.

Sales Representative	Sales Calls	Units Sold	Estimated Sales	$(y - y')$	$(y - y')^2$
Tom Keller	20	30	42.6316	−12.6316	159.5573
Jeff Hall	40	60	66.3156	−6.3156	39.8868
Brian Virost	20	40	42.6316	−2.6316	6.9253
Greg Fish	30	60	54.4736	5.5264	30.5411
Susan Welch	10	30	30.7896	−0.7896	0.6235
Carlos Ramirez	10	40	30.7896	9.2104	84.8315
Rich Niles	20	40	42.6316	−2.6316	6.9253
Mike Kiel	20	50	42.6316	7.3684	54.2933
Mark Reynolds	20	30	42.6316	−12.6316	159.5573
Soni Jones	30	70	54.4736	15.5264	241.0691
					784.2105

In the column $(y - y')$ above, we calculated the **residuals,** or error values. This is the difference between the actual values and the predicted values. For Soni Jones:

$$y' = 18.9476 + (1.1842 \times 30) = 54.4736$$

Her actual number of sales is 70. So, the residual, or error estimate, is $(y - y') = (70 - 54.4736) =$ 15.5264. This value reflects the amount the predicted value of sales is "off" from the actual sales value.

The next column squares the residuals for each of the sales representatives and then totals the result. The total is 784.2105. This is the sum of the squared differences or the least squares value. There is no other line through these 10 data points where the sum of the squared differences is smaller.

self-review 12–2   Refer to self-review 12–1, where the owner of the Reliable Furniture Company was studying the relationship between sales and the amount spent on advertising. The sales information for the last four months is repeated below:

Month	Advertising Expense ($ millions)	Sales Revenue ($ millions)
July	$2	$7
August	1	3
September	3	8
October	4	10

(a) Determine the regression equation.
(b) Interpret the values of a and b.
(c) Estimate sales when $3 million is spent on advertising.

EXERCISES

Note: It is suggested that you save your values, as these exercises will be referred to later in the chapter.

1. The Sally Coffee Shop is considering closing one hour earlier in the evening through the week. Sally obtained the following data from a study taken last week of the number of customers between the hours of 10 and 11 p.m., and the dollar value spent.

x:	4	5	3	6	10
y:	4	6	5	7	7

  a. Draw a scatter diagram.
  b. Determine the regression equation.
  c. Determine the value of y' when x is 7.

2. The following sample observations were randomly selected:

x:	5	3	6	3	4	4	6	8
y:	13	15	7	12	13	11	9	5

    a. Draw a scatter diagram.

    b. Determine the regression equation.

    c. Determine the value of y' when x is 7.

3. Bradford Electric Illuminating Company is studying the relationship between kilowatt-hours (thousands) used and the number of rooms in a private single-family residence. A random sample of 10 homes yielded the following:

Number of Rooms	Kilowatt-Hours (thousands)	Number of Rooms	Kilowatt-Hours (thousands)
12	9	8	6
9	7	10	8
14	10	10	10
6	5	5	4
10	8	7	7

    a. Draw a scatter diagram.

    b. Determine the regression equation.

    c. Determine the number of kilowatt-hours, in thousands, for a six-room house.

4. Mr. James McWhinney, president of Daniel-James Financial Services, believes there is a relationship between the number of client contacts and the dollar amount of sales. To document this assertion, Mr. McWhinney gathered the following sample information. The x column indicates the number of client contacts last month, and the y column shows the value of sales ($ thousands) last month for each client sampled.

Number of Contacts, x	Sales ($ thousands), y	Number of Contacts, x	Sales ($ thousands), y
14	$24	23	$30
12	14	48	90
20	28	50	85
16	30	55	120
46	80	50	110

    a. Draw a scatter diagram.

    b. Determine the regression equation.

    c. Determine the estimated sales if 40 contacts are made.

5. In a recent poll concerning sales, earnings, and job creation, 12 companies responded with the following information:

Company	Sales ($ thousands)	Earnings ($ thousands)	Company	Sales ($ thousands)	Earnings ($ thousands)
M Studios	$89.2	$4.9	Armstrong Aircraft	$17.5	$2.6
Monica's Kitchen	18.6	4.4	WWW Snow Removal	11.9	1.7
ABC Tutoring Services	18.2	1.3	Ice Skaters Group	19.6	3.5
Larry's Motorcycles	71.7	8.0	The Knitting Club	51.2	8.2
Comeau Karts	58.6	6.6	Summer Games	28.6	6.0
Marion Florence Jewellery	46.8	4.1	Skiing with Marilyn	69.2	12.8

Let sales be the independent variable and earnings be the dependent variable.

    a. Draw a scatter diagram.

    b. Determine the regression equation.

    c. For a small company with $50 000 in sales, estimate the earnings.

6. We are studying mutual bond funds for the purpose of investing in several funds. For this particular study, we want to focus on the assets of a fund and its five-year performance. The question is: can the five-year rate of return be estimated based on the assets of the fund? Nine mutual funds were selected at random, and their assets and rates of return are shown below:

Fund	Assets ($ millions)	Return (%)	Fund	Assets ($ millions)	Return (%)
AARP High Quality Bond	$622.2	10.8%	MFS Bond A	$494.5	11.6%
Babson Bond L	160.4	11.3	Nichols Income	158.3	9.5
Compass Capital Fixed Income	275.7	11.4	T. Raive Price Short-term	681.0	8.2
Galaxy Bond Retail	433.2	9.1	Thompson Income B	241.3	6.8
Keystone Custodian B-1	437.9	9.2			

a. Draw a scatter diagram.
b. Determine the regression equation. Use assets as the independent variable.
c. For a fund with $400 million in sales, determine the five-year rate of return (in percentage).

7. The city council of Pine Bluffs is considering increasing the number of police in an effort to reduce crime. Before making a final decision, the council asks the chief of police to survey other cities of similar size to determine the relationship between the number of police and the number of crimes reported. The chief gathered the following sample information:

City	Police	Number of Crimes	City	Police	Number of Crimes
Oxford	15	17	Holgate	17	7
Starksville	17	13	Carey	12	21
Danville	25	5	Whistler	11	19
Athens	27	7	Woodville	22	6

a. If we want to estimate crimes on the basis of number of police officers, which variable is the dependent variable, and which is the independent variable?
b. Draw a scatter diagram.
c. Determine the regression equation.
d. Estimate the number of crimes for a city with 20 police officers.
e. Interpret the regression equation.

8. The owner of Maumee Motors wants to study the relationship between the age of a car and its selling price. Listed below is a random sample of 12 used cars sold at Maumee Motors last year:

Car	Age (years)	Selling Price ($ thousands)	Car	Age (years)	Selling Price ($ thousands)
1	9	$8.1	7	8	$7.6
2	7	6.0	8	11	8.0
3	11	3.6	9	10	8.0
4	12	4.0	10	12	6.0
5	8	5.0	11	6	8.6
6	7	10.0	12	6	8.0

a. If we want to estimate selling price on the basis of the age of the car, which variable is the dependent variable, and which is the independent variable?
b. Draw a scatter diagram.
c. Determine the regression equation.
d. Estimate the selling price of a 10-year-old car.
e. Interpret the regression equation.

LO12-2 12.3 THE STANDARD ERROR OF ESTIMATE

The results of the regression analysis for Copier Sales of America show a significant relationship between number of sales calls and the number of copiers sold. By substituting the names of the variables into the equation, it can be written as:

Number of copiers sold = 18.9476 + 1.1842 (Number of sales calls)

The equation can be used to estimate the number of copiers sold for any given "number of sales calls" within the range of the data. For example, if the number of sales calls is 30, then we can estimate the number of copiers sold. It is 54.4736, found by: 18.9476 + 1.1842(30). However, the sample data show that two sales representatives, Fish and Jones, each made 30 sales calls. However, they did not sell the same number of copiers. Fish sold 60 copiers, and Jones sold 70 copiers. So, is the number of sales calls a good predictor of the number of copiers sold?

Perfect prediction, which is finding the *exact outcome*, in economics and business is practically impossible (Chart 12–9). For example:

- A large electronics firm, with production facilities throughout North America, has a stock option plan for employees. Suppose that there is a relationship between the employee years with the company and the number of shares owned. This relationship is likely because, as employee years of service increases, the number of shares that an employee earns also increases. If we observe all employees with 20 years of service, they would most likely own different numbers of shares.
- A real estate developer on the West Coast studied the relationship between the income of buyers and the size, in square feet, of the home they purchased. The developer reasons that as the incomes of the buyers increase, the sizes of the homes purchased will also increase. However, all buyers with an income of $170 000 will not purchase a home of exactly the same size.

CHART 12–9 Example of Perfect Prediction: Horsepower and Cost of Electricity

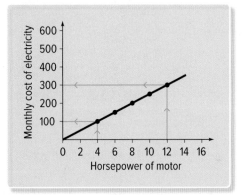

What is needed, then, is a measure that describes how precise the prediction of y is based on x or, conversely, how inaccurate the estimate might be. This measure is called the **standard error of estimate**. The standard error of estimate, symbolized by S_e, is the same concept as the standard deviation discussed in Chapter 3. The standard deviation measures the dispersion around the mean. The standard error of estimate measures the dispersion about the regression line for a given value of x.

The standard error of estimate is found by the following formula (12–4):

Standard error of estimate A measure of the scatter, or dispersion, of the observed values around the line of regression.

STANDARD ERROR OF ESTIMATE $$S_e = \sqrt{\frac{\Sigma(y - y')^2}{n - 2}}$$ [12–4]

Note the following important features:

1. It is similar to the standard deviation in that it is based on squared deviations. The numerator of the standard deviation is based on squared deviations from the mean. The numerator of the standard error is based on squared deviations from the regression line.
2. The sum of the squared deviations is the least square value used to find the best-fitting regression line. Recall in the previous section we described how to find the least squares value.
3. The denominator of the equation is $n - 2$. As usual, n is the number of sample observations. We lose two degrees of freedom because we are estimating two parameters. So, the values of b, the slope of the line, and a, the Y-intercept, are sample values we use to estimate their corresponding population values. We are sampling from a population and are estimating the slope of the line and the intercept with the Y-axis. Hence, the denominator is $n - 2$.

If S_e is small, this means that the data are relatively close to the regression line and the regression equation can be used to predict y with little error. If S_e is large, this means that the data are widely scattered around the regression line and the regression equation will not provide a precise estimate y.

Example

Recall the example involving Copier Sales Inc. The sales manager determined the least squares regression equation to be $y' = 18.9476 + 1.1842x$, where y' refers to the number of copiers sold and x the number of sales calls made. Determine the standard error of estimate as a measure of how well the values fit the regression line.

Solution

To find the standard error, we begin by finding the difference between the value, y, and the value estimated from the regression equation, y'. Next, we square this difference, that is, $(y - y')^2$. We do this for each of the n observations and sum the results. That is, we compute $\Sigma(y - y')^2$, which is the numerator of formula (12–4). Finally, we divide by the number of observations minus 2. The details of the calculations are summarized in Table 12–3.

TABLE 12–3 Computations Needed for the Standard Error of Estimate

Sales Representative	Actual Sales (y)	Estimated Sales (y')	Deviation ($y - y'$)	Deviation Squared ($y - y'$)^2
Tom Keller	30	42.6316	−12.6316	159.557
Jeff Hall	60	66.3156	−6.3156	39.887
Brian Virost	40	42.6316	−2.6316	6.925
Greg Fish	60	54.4736	5.5264	30.541
Susan Welch	30	30.7896	−0.7896	0.623
Carlos Ramirez	40	30.7896	9.2104	84.831
Rich Niles	40	42.6316	−2.6316	6.925
Mike Kiel	50	42.6316	7.3684	54.293
Mark Reynolds	30	42.6316	−12.6316	159.557
Soni Jones	70	54.4736	15.5264	241.069
			0.0000	784.208

The standard error of estimate is 9.901, found by using formula (12–4).

$$S_e = \sqrt{\frac{\Sigma(y - y')^2}{n - 2}} = \sqrt{\frac{784.208}{10 - 2}} = 9.901$$

The deviations $(y - y')$ are the vertical deviations from the regression line. To illustrate, the 10 deviations from Table 12–3 are shown in Chart 12–10. In Table 12–3, note that the sum of the signed deviations is zero. This indicates that the positive deviations (above the regression line) are offset by the negative deviations (below the regression line).

CHART 12–10 Sales Calls and Copiers Sold for 10 Sales Representatives

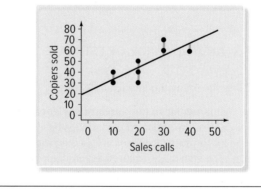

Formula (12–4) for the standard error of estimate was applied to show the similarity in concept and computation between the standard deviation and the standard error of estimate. Suppose that a large number of observations are being studied, and the numbers are large. Computing each y' point on the regression line and then squaring the differences—that is,

$(y - y')$—would be rather tedious. The following formula is algebraically equivalent to formula (12–4) but is much easier to use:

COMPUTATION FORMULA FOR THE STANDARD ERROR OF ESTIMATE	$S_e = \sqrt{\dfrac{\sum y^2 - a(\sum y) - b(\sum xy)}{n - 2}}$	[12–5]

The squares, sums, and other numbers for the Copier Sales Inc. example were calculated in Table 12–2. By inserting these values into the formula, we find:

$$S_e = \sqrt{\frac{22\,100 - 18.9476(450) - 1.1842(10\,800)}{10 - 2}}$$

$$= 9.901$$

This is the same standard error of estimate as computed previously. How do we interpret 9.901? Think of it as the typical vertical distance of the observation from the regression line.

Statistical Software eases computation when finding the least squares regression line, calculating fitted values, or finding the standard error of the estimate. The **Excel** output from the Copier Sales Inc. example is included below. The slope and intercept are in the column "Coefficients" (cells F17 and F18). The fitted values for each sales representative are the column "Predicted Sales" (cells F23:F32). The "Residuals" or differences between the actual and the estimated values are in the next column (cells G23:G32). The standard error of estimate is in cell F7. All of these values are shown below:

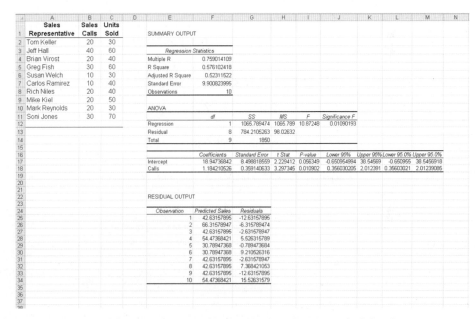

Excel steps to create the regression statistics can be found at the end of the chapter.

Thus far, we have presented linear regression only as a descriptive tool. In other words, it is a simple summary ($y' = a + bx$) of the relationship between the dependent y variable and the independent x variable. When we make conclusions about a population on the basis of the sample data, we are using inferential statistics. Then, we need to recall the distinction between population parameters and sample statistics. In this case, we "model" the linear relationship in the population by the equation:

$$Y = \alpha + \beta X$$

where:

> Y is any value of the dependent variable.
> α is the Y-intercept (the value of Y when $X = 0$) in the population.
> β is the slope (the amount by which Y changes when X increases by one unit) of the population values.
> X is any value of the independent variable.

Now, α and β are population parameters, and a and b, respectively, are estimates of those parameters. They are computed from a particular sample taken from the population. Fortunately, the formulas given earlier in the chapter for a and b do not change when we move from using regression as a descriptive tool to regression in statistical inference.

It should be noted that the linear regression equation for the sample of sales representatives is only an estimate of the relationship between two variables for the population. Thus, the values of a and b in the regression equation are usually referred to as the **estimated regression coefficients,** or simply the **regression coefficients.**

12.4 ASSUMPTIONS UNDERLYING LINEAR REGRESSION

To properly apply linear regression, several assumptions must be met. Chart 12–11 illustrates these assumptions.

CHART 12–11 Regression Assumptions Shown Graphically

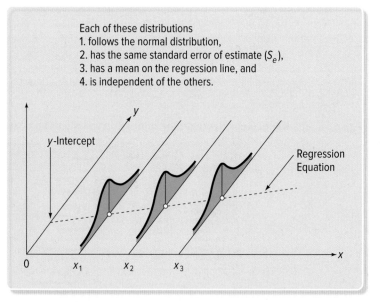

1. For each value of x, there are corresponding y values. These y values follow the normal distribution.
2. The means of these normal distributions lie on the regression line.
3. The standard deviations of these normal distributions are all the same. The best estimate we have of this common standard deviation is the standard error of estimate (S_e).

4. The y values are statistically independent. This means that in selecting a sample a particular x does not depend on any other value of x. This assumption is particularly important when data are collected over a period of time. In such situations, the errors for a particular period are often correlated with those of other periods.

Recall from Chapter 6 that if the values follow a normal distribution, the mean plus or minus one standard deviation will encompass about 68% of the observations, the mean plus or minus two standard deviations will encompass about 95% of the observations, and the mean plus or minus three standard deviations will encompass virtually all of the observations. The same relationship exists between the predicted values y' and the standard error of estimate (S_e).

1. $y' \pm S_e$ will include the middle 68% of the observations.
2. $y' \pm 2S_e$ will include the middle 95% of the observations.
3. $y' \pm 3S_e$ will include virtually all the observations.

We can now relate these assumptions to Copier Sales Inc., where we studied the relationship between the number of sales calls and the number of copiers sold. Assume that we took a much larger sample than $n = 10$, but that the standard error of estimate was still 9.901. If we drew a parallel line 9.901 units above the regression line and another 9.901 units below the regression line, about 68% of the points would fall between the two lines. Similarly, a line 19.802 $[2S_e = 2(9.901)]$ units above the regression line and another 19.802 units below the regression line should include about 95% of the data values.

As a rough check, refer to the second column from the right in Table 12–3, that is, the column headed "Deviation." Three of the 10 deviations exceed one standard error of estimate. That is, the deviation of -12.6316 for Tom Keller, -12.6316 for Mark Reynolds, and $+15.5264$ for Soni Jones all exceed the value of 9.901, which is 1 standard error from the regression line. All of the values are within 19.802 units of the regression line. In short, 7 of the 10 deviations are within one standard error of the regression line and all are within two standard errors. This is a good result for a relatively small sample.

---

self-review 12–3   Refer to self-reviews 12–1 and 12–2, where the owner of Reliable Furniture was studying the relationship between sales and the amount spent on advertising. Determine the standard error of estimate.

EXERCISES

9. Refer to Exercise 1.
   a. Determine the standard error of estimate.
   b. Suppose a large sample is selected (instead of just five). About 68% of the predictions would be between what two values?

10. Refer to Exercise 2.
    a. Determine the standard error of estimate.
    b. Suppose a large sample is selected (instead of just eight). About 95% of the predictions would be between what two values?

11. Refer to Exercise 3.
    a. Determine the standard error of estimate.
    b. Suppose a large sample is selected (instead of just 10). About 95% of the predictions regarding kilowatt-hours would occur between what two values?

12. Refer to Exercise 4.
    a. Determine the standard error of estimate.
    b. Suppose a large sample is selected (instead of just 10). About 95% of the predictions regarding sales would occur between what two values?

13. Refer to Exercise 7. Determine the standard error of estimate.

14. Refer to Exercise 8. Determine the standard error of estimate.

LO12-3 12.5 CONFIDENCE INTERVALS AND PREDICTION INTERVALS

The standard error of estimate is a statistic that provides an overall evaluation of the ability of a regression equation to predict a dependent variable. Another way to report the ability of a regression equation to predict is specific to a stated value of the independent variable. For example, we can predict the number of copiers sold (y) for a selected value of the sales calls made (x). In fact, we can calculate a confidence interval for the predicted value of the dependent variable for a selected value of the independent variable.

When using a regression equation, two different predictions can be made for a selected value of the independent variable. The differences are subtle but very important and are related to the assumptions stated in the last section. Recall that for any selected value of the independent variable (X), the dependent variable (Y) is a random variable that is normally distributed with a mean, Y'. Each distribution of Y has a standard deviation equal to the regression analysis' standard error of the estimate.

The first interval estimate is called a **confidence interval.** This is used when the regression equation is used to predict the mean value of y for a given value of x. For example, we would use a confidence interval to estimate the mean salary of all executives in the retail industry on the basis of their years of experience. To determine the confidence interval for the mean value of y for a given x, the formula is:

CONFIDENCE INTERVAL FOR THE MEAN OF Y, GIVEN X	$$y' \pm tS_e \sqrt{\frac{1}{n} + \frac{(x - \bar{x})^2}{\sum(x - \bar{x})^2}}$$	[12–6]

where:

    y' is the predicted value for any selected independent variable, X.
    x is any selected value of X.
    $\bar{x}$ is the mean of the x-values, found by $\Sigma x/n$.
    n is the number of observations.
    S_e is the standard error of estimate.
    t is the value of t from Appendix B.2 with $n - 2$ degrees of freedom.

The second interval estimate is called a prediction interval. This is used when the regression equation is used to predict an individual y ($n = 1$) for a given value of x. For example, we would estimate the salary of a particular retail executive who has 20 years of experience. To determine the prediction interval for an estimate of an individual for a given x, the formula is:

PREDICTION INTERVAL FOR Y, GIVEN X	$$y' \pm tS_e \sqrt{1 + \frac{1}{n} + \frac{(x - \bar{x})^2}{\sum(x - \bar{x})^2}}$$	[12–7]

Example	We return to the Copier Sales Inc. example. Determine a 95% confidence interval for all sales representatives who make 25 calls and for Sheila Baker, a West Coast sales representative who made 25 calls.
Solution	We use formula (12–6) to determine a confidence interval. Table 12–4 includes the necessary totals.

TABLE 12–4 Calculations Needed for Determining the Confidence Interval and Prediction Interval

Sales Representative	Sales Calls (x)	Copiers Sold (y)	x^2	$(x - \bar{x})$	$(x - \bar{x})^2$
Tom Keller	20	30	400	−2	4
Jeff Hall	40	60	1600	18	324
Brian Virost	20	40	400	−2	4
Greg Fish	30	60	900	8	64
Susan Welch	10	30	100	−12	144
Carlos Ramirez	10	40	100	−12	144
Rich Niles	20	40	400	−2	4
Mike Kiel	20	50	400	−2	4
Mark Reynolds	20	30	400	−2	4
Soni Jones	30	70	900	8	64
Total	220	450	5600	0	760

The first step is to determine the number of copiers we expect a sales representative to sell if he or she makes 25 calls. It is 48.5526, found by: $y' = 18.9476 + 1.1842x = 18.9476 + 1.1842(25)$.

To find the t-value, we need to first know the number of degrees of freedom. In this case, the degrees of freedom is: $n - 2 = 10 - 2 = 8$. We set the confidence level at 95%. To find the value of t, move down the left-hand column of Appendix B.2 to 8 degrees of freedom, then move across to the column with the 95% level of confidence. The value of t is 2.306.

In the previous section, we calculated the standard error of estimate to be 9.901. We let $x = 25$, and from Table 12–4, the mean number of sales is 22 (220/10). Insert the required values in formula (12–6) to determine the confidence interval.

$$\text{Confidence interval} = y' \pm tS_e \sqrt{\frac{1}{n} + \frac{(x - \bar{x})^2}{\sum(x - \bar{x})^2}}$$

$$= 48.5526 \pm 2.306(9.901) \sqrt{\frac{1}{10} + \frac{(25 - 22)^2}{760}}$$

$$= 48.5526 \pm 7.6356$$

Thus, the 95% confidence interval of copiers sold for all sales representatives who make 25 calls is from 40.9170 up to 56.1882. To interpret, let us round the values. If a sales representative makes 25 calls, he or she can expect to sell 48.6 copiers. It is likely that copiers sold will range from 40.9 to 56.2 copiers.

Suppose that we want to estimate the number of copiers sold by Sheila Baker, who made 25 sales calls. The 95% prediction interval is determined as follows:

$$\text{Prediction interval} = y' \pm tS_e \sqrt{1 + \frac{1}{n} + \frac{(x - \bar{x})^2}{\sum(x - \bar{x})^2}}$$

$$= 48.5526 \pm 2.306(9.901) \sqrt{1 + \frac{1}{10} + \frac{(25 - 22)^2}{760}}$$

$$= 48.5526 \pm 24.0746$$

Thus, the interval is from 24.478 up to 72.627 copiers. We conclude that the number of copiers sold will be between about 24 and 73 for a particular sales representative who makes 25 calls. This interval is quite large. It is much larger than the confidence interval for the mean of all sales representatives who made 25 calls. It is logical, however, that there should be more variation in the sales estimate for an individual than for the mean of a group.

The following graph shows the relationship between the regression line (in the centre), the confidence interval (green dashed lines), and the prediction interval (black dashed lines). The bands for the prediction interval are always further from the regression line than for the confidence interval. Also, as the values of x move away from the mean number of calls (22) in the positive or negative direction, the confidence interval and prediction interval bands widen. This is caused by the numerator of the right-hand term in formulas (12–6) and (12–7). That is, as the term $(x - \bar{x})^2$ increases, the widths of the confidence interval and prediction interval also increase. To put it another way, our estimates are less precise as we move away, in either direction, from the mean of the independent variable.

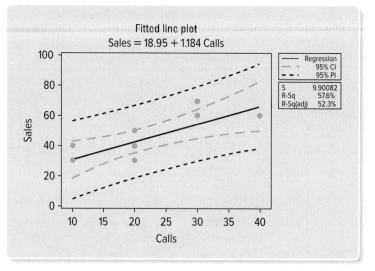

We wish to emphasize again the distinction between a **confidence interval** and a **prediction interval**.

- A confidence interval refers to all observations with a given value of x and is computed using formula (12–6).
- A prediction interval refers to a particular observation for a given value of x and is computed using formula (12–7). The prediction interval will always be wider because of the addition of 1 under the radical in the second equation.

self-review 12–4

Refer to the sample data in self-reviews 12–1, 12–2, and 12–3, where the owner of Reliable Furniture was studying the relationship between sales and the amount spent on advertising. The sales information for the last four months is repeated below:

Month	Advertising Expense ($ millions)	Sales Revenue ($ millions)
July	$2	$7
August	1	3
September	3	8
October	4	10

The regression equation was computed to be $y' = 1.5 + 2.2x$, and the standard error is 0.9487. Both variables are reported in millions of dollars. Determine the 90% confidence interval for the typical month in which $3 million was spent on advertising.

EXERCISES

15. Refer to Exercise 1.
  a. Determine the 95% confidence interval for the mean predicted when $x = 7$.
  b. Determine the 95% prediction interval for an individual predicted when $x = 7$.

16. Refer to Exercise 2.
  a. Determine the 95% confidence interval for the mean predicted when $x = 7$.
  b. Determine the 95% prediction interval for an individual predicted when $x = 7$.

17. Refer to Exercise 3.
  a. Determine the 90% confidence interval, in thousands of kilowatt-hours, for the mean of all six-room homes.
  b. Determine the 90% prediction interval, in thousands of kilowatt-hours, for a particular six-room home.

18. Refer to Exercise 4.
  a. Determine the 98% confidence interval, in thousands of dollars, for the mean of all sales personnel who make 40 contacts.
  b. Determine the 98% prediction interval, in thousands of dollars, for a particular salesperson who makes 40 contacts.

LO12-4   12.6 WHAT IS CORRELATION ANALYSIS?

Correlation coefficient A measure of the strength of the linear relationship between two variables.

Originated by Karl Pearson about 1900, the **correlation coefficient** describes the strength of the linear relationship between two sets of interval-scaled or ratio-scaled variables. Designated r, it is often referred to as *Pearson's r* and as the *Pearson product-moment correlation coefficient*. It can assume any value from -1.00 to $+1.00$ inclusive. A correlation coefficient of -1.00 or $+1.00$ indicates *perfect correlation*. For example, a correlation coefficient for the preceding example computed to be $+1.00$ would indicate that the number of sales calls and the number of copiers sold are perfectly related in a positive linear sense. A computed value of -1.00 reveals that sales calls and the number of copiers sold are perfectly related in a negative linear sense. How the scatter diagram would appear if the relationship between the two sets of data were linear and perfect is shown in Chart 12–12.

CHART 12–12 Scatter Diagrams Showing Perfect Negative Correlation and Perfect Positive Correlation

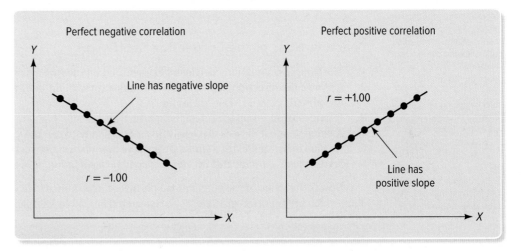

If there is absolutely no relationship between the two sets of variables, Pearson's r is zero. A coefficient of correlation r close to 0 (say, 0.08) shows that the linear relationship is quite weak. The same conclusion is drawn if $r = -0.08$. Coefficients of -0.91 and 0.91 have equal strength; both indicate very strong correlation between the two variables. Thus, *the strength of the correlation does not depend on the direction (either − or +).*

Scatter diagrams for $r = 0$, a weak r (say, -0.23), and a strong r (say, $+0.87$) are shown in Chart 12–13. Note that if the correlation is weak, there is considerable scatter about a line drawn through the centre of the data. For the scatter diagram representing a strong relationship, there is very little scatter about the line. This indicates, in the example shown on the chart, that hours studied is a good predictor of exam score.

CHART 12–13 Scatter Diagrams Depicting Zero, Weak, and Strong Correlations

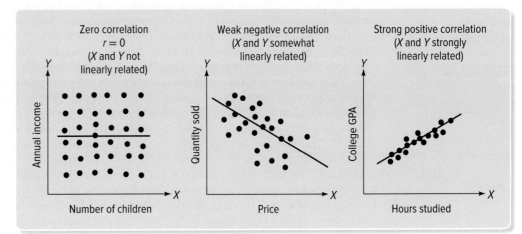

The following drawing summarizes the strength and direction of the coefficient of correlation:

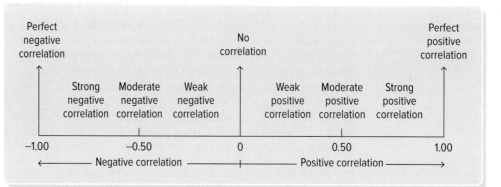

Characteristics of the Correlation Coefficient

1. The sample correlation coefficient is identified by the lowercase letter r.
2. It shows the direction and strength of the linear (straight line) relationship between two in-
    terval-scale or ratio-scale variables.
3. It ranges from -1 up to and including $+1$.
4. A value near 0 indicates there is little association between the variables.
5. A value near 1 indicates a direct or positive association between the variables.
6. A value near -1 indicates inverse or negative association between the variables.

How is the value of the correlation coefficient determined? We will use the Copier Sales Inc.
data, which are reported in Table 12–5, repeated from Table 12–1, as an example.

TABLE 12–5 Sales Calls and Copiers Sold for 10 Sales Representatives

Sales Representative	Number of Sales Calls	Number of Copiers Sold
Tom Keller	20	30
Jeff Hall	40	60
Brian Virost	20	40
Greg Fish	30	60
Susan Welch	10	30
Carlos Ramirez	10	40
Rich Niles	20	40
Mike Kiel	20	50
Mark Reynolds	20	30
Soni Jones	30	70

We begin with a scatter diagram, similar to Chart 12–2. Draw a vertical line through the data
values at the mean of the x-values and a horizontal line at the mean of the y-values. In Chart 12–14,
we have added a vertical line at 22.0 calls ($\bar{x} = \sum x/n = 220/10 = 22$) and a horizontal line at 45.0
copiers ($\bar{y} = \sum y/n = 450/10 = 45.0$). These lines pass through the "centre" of the data and divide
the scatter diagram into four quadrants. Think of moving the origin from (0, 0) to (22, 45).

Two variables are positively related when the number of copiers sold is above the mean and
the number of sales calls is also above the mean. These points appear in the upper-right quadrant
(labelled Quadrant I) of Chart 12–14. Similarly, when the number of copiers sold is less than the
mean, so is the number of sales calls. These points fall in the lower-left quadrant (labelled Quadrant III). For example, the last person on the list in Table 12–6, Soni Jones, made 30 sales calls
and sold 70 copiers. These values are above their respective means, so this point is located in
Quadrant I. She made 8 ($x - \bar{x} = 30 - 22$) more sales calls than the mean and sold 25 ($y - \bar{y} =
70 - 45$) more copiers than the mean. Tom Keller, the first name on the list in Table 12–5, re-
peated from Table 12–1, made 20 sales calls and sold 30 copiers. Both of these values are less
than their respective means; hence, this point is in the lower-left quadrant. Tom made 2 less sales

CHART 12–14 Computation of the Correlation Coefficient

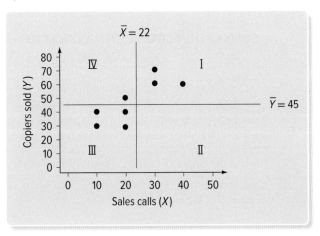

calls and sold 15 less copiers than the respective means. The deviations from the mean number of sales calls and for the mean number of copiers sold are summarized in Table 12–6 for the 10 sales representatives. The sum of the products of the deviations from the respective means is 900. That is, the term is: $\sum(x - \bar{x})(y - \bar{y}) = 900$.

TABLE 12–6 Deviations from the Mean and Their Products

Sales Representative	Calls y	Sales x	$x - \bar{x}$	$y - \bar{y}$	$(x - \bar{x})(y - \bar{y})$
Tom Keller	20	30	−2	15	30
Jeff Hall	40	60	18	15	270
Brian Virost	20	40	−2	−5	10
Greg Fish	30	60	8	15	120
Susan Welch	10	30	−12	−15	180
Carlos Ramirez	10	40	−12	−5	60
Rich Niles	20	40	−2	−5	10
Mike Kiel	20	50	−2	5	−10
Mark Reynolds	20	30	−2	−15	30
Soni Jones	30	70	8	25	200
					900

In both the upper-right and the lower-left quadrants, the product of $(x - x)(y - \bar{y})$ is positive because both of the factors have the same sign. In our example, this happens for all sales representatives except Mike Kiel. We can, therefore, expect the coefficient of correlation to have a positive value.

If the two variables are inversely related, one variable will be above its mean and the other below its mean. Most of the points in this case occur in the upper-left and lower-right quadrants, that is, Quadrant IV and Quadrant II. Now $(x - \bar{x})$ and $(y - \bar{y})$ will have opposite signs, so their product is negative. The resulting correlation coefficient is negative.

What happens if there is no linear relationship between the two variables? The points in the scatter diagram will appear in all four quadrants. The negative products of $(x - \bar{x})(y - \bar{y})$ offset the positive products, so the sum is near zero. This leads to a correlation coefficient near zero. So, the term $\sum(x - \bar{x})(y - \bar{y})$ drives the strength as well as the sign of the relationship between the two variables.

The correlation coefficient also needs to be unaffected by the units of the two variables. For example, if we had used hundreds of copiers sold instead of the number sold, the coefficient of correlation would be the same. The coefficient of correlation is independent of the scale used if we divide the term $\sum(x - \bar{x})(y - \bar{y})$ by the sample standard deviations. It is also made independent of the sample size and bounded by the values +1.00 and −1.00 if we divide by $(n - 1)$.

This reasoning leads to the following formula:

CORRELATION COEFFICIENT—CONCEPTUAL FORM $r = \dfrac{\sum(x - \bar{x})(y - \bar{y})}{(n-1)s_x s_y}$ [12–8]

excel

To compute the correlation coefficient, we use the standard deviations of the sample of 10 sales calls and 10 copiers sold. We could use formula (3–12) to calculate the sample standard deviations or we could use a software package. The following is the **Excel** output. The standard deviation of the number of sales calls is 9.189 and of the number of copiers sold 14.337.

Computer commands to find the following output and the correlation coefficient can be found at the end of the chapter.

J	K	L	M
Sales Calls		*Units Sold*	
Mean	22	Mean	45
Standard Error	2.905933	Standard Error	4.533823503
Median	20	Median	40
Mode	20	Mode	30
Standard Deviation	9.189366	Standard Deviation	14.33720878
Sample Variance	84.44444	Sample Variance	205.5555556
Kurtosis	0.396221	Kurtosis	-1.001147866
Skewness	0.601382	Skewness	0.565529053
Range	30	Range	40
Minimum	10	Minimum	30
Maximum	40	Maximum	70
Sum	220	Sum	450
Count	10	Count	10

We now insert these values into formula (12–8) to determine the correlation coefficient:

$$r = \frac{\sum(x - \bar{x})(y - \bar{y})}{(n-1)s_x s_y} = \frac{900}{(10-1)(9.189)(14.337)} = 0.759$$

The correlation coefficient can also be determined from a computational formula based on the actual values of X and Y. The formula is:

CORRELATION COEFFICIENT $r = \dfrac{n(\sum xy) - (\sum x)(\sum y)}{\sqrt{[n(\sum x^2) - (\sum x)^2][n(\sum y^2) - (\sum y)^2]}}$ [12–9]

where:
    n is the number of paired observations.
    $\sum x$ is the x variable summed.
    $\sum y$ is the y variable summed.
    $(\sum x^2)$ is the x variable squared and the squares summed.
    $(\sum x)^2$ is the x variable summed and the sum squared.
    $(\sum y^2)$ is the y variable squared and the squares summed.
    $(\sum y)^2$ is the y variable summed and the sum squared.
    $\sum xy$ is the sum of the products of x and y.

Note: calculators and computer software can provide the value of r directly from data.

Example

Refer to the Copier Sales Inc. example where we developed a scatter diagram depicting the relationship between the number of sales calls and the number of copiers sold. Determine the correlation coefficient and interpret its value.

Solution

Table 12–2 repeats the information on the number of sales calls and the number of copiers sold. Also included are additional totals necessary to determine the correlation coefficient.

The correlation coefficient is 0.759, found by using formula (12–9).

$$r = \frac{n(\sum xy) - (\sum x)(\sum y)}{\sqrt{[n(\sum x^2) - (\sum x)^2][n(\sum y^2) - (\sum y)^2]}}$$

$$= \frac{10(10\ 800) - (220)(450)}{\sqrt{[10(5600) - (220)^2][10(22\ 100) - (450)^2]}}$$

$$= 0.759$$

We must be careful with the interpretation. The correlation of 0.759 indicates a strong positive association between the variables. Ms. Bancer would be correct to encourage the sales personnel to make those extra sales calls because the number of sales calls is related to the number of copiers sold. However, does this mean that more sales calls *cause* more sales? No, we have not demonstrated cause and effect here, only that the two variables—sales calls and copiers sold—are related.

excel

Computer commands to find the *p*-value for the above example can be found at the end of the chapter.

Correlation and Cause

If there is a strong relationship (say, $r^2 = 0.91$) between two variables, we are tempted to assume that an increase or decrease in one variable *causes* a change in the other variable. For example, it can be shown that the consumption of peanuts and the consumption of aspirin have a strong correlation. However, this does not indicate that an increase in the consumption of peanuts *caused* the consumption of aspirin to increase. Likewise, the incomes of professors and the number of inmates in mental institutions have increased proportionately. Further, as the population of donkeys has decreased, there has been an increase in the number of doctoral degrees granted. Relationships such as these are called **spurious correlations**. What we can conclude when we find two variables with a strong correlation is that there is a relationship between the two variables, not that a change in one causes a change in the other.

12.7 THE COEFFICIENT OF DETERMINATION

Coefficient of determination The proportion of the total variation in the dependent variable, *Y*, that is explained, or accounted for, by the variation in the independent variable, *X*.

In the previous example regarding the relationship between the number of sales calls and the units sold, the coefficient of correlation, 0.759, was interpreted as being "strong." Terms such as *weak, moderate,* and *strong,* however, do not have precise meaning. A measure that has a more easily interpreted meaning is the **coefficient of determination**. It is computed by squaring the correlation coefficient. In the example, the coefficient of determination, r^2, is 0.576, found by $(0.759)^2$. This is a proportion or a percentage; hence, we can say that 57.6% of the variation in the number of copiers sold is explained, or accounted for, by the variation in the number of sales calls.

Further discussion of the coefficient of determination is found later in the chapter.

self-review 12–5

Refer to self-review 12–1, where the owner of Reliable Furniture was studying the relationship between sales and the amount spent on advertising. The information on sales and advertising for the last four months is repeated below:

Month	Advertising Expense ($ millions)	Sales Revenue ($ millions)
July	$2	$7
August	1	3
September	3	8
October	4	10

(a) Determine the correlation coefficient.
(b) Interpret the strength of the correlation coefficient.
(c) Determine the coefficient of determination. Interpret.

EXERCISES

19. The Sally Coffee Shop is considering closing one hour earlier in the evening through the week. Sally obtained the following data from a study taken last week of the number of customers between the hours of 10 and 11 p.m., and the dollar value spent.

x:	4	5	3	6	10
y:	4	6	5	7	7

Determine the correlation coefficient and the coefficient of determination. Interpret.

20. The following sample observations were randomly selected:

x:	5	3	6	3	4	4	6	8
y:	13	15	7	12	13	11	9	5

Determine the correlation coefficient and the coefficient of determination. Interpret.

21. Bi-lo Appliance Super Store has outlets in several large Canadian cities. The general sales manager plans to air a commercial for a digital camera on selected TV stations prior to a sale starting on Saturday and ending Sunday. She plans to get the information for the Saturday–Sunday digital camera sales at the various outlets and pair them with the number of times the advertisement was shown on the local TV stations. The purpose is to find whether there is any relationship between the number of times the advertisement was aired and digital camera sales. The pairings are as follows:

Location of TV Station	Number of Airings	Sales ($ thousands)
Calgary	4	$15
Edmonton	2	8
Quebec City	5	21
Halifax	6	24
St John's	3	17

a. Determine the correlation coefficient.

b. Determine the coefficient of determination.

c. Interpret these statistical measures.

22. The production department of Celltronics International wants to explore the relationship between the number of employees who assemble a subassembly and the number produced. As an experiment, two employees were assigned to assemble the parts. They produced 15 during a one-hour period. Then, four employees assembled them. They produced 25 during a one-hour period. The complete set of paired observations follows:

Number of Assemblers	One-Hour Production (units)
2	15
4	25
1	10
5	40
3	30

The dependent variable is production; that is, it is assumed that the level of production depends on the number of employees.

a. Compute the correlation coefficient.

b. Evaluate the strength of the relationship by computing the coefficient of determination.

23. The city council of Pine Bluffs is considering increasing the number of police officers in an effort to reduce crime. Before making a final decision, the council asks the chief of police to survey other cities of similar size to determine the relationship between the number of police officers and the number of crimes reported. The chief gathered the following sample information:

City	Police Officers	Number of Crimes	City	Police Officers	Number of Crimes
Oxford	15	17	Holgate	17	7
Starksville	17	13	Carey	12	21
Danville	25	5	Whistler	11	19
Athens	27	7	Woodville	22	6

    a. Determine the correlation coefficient.

    b. Determine the coefficient of determination.

    c. Interpret these statistical measures. Does it surprise you that an inverse relationship exists?

24. The owner of Maumee Motors wants to study the relationship between the age of a car and its selling price. Listed below is a random sample of 12 used cars sold at Maumee Motors during the last year:

Car	Age (years)	Selling Price ($ thousands)	Car	Age (years)	Selling Price ($ thousands)
1	9	$8.1	7	8	$7.6
2	7	6.0	8	11	8.0
3	11	3.6	9	10	8.0
4	12	4.0	10	12	6.0
5	8	5.0	11	6	8.6
6	7	10.0	12	6	8.0

    a. Determine the correlation coefficient.

    b. Determine the coefficient of determination.

    c. Interpret these statistical measures. Does it surprise you that an inverse relationship exists?

LO12-5   12.8 TESTING THE SIGNIFICANCE OF THE CORRELATION COEFFICIENT

Recall that the sales manager of Copier Sales Inc. found the correlation between the number of sales calls and the number of copiers sold was 0.759. This indicated a strong positive association between the two variables. However, only 10 sales representatives were sampled. Could it be that the correlation in the population is actually 0? This would mean the correlation of 0.759 was due to chance. The population in this example is all the salespeople employed by the firm.

Resolving this dilemma requires a test to answer the question: could there be zero correlation in the population from which the sample was selected? To put it another way, did the computed r come from a population of paired observations with zero correlation? To continue our convention of allowing Greek letters to represent a population parameter, we will let ρ represent the correlation in the population. It is pronounced "rho."

We will continue with the example involving sales calls and copiers sold. We employ the same hypothesis testing steps described in previous chapters. The null hypothesis and the alternative hypothesis are:

H_0: $\rho = 0$ (The correlation in the population is zero.)
H_1: $\rho \neq 0$ (The correlation in the population is different from zero.)

From the way H_1 is stated, we know that the test is two-tailed. It is a t test. The formula for t is:

t TEST FOR THE CORRELATION COEFFICIENT	$t = \dfrac{r\sqrt{n-2}}{\sqrt{1-r^2}}$ with $n-2$ degrees of freedom [12–10]

Using the 0.05 level of significance, the decision rule in this instance states that if the computed t falls in the area between plus 2.306 and minus 2.306, the null hypothesis is not rejected. To locate the critical value of 2.306, refer to Appendix B.2 for $df = n - 2 = 10 - 2 = 8$. See Chart 12–15.

CHART 12–15 Decision Rule for Test of Hypothesis at 0.05 Significance Level and 8 df

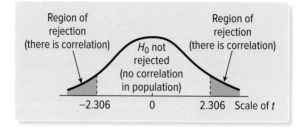

Applying formula (12–10) to the example regarding the number of sales calls and units sold:

$$t = \frac{r\sqrt{n-2}}{\sqrt{1-r^2}} = \frac{0.759\sqrt{10-2}}{\sqrt{1-0.759^2}} = 3.297$$

The computed t is in the rejection region. Thus, H_0 is rejected at the 0.05 significance level. Therefore, we conclude the correlation in the population is not zero. From a practical standpoint, it indicates to the sales manager that there is correlation with respect to the number of sales calls made and the number of copiers sold in the population of sales representatives.

We can also interpret the test of hypothesis in terms of p-values. A p-value is the likelihood of finding a value of the test statistic more extreme than the one computed, when H_0 is true. To determine the p-value, go to the t distribution in Appendix B.2, and find the row for 8 degrees of freedom. The value of the test statistic is 3.297, so in the row for 8 degrees of freedom and a two-tailed test, find the value closest to 3.297. For a two-tailed test at the 0.02 significance level, the critical value is 2.896, and the critical value at the 0.01 significance level is 3.355. Because 3.297 is between 2.896 and 3.355, we conclude that the p-value is between (0.01) and (0.02), which is less than the significance level of 0.05. Therefore, the test statistic lies in the rejection region.

Excel and **MegaStat** will report the correlation between two variables. In addition to the correlation, they also report the p-value for the test of hypothesis that the correlation in the population between the two variables is 0.

self-review 12–6

A sample of 25 mayoral campaigns in cities with populations larger than 50 000 showed that the correlation between the percent of the vote received and the amount spent on the campaign by the candidate was 0.43. At the 0.05 significance level, is there a positive association between the variables?

EXERCISES

25. The following hypotheses are given:

$$H_0: \rho \leq 0$$
$$H_1: \rho > 0$$

A random sample of 12 paired observations indicated a correlation of 0.32. Can we conclude that the correlation in the population is greater than zero? Use the 0.05 significance level.

26. The following hypotheses are given:

$$H_0: \rho \geq 0$$
$$H_1: \rho < 0$$

A random sample of 15 paired observations has a correlation of –0.46. Can we conclude that the correlation in the population is less than zero? Use the 0.05 significance level.

27. A refining company is studying the relationship between the pump price of gasoline and the number of litres sold. For a sample of 20 stations last Tuesday, the correlation was −0.78. At the 0.01 significance level, is the correlation in the population less than zero?

28. A study of 20 worldwide financial institutions showed the correlation between their assets and pretax profit to be 0.86. At the 0.05 significance level, can we conclude that there is positive correlation in the population?

29. The Airline Passenger Association studied the relationship between the number of passengers on a particular flight and the cost of the flight. It seems logical that more passengers being on the flight will result in more weight and more luggage, which, in turn, will result in higher fuel costs. For a sample of 15 flights, the correlation between the number of passengers and total fuel cost was 0.667. Is it reasonable to conclude that there is positive association in the population between the two variables? Use the 0.01 significance level.

30. The SU (Student Union) Association at a local college wanted to demonstrate the relationship between the numbers of beers a student drinks and their blood alcohol content (BAC). A random sample of 18 students participated in the study in which each participating student was randomly assigned a number of 341-millilitre (mL) cans of beer to drink. Thirty minutes after consuming their assigned number of beers, a member of the local sheriff's office measured their BAC. The sample information is reported below:

Student	Beers	BAC	Student	Beers	BAC
1	6	0.10	10	3	0.07
2	7	0.09	11	3	0.05
3	7	0.09	12	7	0.08
4	4	0.10	13	1	0.04
5	5	0.10	14	4	0.07
6	3	0.07	15	2	0.06
7	3	0.10	16	7	0.12
8	6	0.12	17	2	0.05
9	6	0.09	18	1	0.02

a. Develop a scatter diagram for the number of beers consumed and the BAC. Comment on the relationship. Does it appear to be strong or weak? Does it appear to be direct or inverse?

b. Determine the coefficient of correlation.

c. Determine the coefficient of determination.

d. At the 0.01 significance level, is it reasonable to conclude that there is a positive relationship in the population between the number of beers consumed and the BAC? What is the p-value?

12.9 MORE ON THE COEFFICIENT OF DETERMINATION

Earlier in the chapter, we defined the coefficient of determination as the percentage of the variation in the dependent variable that is accounted for by the independent variable. We indicated it is the square of the coefficient of correlation and that it is written r^2.

To further examine the basic concept of the coefficient of determination, suppose that there is interest in the relationship between years on the job, x, and weekly production, y. Sample data revealed the following:

Employee	Years on Job, x	Weekly Production, y
Gordon	14	6
James	7	5
Ford	3	3
Salter	15	9
Artes	11	7

The sample data were plotted in a scatter diagram. Since the relationship between x and y appears to be linear, a line was drawn through the points (Chart 12–16). The equation is $y' = 2 + 0.4x$.

CHART 12–16 Observed Data and the Least Squares Line

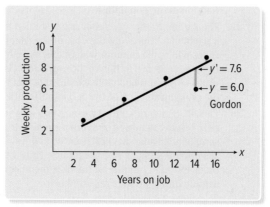

Note in Chart 12–16 that if we were to use that line to predict weekly production for an employee, in no case would our prediction be exact. That is, there would be some error in each of our predictions. As an example, for Gordon, who has been with the company 14 years, we would predict weekly production to be 7.6 units; however, he produces only 6 units.

To measure the overall error in our prediction, every deviation from the line is squared and the squares summed. The predicted point on the line is designated y', and the observed point is designated y. For Gordon, $(y - y')^2 = (6 - 7.6)^2 = (-1.6)^2 = 2.56$. Logically, **this variation cannot be explained by the independent variable, so it is referred to as the *unexplained variation*.** Specifically, we cannot explain why Gordon's production of 6 units is 1.6 units below his predicted production of 7.6 units, based on the number of years he has been on the job.

The sum of the squared deviations, $\Sigma(y - y')^2$, is 4.00. (See Table 12–7.) The term $\Sigma(y - y')^2 = 4.00$ is the variation in y (production) that cannot be predicted from x. It is the "unexplained" variation in y.

TABLE 12–7 Computations Needed for the Unexplained Variation and Explained Variation

	x	y	y'	$y - y'$	$(y - y')^2$	$y' - \bar{y}$	$(y' - \bar{y})^2$
Gordon	14	6	7.6	−1.6	2.56	1.6	2.56
James	7	5	4.8	0.2	0.04	−1.2	1.44
Ford	3	3	3.2	−0.2	0.04	−2.8	7.84
Salter	15	9	8.0	1.0	1.00	2.0	4.0
Artes	11	7	6.4	0.6	0.36	0.4	0.16
Total	50	30		0.0*	4.00	0.0	16.00

*Must be 0.

Now, suppose *only* the Y values (weekly production, in this problem) are known and we want to predict production for every employee. The actual production figures for the employees are 6, 5, 3, 9, and 7 (from Table 12–7). To make these predictions, we could assign the mean weekly production (6 units, found by: $\Sigma y/n = 30/5 = 6$) to each employee. This would keep the sum of the squared prediction errors at a minimum. (Recall from Chapter 3 that the sum of the squared deviations from the arithmetic mean for a set of numbers is smaller than the sum of the squared deviations from any other value, such as the median.) Table 12–8 shows the necessary calculations. The sum of the squared deviations is 20, as shown in Table 12–8. The value 20 is referred to as the *total variation in y*. What we did to arrive at the total variation in y is shown diagrammatically in Chart 12–17.

TABLE 12–8 Calculations Needed for the Total Variation in y

Name	Weekly Production, y	Mean Weekly Production	$y - \bar{y}$	$(y - \bar{y})^2$
Gordon	6	6	0	0
James	5	6	−1	1
Ford	3	6	−3	9
Salter	9	6	3	9
Artes	7	6	1	1
Total			0*	20

*Must be 0.

CHART 12–17 Plots Showing Deviations from the Mean of y

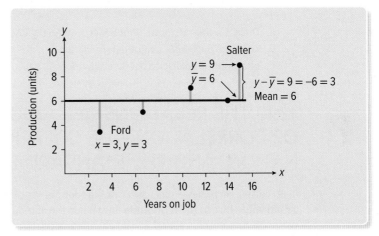

Logically, the total variation in y can be subdivided into unexplained variation and explained variation. To arrive at the explained variation, since we know the total variation and unexplained variation, we simply subtract: Explained variation = Total variation − Unexplained variation. Dividing the explained variation by the total variation gives the coefficient of determination, r^2, which is a proportion. In terms of a formula:

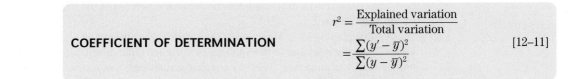

COEFFICIENT OF DETERMINATION
$$r^2 = \frac{\text{Explained variation}}{\text{Total variation}} = \frac{\sum(y' - \bar{y})^2}{\sum(y - \bar{y})^2} \qquad [12\text{–}11]$$

In this problem:

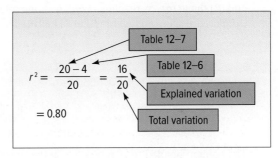

As mentioned, 0.80 is a proportion. We say that 80% of the variation in weekly production, y, is determined, or accounted for, by its linear relationship with x (years on the job).

As a check, the computational formula (12–9) for the coefficient of correlation could be used. Squaring r gives the coefficient of determination. Exercise 31 offers a check on the preceding problem.

EXERCISES

31. Using the preceding problem, involving years on the job and weekly production, verify that the coefficient of determination is, in fact, 0.80.

32. The number of shares of Icom Inc. turned over during a month and the prices at the end of the month are listed in the following table. Also, the y' values on the line going through observed data are given below:

Turnover (thousands of shares), x	Actual Price, y	Estimated Price, y'
4	$2	$2.7
1	1	0.6
5	4	3.4
3	2	2.0
2	1	1.3

a. Draw a scatter diagram. Plot a line through the dots.
b. Compute the coefficient of determination.
c. Interpret the coefficient of determination.

12.10 THE RELATIONSHIPS AMONG THE COEFFICIENT OF CORRELATION, THE COEFFICIENT OF DETERMINATION, AND THE STANDARD ERROR OF ESTIMATE

In an earlier section, we discussed the standard error of estimate, which measures how close the actual values are to the regression line. When the standard error is small, it indicates that the two variables are closely related. In the calculation of the standard error, the key term is $\Sigma(y - y')^2$. If the value of this term is small, then the standard error will also be small.

The correlation coefficient measures the strength of the association between two variables. When the points on the scatter diagram appear close to the line, we note that the correlation coefficient tends to be large. Therefore, the correlation coefficient and the standard error of estimate are inversely related. As the strength of a linear relationship between two variables increases, the correlation coefficient increases and the standard error of the estimate decreases.

We also noted that the square of the correlation coefficient is the coefficient of determination. The coefficient of determination measures the percent of the variation in Y that is explained by the variation in X.

A convenient vehicle for showing the relationship among these three measures is an ANOVA table. This table is similar to the analysis of variance table developed in Chapter 11. In that chapter, the total variation was divided into two components: that due to the *treatments* and that due to *random error*. The concept is similar in regression analysis. The total variation is divided into two components: (1) that explained by the *regression* (explained by the independent variable) and (2) the *error*, or residual—which is unexplained variation. These three sources of variance (total, regression, and residual) are identified in the first column of the ANOVA table below:

Source	df	SS	MS
Regression	1	SSR	SSR/1
Error	$n - 2$	SSE	SSE/$(n - 2)$
Total	$n - 1$	SST*	

*SST = SSR + SSE.

The column headed "df" refers to the degrees of freedom associated with each category. The total number of degrees of freedom is $n - 1$. The number of degrees of freedom in the regression is 1, since there is only one independent variable. The number of degrees of freedom associated with the error term is $n - 2$. The term "SS" located in the middle of the ANOVA table refers to the sum of squares—the variation. Note that the total degrees of freedom are equal to the sum of the regression and residual (error) degrees of freedom, and the total sum of squares is equal to the sum of the regression and residual (error) sum of squares. This is true for any ANOVA table. The terms are computed as follows:

$$\text{Regression} = \text{SSR} = \sum(y' - \bar{y})^2$$
$$\text{Residual or Error variation} = \text{SSE} = \sum(y - y')^2$$
$$\text{Total variation} = \text{SST} = \sum(y - \bar{y})^2$$

Recall that the coefficient of determination is defined as the percentage of the total variation (SST) explained by the regression equation (SSR). Hence, coefficient of determination, r^2, can be obtained directly from the ANOVA table by:

COEFFICIENT OF DETERMINATION	$r^2 = \dfrac{\text{SSR}}{\text{SST}} = 1 - \dfrac{\text{SSE}}{\text{SST}}$	[12–12]

The term "SSR/SST" is the proportion of the variation in Y *explained* by the independent variable, X. Note the effect of the SSE term on r^2. As SSE decreases, r^2 will increase. To put it another way, as the standard error increases, the r^2 term decreases.

The standard error of estimate can also be obtained from the ANOVA table using the following equation:

STANDARD ERROR OF ESTIMATE	$S_e = \sqrt{\dfrac{\text{SSE}}{n - 2}}$	[12–13]

The Copier Sales Inc. example below is used to illustrate the computations of the coefficient of determination and the standard error of estimate from an ANOVA table.

Example

In the Copier Sales Inc. example we studied the relationship between the number of sales calls made and the number of copiers sold. Use a computer software package to determine the least squares regression equation and the ANOVA table. Identify the regression equation, the standard error of estimate, and the coefficient of determination on the computer output. From the ANOVA table on the computer output, determine the coefficient of determination and the standard error of estimate using formulas (12–12) and (12–13).

Solution

The output from **Excel** is:

	A	B	C	D	E	F	G	H	I	J	K
1	**Sales Representative**	**Sales Calls**	**Units Sold**		SUMMARY OUTPUT						
2	Tom Keller	20	30								
3	Jeff Hall	40	60		*Regression Statistics*						
4	Brian Virost	20	40		Multiple R	0.759014109					
5	Greg Fish	30	60		R Square	0.576102418					
6	Susan Welch	10	30		Adjusted R Square	0.52311522					
7	Carlos Ramirez	10	40		Standard Error	9.900823995					
8	Rich Niles	20	40		Observations	10					
9	Mike Kiel	20	50								
10	Mark Reynolds	20	30		ANOVA						
11	Soni Jones	30	70			*df*	*SS*	*MS*	*F*	*Significance F*	
12					Regression	1	1065.789474	1065.789	10.87248	0.01090193	
13					Residual	8	784.2105263	98.02632			
14					Total	9	1850				
15											

Using formula (12–12) the coefficient of determination is 0.576, found by:

$$r^2 = \frac{\text{SSR}}{\text{SST}} = \frac{1066}{1850} = 0.576$$

This is the same value we computed earlier in the chapter, when we found the coefficient of determination by squaring the coefficient of correlation. Again, the interpretation is that the independent variable, *Calls*, explains 57.6% of the variation in the number of copiers sold. If we needed the coefficient of correlation, we could find it by taking the square root of the coefficient of determination:

$$r = \sqrt{r^2} = \sqrt{0.576} = 0.759$$

A problem does remain, and that involves the sign for the coefficient of correlation. Recall that the square root of a value could have either a positive or a negative sign. The sign of the coefficient of correlation will always be the same as that of the slope. That is, b and r will always have the same sign. In this case, the sign is positive, so the coefficient of correlation is 0.759.

To find the standard error of estimate, we use formula (12–13):

$$S_e = \sqrt{\frac{SSE}{n-2}} = \sqrt{\frac{784.2}{10-2}} = 9.901$$

Again, this is the same value calculated earlier in the chapter. These values are identified on the **Excel** output.

To summarize, regression analysis provides two statistics to evaluate the predictive ability of a regression equation: the standard error of the estimate and the coefficient of determination. When reporting the results of a regression analysis, the findings must be clearly explained, especially when using the results to make predictions of the dependent variable. The report must always include a statement regarding the coefficient of determination so that the relative precision of the prediction is known to the reader of the report.

excel

Computer commands to produce the ANOVA table for the above example can be found at the end of the chapter.

EXERCISES

33. Given the following ANOVA table:

SOURCE	df	SS	MS	F
Regression	1	1000.0	1000.00	26.00
Error	13	500.0	38.46	
Total	14	1500.0		

  a. Determine the coefficient of determination.
  b. Assuming a direct relationship between the variables, what is the coefficient of correlation?
  c. Determine the standard error of estimate.

34. On the first statistics exam, the coefficient of determination between the hours studied and the grade earned was 80%. The standard error of estimate was 10. There were 20 students in the class. Develop an ANOVA table.

35. Given the following sample observations, develop a scatter diagram:

x:	−8	−16	12	2	18
y:	58	247	153	3	341

  a. Does the relationship between the variables appear to be linear?
  b. Compute the coefficient of correlation.
  c. Determine the standard error of estimate.

36. According to basic economics, as the demand for a product increases, the price will decrease. Listed below is the number of units demanded and the price:

Demand	Price
2	$120
5	90
8	80
12	70
16	50
21	45
27	31
35	30
45	25
60	21

  a. Determine the correlation between price and demand. Plot the data in a scatter diagram. Does the relationship seem to be linear?
  b. Determine the standard error of estimate.

Chapter Summary

I. A scatter diagram is a graphical tool to portray the relationship between two variables.

    A. The dependent variable is scaled on the Y-axis and is the variable being estimated.

    B. The independent variable is scaled on the X-axis and is the variable used as the estimator.

II. In regression analysis we estimate one variable based on another variable.

    A. The variable being estimated is the dependent variable.

    B. The variable used to make the estimate is the independent variable.

        1. The relationship between the variables is linear.

        2. Both the independent and the dependent variable must be interval or ratio level.

        3. The least squares criterion is used to determine the regression equation.

III. The least squares regression line is of the form $y' = a + bx$.

    A. y' is the estimated value of y for a selected value of x.

    B. b is the slope of the fitted line.

        1. It shows the amount of change in y' for a change of one unit in x.

        2. A positive value for b indicates a direct relationship between two variables and a negative value an inverse relationship.

        3. The sign of b and the sign of r, the coefficient of correlation, are always the same.

        4. b is computed using the following equation:

$$b = \frac{n(\Sigma xy) - (\Sigma x)(\Sigma y)}{n(\Sigma x^2) - (\Sigma x)^2} \qquad \text{[12–2]}$$

    C. a is the constant or intercept.

        1. It is the value of y' when $x = 0$.

        2. a is computed using the following equation:

$$a = \frac{\Sigma y}{n} - b\frac{\Sigma x}{n} \qquad \text{[12–3]}$$

    D. x is the value of the independent variable.

IV. The standard error of estimate measures the variation around the regression line.

    A. It is in the same units as the dependent variable.

    B. It is based on squared deviations from the regression line.

    C. Small values indicate that the points cluster closely about the regression line.

    D. It is computed using the following formula:

$$S_e = \sqrt{\frac{\Sigma(y - y')^2}{n - 2}} = \sqrt{\frac{\Sigma y^2 - a(\Sigma y) - b(\Sigma xy)}{n - 2}} \qquad \text{[12–4, 12–5]}$$

V. Inference about linear regression is based on the following assumptions:

    A. For a given value of x, the values of y are normally distributed about the line of regression.

    B. The standard deviation of each of the normal distributions is the same for all values of x and is estimated by the standard error of estimate.

    C. The deviations from the regression line are independent, with no pattern to the size or direction.

VI. There are two types of interval estimates.

    A. In a confidence interval, the mean value of y is estimated for a given value of x.

        1. It is computed from the following formula:

$$y' \pm tS_e\sqrt{\frac{1}{n} + \frac{(x - \bar{x})^2}{\Sigma(x - \bar{x})^2}} \qquad \text{[12–6]}$$

        2. The width of the interval is affected by the level of confidence, the size of the standard error of estimate, and the size of the sample, as well as the value of the independent variable.

    B. In a prediction interval, the individual value of y is estimated for a given value of x.

        1. It is computed from the following formula:

$$y' \pm tS_e\sqrt{1 + \frac{1}{n} + \frac{(x - \bar{x})^2}{\Sigma(x - \bar{x})^2}} \qquad \text{[12–7]}$$

   2. The difference between formulas (12–6) and (12–7) is the 1 under the radical.

   a. The prediction interval will be wider than the confidence interval.

   b. The prediction interval is also based on the level of confidence, the size of the standard error of estimate, the size of the sample, and the value of the independent variable.

VII. The correlation coefficient measures the strength of the linear association between two variables.

   A. Both variables must be at least the interval level of measurement.

   B. The coefficient of correlation can range from -1.00 up to 1.00.

   C. If the correlation between two variables is 0, there is no association between them.

   D. A value of 1.00 indicates perfect positive correlation, and -1.00 perfect negative correlation.

   E. A positive sign means there is a direct relationship between the variables, and a negative sign means there is an inverse relationship.

   F. It is designated by the letter r and found by the following equations:

$$r = \frac{\Sigma(x - \bar{x})(y - \bar{y})}{(n-1)s_x s_y} = \frac{n(\Sigma xy) - (\Sigma x)(\Sigma y)}{\sqrt{[n(\Sigma x^2) - (\Sigma x)^2][n(\Sigma y^2) - (\Sigma y)^2]}} \qquad \text{[12–8, 12–9]}$$

   G. To test a hypothesis that a population correlation is different from 0, we use the following statistic:

$$t = \frac{r\sqrt{n-2}}{\sqrt{1 - r^2}} \qquad \text{[12–10]}$$

VIII. The coefficient of determination is the proportion of the variation of a dependent variable explained by the independent variable.

   A. It ranges from 0 to 1.0.

   B. It is the square of the correlation coefficient.

Chapter Exercises

37. A regional commuter airline selected a random sample of 25 flights and found that the correlation between the number of passengers and the total mass, in kilograms, of luggage stored in the luggage compartment is 0.94. Using the 0.05 significance level, can we conclude that there is a positive association between the two variables?

38. A sociologist claims that the success of students in college (measured by their grade point average [GPA]) is related to their family's income. For a sample of 20 students, the coefficient of correlation is 0.40. Using the 0.01 significance level, can we conclude that there is a positive correlation between the variables?

39. A Canadian Automobile Association (CAA) study of 12 automobiles revealed a correlation of 0.47 between the engine size and performance. At the 0.01 significance level, can we conclude that there is a positive association between these variables? What is the p-value? Interpret.

40. A study of college soccer games revealed the correlation between the number of shots attempted and the number of goals scored to be 0.21 for a sample of 20 games. Is it reasonable to conclude that there is a positive correlation between the two variables? Use the 0.05 significance level. Determine the p-value.

41. A sample of 30 used cars sold by Northcut Motors in 2009 revealed that the correlation between the selling price and the number of kilometres driven was -0.45. At the 0.05 significance level, can we conclude that there is a negative association in the population between the two variables?

42. A sample of 15 financial executives in the pharmaceutical industry revealed the correlation between the amount of fat (in grams) an executive consumed the previous day and that executive's cholesterol level; the correlation was 0.345.

   a. Does the cholesterol level in blood seem to increase in those who consumed more fat?

   b. How much of the variation in cholesterol level is accounted for by the number of fat grams consumed?

   c. At the 0.05 significance level, is it reasonable to conclude there is a positive association between fat consumed and the cholesterol level? What is the p-value?

43. A suburban hotel derives its gross income from its hotel and restaurant operations. The owners are interested in the relationship between the number of rooms occupied on a nightly basis and the revenue per day in the restaurant. Below is a sample of 25 days (Monday through Thursday) from last year showing the restaurant income at breakfast and number of rooms occupied:

Day	Income	Occupied	Day	Income	Occupied
1	$1452	23	14	$1425	27
2	1361	47	15	1445	34
3	1426	21	16	1439	15
4	1470	39	17	1348	19
5	1456	37	18	1450	38
6	1430	29	19	1431	44
7	1354	23	20	1446	47
8	1442	44	21	1485	43
9	1394	45	22	1405	38
10	1459	16	23	1461	51
11	1399	30	24	1490	61
12	1458	42	25	1426	39
13	1537	54			

a. Does the breakfast revenue seem to increase as the number of occupied rooms increases? Draw a scatter diagram to support your conclusions.

b. Determine the correlation coefficient between the two variables. Interpret the value.

c. Is it reasonable to conclude that there is a positive relationship between revenue and occupied rooms? Use the 0.10 significance level.

d. What percentage of the variation in revenue in the restaurant is accounted for by the number of rooms occupied?

44. Dr. Raymond Lim wants to investigate the relationship between stress and job satisfaction. To begin, he developed a profile for stress based on assigning points for significant events, such as the death of a spouse, a change in sleeping habits, a change in eating habits, and the addition of a family member. Job satisfaction was also based on points assigned for salary, ability to get along with co-workers, and the job environment. Dr. Lim sampled 25 workers in the technology sector and found that the correlation between stress and job satisfaction was −0.536.

a. Does job satisfaction seem to increase or decrease as stress increases?

b. How much of the variation in stress is accounted for by the variation in job satisfaction?

c. At the 0.05 significance level, is it reasonable to conclude there is negative association between stress and job satisfaction?

45. The following output shows the relationship between units sold and price:

Regression Analysis

ANOVA table

Source	SS	df	MS
Regression	3119.4256	1	3119.4256
Residual	840.5744	14	60.0410
Total	3960.0000	15	

Regression Output

Variables	Coefficients	Std. error	$t(df = 14)$
Intercept	51.0218	4.9740	10.258
Price	−0.5170	0.0717	−7.211

a. Does the number of units sold seem to increase as the price increases?

b. How much of the variation in the units sold is accounted for by price?

c. What is the correlation coefficient? Describe the type and the strength of the relationship between units sold and price.

d. What is the estimated number of units sold for a price of $10? Is this value reasonable?

46. The following output shows the relationship between the number of hours studied and the final grade in a statistics course:

Regression Analysis

ANOVA table

Source	SS	df	MS
Regression	1569.0299	1	1569.0299
Residual	1163.9701	14	83.1407
Total	2733.0000	15	

Regression Output

Variables	Coefficients	Std. error	$t(df = 14)$
Intercept	60.1418	4.06725	14.787
Hours of Study	4.3284	0.9964	4.344

a. Does the final grade seem to increase as the number of hours studied increases?

b. How much of the variation in the final grade is accounted for by the hours studied?

c. What is the correlation coefficient? Describe the type and the strength of the relationship between the final grade and hours studied.

d. What is the estimated final grade for five hours studied? Is this final grade reasonable?

47. What is the relationship between the amount spent per week on food and the size of the family? Do larger families spend more on food? A sample of 10 families revealed the following figures for family size and the amount spent on food per week:

Family Size	Amount Spent on Food ($)	Family Size	Amount Spent on Food ($)
3	$99	3	$111
6	104	4	74
5	151	4	91
6	129	5	119
6	142	3	91

a. Compute the correlation coefficient.

b. Determine the coefficient of determination.

c. Can we conclude that there is a positive association between the amount spent on food and the family size? Use the 0.05 significance level.

48. A sample of 12 condominiums sold last week is given below. Can we conclude that as the number of bedrooms increases, the selling price (reported in $ thousands) also increases?

Number of Bedrooms	Selling Price ($ thousands)	Number of Bedrooms	Selling Price ($ thousands)
3	$200	2	$210
3	210	3	185
2	205	1	205
4	220	2	175
2	180	2	170
3	205	1	195

a. Compute the correlation coefficient.

b. Determine the coefficient of determination.

c. Can we conclude that there is a positive association between the number of bedrooms and the selling price? Use the 0.05 significance level.

49. The manufacturer of Cardio Glide exercise equipment wants to study the relationship between the number of months since the glide was purchased and the length of time the equipment was used last week.

Person	Months Owned	Hours Exercised	Person	Months Owned	Hours Exercised
Rupple	12	4	Massa	2	8
Hall	2	10	Sass	8	3
Bennett	6	8	Karl	4	8
Longnecker	9	5	Malrooney	10	2
Phillips	7	5	Veights	5	5

    a. Plot the information on a scatter diagram. Let the hours of exercise be the dependent variable. Comment on the graph.

    b. Determine the correlation coefficient. Interpret.

    c. At the 0.01 significance level, can we conclude that there is a negative association between the variables?

50. The following regression equation was computed from a sample of 20 observations:

$$y' = 15 - 5x$$

SSE was found to be 100, and SS Total 400.

    a. Determine the standard error of estimate.

    b. Determine the coefficient of determination.

    c. Determine the correlation coefficient. (*Caution:* Watch the sign!)

51. An ANOVA table is given:

SOURCE	DF	SS	MS	F
Regression	1	50		
Error				
Total	24	500		

    a. Complete the ANOVA table.

    b. How large was the sample?

    c. Determine the standard error of estimate.

    d. Determine the coefficient of determination.

52. Following is a regression equation:

$$y' = 17.08 + 0.16x$$

This information is also available: $S_e = 4.05$, $\sum x = 210$, $\sum (x - \bar{x})^2 = 1030$, and $n = 5$.

    a. Estimate the value of y' when $x = 50$.

    b. Develop a 95% prediction interval for an individual value of y for $x = 50$.

53. The relationship between the number of bidders on a highway project and the winning (lowest) bid for the project has been studied. Of particular interest is whether the number of bidders increases or decreases the amount of the winning bid.

Project	Number of Bidders, x	Winning Bid ($ millions), y	Project	Number of Bidders, x	Winning Bid ($ millions), y
1	9	$5.1	9	6	$10.3
2	9	8.0	10	6	8.0
3	3	9.7	11	4	8.8
4	10	7.8	12	7	9.4
5	5	7.7	13	7	8.6
6	10	5.5	14	7	8.1
7	7	8.3	15	6	7.8
8	11	5.5			

    a. Determine the regression equation. Interpret the equation. Do more bidders tend to increase or decrease the amount of the winning bid?

    b. Estimate the amount of the winning bid if there were seven bidders.

    c. A new entrance is to be constructed onto the highway. There are seven bidders on the project. Develop a 95% prediction interval for the winning bid.

    d. Determine the coefficient of determination. Interpret its value.

54. Mr. William Profit is studying companies going public for the first time. He is particularly interested in the relationship between the size of the offering and the price per share. A sample of 15 companies that recently went public revealed the following information:

Company	Size ($ millions), x	Price per Share ($), y	Company	Size ($ millions), x	Price per Share ($), y
1	$9.0	$10.8	9	$160.7	$11.3
2	94.4	11.3	10	96.5	10.6
3	27.3	11.2	11	83.0	10.5
4	179.2	11.1	12	23.5	10.3
5	71.9	11.1	13	58.7	10.7
6	97.9	11.2	14	93.8	11.0
7	93.5	11.0	15	34.4	10.8
8	70.0	10.7			

a. Determine the regression equation.

b. Determine the coefficient of determination. Do you think Mr. Profit should be satisfied with using the size of the offering as the independent variable?

55. Below is information on the price per share and the dividend for a sample of 30 companies:

Company	Price per Share ($)	Dividend ($)	Company	Price per Share ($)	Dividend ($)
1	$20.00	$3.14	16	$57.06	$9.53
2	22.01	3.36	17	57.40	12.60
3	31.39	0.46	18	58.30	10.43
4	33.57	7.99	19	59.51	7.97
5	35.86	0.77	20	60.60	9.19
6	36.12	8.46	21	64.01	16.50
7	36.16	7.62	22	64.66	16.10
8	37.99	8.03	23	64.74	13.76
9	38.85	6.33	24	64.95	10.54
10	39.65	7.96	25	66.43	21.15
11	43.44	8.95	26	68.18	14.30
12	49.08	9.61	27	69.56	24.42
13	53.73	11.11	28	74.90	11.54
14	54.41	13.28	29	77.91	17.65
15	55.10	10.22	30	80.00	17.36

a. Calculate the regression equation using selling price based on the annual dividend. Interpret the slope value.

b. Determine the coefficient of determination. Interpret its value.

c. Determine the correlation coefficient. Can you conclude that it is greater than 0 using the 0.05 significance level?

56. A highway employee performed a regression analysis of the relationship between the number of construction work-zone fatalities and the number of unemployed people in a city. The regression equation is shown as: Fatalities = 12.7 + 0.000114 (Unemp), and some more of the output is as follows:

Predictor	Coef	SE Coef	T	P
Constant	12.726	8.115	1.57	0.134
Unemp	0.00011386	0.00002896	3.93	0.001

Analysis of Variance

Source	DF	SS	MS	F	P
Regression	1	10354	10354	15.46	0.001
Residual Error	18	12054	670		
Total	19	22408			

a. How many cities were in the sample?

b. Determine the standard error of estimate.

c. Determine the coefficient of determination.

d. Determine the correlation coefficient.

e. At the 0.05 significance level does the evidence suggest there is a positive association between fatalities and the number unemployed?

57. Regression analysis relating the current market value in dollars to the size of homes in Greene County has been developed. The computer output follows. The regression equation is shown as follows: Value = −37 186 + 65.0 Size.

Predictor	Coef	SE Coef	T	P
Constant	−37186	4629	−8.03	0.000
Size	64.993	3.047	21.33	0.000

Analysis of Variance

Source	DF	SS	MS	F	P
Regression	1	13548662082	13548662082	454.98	0.000
Residual Error	33	9826687392	29778406		
Total	34	14531349474			

a. How many homes were in the sample?

b. Compute the standard error of estimate.

c. Compute the coefficient of determination.

d. Compute the correlation coefficient.

e. At the 0.05 significance level does the evidence suggest a positive association between the market value of homes and the size of the home?

58. The Bardi Trucking Company makes deliveries from Manitoba to the Great Lakes region. Zack Bardi, the president, is studying the relationship between the distance a shipment must travel and the length of time, in days, it takes the shipment to arrive at its destination. To investigate, Zack selected a random sample of 20 shipments made last month. The results are as follows:

Distance (km)	Time (days)	Distance (km)	Time (days)
656	5	862	7
853	14	679	5
646	6	835	13
783	11	607	3
610	8	665	8
841	10	647	7
785	9	685	10
639	9	720	8
762	10	652	6
762	9	828	10

a. Draw a scatter diagram. On the basis of these data, does it appear that there is a relationship between how many kilometres a shipment has to go and the time it takes to arrive at its destination?

b. Determine the correlation coefficient. Can we conclude there is a positive correlation between distance and time? Use the 0.05 significance level.

c. Determine and interpret the coefficient of determination.

d. Determine the standard error of the estimate.

59. Super Markets is considering expanding into the Northwest Territories. Luann Miller, the director of planning, must present an analysis of the proposed expansion to the board of directors. As part of her proposal, she needs to include information on the amount people in the region spend per month on grocery items. She would also like to include information on the relationship between the amount spent for grocery items and income. She gathered the following data:

Monthly Amount ($)	Monthly Income ($)	Monthly Amount ($)	Monthly Income ($)
$555	$4388	$913	$6688
489	4558	918	6752
458	4793	710	6837
613	4856	1083	7242
647	4856	937	7263
661	4899	839	7540
662	4899	1030	8009
675	5091	1065	8094
549	5133	1069	8264
606	5304	1064	8392
668	5304	1015	8414
740	5304	1148	8882
592	5346	1125	8925
720	5495	1090	8989
680	5581	1208	9053
540	5730	1217	9138
693	5943	1140	9329
541	5943	1265	9649
673	6156	1206	9862
676	6603	1145	9880

a. Create a scatter diagram.

b. Determine the regression equation. Interpret the slope value.

c. Determine the correlation coefficient. Interpret your findings.

d. On the basis of these data, would you recommend the expansion? Explain.

60. A dog trainer is exploring the relationship between the size of the dog (weight in kilometres [km]) and its daily food consumption (measured in cups). Below is the result of a sample of 18 observations:

Km	Cups	Km	Cups	Km	Cups
41	3	37	3	49	3
148	8	111	6	113	6
79	5	41	3	84	5
41	4	91	5	95	5
85	5	109	6	57	4
111	6	207	10	168	9

a. Compute the correlation coefficient. Is it reasonable to conclude that the correlation in the population is greater than zero? Use the 0.05 significance level.

b. Develop the regression equation for cups on the basis of the dog's weight. How much does each additional cup change the estimated weight of the dog?

61. Waterbury Insurance Company wants to study the relationship between the amount of fire damage and the distance between the burning house and the nearest fire station. This information will be used in setting rates for insurance coverage. For a sample of 30 claims for the last year, the director of the actuarial department determined the distance from the fire station (x) and the amount of fire damage, in thousands of dollars (y). The computer output is as follows:

ANOVA table				
Source	SS	df	MS	F
Regression	1,864.5782	1	1,864.5782	38.83
Residual	1,344.4934	28	48.0176	
Total	3,209.0716	29		

Regression output				
Variables	Coefficients	Std. Error	t(df = 28)	
Intercept	12.3601	3.2915	3.755	
Distance–X	4.7956	0.7696	6.231	

   a. Write out the regression equation. Is there a direct or indirect relationship between the distance from the fire station and the amount of fire damage?
   b. How much damage would you estimate for a fire 5 km from the nearest fire station?
   c. Determine and interpret the coefficient of determination.
   d. Determine the correlation coefficient. Interpret its value. How did you determine the sign of the correlation coefficient?
   e. Conduct a test of hypothesis to determine if there is a significant relationship between the distance from the fire station and the amount of damage. Use the 0.01 significance level and a two-tailed test.

62. The following table shows the mean annual percentage return on capital (profitability) and the mean annual percentage sales growth for eight aerospace and defence companies:

Company	Profitability	Growth
Alliant Techsystems	23.10	8.00
Boeing	13.20	15.60
General Dynamics	24.20	31.20
Honeywell	11.10	2.50
L-3 Communications	10.10	35.40
Northrop Grunmman	10.80	6.00
Rockwell Collins	27.30	8.70
United Technologies	20.10	3.20

   a. Compute the correlation coefficient. Conduct a test of hypothesis to determine if it is reasonable to conclude that the population correlation is greater than zero. Use the 0.05 significance level.
   b. Develop the regression equation for profitability based on growth. Can we conclude that the slope of the regression line is negative?

63. The following data show the retail price for 12 randomly selected laptop computers along with their corresponding processor speeds in gigahertz:

Computer	Speed	Price
1	2.0	$2017
2	1.6	922
3	1.6	1064
4	1.8	1942
5	2.0	2137
6	1.2	1012
7	2.0	2197
8	1.6	1387
9	2.0	2114
10	1.6	2002
11	1.0	937
12	1.4	869

   a. Develop a linear equation that can be used to describe how the price depends on the processor speed.
   b. Compute the correlation coefficient between the two variables. At the 0.05 significance level, conduct a test of hypothesis to determine if the population correlation is greater than zero.

64. A consumer buying cooperative tested the effective heating area of 20 different electric space heaters with different wattages. Here are the results:

Heater	Wattage	Area
1	1500	205
2	750	70
3	1500	199
4	1250	151
5	1250	181
6	1250	217
7	1000	94
8	2000	298
9	1000	135
10	1500	211
11	1250	116
12	500	72
13	500	82
14	1500	206
15	2000	245
16	1500	219
17	750	63
18	1500	200
19	1250	151
20	500	44

a. Compute the correlation between the wattage and heating area. Is there a direct or an indirect relationship?

b. Conduct a test of hypothesis to determine if it is reasonable that the coefficient is greater than zero. Use the 0.05 significance level.

c. Develop the regression equation for effective heating based on wattage.

65. An air travel service samples domestic airline flights to explore the relationship between airfare and distance. The service would like to know if there is a correlation between airfare and flight distance. If there is a correlation, what percentage of the variation in airfare is accounted for by distance? How much does each additional mile add to the fare? The data are as follows:

Distance	636	2395	2176	605	403	1258	264	627	2342	177	2521	1050
Fare	$109	252	221	151	138	209	254	259	215	128	348	224

a. Draw a scatter diagram with *Distance* as the independent variable and *Fare* as the dependent variable. Is the relationship direct or indirect?

b. Compute the correlation coefficient. At the 0.05 significance level, is it reasonable to conclude that the correlation coefficient is greater than zero?

c. What percentage of the variation in *Fare* is accounted for by *Distance* of a flight?

d. Determine the regression equation. How much does each additional mile add to the fare? Estimate the fare for a 1500-mile flight.

e. A traveller is planning to fly from Atlanta to London (Heathrow). The distance is 4218 miles. She wants to use the regression equation to estimate the fare. Explain why it would not be a good idea to estimate the fare for this international flight with the regression equation.

66. For a sample of 32 large cities, the correlation between the mean number of square feet per office worker and the mean monthly rental rate in the central business district is –0.363. At the 0.05 significance level, can we conclude that there is a negative association in the population between the two variables?

67. Meryl's Apparel is an upscale chain of women's clothing stores. Due to recent success, Meryl's top management is planning to expand by locating new stores in other regions of the country. The director of planning has been asked to study the relationship between yearly sales and the store size. As part of the study, the director selects a sample of 13 stores and determines the size of the store in square feet and the sales for last year. The sample data are as follows:

Square Feet (000)	Sales (millions $)
3.7	9.18
2.0	4.58
5.0	8.22
0.7	1.45
2.6	6.51
2.9	2.82
5.2	10.45
5.9	9.94
3.0	4.43
2.4	4.75
2.4	7.30
0.5	3.33
5.0	6.76

  a. Draw a scatter diagram. Use store size as the independent variable. Does there appear to be a relationship between the two variables? Is it positive or negative?
  b. Determine the correlation coefficient and the coefficient of determination. Is the relationship strong or weak? Explain your reasoning?
  c. At the 0.05 significance level, can we conclude there is a significant positive correlation?

68. City planners believe that larger cities are populated by older residents. To investigate the relationship, data on population and median age in 10 large cities were collected.

Population (in thousands)	Median Age
2.833	31.5
1.233	30.5
2.144	30.9
3.849	31.6
8.214	34.2
1.448	34.2
1.513	30.7
1.297	31.7
1.257	32.5
0.930	32.6

  a. Plot this data on a scatter diagram with median age as the dependent variable.
  b. Find the correlation coefficient.
  c. A regression analysis was performed and the resulting regression equation is: Median age $= 31.4 + 0.272$ population. Interpret the meaning of the slope.
  d. Estimate the median age for a city of 250 000 people.
  e. Here is a portion of the regression software output. What does it tell you?

Predictor	Coef	SE Coef	T	P
Constant	31.3672	0.61585	0.940	0.000
Population	0.2722	0.1901	1.430	0.190

69. Emily Smith decides to buy a fuel-efficient used car. Here are several vehicles she is considering, with the estimated cost to purchase and the age of the vehicle:

Vehicle	Estimated Cost	Age
Honda Insight	$5 555	8
Toyota Prius	17 888	3
Toyota Prius	9 963	6
Toyota Echo	6 793	5
Honda Civic Hybrid	10 774	5
Honda Civic Hybrid	16 310	2
Chevrolet Prizm	2 475	8
Mazda Protege	2 808	10
Toyota Corolla	7 073	9
Acura Integra	8 978	8
Scion xB	11 213	2
Scion xA	9463	3
Mazda3	15 055	2
Mini Cooper	20 705	2

a. Plot these data on a scatter diagram, with estimated cost as the dependent variable.

b. Find the correlation coefficient.

c. A regression analysis was performed and the resulting regression equation is: Estimated cost = 18358 − 1534 age. Interpret the meaning of the slope.

d. Estimate the cost of a five-year-old car.

e. Here is a portion of the regression software output. What does it tell you?

Predictor	Coef	SE Coef	T	P
Constant	18358	1817	10.100	0.000
Age	−1533.6	306.3	−5.010	0.000

Data Set Exercises

Questions marked with ⚡ have data sets available on McGraw-Hill's online resource for *Basic Statistics*.

70. Refer to the Real Estate Data—Halifax Area online, which reports information on home listings.
   a. Let list price be the dependent variable and size (square feet) of the home the independent variable. Determine the regression equation. Estimate the list price for a home with an area of 2200 square feet. Determine the 95% confidence interval and the 95% prediction interval for the list price of a home with 2200 square feet.
   b. Let list price be the dependent variable and number of bedrooms the independent variable. Determine the regression equation. Estimate the list price of a house with three bedrooms. Determine the 95% confidence interval and the 95% prediction interval for a house with three bedrooms.
   c. Can you conclude that the independent variables "number of bedrooms" and "list price" are positively correlated and that the size of the home and the list price are also positively correlated? Use the 0.05 significance level. Determine the p-value of the test.

71. Refer to the Real Estate Data—Saskatoon online, which reports information on home listings.
   a. Let list price be the dependent variable and size (square feet) of the home the independent variable. Determine the regression equation. Estimate the list price for a home with an area of 2000 square feet. Determine the 95% confidence interval and the 95% prediction interval for the list price of a home with 2000 square feet.
   b. Let list price be the dependent variable and number of bedrooms the independent variable. Determine the regression equation. Estimate the list price of a house with four bedrooms. Determine the 95% confidence interval and the 95% prediction interval for a house with four bedrooms.
   c. Can you conclude that the independent variables "number of bedrooms" and "list price" are positively correlated and that the size of the home and the list price are also positively correlated? Use the 0.05 significance level. Determine the p-value of the test.

Practice Test

Part I Objective

1. The first step in correlation analysis is to plot the data in a _____.

2. The range of the coefficient of correlation is between _____.

3. In studying the relationship between two variables, if the value of one variable decreases with increases in the other variable, the coefficient of correlation is _____. (less than zero, zero, greater than zero)

4. The proportion of total variation in the dependent variable that is explained by the variation in the independent variable is measured by the _____.

5. To test the hypothesis that the coefficient of correlation is zero, the test statistic is the _____ distribution.

6. The least squares regression line minimizes the sum of the squared differences between the actual value of the dependent variable and the _____ value.

7. For a given set of data, the coefficient of correlation and the slope of the regression line have the same _____ values, signs, units, squares).

8. For a regression analysis, a small standard error of the estimate indicates that the coefficient of determination will be _____. (large, small, always 0)

9. In regression analysis, confidence and prediction intervals show the _____ associated with an estimated value of the dependent variable. (error, association, convergence, sample size)

10. A prediction interval is based on an individual value of the _____ variable. (dependent, independent, correlated, estimated)

Part II Problems

1. Quick-print firms in urban centres spend most of their advertising dollars on displays on transit benches. A research project involves predicting monthly sales on the basis of the annual amount spent on placing ads on these benches. A sample of quick-print firms revealed the following information:

Company	Annual Advertising ($000)	Monthly Sales ($000)
A	2	10
B	4	40
C	5	30
D	7	50
E	3	20

   a. Draw a scatter diagram.
   b. Compute the coefficient of correlation.
   c. Compute the coefficient of determination.
   d. Compute the regression equation.
   e. On the basis of the regression equation, will an increase in advertising result in an increase or decrease in monthly sales?
   f. How much will an additional $1000 in annual transit bench advertising increase/decrease monthly sales?
   g. Estimate the monthly sales of a quick-print firm that spends nothing on transit bench advertising.
   h. Estimate the monthly sales of a quick-print firm that spends $4500 on transit bench advertising.

Computer Commands

For the Copier Sales Inc. example, enter the data into a spreadsheet as shown:

	A	B	C
1	**Sales Representative**	**Sales Calls**	**Units Sold**
2	Tom Keller	20	30
3	Jeff Hall	40	60
4	Brian Virost	20	40
5	Greg Fish	30	60
6	Susan Welch	10	30
7	Carlos Ramirez	10	40
8	Rich Niles	20	40
9	Mike Kiel	20	50
10	Mark Reynolds	20	30
11	Soni Jones	30	70

1. **Excel** steps to find the slope and intercept for the Copier Sales Inc. example are as follows:

   a. In an **Excel** spreadsheet, enter the data as shown. In cell A13, enter *Slope*. Click B13 to make it the active cell.

   b. Select **Insert Function** and from the **Or select a category** list, select **Statistical**. From the **Select a function** list, select **Slope**. Click **OK**.

   c. Enter *C1:C11* as the **Known_y's** range and *B1:B11* for the **Known_x's** range. Click **OK**. The value of the slope will be in the active cell, B13.

Function Arguments

SLOPE

Known_y's	C1:C11	= {"Units Sold";30;60;40;60;30;40;40;...
Known_x's	B1:B11	= {"Sales Calls";20;40;20;30;10;10;20;...

= 1.184210526

Returns the slope of the linear regression line through the given data points.

Known_x's is the set of independent data points and can be numbers or names, arrays, or references that contain numbers.

Formula result = 1.184210526

Help on this function   OK   Cancel

   d. In cell *A14* enter *Intercept*. Click B14 to make it the active cell.

   e. From the **Select a function** list, select **Intercept**. Click **OK**. Enter *C1:C11* as the **Known_y's** range and *B1:B11* for the **Known_x's** range. Click **OK**. The value of the intercept will be in the active cell, B14.

Function Arguments

INTERCEPT

Known_y's	C1:C11	= {"Units Sold";30;60;40;60;30;40;40;...
Known_x's	B1:B11	= {"Sales Calls";20;40;20;30;10;10;20;...

= 18.94736842

Calculates the point at which a line will intersect the y-axis by using a best-fit regression line plotted through the known x-values and y-values.

Known_x's is the independent set of observations or data and can be numbers or names, arrays, or references that contain numbers.

Formula result = 18.94736842

Help on this function   OK   Cancel

2. **Excel** steps to create the scatter plot and regression equation for the Copier Sales Inc. example are as follows:

   a. In an **Excel** spreadsheet, enter the data as shown.

   b. Select the range *B1:C11*. Select **INSERT**, and in the Recommended Charts section, click **Insert Scatter (x, y)**. and **Scatter with Straight Lines and Markers.**

   c. Right click any marker, and select **Add Trendline**. Select **Linear** and check **Display Equation on chart**. Click **Close**. Add/edit the titles. Move the equation to the top or side.

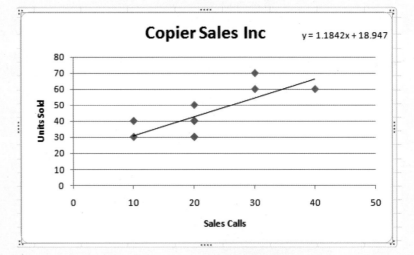

3. **MegaStat** steps to create the scatter plot and regression equation for the Copier Sales Inc. example are as follows:

   a. In an **Excel** spreadsheet, enter the data as shown.

   b. Select **MegaStat**, and **Correlation/Regression** and **Scatterplot**.

   c. Under **Input range** enter *B1:B11* for the **horizontal axis** *and C1:C11* for the **vertical axis.** Enter *Copier Sales Inc.* in the **chart title** box. Check **Plot linear regression line**, and select **Markers.** Click **OK.**

Scatterplot

Input ranges:

'Copier Sales'!$B$1:$B$11 — horizontal axis

'Copier Sales'!$C$1:$C$11 — vertical axis

Copier Sales Inc — chart title

OK   Clear   Cancel   Help

☑ Plot linear regression line   ☐ Force zero intercept

Display:

⦿ Markers   ○ Markers and lines   ○ Lines only

4. **Excel** steps to create the regression statistics for the Copier Sales Inc. example are as follows:

   a. In an **Excel** spreadsheet, enter the data as shown.

   b. Select **Data Analysis** and **Regression.** Click **OK.**

   c. Under **Input,** enter *C1:C11* as the **Input Y Range** and *B1:B11* **as** the **Input X Range.** Check **Labels**, and select the **Output Range** as B19; click **OK.**

5. **Excel** steps to create the output needed to calculate the correlation coefficient for the Copier Sales Inc. example are as follows:

   a. In an **Excel** spreadsheet, enter the data as shown.

   b. Select **Data Analysis** and **Descriptive Statistics.** Click **OK.**

   c. Under **Input,** enter *B1:C11* as the **Input Range** and select **Grouped By Columns.** Check **Labels in First Row**, and select the **Output Range** as J1. Check **Summary statistics**, and click **OK.**

Regression

Input

Input Y Range: $C$1:$C$11

Input X Range: $B$1:$B$11

☑ Labels   ☐ Constant is Zero

☐ Confidence Level: 95 %

OK   Cancel   Help

Output options

⦿ Output Range: $B$19

○ New Worksheet Ply:

○ New Workbook

Residuals

☐ Residuals   ☐ Residual Plots

☐ Standardized Residuals   ☐ Line Fit Plots

Normal Probability

☐ Normal Probability Plots

Descriptive Statistics

Input

Input Range: $B$1:$C$11

Grouped By: ⦿ Columns   ○ Rows

☑ Labels in first row

OK   Cancel   Help

Output options

⦿ Output Range: $J$1

○ New Worksheet Ply:

○ New Workbook

☑ Summary statistics

☐ Confidence Level for Mean: 95 %

☐ Kth Largest: 1

☐ Kth Smallest: 1

Note: you can also use **Excel's** CORREL function to find the correlation coefficient as follows:

Function Arguments

CORREL

Array1   B1:B11   = {"Sales Calls";20;40;20;30;10;10;20;...

Array2   C1:C11   = {"Units Sold";30;60;40;60;30;40;40;...

= 0.759014109

Returns the correlation coefficient between two data sets.

              Array2   is a second cell range of values. The values should be numbers, names, arrays, or references that contain numbers.

Formula result =   0.759014109

Help on this function   OK   Cancel

6. **MegaStat** steps to find the correlation coefficient for the Copier Sales Inc. example are as follows:

    a. In an **Excel** spreadsheet, enter the data as shown.

b. Select **MegaStat**, **Correlation/Regression** and **Correlation Matrix**.

c. Enter *B1:C11* for the **Input range**, and click **OK.** The result is 0.759.

Correlation Matrix

'Copier Sales'!$B$1:$C$11   Input range   OK

Clear

Cancel

Help

7. **MegaStat** steps to find the *p*-value for the Copier Sales Inc. example are as follows:

    a. In an **Excel** spreadsheet, enter the data as shown.

    b. Select **MegaStat**, and **Correlation/Regression** and **Regression Analysis.**

c. Under **Input ranges** enter *B1:B11* for **X, Independent variable(s)** and *C1:C11* for **Y, Dependent variable.** Remove the check beside **Test Intercept.** Click **OK.** The *p*-value will be on the output sheet.

Regression Analysis

Input ranges:

'Copier Sales'!$B$1:$B$11   X, Independent variable(s)   OK

'Copier Sales'!$C$1:$C$11   Y, Dependent variable   Clear

No predictions   Cancel

                          predictor values   Help

Options

95%   Confidence Level

☐ Variance Inflation Factors

☐ Standardized Coefficients (betas)

☐ Test Intercept   ☐ Force Zero Intercept

☐ All Possible Regressions

☐ Stepwise Selection   1 best model of each size

Residuals:

☐ Output Residuals

☐ Diagnostics and Influential Residuals

☐ Durbin-Watson   ☐ Cook's D

☐ Plot Residuals by Observation

☐ Plot Residuals by Predicted Y and X

☐ Normal Probabilty Plot of Residuals

8. **Excel** steps to find the p-value for the Copier Sales Inc. example, see 4 above. The p-value is part of the output as follows:

ANOVA

	DF	SS	MS	F	Significance F
Regression	1	1065.789474	1065.789	10.87248	0.01090193

Answers to Self-Reviews

12–1 **(a)** Advertising expense is the independent variable, and sales revenue is the dependent variable.

(b)

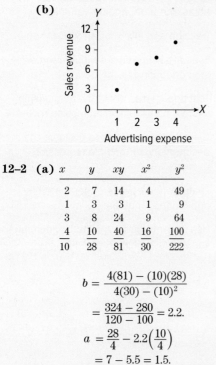

12–2 **(a)**

x	y	xy	x^2	y^2
2	7	14	4	49
1	3	3	1	9
3	8	24	9	64
4	10	40	16	100
10	28	81	30	222

$$b = \frac{4(81) - (10)(28)}{4(30) - (10)^2}$$

$$= \frac{324 - 280}{120 - 100} = 2.2.$$

$$a = \frac{28}{4} - 2.2\left(\frac{10}{4}\right)$$

$$= 7 - 5.5 = 1.5.$$

(b) The slope is 2.2. This indicates that an increase of $1 million in advertising will result in an increase of $2.2 million in sales. The intercept is 1.5. If there was no expenditure for advertising, sales would be $1.5 million.

(c) $y' = 1.5 + 2.2(3) = 8.1$.

12–3 0.9487, found by:

$$S_e = \sqrt{\frac{\Sigma y^2 - a(\Sigma y) - b(\Sigma xy)}{n - 2}}$$

$$= \sqrt{\frac{222 - 1.5(28) - 2.2(81)}{4 - 2}}$$

$$= \sqrt{\frac{1.8}{2}} = 0.9487.$$

12–4 6.58 and 9.62, since y' for an x of 3 is 8.1, found by: $y' = 1.5 + 2.2(3) = 8.1$, then $\bar{x} = 2.5$ and $\Sigma x^2 = 30$ and $\Sigma x = 10$.

t from Appendix B.2 for $4 - 2 = 2$ degrees of freedom at the 0.10 level is 2.920.

$$y' \pm tS_e\sqrt{\frac{1}{n} + \frac{(x - \bar{x})^2}{\Sigma(x - \bar{x})^2}}$$

$$= 8.1 \pm 2.920(0.9487)\sqrt{\frac{1}{4} + \frac{(3 - 2.5)^2}{5}}$$

$$= 8.1 \pm 2.920(0.9487)(0.5477)$$

$$= 6.58 \text{ and } 9.62 \text{ (in \$ millions)}.$$

12–5 See the calculations from self-review 12–2, part (a).

(a) $r = 0.96$, found by:

$$r = \frac{4(81) - (10)(28)}{\sqrt{[4(30) - (10)^2][4(222) - (28)^2]}}$$

$$= \frac{44}{\sqrt{2080}} = \frac{44}{45.607017} = 0.9648.$$

(b) There is a strong correlation between the advertising expense and sales.

(c) $r^2 = 0.93$, 93% of the variation in sales is "explained" by variation in advertising.

12–6 $H_0: \rho \leq 0, H_1: \rho > 0$. H_0 is rejected if $t > 1.714$.

$$t = \frac{0.43\sqrt{25 - 2}}{\sqrt{1 - (0.43)^2}} = 2.284.$$

H_0 is rejected. There is a positive correlation between the percentage of the vote received and the amount spent on the campaign.

The mortgage department of a financial institution is studying its recent loans. A random sample of 25 recent loans is obtained and searched for such factors as the value of the home, education level of borrower, age, monthly mortgage payment, and gender relate to the family income. Are these variables effective predictors of the income of the household? (Exercise 24, LO13-1)

LEARNING OBJECTIVES

When you have completed this chapter, you will be able to:

LO13-1 Use multiple regression analysis to describe and interpret a relationship between several independent variables and a dependent variable.

LO13-2 Develop and interpret an ANOVA table.

LO13-3 Evaluate how well a multiple regression equation fits the data.

LO13-4 Test hypotheses about the relationship inferred by a multiple regression model.

LO13-5 Use residual analysis to evaluate the assumptions of multiple regression analysis.

LO13-6 Evaluate the effects of correlated independent variables.

LO13-7 Use and interpret a qualitative, dummy variable in multiple regression.

13.1 INTRODUCTION

In Chapter 12, we described the relationship between a pair of interval-level or ratio-level variables. We began the chapter by developing a procedure to determine a linear equation to express the relationship between two variables. We referred to this as a *regression equation*. This equation describes the relationship between the variables. It also describes the overall pattern of a dependent variable (y) to a single independent variable (x). Next, we studied the correlation coefficient, which measures the strength of the linear relationship between two variables. A coefficient near plus or minus 1.00 (e.g., -0.88 or 0.78) indicates a very strong linear relationship, whereas a value near 0 (e.g., -0.12 or 0.18) means that the relationship is weak.

In multiple linear correlation and regression, we use additional independent variables (denoted x_1, x_2, etc.), which help us better explain or predict the dependent variable (y). Almost all of the ideas we saw in simple linear correlation and regression extend to this more general situation. However, the additional independent variables do lead to some new considerations. Multiple regression analysis can be used either as a descriptive technique or as an inferential technique.

LO13-1 13.2 MULTIPLE REGRESSION ANALYSIS

The general descriptive form of a multiple linear equation is shown in formula (13–1). We use k to represent the number of independent variables. So, k can be any positive integer.

GENERAL MULTIPLE REGRESSION EQUATION	$y' = a + b_1 x_1 + b_2 x_2 + \cdots + b_k x_k$	[13–1]

where:

a is the y-intercept, the value of y' when all the X-values are zero.

b_j is the amount by which y' changes when that particular x_j increases by one unit, with the values of all other independent variables held constant. The subscript j is simply a label that helps identify each independent variable; it is not used in any calculations. Usually, the subscript is an integer value between 1 and k, which is the number of independent variables. However, the subscript can also be a short or abbreviated label. For example, age could be used as a subscript.

In Chapter 12, the regression analysis described and tested the relationship between a dependent variable, y', and a single independent variable, x. The relationship between y' and x was graphically portrayed by a line. When there are two independent variables, the regression equation is:

$$y' = a + b_1 x_1 + b_2 x_2$$

Because there are two independent variables, this relationship is graphically portrayed as a plane and is shown in Chart 13–1. This chart shows the residuals as the difference between the actual y and the fitted y' on the plane. If a multiple regression analysis includes more than two independent variables, we cannot use a graph to illustrate the analysis, since graphs are limited to three dimensions.

CHART 13–1 Regression Plane with 10 Sample Points

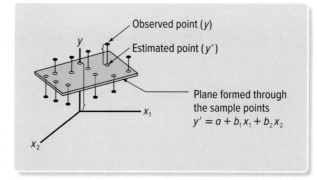

To illustrate the interpretation of the intercept and the two regression coefficients, suppose the selling price of a home is directly related to the number of rooms and inversely related to its age. We let x_1 refer to the number of rooms, x_2 to the age of the home in years, and y to the selling price of the home in \$000. Suppose the regression equation, calculated using statistical software, is:

$$y' = 21.2 + 18.7x_1 - 0.25x_2$$

The intercept, 21.2, indicates the regression equation intersects the y-axis at 21.2. This happens when both the number of rooms and the age of the home are zero. We could say that \$21 200 is the average value of a property without a house. Of course, it does not make any sense to own a house with zero rooms and a zero age. It is important to keep in mind that a regression equation is not generally used outside the range of the sample values.

The first regression coefficient, 18.7, indicates that for each increase of one room in the size of a home, the selling price will increase by 18.7 (\$18 700) *regardless of the age of the home.*

The second regression coefficient, −0.25, indicates that for each increase of one year in age, the selling price will decrease by 0.25 ($250), *regardless of the number of rooms.* As an example, a seven-room home that is 30 years old will sell for $144 600, found by:

$$y' = 21.2 + 18.7x_1 - 0.25x_2 = 21.2 + 18.7(7) - 0.25(30) = 144.6$$

The values for the coefficients in the multiple linear equation are found by using the method of least squares. Recall from the previous chapter that the least squares method makes the sum of the squared differences between the fitted and actual values of y as small as possible; that is, the term $\sum(y - y')^2$ is minimized. The calculations are very tedious, even using a calculator. As an example, for two independent variables, three equations must be solved simultaneously, namely:

$$\sum y = na + b_1 \sum x_1 + b_2 \sum x_2$$
$$\sum x_1 y = a \sum x_1 + b_1 \sum x_1^2 + b_2 \sum x_1 x_2$$
$$\sum x_2 y = a \sum x_2 + b_1 \sum x_1 x_2 + b_2 \sum x_2^2$$

As the calculations are so tedious, they are usually performed by a statistical software package, such as **Excel, Minitab,** or **MegaStat.**

In the following example, we show a multiple regression analysis using three independent variables and use a statistical software package to produce the results.

Example

Superior Realty sells homes in Eastern Canada. One of the questions most frequently asked by prospective buyers is: if we purchase this home, how much can we expect to pay to heat it during the winter? The research department at Superior has been asked to develop some guidelines regarding heating costs for single-family homes. Three variables are thought to relate to the heating costs: (1) the mean daily outside temperature (in degrees Celsius [°C]), (2) insulation (in centimetres [cm]) in the attic, and (3) the age of the furnace (in years). To investigate, Superior's research department selected a random sample of 20 recently sold homes. They determined the cost to heat the home last January, as well as the January outside temperature in the region, insulation in the attic, and the age of the furnace. The sample information is reported in Table 13–1.

TABLE 13–1 Factors in January Heating Cost for a Sample of 20 Homes

Home	Heating Cost ($)	Mean Outside Temperature (°C)	Attic Insulation (cm)	Age of Furnace (years)
1	$250	−8	7.5	6
2	360	−13	10	10
3	165	−9	17.5	3
4	143	−2	15	9
5	192	−7	12.5	6
6	200	−8	12.5	5
7	355	−14	15	7
8	290	−15	22.5	10
9	230	−10	22.5	11
10	120	0	5	5
11	173	−6	30	4
12	205	−10	12.5	1
13	400	−12	12.5	15
14	320	−6	10	7
15	172	−5	20	6
16	272	−5	12.5	8
17	194	−7	17.5	3
18	190	−9	20	11
19	235	−8	22.5	8
20	139	0	17.5	5

The data in Table 13–1 are available on Connect in an **Excel** format.

Determine the multiple regression equation. Which variables are the independent variables? Which variable is the dependent variable? Discuss the regression coefficients. What does it indicate that some are positive and some are negative? What is the intercept value? What is the estimated heating cost for a home if the mean outside temperature is $-8°C$, there are 7.5 cm of insulation in the attic, and the furnace is 6 years old?

Solution

Statistics in Action

Many studies indicate a woman will earn about 70% of what a man would for the same work. Researchers have found that about one-third of the difference can be explained by such social factors as differences in education, seniority, and work interruptions. The remaining two-thirds are not explained by these social factors.

We begin the analysis by defining the dependent and independent variables. The dependent variable is the January heating cost. It is represented by y. There are three independent variables:

- The mean outside temperature in January, represented by x_1.
- The centimetres of insulation in the attic, represented by x_2.
- The age in years of the furnace, represented by x_3.

Given these definitions, the general form of the multiple regression equation follows. The value y' is used to estimate the value of Y.

$$y' = a + b_1 x_1 + b_2 x_2 + b_3 x_3$$

To use the regression equation to predict the January heating cost, we need to know the values of the regression coefficients, b_1, b_2, and b_3. Refer to the following **MegaStat** output. Note that the software used the variable name or labels associated with each independent variable. The regression equation intercept, a, is labelled "Intercept" in the **MegaStat** output. In this case, the multiple regression equation is: $y' = 140.3187 - 12.3168x_1 - 4.1013x_2 + 8.5268x_3$. We can now estimate or predict the January heating cost for a home if we know the mean outside temperature, the number of centimetres of insulation, and the age of the furnace. For the first example home, the mean outside temperature for the month is $-8°C$, (x_1), with 7.5 cm of insulation (x_2), and the furnace is 6 years old (x_3). By substituting the values for the independent variables:

$$y' = 140.3187 - 12.3168(-8) - 4.1013(7.5) + 8.5268(6) = 259.25$$

The estimated January heating cost is $259.25.

Regression Analysis

R^2	0.733		
Adjusted R^2	0.683	n	20
R	0.856	k	3
Std. Error	44.739	Dep. Var.	**Cost**

ANOVA table

Source	SS	df	MS	F	p-value
Regression	87,941.0612	3	29,313.6871	14.65	.0001
Residual	32,024.6888	16	2,001.5431		
Total	119,965.7500	19			

Regression output — confidence interval

variables	coefficients	std. error	t (df = 16)	p-value	95% lower	95% upper
Intercept	140.3187	36.1172	3.885	.0013	63.7536	216.8839
Temp	−12.3168	2.6850	−4.587	.0003	−18.0087	−6.6249
Insul	−4.1013	1.7248	−2.378	.0302	−7.7578	−0.4449
Age	8.5268	3.2954	2.588	.0198	1.5409	15.5126

The regression coefficients and their algebraic signs also provide information about the individual relationships with the January heating cost. The regression coefficient for the mean outside temperature is -12.3168. The coefficient is negative and shows an inverse relationship between heating cost and temperature. This is not surprising. As the outside temperature increases, the cost to heat the home decreases. The numeric value of the regression coefficient provides more information. If we increase the temperature by $1°C$ and hold the other two independent variables constant, we can estimate a decrease of $12.32 in monthly heating cost. So, if the mean temperature in Charlottetown is $-3.4°C$ and it is $-4°C$ in Fredericton, all other things being the same, we expect the heating cost would be $7.39 less in Charlottetown, found by -12.3168 times the difference in the mean temperature, 0.6.

The attic insulation variable also shows an inverse relationship: the more insulation there is in the attic, the less it costs to heat the home. So, the negative sign for this coefficient is logical. For each additional centimetre of insulation, we expect the cost to heat the home to decline $4.10 per month, holding the outside temperature and the age of the furnace constant.

The age of furnace variable shows a direct relationship. With an older furnace, the cost to heat the home increases. Specifically, for each additional year old the furnace is, we expect the cost to increase by $8.53 per month.

excel

Computer commands to produce the output for the heating costs example are at the end of the chapter.

self-review 13–1

Many restaurants in South Carolina (SC) serve beach vacationers in the summer, golfers in the fall and spring, and Canadian snowbirds in the winter. Bill and Joyce Tuneall manage several of the restaurants in the area and are considering moving to Myrtle Beach, SC, to open a new restaurant. Before making a final decision, they wish to investigate existing restaurants and what variables seem to be related to profitability. They gather sample information where profit (reported in $000) is the dependent variable and the independent variables are as follows:

x_1 is the number of parking spaces near the restaurant.
x_2 is the number of hours the restaurant is open per week.
x_3 is the distance from Broadway at the Beach, a landmark in Myrtle Beach.
x_4 is the number of servers employed.
x_5 is the number of years the current owner has owned the restaurant.

The following is part of the output obtained using statistical software:

Predictor	Coef	SE Coef	T
Constant	2.50	1.50	1.667
x_1	3.00	1.500	2.000
x_2	4.00	3.000	1.333
x_3	−5.00	0.20	−15.00
x_4	0.20	.05	4.00
x_5	1.00	1.50	0.667

(a) What is the amount of profit for a restaurant with 40 parking spaces and that is open 72 hours per week, is 16 kilometres (km) from Broadway at the Beach, has 20 servers, and has been open five years?
(b) Interpret the values of b_2 and b_3 in the multiple regression equation.

EXERCISES

1. The director of marketing at Reeves Wholesale Products is studying the monthly sales. Three independent variables were selected as estimators of sales: regional population (x_1), per-capita income (x_2), and regional unemployment rate (x_3). The regression equation was computed (in dollars) as follows:

$$y' = 64\,100 + 0.394x_1 + 9.6x_2 - 11\,600x_3$$

   a. What is the full name of the equation?
   b. Interpret the number 64 100.
   c. What are the estimated monthly sales for a particular region with a population of 796 000, per-capita income of $6940, and an unemployment rate of 6%?

2. Thompson Photo Works purchased several new, highly sophisticated machines. The production department needed some guidance with respect to qualifications needed by an operator. Is age a factor? Is the length of service as a machine operator important? To further explore the factors needed to estimate performance on the new machines, four variables were listed:

x_1 = Length of time employee was a machinist x_3 = Prior on-the-job rating
x_2 = Mechanical aptitude test score x_4 = Age

Performance on the new machine is designated y.

Thirty machinists were selected at random. Data were collected for each, and their performances on the new machines were recorded. A few results are as follows:

Name	Performance on New Machine, y	Length of Time as a Machinist, x_1	Mechanical Aptitude Score, x_2	Prior On-the-Job Performance, x_3	Age, x_4
Andy Kosin	112	12	312	121	52
Sue Annis	113	2	380	123	27

The equation is:

$$y' = 11.6 + 0.4x_1 + 0.286x_2 + 0.112x_3 + 0.002x_4$$

a. What is this equation called?
b. How many dependent variables are there? Independent variables?
c. What is the number 0.286 called?
d. As age increases by one year, how much does estimated performance on the new machine increase?
e. Carl Knox applied for a job at Photo Works. He has been a machinist for six years, and scored 280 on the mechanical aptitude test. Carl's prior on-the-job performance rating is 97, and he is 35 years old. Estimate Carl's performance on the new machine.

3. A consulting group surveyed General Mills Inc. employees to research the factors that affect their satisfaction with their quality of life. A special index, called the *index of satisfaction*, was used to measure satisfaction. Six factors were studied, namely, age at the time of first marriage (x_1), annual income (x_2), number of children living (x_3), value of all assets (x_4), status of health in the form of an index (x_5), and the average number of social activities per week—such as bowling and dancing (x_6). Suppose that the multiple regression equation is:

$$y' = 16.24 + 0.017x_1 + 0.0028x_2 + 42x_3 + 0.0012x_4 + 0.19x_5 + 26.8x_6$$

a. What is the estimated index of satisfaction for a person who first married at age 18, has an annual income of $26 500, has three children living, has assets of $156 000, has an index of health status of 141, and has 2.5 social activities a week on the average?
b. Which would add more to satisfaction, an additional income of $10 000 a year or two more social activities a week?

4. Cellulon, a manufacturer of a new type of home insulation, wants to develop guidelines for builders and consumers on how the thickness of the insulation in the attic of a home and the outside temperature affects gas consumption. In the laboratory, it varied the insulation thickness and temperature. A few of the findings are as follows:

Monthly Natural Gas Consumption (cubic feet), y	Thickness of Insulation (cm), x_1	Outside Temperature (°C), x_2
30.3	12.5	4
26.9	30	4
22.1	20	9

Based on the sample results, the regression equation is:

$$y' = 38.12 - 0.194x_1 - 1.349x_2$$

    a. How much natural gas can homeowners expect to use per month if they install 15 cm of insulation and the outside temperature is 10°C?

    b. What effect would installing 18 cm of insulation instead of 15 have on the monthly natural gas consumption (assuming that the outside temperature remains at 10°C)?

    c. Why are the regression coefficients, b_1 and b_2, negative? Is this logical?

13.3 EVALUATING A MULTIPLE REGRESSION EQUATION

Many statistics and statistical methods are used to evaluate the relationship between a dependent variable and more than one independent variable. Our first step is to express the relationship in terms of a multiple regression equation. The next step follows on the concepts presented in Chapter 12 by using the information in an ANOVA table to evaluate how well the equation fits the data.

LO13-2   The ANOVA Table

As in Chapter 12, the statistical analysis of a multiple regression equation is summarized in an ANOVA table. To review, the total variation of the dependent variable, y, is divided into two components: (1) *regression,* or the variation of y explained by all the independent variables and (2) *the error or residual,* or unexplained variation of y. These two categories are identified in the first column of the ANOVA table below. The column headed "*df*" refers to the degrees of freedom associated with each category. The total number of degrees of freedom is $n - 1$. The number of degrees of freedom in the regression is equal to the number of independent variables in the multiple regression equation. We call the regression degrees of freedom k. The number of degrees of freedom associated with the error term is equal to the total degrees of freedom minus the regression degrees of freedom. In multiple regression, the degrees of freedom are $n - (k + 1)$.

ANOVA				
Source	*df*	**SS**	**MS**	**F**
Regression	k	SSR	MSR = SSR/k	MSR/MSE
Residual	$n - k - 1$	SSE	MSE = SSE/$[n - k - 1]$	
Total	$n - 1$	SS total		

The term "SS" located in the middle of the ANOVA table refers to the sum of squares. Note that there is a sum of squares for each source of variation. The sum of squares column shows the amount of variation attributable to each source. The total variation of the dependent variable, y, is summarized in SS total. This is simply the numerator of the usual formula to calculate any variation—in other words, the sum of the squared deviations from the mean. It is computed as:

$$\text{Total Sum of Squares} = \text{SS total} = \sum(y - \bar{y})^2$$

As we have seen, the total sum of squares is the sum of the regression and residual sum of squares. The regression sum of squares is the sum of the squared differences between the estimated or predicted values, y', and the overall mean of y. The regression sum of squares is found by:

$$\text{Regression Sum of Squares} = \text{SSR} = \sum(y' - \bar{y})^2$$

The residual sum of squares is the sum of the squared differences between the observed values of the dependent variable, y, and their corresponding estimated or predicted values, y'. Note that this difference is the error of estimating or predicting the dependent variable with the multiple regression equation. It is calculated as:

$$\text{Residual or Error Sum of Squares} = \text{SSE} = \sum(y - y')^2$$

We will use the ANOVA table information from the previous example to evaluate the regression equation to estimate January heating costs.

Regression output					confidence interval	
variables	*coefficients*	*std. error*	*t (df=16)*	*p-value*	*95% lower*	*95% upper*
Intercept	140.3187	36.1172	3.885	.0013	63.7536	216.8839
Temp	−12.3168	2.6850	−4.587	.0003	−18.0087	−6.6249
Insul	−4.1013	1.7248	−2.378	.0302	−7.7578	−0.4449
Age	8.5268	3.2954	2.588	.0198	1.5409	15.5126

LO13-3 Multiple Standard Error of Estimate

We begin with the **multiple standard error of estimate**. Recall that the standard error of estimate is comparable with the standard deviation. The standard deviation uses squared deviations from the mean, $(y - \bar{y})^2$, whereas the standard error of estimate utilizes squared deviations from the regression line, $(y - y')^2$. To explain the details of the standard error of estimate, refer to the first sampled home in Table 13–1 in the previous example. The actual heating cost for the first observation, y, is $250; the outside temperature x_1 is −8°C, the depth of insulation x_2, is 7.5 cm, and the age of the furnace x_3, 6 years. Using the regression equation developed in the previous section, the estimated heating cost y' is found by:

$$y' = 140.3187 - 12.3168(-8) - 4.1013(7.5) + 8.5268(6) = 259.25$$

So, we would estimate that a home with a mean outside January temperature of −8°C, 7.5 cm of insulation, and a six-year-old furnace would cost $259.25 for the month. The actual heating cost was $250, so the residual—which is the difference between the actual value and the estimated value—is $(y - y') = 250 - 259.25 = -9.25$. This difference of $9.25 is the random or unexplained error for the first home sampled. Our next step is to square this difference—that is, find $(y - y')^2 = (250 - 259.25)^2 = (-9.25)^2 = 85.5625$. If we repeat these calculations for the other 19 observations and sum all 20 squared differences, the total will be the residual or error sum of squares from the ANOVA table. Using this information, we can calculate the multiple standard error of estimate as:

MULTIPLE STANDARD ERROR OF ESTIMATE $S_{e\cdot 12\ldots k} = \sqrt{\dfrac{\sum(y - y')^2}{n - k - 1}}$ [13–2]

where:

y is the observation.
y' is the value estimated from the regression equation.
n is the number of observations in the sample.
k is the number of independent variables.

In this example, $n = 20$ and $k = 3$ (three independent variables), so the multiple standard error of estimate is:

$$S_{e\cdot 123} = \sqrt{\frac{\sum(y - y')^2}{n - k - 1}} = \sqrt{\frac{32\,025.45}{20 - 3 - 1}} = 44.739$$

Since we have three independent variables, we identify the multiple standard error as $S_{e\cdot 123}$. The subscripts indicate that three independent variables are being used to estimate Y. This value also appears in the previous **MegaStat** output labelled as "Std. Error."

How do we interpret the standard error of estimate of 44.739? It is the typical "error" we make when we use this equation to predict the cost. First, the units are the same as the dependent variable, so the standard error is in dollars, $44.739. Second, we expect the residuals to be approximately normally distributed, so about 68% of the residuals will be within ±$44.739 and about 95% within ±2(44.739) = ±$89.478. As before, with similar measures of dispersion, such as the standard error of the estimate in Chapter 12, a smaller multiple standard error indicates a better or more effective predictive equation (Table 13–2).

TABLE 13-2 Calculations Needed for the Multiple Standard Error of Estimate

Home	Temperature °C	Insulation (cm)	Age (years)	Actual Cost ($) y	Estimated Cost ($) y'	Residual ($) $(y - y')$	$(y - y')^2$
1	−8	7.5	6	$250	$259.25	−$9.25	85.56
2	−13	10	10	360	344.69	15.31	234.40
3	−9	17.5	3	165	204.98	−39.98	1598.40
4	−2	15	9	143	180.17	37.17	1381.61
5	−7	12.5	6	192	226.43	−34.43	1185.42
6	−8	12.5	5	200	230.22	−30.22	913.25
7	−14	15	7	355	310.92	44.08	1943.05
8	−15	22.5	10	290	318.06	−28.06	787.36
9	−10	22.5	11	230	265.00	−35.00	1225.00
10	0	5	5	120	162.45	−42.45	1802.00
11	−6	30	4	173	125.29	47.71	2276.24
12	−10	12.5	1	205	220.75	−15.75	248.06
13	−12	12.5	15	400	364.76	35.24	1241.86
14	−6	10	7	320	232.89	87.11	7588.15
15	−5	20	6	172	171.04	0.96	0.92
16	−5	12.5	8	272	218.85	53.15	2824.92
17	−7	17.5	3	194	180.34	13.66	186.60
18	−9	20	11	190	262.94	−72.94	5320.24
19	−8	22.5	8	235	214.79	20.21	408.44
20	0	17.5	5	139	111.18	27.82	773.95
Total							32 025.45

Coefficient of Multiple Determination

Coefficient of multiple determination The percent of variation in the dependent variable, y, explained by the set of independent variables, $x_1, x_2, x_3, \ldots, x_k$.

Next, let us look at the **coefficient of multiple determination**. Recall from the previous chapter that the coefficient of determination is defined as the percent of variation in the dependent variable explained, or accounted for, by the independent variable.

The characteristics of the coefficient of multiple determination are:

1. **It is symbolized by a capital R squared (R^2).** In other words, it is written as R^2, as it behaves like the square of a correlation coefficient.
2. **It can range from 0 to 1.** A value near 0 indicates little association between the set of independent variables and the dependent variable. A value near 1 means a strong association.
3. **It cannot assume negative values.** Any number that is squared or raised to the second power cannot be negative.
4. **It is easy to interpret.** Because R^2 is a value between 0 and 1 it is easy to interpret, compare, and understand.

We can calculate the coefficient of determination from the information found in the ANOVA table. We look in the sum of squares column, which is labelled SS in the output, and use the regression sum of squares, SSR, then divide by SS total, the total sum of squares.

COEFFICIENT OF MULTIPLE DETERMINATION $R^2 = \dfrac{\text{SSR}}{\text{SS total}}$ [13–3]

The ANOVA table in the heating cost example is repeated below:

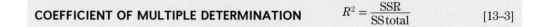

ANOVA table

Source	SS	df	MS	F	p-value
Regression	87,941.0612	3	29,313.6871	14.65	.0001
Residual	32,024.6888	16	2,001.5431		
Total	119,965.7500	19			

$$R^2 = \frac{\text{SSR}}{\text{SS total}} = \frac{87\,941.0612}{119\,965.75} = 0.733$$

How do we interpret this value? We conclude that the independent variables (outside temperature, amount of insulation, and age of furnace) explain, or account for, 73.3% of the variation in heating cost. To put it another way, 26.7% of the variation is due to other sources, such as random error or variables not included in the analysis. Using the ANOVA table, 26.7% is the error sum of squares divided by the total sum of squares. Knowing that SSR + SSE = SS Total, the following relationship is true:

$$1 - R^2 = 1 - \frac{\text{SSR}}{\text{SS total}} = \frac{\text{SSE}}{\text{SS total}} = \frac{32\,024.6888}{119\,965.75} = 0.267$$

The multiple standard error of estimate may also be found directly from the ANOVA table.

$$S_{e\cdot123} = \sqrt{\frac{\text{SSE}}{n - k - 1}} = \sqrt{\frac{32\,024.6888}{20 - 3 - 1}} = 44.739$$

As mentioned previously, the multiple standard error of estimate is also the square root of MS Residual: $\sqrt{2001.5431} = 44.739$. *Note*: ANOVA table values may be slightly different from those of a calculator due to rounding.

---

self-review 13–2

Refer to self-review 13–1 concerning restaurants in Myrtle Beach. The following ANOVA table is part of the regression output:

Source	df	SS	MS
Regression	5	100	20
Residual	20	40	2
Total	25	140	

(a) How large was the sample?
(b) How many independent variables are there?
(c) How many dependent variables are there?
(d) Compute the standard error of estimate. About 95% of the residuals will be between what two values?
(e) Determine the coefficient of multiple determination. Interpret this value.

EXERCISES

5. Refer to the following ANOVA table:

Source	DF	SS	MS	F
Regression	2	77.907	38.954	0.021
Residual Error	62	583.693	9.414	
Total	64	661.600		

   a. How large was the sample?
   b. How many independent variables are there?
   c. How many dependent variables are there?
   d. Compute the standard error of estimate. About 95% of the residuals will be between what two values?
   e. Determine the coefficient of multiple determination. Interpret this value.

6. Refer to the following ANOVA table:

Source	DF	SS	MS	F
Regression	5	3710.00	742.00	12.89
Residual Error	46	2647.38	57.55	
Total	51	6357.38		

a. How large was the sample?

b. How many independent variables are there?

c. How many dependent variables are there?

d. Compute the standard error of estimate. About 95% of the residuals will be between what two values?

e. Determine the coefficient of multiple determination. Interpret this value.

13.4 INFERENCES IN MULTIPLE LINEAR REGRESSION

Thus far, multiple regression analysis has been viewed only as a way to describe the relationship between a dependent variable and several independent variables. However, the least squares method also has the ability to draw inferences or generalizations about the relationship for an entire population. Recall that when you create confidence intervals or perform hypothesis tests as part of inferential statistics, you view the data as a random sample taken from some population.

In the multiple regression setting, we assume that there is an unknown population regression equation that relates the dependent variable to the k independent variables. This is sometimes called a **model** of the relationship. In symbols, we write:

$$Y' = \alpha + \beta_1 X_1 + \beta_2 X_2 + \cdots + \beta_k X_k$$

This equation is analogous to formula (13–1) except the coefficients are now reported as Greek letters. We use Greek letters to denote *population parameters*. Then, under a certain set of assumptions, which will be discussed shortly, the computed values of a and bj are sample statistics. These sample statistics are point estimates of the corresponding population parameters α and β_j. For example, the sample regression coefficient b_2, is a point estimate of the population parameter β_2. The sampling distribution of these point estimates follows the normal probability distribution. These sampling distributions are each centred at their respective parameter values. To put it another way, the means of the sampling distributions are equal to the parameter values to be estimated. Thus, by using the properties of the sampling distributions of these statistics, inferences about the population parameters are possible.

LO13-4   Global Test: Testing the Multiple Regression Model

We can test the ability of the independent variables, $X_1, X_2, \ldots, X_k$, to explain the behaviour of the dependent variable, Y. To put this in question form: can the dependent variable be estimated without relying on the independent variables? The test used is referred to as the **global test**. Basically, it investigates whether it is possible all the independent variables have zero regression coefficients. To put it another way, could the amount of explained variation, R^2, occur by chance?

To relate this question to the heating cost example, we will test whether the independent variables (mean daily outside temperature, amount of insulation in the attic and age of furnace) effectively estimate home heating costs. In testing a hypothesis, we first state the null hypothesis and the alternative hypothesis. In the heating cost example, there are three independent variables. Recall that b_1, b_2, and b_3 are sample regression coefficients. The corresponding coefficients in the population are given the symbols β_1, β_2, and β_3. We now test whether the regression coefficients in the population are all zero. The null hypothesis is:

$$H_0: \beta_1 = \beta_2 = \beta_3 = 0$$

The alternative hypothesis is:

$$H_1: \text{Not all the } \beta\text{s are 0}$$

If the null hypothesis is true, it implies the regression coefficients are all zero and, logically, are of no value in estimating the dependent variable, heating cost. Should that be the case, we would have to search for some other independent variables—or take a different approach—to predict home heating costs.

To test the null hypothesis that the multiple regression coefficients are all zero, we employ the F distribution introduced in Chapter 11. We will use the 0.05 level of significance. Recall these characteristics of the F distribution:

Characteristics of the *F* Distribution

1. **There is a family of F distributions.** Each time the degrees of freedom in either the numerator or denominator changes, a new F distribution is created.
2. **The F distribution cannot be negative.** The smallest possible value is 0.
3. **It is a continuous distribution.** The distribution can assume an infinite number of values between 0 and positive infinity.
4. **It is positively skewed.** The long tail of the distribution is to the right-hand side. As the number of degrees of freedom increases in both the numerator and the denominator, the distribution approaches the normal probability distribution. That is, the distribution will move toward a symmetric distribution.
5. **It is asymptotic.** As the values of X increase, the F curve will approach the horizontal axis but will never touch it.

The F statistic to test the global hypothesis follows. As in Chapter 11, it is the ratio of two variances. In this case, the numerator is the regression sum of squares divided by its degrees of freedom, k. The denominator is the residual sum of squares divided by its degrees of freedom, $n - k - 1$. The formula follows.

GLOBAL TEST	$$F = \frac{\text{MSR}}{\text{MSE}} = \frac{\text{SSR}/k}{\text{SSE}/[n - k - 1]}$$	[13–4]

Using the ANOVA table, the F statistic is:

$$F = \frac{\text{SSR}/k}{\text{SSE}/[n - k - 1]} = \frac{87\ 941.06/3}{32\ 024.69/[20 - 3 - 1]} = 14.65$$

Remember that the F statistic tests the basic null hypothesis that two variances or, in this case, two mean squares are equal. In our global multiple regression hypothesis test, we will reject the null hypothesis, H_0, that all regression coefficients are zero when the regression mean square is larger in comparison to the residual mean square. If this is true, the F statistic will be relatively large and in the far right tail of the F distribution, and the p-value will be small, that is, less than our choice of our significance level of 0.05. Thus, we will reject the null hypothesis.

As with other hypothesis-testing methods, the decision rule can be based on either of two methods: (1) comparing the test statistic to a critical value or (2) calculating a p-value on the basis of the test statistic and comparing the p-value to the significance level. The critical value method using the F statistic requires three pieces of information: (1) the numerator degrees of freedom, (2) the denominator degrees of freedom, and (3) the significance level. The degrees of freedom for the numerator and the denominator are reported in the ANOVA table that follows.

ANOVA table					
Source	*SS*	*df*	*MS*	*F*	*p-value*
Regression	87,941.0612	3	29,313.6871	14.65	.0001
Residual	32,024.6888	16	2,001.5431		
Total	119,965.7500	19			

The top number in the column marked "*df* " is 3, indicating that there are 3 degrees of freedom in the numerator. This value corresponds to the number of independent variables. The middle number in the "*df*" column (16) indicates that there are 16 degrees of freedom in the denominator. The number 16 is found by: $n - k - 1 = 20 - 3 - 1 = 16$.

The critical value of F is found in Appendix B.7. Using the table for the 0.05 level, move horizontally to 3 degrees of freedom in the numerator, then down to 16 degrees of freedom in the denominator, and read the critical value. It is 3.24. The region where H_0 is not rejected and the region where H_0 is rejected are shown in the following diagram.

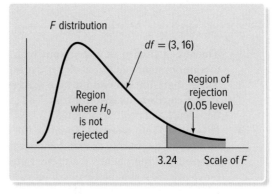

Continuing with the global test, the decision rule is: do not reject the null hypothesis that all the regression coefficients are 0 if the computed value of F is less than or equal to 3.24. If the computed F is greater than 3.24, reject H_0 and accept the alternative hypothesis, H_1.

The computed value of F is 14.65, which is in the rejection region. The null hypothesis that all the multiple regression coefficients are zero is therefore rejected. That is at least one of the independent variables has the ability to explain the variation in the dependent variable (heating cost). We expected this decision. Logically, the outside temperature, the amount of insulation and age of the furnace have a great bearing on heating costs. The global test assures us that they do.

Testing the null hypothesis can also be based on a p-value, which is reported in the statistical software output for all hypothesis tests. In the case of the F statistic, the p-value is defined as the probability of observing an F-value as large or larger than the F test statistic, assuming that the null hypothesis is true. If the p-value is less than our selected significance level, then we decide to reject the null hypothesis. The ANOVA shows the F statistic's p-value is very close to zero. It is clearly less than our significance level of 0.05. Therefore, we reject the global null hypothesis and conclude that at least one of the regression coefficients is not equal to zero.

The decision is the same as when we used the critical value approach. The advantage to using the p-value approach is that the p-value gives us the probability of making a Type I error. The computed p-value is much smaller than our significance level (nearly zero versus 0.05). We reject the null hypothesis that all the regression coefficients are 0 and, on the basis of the p-value, there is little likelihood this hypothesis is true.

Evaluating Individual Regression Coefficients

So far, we have shown that at least one, but not necessarily all, of the regression coefficients are not equal to zero and thus useful for predictions. The next step is to test the independent variables *individually* to determine which regression coefficients may be 0 and which are not.

Why is it important to know if any of the βs equal 0? If a β could equal 0, it implies that this particular independent variable is of no value in explaining any variation in the dependent variable. If there are coefficients for which H_0 cannot be rejected, we may want to eliminate them from the regression equation.

Our strategy is to establish three sets of hypotheses—one for temperature, one for insulation, and one for age of the furnace.

Step 1:   Is to state the null and alternative hypothesis.

For temperature:	For insulation:	For furnace age:
$H_0: \beta_1 = 0$	$H_0: \beta_2 = 0$	$H_0: \beta_3 = 0$
$H_1: \beta_1 \neq 0$	$H_1: \beta_2 \neq 0$	$H_1: \beta_3 \neq 0$

Step 2:   We will test the hypotheses at the 0.05 level. Note that these are two-tailed tests.

Step 3:   The test statistic follows the Student's t distribution with $n - k - 1$ degrees of freedom. The number of sample observations is n. There are 20 homes in the study, so $n = 20$. The number of independent variables is k, which is 3. Thus, there are $n - k - 1 = 20 - 3 - 1 = 16$ degrees of freedom.

Step 4: The critical value for t is in Appendix B.2. For a two-tailed test with 16 degrees of freedom using the 0.05 significance level, H_0 is rejected if t is less than -2.120 or greater than 2.120.

Refer to the following **MegaStat** output.

variables	coefficients	std. error	t (df = 16)	p-value
Intercept	140.3187	36.1172	3.885	.0013
Temp	−12.3168	2.6850	−4.587	.0003
Insul	−4.1013	1.7248	−2.378	.0302
Age	8.5268	3.2954	2.588	.0198

The column headed "coefficients" lists the values for the multiple regression equation.

$$y' = 140.3187 - 12.3168x_1 - 4.1013x_2 + 8.5268x_3$$

The term $-12.3168\,x_1$ in the equation is interpreted as follows: it is expected that the heating cost will decrease about \$12.32 for each degree increase in temperature holding the insulation and age of furnace variables constant.

The column in the **MegaStat** output labelled "std. error" indicates the standard error of the sample regression coefficients. Recall that Superior Realty selected a sample of 20 homes in Eastern Canada. If Superior Realty were to select a second sample at random and compute the regression coefficients of that sample, the values would not be exactly the same. If the sampling process was repeated many times, we could design a sampling distribution for each these regression coefficients. The column labelled "std. error" estimates the variability for each of these regression coefficients. The sampling distribution of the coefficients follow the t distribution with $n - k - 1$ degrees of freedom. Hence, we are able to test the independent variables individually to determine whether the net regression coefficients differ from zero. The formula is:

TESTING INDIVIDUAL REGRESSION COEFFICIENTS	$t = \dfrac{b_i - 0}{s_{b_i}}$	[13–5]

The b_i refers to any one of the regression coefficients and s_{b_i} refers to the standard deviation of that distribution of the regression coefficient. We include 0 in the equation because the null hypothesis is $\beta_i = 0$.

To illustrate this formula, refer to the test of the regression coefficient for the independent variable, temperature. From the computer output, the regression coefficient is -12.32. The standard deviation of the sampling distribution of the regression coefficient for the independent variable temperature is 2.68. Inserting these values in formula (13–5):

$$t = \frac{b_1 - 0}{s_{b_1}} = \frac{-12.32 - 0}{2.68} = -4.59$$

This is the value found in the $t(df = 16)$ column of the **MegaStat** output.

The computed value of t is -4.587 for temperature (the small difference between the computed value and that shown on the **MegaStat** output is due to rounding), -2.378 for insulation, and 2.588 for age of the furnace. These t-values are in the rejection regions. Thus, we conclude that all the regression coefficients are *not* zero. Therefore, all variables are significant predictors of heating cost.

We can also use p-values to test the individual regression coefficients. Again, these are commonly reported in computer software output. The computed t ratio for temperature on the computer output is -4.587 and the p-value is 0.000. Because the p-value is less than 0.05, the regression coefficient for the independent variable "temperature" is not equal to zero and should be included in the equation to predict heating costs. For insulation, the t ratio is -2.378 and has a p-value of 0.0302. As with temperature, the p-value is less than 0.05, so we conclude that the insulation regression coefficient is not equal to zero and should be included in the equation to predict heating cost. Likewise, the p-value to test the "age of the furnace" regression coefficient is 0.020, so we conclude that the "age of furnace" regression coefficient is also a significant predictor of heating cost.

At this point, we need to develop a strategy for deleting independent variables. In the Superior Realty case, the three independent variables were significant. If an independent variable were found not to be significant, we should drop that variable. Then we delete that variable and rerun the regression equation. However, in some instances, it may not be as clear-cut which variable to delete.

To explain, suppose we developed a multiple regression equation based on five independent variables. We conducted the global test and found that some of the regression coefficients were different from zero. Next, we tested the regression coefficients individually and found that three were significant and two were not. The preferred procedure is to drop the single independent variable with the *smallest absolute t-value* or *largest p-value* and rerun the regression analysis with the four remaining variables. Then, on the new regression equation with four independent variables, conduct the individual tests. If there are still regression coefficients that are not significant, again drop the variable with the smallest absolute t-value. To describe the process in another way, we should delete only one variable at a time. Each time we delete a variable, we need to rerun the regression analysis and check the remaining variables.

This process of selecting variables to include in a regression model can be automated, using statistical software. Most statistical software includes methods to sequentially remove and/or add independent variables and at the same time provide estimates of the percentage of variation explained (the R-square term). Two of the common methods are **stepwise regression** and **best subset regression**. It may take a long time, but in the extreme, we could compute every possible regression between the dependent variable and any subset of the independent variables.

Unfortunately, on occasion, the software may work "too hard" to find an equation that fits all the quirks of your particular data set. The resultant equation may not represent the relationship in the population. Judgment is needed to choose among the relationships presented. Consider whether the results are logical. They should have a simple interpretation and be consistent with your knowledge of the application under study.

---

self-review 13–3

The regression output concerning eating places in Myrtle Beach is repeated below:

Predictor	Coef	SE Coef	T	p-value
Constant	2.50	1.50	1.667	
x_1	3.00	1.500	2.000	0.054
x_2	4.00	3.000	1.333	0.194
x_3	−5.00	0.20	−15.00	0.000
x_4	0.20	.05	4.00	0.000
x_5	1.00	1.50	0.667	0.511

ANOVA

SOURCE	df	SS	MS	F	p-value
Regression	5	100	20	10	0.000
Residual Error	20	40	2		
Total	25	140			

(a) Perform a global test of hypothesis to check if any of the regression coefficients are different from 0. What do you decide? Use the 0.05 significance level.
(b) Do an individual test of each independent variable. Which variables would you consider eliminating? Use the 0.05 significance level.
(c) Outline a plan for possibly removing independent variables.

EXERCISES

7. Refer to the following regression output:

Predictor	Coef	SE Coef
Constant	20.00	10.00
X_1	−1.00	0.25
X_2	12.00	8.00
X_3	−15.00	5.00

Source	DF	SS	MS	F
Regression	3	7500.00		
Error	18			
Total	21	10000.0		

a. What is the regression equation?

b. If $X_1 = 4$, $X_2 = 6$, and $X_3 = 8$, what is the value of the dependent variable?

c. How large is the sample? How many independent variables are there?

d. Complete the ANOVA table.

e. Conduct a global test of hypothesis, using the 0.05 significance level. Can you conclude that any of the regression coefficients are different from zero?

f. Conduct a test of hypothesis on each of the regression coefficients. Could you delete any of the variables?

8. Refer to the following information:

Predictor	Coef	SE Coef
Constant	−150	90
X_1	2000	500
X_2	−25	30
X_3	5	5
X_4	−300	100
X_5	0.60	0.15

Source	df	SS	MS	F
Regression	5	1500.0		
Error	15			
Total	20	2000.0		

a. What is the regression equation?

b. If $X_1 = 4$, $X_2 = 6$, $X_3 = 8$, $X_4 = 6$, and $X_5 = 8$, what is the value of the dependent variable?

c. How large is the sample? How many independent variables are there?

d. Complete the ANOVA table.

e. Conduct a global test of hypothesis, using the 0.05 significance level. Can you conclude that any of the regression coefficients are different from zero?

f. Conduct a test of hypothesis on each of the regression coefficients. Could you delete any of the variables?

13.5 EVALUATING THE ASSUMPTIONS OF MULTIPLE REGRESSION

In the previous section, we described the methods to statistically evaluate the multiple regression equation. The results of the test let us know if at least one of the coefficients was not equal to zero, and we described a procedure of evaluating each regression coefficient. We also discussed the decision-making process for including and excluding independent variables in the multiple regression equation.

It is important to know that the validity of the global and individual tests rely on several assumptions. So, if the assumptions are not true, the results might be biased or misleading. However, strict adherence to the following assumptions is not always possible. Fortunately, the statistical techniques discussed in this chapter appear to work well even when one or more of the assumptions are violated. Even if the values in the multiple regression equation are "off " slightly, our estimates using a multiple regression equation will be closer than any that could be made otherwise. *Usually, the statistical procedures are robust enough to overcome violations of some assumptions.*

In Chapter 12, we listed the necessary assumptions for regression when we considered only a single independent variable. The assumptions for multiple regression are similar.

1. **There is a linear relationship.** That is, there is a straight-line relationship between the dependent variable and the set of independent variables.
2. **The variation in the residuals is the same for both large and small values of y'.** To put it another way, $(y - y')$ is unrelated to whether y' is large or small.
3. **The residuals follow the normal probability distribution.** Recall the residual is the difference between the actual value of y and the estimated value, y'. So, the term $(y - y')$ is computed for every observation in the data set. These residuals should approximately follow a normal probability distribution. In addition, the mean of the residuals is 0.
4. **The independent variables should not be correlated.** That is, we would like to select a set of independent variables that are not themselves correlated.
5. **The residuals are independent.** This means that successive observations of the dependent variable are not correlated. This assumption is often violated when time is involved with the sampled observations. Violation of this assumption is called **autocorrelation**.

In this section, we present a brief discussion of each of these assumptions. In addition, we provide methods to validate these assumptions and indicate the consequences if these assumptions cannot be met.

LINEAR RELATIONSHIP

Let's begin with the linearity assumption. The idea is that the relationship between the set of independent variables and the dependent variable is linear. If we are considering two independent variables, we can visualize this assumption. The two independent variables and the dependent variable would form a three-dimensional space. The regression equation would then form a plane, as shown previously. We can evaluate this assumption with scatter diagrams and residual plots.

Using Scatter Diagrams

The evaluation of a multiple regression equation should always include a scatter diagram that plots the dependent variable against each independent variable. These graphs help us visualize the relationships and provide some initial information about the direction (positive or negative), linearity, and strength of the relationship. For example, the scatter diagrams for home heating example are as follows.

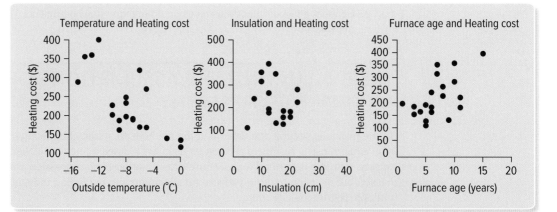

The plots suggest the strongest association is between heating cost and temperature. The relationships between cost and temperature and cost and insulation are both inverse. That is, as the independent variable increases, the dependent variable decreases. The relationship between the heating cost and the age of the furnace is direct. As the furnace gets older, it costs more to heat the home.

LO13-5 USING RESIDUAL PLOTS

Recall that a residual $(y - y')$ is computed using the multiple regression equation for each observation in a data set, as is shown in Table 13–3. In Chapter 12, we discussed the idea that the best regression line passed through the centre of the data in a scatter plot. In this case, you would find a good number of the observations above the regression line (these residuals would have a positive sign), and a good number of the observations below the line (these residuals would have a negative sign). Further, the observations would be scattered above and below the line over the entire range of the independent variable.

TABLE 13–3 Summary of Actual Costs, Estimated Costs, and Residuals for Superior Realty Problem

Observation	Actual Cost ($)	Estimated Cost ($)	Residual
1	$250.0	$259.25	−9.25
2	$360.0	344.69	15.31
3	$165.0	204.98	−39.98
4	$143.0	180.17	−37.17
5	$192.0	226.43	−34.43
6	$200.0	230.22	−30.22
7	$355.0	310.92	44.08
8	$290.0	318.06	−28.06
9	$230.0	265.00	−35.00
10	$120.0	162.45	−42.45
11	$173.0	125.29	47.71
12	$205.0	220.75	−15.75
13	$400.0	364.76	35.24
14	$320.0	232.89	87.11
15	$172.0	171.04	0.96
16	$272.0	218.85	53.15
17	$194.0	180.34	13.66
18	$190.0	262.94	−72.94
19	$235.0	214.79	20.21
20	$139.0	111.18	27.82

The same concept is true for multiple regression, but we cannot graphically portray the multiple regression. However, plots of the residuals can help us evaluate the linearity of the multiple regression equation. To investigate, the residuals are plotted on the vertical axis against the predictor variable, y'. The graph on the left below shows the residual plot for the home heating cost example.

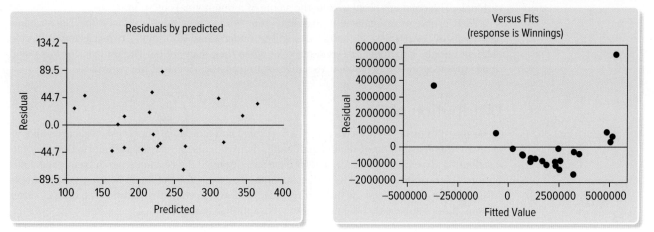

Note the following:

- The residuals are plotted on the vertical axis and are centred around zero. There are both positive and negative residuals.
- The residual plot shows a random distribution of positive and negative values across the entire range of the variable plotted on the horizontal axis.
- The points are scattered and there is no obvious pattern, so there is no reason to doubt the linearity assumption.

If there is a pattern to the points in the scatter plot, further investigation is necessary. For example, if the graph shows a curvature to the residual plots, the relationship may not be linear. For example, the graph on the right above shows nonrandom residuals. Note that the residual plot does not show a random distribution of positive and negative values across the entire range of the variable plotted on the horizontal axis. In fact, the graph shows a curvature to the residual plots. This indicates the relationship may not be linear. In this case, we would need to evaluate different transformations of the equation, as discussed in Chapter 12.

Variation in Residuals Same for Large and Small y' Values

This requirement indicates that the variation about the predicted values is constant regardless of whether the predicted values are large or small. To cite a specific example, which may violate the assumption, suppose that we use the single independent variable, age, to explain the variation in income. We suspect that as age increases so does income, but it also seems reasonable that as age increases there may be more variation around the regression line. That is, there will likely more variation in income for a 50-year-old person than for a 35-year-old person. The requirement for constant variation around the regression line is called **homoscedasticity**.

Homoscedasticity The variation around the regression equation is the same for all of the values of the independent variables.

To check for homoscedasticity, the residuals are plotted against the fitted values of y. This is the same graph that we used to evaluate the assumption of linearity. On the basis of the scatter diagram, it is reasonable to conclude that this assumption has not been violated.

Following are two examples in which the homoscedasticity requirement is not met.

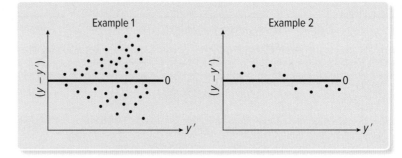

Note that in the first example, the plot of residuals is funnel shaped. That is, as the fitted y-values increase, so does the variation in the residuals. In the second example, there is a pattern to the residuals. The residuals seem to take the shape of a polynomial equation.

What problems are caused by residuals that fail to show homoscedasticity? The standard deviations of the regression coefficients will be understated (too small), causing potential independent variables to appear to be significant when they may not be. The remedy for this condition is to select other independent variables or to transform some of the variables.

Distribution of Residuals

To be sure that the inferences we make in the global and individual hypothesis tests are valid, we evaluate the distribution of residuals. Ideally, the residuals should follow a normal probability distribution. To evaluate this assumption, we can organize the residuals into a frequency distribution. The histogram on the left side shows the residuals for the home heating cost example. Although it is difficult to show that the residuals follow a normal distribution with only 20 observations, it does appear that the normality assumption is reasonable.

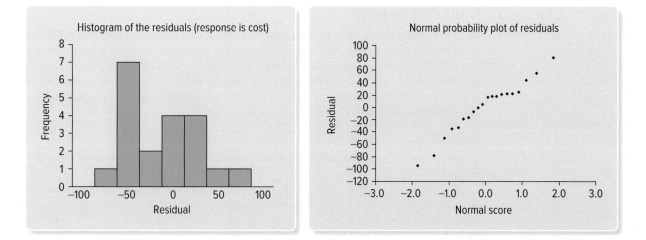

Another graph that helps to evaluate the assumption of normally distributed residuals is called a **normal probability plot**, shown to the right of the histogram. The normal probability plot supports the assumption of normally distributed residuals if the plotted points are fairly close to a straight line drawn from the lower left to the upper right of the graph.

In this case, both graphs support the assumption that the residuals follow the normal probability distribution. Therefore, the inferences that we made based on the global and individual hypothesis tests are supported with the results of this evaluation.

excel   Computer commands to produce the plots of residuals can be found at the end of the chapter.

Correlation matrix A matrix showing the coefficients of correlation between all pairs of variables.

Correlation Matrix

A **correlation matrix** is also useful in analyzing the factors involved in the cost to heat a home.

The correlation matrix of the Superior Realty example, developed using **MegaStat,** is given below:

	Cost	Temp	Insul	Age
Cost	1.000			
Temp	−.725	1.000		
Insul	−.197	−.152	1.000	
Age	.576	−.361	.046	1.000

excel   Computer commands to develop the above correlation matrix can be found at the end of the chapter.

Cost is the dependent variable, y. We are particularly interested in independent variables that have a strong correlation with the dependent variable. We may wish to develop a simpler multiple regression equation using fewer independent variables and the correlation matrix helps us identify which variables may be relatively more important. As indicated in the output, temperature has the strongest correlation with cost, -0.725. The negative sign indicates the inverse relationship we were expecting. Age has a stronger correlation with cost than insulation and, again as we expected, the correlation between cost and the age of the furnace is direct. It is 0.576.

Multicollinearity Correlation among the independent variables.

A second use of the correlation matrix is to check for **multicollinearity.**

LO13-6   Multicollinearity

Multicollinearity exists when independent variables are correlated. Correlated independent variables make it difficult to make inferences about the individual regression coefficients and their individual effects on the dependent variable. In practice, it is nearly impossible to select variables that are completely unrelated. To put it another way, it is nearly impossible to create a set of independent variables that are not correlated to some degree. However, a general understanding of the issue of multicollinearity is important.

Fist, multicollinearity does not affect a multiple regression equation's ability to predict the dependent variable. However, when we are interested in evaluating the relationship between each independent variable and the dependent variable, multicollinearity may show unexpected results.

For example, if we use two highly correlated variables, high school GPA and high school class rank, to predict the GPA of incoming college students (dependent variable), we would expect that both independent variables would be positively related to the dependent variable. However, because the independent variables are highly correlated, one of the independent variables may have an unexpected and inexplicable negative sign. In essence, these two independent variables are redundant in that they explain the same variation in the dependent variable.

A second reason for avoiding correlated independent variables is they may lead to erroneous results in the hypothesis tests for the individual independent variables. This is due to the instability of the standard error of estimate. Several clues that indicate problems with multicollinearity include the following:

1. An independent variable known to be an important predictor ends up having a regression coefficient that is not significant.
2. A regression coefficient that should have a positive sign turns out to be negative, or vice versa.
3. When an independent variable is added or removed, there is a drastic change in the values of the remaining regression coefficients.

In our evaluation of a multiple regression equation, an approach to reducing the effects of multicollinearity is to carefully select the independent variables that are included in the regression equation. A general rule is if the correlation between two independent variables is between −0.70 and 0.70, there is likely not a problem using both of the independent variables.

Recall that multicollinearity exists when independent variables are highly correlated. From our correlation matrix developed earlier in a previous section, none of the correlations among the independent variables exceed −0.70 or 0.70, so we do not suspect problems with multicollinearity. The largest correlation among the independent variables is −0.361, between temperature and age, but it is not large enough to cause a problem. Therefore, our fourth assumption is not violated.

Independent Observations

The fifth assumption about regression and correlation analysis is that successive residuals should be independent. This means that there is not a pattern to the residuals, the residuals are not highly correlated, and there are not long runs of positive or negative residuals. When successive residuals are correlated we refer to this condition as **autocorrelation**.

Autocorrelation frequently occurs when the data are collected over a period of time. For example, we wish to predict yearly sales of Ages Software Inc., based on the time and the amount spent on advertising. The dependent variable is yearly sales and the independent variables are time and amount spent on advertising. It is likely that for a period of time the actual points will be above the regression plane (remember, there are two independent variables), and then for another period of time, the points will be below the regression plane. The graph below shows the residuals plotted on the vertical axis and the fitted values, y', on the horizontal axis. Note a run of the residuals above the mean of the residuals is followed by a run below the mean. A scatter plot such as this would indicate possible autocorrelation. There is a formal statistical test for autocorrelation, called the *Durbin-Watson* test.

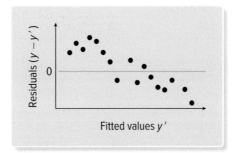

LO13-7 13.6 Qualitative Independent Variables

In the previous example regarding heating cost, the three independent variables were all quantitative, that is, numerical in nature. Frequently, we wish to use nominal-level variables—for example, gender, whether or not the home has a swimming pool, or whether the sports team was the home or the visiting team—in our analysis. These are called **qualitative variables** because they describe a particular quality, such as male or female. To use a qualitative variable in regression analysis, we use a scheme of **dummy variables** in which one of the two possible conditions is coded 0 and the other 1.

For example, we might be interested in estimating an executive's salary on the basis of years of job experience and whether he or she graduated from college. "Graduation from college" can take on only one of two conditions: yes or no. Thus, it is considered a qualitative variable.

Suppose in the Superior Realty example that the independent variable "garage" is added. For those homes without an attached garage, 0 is used; for homes with an attached garage, a 1 is used. We will refer to the "garage" variable as x_4. The data from Table 13–4 are entered into an **Excel** worksheet.

> **Dummy variable** A variable in which there are only two possible outcomes. For analysis, one of the outcomes is coded a 0 and the other a 1.

Statistics in Action

In recent years, multiple regression has been used in a variety of legal proceedings. It is particularly useful in cases alleging discrimination by gender or race. As an example, suppose that a woman alleges that Company AB's wage rates are unfair to women. To support the claim, the plaintiff produces data showing that, on average, women earn less than men. In response, Company AB argues that its wage rates are based on experience, training, and skill and that its female employees, on average, are younger and less experienced than the male employees. In fact, the company might further argue that the current situation is actually due to its recent successful efforts to hire more women.

TABLE 13–4 Home Heating Costs, Temperature, Insulation, and Presence of a Garage for a Sample of 20 Homes

Cost, ($) y	Temperature, x_1	Insulation, x_2	Garage, x_4
$250	−8	7.5	0
360	−13	10	1
165	−9	17.5	0
143	−2	15	0
192	−7	12.5	0
200	−8	12.5	0
355	−14	15	1
290	−15	22.5	1
230	−10	22.5	0
120	0	5	0
173	−6	30	0
205	−10	12.5	1
400	−12	12.5	1
320	−6	10	1
172	−5	20	0
272	−5	12.5	1
194	−7	17.5	0
190	−9	20	1
235	−8	22.5	0
139	0	17.5	0

The output follows.

ANOVA table

Source	SS	df	MS	F	p-value
Regression	84,877.4926	3	28,292.4975	12.90	.0002
Residual	35,088.2574	16	2,193.0161		
Total	119,965.7500	19			

Regression output   *confidence interval*

variable	coefficients	std. error	t (df = 16)	p-value	95% lower	95% upper
Intercept	169.2780	34.4003	4.921	.0002	96.3526	242.2033
Temp	−10.3855	3.3218	−3.126	.0065	−17.4274	−3.3435
Insul	−2.7266	1.9200	−1.420	.1748	−6.7967	1.3435
Garage	59.8693	27.5756	2.171	.0453	1.4118	118.3269

What is the effect of the variable garage? Should it be included in the analysis? To show the effect of the variable, suppose we have two houses exactly alike next to each other in Charlotte-town, Prince Edward Island (PEI), one has an attached garage, and the other does not. Both homes have 7.5 cm of insulation, and the mean January temperature in Charlottetown is −3.4°C. For the house without an attached garage, a 0 is substituted for x_4 in the regression equation. The estimated heating cost is \$184.14, found by:

$$y' = 169.2780 - 10.3855x_1 - 2.7266x_2 + 59.8693x_4$$
$$= 169.2780 - 10.3855(-3.4) - 2.7266(7.5) + 59.8693(0) = 184.14$$

For the house with an attached garage, a 1 is substituted for x_4 in the regression equation. The estimated heating cost is \$244.01, found by:

$$y' = 169.2780 - 10.3855x_1 - 2.7266x_2 + 59.8693x_4$$
$$= 169.2780 - 10.3855(-3.4) - 2.7266(7.5) + 59.8693(1) = 244.01$$

The difference between the estimated heating costs is \$59.87 (\$244.01 − \$184.14). Therefore, we can expect the cost to heat a house with an attached garage to be \$59.87 more than the cost for an equivalent house without a garage.

We have shown the difference between the two types of homes to be \$59.87, but is the difference significant? We conduct the following test of hypothesis:

$$H_0: \beta_4 = 0$$
$$H_1: \beta_4 \neq 0$$

The information necessary to answer this question is on the previous **Excel** output. The regression coefficient for the independent variable garage is 59.88, the standard deviation of the distribution of sampling distribution is 27.575. We identify this as the fourth independent variable, so we use a subscript of 4. Finally, we insert these values in formula (13–5).

$$t = \frac{b_4 - 0}{S_{b_4}} = \frac{59.8693 - 0}{27.5756} = 2.17$$

There are three independent variables in the analysis, so there are 16 degrees of freedom ($n - k - 1 = 20 - 3 - 1$). The critical value from Appendix B.2 is 2.120. The decision rule, using a two-tailed test and the 0.05 significance level, is to reject H_0 if the computed t is to the left of −2.120 or to the right of 2.120. Since the computed value of 2.17 is to the right of 2.120, the null hypothesis is rejected. It is concluded that the regression coefficient is not zero. The independent variable garage should be included in the analysis.

Using the p-value approach for the variable garage, the value is 0.0453 as found in the fifth column of the **MegaStat** output. This is less than the significance level of 0.05, so the null hypothesis is rejected, and the variable garage should be included in the analysis.

Is it possible to use a qualitative variable with more than two possible outcomes? Yes, but the coding scheme becomes more complex and will require a series of dummy variables. To explain, suppose a company is studying its sales as they relate to advertising expense by quarter for the last five years. Let "sales" be the dependent variable and "advertising expense" be the first independent variable, x_1. To include the qualitative information regarding the quarter, we use three additional independent variables. For the variable x_2, the five observations referring to the first quarter of each of the five years are coded 1 and the other quarters 0. Similarly, for x_3 the five observations referring to the second quarter are coded 1 and the other quarters 0. For x_4 the five observations referring to the third quarter are coded 1 and the other quarters 0. An observation that does not refer to any of the first three quarters must refer to the fourth quarter, so a distinct independent variable referring to this quarter is not necessary.

self-review 13–4

A study by the Realtors Association investigated the relationship between the commissions earned by sales associates last year and the number of months since the associates earned their real estate licences. Also of interest in the study is the gender of the sales associate. Below is a portion of the regression output. The dependent variable is commissions, which is reported in $000, and the independent variables are months since the licence was earned and gender (female = 1 and male = 0).

Regression Analysis

	R^2 0.642			
			n	20
	R 0.801		k	2
	Std. Error 3.219		Dep. Var.	**Commissions**

ANOVA table

Source	SS	df	MS	F	p-value
Regression	315.9291	2	157.9645	15.25	.0002
Residual error	176.1284	17	10.3605		
Total	492.0575	19			

Regression output

Variables	coefficients	std. error	t	p-value
Intercept	15.7625	3.0782	5.121	.0001
Months	0.4415	0.0839	5.263	.0001
Gender	3.8598	1.4724	2.621	.0179

(a) Write out the regression equation. How much commission would you expect a female agent to make who earned her licence 30 months ago?

(b) Do the female agents on the average make more or less than the male agents? How much more?

(c) Conduct a test of hypothesis to determine if the independent variable gender should be included in the analysis. Use the 0.05 significance level. What is your conclusion?

EXERCISES

9. Refer to the following correlation matrix:

	y	x_1	x_2	x_3	x_4
y	1.000				
x_1	.192	1.000			
x_2	.510	.124	1.000		
x_3	.806	.062	.438	1.000	
x_4	−.819	.650	−.481	−.729	1.00

a. Which independent variable has the strongest correlation with the dependent variable?

b. Suppose you could only use three of the four independent variables in your regression equation to estimate the dependent variable. On the basis of the correlation matrix above, which would you use? Explain.

c. Is there evidence of multicollinearity? If so, where does it occur?

10. Refer to the following correlation matrix:

	Sales	Advertising ($)	Population	Income
Sales	1.000			
Advertising ($)	.192	1.000		
Population	.510	.124	1.000	
Income	.806	.062	.438	1.000

a. Which independent variable has the strongest correlation with the dependent variable?

b. Suppose you could only use two of Advertising ($), Population, and Income in your regression equation to estimate Sales. On the basis of the correlation matrix above, which would you use? Explain.

c. Is there evidence of multicollinearity? If so, where does it occur?

11. The speed of a car can be estimated using many factors, three of which are horsepower, the weight of the car, and the age of the car. A study was done on 35 cars and the following correlation matrix was developed from the sample data:

	Speed	H-Power	Weight	Age
Speed	1			
H-Power	0.83	1		
Weight	−0.197	−0.15	1	
Age	0.15	0.13	0.05	1

a. Suppose that you could only use horsepower or weight in your regression equation to estimate speed. On the basis of the correlation matrix above, which would you use? Explain.

b. Weight has an inverse relationship with speed. Does this seem reasonable?

c. Is there evidence of multicollinearity?

12. The selling price of a residence can be estimated by using many factors, three of which are the square footage, number of bedrooms and bathrooms, and the location. A study was conducted on 50 homes and the following correlation matrix was developed from the sample data:

	Price	Sq. Ft.	Bath	Bed	Location
Price	1				
Square Feet	0.63	1			
Bathrooms	0.78	0.56	1		
Bedrooms	0.84	0.66	0.88	1	
Location	0.85	0.24	0.09	0.08	1

a. Suppose that you could only use one of the four independent variables to estimate the selling price. On the basis of the correlation matrix above, which would you use? Explain.

b. Is there evidence of multicollinearity? If so, how would this affect your regression equation?

Chapter Summary

I. The general form of the multiple regression equation is:

$$y' = a + b_1x_1 + b_2x_2 + b_3x_3 + \cdots + b_kx_k \qquad [13\text{--}1]$$

where a is the y-intercept when all x's are zero, b_i refers to the sample regression coefficients, and x_i refers to the value of the various independent variables.

  A. There can be any number of independent variables.

  B. The least squares criterion is used to develop the equation.

  C. A statistical software package is very helpful in performing the calculations.

II. There are two measures of the effectiveness of the regression equation.

  A. The multiple standard error of estimate is similar to the standard deviation.

   1. It is measured in the same units as the dependent variable.

   2. It is based on squared deviations from the regression equation.

   3. It ranges from 0 to plus infinity.

   4. It is calculated from the following equation:

$$S_{e \cdot 123 \cdots k} = \sqrt{\frac{\sum(y - y')^2}{n - k - 1}} \text{ also, } = \sqrt{\text{MSE}} \qquad [13\text{--}2]$$

  B. The coefficient of multiple determination reports the percent of the variation in the dependent variable explained by the set of independent variables.

   1. It may range from 0 to 1.

   2. It is also based on squared deviations from the regression equation.

   3. It is found by the following equation:

$$R^2 = \frac{\text{SSR}}{\text{SS total}} \qquad [13\text{--}3]$$

III. An ANOVA table summarizes the multiple regression analysis.

  A. It reports the total amount of the variation in the dependent variable and divides this variation into that explained by the set of independent variables and that not explained.

  B. It reports the degrees of freedom associated with the independent variables, the error variation, and the total variation.

IV. A correlation matrix shows all possible simple correlation coefficients between pairs of variables.

  A. It shows the correlation between each independent variable and the dependent variable.

  B. It shows the correlation between each pair of independent variables.

V. A global test is used to investigate whether any of the independent variables have a regression coefficient that differs significantly from zero.

  A. The null hypothesis is: All the regression coefficients are zero.

  B. The alternative hypothesis is: At least one regression coefficient is not zero.

  C. The test statistic is the F distribution with k (the number of independent variables) degrees of freedom in the numerator and $n - k - 1$ degrees of freedom in the denominator, where n is the sample size.

  D. The formula to calculate the value of the test statistic for the global test is:

$$F = \frac{\text{SSR/k}}{\text{SSE/}[n - k - 1]} \qquad [13\text{--}4]$$

VI. The test for individual variables determines which independent variables have regression coefficients that differ significantly from zero.

  A. The variables that have zero regression coefficients are usually dropped from the analysis.

  B. The test statistic is the t distribution with $n - k - 1$ degrees of freedom.

  C. The formula to calculate the value of the test statistic for the individual test is:

$$t = \frac{b_i - 0}{s_{b_i}} \qquad [13\text{--}5]$$

VII. Dummy variables or qualitative independent variables and can assume only one of two possible outcomes. A value of 1 is assigned to one outcome and a 0 to the other.

VIII. There are five assumptions to use multiple regression analysis.

  A. The relationship between the dependent variable and the set of independent variables must be linear.

   1. To verify this assumption, develop a scatter diagram and plot the residuals on the vertical axis and the fitted values on the horizontal axis.

   2. If the plots appear random, we conclude the relationship is linear.

B. The variation is the same for both large and small values of y'.
   1. Homoscedasticity means the variation is the same for all fitted values of the dependent variable.
   2. This condition is checked by developing a scatter diagram with the residuals on the vertical axis and the fitted values on the horizontal axis.
   3. If there is no pattern to the plots—that is, they appear random—the residuals meet the homoscedasticity requirement.

C. The residuals follow the normal probability distribution.
   1. This condition is checked by developing a histogram of the residuals to see if they follow a normal distribution.
   2. The mean of the distribution of the residuals is 0.

D. The independent variables are not correlated.
   1. A correlation matrix will show all possible correlations among independent variables. An indication of difficulty is a correlation larger than 0.70 or less than −0.070.
   2. Signs of correlated independent variables include when an important predictor variable is found insignificant, when an obvious reversal occurs in signs in one or more of the independent variables, or when a variable is removed from the solution, there is a large change in the regression coefficients.

E. Each residual is independent of other residuals.
   1. Autocorrelation occurs when successive residuals are correlated.
   2. When autocorrelation exists, the value of the standard error will be biased and will return poor results for tests of hypothesis regarding the regression coefficients.

Chapter Exercises

13. A multiple regression equation yields the following partial results:

Source	Sum of Squares	df
Regression	750	4
Error	500	35

    a. What is the total sample size?
    b. How many independent variables are being considered?
    c. Compute the coefficient of determination.
    d. Compute the standard error of estimate.
    e. Test the hypothesis that none of the regression coefficients is equal to zero. Let $\alpha = 0.05$.

14. In a multiple regression equation two independent variables are considered, and the sample size is 25. The regression coefficients and the standard errors are as follows:

$$b_1 = 2.676 \qquad s_{b_1} = 0.56$$
$$b_2 = -0.880 \qquad s_{b_2} = 0.71$$

Conduct a test of hypothesis to determine whether either independent variable has a coefficient equal to zero. Would you consider deleting either variable from the regression equation? Use the 0.05 significance level.

15. The following output was obtained:

Analysis of variance

Source	df	SS	MS
Regression	5	100	20
Error	20	40	2
Total	25	140	

Predictor	Coef	StDev	t-ratio
Constant	3.00	1.50	2.00
X_1	4.00	3.00	1.33
X_2	3.00	0.20	15.00
X_3	0.20	0.05	4.00
X_4	−2.50	1.00	−2.50
X_5	3.00	4.00	0.75

a. What is the sample size?
b. Compute the value of R^2.
c. Compute the multiple standard error of estimate.
d. Conduct a global test of hypothesis to determine whether any of the regression coefficients are significant. Use the 0.05 significance level.
e. Test the regression coefficients individually. Would you consider omitting any variable(s)? If so, which one(s)? Use the 0.05 significance level.

16. In a multiple regression equation $k = 5$ and $n = 20$, the MSE value is 5.10, and SST is 519.68. At the 0.05 significance level, can we conclude that any of the regression coefficients are not equal to 0?

17. The district manager of Jason's, a large discount retail chain, is investigating why certain stores in her region are performing better than others. She believes that three factors are related to total sales: the number of competitors in the region, the population in the surrounding area, and the amount spent on advertising. From her district, consisting of several hundred stores, she selects a random sample of 30 stores. For each store she gathered the following information:

y = total sales last year (in $000).
X_1 = number of competitors in the region.
X_2 = population of the region (in millions).
X_3 = advertising expense (in $000).

The sample data produces the following results:

Analysis of variance

Source	df	SS	MS
Regression	3	3050.00	1016.67
Error	26	2200.00	84.62
Total	29	5250.00	

Predictor	Coef	StDev	t-ratio
Constant	14.00	7.00	2.00
X_1	−1.00	0.70	−1.43
X_2	30.00	5.20	5.77
X_3	0.20	0.08	2.50

a. What are the estimated sales for the Bryne Store, which has four competitors, a regional population of 0.4 (400 000), and advertising expense of 30 ($30 000)?
b. Compute the R^2 value.
c. Compute the multiple standard error of estimate.
d. Conduct a global test of hypothesis to determine whether any of the regression coefficients are not equal to zero. Use the 0.05 level of significance.
e. Conduct tests of hypotheses to determine which of the independent variables have significant regression coefficients. Which variables would you consider eliminating? Use the 0.05 significance level.

18. The administrator of a new paralegal program at a college wants to estimate a student's GPA in the new program. He thought that high school marks, and the verbal and mathematical scores on the entrance examinations would be good predictors of student GPAs. A study of nine students was done. The data on the nine students are as follows:

Student	HS Marks	Verbal	Math	GPA
1	75	480	410	3.21
2	58	290	270	1.68
3	68	420	410	3.58
4	78	500	600	3.92
5	72	500	490	3.00
6	68	430	460	2.82
7	64	320	490	1.65
8	62	530	480	2.30
9	66	469	440	2.33

a. Consider the following correlation matrix. Which single variable has the strongest correlation with the dependent variable? Some of the correlations between the independent variables are strong. Could this be a problem?

	HS Marks	Verbal	Math	GPA
HS Marks	1.000			
Verbal	.595	1.000		
Math	.639	.599	1.000	
GPA	.857	.616	.487	1.000

b. Consider the following output. Compute the coefficient of multiple determination.

ANOVA table

Source	SS	df	MS	F	p-value
Regression	3.8967	3	1.2989	5.57	.0474
Residual	1.1664	5	0.2333		
Total	5.0631	8			

c. Conduct a global test of hypothesis from the preceding output. Does it appear that any of the regression coefficients are not equal to zero? Test at a significance level of 0.05.

d. Conduct a test of hypothesis on each independent variable. Would you consider eliminating the variables verbal or math? Test at a 0.05 significance level.

Regression output

Variables	coefficients	std. error	$t\ (df = 5)$	p-value
Intercept	−4.6451	1.8812	−2.469	.0566
HS Marks	0.1055	0.0373	2.826	.0368
Verbal	0.0022	0.0027	0.801	.4595
Math	−0.0017	0.0027	−0.625	.5595

e. The analysis has been rerun without the variables Verbal and Math. See the following output. Compute the coefficient of determination. How much has R^2 changed from the previous analysis? Which model is the better predictor of GPA?

ANOVA table

Source	SS	df	MS	F	p-value
Regression	3.7159	1	3.7159	19.31	.0032
Residual	1.3472	7	0.1925		
Total	5.0631	8			

f. Following is a normal probability plot of residuals from the first model. Does the normality assumption for the residuals seem reasonable?

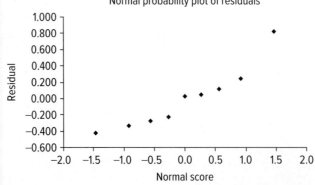

Normal probability plot of residuals

g. Following is a plot of the residuals and the y' values. Do you see any violation of the assumptions?

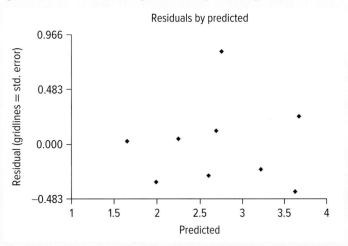

Residuals by predicted

19. Suppose that the sales manager of a large automotive parts distributor wants to estimate as early as April the total annual sales of a region. On the basis of regional sales, the total sales for the company can also be estimated. If, on the basis of past experience, it is found that the April estimates of annual sales are reasonably accurate, then in future years the April forecast could be used to revise production schedules and maintain the correct inventory at the retail outlets.

  Several factors appear to be related to sales, included the number of retail outlets in the region stocking the company's parts, the number of automobiles in the region registered as of April 1, and the total personal income for the first quarter of the year. Five independent variables were finally selected as being the most important (according to the sales manager). Then, the data were gathered for a recent year. The total annual sales for that year for each region were also recorded. In the following table, note that for region 1, there were 1739 retail outlets stocking the company's automotive parts, 9 270 000 (9.27 million) registered automobiles in the region as of April 1, and so on. The sales for that region for that year were $37 702 000 ($37.702 million).

y is annual sales ($ millions)
x_1 is number of retail outlets
x_2 is number of automobiles registered (millions)
x_3 is personal income ($ billions)
x_4 is average age of automobiles (years)
x_5 is number of supervisors

y	x_1	x_2	x_3	x_4	x_5
$37.702	1739	9.27	$85.4	3.5	9.0
24.196	1221	5.86	60.7	5.0	5.0
32.055	1846	8.81	68.1	4.4	7.0
3.611	120	3.81	20.2	4.0	5.0
17.625	1096	10.31	33.8	3.5	7.0
45.919	2290	11.62	95.1	4.1	13.0
29.600	1687	8.96	69.3	4.1	15.0
8.114	241	6.28	16.3	5.9	11.0
20.116	649	7.77	34.9	5.5	16.0
12.994	1427	10.92	15.1	4.1	10.0

a. Consider the following correlation matrix. Which single variable has the strongest correlation with the dependent variable? The correlations between the independent variables "outlets" and "income" and between "cars" and "outlets" are fairly strong. What is this condition called? Could this be a problem?

	y	x_1	x_2	x_3	x_4	x_5
x_1	.899	1.000				
x_2	.605	.775	1.000			
x_3	.964	.825	.409	1.000		
x_4	−.323	−.489	−.447	−.349	1.000	
x_5	.286	.183	.395	.155	.291	1.000

b. The following regression output was obtained using the five independent variables:

ANOVA

Source	SS	df	MS	F	p-value
Regression	1593.8097	5	318.7619	140.36	.0001
Residual	9.0843	4	2.2711		
Total	1602.8940	9			

Regression output

variables	coefficients	std. error	$t\,(df=4)$	p-value
Intercept	−19.6715			
x_1	−0.0006	0.0026	−0.238	.8234
x_2	1.7399	0.5530	3.146	.0346
x_3	0.4099	0.0439	9.348	.0007
x_4	2.0357	0.8779	2.319	.0812
x_5	−0.0344	0.1880	−0.183	.8635

What is the regression equation? What percentage of the variation is explained by the regression equation?

c. Conduct a global test of hypothesis to determine whether any of the regression coefficients are not zero. Use the 0.05 significance level.

d. Conduct a test of hypothesis on each of the independent variables. Would you consider eliminating "outlets" and "supervisors?" Use the 0.05 significance level.

e. The regression equation has been rerun below with "outlets" and "supervisors" eliminated. Compute the coefficient of determination. How much has R^2 changed from the previous analysis? Which model is the better predictor of Annual Sales?

ANOVA table

Source	SS	df	MS	F	p-value
Regression	1593.6621	3	531.2207	345.25	4.17E−07
Residual	9.2319	6	1.5387		
Total	1602.8940	9			

Regression output

variables	coefficients	Std. Error	$t(df=6)$	p-value
Intercept	−18.9239			
x_2	1.6129	0.1979	8.152	.0002
x_3	0.4003	0.0157	25.517	2.39E − 07
x_4	1.9637	0.5846	3.359	.0152

f. Below is a normal probability plot of residuals from the first model. Does the normality assumption for the residuals seem reasonable?

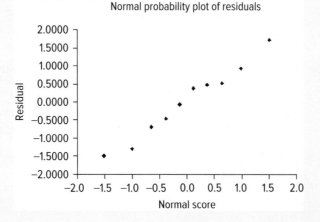

Normal probability plot of residuals

g. Below is a plot of the residuals and the y' values. Do you see any violation of the assumptions?

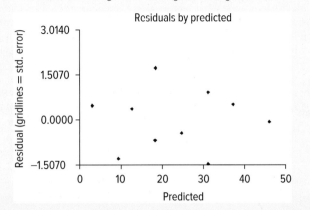

Residuals by predicted

20. Mike Wilde is president of the teachers' union for Otsego School District. In preparing for upcoming negotiations, he would like to investigate the salary structure of classroom teachers in the district. He believes there are three factors that affect a teacher's salary: years of experience, a rating of teaching effectiveness given by the principal, and whether the teacher has a master's degree. A random sample of 20 teachers resulted in the following data:

Salary ($000), y	Years of Experience, x_1	Principal's Rating, x_2	Master's Degree,* x_3
$55.1	8	35	0
57.6	5	43	0
53.3	2	51	1
67.0	15	60	1
62.6	11	73	0
69.0	14	80	1
66.0	9	76	0
60.8	7	54	1
72.6	22	55	1
55.7	3	90	1
49.7	1	30	0
54.6	5	44	0
75.8	23	84	1
70.7	17	76	0
62.4	12	68	1
57.6	14	25	0
65.8	8	90	1
54.7	4	62	0
56.8	2	80	1
66.8	8	72	0

*1 = yes, 0 = no.

a. Develop a correlation matrix. Which independent variable has the strongest correlation with the dependent variable? Does it appear there will be any problems with multicollinearity?

b. Determine the regression equation. What salary would you estimate for a teacher with five years' experience, a rating by the principal of 60, and no master's degree?

c. Conduct a global test of hypothesis to determine whether any of the net regression coefficients differ from zero. Use the 0.05 significance level.

d. Conduct a test of hypothesis for the individual regression coefficients. Would you consider deleting any of the independent variables? Use the 0.05 significance level.

e. If your conclusion in part (d) was to delete one or more independent variables, run the regression equation again without those variables.

f. Determine the residuals for the equation of part (e). Plot the residuals by observation to verify that the distribution of the residuals is approximately normal.

g. Plot the residuals computed in part (f) in a scatter diagram with the residuals on the y-axis and the y' values on the x-axis. Does the plot reveal any violations of the assumptions of regression?

21. The district sales manager for a major automobile manufacturer is studying car sales. Specifically, he would like to determine what factors affect the number of cars sold at a dealership. To investigate, he randomly selects 12 dealers. From these dealers, he obtains the number of cars sold last month, the minutes of radio advertising purchased last month, the number of full-time salespeople employed in the dealership, and whether the dealer is located in the city. The information is as follows:

Cars Sold Last Month, y	Advertising, x_1	Sales Force, x_2	City, x_3	Cars Sold Last Month, y	Advertising, x_1	Sales Force, x_2	City, x_3
127	18	10	Yes	161	25	14	Yes
138	15	15	No	180	26	17	Yes
159	22	14	Yes	102	15	7	No
144	23	12	Yes	163	24	16	Yes
139	17	12	No	106	18	10	No
128	16	12	Yes	149	25	11	Yes

a. Develop a correlation matrix. Which independent variable has the strongest correlation with the dependent variable? Does it appear there will be any problems with multicollinearity?

b. Determine the regression equation. How many cars would you expect to be sold by a dealership employing 20 salespeople, purchasing 15 minutes of advertising, and located in a city?

c. Conduct a global test of hypothesis to determine whether any of the net regression coefficients differ from zero. Let $\alpha = 0.05$.

d. Conduct a test of hypothesis for the individual regression coefficients. Would you consider deleting any of the independent variables? Let $\alpha = 0.05$.

e. If your conclusion in part (d) was to delete one or more independent variables, run the regression equation again without those variables.

f. Determine the residuals for the equation of part (e). Plot the residuals by observation to verify that the distribution of the residuals is approximately normal.

g. Plot the residuals computed in part (f) in a scatter diagram with the residuals on the y-axis and the y' values on the x-axis. Does the plot reveal any violations of the assumptions of regression?

22. Fran's Convenience Marts are located throughout a metropolitan area. Fran, the owner, would like to expand into other communities. As part of her presentation to the local bank, she would like to better understand the factors that make a particular outlet profitable. She must do all the work herself, so she will not be able to study all her outlets. She selects a random sample of 15 marts and records the average daily sales (y), the floor space (area), the number of parking spaces, and the median income of families in each region. The sample information is reported below:

Sampled Mart	Daily Sales ($)	Store Area	Parking Spaces	Income ($000)
1	$1840	532	6	$44
2	1746	478	4	51
3	1812	530	7	45
4	1806	508	7	46
5	1792	514	5	44
6	1825	556	6	46
7	1811	541	4	49
8	1803	513	6	52
9	1830	532	5	46
10	1827	537	5	46
11	1764	499	3	48
12	1825	510	8	47
13	1763	490	4	48
14	1846	516	8	45
15	1815	482	7	43

a. Determine the regression equation.

b. What is the value of R^2? Comment on the value.

c. Conduct a global hypothesis test to determine if any of the independent variables are different from zero. Test at a significance level of 0.05.

d. Conduct individual hypothesis tests to determine if any of the independent variables can be dropped. Test at a significance level of 0.05.

e. If variables are dropped, recompute the regression equation and R^2.

23. Steve Douglas has been hired as a management trainee by a large brokerage firm. As his first project, he is asked to study the gross profit of firms in the chemical industry. What factors affect profitability in that industry? Steve selects a random sample of 16 firms and obtains data on the number of employees, number of consecutive common stock dividends paid, the total value of inventory at the start of the current year, and the gross profit for each firm. His findings are as follows:

Company	Gross Profit ($000), y	Number of Employees, x_1	Consecutive Dividends, x_2	Beginning Inventory ($000), x_3
1	$2800	140	12	$1800
2	1300	65	21	320
3	1230	130	42	820
4	1600	115	80	76
5	4500	390	120	3600
6	5700	670	64	8400
7	3150	205	43	508
8	640	40	14	870
9	3400	480	88	5500
10	6700	810	98	9875
11	3700	120	44	6500
12	6440	590	110	9130
13	1280	440	38	1200
14	4160	280	24	890
15	3870	650	60	1200
16	980	150	24	1300

a. Determine the regression equation. The Master Chemical Company employs 220 people, has paid 64 consecutive common stock dividends, and has an inventory valued at $1 500 000 at the start of the year. What is the estimate of the gross profit?

b. Conduct a global test of hypothesis to determine whether any of the net regression coefficients differ from zero. Test at a significance level of 0.05.

c. Conduct a test of hypothesis for the individual regression coefficients. Would you consider deleting any of the independent variables? Test at a significance level of 0.05.

d. If your conclusion in part (c) was to delete one or more independent variables, run the regression equation again, deleting those variables.

e. Determine the residuals for the equation of part (d). Plot the residuals by observation to verify that the distribution of the residuals is approximately normal.

f. Plot the residuals computed in part (e) in a scatter diagram with the residuals on the y-axis and the y' values on the x-axis. Does the plot reveal any violations of the assumptions of regression?

24. The mortgage department of a financial institution is studying its recent loans. Of particular interest is how such factors as the value of the home (in thousands of dollars), education level of the head of the household, age of the head of the household, current monthly mortgage payment (in dollars), and gender of the head of the household (male = 1, female = 0) relate to the family income. Are these variables effective predictors of the income of the household? A random sample of 25 recent loans is obtained.

a. Determine the regression equation.

b. What is the value of R^2? Comment on the value.

c. Conduct a global hypothesis test to determine whether any of the independent variables are different from zero. Test at a significance level of 0.05.

d. Conduct individual hypothesis tests to determine whether any of the independent variables can be dropped. Test at a significance level of 0.05.

e. If variables are dropped, recompute the regression equation and R^2.

Income ($000)	Value ($000)	Years of Education	Age	Mortgage Payment ($)	Gender
$40.3	$190	14	53	$230	1
39.6	121	15	49	370	1
40.8	161	14	44	397	1
40.3	161	14	39	181	1
40.0	179	14	53	378	0
38.1	99	14	46	304	0
40.4	114	15	42	285	1
40.7	202	14	49	551	0
40.8	184	13	37	370	0
37.1	90	14	43	135	0
39.9	181	14	48	332	1
40.4	143	15	54	217	1
38.0	132	14	44	490	0
39.0	127	14	37	220	0
39.5	153	14	50	270	1
40.6	145	14	50	279	1
40.3	174	15	52	329	1
40.1	177	15	47	274	0
41.7	188	15	49	433	1
40.1	153	15	53	333	1
40.6	150	16	58	148	0
40.4	173	13	42	390	1
40.9	163	14	46	142	1
40.1	150	15	50	343	0
38.5	139	14	45	373	0

25. A regional planner is studying the demographics in a region of a particular province. She has gathered the following data on nine counties:

County	Median Income ($)	Median Age	Population >400 000
A	$48 157	57.7	1
B	48 568	60.7	1
C	46 816	47.9	1
D	34 876	38.4	0
E	35 478	42.8	0
F	34 465	35.4	0
G	35 026	39.5	1
H	38 599	65.6	0
J	33 315	27.0	0

a. Is there a linear relationship between the median income and median age?

b. Which variable is the "dependent" variable?

c. Use statistical software to determine the regression equation. Interpret the value of the slope in a simple regression equation.

d. Include the aspect that the population of the county is greater than 400 000 or not in a multiple linear regression analysis using a "dummy" variable. Does it appear to be a significant influence on incomes?

e. Test each of the individual coefficients to see if they are significant.

f. Make a plot of the residuals and comment on whether they appear to follow a normal distribution.

g. Plot the residuals versus the fitted values. Do they seem to have the same amount of variation?

26. Many urban regions have experienced rapid population growth over the last 10 years. It is expected that growth will continue over the next 10 years. This has resulted in many of the large grocery store chains building new stores. The Kelley's Super Grocery Stores Inc. chain is no exception. The director of planning for Kelley's Super Grocery Stores wants to study adding more stores. He believes there are two main factors that indicate the amount families spend on groceries. The first is their income and the other is the number of people in the family. The director gathered the following sample information:

Family	Food ($)	Income ($)	Size
1	$5.04	$73.98	4
2	4.08	54.90	2
3	5.76	94.14	4
4	3.48	52.02	1
5	4.20	65.70	2
6	4.80	53.64	4
7	4.32	79.74	3
8	5.04	68.58	4
9	6.12	165.60	5
10	3.24	64.80	1
11	4.80	138.42	3
12	3.24	125.82	1
13	6.60	77.58	7
14	4.92	171.36	2
15	6.60	82.08	9
16	5.40	141.30	3
17	6.00	36.90	5
18	5.40	56.88	4
19	3.36	71.82	1
20	4.68	69.48	3
21	4.32	54.36	2
22	5.52	87.66	5
23	4.56	38.16	3
24	5.40	43.74	7
25	4.80	48.42	5

Food and income are reported in thousands of dollars per year, and the variable "size" refers to the number of people in the household.

a. Develop a correlation matrix. Do you see any problems with multicollinearity?

b. Determine the regression equation. Discuss the regression equation. How much does an additional family member add to the amount spent on food?

c. What is the value of R^2? Can we conclude that this value is greater than 0?

d. Would you consider deleting either of the independent variables?

e. Plot the residuals by observation. Is there any problem with the normality assumption?

f. Plot the fitted values against the residuals. Does this plot indicate any problems with homoscedasticity?

27. How important is GPA in determining the starting salary of recent business school graduates? Does graduating from a business program increase the starting salary? The placement officer at a local college wanted to study these questions. She gathered the following sample information on 15 graduates last spring to investigate these questions:

Student	Salary ($)	GPA	Business	Student	Salary ($)	GPA	Business
1	$31.5	3.245	0	9	$34.7	3.355	1
2	33	3.278	0	10	32.5	3.08	0
3	34.1	3.52	1	11	31.5	3.025	0
4	35.4	3.74	1	12	32.2	3.146	0
5	34.2	3.52	1	13	34	3.465	1
6	34	3.421	1	14	32.8	3.245	0
7	34.5	3.41	1	15	31.8	3.025	0
8	35	3.63	1				

The salary is reported in thousands of dollars. The Business column indicates a "1" if the student graduated from a school of business, and a "0" if the student graduated from another program.

a. Develop a correlation matrix. Do you see any problems with multicollinearity?

b. Determine the regression equation. How much does graduating from a college business school add to a starting salary? What is the estimate of the starting salary for a student with a GPA of 3.00 who graduated from a business school?

   c. What is the value of the coefficient of determination? What does this value tell us?

   d. Would you consider deleting either of the independent variables?

   e. Develop a normal probability plot of residuals. Is there any problem with the normality assumption?

   f. Plot the fitted values against the residuals. Does this plot indicate any problems with homoscedasticity?

28. An investment advisor is studying the relationship between a common stock's price to earnings (P/E) ratio and factors that she thinks would influence it. She has the following data on the earnings per share (EPS) and the dividend percentage (Yield) for a sample of 20 stocks:

Stock	P/E	EPS ($)	Yield	Stock	P/E	EPS ($)	Yield
1	20.79	$2.46	1.42	11	1.35	$2.93	2.59
2	3.03	2.69	4.05	12	25.43	2.07	1.04
3	44.46	−0.28	4.16	13	22.14	2.19	3.52
4	41.72	−0.45	1.27	14	24.21	−0.83	1.56
5	18.96	1.60	3.39	15	30.91	2.29	2.23
6	18.42	2.32	3.86	16	35.79	1.64	3.36
7	34.82	0.81	4.56	17	18.99	3.07	1.98
8	30.43	2.13	1.62	18	30.21	1.71	3.07
9	29.97	2.22	5.10	19	32.88	0.35	2.21
10	10.86	1.44	1.17	20	15.19	5.02	3.50

   a. Develop a multiple linear regression equation with P/E as the dependent variable.

   b. Are either of the two independent variables an effective predictor of P/E?

   c. Interpret the regression coefficients.

   d. Do any of the stocks look undervalued?

   e. Develop a normal probability plot of residuals. Is there any problem with the normality assumption?

   f. Plot the fitted values against the residuals. Does this plot indicate any problems with homoscedasticity?

   g. Develop a correlation matrix. Do any of the correlations indicate multicollinearity?

29. The president of Blitz Sales Enterprises sells kitchen products through television commercials, often called *Infomercials*. He gathered data from the last 15 weeks of sales to determine the relationship between sales and the number of infomercials:

Infomercials	Sales ($000)	Infomercials	Sales ($000)
20	$3.2	22	$2.5
15	2.6	15	2.4
25	3.4	25	3.0
10	1.8	16	2.7
18	2.2	12	2.0
18	2.4	20	2.6
15	2.4	25	2.8
12	1.5		

   a. Determine the regression equation.

   b. Are the sales predictable from the number of commercials? Test at a significance level of 0.01.

   c. Develop a normal probability plot of the residuals.

   d. Does the normality assumption seem reasonable?

30. The *Times-Observer* is a daily newspaper in Metro City. Like many city newspapers, the *Times-Observer* is suffering through difficult financial times. The circulation manager is studying other papers in similar cities in Canada and the United States. She is particularly interested in what variables relate to the number of subscriptions to the paper. She is able to obtain the following sample information on 25 newspapers in similar cities. The following notation is used:

   Sub: Number of subscriptions (in thousands)

   Popul: The metropolitan population (in thousands)

   Adv: The advertising budget of the paper (in $00)

   Income: The median family income in the metropolitan area (in $000)

Sub.	Popul.	Adv. ($)	Income ($)	Sub.	Popul.	Adv. ($)	Income ($)
37.95	588.9	$13.2	$35.1	38.39	586.5	$15.4	$35.5
37.66	585.3	13.2	34.7	37.29	544.0	11.0	34.9
37.55	566.3	19.8	34.8	39.15	611.1	24.2	35.0
38.78	642.9	17.6	35.1	38.29	643.3	17.6	35.3
37.67	624.2	17.6	34.6	38.09	635.6	19.8	34.8
38.23	603.9	15.4	34.8	37.83	598.9	15.4	35.1
36.90	571.9	11.0	34.7	39.37	657.0	22.0	35.3
38.28	584.3	28.6	35.3	37.81	595.2	15.4	35.1
38.95	605.0	28.6	35.1	37.42	520.0	19.8	35.1
39.27	676.3	17.6	35.6	38.83	629.6	22.0	35.3
38.30	587.4	17.6	34.9	38.33	680.0	24.2	34.7
38.84	576.4	22.0	35.4	40.24	651.2	33.0	35.8
38.14	570.8	17.6	35.0				

a. Determine the regression equation.

b. Conduct a global test of hypothesis to determine whether any of the regression coefficients are not equal to zero. Use a significance level of 0.05.

c. Conduct a test for the individual coefficients. Would you consider deleting any coefficients?

d. Plot the fitted values against the residuals. Does this plot indicate any problems?

e. Develop a normal probability plot of residuals. Is there any problem with the normality assumption?

31. A consumer analyst collected the following data on the screen sizes of popular LCD (liquid crystal display) televisions sold recently at a large retailer:

Manufacturer	Screen	Price
Sharp	46	$1473.00
Samsung	52	2300.00
Samsung	46	1790.00
Sony	40	1250.00
Sharp	42	1546.50
Samsung	46	1922.50
Samsung	40	1372.00
Sharp	37	1149.50
Sharp	46	2000.00
Sony	40	1444.50
Sony	52	2615.00
Samsung	32	747.50
Sharp	37	1314.50
Sharp	32	853.50
Sharp	52	2778.00
Samsung	40	1749.50
Sharp	32	1035.00
Samsung	52	2950.00
Sony	40	1908.50
Sony	52	3103.00
Sony	46	2606.00
Sony	46	2861.00
Sony	52	3434.00

a. Does there appear to be a linear relationship between the screen size and the price?

b. Which variable is the "dependent" variable?

c. Using statistical software, determine the regression equation. Interpret the value of the slope in the regression equation.

d. Include the manufacturer in a multiple linear regression analysis using a "dummy" variable. Does it appear that some manufacturers can command a premium price? *Hint:* you will need to use a set of indicator variables.

e. Test each of the individual coefficients to see if they are significant.

f. Make a plot of the residuals and comment on whether they appear to follow a normal distribution.

g. Plot the residuals versus the fitted values. Do they seem to have the same amount of variation?

32. Great Plains Roofing and Siding Company Inc. sells roofing and siding products to home repair retailers, such as Lowe's and Home Depot, and commercial contractors. The owner is interested in studying the effects of several variables on the value of shingles sold ($000). The marketing manager is arguing that the company should spend more money on advertising, while a market researcher suggests it should focus more on making its brand and product more distinct from its competitors.

The company has divided their target marketing areas into districts. In each district, it collected information on the following variables: volume of sales (in thousands of dollars), advertising dollars (in thousands), number of active accounts, number of competing brands, and a rating of district potential.

Sales ($000s)	Advertising Dollars ($000s)	Number of Accounts	Number of Competitors	Market Potential
79.3	5.5	31	10	8
200.1	2.5	55	8	6
163.2	8.0	67	12	9
200.1	3.0	50	7	16
146.0	3.0	38	8	15
177.7	2.9	71	12	17
⋮	⋮	⋮	⋮	⋮
93.5	4.2	26	8	3
259.0	4.5	75	8	19
331.2	5.6	71	4	9

Conduct a multiple regression analysis to find the best predictors of sales. Additional data found in the Great Plains Excel file available on McGraw-Hill's online resource, Data Files.

a. Draw a scatter diagram comparing sales volume with each of the independent variables. Comment on the results.

b. Develop a correlation matrix. Do you see any problems? Does it appear there are any redundant independent variables?

c. Develop a regression equation. Conduct the global test. Can we conclude that some of the independent variables are useful in explaining the variation in the dependent variable?

d. Conduct a test of each of the independent variables. Are there any that should be dropped?

e. Refine the regression equation so the remaining variables are all significant.

f. Develop a histogram of the residuals and a normal probability plot. Are there any problems?

Data Set Exercises

Questions marked with ⤴ have data sets available on McGraw-Hill's online resource for *Basic Statistics*.

33. Refer to the Real Estate Data—Halifax Area online, which reports information on home listings. Use the list price of the home as the dependent variable and determine the regression equation with number of bedrooms, number of full bathrooms, number of square feet, and type as independent variables.

a. Write out the regression equation. Discuss each of the variables. For example, are any of the coefficients negative? *Note:* code House or Townhouse as 1, and Apartment as 0.

b. Determine the value of R^2. Interpret.

c. Develop a correlation matrix. Which independent variables have strong or weak correlations with the dependent variable? Do you see any problems with multicollinearity?

d. Conduct the global test on the set of independent variables. Interpret. Test at a significance level of 0.05.

e. Conduct a test of hypothesis on each of the independent variables. Would you consider deleting any of the variables? If so, which ones? Test at a significance level of 0.05.

f. Rerun the regression equation until only significant regression coefficients remain in the analysis. Identify these variables. Test at a significance level of 0.05.

g. Develop a normal probability plot of residuals from the final regression equation developed in part (f). Is it reasonable to conclude that the normality assumption has been met?

34. Refer to the Real Estate Data—Saskatoon online, which reports information on home listings. Use the list price of the home as the dependent variable and determine the regression equation with number of bedrooms, number of full bathrooms, number of square feet, and type as independent variables.

a. Write out the regression equation. Discuss each of the variables. For example, are any of the coefficients negative? *Note:* code House or Townhouse as 1, and Apartment as 0.

   b. Determine the value of R^2. Interpret.

   c. Develop a correlation matrix. Which independent variables have strong or weak correlations with the dependent variable? Do you see any problems with multicollinearity?

   d. Conduct the global test on the set of independent variables. Interpret. Test at a significance level of 0.05.

   e. Conduct a test of hypothesis on each of the independent variables. Would you consider deleting any of the variables? If so, which ones? Test at a significance level of 0.05.

   f. Rerun the regression equation until only significant regression coefficients remain in the analysis. Identify these variables. Test at a significance level of 0.05.

   g. Develop a normal probability plot of residuals from the final regression equation developed in part (f). Is it reasonable to conclude that the normality assumption has been met?

Practice Test

Part I Objective

1. Multiple regression analysis describes the relationship between one dependent variable and two or more _____ .

2. In multiple regression analysis, the regression coefficients are computed using the method of _____ . (residuals, normality, least squares, standardized)

3. In multiple regression analysis, the multiple standard error of the estimate is the square root of the _____ . (mean square error, residual, residual squared, explained variation)

4. The coefficient of multiple determination is the percent of variation in the dependent variable that is explained by the set of _____ .

5. The adjusted coefficient of determination compensates for the number of _____ . (dependent variables, errors, independent variables, explained variation)

6. In the Global Test of the regression coefficients, when the hypothesis is rejected, at least one coefficient is _____ .

7. The test statistic for the Global Test of regression coefficients is the _____ .

8. The test statistic for testing individual regression coefficients is the _____ .

9. A scatter plot of the residuals versus the fitted values of the dependent variable evaluates the assumption of _____ .

10. Multicollinearity exists when independent variables are _____ .

11. Another term for a qualitative variable is a _____ .

Part II Problems

1. Given the following ANOVA output:

Source	Sum of Squares	df	MS
Regression	1050.8	4	262.70
Error	83.8	20	4.19
Total	1134.6	24	

Predictor	Coefficient	St. Dev	*t*-ratio
Constant	70.06	2.13	32.89
X_1	0.42	0.17	2.47
X_2	0.27	0.21	1.29
X_3	0.75	0.30	2.50
X_4	0.42	0.07	6.00

   a. How many independent variables are there in the regression equation?

   b. Write out the regression equation.

   c. Compute the coefficient of multiple determination.

   d. Compute the multiple standard error of estimate. Use the 0.05 significance level.

   e. Conduct a test of hypothesis to determine if any of the regression coefficients are different from zero. Use the 0.05 significance level.

   f. Conduct a test of hypothesis on each of the regression coefficients. Can any of them be deleted? Test at a 5% significance level.

Computer Commands

1. **MegaStat** steps to produce the multiple regression output for the heating cost example are as follows:

    a. Import the data from McGraw-Hill's online resource. Select **Data Files** and Table 13–1, **Superior Realty.**

    b. Select **MegaStat**, **Correlation/Regression**, and **Regression Analysis.**

    c. For **Input ranges** enter *B3:D23* for **X, Independent variable(s)** and *A3:A23* for **Y, Dependent variable.**

    d. Click the **No predictions** box to select **Type in predictor values.** Enter the values *−5,12.5,10.*

    e. Remove the check beside **Test Intercept.** Click **OK.**

Regression Analysis			X
Input ranges:			
Cost!$B$3:$D$23	·	X, Independent variable(s)	OK
Cost!$A$3:$A$23	·	Y, Dependent variable	Clear
			Cancel
Type in predictor values ▼			Help
-5,12.5,10		predictor	

Options
- 95% ▼ Confidence Level
- ☐ Variance Inflation Factors
- ☐ Standardized Coefficients (betas)
- ☐ Test Intercept   ☐ Force Zero Intercept
- ☐ All Possible Regressions
- ☐ Stepwise Selection   ▲▼ 1 best model of each size

Residuals:
- ☐ Output Residuals
- ☐ Diagnostics and Influential Residuals
- ☐ Durbin-Watson   ☐ Cook's D
- ☐ Plot Residuals by Observation
- ☐ Plot Residuals by Predicted Y and X
- ☐ Normal Probability Plot of Residuals

2. **Excel** steps to produce the multiple regression output for the heating cost example are as follows:

    a. Import the data from McGraw-Hill's online resource. Select **Data Files** and Table 13–1, **Superior Realty.**

    b. Select **DATA** from the toolbar, **Data Analysis, Regression,** and click **OK.**

    c. For the **Input Y Range,** enter *A3:A23*, and for the **Input X Range,** enter *B3:D23*, check the **Labels** box, enter the **Output Range** as *G1*, and click **OK.**

Regression		? X
Input		OK
Input Y Range:	$A$3:$A$23	Cancel
Input X Range:	$B$3:$D$23	Help
☑ Labels ☐ Constant is Zero		
☐ Confidence Level:	95 %	
Output options		
⦿ Output Range:	$G$1	
○ New Worksheet Ply:		
○ New Workbook		
Residuals		
☐ Residuals ☐ Residual Plots		
☐ Standardized Residuals ☐ Line Fit Plots		
Normal Probability		
☐ Normal Probability Plots		

3. **MegaStat** steps to produce the plots of the residuals for the heating cost example are as follows:

a. Follow the steps in #1 above. Then check the following boxes for residual plots on the bottom right as shown:

4. **Excel** steps to produce the plots of the residuals for the heating cost example are as follows:

a. Follow the steps in #2 above. Then check the boxes for residual plots as shown:

5. **MegaStat** steps to produce the correlation matrix for the heating cost example are as follows:

a. Import the data from McGraw-Hill's online resource. Select **Data Files** and Table 13–1, **Superior Realty.**

b. Select **MegaStat**, and then **Correlation/Regression** and **Correlation Matrix.**

c. For the **Input range,** enter *A3:D23*. Click **OK.**

Correlation Matrix

Cost!$A$3:$D$23   —   Input

OK

Clear

Cancel

Help

6. Excel steps to produce the correlation matrix for the heating cost example are as follows:

    a. Import the data from McGraw-Hill's online resource. Select **Data Files** and Table 13–1, **Superior Realty.**

    b. Select **DATA** from the toolbar, **Data Analysis, Correlation,** and click **OK.**

    c. Enter the **Input Range** as *A3:D23*, select **Grouped by Columns** and the **Output Range** as *D25*, and click **OK.**

Correlation

Input

Input Range: $A$3:$D$23

Grouped By: ⦿ Columns   ○ Rows

☐ Labels in first row

Output options

⦿ Output Range: $D$25

○ New Worksheet Ply:

○ New Workbook

OK   Cancel   Help

Answers to Self-Reviews

13–1 **(a)** $339 500 or 339.5 (in $000) found by $y' = 2.5 + 3(40) + 4(72) - 5(16) + 0.2(20) + 1(5) = 339.50$.

    (b) The b_2 of 4 shows profit will go up $4000 for each extra hour the restaurant is open (if none of the other variables change). The b_3 of -5 implies profit will fall $5000 for each added kilometre away from the central area (if none of the other variables change).

13–2 **(a)** $n =$ The total degrees of freedom $(n - 1)$ is 25. The sample size is then 26.

    (b) 5

    (c) 1

    (d) $S_{e12345} = 1.414$, found by $\sqrt{2}$. Ninety-five percent of the residuals will be between -2.828 and 2.828, found by $\pm 2(1.414)$.

    (e) $R^2 = 0.714$, found by 100/140. 71.4% of the deviation in profit is accounted for by these five variables.

13–3 **(a)** $H_0: \beta_1 = \beta_2 = \beta_3 = \beta_4 = \beta_5 = 0$
        $H_1:$ Not all of the βs are 0.
        The decision rule is to reject H_0 if $F > 2.71$. The computed value of F is 10, found by 20/2. So, we reject H_0, which indicates at least one of the regression coefficients is different from zero.

    (b) For variable 1: $H_0: \beta_1 = 0$ and. $H_1: \beta_1 \neq 0$; the decision rule is: Reject H_0 if $t < -2.086$ or $t > 2.086$. Since 2.000 does not go beyond either of these limits, we fail to reject the null hypothesis. In addition, the *p*-value > 0.05, so there is not enough evidence to reject the null hypothesis. This regression coefficient could be zero. We can consider dropping this variable. By parallel logic the null hypothesis is rejected for variables 3 and 4.

    (c) We should consider dropping variables 1, 2, and 5. Variable 5 has the smallest absolute value of t, so delete it first and rerun the regression model.

13–4 **(a)** $y' = 15.7625 + 0.4415x_1 + 3.8598x_2$
           $= 15.7625 + 0.4415(30) + 3.8598$
           $= 32.87$

    (b) Female agents make $3860 more than male agents do.

    (c) $H_0: \beta_3 = 0$ & and $H_1: \beta_3 \neq 0$ $df = 17$, reject H_0 if $t < -2.110$ or $t > 2.110$
        $t = \dfrac{3.8598 - 0}{1.4724} = 2.621$
        Reject H_0. Gender should be included in the regression equation.

CHAPTER 14
Chi-Square Applications

For many years, TV executives used the guideline that 30% of the audience was watching each of the traditional big three prime-time networks and 10% was watching cable stations on a weekday night. A random sample of 500 viewers last Monday night showed that 165 homes were tuned in to the ABC affiliate, 140 to the CBS affiliate, 125 to the NBC affiliate, and the remainder was viewing a cable station. At the 0.05 significance level, can we conclude that the guideline is still reasonable? (Exercise 12, LO14-3)

LEARNING OBJECTIVES

When you have completed this chapter, you will be able to:

LO14-1 Test a hypothesis comparing an observed set of frequencies to an expected frequency distribution.

LO14-2 List and explain the characteristics and limitations of using of the chi-square statistic in goodness-of-fit tests.

LO14-3 Compute a goodness-of-fit test for unequal expected frequencies.

LO14-4 Perform a chi-square test for independence on a contingency table.

14.1 INTRODUCTION

Chapters 8 through 11 described tests of hypothesis for data of interval or ratio scale. Examples of interval and ratio scale include the grades on the first statistics test in your class, the incomes of corporate executives in technology companies, or years of employment of production workers in the Ford plant in Oakville, Ontario.

We conducted hypothesis tests about a single population mean, two population means, and three or more population means. For these tests we use interval or ratio data and assume that the populations follow the normal probability distribution. However there are hypothesis tests that do not require any assumption regarding the shape of the population. Hence, the assumption of a normal population is not necessary. These tests are referred to as *nonparametric* tests.

In this chapter, we discuss tests of hypothesis for nominal scale data. Recall that nominal data are simply classified into mutually exclusive categories. Examples include gender, province of birth, or brand of peanut butter purchased. In this chapter, we introduce a new test statistic, the chi-square statistic. It is most often used when there are more than two nominal scale categories.

LO14-1
14.2 GOODNESS-OF-FIT TEST: EQUAL EXPECTED FREQUENCIES

The goodness-of-fit test is one of the most commonly used statistical tests. It is particularly useful because it requires only the nominal level of measurement. So, we are able to conduct a test of hypothesis on data that have been classified into groups. The first illustration of this test involves the case in which the expected cell frequencies are equal.

As the full name implies, the purpose of the goodness-of-fit test is to compare an observed distribution to an expected distribution. An example will describe the hypothesis testing situation.

Example

Bubba's Fish and Pasta is a chain of restaurants located along the Gulf Coast. Bubba, the owner, is considering adding steak to his menu. Before doing so, he decides to hire Magnolia Research, LLC, to conduct a survey of adults as to their favorite meal when eating out. Magnolia selected a sample 120 adults and asked each to indicate their favourite meal when dining out. The results are reported in Table 14–1.

TABLE 14–1 Favourite Entrée as Selected by a Sample of 120 Adults

Favourite Entrée	Frequency
Chicken	32
Fish	24
Meat	35
Pasta	29
Total	120

Is it reasonable to conclude there is no preference for any one of the four entrées?

Solution

If there is no difference in the popularity of the four entrées, we would expect the observed frequencies to be equal—or nearly equal. To put it another way, we would expect as many adults to indicate they preferred chicken as fish. Thus, any discrepancy in the observed and expected frequencies is attributed to sampling error or chance.

What is the level of measurement in this problem? Note that when a person is selected, we can only classify the selected adult as to the entrée preferred. We do not get a reading or a measurement of any kind. The "measurement" or "classification" is based on the selected entrée. In addition, there is no natural order to the favourite entrée. No one entrée is assumed to be better than another. Therefore, the nominal scale is appropriate.

©Valerie Martin

If the entrées are equally popular, we would expect 30 adults to select each meal. Why is this so? If there are 120 adults in the sample and four categories, we expect that one-fourth of those surveyed would select each entrée. So, 30, found by 120/4, is the expected frequency for each category or cell, assuming that there is no preference for any of the entrées. This information is summarized in Table 14–2. An examination of the data indicates meat is the entrée selected most frequently (35 out of 120) and fish is selected least frequently (24 out of 120). Is the difference in the number of times each entrée is selected due to chance, or should we conclude that the entrées are not equally preferred?

TABLE 14–2 Observed and Expected Frequency for Survey of 120 Adults

Favourite Meal	Frequency Observed, f_o	Frequency Expected, f_e
Chicken	32	30
Fish	24	30
Meat	35	30
Pasta	29	30
Total	120	120

To investigate the issue, we use the five-step hypothesis-testing procedure.

Step 1: **State the null hypothesis and the alternative hypothesis.** The null hypothesis, H_0, is that there is no difference between the set of observed frequencies and the set of expected frequencies. In other words, any difference between the two sets of frequencies is attributed to sampling error. The alternative hypothesis, H_1, is that there is a difference between the observed and expected sets of frequencies. If the null hypothesis is rejected and the alternative hypothesis is accepted, we conclude the preferences are not equally distributed among the four categories (cells).

H_0: There is no difference in the proportion of adults selecting each entrée.
H_1: There is a difference in the proportion of adults selecting each entrée.

Step 2: **Select the level of significance.** We selected the 0.05 significance level. The probability is 0.05 that a true null hypothesis is rejected.

Step 3: **Select the test statistic.** The test statistic follows the chi-square distribution, designated by χ^2.

CHI-SQUARE TEST STATISTIC
$$\chi^2 = \sum \left[\frac{(f_o - f_e)^2}{f_e} \right]$$
[14–1]

with $k - 1$ degrees of freedom, where:

k is the number of categories.
f_o is an observed frequency in a particular category.
f_e is an expected frequency in a particular category.

We will examine the characteristics of the chi-square distribution in more detail shortly.

Step 4: **Formulate the decision rule.** Recall that the decision rule in hypothesis testing is the value that separates the region where we do not reject H_0 from the region where H_0 is rejected. This number is called the *critical value*. As we will soon see, the chi-square distribution is really a family of distributions. Each distribution has a slightly different shape, depending on the number of degrees of freedom. The number of degrees of freedom is $k - 1$, where k is the number of categories. In this particular problem, there are four categories, the four meal entrées. Because there are four categories, there is $k - 1 = 4 - 1 = 3$ degrees of freedom. As noted, a category is called a *cell*, and there are four cells. The critical value for 3 degrees of freedom and the 0.05 level of significance is found in Appendix B.6. A portion of that table is shown in Table 14–3. The critical value is 7.815, found by locating 3 degrees of freedom in the left margin and then moving horizontally (to the right) and reading the critical value in the 0.05 column.

TABLE 14–3 A Portion of the Chi-Square Table

Degrees of Freedom *df*	Right-Tail Area			
	0.10	**0.05**	**0.02**	**0.01**
1	2.706	3.841	5.412	6.635
2	4.605	5.991	7.824	9.210
3	6.251	7.815	9.837	11.345
4	7.779	9.488	11.668	13.277
5	9.236	11.070	13.388	15.086

The decision rule is to reject H_0 if the computed value of chi-square is greater than 7.815. If it is less than or equal to 7.815, do not reject H_0. Chart 14–1 shows the decision rule.

CHART 14–1 Chi-Square Probability Distribution for 3 Degrees of Freedom, Showing the Region of Rejection, 0.05 Level of Significance

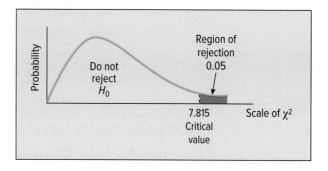

The decision rule indicates that if there are large differences between the observed and expected frequencies, resulting in a computed χ^2 of more than 7.815, the null hypothesis should be rejected. However, if the differences between f_o and f_e are small, the computed χ^2 value will be 7.815 or less, and the null hypothesis should not be rejected. The reasoning is that such small differences between the observed and expected frequencies are probably due to chance.

Step 5: **Compute the value of chi-square and make a decision.** Of the 120 adults in the sample, 32 indicated their favorite entrée was chicken. The counts were reported in Table 14–1. The calculations for chi-square follow. (Note, again, that the expected frequencies are the same for each cell.)

Column 1: Determine the differences between each f_o and f_e. That is, $f_o - f_e$. The sum of these differences will always be zero.

Column 2: Square the difference between each observed and expected frequency, that is, $(f_o - f_e)^2$.

Column 3: Divide the result for each observation by the expected frequency, that is, $\dfrac{(f_o - f_e)^2}{f_e}$. Finally, sum these values.

Favourite Entrée	f_o	f_e	(1) $(f_o - f_e)$	(2) $(f_o - f_e)^2$	(3) $\dfrac{(f_o - f_e)^2}{f_e}$
Chicken	32	30	2	4	0.133
Fish	24	30	−6	36	1.200
Meat	35	30	5	25	0.833
Pasta	29	30	−1	1	0.033
Total	120	120	0		2.200

The result is the value of χ^2, which is 2.20.

The computed χ^2 of 2.200 is not in the rejection region. It is less than the critical value of 7.815. The decision, therefore, is to not reject the null hypothesis. We conclude that the differences between the observed and the expected frequencies could be due to chance. The data do not suggest that the preference among the four entrées is different.

We can use software to compute the value of chi-square. The output of **MegaStat** follows. The steps are shown in the **Software Commands** section at the end of the chapter. The computed value of chi-square is 2.200, the same value obtained in our earlier calculations. Also, note the p-value is 0.5319, much larger than 0.05.

Goodness-of-Fit Test

observed	expected	O − E	(O − E)²/E	% of chisq
32	30.000	2.000	0.133	6.06
24	30.000	−6.000	1.200	54.55
35	30.000	5.000	0.833	37.88
29	30.000	−1.000	0.033	1.52
120	120.000	0.000	2.200	100.00

2.20	chi-square
3	df
0.5319	p-value

excel   Computer commands to produce the previous Chi-Square output can be found at the end of the chapter.

LO14-2   The chi-square distribution, which is used as the test statistic in this chapter, has the following characteristics:

1. **Chi-square is never negative.** This is because the difference between f_o and f_e is squared, that is, $(f_o - f_e)^2$.
2. **There is a family of chi-square distributions.** There is a chi-square distribution for 1 degree of freedom, another for 2 degrees of freedom, another for 3 degrees of freedom, and so on. In this type of problem, the number of degrees of freedom is determined by $k - 1$, where k is the number of categories. Therefore, the shape of the chi-square distribution does *not* depend on the size of the sample but on the number of categories used. For example, if 200 employees of an airline were classified into one of three categories—flight personnel, ground support, and administrative personnel—there would be 2 degrees of freedom ($k - 1 = 3 - 1 = 2$).
3. **The chi-square distribution is positively skewed.** However, **as the number of degrees of freedom increases, the distribution begins to approximate the normal probability distribution.** Chart 14–2 shows the distributions for selected degrees of freedom. Note that for 10 degrees of freedom, the curve is approaching a normal distribution.

CHART 14–2 Chi-Square Distributions for Selected Degrees of Freedom

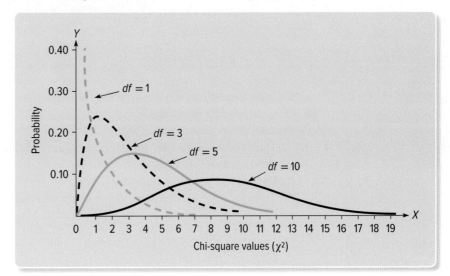

The human resources director at Georgetown Paper Inc. is concerned about absenteeism among workers on hourly wages. She decides to sample the records to determine whether absenteeism is distributed evenly throughout the six-day work week. The hypotheses are:

H_0: Absenteeism is evenly distributed throughout the work week.
H_1: Absenteeism is *not* evenly distributed throughout the work week.

The sample results are:

	Number Absent
Monday	12
Tuesday	9
Wednesday	11
Thursday	10
Friday	9
Saturday	9

(a) What are the numbers 12, 9, 11, 10, 9, and 9 called?
(b) How many categories (cells) are there?
(c) What is the *expected* frequency for each day?
(d) How many degrees of freedom are there?
(e) What is the chi-square critical value at the 1% significance level?
(f) Compute the χ^2 test statistic.
(g) What is the decision regarding the null hypothesis?
(h) Specifically, what does this indicate to the human resources director?

EXERCISES

1. In a particular chi-square goodness-of-fit test, there are four categories and 200 observations. Use the 0.05 significance level.
   a. How many degrees of freedom are there?
   b. What is the critical value of chi-square?

2. In a particular chi-square goodness-of-fit test, there are six categories and 500 observations. Use the 0.01 significance level.
   a. How many degrees of freedom are there?
   b. What is the critical value of chi-square?

3. The null hypothesis and the alternative hypothesis are as follows:

   H_0: The frequencies are equal.

   H_1: The frequencies are not equal.

Category	f_o
A	10
B	20
C	30
D	20

   a. State the decision rule, using the 0.05 significance level.
   b. Compute the value of chi-square.
   c. What is your decision regarding H_0?

4. The null hypothesis and the alternative hypothesis are as follows:

   H_0: The frequencies are equal.

   H_1: The frequencies are not equal.

Category	f_o
A	10
B	20
C	30

a. State the decision rule, using the 0.05 significance level.
b. Compute the value of chi-square.
c. What is your decision regarding H_0?

5. A six-sided die is rolled 30 times, and the numbers 1 through 6 appear as shown in the following frequency distribution. At the 0.10 significance level, can we conclude that the die is fair?

Outcome	Frequency	Outcome	Frequency
1	3	4	3
2	6	5	9
3	2	6	7

6. Classic Gold Inc. manages five golf courses. The director of golf for Classic Golf Inc. wishes to study the number of rounds of golf played per weekday at the five courses. He gathered the following sample information for 520 rounds:

Day	Rounds
Monday	124
Tuesday	74
Wednesday	104
Thursday	98
Friday	120

At the 0.05 significance level, is there a difference in the number of rounds played by day of the week?

7. A group of department store buyers viewed a new line of dresses and gave their opinions of them. The results were:

Opinion	Number of Buyers	Opinion	Number of Buyers
Outstanding	47	Good	39
Excellent	45	Fair	35
Very good	40	Undesirable	34

Because the largest number (47) indicated the new line is outstanding, the head designer thinks that this is a mandate to go into mass production of the dresses. The head sweeper (who somehow became involved in this) believes that there is not a clear mandate and claims that the opinions are evenly distributed among the six categories. He further states that the slight differences among the various counts are probably due to chance. Test the null hypothesis that there is no significant difference among the opinions of the buyers. Test at the 0.01 level of risk. Follow a formal approach; that is, state the null hypothesis, the alternative hypothesis, and so on.

8. The safety director of Honda took samples at random from the file of minor work-related accidents and classified them according to the time the accident took place.

Time	Number of Accidents	Time	Number of Accidents
8 a.m. up to 9 a.m.	6	1 p.m. up to 2 p.m.	7
9 a.m. up to 10 a.m.	6	2 p.m. up to 3 p.m.	8
10 a.m. up to 11 a.m.	20	3 p.m. up to 4 p.m.	19
11 a.m. up to 12 noon	8	4 p.m. up to 5 p.m.	6

Using the goodness-of-fit test and the 0.01 level of significance, determine whether the accidents are evenly distributed throughout the day. Write a brief explanation of your conclusion.

LO14-3 14.3 GOODNESS-OF-FIT TEST: UNEQUAL EXPECTED FREQUENCIES

The expected frequencies (f_e) in the previous example involving preferred entrées were all equal. According to the null hypothesis, it was expected that of the 120 adults in the study, an equal number would select each of the four entrées. So, we expect 30 to select chicken, 30 to select fish, and so on. The chi-square test can also be used if the expected frequencies are not equal.

The following example illustrates the case of unequal frequencies and also gives a practical use of chi-square, namely, to find whether a local experience differs from the national experience.

Example

The following information reports the number of times senior citizens are admitted to a hospital during a one-year period: 40% are not admitted, 30% are admitted once, 20% are admitted twice, and the remaining 10% are admitted three or more times.

A survey of 150 residents of Bartow Estates, a community devoted to active seniors, revealed 55 residents were not admitted during the last year, 50 were admitted to a hospital once, 32 were admitted twice, and the rest of those in the survey were admitted three or more times. Can we conclude the survey at Bartow Estates is consistent with the information suggested by the report? Use the 0.05 significance level.

Solution

We begin by organizing the above information into Table 14–4. Clearly, we cannot compare percentages given in the study to the frequencies reported for the Bartow Estates. However, these percentages can be converted to expected frequencies, f_e. According to the report, 40% of the Bartow residents in the survey did not require hospitalization. Thus, if there is no difference between the national experience and those of Bartow Estates, then 40% of the 150 seniors surveyed (60 residents) would not have been hospitalized. Further, 30% of those surveyed (45 residents) would have been admitted once, and so on. The observed frequencies for Bartow residents and the expected frequencies based on the percentages in the national study are given in Table 14–4.

TABLE 14–4 Summary of the Report and of Bartow Estates Residents

Number of Times Admitted	Reported Percentage of Total (%)	Number of Bartow Residents (f_o)	Expected Number of Residents (f_e)
0	40	55	60
1	30	50	45
2	20	32	30
3 or more	10	13	15
Total	100	150	150

The null hypothesis and the alternative hypotheses are as follows:

H_0: There is no difference between local and national experience for hospital admissions.
H_1: There is a difference between local and national experience for hospital admissions.

To find the decision rule we use Appendix B.6. There are four categories, so the degrees of freedom are $df = 4 - 1 = 3$. The critical value is 7.815. Therefore, the decision rule is to reject the null hypothesis if $\chi^2 > 7.815$. The decision rule is portrayed in Chart 14–3.

CHART 14–3 Decision Criteria for the Bartow Estates Study

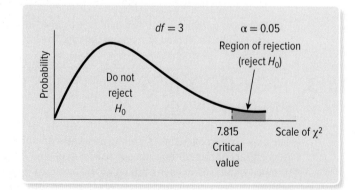

Statistics in Action

Many provincial governments operate lotteries to help fund hospitals, health care, and education, and amateur sport among other activities. In many lotteries, numbered balls are mixed and selected randomly from three groups of balls numbered zero through nine. Randomness would predict that the frequency of each number is equal. How would you prove that the selection machine ensured randomness? A chi-square, goodness-of-fit test could be used to prove or disprove randomness.

Now, to compute the chi-square test statistic:

Number of Times Admitted	(f_o)	(f_e)	$f_o - f_e$	$(f_o - f_e)^2/f_e$
0	55	60	−5	0.4167
1	50	45	5	0.5556
2	32	30	2	0.1333
3 or more	13	15	−2	0.2667
Total	150	150	0	1.3723

The computed values of χ^2 (1.3723) lies to the left of 7.815. Thus, there is not enough evidence to reject the null hypothesis. We conclude that there is no evidence of a difference between local and national experiences in hospital admissions.

MegaStat output is as follows:

Goodness-of-Fit Test

Observed	Expected	O − E	(O − E)²/E	% of chisq
55	60.000	−5.000	0.417	30.36
50	45.000	5.000	0.556	40.49
32	30.000	2.000	0.133	9.72
13	15.000	−2.000	0.267	19.43
150	150.000	0.000	1.372	100.00

1.37	chi-square
3	*df*
.7121	*p*-value

MegaStat returns the chi-square value of 1.37 as expected and a *p*-value of 0.7121. As the *p*-value is greater than the significance level, there is not enough evidence to reject the null hypothesis, and we conclude that there is no difference between local and national experiences in hospital admissions.

LO14-2 14.4 LIMITATIONS OF CHI-SQUARE

If there is an unusually small expected frequency in a cell, chi-square (if applied) might result in an erroneous conclusion. This can happen because f_e appears in the denominator, and dividing by a very small number makes the quotient quite large! Two generally accepted rules regarding small cell frequencies are as follows:

1. **If there are only two cells, the *expected* frequency in each cell should be 5 or more.** The computation of chi-square would be permissible in the following problem, involving a minimum f_e of 6:

Individual	f_o	f_e
Literate	643	642
Illiterate	7	6

2. **For more than two cells, chi-square should *not* be used if more than 20% of the f_e cells have expected frequencies less than 5.** According to this policy, it would not be appropriate to use the goodness-of-fit test on the following data. Three of the seven cells, or 43%, have expected frequencies (f_e) of less than 5.

Level of Management	f_o	f_e
Foreman	30	32
Supervisor	110	113
Manager	86	87
Middle management	23	24
Assistant vice-president	5	2
Vice-president	5	4
Senior vice president	4	1
Total	263	263

To show the reason for the 20% policy, we conducted the goodness-of-fit test on the above data on the levels of management. The hypothesis is that the observed and expected frequency distributions are the same. The **MegaStat** output follows.

Observed	Expected	O − E	$(O − E)^2/E$	% of Chi-Square
30	32.000	−2.000	0.125	0.89
110	113.000	−3.000	0.080	0.57
86	87.000	−1.000	0.011	0.08
23	24.000	−1.000	0.042	0.30
5	2.000	3.000	4.500	32.12
5	4.000	1.000	0.250	1.78
4	1.000	3.000	9.000	64.25
263	263.000	0.000	14.008	100.00

14.01	chi-square	
6	df	
.0295	p-value	

For this test at the 0.05 significance level, H_0 is rejected if the computed value of chi-square is greater than 12.592. The computed value is 14.01, with a p-value of 0.0295. So, we reject the null hypothesis that the observed frequencies represent a random sample from the population of the expected values. Examine the **MegaStat** output. More than 98% of the computed chi-square value is accounted for by the three vice-president categories ([4.500 + 0.250 + 9.000]/14.008 = 0.9815). Logically, too much weight is being given to these categories.

The dilemma can be resolved by combining categories if it is logical to do so. In the above example, combining the three vice-presidential categories satisfies the 20% policy.

Level of Management	f_o	f_e
Foreman	30	32
Supervisor	110	113
Manager	86	87
Middle management	23	24
Vice-president	14	7
Total	263	263

The computed value of chi-square with the revised categories is 7.26. See the following **MegaStat** output. This value is less than the critical value of 9.488 for the 0.05 significance level. The null hypothesis is, therefore, not rejected at the 0.05 significance level. This indicates that there is no significant difference between the observed distribution and the expected distribution.

Observed	Expected	O − E	$(O − E)^2/E$	% of Chi-Square
30	32.000	−2.000	0.125	1.72
110	113.000	−3.000	0.080	1.10
86	87.000	−1.000	0.011	0.16
23	24.000	−1.000	0.042	0.57
14	7.000	7.000	7.000	96.45
263	263.000	0.000	7.258	100.00

7.26	chi-square	
4	df	
.1229	p-value	

Note that the *p*-value is 0.1229. As the *p*-value is greater than the significance level, there is not enough evidence to reject the null hypothesis, and we conclude that there is no difference between the observed distribution and the expected distribution.

---

self-review 14–2

Accounts receivable are classified as "current," "late," and "not collectible." Industry figures show that 60% of accounts receivable are current, 30% are late, and 10% are not collectible. Massa and Barr, attorneys in Devon, Alberta, have 500 accounts receivable: 320 are current, 120 are late, and 60 are not collectible. Are these numbers in agreement with the industry distribution? Use the 0.05 significance level.

EXERCISES

9. The following hypotheses are given:

    H_0: Forty percent of the observations are in category A, 40% are in B, and 20% are in C.
    H_1: The distribution of the observations are not as described in H_0.

    We took a sample of 60, with the following results:

Category	f_o
A	30
B	20
C	10

    a. State the decision rule using the 0.01 significance level.
    b. Compute the value of chi-square.
    c. What is your decision regarding H_0?

10. The chief of security for a shopping mall in Calgary, Alberta, was directed to study the problem of missing goods. He selected a sample of 100 boxes that had been tampered with and ascertained that for 60 of the boxes, the missing pants, shoes, and so on were attributed to shoplifting. For 30 other boxes, employees had stolen the goods, and for the remaining 10 boxes, he blamed poor inventory control. In his report to the mall management, can he say that shoplifting is *twice* as likely to be the cause of the loss compared with either employee theft or poor inventory control and that employee theft and poor inventory control are equally likely? Use the 0.02 level.

11. A bank credit card department knows from experience that 5% of the cardholders have had some high school, 15% have completed high school, 25% have had some college or university, and 55% have completed college or university. Of the 500 cardholders whose cards have been called in for failure to pay their charges this month, 50 had some high school, 100 had completed high school, 190 had some college or university, and 160 had completed college or university. Can we conclude that the distribution of cardholders who do not pay their charges is different from all others? Use the 0.01 significance level.

12. For many years, U.S. TV executives used the guideline that 30% of the audience was watching each of the prime-time networks and 10% cable stations on a weekday night. A random sample of 500 viewers last Monday night showed that 165 homes were tuned in to the ABC affiliate, 140 to the CBS affiliate, 125 to the NBC affiliate, and the remainder was viewing a cable station. At the 0.05 significance level, can we conclude that the guideline is still reasonable?

LO14-4 ## 14.5 CONTINGENCY TABLE ANALYSIS

In Chapter 4, where we discussed bivariate data, we studied the relationship between two variables. We described a contingency table that simultaneously summarizes two nominal scale variables of interest. For example, a sample of students enrolled in the School of Business is classified by gender (male or female) and major (accounting, finance, marketing, or human resources). This classification is based on the nominal scale because there is no natural order to the classifications.

In Chapter 4, we also discussed contingency tables. We illustrated the relationship between loyalty to a company and length of employment. We can use the chi-square statistic to test whether tow nominal-scaled variables are related or not. To put it another way, is one variable independent of the other?

Here are some examples where we are interested in testing whether two variables are related:

- A sample of 100 drivers who were stopped for speeding violations was classified by gender and whether or not they were wearing a seat belt. For this sample, is wearing a seat belt related to gender?
- The Ford Motor Company operates several assembly plants. One such plant operates three shifts per day, five days per week. The quality control manager wishes to compare the quality level on the three shifts. Vehicles are classified by quality level (acceptable, unacceptable) and shift (day, afternoon, or night). Is there a difference in the quality level on the three shifts? That is, is the quality of the product related to the shift when it was manufactured? Or, is the quality of the product independent of the shift on which it was manufactured?
- Does a male released from federal prison make a different adjustment to civilian life if he returns to his hometown or if he goes elsewhere to live? The two variables are adjustment to civilian life and place of residence. Note that both variables are measured at the nominal level.

The following example illustrates the study of the relationship between two nominal-scale variables using the chi-square distribution:

Example	Does an individual released from federal prison make a different adjustment to civilian life if he returns to his hometown or if he goes elsewhere to live? To put it another way, is there a relationship between adjustment to civilian life and place of residence after release from prison? Use the 0.01 level of significance.
Solution	As before, the first step in hypothesis testing is to state the null and alternative hypotheses.

H_0: There is no relationship between adjustment to civilian life and where the individual lives after being released from prison.

H_1: There is a relationship between adjustment to civilian life and where the individual lives after being released from prison.

Psychologists interviewed 200 randomly selected former prisoners. Using a series of questions, the psychologists classified the adjustment of each individual to civilian life as outstanding, good, fair, or unsatisfactory. The classifications for the 200 former prisoners were tallied as follows. Joseph Camden, for example, returned to his hometown and has shown outstanding adjustment to civilian life. His case is one of the 27 tallies in the upper left box.

Residence after Release from Prison	Adjustment to Civilian Life			
	Outstanding	**Good**	**Fair**	**Unsatisfactory**
Hometown	JHT JHT JHT JHT JHT II	JHT JHT JHT JHT JHT JHT JHT	JHT JHT JHT JHT JHT JHT III	JHT JHT JHT JHT JHT
Not hometown	JHT JHT III	JHT JHT JHT	JHT JHT JHT JHT JHT II	JHT JHT JHT JHT JHT

The tallies in each box, or *cell*, were counted. The counts are given in Table 14–5. In this case, the psychologists wondered whether adjustment to civilian life is *contingent* on or related to where the prisoner goes after release from prison.

TABLE 14–5 Adjustment to Civilian Life and Place of Residence

Residence after Release from Prison	Adjustment to Civilian Life				
	Outstanding	Good	Fair	Unsatisfactory	Total
Hometown	27	35	33	25	120
Not hometown	13	15	27	25	80
Total	40	50	60	50	200

Once we know how many rows (2) and columns (4) there are in the contingency table, we can determine the critical value and the decision rule. For a chi-square test of significance where two traits are classified in a contingency table, the degrees of freedom are found by:

$$df = (\text{number of rows} - 1)(\text{number of columns} - 1) = (r - 1)(c - 1)$$

In this problem:

$$df = (r - 1)(c - 1) = (2 - 1)(4 - 1) = 3$$

To find the critical value for 3 degrees of freedom and the 0.01 level (selected earlier), refer to Appendix B.6. It is 11.345. The decision rule is to reject the null hypothesis if the computed value of χ^2 is greater than 11.345. The decision rule is portrayed graphically in Chart 14–4.

CHART 14–4 Chi-Square Distribution for 3 Degrees of Freedom

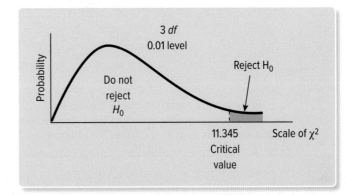

Next, we find the computed value of χ^2. The observed frequencies, f_o, are shown in Table 14–5. How are the corresponding expected frequencies, f_e, determined? Note in the "Total" column of Table 14–5 that 120 of the 200 former prisoners (60%) returned to their hometowns. *If there were no relationship* between adjustment and residency after release from prison, we would expect 60% of the 40 ex-prisoners who made outstanding adjustment to civilian life to reside in their hometowns. Thus, the expected frequency f_e for the upper left cell is $0.60 \times 40 = 24$. Likewise, if there were no relationship between adjustment and present residence, we would expect 60% of the 50 ex-prisoners (30) who had "good" adjustment to civilian life to reside in their hometowns.

Further, note that 80 of the 200 ex-prisoners studied (40%) did not return to their hometowns. Thus, of the 60 considered by the psychologists to have made "fair" adjustment to civilian life, 0.40×60, or 24, would be expected not to return to their hometowns.

The expected frequency for any cell can be determined by:

EXPECTED FREQUENCY $$f_e = \frac{(\text{Row total})(\text{Column total})}{\text{Grand total}}$$ [14–2]

Using this formula, the expected frequency for the upper left cell in Table 14–5 is:

$$\text{Expected frequency} = \frac{(\text{Row total})(\text{Column total})}{\text{Grand total}} = \frac{(120)(40)}{200} = 24$$

The observed frequencies, f_o, and the expected frequencies, f_e, for all of the cells in the contingency table are listed in Table 14–6.

TABLE 14–6 Observed and Expected Frequencies

Residence after Release from Prison	Adjustment to Civilian Life									
	Outstanding		Good		Fair		Unsatisfactory		Total	
	f_o	f_e	f_o	f_e	f_o	f_e	f_o	f_e	f_o	f_e
Hometown	27	24	35	30	33	36	25	30	120	120
Not hometown	13	16	15	20	27	24	25	20	80	80
Total	40	40	50	50	60	60	50	50	200	200

Must be equal

$\dfrac{(80)(50)}{200}$

Must be equal

Recall that the computed value of chi-square using formula (14–1) is found by:

$$\chi^2 = \Sigma \left[\frac{(f_o - f_e)^2}{f_e} \right]$$

Starting with the upper left cell:

$$\chi^2 = \frac{(27 - 24)^2}{24} + \frac{(35 - 30)^2}{30} + \frac{(33 - 36)^2}{36} + \frac{(25 - 30)^2}{30}$$
$$+ \frac{(13 - 16)^2}{16} + \frac{(15 - 20)^2}{20} + \frac{(27 - 24)^2}{24} + \frac{(25 - 20)^2}{20}$$
$$= 0.375 + 0.833 + 0.250 + 0.833 + 0.563 + 1.250 + 0.375 + 1.250$$
$$= 5.729$$

Because the computed value of chi-square (5.729) lies in the region to the left of 11.345, the null hypothesis is not rejected at the 0.01 level. We conclude there is no evidence of a relationship between adjustment to civilian life and where the prisoner resides after being released from prison.

excel

Computer commands to produce the above output can be found at the end of the chapter.

MegaStat output follows.

Chi-square Contingency Table Test for Independence

	Outstanding	Good	Fair	Unsatisfactory	Total
Hometown	27	35	33	25	120
Not hometown	13	15	27	25	80
Total	40	50	60	50	200

5.73 chi-square
3 df
.1256 p-value

Observe that the value of chi-square is the same as that calculated earlier. **MegaStat** also reports the p-value as 0.1256. Therefore, the probability of finding a value of the test statistic as large or larger is 0.1256 when the null hypothesis is true. Therefore, there is not enough evidence to reject the null hypothesis.

self-review 14–3

A social scientist sampled 140 people and classified them according to income level and whether or not they played a provincial lottery in the last month. The sample information is reported below. Is it reasonable to conclude that playing the lottery is related to income level? Use the 0.05 significance level.

(a) What is this table called?
(b) State the null hypothesis and the alternative hypothesis.
(c) What is the decision rule?
(d) Determine the value of chi-square.
(e) Make a decision on the null hypothesis. Interpret the result.

	Income			
	Low	Middle	High	Total
Played	46	28	21	95
Did not play	14	12	19	45
Total	60	40	40	140

EXERCISES

13. The director of advertising for a large newspaper is studying the relationship between the type of community in which a subscriber resides and the portion of the newspaper he or she reads first. For a sample of readers, she collected the following sample information:

	National News	Sports	Comics
City	170	124	90
Suburb	120	112	100
Rural	130	90	88

At the 0.05 significance level, can we conclude there is a relationship between the type of community where the person resides and the portion of the paper read first?

14. Four brands of light bulbs are being considered for use in a large manufacturing plant. The director of purchasing asked for samples of 100 from each manufacturer. The numbers of acceptable and unacceptable bulbs from each manufacturer are shown below. At the 0.05 significance level, is there a difference in the quality of the bulbs?

	Manufacturer			
	A	B	C	D
Unacceptable	12	8	5	11
Acceptable	88	92	95	89
Total	100	100	100	100

15. The quality control department at Food Town Inc. conducts a monthly check on the comparison of scanned prices to posted prices. The chart below summarizes the results of a sample of 500 items last month. Company management would like to know whether there is any relationship between error rates on regular priced items and specially priced items. Use the 0.01 significance level.

	Regular Price	Advertised Special Price
Undercharged	20	10
Overcharged	15	30
Correct price	200	225

16. The use of cellular phones in automobiles has increased dramatically in the last few years. Of concern to traffic experts, as well as manufacturers of cellular phones, is the effect on accident rates. Is someone who is using a cellular phone more likely to be involved in a traffic accident? What is your conclusion from the following sample information? Use the 0.05 significance level.

	Had Accident in the Last Year	Did Not Have an Accident in the Last Year
Cellular phone in use	25	300
Cellular phone not in use	50	400

Chapter Summary

I. The characteristics of the chi-square distribution are as follows:

  A. The value of chi-square is never negative.

  B. The chi-square distribution is positively skewed.

  C. There is a family of chi-square distributions.
     1. Each time the degrees of freedom change, a new distribution is formed.
     2. As the degrees of freedom increase, the distribution approaches a normal distribution.

II. A goodness-of-fit test will show whether an observed set of frequencies could have come from a hypothesized population distribution.

  A. The degrees of freedom are $k - 1$, where k is the number of categories.

  B. The formula for computing the value of chi-square is:

$$\chi^2 = \Sigma \left[\frac{(f_o - f_e)^2}{f_e} \right]$$
  [14–1]

III. A contingency table is used to test whether two traits or characteristics are related.

  A. Each observation is classified according to two traits.

  B. The expected frequency is determined as follows:

$$f_e = \frac{(\text{Row total})(\text{Column total})}{\text{Grand total}}$$
  [14–2]

  C. The degrees of freedom are found by:

$$df = (\text{Rows} - 1)(\text{Columns} - 1)$$

  D. The usual hypothesis testing procedure is used.

Chapter Exercises

17. Vehicles heading west on Front Street may turn right, left, or go straight ahead at Elm Street. The city traffic engineer believes that half of the vehicles will continue straight through the intersection. Of the remaining half, equal proportions will turn right and left. Two hundred vehicles were observed, with the following results. Use the 0.10 significance level. Can we conclude that the traffic engineer is correct?

	Straight	Right Turn	Left Turn
Frequency	112	48	40

18. The publisher of a sports magazine plans to offer new subscribers one of three gifts: a sweatshirt with the logo of their favourite team, a coffee cup with the logo of their favourite team, or a pair of earrings also with the logo of their favourite team. In a sample of 500 new subscribers, the number selecting each gift is

reported below. At the 0.05 significance level, is there a preference for the gifts, or should we conclude that the gifts are equally well liked?

Gift	Frequency
Sweatshirt	183
Coffee cup	175
Earrings	142

19. In a particular market there are three commercial television stations, each with its own evening news program from 6:00 to 6:30 p.m. According to a report in this morning's local newspaper, a random sample of 150 viewers last night revealed 53 watched the news on CTV Television, 64 watched on Global Television, and 33 on CityTV. At the 0.05 significance level, is there a difference in the proportion of viewers watching the three channels?

20. There are four entrances to a large office building in downtown Halifax. The building maintenance supervisor would like to know if the entrances are equally utilized. To investigate, 400 people were observed entering the building. The number using each entrance is reported below. At the 0.01 significance level, is there a difference in the use of the four entrances?

Entrance	Frequency
Main Street	140
Broad Street	120
Cherry Street	90
Walnut Street	50
Total	400

21. To update her marketing strategies, the owner of a private ski club in Collingwood, Ontario, wants to compare the current geographical distribution of her club members to those of 10 years ago. According to her past records, 21% are from New York State, 24% from Ontario (excluding the GTA), 35% from the GTA, and 20% from other areas. Listed below is a breakdown of a sample of 400 current members, randomly selected from all club members:

At the 0.01 significance level, has the geographical distribution of her club members changed?

Area	Frequency
New York State	68
Ontario (excluding GTA)	104
GTA	155
Other	73
Total	400

22. Banner Mattress and Furniture Company wishes to study the number of credit applications received per day for the last 300 days. The information follows:

Number of Credit Applications	Frequency (Number of Days)
0	50
1	77
2	81
3	48
4	31
5 or more	13

To interpret, there were 50 days on which no credit applications were received, 77 days on which only one application was received, and so on. Would it be reasonable to conclude that the population distribution is Poisson with a mean of 2.0? Use the 0.05 significance level. *Hint:* To find the expected frequencies, use the Poisson distribution with a mean of 2.0. Find the probability of exactly one success given a Poisson distribution with a mean of 2.0. Multiply this probability by 300 to find the expected frequency for the number of days in which there was exactly one application. Determine the expected frequency for the other days in a similar manner.

23. In the early 2000s, the Deep Down Mining Company implemented new safety guidelines. Prior to these new guidelines, management expected there to be 0 accidents in 40% of the months, 1 accident in 30% of the months, 2 accidents in 20% of the months, and 3 accidents in 10% of the months. Over the last 10 years, or 120 months, there have been 46 months in which there were no accidents, 40 months in which there was 1 accident, 22 months in which there were 2 accidents, and 12 months in which there were 3 accidents. At the

0.05 significance level, can the management at Deep Down conclude that there has been a change in the monthly accident distribution?

24. A recent study by a large retailer designed to determine whether there was a relationship between the importance a store manager placed on advertising and the size of the store revealed the following sample information:

	Important	Not Important
Small	40	52
Medium	106	47
Large	67	32

What is your conclusion? Use the 0.05 significance level.

25. Two hundred managers from various levels were randomly selected and interviewed regarding their concern about environmental issues. The response of each person was tallied into one of three categories: no concern, some concern, and great concern. The results were:

Level of Management	No Concern	Some Concern	Great Concern
Top management	15	13	12
Middle management	20	19	21
Supervisor	7	7	6
Group leader	28	21	31

Use the 0.01 significance level to determine whether there is a relationship between management level and environmental concern.

26. A study regarding the relationship between age and the amount of pressure sales personnel feel in relation to their jobs revealed the following sample information. At the 0.01 significance level, is there a relationship between job pressure and age?

	Degree of Job Pressure		
Age (years)	Low	Medium	High
Less than 25	20	18	22
25 up to <40	50	46	44
40 up to <60	58	63	59
60 and older	34	43	43

27. The claims department at the Wise Insurance Company believes that younger drivers have more accidents and, therefore, should be charged higher insurance rates. Investigating a sample of 1200 Wise policyholders revealed the following breakdown on whether a claim had been filed in the last three years and the age of the policyholder. Is it reasonable to conclude that there is a relationship between the age of the policyholder and whether or not the person filed a claim? Use the 0.05 significance level.

Age Group	No Claim	Claim
16 up to <25	170	74
25 up to <40	240	58
40 up to <55	400	44
55 or older	190	24
Total	1000	200

28. A sample of employees at a large chemical plant was asked to indicate a preference for one of three pension plans. The results are given in the following table. Does it seem that there is a relationship between the pension plan selected and the job classification of the employees? Use the 0.01 significance level.

	Pension Plan		
Job Class	Plan A	Plan B	Plan C
Supervisor	10	13	29
Clerical	19	80	19
Labour	81	57	22

29. A recent survey suggested that 55% of all adults favoured legislation requiring restaurants to include information on their menus regarding calories, fat, and carbohydrates of the menu items. The same survey indicated that 28% of all adult respondents were opposed to such legislation. The remainder of those surveyed was unsure of the need. A sample of 450 young adults revealed 220 favoured the proposed legislation, 158 opposed it, and the remaining 72 were unsure. At the 0.05 significance level, is it reasonable to conclude the position of young adults regarding adding dietary information to restaurant menus is different from the total population?

30. Is it proper to respond with an email after a job interview thanking the prospective employer for the interview? This question was asked of a sample of 200 human resource professionals and 250 technical personnel who were a part of the interview process. The results are reported below. At the 0.01 significance level, is it reasonable to conclude that human resource and technical personnel differ on whether an email response is appropriate?

Email response	Human Resource	Technical
Very appropriate	35	98
Somewhat appropriate	95	114
Somewhat inappropriate	40	22
Very inappropriate	30	16
Total	200	250

31. Each of the digits in a raffle is thought to have the same chance of occurrence. The table shows the frequency of each digit for consecutive drawings in an Alberta lottery. Perform the chi-square test to see if you reject the hypothesis at the 0.05 significance level that the digits are from a uniform population.

Digit	Frequency	Digit	Frequency
0	44	5	24
1	32	6	31
2	23	7	27
3	27	8	28
4	23	9	21

32. John Isaac Inc., a designer and installer of industrial signs, employs 60 people. The company recorded the type of the most recent visit to a doctor by each employee. A national assessment conducted in 2010 found that 53% of all physician visits were to primary care physicians, 19% to medical specialists, 17% to surgical specialists, and 11% to emergency departments. Test at the 0.01 significance level if Isaac employees differ significantly from the survey distribution. Here are their results:

Visit Type	Number of Visits
Primary care	29
Medical specialist	11
Surgical specialist	16
Emergency	4

33. A survey by the *Chronicle* investigated the public's attitude toward the federal deficit. Each sampled citizen was classified as to whether he or she felt the government should reduce the deficit, increase the deficit, or if he or she had no opinion. The sample results of the study by gender are reported below:

Gender	Reduce the Deficit	Increase the Deficit	No Opinion
Male	244	194	68
Female	305	114	25

At the 0.05 significance level, is it reasonable to conclude that gender is independent of a person's position on the deficit?

34. Did you ever purchase a bag of M&M's candies and wonder about the distribution of colours? For peanut M&M's, 12% are brown, 15% yellow, 12% red, 23% blue, 23% orange, and 15% green. A bag purchased at the college book store had 12 blue, 14 brown, 13 yellow, 14 red, 7 orange, and 12 green. Is it reasonable to conclude that the actual distribution agrees with the expected distribution? Use the 0.05 significance level.

35. A survey of movie ticket purchases made last Sunday afternoon showed the following:

	Type of Movie			
Gender	Action	Documentary	Romantic	Comedy
Male	75	50	60	60
Female	50	50	95	60
Total	125	100	155	120

Is there a relationship between the type of movie ticket purchased and gender? Use the 0.01 significance level.

36. The Coffee Producers Association reports the following information on age and the amount of coffee consumed in a month. Each of the 300 respondents is classified according to two criteria: (1) his or her age and (2) the amount of coffee consumed. The results are as follows:

	Coffee Consumption			
Age (years)	Low	Moderate	High	Total
Under 30	36	32	24	92
30 to under 50	28	54	47	129
50 or more	26	24	29	79
Total	90	110	100	300

Is there a relationship between coffee consumption and age? Test at the 0.05 significance level.

37. A sample of executives was surveyed about loyalty to their company. One of the questions was, "If you were given an offer by another company equal to or slightly better than your present position, would you remain with the company or take the other position"? The responses of the 200 executives in the survey were cross-tabulated with their length of service with the company. The results are as follows:

	Length of Service (in Years)				
Loyalty	Less than 1	1–5 Years	6–10 Years	More than 10	Total
Would remain	10	30	5	75	120
Would not remain	25	15	10	30	80
	35	45	15	105	200

Is there a relationship between loyalty and years of service? Test at the 0.05 significance level.

38. A dairy producer is developing ice cream flavours. At a recent country fair, 300 adults were asked to taste test four of the latest flavours: carrot cake, coffee walnut, apple-taffy and coconut cream. The results are 30 preferred carrot cake, 115 coffee walnut, 50 apple-taffy and 105 coconut cream. At the 10% level of significance, is there a difference in preference for ice cream flavours?

39. Are students more likely to be absent from classes on Fridays? A count was taken in Mr. Smythe's statistics class over the past four weeks. The results are as follows:

Day of the Week	Number Absent
Monday	11
Tuesday	6
Wednesday	8
Thursday	7
Friday	12

Test at the 0.05 level of significance. Can we conclude that students are more likely to be absent on Fridays?

40. From a recent survey of 1500 households in Canada, the Cable and Telecommunications Association reported that the numbers of HDTVs per household are as follows:

Number of HDTVs	Number of Households
0	120
1–2	840
3–4	420
5 or more	120
Total	1500

The manager at the Best Buy store in Rosemere wanted to find out if the reported results were the same for his city. He decided to sample 100 customers who came into his store last week. He found that 7 households had 0 HDTVs, 55 had 1 to 2 HDTVs, 28 had 3 to 4 HDTVs, and 10 had 5 or more HDTVs. At the 0.10 level of significance, is it reasonable to conclude that the number of HDTVs per household in Rosemere is the same as that reported by the Cable and Telecommunications Association?

41. Professor Brown has been teaching Statistics 201 for 20 years. In the past, student grades for the 40 students in his classes have been distributed with the breakdown shown in the following table in the column labelled "Statistics 201." His fall class last semester achieved the grades as shown in the column labelled "Fall Class." At the 0.05 level of significance, is there is difference in the distribution of grades for his fall class?

Grade	Statistics 201	Fall Class
A	3	7
B	8	11
C	21	16
D	5	3
F	3	3
	40	40

Data Set Exercises

Questions marked with 📈 have data sets available on McGraw-Hill's online resource for *Basic Statistics*.

📈 **42.** Refer to the Real Estate Data—Saskatoon area online, which include reports on home listings.
  a. Develop a contingency table that shows the type of listing (apartment + townhouse, or house). Is there an association between the variable type and list price? Use under $300 000, $300 000 to under $500 000, $500 000 to under $700 000, and over $700 000 as the list price categories. Use the 0.05 significance level.
  b. Develop a contingency table that shows whether a listing has three or fewer bedrooms and list price. Is there an association between the variables three or fewer bedrooms and price? Use under $300 000, $300 000 to under $500 000, $500 000 to under $700 000, and over $700 000 as the list price categories. Use the 0.05 significance level.

📈 **43.** Refer to the Real Estate Data—Halifax Area online, which reports information on home listings.
  a. Develop a contingency table that shows the type of listing (apartment, townhouse, or house). Is there an association between the variable type and list price? Use under $400 000, $400 000 to under $600 000, $600 000 to under $800 000, and over $800 000 as the list price categories. Use the 0.05 significance level.
  b. Develop a contingency table that shows whether a listing has three or fewer bedrooms and list price. Is there an association between the variables three or fewer bedrooms and price? Use under $400 000, $400 000 to under $600 000, $600 000 to under $800 000, and over $800 000 as the list price categories. Use the 0.05 significance level.

📈 **44.** Refer to the Whitner Autoplex file online, which reports information on car sales.
  a. Develop a contingency table that shows the code and selling price. Is there an association between the variables code and selling price? Use under $25 000, $25 000 to under $35 000, and over $35 000 as the selling price categories. Use the 0.05 significance level.
  b. Develop a contingency table that shows the age of the buyer and the selling price. Is there an association between the age of the buyer and the selling price? Use under $25 000, $25 000 to under $35 000, and over $35 000 as the selling price categories. Use the 0.05 significance level.

Practice Test

Part I Objective

1. The _____ level of measurement is required for the chi-square goodness-of-fit test.

2. To use the chi-square distribution as the test statistic, we assume that the population _____. (follows the normal distribution, meets the binomial conditions, or no assumption is necessary about the population shape)

3. Which of the following is not a characteristic of the chi-square distribution? _____ (positively skewed, based on degrees of freedom, cannot be negative, at least 30 observations)

4. In a contingency table, how many variables are summarized? (two, four, fifty)

5. If a contingency table has four columns and three rows, it will have _____ degrees of freedom.

6. In a contingency table, we test the null hypothesis that the variables are _____. (independent, dependent, mutually exclusive, normally distributed)

7. A sample of 100 undergraduate business students is classified by major (five groups); hence, there are _____ degrees of freedom.

8. The sum of the observed and expected frequencies _____.(are the same, must be more than 30, can assume negative values, must be at least 5%.)

9. In a goodness-of-fit test with 200 observations and 4 degrees of freedom, the critical value of chi-square is _____ assuming the 0.05 significance level.

10. The shape of the chi-square distribution is based on _____. (shape of the population, degrees of freedom, level of significance, level of measurement)

Part II Problems

1. A recent census report indicated 65% of families have two parents, 20% have a mother only present, 10% have a father only present, and 5% have no parent present. A random sample of 200 children from a rural school district revealed the following:

Two Parents	Mother Only	Father Only	No Parent	Total
120	40	30	10	200

Is there sufficient evidence to conclude that the proportion of families by type of parent present in the particular rural school district differs from that reported in the recent census? Use the 0.05 significance level.

2. A book publisher wants to investigate the type of books selected for recreational reading by adult men and women. A random sample provided the following information. At the 0.05 significance level, should we conclude that gender is related or unrelated to the type of book selected?

Gender	Mystery	Romance	Self-Help	Total
Men	250	100	190	540
Women	130	170	200	500

Computer Commands

1. **MegaStat** commands to create the chi-square goodness-of-fit test for Bubba's Fish and Pasta example are as follows:

   a. Enter the information from Table 14–2 into a worksheet as shown.

   b. Select **MegaStat**, **Chi-Square/Crosstab** and **Goodness of Fit Test**.

   c. In the dialog box enter *B2:B5* as the **Observed values** and *C2:C5* as the **Expected values**. Click **OK**.

	A	B	C
1	Favourite Meat	Observed Frequency (f_o)	Expected Frequency (f_e)
2	Chicken	32	30
3	Fish	24	30
4	meat	35	30
5	Pasta	29	30
6	Total	120	120
7			
8			

2. The **Excel** function **CHISQ.DIST.RT** will return the p-value. It is necessary to know the chi-square value and the degrees of freedom to use this function. Enter the values into the dialogue box as follows:

Function Arguments

CHISQ.DIST.RT

X 2.20 = 2.2

Deg_freedom 3 = 3

= 0.531948371

Returns the right-tailed probability of the chi-squared distribution.

Deg_freedom is the number of degrees of freedom, a number between 1 and 10^10, excluding 10^10.

Formula result = 0.531948371

Help on this function   OK   Cancel

3. **MegaStat** commands to create the chi-square test for the Adjustment to Civilian Life example are as follows:

	A	B	C	D	E	F
1		Outstanding	Good	Fair	Unsatisfactory	Total
2	Hometown	27	35	33	25	120
3	Not hometown	13	15	27	25	80
4	Total	40	50	60	50	200

a. Enter the information as shown.

b. Select **MegaStat**, **Chi-Square/Crosstab**, and **Contingency Table**.

c. In the dialog box enter *A1:E3* as the **Input range,** and select **chi-square.** Click **OK.**

Answers to Self-Reviews

14–1 (a) Observed frequencies.

(b) Six (six days of the week).

(c) 10. Total observed frequencies $\div$ 6 = 60/6 = 10.

(d) 5; $k - 1 = 6 - 1 = 5$.

(e) 15.086 (from the chi-square table in Appendix B.6).

(f)

$$\chi^2 = \Sigma\left[\frac{(f_o - f_e)^2}{f_e}\right] = \frac{(12-10)^2}{10} + \cdots + \frac{(9-10)^2}{10} = 0.8.$$

(g) No. We do not reject H_0.

(h) Absenteeism is distributed evenly throughout the week. The observed differences are due to sampling variation.

14–2

H_0: $P_C = 0.60$, $P_L = 0.30$, and $P_U = 0.10$.
H_1: Distribution is not as above.
Reject H_0 if $\chi^2 > 5.991$.

Category	f_o	f_e	$\frac{(f_o - f_e)^2}{f_e}$
Current	320	300	1.33
Late	120	150	6.00
Uncollectible	60	50	2.00
	500	500	9.33

Reject H_0. The accounts receivable data do not reflect the national average.

14–3 **(a)** Contingency table

(b) H_0: There is no relationship between income and whether the person played the lottery.
H_1: There is a relationship between income and whether the person played the lottery.

(c) Reject H_0 if $\chi^2 > 5.991$.

(d) $\chi^2 = \dfrac{(46 - 40.71)^2}{40.71} + \dfrac{(28 - 27.14)^2}{27.14} + \dfrac{(21 - 27.14)^2}{27.14}$
$\qquad + \dfrac{(14 - 19.29)^2}{19.29} + \dfrac{(12 - 12.86)^2}{12.86} + \dfrac{(19 - 12.86)^2}{12.86}$
$\qquad = 6.544$

(e) Reject H_0. There is a relationship between income level and playing the lottery.

Appendices

Appendix A: Answers

A.1 Answers to Odd-Numbered Chapter Exercises

Chapter 1

1. **a.** Interval
   b. Ratio
   c. Ratio
   d. Nominal
   e. Ordinal
   f. Ratio
   g. Nominal
   h. Ordinal
   i. Nominal
   j. Ratio

3. Answers will vary

5. Qualitative data are not numerical, whereas quantitative data are numerical. Examples will vary by student.

7. Discrete variables can assume only certain values, whereas continuous variables can assume any value within a specific range. Examples will vary.

9. If you were using one store as typical of all of the stores selling electronic book readers in the mall then it would be sample data. However, if you were considering all of the stores selling electronic book readers in the mall, then the data would be population data.

11. Based on these findings, we can infer that 270/300 or 90 percent of the executives would move.

13. **a.** This year total sales = 1 000 772; last year total sales = 942 973; total sales increased about 6% from last year to this year.
    b. Increases: Hockey Men's Finals by 19.9% and Hockey Women's by 23.5%. It appears that there has been a significant shift within the market from last year to this year.

15. **a.** quantitative
    b. discrete
    c. interval

17. **a.** quantitative
    b. discrete
    c. ratio

19. **a.** quantitative
    b. continuous
    c. ratio

21. sample

23. **a.** qualitative
    b. nominal

25. **a.** continuous, quantitative, ratio
    b. discrete, qualitative, nominal
    c. discrete, quantitative, ratio
    d. discrete, qualitative, nominal
    e. continuous, quantitative, interval
    f. continuous, quantitative, interval

   g. discrete, qualitative, ordinal
   h. discrete, qualitative, ordinal
   i. discrete, quantitative, ratio

27. **a.** Qualitative: region
    Quantitative: average house prices
    b. Nominal: region
    Ratio: average house prices

Chapter 2

1. Maxwell Heating & Air Conditioning far exceeds the other corporations in sales. Mancell Electric & Plumbing and Mizelle Roofing & Sheet Metals are the two corporations with the least amount of fourth quarter sales.

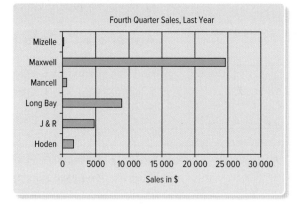

Maxwell has the highest sales, and Mizelle the lowest.

3. There are four classes: winter, spring, summer, and fall. The relative frequencies are 0.1, 0.3, 0.4, and 0.2, respectively.

5. **a.**

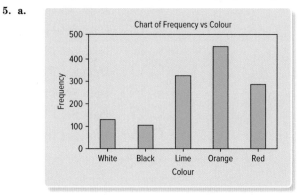

   b.

Type	Number	Relative Frequencies
Bright white	130	0.10
Metallic black	104	0.08
Magnetic lime	325	0.25
Tangerine orange	455	0.35
Fusion red	286	0.22
Total	1300	1.00

c.

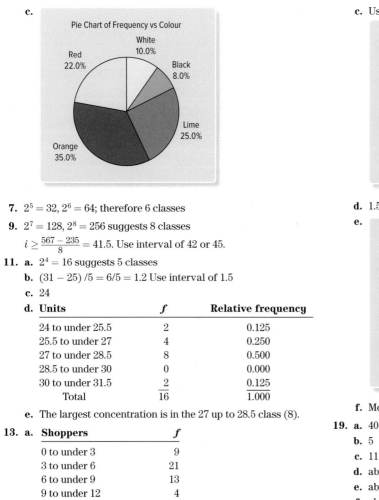

Pie Chart of Frequency vs Colour

White 10.0%
Red 22.0%
Black 8.0%
Lime 25.0%
Orange 35.0%

7. $2^5 = 32$, $2^6 = 64$; therefore 6 classes

9. $2^7 = 128$, $2^8 = 256$ suggests 8 classes

$i \geq \frac{567 - 235}{8} = 41.5$. Use interval of 42 or 45.

11. a. $2^4 = 16$ suggests 5 classes

b. $(31 - 25) / 5 = 6/5 = 1.2$ Use interval of 1.5

c. 24

d.

Units	f	Relative frequency
24 to under 25.5	2	0.125
25.5 to under 27	4	0.250
27 to under 28.5	8	0.500
28.5 to under 30	0	0.000
30 to under 31.5	2	0.125
Total	16	1.000

e. The largest concentration is in the 27 up to 28.5 class (8).

13. a.

Shoppers	f
0 to under 3	9
3 to under 6	21
6 to under 9	13
9 to under 12	4
12 to under 15	3
15 to under 18	1
Total	51

b. The largest group of shoppers (21) shop at BiLo Supermarket 3, 4, or 5 times during a month and only one customer visits the store as many as 15 times in a month.

c.

Number of Shoppers	Relative Frequency
0 to under 3	0.1765
3 to under 6	0.41180
6 to under 9	0.2549
9 to under 12	0.0784
12 to under 15	0.0588
15 to under 18	0.1960
Total	1.0000

15. a. Histogram

b. 100

c. 5

d. 28

e. 0.28

f. 12.5

g. 13

17. a. 50

b. 1.5 thousands or 1500 miles

c. Using lower limits on the X-axis

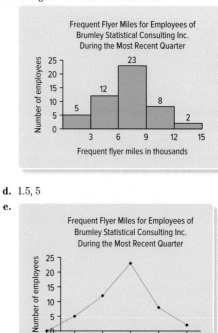

Frequent Flyer Miles for Employees of Brumley Statistical Consulting Inc. During the Most Recent Quarter

d. 1.5, 5

e.

Frequent Flyer Miles for Employees of Brumley Statistical Consulting Inc. During the Most Recent Quarter

f. Most between 6000 and 9000, even spread on both sides

19. a. 40

b. 5

c. 11 or 12

d. about $18 per hour

e. about $9 per hour

f. about 75%

21. a. 5

b.

Miles	f	Cumulative Frequency Less than
0 to under 3	5	5
3 to under 6	12	17
6 to under 9	23	40
9 to under 12	8	48
12 to under 15	2	50

c.

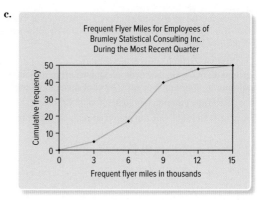

Frequent Flyer Miles for Employees of Brumley Statistical Consulting Inc. During the Most Recent Quarter

d. about 8500 miles

23. a. 13, 25

b.

Lead Time	f	Cumulative Frequency Less-than
0 to under 5	6	6
5 to under 10	7	13
10 to under 15	12	25
15 to under 20	8	33
20 to under 25	7	40

c.

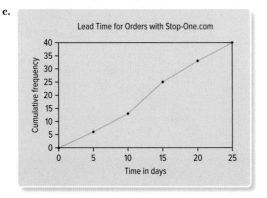

d. About 14 days

25. a. 621 to 629

b. 5

c. 621, 623, 623, 627, 629

27. a. 25

b. 1

c. 38, 106

d. 60, 61, 63, 63, 65, 65, 69

e. No values

f. 9

g. 9

h. 76

i. 16

29.

Stem	Leaves
0	5
1	28
2	—
3	0024789
4	12366
5	2

There were a total of 16 calls studied. The number of calls ranged from 5 to 52 received. Typical was 30–39 calls; smallest was 5; largest was 52.

31. a. Qualitative variables are ordinarily nominal level of measurement, but some are ordinal. Quantitative variables are commonly of interval or ratio level of measurement.

b. Yes, both types depict samples and populations.

c. Both are readable, but the pie chart may be easier to comprehend.

33. $2^6 = 64$ and $2^7 = 128$ suggest 7 classes

35.

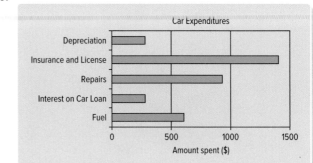

A pie chart is also acceptable. From the graph we can see that insurance and license fees are the highest expense at close to $1500 per year.

37.

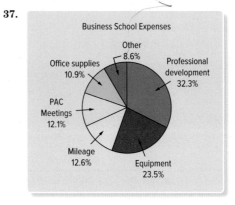

Professional development is the largest expense.

39.

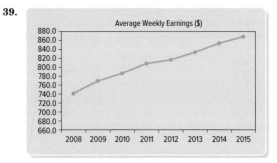

41.

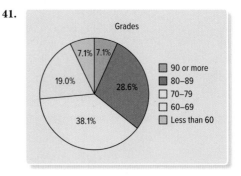

The largest group had grades between 70 and 79 (38.1%). Three students (7.1%) had grades at 90 or more and 3 students (7.1%) had grades less than 60.

43.

City	Frequency	Relative Frequency
Vancouver	100	0.05
Calgary	450	0.225
Edmonton	1300	0.65
Saskatoon	150	0.075
	2000	

The preference among frequent business travelers is definitely Edmonton (65%). The least preferred is Vancouver (5%).

45. a. 5 because $2^4 = 16 < 25$ and $2^5 = 32 > 25$

b. $i \geq \frac{48 - 16}{5} = 6.4$ use interval of 7.

c. 15

d.

Class	Frequency
15 to under 22	3
22 to under 29	8
29 to under 36	7
36 to under 43	5
43 to under 50	2
	25

e. The values are clustered between 22 and 36.

47. a. 70

b. 1

c. 0, 145

d. 30, 30, 32, 39

e. 24

f. 21

g. 77.5

h. 25

49. a. $36.60, (found by 265 − 82)/5

b. approx $40

c.

$80 to under $120	8
120 to under 160	19
160 to under 200	10
200 to under 240	6
240 to under 280	1
Total	44

d. The purchases ranged from a low of about $80 to a high of about $280. The concentration is in the $120 to under $160 class.

51. a. Since $2^6 = 64 < 70 < 128 = 2^7$, 7 classes are recommended. The interval should be at least $(1002.2 − 3.3)/7 = 142.7$; use 150 as a convenient value.

b.

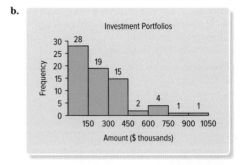

There will be many answers for the interpretation.

53. a. $2^5 = 32 < 36 < 64 = 2^6$. Thus 6 classes are recommended.

b. The interval width should be at least 2, found by $(15 − 3)/6$. Use 2.2 for convenience and to ensure there are only 6 classes

c. 2.2

d.

Class	Frequency
2.2 to under 4.4	2
4.4 to under 6.6	7
6.6 to under 8.8	11
8.8 to under 11	7
11 to under 13.2	7
13.2 to under 15.4	2

e. The distribution is slightly right-skewed with the largest concentration in the class of 6.6 up to 8.8.

55. a. $2^5 = 32 < 33 < 64 = 2^6$. Thus 6 classes are recommended.

b. The interval width should be at least 1253, found by $(7829 − 312)/6$. Use 1500 for simplicity.

c. 0

d.

Class	Frequency
0 to under 1500	1
1500 to under 3000	2
3000 to under 4500	0
4500 to under 6000	7
6000 to under 7500	20
7500 to under 9000	3

Investment Portfolios

lower		upper	midpoint	width	frequency	percent	cumulative frequency	percent
0	<	150	75	150	28	40.0	28	40.0
150	<	300	225	150	19	27.1	47	67.1
300	<	450	375	150	15	21.4	62	88.6
450	<	600	525	150	2	2.9	64	91.4
600	<	750	675	150	4	5.7	68	97.1
750	<	900	825	150	1	1.4	69	98.6
900	<	1050	975	150	1	1.4	70	100.0
					70	100.0		

e. This distribution is skewed with a few very small values, which likely correspond to the "start up" phase of this publication. Most observations fall in the 6000 up to 7500 class, which contains 20 of the 33 (60.6%) months.

57. There are 50 observations so the recommended number of classes is 6.

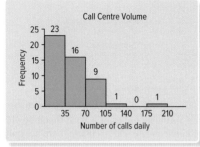

Twenty-three of the 50 days, or 46%, have fewer than 35 calls waiting. There are two days that have more than 105 calls waiting.

59. a. 56
   b. 10 (found by 60 − 50)
   c. 55
   d. 17

61. a. $2^5 = 32 < 45 < 64 = 2^6$. Thus 6 classes are recommended.
   b. The interval width should be at least 1.5, found by $(10 − 1)/6$. Use 2 for simplicity.
   c. 0

Class	Frequency
0 to under 2	1
2 to under 4	5
4 to under 6	12
6 to under 8	17
8 to under 10	8
10 to under 12	2

   d. The distribution is fairly symmetric or "bell-shaped" with a large peak in the middle two classes of 4 up to 8.

e.

Class	Frequency
Less than 2	1
Less than 4	6
Less than 6	18
Less than 8	35
Less than 10	43
Less than 12	45

f.

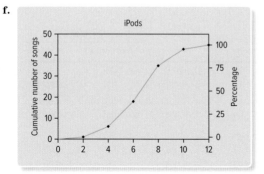

g. About 28

h.

Class	Frequency
More than 0	45
More than 2	44
More than 4	39
More than 6	27
More than 8	10
More than 10	2
More than 12	0

i.

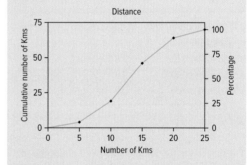

j. About 32

63. a.

	Cumulative Frequency
Less than 5	4
Less than 10	19
Less than 15	46
Less than 20	64
Less than 25	70

b.

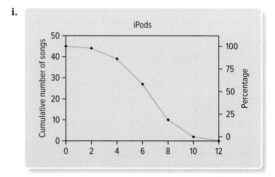

c. About 30; about 60

d.

	Cumulative Frequency
More than 0	70
More than 5	66
More than 10	51
More than 15	24
More than 20	6
More than 25	0

e.

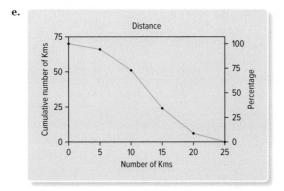

f. About 25%

65. a. min = 500

max = 5200   interval = $(5200 - 500)/7 = 671$

use 750 as the interval

Total Square Feet

Lower		Upper	Frequency
0	<	750	11
750	<	1500	48
1500	<	2250	18
2250	<	3000	8
3000	<	3750	6
3750	<	4500	2
4500	<	5250	5
			98

1. A typical size is from 750 to 1500. The range of the data is from about 0 to under 5250.

2. There are 7 values between 3750 and 5250 square feet. These values are much larger than the typical number of square feet.

b.   **Total Square Feet**

Lower		Upper	Frequency	Less-than	More-than
0	<	750	11	11	98
750	<	1500	48	59	87
1500	<	2250	18	77	39
2250	<	3000	8	85	21
3000	<	3750	6	91	13
3750	<	4500	2	93	7
4500	<	5250	5	98	5

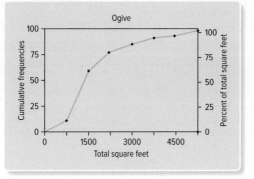

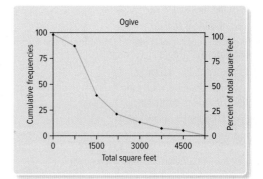

1. less than 1500 sq ft.

2. about 75

3. about 75%

c.   Stem and Leaf plot for   List Price

stem unit = 1000000

leaf unit = 100000

Frequency	Stem	Leaf
88	0	1 1 1 1 1 1 2 2 2 2 2 2 2 2 2 2 2 2 2 2 2 2 2 2 2 2 2 3 3 3 3 3 3 3 3 3 3 3 3 4 4 4 4
	0	4 4 4 4 4 4 4 4 4 4 4 4 4 4 4 4 4 4 4 5 5 5 5 5 5 6 6 6 6 7 7 7 7 7 8 9 9 9 9 9
9	1	1 3 3 3 4 5 5 5 8
1	2	4
98		

1. The values are clustered between $100 000 and $900 000.

2. Smallest value – 100 000 Largest value – 2 400 000

3. There are 10 homes listed for more than $900 000.

d. Stem and   Total
Leaf plot for   Square Feet

stem unit = 1000

leaf unit = 100

Frequency	Stem	Leaf
19	0	5 5 5 5 6 6 7 7 7 7 7 7 8 8 8 8 9 9
53	1	0 0 0 0 0 0 0 0 0 0 0 1 1 1 1 1 1 1 1 2 2 2 2 2
13	1	3 3 3 3 3 3 3 3 3 3 3 3 3 4 4 5 5 6 6 6 6 6 6 7 8 9 9
6	2	1 1 1 1 1 2 2 2 3 4 4 5 8
4	3	0 2 2 3 5 6
3	4	0 3 7 8
98	5	0 2 2

1. The values are clustered between 1000 and 1900.

2. Smallest value – 500 sq ft
Largest value – 5200 sq ft

3. There are 6 homes with square footage more than 4000 sq ft.

Chapter 3

1. $\mu = 5.4$ found by 27/5

3. a. Mean = 7.0, found by 2 = 8/4

b. $(5 - 7) + (9 - 7) + (4 - 7) + (10 - 7) = 0$

5. 14.58, found by 43.74/3

7. a. 15.4, found by 154/10

   b. Population parameter since it includes all the salespersons at Midtown Ford.

9. a. \$54.55, found by \$1091/20

   b. A sample statistic, assuming that the power company serves more than 20 customers.

11. Yes, \$162 900 found by 30(\$5430)

13. \$22.91, found by $\dfrac{300(\$20)+400(\$25)+400(\$23)}{300+400+400}=\dfrac{\$25\,200}{1100}$

15. \$23.00, found by (\$800 + \$1000 + \$2800)/200

17. a. no mode

   b. The given value would be the mode

   c. 3 and 4; bimodal

19. Median = 5 Mode = 5

21. a. Median = (64.3 + 64.7)/2 = 64.5

   b. Mode = no mode

22. Mean = 58.82; Median = 58.00; Mode = 58.00. All three measures are nearly identical.

25. a. 6.72, found by 80.6/12

   b. 6.6 is both the median and the mode

   c. positively skewed; the mean is the highest value

27. 12.78% increase found by
$$\sqrt[5]{(1.08)(1.12)(1.14)(1.26)(1.05)}-1$$

29. 12.28% increase found by
$$\sqrt[5]{(1.094)(1.138)(1.117)(1.119)(1.147)}-1$$

31. 1.11% increase found by $\sqrt[45]{\dfrac{36\,155\,48}{21\,961\,999}}-1$

33. 10.76% found by $\sqrt[5]{\dfrac{70}{42}}-1$

35. a. 7, found by 10 − 3

   b. 6, found by 30/5

   c. 2.4, found by 12/5

   d. The difference between the highest number sold (10) and the smallest number sold (3) is 7. On the average the number of service reps on duty deviates by 2.4 from the mean of 6.

37. a. 30, found by 54 − 24

   b. 38, found by 380/10

   c. 7.2, found by 72/10

   d. The difference between 54 and 24 is 30. On the average the number of minutes required to install a door deviates 7.2 minutes from the mean of 38 minutes.

39. British Columbia: Median = 34, Mean = 33.1 Mode = 34 and Range = 32

Manitoba: Median = 25, Mean = 24.5, Mode = 25, and Range = 19

In BC, there was a greater average preference for the pizza than in Manitoba, however BC also had a greater dispersion in preference.

41 a. 5

   b. 4.4 found by $\dfrac{(8-5)^2+(3-5)^2+(7-5)^2+(3-5)^2+(4-5)^2}{5}$

43 a. \$2.77

   b. $\sigma^2=\dfrac{(2.68-2.77)^2+\dots+(4.30-2.77)^2+(3.58-2.77)^2}{5}=1.26$

45. a. Range = 7.3, found by 11.6 − 4.3

   Arithmetic mean = 6.94, found by 34.7/5

   Variance = 6.5944, found by 32.972/5

   Standard deviation = 2.568

   b. Dennis has a higher mean return (11.76 > 6.94). However, Dennis has greater spread in their returns on equity (16.89 > 6.59).

47. a. mean = 4 $s^2=\dfrac{(7-4)^2+\dots+(3-4)^2}{5-1}=5.5$

   b. $s=2.3452$

49. a. mean = 38 $s^2=\dfrac{(28-38)^2+\dots+(42-38)^2}{10-1}=82.67$

   b. $s=9.0921$

51. mean = 95.1 $s^2=\dfrac{(101-95.1)^2+(97-95.1)^2+\dots+(88-95.1)^2}{10-1}$
$=123.66$

   b. 11.1201

53. $1-1/(1.8)^2=0.69136=69.14\%$

55. a. About 95 %

   b. 47.5%, 2.5%

57. 8.06%, found by (0.25/3.10)(100)

59. a. Because the two series are in different units of measurement.

   b. P.E. ratio = 36.73 % ; ROI 52 % , less spread in the P.E. ratios

61. a. The mean is 30.8, found by 154/5. The median is 31.0 and the standard deviation is 3.96, found as
$$\sqrt{\dfrac{4806-\dfrac{154^2}{5}}{4}}.$$

   b. −0.151, found by $\dfrac{3(30.8-31.0)}{3.96}$.

63. a. The mean is 21.93, found by 328.9 / 15. The median is 15.8 and the standard deviation is 21.18, found as
$$\sqrt{\dfrac{13\,494.67-\dfrac{328.9^2}{15}}{14}}.$$

   b. 0.868, found by $\dfrac{3(21.93-15.8)}{21.18}$.

65. Median = 53 found by (11 + 1)(1/2); therefore 6th value in from lowest.

   $Q_1=49$ found by (11 + 1)(1/4); therefore 3rd value in from lowest

   $Q_3=55$ found by (11 + 1)(3/4); therefore 9th value in from lowest

67. a. $Q_1=33.25\ Q_3=50.25$

   b. $D_2=27.8\ D_8=52.6$

   c. $P_{67}=47$

69. a. 350

   b. $Q_1=175\ Q_3=933$

   c. 758, found by 933 − 175

   d. Less than zero, or more than about 2070

   e. There are no outliers

   f. The distribution is positively skewed.

71. The distribution is somewhat positively skewed. Note that the line above 15.5 is longer than below 7.8.

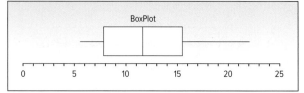

73. Because the exact values in a frequency distribution are not known, the midpoint of the class is used for every member of that class.

75.

Class	f	M	fM	fM^2
20 to under 30	7	25	175	4375
30 to under 40	12	35	420	14 700
40 to under 50	21	45	945	42 525
50 to under 60	18	55	990	54 450
60 to under 70	12	65	780	50 700
Total	70		3310	166 750

$$\bar{x} = \frac{3310}{70} = 47.2857 \quad s = \sqrt{\frac{166\,750 - (3310)^2/70}{69}} = 12.179$$

$$\text{Median} = 40 + \frac{\frac{70}{2} - 19}{21}(10) = 47.6$$

77.

Amount	f	M	fM	fM^2
20 to under 30	1	25	25	625
30 to under 40	15	35	525	18 375
40 to under 50	22	45	990	44 550
50 to under 60	8	55	440	24 200
60 to under 70	4	65	260	16 900
Total	50		2240	104 650

$$\text{Mean} = 2240/50 = 44.8 \quad s = \sqrt{\frac{104\,650 - (2240)^2/50}{50 - 1}} = 9.37$$

$$\text{Median} = 40 + \frac{\frac{50}{2} - 16}{22}(10) = 44.1$$

79. a. Mean = 5, found by $(6 + 4 + 3 + 7 + 5)/5$

Median is 5, found by ordering the values and selecting the middle value.

b. Population because all partners were included.

c. $\sum(x - \mu) = (6 - 5) + (4 - 5) + (3 - 5) + (7 - 5) + (5 - 5) = 0$

81. mean = 545/16 = 34.06, Median = 37.50

83. The Communications industry has older workers than the Retail Trade. Production workers have the most age difference.

85. $\bar{x}_w = \dfrac{5.00(270) + 6.50(300) + 8.00(100)}{270 + 300 + 100} = \$6.12$

87. $\bar{x}_w = \dfrac{15\,300(4.5) + 10\,400(3.0) + 150\,600(10.2)}{176\,300} = 9.28$

89.

Wage (x)	Freq (f)	fx	fx^2
13.00	20	260	3380
15.50	12	186	2883
18.00	8	144	2592
Totals:	40	590	8855

Mean = 590/40 = 14.75

$$\text{Variance} = \frac{8855 - \frac{(590)^2}{40}}{40} = 3.8125$$

Standard deviation = 1.95

91. a. population

b. 183.47

c. 94.92 %; a lot of variability compared to the mean

93. Comments may vary. The following results were found using statistical software.

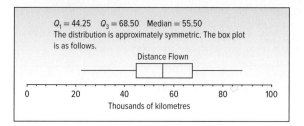

$Q_1 = 44.25 \quad Q_3 = 68.50 \quad \text{Median} = 55.50$
The distribution is approximately symmetric. The box plot is as follows.

Distance Flown

0   20   40   60   80   100
Thousands of kilometres

95. The distribution is positively skewed. The first quartile is approximately \$20 and the third quartile is approximately \$90. There is one outlier located at approx \$255. The median is about 50.

97. Mean is 13, found by 910/70

$$s = \sqrt{\frac{13\,637.50 - \frac{(910)^2}{70}}{69}} = 5.118$$

$$\text{Median} = 10 + \frac{\frac{70}{2} - 19}{27}(5) = 12.96 \text{ km.}$$

99. $Q_3 + 1.5(\text{IQR}) = 100 + 1.5(20) = 130;$

$Q_1 - 1.5(\text{IQR}) = 80 - 1.5(20) = 50;$

Low outliers: 35 & 48; not an outlier: 52, 66, 105, & 108;

101. a. The mean is 173.77 hours, found by 2259/13. The median is 195 hours.

$$s = 105.61 \text{ hours, found by } \sqrt{\frac{526\,391 - \frac{2259^2}{13}}{12}}.$$

b. CV = 60.78%, found by $(105.61/173.77) \times 100$

Coefficient of skewness is -0.697; slight negative skewness

c. $L_{45} = (14)(0.45) = 6.3.$ So the 45th percentile is $192 + 0.3(195 - 192) = 192.9.$

$L_{82} = (14)(0.82) = 11.48.$ So the 82nd percentile is $260 + 0.48(295 - 260) = 276.8.$

d.

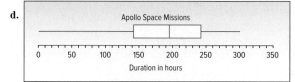

Apollo Space Missions

0   50   100   150   200   250   300   350
Duration in hours

There is a slight negative skewness visible, but no outliers.

103.

Grade	Number of Students	fx
3	4	12
4	4	16
5	6	30
7	20	140
8	6	48
10	1	10
	41	256

Mean = 256/41 = 6.24

Mode = 7

Median = 7

$$s = \sqrt{\frac{1714 - \frac{256^2}{41}}{40}} = 1.70;$$

IQR = 7 − 5 = 2

105.

Class	f	x	fx	fx^2
0 to under 200	18	100	1800	180 000
200 to under 400	5	300	1500	450 000
400 to under 600	4	500	2000	1 000 000
600 to under 800	4	700	2800	1 960 000
800 to under 1000	2	900	1800	1 620 000
	33		9900	5 210 000

Mean = 9900/33 = 300.00

Median observation = $(33 + 1) * 50/100 = 17$th observation; Median class = 1st class

Median = 0 + (33/2 – 0)/18 (200) = 183.33

$$\text{Standard deviation} = \sqrt{\frac{5\,210\,000 - \frac{(9900)^2}{33}}{33 - 1}} = 264.575$$

The median is a smaller value than the mean, so positively skewed.

107. CV(Calgary) = 7.12/112.50(100) = 6.33%

CV(Vaughan) = 7.84/66.33(100) = 11.82%

The variability in production is lower at the Calgary plant. A manager may want to investigate why this is the case.

109. a. 55, found by 72 –17

b. 14.4, found by 144/10 where $\bar{X} = 43.2$

c. 17.62

d. $1 - 1/k^2 = 1 - \frac{1}{4} = 0.75 = 75\%$

e. $43.2 \pm 2(17.6245) = 7.95$ to 78.45, all the values are.

111. a. mean = 857.90/50 = 17.158 Median = 16.35

b. $s = \sqrt{\dfrac{20\,206.73 - \dfrac{(857.90)^2}{50}}{50 - 1}} = 10.58$

c. $17.158 \pm (2)(10.58) = -4.01$ and 38.318

d. $CV = \dfrac{10.58}{17.158}(100) = 61.67\%$

e. $sk = \dfrac{3(17.158 - 16.35)}{10.58} = 0.23$

f. $L_p = (50 + 1)\dfrac{25}{100} = 12.75$ $L_p = (50 + 1)\dfrac{75}{100} = 38.25$
Excel will give you 8.075 & 27.025
$Q_1 = 7.825$ $Q_3 = 27.400$

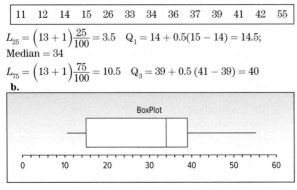

Auto Parts Company Market Values

g. The distribution is nearly symmetrical. The mean is 17.158, the median is 16.35 and the standard deviation is 10.58. About 75 percent of the companies have a value less than 27.4 and 25 percent have a value less than 7.825.

113. a. 68%

b. 95%

c. 99.7%

d. 2.5%

e. 0.15%

f. 2.5% + 0.15% = 2.65%

115. a. sort the data:

11	12	14	15	26	33	34	36	37	39	41	42	55

$L_{25} = \left(13 + 1\right)\dfrac{25}{100} = 3.5$ $Q_1 = 14 + 0.5(15 - 14) = 14.5$;
Median = 34

$L_{75} = \left(13 + 1\right)\dfrac{75}{100} = 10.5$ $Q_3 = 39 + 0.5(41 - 39) = 40$

b.

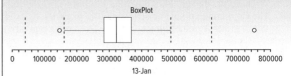

BoxPlot

c. $14.5 -1.5(40 - 14.5) = -23.75$; $40 + 1.5(40 - 14.5) = 78.25$;
an outlier would be less than −23.75 or more than 78.25

d. There are no outliers.

e. $L_{90} = (13 + 1)\dfrac{20}{100} = 2.8$ $P_{90} = 12 + 0.8(14 - 12) = 13.6$

$L_{60} = (13 + 1)\dfrac{60}{100} = 8.4$ $P_{60} = 36 + 0.4(37 - 36) = 36.4$

117. a.

mean	415 239.25
median	344 032.00
population variance	44 697 839 565.44
population standard deviation	211 418.64
skewness	1.73
1st quartile	293 569.50
3rd quartile	478 530.50

The data is positively skewed. There is one outlier. The value is from Vancouver listed at $1 026 207.

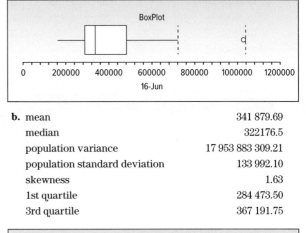

b.

mean	341 879.69
median	322176.5
population variance	17 953 883 309.21
population standard deviation	133 992.10
skewness	1.63
1st quartile	284 473.50
3rd quartile	367 191.75

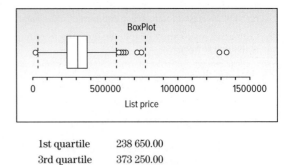

The data is positively skewed. There are two outliers, one low and one high.

The high outlier is from Vancouver listed at $748 651.
The low outlier is from Saint John listed at $148 320.

The mean of the house prices has increased in June 2016 as compared to January 2013.

119. a. 1.

mean	330 503.48
median	308 482.50
standard deviation	161 110.89

2. skewness 3.05

the distribution is extremely positively skewed

BoxPlot

1st quartile	238 650.00
3rd quartile	373 250.00

3. There are several high mild outliers and two high extreme outliers.

There is one low mild outlier.

4. The high outliers pull the mean up. In this case, the median would be a more representative measure of location than the mean.

b. 1.

mean	3.15
median	3.00
standard deviation	0.92
skewness	0.86

2. The distribution is positively skewed.

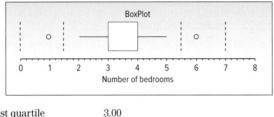

1st quartile	3.00
3rd quartile	4.00

3. There is one low mild outlier and 1 high mild outlier.

4. The middle 50% of the houses have either 3 or 4 bedrooms.

Chapter 4

1.

Outcome	1	2
1	A	A
2	A	F
3	F	A
4	F	F

3. **a.** 0.176 found by 6/34   **b.** Empirical

5. **a.** Empirical **c.** Classical
   b. Classical **d.** Subjective

7. **a.** The survey of 40 people about environmental issues
   b. 26 or more, respond yes for example
   c. 0.25 found by 10/40
   d. Empirical
   e. The events are probably not equally likely (we don't know for sure) but they are mutually exclusive.

9. **a.** Answers will vary, here are some possibilities: 1234, 1248, 1251, 9999
   b. $\left(\frac{1}{10}\right)^4$
   c. Classical

11. **a.** 78 960 960
    b. 840, found by (7)(6)(5)(4). That is 7!/3!
    c. 10, found by 5!/3!2!

13. 210, found by (10)(9)(8)(7)/(4)(3)(2)

15. 120, found by 5!

17. 10 897 286 400 found by
    $_{15}P_{10} = 15 \times 14 \times 13 \times 12 \times 11 \times 10 \times 9 \times 8 \times 7 \times 6$

19. $P(A \text{ or } B) = P(A) + P(B) = 0.30 + 0.20 = 0.50$

    $P(\text{neither}) = 1 - 0.50 = 0.50$

21. **a.** 0.51 found by 102/200
    b. 0.49 found by (1 − 0.51) or *by*
        61/200 + 37/200 = 0.305 + 0.185 Special rule of addition

23. 0.75, found by 0.25 + 0.50

25. $P(A \text{ or } B) = P(A) + P(B) - P(A \text{ and } B)$
        $= 0.20 + 0.30 - 0.15$
        $= 0.35$

27. When two events are mutually exclusive it means that if one occurs the other event cannot occur. Therefore, the probability of their joint occurrence is zero.

29. **a.** 0.20
    b. 0.30
    c. No, because a store could have both.
    d. Joint probability
    e. 0.90, found by 1.0 − 0.10

31. $P(A \text{ and } B) = P(A) \times P(B|A)$
        $= 0.40 \times 0.30.$
        $= 0.12$

33. 0.90, found by (0.80 + 0.60) − 0.50   0.10, found by (1 − 0.90)

35. **a.** $P(\text{Red}) = 3/10 = 0.30$
    b. $P(\text{Clear|Blue}) = 1/3 = 0.33$
    c. $P(\text{Solid and Green}) = 1/10 = 0.10$

37. **a.** A contingency table
    b. 0.27, found by 300/500 × 135 ÷ 300
    c. A tree diagram would appear as:

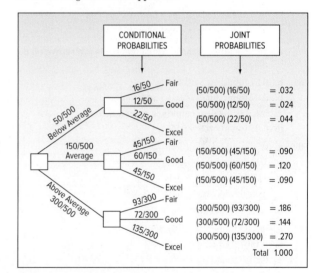

39. No.
    Probability the 1st presentation wins 3/5 = 0.60
    Probability the 2nd presentation wins 2/5 (3/4) = 0.30
    Probability the 3rd presentation wins (2/5) (1/4) (3/3) = 0.10

41. **a.** nominal
    b. 32/200 = 16%
    c. 85/200 = 42.5%
    d. Yes, as 32% of men ordered dessert compared to 15% of women

43. **a.** 106/659 = 16.1%
    b. 143/659 = 21.7%
    c. 12/659 = 1.8%
    d. 233/659 + 233/659 − 87/659 = 57.5%
    e. 40/161 = 24.8%

45. a. Asking teenagers their reactions to a newly developed soft drink.

    b. Answers will vary. One possibility is more than half of the respondents like it.

47. Subjective

49. a. The likelihood an event will occur, assuming that another event has already occurred.

    b. The collection of one or more outcomes of an experiment.

    c. A measure of the likelihood that two or more events will happen concurrently.

51. 456 976 found by 26^4

53. $C(52,7) = 133\,784\,560$ ways

55. $P(15,6) = 3\,603\,600$ ways

57. a. 0.8145, found by $(0.95)^4$

    b. Special rule of multiplication

    c. $P(A \text{ and } B \text{ and } C \text{ and } D) = P(A) \times P(B) \times P(C) \times P(D)$

59. a. 0.08, found by 0.80×0.10

    b. The text answer is labelled.

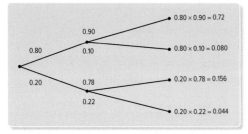

    c. Yes, because all the possible outcomes are shown on the tree diagram.

61. a. 0.57 found by 57/100

    b. 0.97 found by $(57/100) + (40/100)$

    c. Yes, because an employee cannot be both.

    d. 0.03 found by $1 - 0.97$

63. a. 0.5 found by $(2/3)(3/4)$

    b. 1/12 found by $(1/3)(1/4)$

    c. 11/12 found by $1 - 1/12$

65. a. 0.9039 found by $(0.98)^5$

    b. 0.0961 found by $1 - 0.9039$

67. a. 0.0333 found by $(4/10)(3/9)(2/8)$

    b. 0.1667 found by $(6/10)(5/9)(4/8)$

    c. 0.8333 found by $1 - 0.1667$

    d. dependent

69. a. 0.3818, found by $(9/12)(8/11)(7/10)$

    b. 0.6182, found by $1 - 0.3818$

71. $C(20,4)\,C(15,3) = (4845)(455) = 2\,204\,475$ ways

73. $C(30,4)\,C(20,4) + C(30,5)\,C(20,3) + C(30,6)\,C(20,2) + C(30,7)$
$C(20,1) + C(30,8)\,C(20,0) = 454\,620\,240$ ways

75. a. 0.30, found by 6/20

    b. 0.45, found by $(6 + 7 - 4)/20$

    c. 0.5714, found by 4/7

    d. 0.0789, found by $(6/20)*(5/19)$

77. 0.2373, found by $(\frac{3}{4})^5$

79. Yes, 256 is found by 2^8

81. a. 0.50, found by 10/20

    b. 0.2368, found by $(10/20)(9/19)$

    c. 0.1053, found by $(10/20)(9/18)(8/18)$

    d. 0.7158, found by $(17/20)(16/19)$

83. a. $_7C_3 = \dfrac{n!}{r!(n/r)!} = \dfrac{n!}{3!(7-3)!} = \dfrac{7!}{3!4!} = 35$
This would be more than adequate to colour code the 42 different lines.

    b. Yes. There are 45 combinations, found by:
$$_{10}C_2 = \frac{n!}{r(n-r)!} = \frac{10!}{2!(10-2)!} = 45$$

85. a. $P(F \text{ and } > 60) = 0.25$, found by solving with the general rule of multiplication:
$$1 = P(F) \cdot P(> 60|F) = (0.50)(0.50)$$

    b. 0

    c. 0.3333, found by 1/3

87. $26 \times 10 \times 26 \times 10 \times 26 \times 10 = 17\,576\,000$ ways

89. a. $60/377 = 0.159$

    b. $(47 + 105)/377 = 0.403$

    c. $1 - 133/377 = 0.647$

    d. $23/377 = 0.061$

    e. $(15 + 55)/377 = 0.186$

    f. $105/377 + 121/377 - 55/377 = 0.454$

91. 0.512, found by $(0.8)^3$

93. 0.525, found by $1 - (0.78)^3$

95. a. $P(P \text{ or } D) = (1/50) + (1/10) = 0.10 + 0.02 = 0.12$

    b. $P(\text{No}) = (49/50)(9/10) = 0.882$

    c. $P(\text{No on 3}) = (0.882)^3 = 0.686$

    d. $P(\text{at least one prize}) = 1 - 0.686 = 0.314$

97. 0.9744, found by $1 - (0.40)^4$

99. a. 0.185, found by $(0.15)(0.95) + (0.05)(0.85)$

    b. 0.0075, found by $(0.15)(0.05)$

101. 3 628 800 matches are possible. So the probability is 1/3 628 800.

103. a. $26/68 = 0.3824$

    b. $(4 + 6)/68 = 0.1471$

    c. $63/68 = 0.9265$

    d. $22/68 = 0.3235$

105.

List Price			Apartment	House	Row/Townhouse	Total
$100 000	to under	$200 000	2	0	2	4
$200 000	to under	$300 000	6	5	11	22
$300 000	to under	$400 000	0	16	8	24
$400 000	to under	$500 000	1	15	0	16
$500 000	to under	$600 000	0	2	0	2
			9	38	21	68

    a. $9/68 = 0.1324$

    b. $2/9 = 0.2222$

    c. $2/68 = 0.0294$

    d. $16/38 = 0.4211$

107. a. $= 24/50 = 0.48$

    b. $= 26/50 = 0.52$

    c. $= 20/50 = 0.40$

    d. $= 3/50 = 0.06$

109. a. $= 15/50 = 0.30$

    b. $= 25/50 + 9/50 = 34/50 = 0.68$

    c. $= 1 - 34/50 = 16/50 = 0.32$

111.

# Bedrooms	List price ($000's) 0 > 500	500 > 1000	1000 > 1500	Totals
1	9	1	0	10
2	17	0	0	17
3	6	2	0	8
4+	9	5	1	15
	41	8	1	50

1. $= 8/50 = 0.16$

2. $= 41/50 = 0.82$

3. 0

4. $= 2/8 = 0.25$

Chapter 5

1. Mean $= 1.3$ Variance $= 0.81$ found by:

$$\sigma^2 = \sum (x - \mu)^2 P(x)$$
$$= (0 - 1.3)^2(0.2) + (1 - 1.3)^2(0.4) + (2 - 1.3)^2(0.3) +$$
$$(3 - 1.3)^2(0.1)$$
$$= 0.81$$
$$\sigma = \sqrt{0.81} = 0.9$$

3. a. the middle one

   b. (1) $0.3 = 30\%$

      (2) $0.3 = 30\%$

      (3) $0.9 = 90\%$

   c. $\mu = 5(0.1) + 10(0.2) + 15(0.3) + 20(0.4) = 15$

$$\sigma^2 = (5 - 15)^2(0.1) + (10 - 15)^2(0.2) + (15 - 15)^2(0.3) +$$
$$(20 - 15)^2(0.4)$$
$$= 25$$
$$\sigma = 5$$

5. a.

Number of Calls	Probability
0	0.16
1	0.20
2	0.44
3	0.18
4	0.02

   b. discrete

   c. 1.7, found by $0.16(0) + 0.20(1) + 0.44(2) + 0.18(3) + 0.02(4)$

   d. 1.005, found by

$$\sqrt{0.16(0 - 1.7)^2 + 0.20(1 - 1.7)^2 + 0.44(2 - 1.7)^2 + 0.18(3 - 1.7)^2 + 0.02(4 - 1.7)^2}$$

7. a. 0.20

   b. 0.55

   c. 0.95

   d. $\mu = 0(0.45) + 10(0.3) + 100(0.2) + 500(0.05) = 48$

$$\sigma^2 = (0 - 48)^2(0.45) + (10 - 48)^2(0.3) + (100 - 48)^2(0.2) +$$
$$(500 - 48)^2(0.05) = 12\,226$$
$$\sigma = 110.57$$

9. a. 21, found by $0.50(10) + 0.40(25) + 0.08(50) + 0.02(100)$

   b. 16.09, found by

$$\sqrt{0.50(10 - 21)^2 + 0.40(25 - 21)^2 + 0.08(50 - 21)^2 + 0.02(100 - 21)^2}$$

11. a. $P(2) = \dfrac{4!}{2!(4 - 2)!}(0.25)^2(0.75)^{4-2} = 0.2109$

   b. $P(3) = \dfrac{4!}{3!(4 - 3)!}(0.25)^3(0.75)^{4-3} = 0.0469$

   c. $P(2) + P(3) + P(4) = 0.2109 + 0.0469 + 0.0039 = 0.2617$

   c. $P(0) + P(1) + P(2) = 0.3164 + 0.4219 + 0.2109 = 0.9492$

13. a.

x	$P(x)$
0	0.064
1	0.288
2	0.432
3	0.216

   b. $\mu = 0(0.064) + ... 3(0.216) = 1.8$

$$\sigma^2 = (0 - 1.8)^2 0.064 + ... + (3 - 1.8)^2 0.216 = 0.72$$
$$\sigma = \sqrt{0.72} = 0.8485$$

15. a. 0.2668, found by $\dfrac{P(2) = 9!}{2!(9/2)!}(0.3)^2(0.7)^7$

   b. 0.1715, found by $\dfrac{P(4) = 9!}{4!(9/4)!}(0.3)^4(0.7)^5$

   c. 0.0404, found by $\dfrac{P(0) = 9!}{0!(9/0)!}(0.3)^0(0.7)^9$

17. a. 0.2824, found by $P(0) = \dfrac{12!}{0!(12 - 0)!}(0.1)^0(0.9)^{12}$

   b. 0.3766, found by $P(1) = \dfrac{12!}{1!(12/1)!}(0.1)^1(0.9)^{11}$

   c. 0.2301, found by $P(2) = \dfrac{12!}{2!(12/2)!}(0.1)^2(0.9)^{10}$

   d. $P(0) + P(1) + P(2) = 0.2824 + 0.3766 + 0.2301 = 0.8891$

   e. $\mu = 1.2$, found by $12(0.1)$, $\sigma^2 = 1.08$, $\sigma = 1.04$

19. a. 0.1858, found by $\dfrac{15!}{2!13!}(0.23)^2(0.77)^{13}$

   b. 0.1416, found by $\dfrac{15!}{5!10!}(0.23)^5(0.77)^{10}$

   c. 3.45 found by $(0.23)(15)$

21. a. 0.296, found by using Appendix B.3 with n of 8, p of 0.30 and x of 2.

   b. $P(x \le 2) = 0.058 + 0.198 + 0.296 = 0.552$

   c. 0.448, found by $P(x \ge 3) = 1 - P(x \le 2) = 1 - 0.552$

23. a. 0.387, found from Appendix B.3 with n of 9, p of 0.90, and an x of 9

   b. $P(x < 5) = 0.001$

   c. 0.992, found by $1 - 0.008$

   d. 0.947, found by $1 - 0.053$

25. a. $\mu = 10.5$, found by $15(0.7)$ and $\sigma = \sqrt{15(0.7)(0.3)} = 1.7748$

   b. 0.2061, found by $\dfrac{15!}{10!5!}(0.7)^{10}(0.3)^5$

   c. 0.4247, found by $0.2061 + 0.2186$

   d. 0.5154, found by $0.2186 + 0.1700 + 0.0916 + 0.0305 + 0.0047$

27 $P(2) = \dfrac{(_6C_2)(_4C_1)}{_{10}C_3} = \dfrac{15(4)}{120} = 0.50$

29. $P(0) = \dfrac{(_3C_0)(_7C_2)}{_{10}C_2} = \dfrac{21(1)}{45} = 0.4667$

31. $P(2) = \dfrac{(_6C_2)(_9C_3)}{_{15}C_5} = \dfrac{84(15)}{3003} = 0.4196$

33. a. 0.6703

   b. 0.3297

35. a. 0.0613

    b. 0.0803

37. $\mu = 6, P(x \geq 5) = 0.7149 = 1 - (0.0025 + 0.0149 + 0.0446 +$
$0.0892 + 0.1339)$

39. A random variable is a quantitative or qualitative outcome, which results from a chance experiment. A probability distribution also includes the likelihood of each possible outcome.

41. The binomial distribution is a discrete probability distribution where the there are only two possible outcomes. A second important part is that data collected is a result of counts. Additionally, one trial is independent from the next and the chance for success remains the same from one trial to the next.

43. $\mu = 0(0.1) + 1(0.2) + 2(0.3) + 3(0.4) = 2.00$
$\sigma^2 = (0 - 2)^2(0.1) + ... + (3 - 2)^2(0.40) = 1.0$
$\sigma = 1$

45. $\mu = 0(0.4) + 1(0.2) + 2(0.2) + 3(0.1) + 4(0.1) = 1.3$
$\sigma^2 = (0 - 1.30)^2(0.4) + ... + (4 - 1.30)^2(0.1) = 1.81$
$\sigma = 1.3454$

47. $\mu = 13.2$, found by $12(0.25) + 13(0.4) + 14(0.25) + 15(0.1)$
$= 3.0 + 5.2 + 3.5 + 1.5$

    $\sigma^2 = 0.86$, found by $0.36 + 0.016 + 0.16 + 0.324$

    $\sigma = \sqrt{0.86} = 0.9274$

49. a. discrete

    b. continuous

    c. discrete

    d. discrete

    e. continuous

51. a. 6, found by $(0.4)(15)$

    b. 0.0245, found by $\dfrac{15!}{10!5!}(0.4)^{10}(0.6)^5$

    c. 0.0338, found by $0.0245 + 0.0074 + 0.0016 + 0.0003 + 0.0000$

    d. 0.4032, found by $0.0005 + 0.0047 + 0.0219 + 0.0634 + 0.1268$
$+ 0.1859$

53. a. $\mu = 20(0.075) = 1.5$ and $\sigma = \sqrt{20(0.075)(0.925)} = 1.1779$

    b. 0.2103, found by $\dfrac{20!}{0!20!}(0.075)^0(0.925)^{20}$

    c. 0.7897, found by $1 - 0.2103$

55. a. 0.1311, found by $\dfrac{16!}{4!12!}(0.15)^4(0.85)^{12}$

    b. 2.4, found by $(0.15)(16)$

    c. 0.2100, found by $1 - 0.0743 - 0.2097 - 0.2775 - 0.2285$

57. a.

0	0.0001
1	0.0019
2	0.0116
3	0.0418
4	0.1020
5	0.1768
6	0.2234
7	0.2075
8	0.1405
9	0.0676
10	0.0220
11	0.0043
12	0.0004

    b. $\mu = 12(0.52) = 6.24$ and $\sigma = \sqrt{12(0.52)(0.48)} = 1.7307$

    c. 0.1768

    d. 0.3342, found by
$0.0001 + 0.0019 + 0.0116 + 0.0418 + 0.1020 + 0.1768$

59. a. 0.0498

    b. 0.7746, found by $(1 - 0.0498)^5$

61. $\mu = 4.0$; from Appendix B.4

    a. 0.0183

    b. 0.1954

    c. 0.6289

    d. 0.5665

63. a. 0.00005, found by $\dfrac{(18.4)^4 e^{-18.4}}{4!}$

    b. almost 0, found by $\dfrac{(18.4)^0 e^{-18.4}}{0!}$

    c. 0.38489, found by $1 - 0.61511$

65. $P(0) = 0.6859$ and $P(2) = 0.0474$

67. Let $n = 34$, and $p = 0.5$

    $P(29) = {}_{34}C_{29}(0.5)^{29}(0.5)^5 = 0.00002$

69. Using the Binomial Probability Distribution Tables with $n = 8$ and a probability of success equal to 0.40:

    a. $P(x = 3) = 0.279$ or $P(x = 3) = {}_8C_3(0.4)^3(0.6)^5 = 0.2787$

    b. $P(x > 1) = 0.983$ or $P(x > 1) = 1 - {}_8C_0(0.4)^0(0.6)^8 = 0.9832$

71. a. 0.262144, found by $\dfrac{6!}{6!0!}(0.8)^6(0.2)^0$

    b. 0.98304, found by $0.08192 + 0.24576 + 0.393216 + 0.262144$
    where

        $P(3) = 0.08192$ found by $\dfrac{6!}{3!3!}(0.8)^3(0.2)^3, ...,$

        $P(6) = 0.262144$

        found by $\dfrac{6!}{6!0!}(0.8)^6(0.2)^0$

    c. 0.000064, found by $(0.2)^6$

73. a. 0.9831, found by $0.8179 + 0.1652$

    b. 0.9401, found by $0.6676 + 0.2725$

    c. 0.7359, found by $0.3585 + 0.3774$

75. a. 2.2059, found by $300(1/136)$.

    b. 0.2680, found by $((2.2059)^2 e^{-2.2059})/2!$

    c. 0.8898, found by $1 - ((2.2059)^0 e^{-2.2059})/0!$

77. a. mean is 10.05 found by $15(0.67)$ and standard deviation is
$1.8211 = \sqrt{15(0.67)(0.33)}$

    b. 0.1114 found by ${}_{15}C_8(0.67)^8(0.33)^7$

    c. 0.9163 found by $1 - [0.0549 + 0.0210 + 0.0062 + 0.0014 +$
$0.0002 + 0.0000]$

79. Let $\mu = 155(1/3709) = 0.042$

    $P(4) = \dfrac{0.042^4 e^{-0.042}}{4!} = 0.0000001$ Very Unlikely!

81. a.

Number of Bedrooms (x)	$P(x)$	Count	$xP(x)$	$(x - \mu)$	$(x - \mu)^2$	$(x - \mu)^2 p(x)$
1	0.059	4	0.059	−2.103	4.422	0.260
2	0.191	13	0.382	−1.103	1.216	0.233
3	0.456	31	1.368	−0.103	0.011	0.005
4	0.176	12	0.706	0.897	0.805	0.142
5	0.118	8	0.588	1.897	3.599	0.423
	1.000	68	3.103			1.063

mean = 3.103
variance = 1.063
standard deviation = 1.031

b.

Number of Bathrooms (x)	$P(x)$	Count	$xP(x)$	$(x - \mu)$	$(x - \mu)^2$	$(x - \mu)^2 p(x)$
1	0.074	5	0.074	−1.735	3.010	0.221
2	0.309	21	0.618	−0.735	0.540	0.167
3	0.441	30	1.324	0.265	0.070	0.031
4	0.162	11	0.647	1.265	1.600	0.259
5	0.015	1	0.074	2.265	5.130	0.075
	1.000	68	2.735			0.753

mean = 2.735
variance = 0.753
standard deviation = 0.868

Chapter 6

1. a. $a = 6\; b = 10$

  b. 8, found by $(6 + 10)/2$

  c. 1.1547 found by $\sqrt{\dfrac{(10 - 6)^2}{12}}$

  d. $[1/(10 - 6)](10 - 6) = 1$

  e. 0.75, found by $[1/(10 - 6)](10 - 7)$

  f. 0.5, found by $[1/(10 - 6)](9 - 7)$

3. a. 0.3 found by $[1/(30 - 20)](30 - 27)$

  b. 0.4 found by $[1/(30 - 20)](24 - 20)$

5. a. $a = 0.5, b = 8.0$

  b. Mean is 4.25, found by $(0.5 + 8.0)/2$

    Standard deviation is 2.17, found by $\sqrt{\dfrac{(8 - 0.5)^2}{12}}$

  c. 0.2, found by $[1/(8.0 - 0.5)](2.0 - 0.5)$

  d. 0.0, found by $[1/(8.0 - 0.5)](3.0 - 3.0)$

  e. 0.4, found by $[1/(8.0 - 0.5)](8.0 - 5.0)$

7. The actual shape of a normal distribution depends on its mean and standard deviation. Thus, there is a normal distribution, and an accompanying normal curve, for a mean of 7 and a standard deviation of 2. There is another normal curve for a mean of $25\,000$ and a standard deviation of \$1742, and so on.

9. a. 490 and 510, found by $500 \pm 1(10)$

  b. 480 and 520, found by $500 \pm 2(10)$

  c. 470 and 530, found by $500 \pm 3(10)$

11. a. 68.26%

  b. 95.44%

  c. 99.7%

13. $Z_{Rob} = \dfrac{50\,000 - 60\,000}{5000} = -2.00$

  $Z_{Rachel} = \dfrac{50\,000 - 35\,000}{8000} = 1.875$

Adjusting for their industries, Rob is well below average and Rachel well above.

15. a. 0.8413; 0.1587

  b. 0.1056; 0.8944

  c. 0.9977; 0.0023

  d. 0.0094; 0.9906

17. a. 1.25 found by $z = \dfrac{25 - 20}{4.0} = 1.25$

  b. $0.3944 = 39.44\%$, found in Appendix B.1

  c. $0.3085 = 30.85\%$, found by $z = \dfrac{18 - 20}{4.0} = -0.5$

  Find 0.1915 in Appendix B.1 for $z = -0.5$; then $0.5000 - 0.1915 = 0.3085$

19. a. 0.3413, found by $z = \dfrac{\$20 - \$16.50}{\$3.50} = 1.00$

  Then find 0.3413 in Appendix B.1 for $z = 1$

  b. 0.1587, found by $0.5000 - 0.3413 = 0.1587$

  c. 0.3336, found by $z = \dfrac{\$15.00 - \$16.50}{\$3.50} = -0.43$

  Find 0.1664 in Appendix B.1, for a $z = -0.43$, then $0.5000 - 0.1664 = 0.3336$

21. a. 0.8276, first find $z = -1.5$, found by $((44 - 50)/4)$ and $z = 1.25 = (55 - 50)/4)$. The area between -1.5 and 0 is 0.4332 and the area between 0 and 1.25 is 0.3944, both from Appendix B.1. Then adding the two areas, we find that $0.4332 + 0.3944 = 0.8276$.

  b. 0.1056, found by $0.5000 - 0.3994$, where $z = 1.25$

  c. 0.2029, recall that the area for $z = 1.25$ is 0.3944, and the area for $z = 0.5$, found by $((52 - 50)/4)$ is 0.1915. Then subtract $0.3944 - 0.1915$ and find 0.2029.

23. a. 0.1525, found by subtracting $0.4938 - 0.3413$, which are the areas associated with z values of 2.5 and 1, respectively.

  b. 0.0062, found by $0.5000 - 0.4938$

c. 0.9710, found by recalling that the area of the z value of 2.5 is 0.4938. Then find $z = -2.00$ found by $((205 - 225)/10)$. Thus, $0.4938 + 0.4772 = 0.9710$

25. a. 0.0764, found by $z = (20 - 15)/3.5 = 1.43$, then $0.5000 - 0.4236 = 0.0764$

    b. 0.9236, found by $0.5000 + 0.4236$, where $z = 1.43$

    c. 0.1185, found by $z = (12 - 15)/3.5 = -0.86$. The area under the curve is 0.3051, then $z = ((10 - 15)/3.5) = -1.43$. The area is 0.4236, finally, $0.4236 - 0.3051 = 0.1185$

27. $x = 56.58$, found by adding 0.5000 (the area left of the mean) and then finding a z value that forces 45% of the data to fall inside the curve. Solving for x: $1.645 = (x - 50)/4 = 56.58$.

29. 200.7; find a z value where 0.4900 of area is between 0 and z. That value is $z = 2.33$, then solve for x:$(x - 200)/0.3$ so $x = 200.7$

31. 1630, found by $2100 - 1.88 (250)$

33 1026, found by $900 + 0.84(150)$

35. a. $\mu = np = 50(0.25) = 12.5$
$\sigma^2 = np(1 - p) = 12.5(1 - 0.25) = 9.375$ $\sigma = \sqrt{9.375} = 3.0619$

    b. 0.2578, found by $(14.5 - 12.5)/3.0619 = 0.65$, the area is 0.2422, then $0.5000 - 0.2422 = 0.2578$

    c. 0.2578, found by $(10.5 - 12.5)/3.0619 = -0.65$. The area is 0.2422. Then $0.5000 - 0.2422 = 0.2578$.

37. a. 0.0192, found by $0.500 - 0.4808$

    b. 0.0694, found by $0.500 - 0.4306$

    c. 0.0502, found by $0.0694 - 0.0192$

39. a. Yes. (1) There are two mutually exclusive outcomes-overweight and not overweight. (2) It is the result of counting the number of successes (overweight members). (3) Each trial is independent. (4) The probability of 0.30 remains the same for each trial.

    b. 0.0084, found by
$\mu = 500(0.30) = 150$ $\sigma^2 = 500(0.30)(0.70) = 105$
$\sigma = \sqrt{105} = 10.24695$ $z = \dfrac{x - \mu}{\sigma} = \dfrac{174.5 - 150}{10.24695} = 2.39$
The area under the curve for 2.39 is 0.4916. Then $0.5000 - 0.4916 = 0.0084$

    c. 0.8461, found by $z = \dfrac{139.5 - 150}{10.24695} = -1.02$
The area between 139.5 and 150 is 0.3461. Adding $0.3461 + 0.5000 = 0.8461$

41. a. 12.005 found by $(11.96 + 12.05)/2$

    b. 0.02598 found by $\sqrt{\dfrac{(12.05 - 11.96)^2}{12}}$

    c. 0.4444 found by $[1/(12.05 - 11.96)](12 - 11.96)$

    d. 0.7778 found by $[1/(12.05 - 11.96)](12.05 - 11.98)$

    e. 11.6667 found by $[1/(12.05 - 11.96)](12.05 - 11.00)$

43. a. 7 found by $(4 + 10)/2$

    b. 1.732 found by $\sqrt{\dfrac{(10 - 4)^2}{12}}$

    c. 0.3333 found by $[1/(10 - 4)](6 - 4)$

    d. 0.8333 found by $[1/(10 - 4)](10 - 5)$

45. a. 0.9406 and 0.0594

    b. 0.9664 and 0.0336

    c. 0.2177 and 0.7823

    d. 0.0071 and 0.9929

47. a. $0.3413 + 0.3413 = 0.6826$

    b. $0.4772 + 0.4772 = 0.9544$

c. $0.4987 + 0.4987 = 0.9974$

d. $0.3413 + 0.4772 = 0.8185$

e. $0.0228 + 0.1587 = 0.1814$

49. a. -0.4 for net sales, found by $(170 - 180)/25$ and 2.92 for employees, found by $(1850 - 1500)/120$

    b. Net sales are 0.4 standard deviations below the mean. Employees is 2.92 standard deviations above the mean.

    c. 65.54% of the aluminum fabricators have greater net sales compared with Clarion, found by $0.1554 + 0.5000$. Only 0.18% have more employees than Clarion, found by $0.5000 - 0.4982$

51. a. almost 0.5000, because $z = \dfrac{30 - 490}{90} = -5.11$

    b. 0.2514, found by $0.5000 - 0.2486$

    c. 0.6374, found by $0.2486 + 0.3888$

    d. 0.3450, found by $0.3888 - 0.0438$

53. a. $0.3015 = 30.15\%$, found by $0.5000 - 0.1985$

    b. $0.2579 = 25.79\%$, found by $0.4564 - 0.1985$

    c. $0.0011 = 0.11\%$, found by $0.5000 - 0.4989$

    d. \$1818, found by $1280 + 1.28(420)$

55. a. 90.82%, found by $z = (40 - 34)/4.5 = 1.33$, then $0.5000 + 0.4082$

    b. 78.23%, found by $0.5000 + 0.2823$, where $z = (25 - 29)/5.1 = -0.78$

    c. Prob $(z > x) = 0.01$ implies Prob $(0 < z < x) = 0.49$ and $x = 2.33$
Women: $34 + 2.33(4.5) = 44.485$
Men: $29 + 2.33(5.1) = 40.883$

57. About 4099 units found by solving for x. $1.645 = (x - 4000)/60$

59. a. 15.39%, found by $(8 - 10.3)/2.25 = -1.02$, then $0.5000 - 0.3461 = 0.1539$

    b. 17.31%, found by: $z = (12 - 10.3)/2.25 = 0.76$. Area is 0.2764 $z = (14 - 10.3)/2.25 = 1.64$. Area is 0.4495
The area between 12 and 14 is 0.1731, found by $0.4495 - 0.2764$.

    c. Yes, but it is rather remote. Reasoning: On 99.73% of the days, returns are between 3.55 and 17.05, found by 10.3 ± 3 (2.25). Thus, the chance of less than 3.55 returns is rather remote.

61. a. $(37 - 39.5)/1.5 = -1.67$. Then $0.4525 + 0.5 = 0.9525$

    b. $(41.5 - 39.5)/1.5 = 1.33$. Then $0.4082 + 0.5 = 0.9082$

    c. $(36 - 39.5)/1.5 = -2.33$. Then $0.4901 - 0.4525 = 0.0376$

    d. $(0.5 - 0.4901) + 0.9525 = 0.9624$

63. a. 0.9678, found by: $\mu = 60(0.64) = 38.4$
$\sigma^2 = 60(0.64)(0.36) = 13.824$ $\sigma = \sqrt{13.824} = 3.72$
Then $(31.5 - 38.4)/3.72 = -1.85$, for which the area is 0.4678.
Then $0.5000 + 0.4678 = 0.9678$

    b. 0.0853, found by $(43.5 - 38.4)/3.72 = 1.37$, for which the area is 0.4147. Then $0.5000 - 0.4147 = 0.0853$

    c. 0.8084, found by $0.4441 + 0.3643$

    d. 0.0348 found by $0.4495 - 0.4147$

65. 0.0968, found by: $\mu = 50(0.40) = 20$
$\sigma^2 = 50(0.40)(0.60) = 12$ $\sigma = \sqrt{12} = 3.46$
$z = (24.5 - 20)/3.46 = 1.30$. The area is 0.4032. Then for 25 or more, $0.5000 - 0.4032 = 0.0968$

67. a. $1.645 = (45 - \mu)/5$ $\mu = 36.78$

    b. $1.645 = (45 - \mu)/10$ $\mu = 28.55$

c. $z = (30 - 28.6)/10 = 0.14$, then $0.5000 + 0.0557 = 0.5557$

69. a. 215, found by $195 + 2.33(8.5)$

   b. 270, found by $290 - 2.33(8.5)$

71. a. $z = (100 - 85)/8 = 1.88$, so $0.5000 - 0.4699 = 0.0301$

   b. Let $z = 0.67$, so $0.67 = (x - 85)/8$ and $x = 90.36$, set mileage at 90 360

   c. $z = (72 - 85)/8 = -1.63$, so $0.5000 - 0.4484 = 0.0516$

73. a. 0.2620; the z-value for 30 is 0.2, found by $((30 - 29)/5$, with a corresponding area of 0.0793, and the z-value for 34 is 1.0, found by $(34 - 29)/5$, with a corresponding area of 0.3413, which leads to $0.3413 - 0.0793 = 0.2620$.

   b. 0.8849, found by $0.3849 + 0.5000$.
   The z-value for 23 is -1.2, found by $(23 - 29)/5$.

   c. 0.0139, found by $0.5000 - 0.4861$.
   The z-value for 40 is 2.2, found by $(40 - 29)/5$.

75. $\mu = 150(0.15) = 22.5$ $\sigma\sqrt{150(0.15)(0.85)} = 4.37$
   $z = (30.5 - 22.5)/4.37 = 1.83$
   $P(z > 1.83) = 0.5000 - 0.4664 = 0.0336$

77. a. $z = (154 - 150)/5 = 0.8$; $p = 0.2881$

   b. $z = (164 - 150)/5 = 2.8$; $p = 0.4974$; $(0.5 - 0.4974) = 0.0026$ $= 0.26\%$

   c. $z = (146 - 150)/5 = -0.8$; $p = 0.2881$; $z = (156 - 150)/5 = 1.2$; $p = 0.3849$ $0.2881 + 0.3849 = 0.6730$

   d. $z = (156 - 150)/5 = 1.2$; $p = 0.3849$; $z = (162 - 150)/5 = 2.4$; $p = 0.4918$; $0.4918 - 0.3849 = 0.1069$

79. $\dfrac{470 - \mu}{\sigma} = 0.25$ $\dfrac{500 - \mu}{\sigma} = 1.28$ $\sigma = 29.126$ and $\mu = 462.718$

81. a. -0.71

   b. $0.2611 + 0.4686 = 0.7297 = 72.97\%$

   c. $0.2611 + 0.5 = 0.7611 = 76.11\%$

   d. $0.4236 + 0.5 = 0.9236 = 92.36\%$

   e. $0.0764 + 0.2389 = 0.3153 = 31.53\%$

   f. $0.84 = (x - 50)/7$; $x = 55.88$

83. a. 21.19 percent found by $z = (3 - 3.1)/0.125 = -0.80$; so $0.5000 - 0.2881 = 0.2119$

   b. Increase the mean. $z = (3 - 3.15)/0.125 = -1.2$; probability is $0.5000 - 0.3849 = 0.1151$ Reduce the standard deviation. $z = (3 - 3.1)/0.1 = -1.0$; the probability $= 0.5000 - 0.3413 = 0.1587$

   Increasing the mean is better because a smaller percent of the hams will be below the limit.

85. 42, found by $12 + 1.645(18)$

87. **Descriptive statistics**

List Price			
Count	50		
Mean	331,233.98		
		Note:	
population variance	38,079,899,213.38	sample standard deviation	197 121.89
population standard deviation	195,140.72		

normal distribution

P(lower)	P(upper)	z	X	mean	std.dev
.5383	.4617	0.10	350000	331234	195140.7

actual number of homes > $350 000 =   15

The actual number of homes listed for more than $350 000 is 15, so the probability is 15/50 =   0.3

The values should be closer, so we will further examine the list prices to see if the distribution is skewed.

We get the following results from MegaStat.

skewness   1.86

We can see that the distribution is fairly positively skewed. This is not a good approximation as a result.

Chapter 7

1. a. 303 Louisiana, 5155 S. Main, 3501 Monroe, 2652 W. Central

   b. Answers will vary

   c. 630 Dixie Hwy, 835 S. McCord Rd., 4624 Woodville Rd.

   d. Answers will vary

3. Systematic random sampling

5. a.

Sample	Values	Sum	Mean
1	12, 12	24	12
2	12, 14	26	13
3	12, 16	28	14
4	12, 14	26	13
5	12, 16	28	14
6	14, 16	30	15

   b. $\mu_{\bar{x}} = (12 + 13 + 14 + 13 + 14 + 15)/6 = 13.5$
   $\mu = (12 + 12 + 14 + 16)/4 = 13.5$

   c. More dispersion with population compared to the sample means. The sample means vary from 12 to 15 whereas the population varies from 12 to 16.

7. a.

Sample	Values	Sum	Mean
1	12, 12, 14	38	12.67
2	12, 12, 15	39	13.0
3	12, 12, 20	44	14.67
4	14, 15, 20	49	16.33
5	12, 14, 15	41	13.67
6	12, 14, 15	41	13.67
7	12, 15, 20	47	15.67
8	12, 15, 20	47	15.67
9	12, 14, 20	46	15.33
10	12, 14, 20	46	15.33

   b. $\mu_{\bar{x}} = (12.66 + 13.0 + \ldots + 15.33 + 15.33)/10 = 14.6$
   $\mu = (12 + 12 + 14 + 15 + 20)/5 = 14.6$

   c. The dispersion of the population is greater than that of the sample means. The sample means vary from 12.67 to 16.33 whereas the population varies from 12 to 20.

9. a. 20 found by $_6C_3$

b.

Sample	Cases	Sum	Mean
Ruud, Austin, Sass	3, 6, 3	12	4.0
Ruud, Sass, Palmer	3, 3, 3	9	3.0
Ruud, Palmer, Wilhelms	3, 3, 0	6	2.0
Ruud, Wilhelms, Schueller	3, 0, 1	4	1.33
Austin, Sass, Palmer	6, 3, 3	12	4.0
Austin, Palmer, Wilhelms	6, 3, 0	9	3.0
Austin, Wilhelms, Schueller	6, 0, 1	7	2.33
Sass, Palmer, Wilhelms	3, 3, 0	6	2.0
Sass, Wilhelms, Schueller	3, 0, 1	4	1.33
Palmer, Wilhelms, Schueller	3, 0, 1	4	1.33
Austin, Sass, Wilhelms	6, 3, 0	9	3.00
Ruud, Austin, Palmer	3, 6, 3	12	4.0
Ruud, Austin, Wilhelms	3, 6, 0	9	3.0
Ruud, Austin, Schueller	3, 6, 1	10	3.33
Ruud, Sass, Wilhelms	3, 3, 0	6	2.0
Ruud, Sass, Schueller	3, 3, 1	7	2.33
Ruud, Palmer, Schueller	3, 3, 1	7	2.33
Austin, Sass, Schueller	6, 3, 1	10	3.33
Austin, Palmer, Schueller	6, 3, 1	10	3.33
Sass, Palmer, Schueller	3, 3, 1	7	2.33

c. $\mu_{\bar{x}} = \frac{53.33}{20} = 2.66 \; \mu = (3+6+3+3+1+0)/6 = 2.7$
They are equal

d.

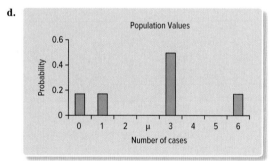

Population Values

Sample Mean	Number of Means	Probability
1.33	3	0.1500
2.00	3	0.1500
2.33	4	0.2000
3.00	4	0.2000
3.33	3	0.1500
4.00	3	0.1500
	20	1.0000

More of a dispersion in population compared to sample means. The sample means vary from 1.33 to 4.0. The population varies from 0 to 6.

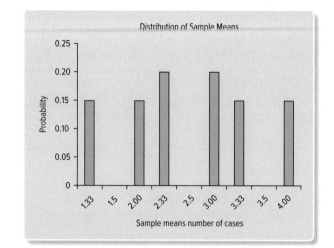

Distribution of Sample Means

11. a. $\mu = \frac{0+1+\ldots+9}{10} = 4.5$

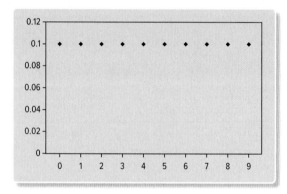

b.

Sample	Sum	$\bar{x}$
1	11	2.2
2	31	6.2
3	21	4.2
4	24	4.8
5	21	4.2
6	20	4.0
7	23	4.6
8	29	5.8
9	35	7.0
10	27	5.4

$\mu_{\bar{x}} = (2.2 + 6.2 + \ldots\ldots + 7.0 + 5.4)/10 = 4.84$

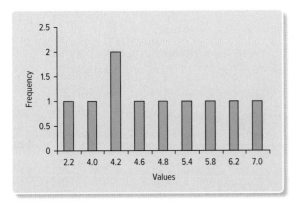

The mean of the 10 sample means is 4.84, which is close to the population mean of 4.5. The sample means range from 2.2 to 7.0, whereas the population values range from 0 to 9. From the above graph, the sample means tend to cluster between 4 and 5.

13. a. Answers will vary

    b. Answers will vary

    c. The sample distribution should be more bell-shaped.

15. a. $z = \dfrac{63 - 60}{12/\sqrt{9}} = 0.75$ So the probability is 0.2266, found by

    $0.5000 - 0.2734$.

    b. $z = \dfrac{56 - 60}{12/\sqrt{9}} = -1$ So the probability is 0.1587, found by

    $0.5000 - 0.3413$

    c. 0.6147, found by $0.3413 + 0.2734$.

17. $z = \dfrac{950 - 1200}{250/\sqrt{50}} = -7.07$ So probability is very close to 1 or virtually certain.

19. $\sqrt{\dfrac{0.45(1 - 0.45)}{200}} = 0.035178$

21. $z = (0.06 - 0.02)/\sqrt{\dfrac{0.02(1 - 0.02)}{50}} = 2.02$;

    then $0.5 - 0.4783 = 0.0217$

23. $z = (0.80 - 0.75)/\sqrt{\dfrac{0.75(1 - 0.75)}{300}} = 2$;

    then $0.5 - 0.4772 = 0.0228$

25. a. Formal Man, Summit Stationers, Bootleggers, Leather Ltd., Petries.

    b. Answers will vary.

    c. Gap, Fredericks, Summit, M Studios, Leather ltd, Things Remembered, County Seat, Coach House Gifts, Regis Hairstylists.

27. The difference between a sample statistic and the population parameter. Yes, the difference could be zero. The sample mean and the population parameter are equal.

29. a. The standard error of the mean declines as the sample size grows because the sample size is in the denominator and as the denominator increases the proportion decreases.

    b. If the sample size is increased, the Central Limit theorem guarantees the distribution of the sample means becomes more normal.

    c. The shape of the distribution becomes narrower since the dispersion is less and estimates of the mean are more precise.

31. Use of either a proportional or nonproportional stratified random sample would be appropriate. For example, suppose the number of banks in the financial district were as follows:

Assets	Number	Percent of Total
$500 million and more	20	2.0
$100–499 million	324	32.4
less than $100 million	656	65.6
	1000	100

For a proportional stratified sample, if the sample size is 100, then two banks with assets of $500 million would be selected, 32 medium-sized banks, and 66 small banks. For a nonproportional sample, 10 or even all 20 large banks could be selected and fewer medium- and small size-banks, and the sample results weighted by the appropriate percents of the total.

33. a. We selected 60, 104, 75, 72, and 48. Answers will vary.

    b. We selected the third observation. So the sample consists of 75, 72, 68, 82, 48. Answers will vary.

    c. Use a stratified random sample.

35. a. 15 found by $_6C_2$

    b.

Sample	Value	Sum	Mean
1	79, 64	143	71.5
2	79, 84	163	81.5
3	79, 82	161	80.5
4	79, 92	171	85.5
5	79, 77	156	78.0
6	64, 84	148	74.0
7	64, 82	146	73.0
8	64, 92	156	78.0
9	64, 77	141	70.5
10	84, 82	166	83.0
11	84, 92	176	88.0
12	84, 77	161	80.5
13	82, 92	174	87.0
14	82, 77	159	79.5
15	92, 77	169	84.5
			1195.0

    c. $\mu_{\bar{x}} = \dfrac{1195}{15} = 79.67$ $\mu = 478/6 = 79.67$ They are equal

    d. No, the student is not graded on all available information. He or she is as likely to get a lower grade based on the sample as a higher grade. By dropping a lower grade, the average is 82.8. This is preferable.

37. a. 10, found by $_5C_2$

    b.

Shutdowns	Mean	Shutdowns	Mean
4, 3	3.5	3, 3	3.0
4, 5	4.5	3, 2	2.5
4, 3	3.5	5, 3	4.0
4, 2	3.0	5, 2	3.5
3, 5	4.0	3, 2	2.5

    c. $\mu_{\bar{x}} = (3.5 + 4.5 + \ldots + 2.5)/10 = 3.4$
    $\mu = (4 + 3 + 5 + 3 + 2)/5 = 3.4$

    The two means are equal.

    d. The population values are uniform in shape. The distribution of the sample means tends toward normality. See the following charts.

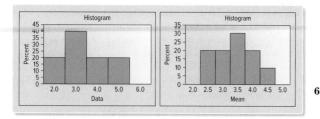

39. a. The distribution will be normal.

b. $\sigma_{\bar{x}} = \dfrac{5.5}{\sqrt{25}} = 1.1$

c. $z = \dfrac{36 - 35}{5.5/\sqrt{25}} = 0.91$ So probability is 0.1814,

found by $0.5000 - 0.3186$.

d. $z = \dfrac{34.5 - 35}{5.5/\sqrt{25}} = -0.45$ So probability is 0.6736,

found by $0.5000 + 0.1736$.

e. 0.4922, found by $0.3186 + 0.1736$

41. $z = \dfrac{335 - 350}{45/\sqrt{40}} = -2.11$ So probability is 0.9826, found by

$0.5000 + 0.4826$.

43. $z = \dfrac{31.5 - 30.6}{2.5/\sqrt{60}} = 2.79$. So probability is 0.9974, found by

$0.5000 + 0.4974$.

45. Between 2679 and 2721, found by $2700 \pm 1.96(68/\sqrt{40})$.

47. $z = \dfrac{900 - 947}{205/\sqrt{60}} = -1.78$ So probability is 0.0375, found by

$0.5000 - 0.4625$.

49. $z = \dfrac{73 - 69}{12.5/\sqrt{50}} = 2.26$

Area $= 0.0119$ found by $0.5 - 0.4881$

51. $z = (0.3 - 0.25)/\sqrt{\dfrac{0.25(1 - 0.25)}{200}} = 1.63;$

then $0.5 + 0.4484 = 0.9484$

53. a. $z = (0.85 - 0.90)/\sqrt{\dfrac{0.90(1 - 0.90)}{300}} = -2.887$

then $0.5 + 0.4981 = 0.9981$

b. $z = (0.92 - 0.90)/\sqrt{\dfrac{0.90(1 - 0.90)}{300}} = 1.15;$

then $0.5 - 0.3749 = 0.1251$

c. $0.4981 + 0.3749 = 0.8730$

55. a. $20/\sqrt{36} = 3.33$

b. $z = (490 - 500)/3.33 = -3.00$ and
$z = (510 - 500)/3.33 = 3.00; p = 0.4987(2) = 0.9974$

c. $0.4987 + 0.5 = 0.9987$

57. a. $0.5 - 0.4525 = 0.0475 = 4.75\%;$
found by $z = (675 - 650)/(120/\sqrt{64}) = 1.67;$
$p = 0.4525$

b. $0.5 + 0.2486 = 0.7486 = 74.86\%;$
found by $z = (660 - 650)/(120/\sqrt{64}) = 0.67;$
$p = 0.2486$

c. $0.4082 - 0.2486 = 0.1596 = 15.96\%;$
found by $z = (670 - 650)/(120/\sqrt{64}) = 1.33;$
$p = 0.4082$

d. $0.5 + 0.0475 = 0.5475 = 54.75\%$

59. a. $\sigma_{\bar{x}} = \dfrac{0.33}{\sqrt{40}} = 0.052$

b. $z_1 = \dfrac{3.46 - 3.50}{0.052} = -0.77$ and $z_2 = \dfrac{3.54 - 3.50}{0.052} = 0.77$

Probability is 0.5588, found by $0.2794 + 0.2794$.

c. $z_1 = \dfrac{0.01}{0.052} = -0.19$ and $z_2 = \dfrac{0.01}{0.052} = 0.19$

Probability is 0.1506, found by $0.0753 + 0.0753$.

d. $z = \dfrac{3.60 - 3.50}{0.052} = 1.92$ Probability is 0.0274,

found by $0.5000 - 0.4726$.

61. a. $\bar{p} = 420/1400 = 0.3$

b. 0.012247, found by $\sqrt{\dfrac{0.3(1 - 0.3)}{1400}}$

c. $0.5 - 0.4599 = 0.0401;$ found by $\dfrac{390/1400 - 0.3}{0.0122} = -1.75;$
$p = 0.4599$

63. a. $0.5 - 0.3212 = 0.1788;$ found by $\dfrac{0.02 - 0.05}{\sqrt{\dfrac{0.05(1 - 0.05)}{45}}} = -0.92;$
$p = 0.3212$

b. $0.5 - 0.4382 = 0.0618;$ found by $\dfrac{0.10 - 0.05}{\sqrt{\dfrac{0.05(1 - 0.05)}{45}}} = 1.54;$
$p = 0.4382$

c. $0.5 - 0.4382 = 0.0618;$ found by $\dfrac{0.0 - 0.05}{\sqrt{\dfrac{0.05(1 - 0.05)}{45}}} = -1.54;$
$p = 0.4382$

65. a. Part of this answer is from Chapter 2.

Descriptive statistics

	List Price
count	98
mean	567,496.76
population variance	171,676,803,157.51
population standard deviation	414,339.00

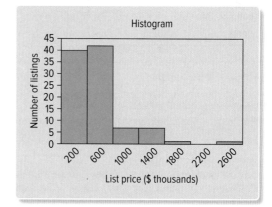

The distribution appears to be positively skewed.

b. Sample list prices

$	179 000
$	184 900
$	189 000
$	192 779
$	214 900
$	219 500
$	220 000
$	222 400
$	227 000
$	229 000
$	237 500

$	239 000
$	241 745
$	244 900
$	249 000
$	249 999
$	269 000
$	274 900
$	274 900
$	479 900
$	484 000
$	489 900
$	495 000
$	495 500
$	499 000
$	499 900
$	499 900
$	509 900
$	515 000
$	535 000
$	539 900
$	575 000
$	585 000
$	599 900
$	639 900

Descriptive statistics

	Sample list prices
count	35
mean	365 774.94

normal distribution

P(lower)	P(upper)	z	X	mean	Standard error
.0020	.9980	−2.88	365774.9	567496.8	70036.07

Chapter 8

1. $51 314.29 and $58 685.71, found by $55 000 $\pm 2.58(\$10\,000/\sqrt{49})$

3. a. 1.581, found by $\sigma_{\bar{X}} = 5/\sqrt{10}$
   b. The population is normally distributed and the population variance is known.
   c. 16.901 and 23.099, found by 20 ± 3.099

5. a. 0.95, found by $4.75/\sqrt{25}$
   b. 14.637 to 19.064, found by $16.85 \pm 2.33(4.75/\sqrt{25})$
   c. decrease the confidence level

7. a. $20. It is our best estimate of the population mean.
   b. $18.60 and $21.40, found by $20 \pm 1.96(\$5/\sqrt{49})$ About 95 percent of the intervals similarly constructed will include the population mean.

9. a. 40 litres
   b. 36.669 and 43.331, found by $40 \pm 2.58(10/\sqrt{60})$

c. If 100 such intervals were determined, the population mean would be included in about 99 intervals.

11. a. 2.201
   b. 1.729
   c. 3.499

13. a. 5.8697, found by $26.25/\sqrt{20}$
   b. 64.85 to 85.15, found by $75 \pm 1.729(5.8697)$
   c. increase

15. a. The population mean is unknown, but the best estimate is 20, the sample mean.
   b. Use the t distribution as the population standard deviation is unknown. However, we must assume that the population is normally distributed.
   c. 2.093
   d. Between 19.06 and 20.94, found by $20 \pm 2.093\left(\frac{2}{\sqrt{20}}\right)$.
   e. Neither value is reasonable because they are not inside the interval.

17. Between 95.39 and 101.81, found by $98.6 \pm 1.833\left(\frac{5.54}{\sqrt{10}}\right)$.

19. a. 0.375, found by 75/200
   b. 0.0342, found by $\sqrt{\frac{(0.375)(1-0.375)}{200}} = 0.0342$
   c. 0.319 to 0.431, found by found by $0.375 \pm 1.645(0.0342)$
   d. If 200 such intervals were determined, the population proportion would be included in about 180 intervals.

21. a. 0.8, found by 80/100.
   b. 0.04, found by $\sqrt{\frac{0.8(1-0.8)}{100}}$.
   c. Between 0.72 and 0.88, found by $0.8 \pm 1.96\left(\sqrt{\frac{0.8(1-0.8)}{100}}\right)$.
   d. We are reasonably sure the population proportion is between 72% and 88%.

23. a. 0.625, found by 250/400.
   b. 0.0242, found by $\sqrt{\frac{0.625(1-0.625)}{400}}$.
   c. Between 0.563 and 0.687, found by
   $0.625 \pm 2.58\left(\sqrt{\frac{0.625(1-0.625)}{400}}\right)$.
   d. We are reasonably sure the population proportion is between 56% and 69%.

25. 33.410 and 36.590, found by $35 \pm 2.03\left(\frac{5}{\sqrt{36}}\right)\sqrt{\frac{300-36}{300-1}}$

27. 1.683 up to 2.037, found by $1.86 \pm 2.68\left(\frac{0.50}{\sqrt{50}}\right)\sqrt{\frac{400-50}{400-1}}$

29. 0.023 to 0.110, found by
   $0.066667 \pm 1.645\sqrt{\frac{0.0667(1-0.0667)}{75}}\sqrt{\frac{500-75}{500-1}}$
   $10/75 = 0.13$; therefore, it would not be reasonable as 0.13 is not in the CI.

31. 55, found by $\left(\frac{1.96 \times 30}{8}\right)^2 = 54.0225$

33. 196, found by $n = 0.15(0.85)\left(\frac{1.96}{0.05}\right)^2 = 195.9216$

35. 554, found by $\left(\frac{1.96 \times 3}{0.25}\right)^2 = 553.19$

37. a. 577, found by $0.60(0.40)\left(\frac{1.96}{0.04}\right)^2 = 576.24$
   b. 601, found by $0.50(0.50)\left(\frac{1.96}{0.04}\right)^2 = 600.25$

39. 6.13 years to 6.87 years, found by $6.5 \pm 1.989(1.7/\sqrt{85})$

41. a. Between $1.27 to $1.33, found by $1.30 \pm 2.680(0.07/\sqrt{50})$

    b. $1.40 is not reasonable because it is outside of the confidence interval.

43. a. Between 7.2 and 8.8, found by $8 \pm 1.685\left(\dfrac{3}{\sqrt{40}}\right)$.

    b. 9 is not reasonable because it is outside of the confidence interval.

45. a. 65.5 up to 71.7 hours, found by $68.6 \pm 2.680(8.2/\sqrt{50})$

    b. The value suggested by the manager is included in the confidence interval. Therefore it is reasonable.

    c. Changing the confidence level to 95% would reduce the width of the interval. The value of 2.608 would change to 2.010.

47. 62, found by $n = \left(\dfrac{1.96 \times 16}{4}\right)^2 = 61.5$

49. Between $13 734 up to $15 028, found by

$14\,381 \pm 1.711\left(\dfrac{1892}{\sqrt{25}}\right)$.

15 000 is reasonable because it is inside of the confidence interval.

51. a. $62.583, found by $751/12.

    b. Between $60.54 and 64.63, found by $62.583 \pm 1.796\left(\dfrac{3.94}{\sqrt{12}}\right)$.

    c. $60 is not reasonable because it is outside of the confidence interval.

53. a. 89.4667, found by $1342/15$.

    b. Between 84.99 and 93.94, found by $89.4667 \pm 2.145\left(\dfrac{8.08}{\sqrt{15}}\right)$.

    c. Yes, because even the lower limit of the confidence interval is above 80.

55. Do not use PCF as $n < 5\% N$. Between 0.647 and 0.753,

found by $0.7 \pm 2.58\left(\sqrt{\dfrac{0.7(1-0.7)}{500}}\right)$.

Yes, because even the lower limit of the confidence interval is above 0.500.

57. $52.51 and $55.50, found by $54.00 \pm 2.032\, \dfrac{\$4.50}{\sqrt{35}}\sqrt{\dfrac{(500-35)}{500-1}}$

59. 369, found by $n = 0.60(1-0.60)[1.96/0.05]^2$

61. 97, found by $\left(\dfrac{1.96 \times 500}{100}\right)^2$

63. a. 708.13, rounded up to 709, found by:
$0.21(1-0.21)[1.96/0.03]^2$

    b. 1068, found by $0.50(0.50)[1.96/0.03]^2$

65. Between 0.573 and 0.653, found by

$0.613 \pm 2.58\left(\sqrt{\dfrac{0.613(1-0.613)}{1000}}\right)$.

Yes, because even the lower limit of the confidence interval is above 0.500.

67. Between 12.69 and 14.11, found by $13.4 \pm 1.96\left(\dfrac{6.8}{\sqrt{352}}\right)$.

69. a. 30, found by $180/\sqrt{36}$

    b. Between $355.10 and 476.90, found by $416 \pm 2.030\left(\dfrac{180}{\sqrt{36}}\right)$

    c. 1245, found by $\left(\dfrac{1.96*180}{10}\right)^2$

71. a. Between $313.41 and 332.59, found by $323 \pm 2.426\left(\dfrac{25}{\sqrt{40}}\right)$.

b. $350 is not reasonable because it is outside of the confidence interval.

73. a. 65.49 up to 71.71 hours, found by $68.6 \pm 2.68(8.2\sqrt{50})$

    b. The value suggested by the NCAA is included in the confidence interval, therefore it is reasonable.

    c. Changing the confidence interval to 95% would reduce the width of the interval. The value of 2.680 would change to 2.010.

75. a. Between 75.44 and 80.56, found by $78 \pm 2.01\left(\dfrac{9}{\sqrt{50}}\right)$.

    b. 220, found by $\{(1.645 \times 9)/1\}^2 = 219.2$

77. The confidence interval is between 0.021 and 0.106, found by $0.064 \pm 2.576\left(\sqrt{\dfrac{0.064(1-0.064)}{220}}\right)$. It would not be reasonable to conclude that more than 10% the applicants are now failing the test because 0.10 is inside the confidence interval.

79. a. Between $10 592 and $11 366, found by $10\,979 \pm 1.729\left(\dfrac{\$1000}{\sqrt{20}}\right)$.

    b. 107, found by $\{(2.576 \times 1000)/250\}^2 = 106.2$

81. a. Answers will vary.

Descriptive statistics

	List Price
Mean	764,432.08
sample standard deviation	588,551.67
Confidence interval − mean	

	95%	confidence level
	764,432.075	Mean
	588,551.6667	std. dev.
	40	n
	2.023	t (df = 39)
	188,227.953	half-width
	952,660.03	upper confidence limit
	576,204.12	lower confidence limit
true mean	567,496.76	

The true mean is not in the 95% confidence interval.

    b. Answers will vary.

	Total Square Feet
Mean	2134.53
sample standard deviation	1534.76
Confidence interval − mean	

	95%	confidence level
	2134.525	Mean
	1534.760651	std. dev.
	40	n
	2.023	t (df = 39)
	490.840	half-width
	2625.37	upper confidence limit
	1643.68	lower confidence limit
true mean	1710.01	

The true mean is in the 95% confidence interval.

    c. Answers will vary

	3 + Bedrooms
sample proportion	0.450
Confidence interval − proportion	

	95%	confidence level

0.45	proportion
40	n
1.960	Z
0.154	half-width
0.60	upper confidence limit
0.30	lower confidence limit

true proportion	0.378

The true proportion is in the 95% confidence interval.

83. This answer was obtained using MegaStat. Your answer may be slightly different due to rounding.

a. Descriptive statistics

	16-Jun
count	16
sample standard deviation	218,352.23
sample variance	47,677,695,536.47
confidence interval 80.% lower	342,058.19
confidence interval 80.% upper	488,420.31
margin of error	73,181.06
t(df = 15)	1.341

b. no, as $300 000 is not in the interval

Chapter 9

1. a. $H_0 : \mu = 2$
$H_1 : \mu \neq 2$
b. $H_0 : \mu \geq 40$
$H_1 : \mu < 40$
c. $H_0 : \mu \leq \$1750$
$H_1 : \mu > \$1750$
d. $H_0 : \mu = 3.25$
$H_1 : \mu \neq 3.25$

3. a. Two-tailed
b. Reject H_0 and accept H_1 when z does not fall in the region from -1.96 and 1.96
c. -1.2, found by $z = \dfrac{49 - 50}{(5/\sqrt{36})}$
d. Not enough evidence to reject H_0 and conclude the mean is not different from 50.
e. $p = 0.2302$, found by $2(0.5000 - 0.3849)$. A 23.02% chance of finding a z value this large when H_0 is true.

5. a. One-tailed
b. Reject H_0 and accept H_1 when $z > 1.645$
c. 1.2, found by $z = \dfrac{21 - 20}{(5/\sqrt{36})}$
d. Not enough evidence to reject H_0 at the 0.05 significance level so we can conclude that wait times have not increased.
e. $p = 0.1151$, found by $0.5000 - 0.3849$. An 11.51% chance of finding a z-value this large or larger.

7. a. $H_0 : \mu = 96\ 600$
$H_1 : \mu \neq 96\ 600$
b. Reject H_0 if $z < -1.96$ or $z > 1.96$
c. -0.69, found by $z = \dfrac{95\ 795 - 96\ 600}{8050/\sqrt{48}}$
d. There is not enough evidence to reject H_0
e. $p = 0.4902$, found by $2(0.5000 - 0.2549)$. Crosset's experience is not different from that claimed by the manufacturer. If the H_0 is true, the probability of finding a value more extreme than this is 0.4902.

9. a. $H_0 : \mu \geq 6.8\ H_1 : \mu < 6.8$
b. Reject H_0 if $z < -1.645$
c. -7.2, found by $z = \dfrac{6.2 - 6.8}{(0.5/\sqrt{36})}$
d. Reject H_0 at a significance level of 0.05.
e. p-value is almost zero; the mean number of DVDs watched is less than 6.8 per month. If H_0 is true, there is virtually no chance of getting a statistic this small.

11. a. Reject H_0 when $t > 1.833$
b. $t = \dfrac{12 - 10}{(3/\sqrt{10})} = 2.108$
c. Reject H_0; the mean delivery time is greater than 10 days.

13. Choose $\alpha = 0.05$
$H_0 : \mu \leq 40\ H_1 : \mu > 40$; Reject H_0 if $t > 1.703$
$t = \dfrac{42 - 40}{(2.1/\sqrt{28})} = 5.040$

Reject H_0 and conclude that the mean number of calls is greater than 40 per week.

15. $H_0 : \mu \leq 35\ 600\ \ H_1 : \mu > 35\ 600$ Reject H_0 if $t > 1.740$
$t = \dfrac{37\ 675 - 35\ 600}{2415/\sqrt{18}} = 3.645$

Reject H_0 and conclude that as the mean life of the spark plugs is greater than 35 600 km, the claim is true.

17. a. Reject H_0 if $t < -3.747$
b. $\bar{x} = 17$ and $s = \sqrt{\dfrac{1495 - \dfrac{(85)^2}{5}}{5 - 1}} = 3.536\ t = \dfrac{17 - 20}{3.536/\sqrt{5}} = -1.90$
c. Do not reject H_0. We cannot conclude the population mean wait time is less than 20.
d. Between 0.05 and 0.10, about 0.065; by computer, the p-value $= 0.0653$.

19. $H_0 : \mu \leq 4.35\ \ H_1 : \mu > 4.35$ Reject H_0 if $t > 2.821$
$t = \dfrac{4.368 - 4.35}{(0.0339/\sqrt{10})} = 1.68$

Do not reject H_0. The additive did not increase the mean weight of the puppies. The p-value is between 0.10 and 0.05. Using a computer, the p-value $= 0.0639$

21. $H_0 : \mu \leq 4.0\ H_1 : \mu > 4.0$ Reject H_0 if $t > 1.796$
$t = \dfrac{4.50 - 4.0}{(2.68/\sqrt{12})} = 0.65$
Do not reject H_0. The mean number of km travelled has not been shown to be greater than 4.0. The p-value is greater than 0.10. Using a computer, the p-value $= 0.2657$.

23. a. H_0 is rejected if $z > 1.645$
b. 1.09, found by $z = \dfrac{0.75 - 0.70}{\sqrt{\dfrac{0.70(0.30)}{100}}}$
c. H_0 is not rejected

25. a. $H_0 : p \leq 0.52\ H_1 : p > 0.52$
b. H_0 is rejected if $z > 2.33$
c. 1.62, found by $z = \dfrac{0.5667 - 0.52}{\sqrt{\dfrac{0.52(0.48)}{300}}}$
d. H_0 is not rejected. We cannot conclude that the proportion of men driving on Hwy 400 is larger than 0.52.

27. a. $H_0 : p \geq 0.90\ H_1 : p < 0.90$
b. H_0 is rejected if $z < -2.33$
c. -2.67, found by $z = \dfrac{0.82 - 0.90}{\sqrt{\dfrac{0.90(0.10)}{100}}}$

d. H_o is rejected. Less than 90% of the customers receive their orders in less than 10 minutes.

29. $H_0: \mu = \$60\,000$ $H_1: \mu \neq \$60\,000$

Reject H_o if $z \leq 1.645$ or $z > 1.645$

$$z = \frac{62\,500 - 60\,000}{6000/\sqrt{120}} = 4.56$$

Reject H_o. We can conclude that the mean salary is not $60 000. The p-value is very close to zero. The confidence interval is from $61 599 to $63 401. As $60 000 falls outside of the confidence interval, the hypothesized mean is rejected.

31. $H_0: \mu \geq 10$ $H_1: \mu < 10$

Reject H_o if $z < -1.645$

$$z = \frac{9.0 - 10.0}{2.8/\sqrt{50}} = -2.53$$

Reject H_o. The mean weight loss is less than 10 pounds. The p-value $= 0.5000 - 0.4943 = 0.0057$.

33. $H_0: \mu \geq 7$ $H_1: \mu < 7$

$$t = \frac{(6.8 - 7)}{0.9/\sqrt{50}} = -1.57$$

The p-value is 0.0613, so at a significance level of 5%, do not reject the null hypothesis. University students sleep no less than the typical adult male.

35. $H_0: \mu \leq 1.25$ $H_1: \mu > 1.25$ Reject H_o if $t > 1.691$

$$z = \frac{1.27 - 1.25}{0.05/\sqrt{35}} = 2.37$$

Reject H_o. The mean price of gasoline is greater than $1.25. The p-value $= 0.0119$ (by computer)

37. $H_0: \mu \leq 14$ $H_1: \mu > 14$ Reject H_o if $t > 2.821$

$$t = \frac{15.64 - 14}{1.561/\sqrt{10}} = 3.32$$

Reject H_o. The mean rate charged is greater than 14 percent.

39. $H_0: \mu = 1.92$ $H_1: \mu \neq 1.92$ Reject H_o if $t < -2.201$ or $t > 2.201$
$\bar{x} = 2.08667$ $s_d = 0.40484$

$$t = \frac{2.08667 - 1.92}{0.40484/\sqrt{12}} = 1.43$$

Do not reject H_o. There is not a difference in the mean amount of water consumed at the college surveyed and the national average.

The confidence interval is from 1.82945 to 2.34389. The hypothesized mean falls in the confidence interval, and so H_o is not rejected.

41. $H_0: \mu \geq 6.5$ $H_1: \mu < 6.5$ Reject H_o if $t < -2.718$
$\bar{x} = 5.1667$ $s = 3.1575$

$$t = \frac{5.1667 - 6.5}{3.1575/\sqrt{12}} = -1.463$$

Do not reject H_o. The mean is not less than 6.5.

43. $H_0: \mu = 0$ $H_1: \mu \neq 0$ Reject H_o if $t < -2.110$ or $t > 2.110$
$\bar{x} = -0.2322$ $s = 0.3120$

$$t = \frac{-0.2322 - 0}{0.3120/\sqrt{18}} = -3.158$$

Reject H_o. The mean gain or loss does not equal 0. The p-value is less than 0.01, but greater than 0.001, so the probability of no time gain or loss is very small. Using a computer, the p-value $= 0.0057$, and as this is less than the significance level, the null hypothesis is rejected.

45. $H_0: \mu \leq 100$ $H_1: \mu > 100$ Reject H_0 if $t > 1.761$.

[Assuming the population is normally distributed]

$$t = \frac{109.4 - 100}{9.96/\sqrt{15}} = 3.65$$

Reject H_0. The mean is greater than 100.

47. $H_0: p \leq 0.60$ $H_1: p > 0.60$ H_0 is rejected if $z > 2.33$

$$z = \frac{0.70 - 0.60}{\sqrt{\dfrac{0.60(0.40)}{200}}} = 2.89$$

H_0 is rejected. Ms. Dennis is correct. More than 60% of the accounts are more than 3 months old.

49. $H_0: p \leq 0.44$ $H_1: p > 0.44$ H_0 is rejected if $z > 1.645$

$$z = \frac{0.480 - 0.44}{\sqrt{\dfrac{0.44(0.56)}{1000}}} = 2.55$$

H_0 is rejected. We conclude that there has been an increase in the proportion of people wanting to go to Europe.

51. $H_0: p \leq 0.20$ $H_1: p > 0.20$ H_0 is rejected if $z > 2.33$

$$z = \frac{\dfrac{56}{200} - 0.20}{\sqrt{\dfrac{0.20(0.80)}{200}}} = 2.83$$

H_0 is rejected. More than 20% of the owners move during a particular year. The p-value$= 0.5000 - 0.4977 = 0.0023$

53. $H_0: \mu \leq 42$ $H_1: \mu > 42$ Reject H_o if $t > 1.796$

$$t = \frac{51 - 42}{8/\sqrt{12}} = 3.90$$

Reject H_o. The mean time for delivery is more than 42 days. The p-value is less than 0.005; using a computer, the p-value $= 0.0012$.

55. $H_0: \mu \geq 8$ $H_1: \mu < 8$ Reject H_o if $t < -1.714$

$$t = \frac{7.5 - 8}{3.2/\sqrt{24}} = -0.77$$

Do not reject H_o. The time is not less than 8.

57. $H_0: \mu \leq 50$ $H_1: \mu > 50$ Reject H_o if $t > 1.796$

$$t = \frac{82.5 - 50}{(59.5/\sqrt{12})} = 1.892$$

Reject H_o and conclude that the mean number of text messages is greater than 50. The p-value (0.0425) is less than 0.05. There is a slight probability (less than one chance in 20) this could happen by chance.

59. $H_0: \mu = 1.5$; $H_1: \mu \neq 1.5$ Reject H_o if t is not between -3.25 and 3.25

$$t = \frac{1.3 - 1.5}{0.9/\sqrt{10}} = -0.703$$

Do not reject H_o. This data does not contradict the publisher.

61. $H_0: p \leq 0.40$ $H_1: p > 0.40$ Reject H_o if z is greater than 2.33

$$z = \frac{(16/30) - 0.40}{\sqrt{(0.40(1 - 0.40))/30}} = 1.49$$

Do not reject the null hypothesis. This data does not show college students are more likely to skip breakfast.

63. $H_0: \mu \leq 370$; $H_1: \mu > 370$ Reject H_o if $t > 2.681$

$$t = \frac{388.31 - 370}{22.46/\sqrt{13}} = 2.939$$

Reject the null. The fare is higher. p-value$= 0.0062 < 0.01$

65. $H_0: p \geq 0.5$; $H_1: p < 0.5$ H_0 is rejected if $z < -1.645$

$$z = \frac{0.4 - 0.5}{\sqrt{\dfrac{0.5(0.5)}{200}}} = -2.828$$

H_0 is rejected. The proportion of alumni who supports the coach is less than 50%.

67. a. 445 469.4846   upper confidence limit

280 435.6404   lower confidence limit

b.

$H_0: \mu = 450\,000$

$H_1: \mu \neq 450\,000$

Hypothesis Test: Mean vs. Hypothesized Value

450 000.000	hypothesized value
362 952.563	mean Jan-14
154 855.971	std. dev.
38 713.993	std. error
16	n
15	df
−2.25	t
.0400	p-value (two-tailed)

Since the p-value > 0.02, there is not enough evidence to reject the null hypothesis,

so we conclude that the mean could be $450 000.

c. $H_0: \mu = 275\,000$

$H_1: \mu \neq 275\,000$

Since the value of $275 000 does not fall within the limits of the 95% CI from part (a), H_0 is rejected and so we conclude that the mean could not be $275 000.

d. Hypothesis Test: Mean vs. Hypothesized Value

275 000.000	hypothesized value
362 952.563	mean Jan-14
154 855.971	std. dev.
38 713.993	std. error
16	n
15	df
2.27	t
.0382	p-value (two-tailed)

Since the p-value < 0.05, the null hypothesis is rejected, so we conclude that the mean could not be $275 000.

69. a. $H_0: \mu = 350\,000$

$H_1: \mu \neq 350\,000$

Hypothesis Test: Mean vs. Hypothesized Value

350 000.000	hypothesized value
331 233.980	mean List Price
197 121.891	std. dev.
27 877.245	std. error
50	N
49	Df
−0.67	T
.5040	p-value (two-tailed)
256 524.302	confidence interval 99.% lower
405 943.658	confidence interval 99.% upper
74 709.678	margin of error

The p-value > 0.01, so there is not enough evidence to reject the null hypothesis.

We conclude that the list price is $350 000.

The mean of $350 000 falls in the 99% CI, which confirms that we do not have enough evidence to reject the null hypothesis.

b. $H_0: \mu = 1500$

$H_1: \mu \neq 1500$

Hypothesis Test: Mean vs. Hypothesized Value

1500.000	hypothesized value
1250.780	mean Total Square Feet
730.875	std. dev.
103.361	std. error
50	n
49	df
−2.41	t
.0197	p-value (two-tailed)
1043.068	confidence interval 95.% lower
1458.492	confidence interval 95.% upper
207.712	margin of error

The p-value < 0.05, so we reject the null hypothesis.

We conclude that the list price is not 1500 square feet.

The mean of 1500 does not fall in the 95% CI, which confirms that we should reject the null hypothesis.

c. # of houses = 24   proportion = 0.48

$H_0: p \leq .50$

$H_1: p > .50$

	Observed	Hypothesized	
	0.48	0.5	p (as decimal)
	24/50	25/50	p (as fraction)
	24.	25.	X
	50	50	n
			std.
		0.0707	error
		−0.28	z
		.6114	p-value (one-tailed, upper)

Note: the p-value is large, so the possibility of the null hypothesis being true is fairly certain.

There is not enough evidence to reject the null hypothesis.

We conclude that the proportion ≤ 0.50.

d. $H_0: p \leq 0.50$

$H_1: p > 0.50$

with more than 2 bedrooms = 23   proportion = .46

	Observed	Hypothesized	
	0.46	0.5	p (as decimal)
	23/50	25/50	p (as fraction)
	23.	25.	X
	50	50	n
		0.0707	std. error
		−0.57	z
		.7142	p-value (one-tailed, upper)

Note: the p-value is large, so the possibility of the null hypothesis being true is good.

There is not enough evidence to reject the null hypothesis.

We conclude that the proportion ≤ 0.50.

Chapter 10

1. a. Two-tailed test

b. Reject H_0 if $z < -2.05$ or $z > 2.05$

c. 2.59, found by $z = \dfrac{102 - 99}{\sqrt{\dfrac{5^2}{40} + \dfrac{6^2}{50}}}$

d. Reject H_0

e. $p = 0.0096$, found by $2(0.5000 - 0.4952)$

3. Step 1: $H_0: \mu_1 - \mu_2 \geq 0$ $H_1: \mu_1 - \mu_2 < 0$

Step 2: The 0.05 significance level was chosen

Step 3: Reject H_0 if $z < -1.645$

Step 4: -0.83, found by $z = \dfrac{3.5 - 3.7}{\sqrt{\dfrac{(1.05)^2}{40} + \dfrac{(1.3)^2}{55}}}$

Step 5: There is not enough evidence to reject H_0. Babies using the Gibbs brand did not gain less weight. $p = 0.2033$ found by $0.5000 - 0.2967$, which is $>$ than the significance level, and so, there is not enough evidence to reject H_0 Using a computer, the p-value $= 0.2037$.

5. Two-tailed test. Because we are trying to show a difference exists between two means.

$H_0: \mu_1 - \mu_2 = 0 \quad H_1: \mu_1 - \mu_2 \neq 0$

Reject H_0 if $z < -2.58$ or $z > 2.58$

-2.66, found by $z = \dfrac{31.4 - 34.9}{\sqrt{\dfrac{(5.1)^2}{32} + \dfrac{(6.7)^2}{49}}}$ Reject H_0 at the 0.01 level.

There is a difference in the mean turnover rate. The p-value $= 2(0.5 - 0.4961) = 0.0078$. Since this is $<$ than the significance level we reject H_0

7. **a.** Reject H_0 if $t > 2.120$ or $t < -2.120$ $df = 10 + 8 - 2 = 16$

b. $s_p^2 = \dfrac{(10 - 1)(4)^2 + (8 - 1)(5)^2}{10 + 8 - 2} = 19.9375$

c. $t = \dfrac{23 - 26}{\sqrt{19.9375\left(\dfrac{1}{10} + \dfrac{1}{8}\right)}} = -1.416$

d. There is not enough evidence to reject H_0.

e. p-value is greater than 0.10 and less than 0.20. The actual p-value $= 0.1759$.

9. $H_0: \mu_f - \mu_m \leq 0 \quad H_1: \mu_f - \mu_m > 0 \ df = 9 + 7 - 2 = 14$
Reject H_0 if $t > 2.624$

$s_p^2 = \dfrac{(7 - 1)(6.88)^2 + (9 - 1)(9.49)^2}{7 + 9 - 2} = 71.749$

$t = \dfrac{79 - 78}{\sqrt{71.749\left(\dfrac{1}{7} + \dfrac{1}{9}\right)}} = 0.234$

There is not enough evidence to reject H_0. The mean grade of women is not higher than that of men. The p-value $= 0.4090$, which is $>$ than the significance level and supports the decision. The actual p-value$= 0.4091$.

11. $H_0: \mu_s - \mu_a \leq 0 \ H_1: \mu_s - \mu_a > 0 \ df = 6 + 7 - 2 = 11$
Reject H_0 if $t > 1.363$

$s_p^2 = \dfrac{(6 - 1)(12.2)^2 + (7 - 1)(15.8)^2}{6 + 7 - 2} = 203.82$

$t = \dfrac{142.5 - 130.3}{\sqrt{203.82\left(\dfrac{1}{6} + \dfrac{1}{7}\right)}} = 1.536$

Reject H_0. The mean daily expenses are greater for the sales staff. The p-value is between 0.05 and 0.10, which is $<$ than the significance level, and so H_0 is rejected. The actual p-value $= 0.0763$.

13. Reject H_0 if $t > 2.353$

$\bar{d} = \dfrac{4}{4} = 1 \ s_d = \sqrt{\dfrac{38 - 4^2/4}{3}} = 3.367$

$t = \dfrac{1}{3.367/\sqrt{4}} = 0.59$

There is not enough evidence to reject the H_0. There is no difference in the defective parts produced on the day or afternoon shift. (The actual p-value $= 0.2971$)

15. $H_0: \mu_d \leq 0 \quad H_1: \mu_d > 0 \quad$ Reject H_0 if $t > 1.796$
$\bar{d} = 25.917 \quad s_d = 40.791$

$t = \dfrac{25.917}{40.791/\sqrt{12}} = 2.20$

Reject H_0. The incentive plan resulted in an increase in daily income. The p-value is 0.0250, which is $<$ than the significance level, and so reject H_0.

17. **a.** H_0 is rejected if $z > 1.645$

b. 0.64, found by $p_c = \dfrac{70 + 90}{100 + 150}$

c. 1.61, found by $z = \dfrac{0.70 - 0.60}{\sqrt{\dfrac{(0.64)(0.36)}{100} + \dfrac{(0.64)(0.36)}{150}}}$

d. There is not enough evidence to reject H_0.

e. p-value $= 0.5 - 0.4463 = 0.0537$. The p-value is 0.0537, which is $>$ than the significance level, and therefore, there is not enough evidence to reject H_0.

19. $H_0: p_1 - p_2 = 0 \quad H_1: p_1 - p_2 \neq 0$
H_0 is rejected if $z < -1.96$ or $z > 1.96$

$P_c = \dfrac{24 + 40}{400 + 400} = 0.08$

-2.09, found by $z = \dfrac{0.06 - 0.10}{\sqrt{\dfrac{(0.08)(0.92)}{400} + \dfrac{(0.08)(0.92)}{400}}}$

H_0 is rejected. The proportion infested is not the same in the two fields. The p-value $= 2(0.5 - 0.4817) = 0.0366$. The p-value is $<$ than the significance level, and therefore, H_0 is rejected. (computer p-value$= 0.0371$)

21. $H_0: p_d - p_r \leq 0 \quad H_1: p_d - p_r > 0$

H_0 is rejected if $z > 2.05 \ p_c = \dfrac{168 + 200}{800 + 1000} = 0.2044$

$z = \dfrac{0.21 - 0.20}{\sqrt{\dfrac{(0.2044)(0.7956)}{800} + \dfrac{(0.2044)(0.7956)}{1000}}} = 0.52$

There is not enough evidence to reject H_0. There is no difference in the proportion of Conservatives and Liberals who favour lowering the standards. The p-value $= 0.5 - 0.1985 = 0.3015$. The p-value is $>$ than the significance level, and therefore, there is not enough evidence to reject H_0.

23. $H_0: \mu_1 - \mu_2 = 0 \quad H_1: \mu_1 - \mu_2 \neq 0 \quad$ Reject H_0 if $z < -2.576$ or $z > 2.576$

$z = \dfrac{24.51 - 22.69}{\sqrt{\dfrac{(448)^2}{35} + \dfrac{(386)^2}{40}}} = 1.87$

There is not enough evidence to reject the null hypothesis. There is no difference in the means. The p-value is 0.0614, which is $>$ than the significance level, and confirms that there is not enough evidence to reject H_0.

25. $H_0: \mu_1 - \mu_2 = 0 \quad H_1: \mu_1 - \mu_2 \neq 0 \quad$ Reject H_0 if $z < -2.58$ or $z > 2.58$

$z = \dfrac{36.2 - 37.0}{\sqrt{\dfrac{(1.14)^2}{35} + \dfrac{(1.30)^2}{40}}} = -2.84$

Reject H_0. There is a difference in the useful life of the two brands of paint. The p-value is 0.0046, found by $2(0.5000 - 0.4977)$. Since the p-value is $<$ than the significance level, H_0 is rejected.

27. $H_0: \mu_1 - \mu_2 = 0 \quad H_1: \mu_1 - \mu_2 \neq 0 \quad$ Reject H_0 if $z < -1.96$ or $z > 1.96$

$z = \dfrac{4.77 - 5.02}{\sqrt{\dfrac{(1.05)^2}{40} + \dfrac{(1.23)^2}{50}}} = -1.04$

There is not enough evidence to reject H_0. There is no difference in the mean number of calls. The p-value $= 2(0.5000 - 0.3508) = 0.2984$, which is $>$ than the significance level, and so, there is not enough evidence to reject H_0.

29. $H_0: \mu_1 - \mu_2 = 0 \quad H_1: \mu_1 - \mu_2 \neq 0$ If t is not between -2.024 and 2.024, reject H_0.

$s_p^2 = \dfrac{(15 - 1)(40\,000)^2 + (25 - 1)(30\,000)^2}{15 + 25 - 2} = 1\,157\,894\,737$

$t = \dfrac{150\,000 - 180\,000}{\sqrt{1\,157\,894\,737\left(\dfrac{1}{15} + \dfrac{1}{25}\right)}} = -2.70$

Reject the null hypothesis. The population means are different. The p-value is almost zero.

31. $H_o: p_1 - p_2 \leq 0$ $H_1: p_1 - p_2 > 0$ Reject H_o if $z > 1.645$

$$P_c = \frac{180 + 261}{200 + 300} = 0.882$$

$$z = \frac{0.90 - 0.87}{\sqrt{\dfrac{0.882(0.118)}{200} + \dfrac{0.882(0.118)}{300}}} = 1.019$$

There is not enough evidence to reject H_o. There is no difference in the proportions that found relief in the new and the old drugs. The p-value is $0.5 - 0.3461 = 0.1539$, which is > than the significance level, and confirms that there is not enough evidence to reject H_o. (Computer p-value = 0.1542)

33. $H_o: p_1 - p_2 \leq 0$ $H_1: p_1 - p_2 > 0$ If $z > 1.645$, reject H_o.

$$p_c = \frac{7 + 13}{67 + 180} = 0.081$$

$$z = \frac{0.10448 - 0.07222}{\sqrt{\dfrac{(0.081)(0.919)}{67} + \dfrac{(0.081)(0.919)}{180}}} = 0.826$$

Do not reject the null. We cannot determine the white board markers from the new supplier are inferior to those in stock.

35. $H_o: p_1 - p_2 = 0$ $H_1: p_1 - p_2 \neq 0$
H_o is rejected if $z < -1.96$ or $z > 1.96$

$$P_c = \frac{68 + 45}{98 + 85} = 0.617$$

$$z = \frac{0.6939 - 0.5294}{\sqrt{\dfrac{(0.617)(0.383)}{98} + \dfrac{(0.617)(0.383)}{85}}} = 2.28$$

H_o is rejected. The proportions are not the same.

37. $H_o: p_1 - p_2 \leq 0$ $H_1: p_1 - p_2 > 0$ If $z > 2.33$, reject H_o.

$$p_c = \frac{990 + 970}{1500 + 1600} = 0.63$$

$$z = \frac{0.6600 - 0.60625}{\sqrt{\dfrac{(0.63)(0.37)}{1500} + \dfrac{(0.63)(0.37)}{1600}}} = 3.10$$

Reject the null. We can conclude the proportion of men who believe the division is fair is greater. The p-value is virtually zero. (Computer p-value = 0.0010)

39. $H_o: \mu_n - \mu_s = 0$ $H_1: \mu_n - \mu_s \neq 0$ Reject H_o if
$t < -2.086$ or $t > 2.086$

$$s_p^2 = \frac{(10 - 1)(10.5)^2 + (12 - 1)(14.25)^2}{10 + 12 - 2} = 161.2969$$

$$t = \frac{83.55 - 78.8}{\sqrt{161.2969\left(\dfrac{1}{10} + \dfrac{1}{12}\right)}} = 0.873$$

There is not enough evidence to reject H_o. There is no difference in the mean number of hamburgers sold at the two locations. The p-value is > than 0.20, which is > than the significance level, and so the decision is supported. (Computer p-value = 0.3928)

41. $H_o: \mu_1 - \mu_2 \leq 0$ $H_1: \mu_1 - \mu_2 > 0$ Reject H_o if
$t > 2.567$

$$s_p^2 = \frac{(8 - 1)(2.2638)^2 + (11 - 1)(2.4606)^2}{8 + 11 - 2} = 5.672$$

$$t = \frac{10.375 - 5.636}{\sqrt{5.672\left(\dfrac{1}{8} + \dfrac{1}{11}\right)}} = 4.28$$

Reject H_o. The mean number of transaction by the young adults is more than for the senior citizens. P-value = 0.0003

43. $H_o: \mu_1 - \mu_2 \leq 0$ $H_1: \mu_1 - \mu_2 > 0$ Reject H_o if $t > 2.650$

$\bar{x}_1 = 125.125$ $s_1 = 15.094$ $\bar{x}_2 = 117.714$ $s_2 = 19.914$

$$s_p^2 = \frac{(8 - 1)(15.094)^2 + (7 - 1)(19.914)^2}{8 + 7 - 2} = 305.708$$

$$t = \frac{125.125 - 117.714}{\sqrt{305.708\left(\dfrac{1}{8} + \dfrac{1}{7}\right)}} = 0.819$$

There is not enough evidence to reject H_o. There is no increase in the mean number sold at the regular price and the mean number sold at reduced price. P-value = 0.2138

45. $H_o: \mu_d \leq 0$; $H_1: \mu_d > 0$ Reject H_o if $t > 1.440$

$\bar{d} = 2$ (post-training-pre-training) $s_d = 2.082$

$$t = \frac{2}{2.082/\sqrt{7}} = 2.54$$

Reject H_o. The survey results show the training program has been effective in improving customer service. P-value = 0.0220

47. $H_o: \mu_A - \mu_B \geq 0$ $H_1: \mu_A - \mu_B < 0$ Reject H_o if $t < -1.668$

$$s_p^2 = \frac{(40 - 1)(9\,200)^2 + (30 - 1)(7\,100)^2}{40 + 30 - 2} = 70\,041\,912$$

$$t = \frac{57\,000 - 61\,000}{\sqrt{70\,041\,912\left(\dfrac{1}{40} + \dfrac{1}{30}\right)}} = -1.98$$

Reject H_o. The mean income of those selecting Plan B is larger. The p-value is 0.0259, which is smaller than the significance level, and confirms that the null hypothesis should be rejected. (Computer p-value = 0.0259)

49. $H_o: \mu_d \leq 0$ $H_1: \mu_d > 0$ Reject H_o if $t > 1.895$

$\bar{d} = 3.11$ $s_d = 2.91$

$$t = \frac{3.11}{2.91/\sqrt{8}} = 3.02$$

Reject H_o. The mean contamination rate is lower.
p-value = 0.0096

51. $H_o: p_1 - p_2 = 0$; $H_1: p_1 - p_2 \neq 0$ H_o is rejected if z is not between -1.96 and 1.96.

$$p_c = \frac{100 + 36}{300 + 200} = 0.272$$

$$z = \frac{\dfrac{100}{300} - \dfrac{36}{200}}{\sqrt{\dfrac{(0.272)(0.728)}{300} + \dfrac{(0.272)(0.728)}{200}}} = 3.775$$

H_o is rejected. There is a difference in the replies of the sexes.

53. $H_o: \mu_d \leq 0$ $H_1: \mu_d > 0$ Reject H_o if $t > 1.895$

$\bar{d} = 1.75$ $s_d = 2.9155$ $t = \dfrac{1.75}{2.9155/\sqrt{8}} = 1.698$

There is not enough evidence to reject H_o. There is no difference in the mean number of absences. The p-value is greater than 0.05. (Actual p-value = 0.0667)

55. $H_o: \mu_1 - \mu_2 \geq 0$ $H_1: \mu_1 - \mu_2 < 0$ Reject H_o if $t < -1.860$
μ_1 new web design μ_2: old web design
$\bar{x}_1 = 18.0$ $s_1 = 5.70$ $\bar{x}_2 = 32.0$ $s_2 = 7.71$

$$s_p^2 = \frac{(5 - 1)(7.71)^2 + (5 - 1)(5.70)^2}{5 + 5 - 2} = 45.967$$

$$t = \frac{18.0 - 32.0}{\sqrt{45.967\left(\dfrac{1}{5} + \dfrac{1}{5}\right)}} = -3.26$$

Reject H_o. The new web design allows users to access web sites faster than the old design.

57. $H_o: p_1 - p_2 \leq 0$ $H_1: p_1 - p_2 > 0$ H_o is rejected if $z > 1.645$

$$p_c = \frac{88.5 + 85.7}{100 + 100} = 0.871$$

$$z = \frac{0.885 - 0.857}{\sqrt{\dfrac{(0.871)(0.129)}{2000} + \dfrac{(0.871)(0.129)}{2000}}} = 2.64$$

H_o is rejected. Conclude there is an increase in the proportion calling conditions "good". The p-value is 0.0041.

59. $H_0: \mu_1 - \mu_2 \geq 0$ $H_1: \mu_1 - \mu_2 < 0$ Reject H_0 if $t < -2.453$

$$s_p^2 = \frac{(15-1)(3.17)^2 + (18-1)(4.38)^2}{15 + 18 - 2} = 15.06$$

$$t = \frac{8.8 - 12.33}{\sqrt{15.06\left(\frac{1}{15} + \frac{1}{18}\right)}} = -2.602$$

Reject H_0. The mean allowance for children in 11 to 14 year age group is more that for children 8 to 10. The p-value is between 0.005 and 0.010.

61. a.

$H_0: \mu_1 - \mu_2 = 0$ $H_1: \mu_1 - \mu_2 \neq 0$

List Price	Group 2	
416,154.63	986,598.04	Mean
235,580.14	516,451.58	std. dev.
72	26	N
	96	Df
	−570,443.413	difference (List Price - Group 2)
	110,504,312,251.332	pooled variance
	332,421.889	pooled std. dev.
	76,058.845	standard error of difference
	0	hypothesized difference
	−7.50	t
	3.20E-11	p-value (two-tailed)

Reject the null hypothesis as the p-value is very close to zero. There is a difference in the list price of homes with more than 2000 square feet.

b.

$H_0: \mu_1 - \mu_2 = 0$ $H_1: \mu_1 - \mu_2 \neq 0$

List Price	Group 2	
402,400.54	839,682.41	Mean
231,549.45	505,624.19	std. dev.
61	37	N
	96	Df
	−437,281.864	difference (List Price - Group 2)
	129,380,399,062.459	pooled variance
	359,694.869	pooled std. dev.
	74,951.702	standard error of difference
	0	hypothesized difference
	−5.83	t
	7.29E-08	p-value (two-tailed)

Reject the null hypothesis as the p-value is very close to zero. There is a difference in the list price of homes with more than 2 bedrooms.

63. a.

$H_0: \mu_1 - \mu_2 = 0$ $H_1: \mu_1 - \mu_2 \neq 0$

	Winnipeg	Calgary			
Nov-12	115.4	106.7	Winnipeg	Calgary	
Nov-13	111.8	108.4	104.120	101.240	mean
Nov-14	106.9	104.0	10.992	8.406	std. dev.
Nov-15	98.4	99.7	5	5	n
Nov-16	88.1	87.4			

	8	df

There is not enough evidence to reject the null hypothesis. Conclude that there is not a difference in the mean gas prices.

2.8800	difference (Winnipeg - Calgary)
95.7400	pooled variance

Note: the p-value > alpha (.05).

9.7847	pooled std. dev.
6.1884	standard error of difference
0	hypothesized difference
0.465	t
.6541	p-value (two-tailed)

b.

$H_0: \mu_1 - \mu_2 = 0$ $H_1: \mu_1 - \mu_2 \neq 0$

	Halifax	St John			
Nov-12	126.1	121.4	Halifax	St John	
Nov-13	126.3	122.3	114.280	112.320	mean
Nov-14	117.8	115.4	12.994	10.729	std. dev.
Nov-15	99.1	97.8	5	5	n
Nov-16	102.1	104.7			

	8	df

There is not enough evidence to reject the null hypothesis. Conclude that there is not a difference in the mean gas prices. Note: the p-value > alpha (.01).

1.9600	difference (Halifax - St John)
141.9745	pooled variance
11.9153	pooled std. dev.
7.5359	standard error of difference
0	hypothesized difference
0.260	t
.8014	p-value (two-tailed)

c.

$H_0: \mu_1 - \mu_2 \geq 0$ $H_1: \mu_1 - \mu_2 < 0$

	Toronto	Montreal			
Nov-12	122.2	133.4	Toronto	Montreal	
Nov-13	124.6	133.2	113.200	122.740	mean
Nov-14	114.8	125.0	10.686	11.197	std. dev.
Nov-15	103.0	110.9	5	5	n
Nov-16	101.4	111.2			

	8	df
	−9.5400	
	119.7890	pooled variance
	10.9448	pooled std. dev.
	6.9221	standard error of difference
	0	hypothesized difference

There is not enough evidence to reject the null hypothesis.

Conclude that Toronto's gas prices are not less than those of Montreal
Note: the p-value > alpha (.05).

−1.378	t
.1027	p-value (one-tailed, lower)

d.

$H_0: \mu_1 - \mu_2 \geq 0$ $H_1: \mu_1 - \mu_2 < 0$

	Edmonton	St John's			
Nov-12	100.9	127.9	Edmonton	St John's	
Nov-13	103.0	126.0	95.300	120.320	mean
Nov-14	99.7	117.8	8.377	11.000	std. dev.
Nov-15	89.1	102.1	5	5	n
Nov-16	83.8	127.8			

8	df
−25.0200	difference (Edmonton - St John's)
95.5860	pooled variance
9.7768	pooled std. dev.
6.1834	standard error of difference
0	hypothesized difference
−4.046	t
.0019	p-value (one-tailed, lower)

There is enough evidence to reject the null hypothesis. Conclude that Edmonton's gas prices are less than those of St John's.

Note: the p-value $<$ alpha(0.02).

Chapter 11

1. 9.01 from Appendix B.7

3. Reject H_o if $F > 10.5$, where df numerator are 7 and 5 in the denominator. $F = 2.04$, found by:

$$F = \frac{s_1^2}{s_2^2} = \frac{(10)^2}{(7)^2} = 2.04$$

There is not enough evidence to reject H_o. There is no difference in the variations of the two populations.

5. $H_o: \sigma_1^2 - \sigma_2^2 = 0 \quad H_1: \sigma_1^2 - \sigma_2^2 \neq 0$

Reject H_o when $F > 3.10$ (3.10 is about halfway between 3.14 and 3.07) $F = 1.44$, found by

$$F = \frac{(12)^2}{(10)^2} = 1.44$$

There is not enough evidence to reject H_o. There is no difference in the variations of the two populations.

7. **a.** $H_o: \mu_1 = \mu_2 = \mu_3 \quad H_1$: Treatment means are not all the same.
   b. Reject H_o if $F > 4.26$
   c. 62.17, 12.75, 74.92
   d.

Source	SS	df	MS	F
Treatment	62.17	2	31.08	21.94
Error	12.75	9	1.42	
Total	74.92	11		

   e. Reject H_o. The treatment means are not all the same.

9. $H_o: \mu_1 = \mu_2 = \mu_3 \quad H_1$: Treatment means are not all the same. Reject H_o if $F > 4.26$

Source	SS	df	MS	F
Treatment	276.50	2	138.25	14.18
Error	87.75	9	9.75	
Total	364.25	11		

Reject H_o. The treatment means are not all the same.

11. **a.** $H_o: \mu_1 = \mu_2 = \mu_3 \quad H_1$: Treatment means are not all the same.
   b. Reject H_o if $F > 4.26$
   c. SST $= 107.20$ SSE $= 9.47$ SS total $= 116.67$
   d.

Source	SS	df	MS	F
Treatment	107.20	2	53.600	50.96
Error	9.47	9	1.052	
Total	116.67	11		

   e. Since $50.96 > 4.26$, H_o is rejected. At least one of the means differs.
   f. $(\bar{x}_1 - \bar{x}_2) \pm t \sqrt{MSE(1/n_1 + 1/n_2)}$
   $= (9.667 - 2.20) \pm 2.262 \sqrt{1.052(1/3 + 1/5)}$
   $= 7.467 \pm 1.69$
   $= [5.777, 9.157]$

   Yes, we can conclude that the treatments 1 and 2 have different means.

13. $H_o: \mu_1 = \mu_2 = \mu_3 = \mu_4 \quad H_1$: Treatment means are not all equal, Reject H_o if $F > 3.71$

Source	SS	df	MS	F
Treatment	32.33	3	10.77	2.36
Error	45.67	10	4.567	
Total	78.00	13		

Since 2.36 is less than 3.71, there is not enough evidence to reject H_o. There is no difference in the mean number of months.

15. $H_o: \sigma_1^2 \leq \sigma_2^2 \quad H_1: \sigma_1^2 > \sigma_2^2$
    $df_1 = 21 - 1 = 20 \; df_2 = 18 - 1 = 17$
    H_o is rejected if $F > 3.16$

$$F = \frac{(45\ 600)^2}{(21\ 330)^2} = 4.57$$

Reject H_o. There is more variation in selling price of waterfront homes.

17. Sharkey: $n = 7 \quad s = 14.79$
    White: $n = 8 \quad s = 22.95$
    $H_o: \sigma_w^2 \leq \sigma_s^2 \quad H_1: \sigma_w^2 > \sigma_s^2$
    $df_s = 7 - 1 = 6 \quad df_w = 8 - 1 = 7 \quad H_o$ is rejected if $F > 8.26$

$$F = \frac{(22.95)^2}{(14.79)^2} = 2.41$$

There is not enough evidence to reject H_o. There is no difference in the variation of the weekly sales.

19. **a.** $H_o: \mu_1 = \mu_2 = \mu_3 = \mu_4 \quad H_1$: Treatment means are not all equal.
   b. $\alpha = 0.05$ Reject if $F > 3.10$
   c.

Source	SS	df	MS	F
Treatment	50	3	50/3	1.67
Error	200	20	10	
Total	250	23		

   d. Do not reject H_o. There is not a difference in the treatment means.

21. $H_o: \mu_1 = \mu_2 = \mu_3 \quad H_1$: Not all means are equal. H_o is rejected if $F > 3.89$

Source	SS	df	MS	F
Treatment	63.33	2	31.667	13.38
Error	28.40	12	2.367	
Total	91.73	14		

H_o is rejected. There is a difference in the treatment means.

23. $H_o: \mu_1 = \mu_2 = \mu_3 = \mu_4 \quad H_1$: Not all means are equal. H_o is rejected if $F > 3.10$

Source	SS	df	MS	F
Factor	87.79	3	29.26	9.12
Error	64.17	20	3.21	
Total	151.96	23		

Since computed F of $9.12 > 3.10$, the null hypothesis of no difference is rejected at the 0.05 level.

25. **a.** $H_o: \mu_1 = \mu_2 \quad H_1: \mu_1 \neq \mu_2$ Critical value of $F = 4.75$

Source	SS	df	MS	F
Treatment	219.43	1	219.43	23.10
Error	114.00	12	9.5	
Total	333.43	13		

   b. $t = \dfrac{19 - 27}{\sqrt{9.5\left(\frac{1}{6} + \frac{1}{8}\right)}} = -4.81$

   Since $t^2 = F$. That is $(-4.81)^2 \approx 23.10$ (actually 23.14, difference due to rounding).

   c. H_o is rejected. There is a difference in the mean scores.

27. $H_o: \mu_1 = \mu_2 = \mu_3 = \mu_4$ H_1: Treatment means are not all equal. Reject H_o if $F > 3.49$. The computed value of F is 9.61.

The null hypothesis of equal means is rejected because the F statistic (9.61) is greater than the critical value (3.49). The p-value (0.0016) is also less than the significance level (0.05). The mean waiting times are different.

29. $H_o: \sigma_1^2 - \sigma_2^2 = 0$ $H_1: \sigma_1^2 - \sigma_2^2 \neq 0$
Reject H_o when $F > 2.85$ (df: 10, 11) $F = 2.25$, found by

$$F = \frac{(12)^2}{(8)^2} = 2.25$$

There is not enough evidence to reject H_o. We conclude there is no difference in the variation at a 10% level of significance.

31. $H_o: \mu_1 = \mu_2 = \mu_3 = \mu_4 = \mu_5 = \mu_6$ H_1: The treatment means are not equal

Reject H_o if $F > 2.37$

ANOVA table

Source	SS	df	MS	F
Treatment	0.03478	5	0.006956	3.86
Error	0.10439	58	0.001800	
Total	0.13917	63		

H_o is rejected. There is a difference in the mean weight of the colours.

33. a. $H_o: \mu_1 = \mu_2 = \mu_3$ H_1: Not all means are equal H_o is rejected if $F > 3.29$

Source	SS	df	MS	F
Treatment	127.1	2	63.6	3.04
Error	669.9	32	20.9	
Total	797.0	34		

H_o is not rejected since $3.04 < 3.29$. There is no difference in the mean flight times.

b. $(52.07 - 55.71) \pm 2.037 \sqrt{20.9\left(\frac{1}{14} + \frac{1}{7}\right)}$

This reduces to -3.64 ± 4.31. So there is no difference as 0 is present in the interval between -7.95 and 0.67 minutes.

35. $H_o: \mu_1 = \mu_2 = \mu_3 = \mu_4 = \mu_5 = \mu_6 = \mu_7$ H_1: At least one mean is different.

The critical value for a F statistic with 6 and 48 degrees of freedom in the numerator and the denominator, respectively, at a 0.05 significance level is 2.295. Since 5.72 is greater than 2.295 the null is rejected. At least one mean is different. Also note the p-value is very close to 0.

37. a. $H_o: \mu_1 = \mu_2 = \mu_3$ H_1: Treatment means are not all equal. Reject H_o if $F > 6.36$. The computed value of F is 11.33.

The null hypothesis of equal means is rejected because the F statistic (11.33) is greater than the critical value (6.36). The p-value (0.0010) is also less than the significance level (0.01). The mean production rates are different.

b. $(43.33 - 41.5) \pm 2.947 \sqrt{0.5444\left(\frac{1}{6} + \frac{1}{6}\right)}$

This reduces to 1.83 ± 1.26. So the difference is between 0.57 and 3.09.

39. $H_o: \mu_1 = \mu_2 = \mu_3$ H_1: Not all means are equal
H_o is rejected if $F > 3.89$

ANOVA table

Source	SS	df	MS	F	p-value
Treatment	62.53	2	31.267	4.86	.0284
Error	77.20	12	6.433		
Total	139.73	14			

Computer $F > 3.89$. Reject the null hypothesis that the production levels are the same on all shifts.

41. $H_0: \mu_1 = \mu_2 = \mu_3 = \mu_4$ H_1: Not all means are equal
H_0 is rejected if $F > 4.07$

ANOVA table

Source	SS	df	MS	F	p-value
Treatment	44.25	3	14.750	5.21	.0276
Error	22.67	8	2.833		
Total	66.92	11			

p-values for pairwise t-tests

		Red	Orange	Green	Blue
		3.7	5.7	7.7	8.7
Red	3.7				
Orange	5.7	.1837			
Green	7.7	.0196	.1837		
Blue	8.7	.0066	.0606	.4876	

The difference in pairs are between Red and Blue and between Green and Red.

43. a. $H_0: \mu_1 = \mu_2 = \mu_3$
H_1: not all population means are equal
$\alpha = 0.05$
One factor ANOVA

Mean	n	Std. Dev	
459,074.7	58	292,294.38	Apartment
904,248.0	26	552,948.91	House
391,278.5	14	137,470.32	Townhouse
567,496.8	98	416,469.29	Total

ANOVA table

Source	SS	df	MS	F	p-value
Treatment	4,064,986,860,294.07	2	2,032,493,430,147.030	15.13	1.97E-06
Error	12,759,339,849,142.10	95	134,308,840,517.285		
Total	16,824,326,709,436.10	97			

The p-value is very close to zero and less than a significance level of 0.01, and so, we reject the null hypothesis and conclude that the variances of list prices of the home styles are different.

b. $H_0: \mu_1 = \mu_2 = \mu_3$
H_1: not all population means are equal
$\alpha = 0.05$
One factor ANOVA

Mean	n	Std. Dev	
402,400.5	61	231,549.45	1 and 2 bedrooms
586,994.7	19	308,194.90	3 bedrooms
1,106,408.3	18	542,334.67	> bedrooms
567,496.8	98	416,469.29	Total

ANOVA table

Source	SS	df	MS	F	p-value
Treatment	6,897,546,936,345.69	2	3,448,773,468,172.850	33.01	1.31E-11
Error	9,926,779,773,090.43	95	104,492,418,664.110		
Total	16,824,326,709,436.10	97			

The p-value is very close to zero and less than a significance level of 0.01, and so, we reject the null hypothesis and conclude that the variances of list prices of homes with 1 and 2 bedrooms, 3 bedrooms, and more than 3 bedrooms are different.

c. $H_0: \sigma_1^2 - \sigma_2^2 = 0$
$H_1: \sigma_1^2 - \sigma_2^2, \neq 0$

Anova: Single Factor

SUMMARY

Groups	Count	Sum	Average	Variance
less than 1500 sq ft	59	22358533	378958.2	3.77E+10
more than 1500 sq ft	39	33256149	852721.8	2.46E+11

ANOVA

Source of Variation	SS	df	MS	F	P-value	F crit
Between Groups	5.27E+12	1	5.27E+12	43.78668	2.09E-09	3.940163
Within Groups	1.16E+13	96	1.2E+11			
Total	1.68E+13	97				

The p-value of the F-test is very close to zero, so we reject the null hypothesis, and conclude that there is a difference in the variability of the list prices of the homes.

45. a. $H_0: \mu_1 = \mu_2 = \mu_3$
H_1: not all population means are equal
One factor ANOVA

Mean	n	Std. Dev	
104.12	5	10.992	Winnipeg
101.24	5	8.406	Calgary
109.74	5	18.167	Saskatoon
105.03	15	12.742	Total

ANOVA table

Source	SS	df	MS	F	p-value
Treatment	186.881	2	93.4407	0.54	.5976
Error	2,086.052	12	173.8377		
Total	2,272.933	14			

The p-value is $>$ the significance level of 0.05, so, there is not enough evidence to reject the null hypothesis and we conclude that the variances of gas prices of the three cities are not different.

b. $H_0: \mu_1 = \mu_2 = \mu_3$
H_1: not all population means are equal
One factor ANOVA

Mean	n	Std. Dev	
114.28	5	12.994	Halifax
101.24	5	8.406	Calgary
112.32	5	10.729	Saint John
109.28	15	11.689	Total

ANOVA table

Source	SS	df	MS	F	p-value
Treatment	494.416	2	247.2080	2.09	.1662
Error	1,418.408	12	118.2007		
Total	1,912.824	14			

The p-value is $>$ the significance level of .05, so, there is not enough evidence to reject the null hypothesis and we conclude that the variances of gas prices of the three cities are not different.

c. $H_0: \mu_1 = \mu_2 = \mu_3$
H_1: not all population means are equal
One factor ANOVA

Mean	n	Std. Dev	
113.20	5	10.686	Toronto
124.54	5	5.381	Vancouver
122.74	5	11.197	Montreal
120.16	15	10.161	Total

ANOVA table

Source	SS	df	MS	F	p-value
Treatment	371.412	2	185.7060	2.07	.1683
Error	1,074.124	12	89.5103		
Total	1,445.536	14			

The p-value is $>$ the significance level of 0.10, so there is not enough evidence to reject the null hypothesis and we conclude that the variances of gas prices of the three cities are not different.

Chapter 12

1. a.

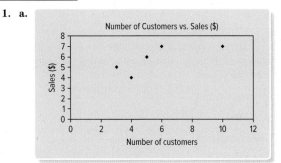

b. $y' = 3.7671 + 0.3630x$
$b = \dfrac{5(173) - (28)(29)}{5(186) - (28)^2} = 0.3630$

$a = \dfrac{29}{5} - (0.363)\dfrac{28}{5} = 3.7671$

c. 6.3081, found by $y' = 3.7671 + 0.3630(7)$

3. a.

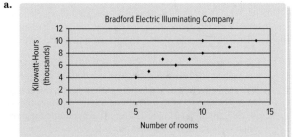

b. $b = \dfrac{10(718) - (91)(74)}{10(895) - (91)^2} = \dfrac{446}{669} = 0.667$

$a = \dfrac{74}{10} - (0.667)\dfrac{91}{10} = 1.333$

c. $y' = 1.333 + 0.667(6) = 5.335$

5. a.

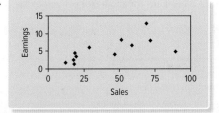

b. $b = \dfrac{12(3306.35) - (501.1)(64.1)}{12(28\,459) - (501.1)^2} = 0.0836$

$a = \dfrac{64.1}{12} - (0.0836)\dfrac{501.10}{12} = 1.8507$

c. $y' = 1.8507 + 0.0836(50.0) = 6.0307$ ($ million)

Note: calculator or computer values may be slightly different due to rounding.

7. **a.** Police is the independent variable and crime is the dependent variable

b.

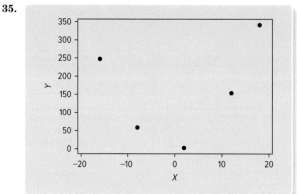

c. $b = \dfrac{8(1502) - (146)(95)}{8(2906) - (146)^2} = -0.95963$

$a = \dfrac{95}{8} - (-0.95963)\left(\dfrac{146}{8}\right) = 29.3882$

$y' = 29.3882 - 0.95963\ Police$

d. $y' = 29.3882 - 0.95963(20) = 10.196$

e. Inverse relationship. As the number of police increase, crime decreases.

9. **a.** 0.993, found by $\sqrt{\dfrac{175 - 3.767(29) - 0.363(173)}{5 - 2}}$

b. $y' \pm 0.993$

11. **a.** 0.898, found by $\sqrt{\dfrac{584 - 1.333(74) - 0.667(718)}{10 - 2}}$

b. $y' \pm 1.796$

13. 3.379, found by $\sqrt{\dfrac{1419 - 29.3877(95) - (-0.9596)(1502)}{8 - 2}}$

15. **a.** $6.308 \pm 3.182(0.993)\sqrt{\dfrac{1}{5} + \dfrac{(7 - 5.6)^2}{29.2}} = 6.308 \pm 1.633$

$= [4.675, 7.941]$

b. $6.308 \pm (3.182)(0.933)\sqrt{1 + 1/5 + 0.0671} = [2.751, 9.865]$

17. **a.** [4.495, 6.171]

b. [3.440, 7.226]

19. **a.** $\sum x = 28 \quad \sum y = 29 \quad \sum x^2 = 186 \quad \sum xy = 173 \quad \sum y^2 = 175$

$r = \dfrac{5(173) - (28)(29)}{\sqrt{[5(186) - (28)^2][5(175) - (29)^2]}} = 0.75$

The 0.75 coefficient indicates a rather strong positive correlation between x and y. The coefficient of determination is 0.5625, found by $(0.75)^2$. Therefore, x accounts for more than 56 percent of the variation in y.

21. **a.** $n = 5 \quad \sum x = 20 \quad \sum y = 85 \quad \sum x^2 = 90 \quad \sum xy = 376 \quad \sum y^2 = 1595$

$r = \dfrac{5(376) - (20)(85)}{\sqrt{[5(90) - (20)^2][5(1595) - (85)^2]}} = 0.9295$

b. $r^2 = (0.9295)^2 = 0.864$

c. The 0.9295 indicates a very strong positive relationship between x and y. The coefficient of determination is 0.864. Therefore, x accounts for about 86.4 percent of the variation in y.

23. **a.** $n = 8 \quad \sum x = 146 \quad \sum y = 95 \quad \sum x^2 = 2906 \quad \sum xy = 1502 \quad \sum y^2 = 1419$

$r = \dfrac{8(1502) - (146)(95)}{\sqrt{[8(2906) - (146)^2][8(1419) - (95)^2]}} = -0.874$

b. 0.76, found by $(-0.874)^2$

c. -0.874 indicates a strong inverse relationship. As the number of police increase, the crime decreases. The coefficient of determination is 0.76. Therefore, x accounts for about 76 percent of the variation in y.

25. Reject H_o if $t > 1.812$

$t = \dfrac{0.32\sqrt{12 - 2}}{\sqrt{1 - (0.32)^2}} = 1.07$

Do not reject H_o.

27. $H_o: \rho \geq 0 \quad H_1: \rho < 0 \quad$ Reject H_o if $t < -2.552 \quad df = 18$

$t = \dfrac{-0.78\sqrt{20 - 2}}{\sqrt{1 - (-0.78)^2}} = -5.288$

Reject H_o. There is a negative correlation between litres sold and the pump price.

29. $H_o: \rho \leq 0 \quad H_1: \rho > 0 \quad$ Reject H_o if $t > 2.650 \quad df = 13$

$t = \dfrac{0.667\sqrt{15 - 2}}{\sqrt{1 - (0.667)^2}} = 3.23$

Reject H_o. There is a positive correlation between passengers and cost.

31. Coefficient of correlation $r = 0.8944$, found by

$\dfrac{(5)(340) - (50)(30)}{\sqrt{[(5)(600) - (50)^2][(5)(200) - (30)^2]}}$

Then $(0.8944)^2 = 0.80$, the coefficient of determination.

33. **a.** $r^2 = 1000/1500 = 0.667$

b. 0.82, found by $\sqrt{0.667}$

c. 6.20, found by $s_e = \sqrt{\dfrac{500}{15 - 2}}$

35.

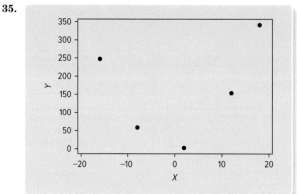

a. The relationship does not appear to be linear.

b. The correlation of X and Y is 0.2975. There is a weak positive correlation between the variables.

c. 151.388

37. $H_o: \rho \leq 0 \quad H_1: \rho > 0 \quad$ Reject H_o if $t > 1.714$

$t = \dfrac{0.94\sqrt{25 - 2}}{\sqrt{1 - (0.94)^2}} = 13.213$

Reject H_o. There is a positive correlation between passengers and weight of luggage.

39. $H_o: \rho \leq 0 \quad H_1: \rho > 0 \quad$ Reject H_o if $t > 2.764$

$t = \dfrac{0.47\sqrt{12 - 2}}{\sqrt{1 - (0.47)^2}} = 1.684$

Do not reject H_o. There is not a positive correlation between engine size and performance.

The p-value (0.0616) is greater than 0.05, but less than 0.10.

41. $H_o: \rho \geq 0 \quad H_1: \rho < 0 \quad$ Reject H_o if $t < -1.701 \quad df = 28$

$t = \dfrac{-0.45\sqrt{30 - 2}}{\sqrt{1 - 0.2025}} = -2.67$

Reject H_o. There is a negative correlation between the selling price and the number of kilometres driven.

43. a.

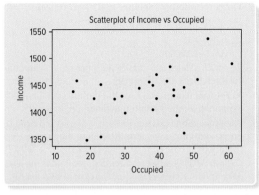

Revenue increases slightly as the number of occupied rooms increases.

b. Pearson correlation of Income and Occupied = 0.423

c. H_o: $\rho \leq 0$ H_1: $\rho > 0$ Reject H_o if $t > 1.319$ $df = 23$

$$t = \frac{0.423 \sqrt{25 - 2}}{\sqrt{1 - (0.423)^2}} = 2.24$$

Reject H_o.

There is a positive correlation between revenue and occupied rooms.

d. 17.9%, found by $(0.423)^2$, of the variation in revenue is explained by variation in occupied rooms.

45. a. No, the coefficient is -0.5170 which indicates a negative relationship between the variables.

b. $r^2 = 3119.4256/3960 = 78.77\%$

c. $r = \sqrt{0.78773} = -0.8875$; strong, negative

d. $y' = 45.85$; 46 units; yes, this is reasonable.

47. a. $r = 0.589$

b. $r^2 = (0.589)^2 = 0.3469$

c. H_o: $\rho \leq 0$ H_1: $\rho > 0$ Reject H_o if $t > 1.860$

$$t = \frac{0.589 \sqrt{10 - 2}}{\sqrt{1 - (0.589)^2}} = 2.061$$

H_o is rejected. There is a positive association between family size and the amount spent on food.

49. a. It looks to be an inverse relationship between the variables. As the months owned increases the number of hours exercised decreases.

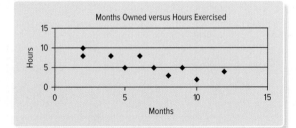

b. $r = \dfrac{10(313) - (65)(58)}{\sqrt{[10(523) - (65)^2][10(396) - (58)^2]}} = -0.827$

c. H_o: $\rho \geq 0$ H_1: $\rho < 0$ Reject H_o if $t < -2.896$

$$t = \frac{-0.827 \sqrt{10 - 2}}{\sqrt{1 - (-0.827)^2}} = -4.16$$

Reject H_o. We can conclude that there is a negative association between months owned and hours exercised.

51. a.

Source	SS	df	MS	F
Regression	50	1	50	2.5556
Error	450	23	19.5652	
Total	500	24		

b. $n = 25$

c. $s_e = \sqrt{19.5652} = 4.4233$

d. $r^2 = 50/500 = 0.10$

53. a. $n = 15$ $\sum x = 107$ $\sum x^2 = 837$ $\sum y = 118.6$

$\sum y^2 = 969.92$ $\sum xy = 811.60$ $s_{y \cdot x} = 1.114$

$$b = \frac{15(811.60) - (107)(118.6)}{15(837.0) - (107)^2} = \frac{-516.2}{1106.0} = -0.4667$$

$$a = \frac{118.6}{15} - (-0.4667)\left(\frac{107}{15}\right) = 11.2358$$

More bidders decrease winning bid.

b. $y' = 11.2358 - 0.4667(7.0) = 7.9689$

c. $7.9689 \pm (2.160)(1.114)\sqrt{1 + \dfrac{1}{15} + \dfrac{(7 - 7.1333)^2}{837 - \dfrac{(107)^2}{15}}}$

$= 7.9689 \pm 2.4854$

$[5.4835 \quad 10.4543]$

d. $r^2 = 0.499$. The number of bidders explains nearly 50 percent of the variation in the amount of the bid.

55. a. $b = \dfrac{30(18\,924) - (320.33)(1575.6)}{30(4292.5) - (320.33)^2} = 2.41$

$$a = \frac{1575.6}{30} - 2.41\left(\frac{320.33}{30}\right) = 26.8$$

The regression equation is: Price = 26.8 + 2.41 dividend. For each additional dollar of dividend, the price increases by $2.41.

b. $r^2 = \dfrac{5057.6}{7682.7} = 0.658$

65.8% of the variation in price is explained by the dividend.

c. $r = \sqrt{0.658} = 0.811$ H_o: $\rho \leq 0$ H_1: $\rho > 0$

At the 5% level, reject H_o when $t > 1.701$.

$$t = \frac{0.811 \sqrt{30 - 2}}{\sqrt{1 - (0.811)^2}} = 7.34$$

Thus H_o is rejected. The population correlation is positive.

57. a. 35, found by one more than the total degrees of freedom $(34 + 1)$

b. 5457, found by the square root of MSE (mean square error) $(\sqrt{29\,778\,406})$.

c. 0.93, found by SSR/SStotal $\dfrac{13\,548\,662\,082}{14\,531\,349\,474}$.

d. 0.97, found by $\sqrt{0.93}$

e. H_o: $\rho \leq 0$ H_1: $\rho > 0$ Reject H_o if $t > 1.692$

Yes, because the t-value (21.43) is greater than the critical value (1.692) and the p-value (0.000) is less than the significance level (0.05). Reject the null hypothesis. There is a positive association between market value and size of the home.

59. a.

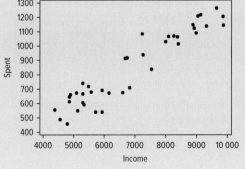

b. $b = \dfrac{40(245\ 792\ 400) - (273\ 384)(33\ 625)}{40(1\ 987\ 816\ 326) - (273\ 384)^2} = 0.13388$

$a = \dfrac{33\ 625}{40} - 0.13388\left(\dfrac{273\ 384}{40}\right) = -74.4$

The regression equation is Spent $= -74.4 + 0.134$ Income. For each additional dollar of income, 13.4 cents more is spent on groceries.

c.

$r = \dfrac{40(245\ 792\ 400) - (273\ 384)(33\ 625)}{\sqrt{[40(1\ 987\ 816\ 326) - (273\ 384)^2][40(30\ 662\ 885) - (33\ 625)^2]}}$

$= 0.945$

$H_o: \rho \le 0 \quad H_1: \rho > 0 \qquad$ At the 5% level, reject H_o when $t > 1.686$.

$t = \dfrac{0.945 \sqrt{40 - 2}}{\sqrt{1 - (0.945)^2}} = 17.8 \qquad$ Thus H_o is rejected. The population correlation is positive.

d. We know is that there is a strong positive association between income and groceries; however, other factors such as location and growth in the area need to be considered.

61. a. $y' = 12.3601 + 4.7956\,x$

The relationship between distance and damage is direct.

b. $36\ 338$ found by $12.3601 + 4.7956(5)$

c. 0.581, found by 1865/3209

58.1% of the variation in damage is explained by variation in distance.

d. 0.762 which is $\sqrt{0.581}$ It is positive because the slope is positive.

There is a fairly solid direct link between the variables.

e. $H_o: \rho = 0 \quad H_1: \rho \ne 0 \quad$ Reject H_o if $t < -2.763$ or $t > 2.763$

$t = \dfrac{0.762 \sqrt{30 - 2}}{\sqrt{1 - (0.762)^2}} = 6.23$ Reject H_o.

There is a connection between distance and fire damage.

63. a. The regression equation is Price $= -773 + 1408$ Speed.

b. The correlation of Speed and Price is 0.835.

$H_0: \rho \le 0 \quad H_1: \rho > 0 \quad$ Reject H_0 if $t > 1.8125$

$t = \dfrac{0.835 \sqrt{12 - 2}}{\sqrt{1 - (0.835)^2}} = 4.799$

Reject H_0 It is reasonable to say the population correlation is positive.

65. a.

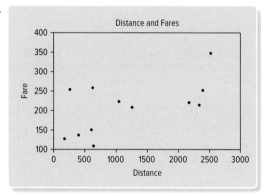

The relationship is direct. Fares increase for longer flights.

b. The correlation of Distance and Fare is 0.606.

$H_o: \rho \le 0 \quad H_1: \rho > 0 \quad$ Reject H_o if $t > 1.812$ $df = 10$

$t = \dfrac{0.606 \sqrt{12 - 2}}{\sqrt{1 - (0.606)^2}} = 2.41$

Reject H_o. There is a significant positive correlation between fares and distances.

c. 36.7%, found by $(0.606)^2$, of the variation in fares is explained by the variation in distance.

d. The regression equation is Fare $= 154.09 + 0.0456$ Distance. Each additional mile adds $0.0456 to the fare. A 1500-mile flight would cost $222.49, found by $154.09 + 0.0456\,(1500)$.

e. A flight of 4218 miles is outside the range of the sampled data. So the regression equation may not be useful.

67. a.

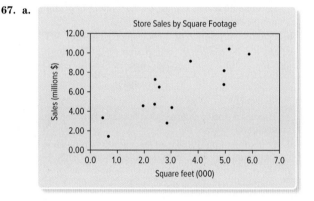

There is a strong positive connection between the two variables. Larger stores have higher sales.

b. The correlation of Square Feet and Sales is 0.824 and the coefficient of determination is 0.679. There exists a strong relationship between the two variables.

c. $H_o: \rho \le 0 \quad H_1: \rho > 0 \quad$ Reject H_o if $t > 1.796 \quad df = 11$

$t = \dfrac{0.824 \sqrt{13 - 2}}{\sqrt{1 - (0.824)^2}} = 4.82$

Reject H_o. There is a significant positive correlation between store size and sales.

69. a.

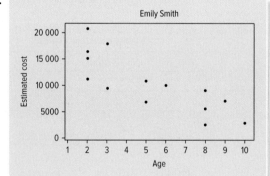

b. $r = -0.822$

c. The slope of -1534 indicates that for each increase of 1 year in the age of the car that the estimated cost decreases on average by $1534.

d. $10\ 688$, found by $18\ 358 - 1534(5)$

e. The p-value (0.000) for the age variable is less than, say 0.05. A test for significance of that coefficient would be rejected. In other words, the coefficient is much different from zero.

71. a.

Regression Analysis

r^2	0.722		n	50
r	0.850		k	1
Std. Error	105034.932		Dep. Var.	List Price

ANOVA table

Source	SS	df	MS	F
Regression	1,374,442,787,920.0700	1	1,374,442,787,920.0700	124.58
Residual	529,552,172,748.9060	48	11,032,336,932.2689	
Total	1,903,994,960,668.9800	49		

Regression output

variables	coefficients	std. error	t (df = 48)	p-value
Intercept	44,616.1734			
Total Square Feet	229.1513	20.5302	11.162	6.14E-15

Predicted values for: List Price

		95% Confidence Interval		95% Prediction Interval	
Total Square Feet	Predicted	lower	upper	Lower	upper
2,000	502,918.683	459,924.893	545,912.473	287,399.853	718437.513809164

95% PI upper:

$Y' = 44\,616.1734 + 229.1513$ Square Feet

Predicted value = \$502 919

95% CI:	\$459 925 to \$545 912
95% PI:	\$287 400 to \$718 438

b.

Regression Analysis

r^2	0.292		n	50
r	0.541		k	1
Std. Error	167552.835		Dep. Var.	**List Price**

ANOVA table

Source	SS	df	MS	F
Regression	556,445,242,159.6050	1	556,445,242,159.6050	19.82
Residual	1,347,549,718,509.3700	48	28,073,952,468.9453	
Total	1,903,994,960,668.9800	49		

Regression output

Variables	coefficients	std. error	t (df = 48)	p-value
Intercept	106,724.2293			
Number of Bedrooms	85,690.7445	19,247.5067	4.452	.0001

Predicted values for: List Price

		95% Confidence Interval		95% Prediction Interval	
Number of Bedrooms	Predicted	lower	upper	Lower	upper
4	449,487.207	377,918.905	521,055.510	105,081.566	793892.848625105

$Y' = 106\,724.23 + 85\,690.74$ Number of Bedrooms

Predicted value = \$449 487

95% CI:	\$377 919 to \$521 056
95% PI:	\$105 082 to \$793 893

c.

| Total Square Feet | *p*-value 6.14E-15 |
| | r 0.850 |

The size of the house and the list price are positively correlated.

The p-value is very close to zero, and therefore, the variable size is significant.

| Number of Bedrooms | *p*-value .0001 |
| | r 0.541 |

The number of bedrooms and the list price are positively correlated.

The p-value is .0001, and therefore, the variable number of bedrooms is significant.

Chapter 13

1. a. Multiple regression equation

b. The *y*-intercept, 64 100 is the value of *y* when the values of independent variables are zero.

c. $374 748 found by $y' = 64\,100 + 0.394(796\,000) + 9.6(6940) - 11\,600(6.0)$

3. a. 497.736, found by $y' = 16.24 + 0.017(18) + 0.0028(26\,500) + 42(3) + 0.0012(156\,000) + 0.19(141) + 26.8(2.5)$

b. Two more social activities. Income added only 28 to the index; social activities added 53.6.

5. a. 65

b. 2

c. 1

d. $s_{Y0.12} = \sqrt{\dfrac{SSE}{n - (k+1)}} = \sqrt{\dfrac{583.693}{65 - (2+1)}} = \sqrt{9.414} = 3.068$

95% of the residuals will be between ± 6.136, found by 2(3.068)

e. $R^2 = \dfrac{SSR}{SStotal} = \dfrac{77.907}{661.6} = 0.118$

The independent variables explain 11.8% of the variation.

7. a. $Y' = 20 - X_1 + 12X_2 - 15X_3$

b. $Y' = 20 - (4) + 12(6) - 15(8) = -32$

c. $n = 22$; 3 independent variables

d.

Source	SS	DF	MS	F
Regression	7500	3	2500	18
Error	2500	18	138.89	
Total	10 000	21		

e. $H_0: \beta_1 = \beta_2 = \beta_3 = 0$ H_1: Not all β's are 0   Reject H_0 if $F > 3.16$

F = 18.0 Reject H_0. Not all net regression coefficients equal zero.

For X_1	for X_2	for X_3
$H_0: \beta_1 = 0$	$H_0: \beta_2 = 0$	$H_0: \beta_3 = 0$
$H_1: \beta_1 \neq 0$	$H_1: \beta_2 \neq 0$	$H_1: \beta_3 \neq 0$
$t = -4.00$	$t = 1.50$	$t = -3.00$

f. Reject H_0 if $t > 2.101$ or $t < -2.101$

Delete variable 2, keep 1 and 3

9. a. x_4 at −0.819 had the strongest correlation with the dependent variable

b. x_2, x_3 and x_4 have the strongest correlation with the dependent variable

c. yes, between x_3 and x_4.

11. a. Horsepower is the most highly correlated with speed at 0.83.

b. It is reasonable as the weight of a car would probably slow it down.

c. No, none of the independent variables is highly correlated with each other.

13. a. $n = 40$

b. 4

c. $\rho^2 = 750/1250 = 0.60$

d. $S_{y \cdot 1234} = \sqrt{500/35} = 3.7796$

e. $H_0: \beta_1 = \beta_2 = \beta_3 = \beta_4 = 0$ H_1: Not all β's equal 0
H_0 is rejected if $F > 2.65$

f. $F = \dfrac{750/4}{500/35} = 13.125$ H_0 is rejected. At least one β_i does not equal zero

15. a. $n = 26$

b. $R^2 = 100/140 = 0.7143$

c. 1.4142, found by $\sqrt{2}$

d. $H_0: \beta_1 = \beta_2 = \beta_3 = \beta_4 = \beta_5 = 0$ H_1: Not all β's are 0
Reject H_0 if $F > 2.71$
Computed $F = 10.0$. Reject H_0. At least one regression coefficient is not zero.

e. H_0 is rejected in each case if $t < -2.086$ or $t > 2.086$. X_1 and X_5 should be dropped.
($X_1 = 1.33$ do not reject; $X_2 = 15$ reject; $X_3 = 4$ reject; $X_4 = -2.5$ reject; $X_5 = 0.75$ do not reject)

17. a. $28 000

b. 0.5810 found by $R^2 = \dfrac{SSR}{SStotal} = \dfrac{3050}{5250}$

c. 9.199 found by $\sqrt{84.62}$

d. H_0 is rejected if $F > 2.98$ (approximately) Computed $F = 1016.67/84.62 = 12.01$

H_0 is rejected. At least one regression coefficient is not zero.

e. If computed t is to the left of −2.056 or to the right of 2.056, the null hypothesis in each of these cases is rejected. Computed t for X_2 and X_3 exceed the critical value. Thus, "population" and "advertising expenses" should be retained and "number of competitors," X_1 dropped.

19. a. The strongest relationship is between sales and income (0.964). A problem could occur if both "outlets" and "income" (0.825) and "cars" and "outlets" (0.775) are part of the final solution. This is called multicollinearity.

b. $y' = -19.6715 - 0.0006(\text{outlets}) + 1.7399(\text{cars}) + 0.4099(\text{income}) + 2.0357(\text{age}) - 0.0344(\text{supervisor})$;
$R^2 = \dfrac{1593.81}{1602.89} = 0.9943$

c. H_0 is rejected. At least one regression coefficient is not zero. The computed value of F is 140.36. Critical value = 6.26; therefore, reject the null hypothesis (Note that the p-value = 0.0001, which is < than the significance level, and supports the decision to reject the null.

d. Delete "outlets" and "supervisors". Critical values are −2.776 and 2.776. Note that "age" is also insignificant.

e. $R^2 = \dfrac{1593.66}{1602.89} = 0.9942$
There was little change in the coefficient of determination. Note that age is now a significant variable.

f. The normality assumption seems reasonable since the graph is fairly linear.

g. There appears to be no violation of homoscedasticity.

21. a. The correlation matrix is:

	Cars	Adv	Sales
Adv	0.808		
Sales	0.872	0.537	
City	0.639	0.713	0.389

Size of sales force (0.872) has strongest correlation with cars sold. Fairly strong relationship between location of dealership and advertising (0.713). Could be a problem.

b. The regression equation is:

$$y' = 31.1328 + 2.1516\text{adv} + 5.0140\text{sales} + 5.6651\text{city}$$
$$y' = 31.1328 + 2.1516(15) + 5.0140(20) + 5.6651(1) = 169.352$$

c. $H_o: \beta_1 = \beta_2 = \beta_3 = 0$ H_1: Not all β's are 0

Reject H_o if computed $F > 4.07$

Analysis of Variance

Source	SS	DF	MS
Regression	5504.4	3	1834.8
Error	420.2	8	52.5
Total	5924.7	11	

$F = 1834.8/52.5 = 34.95$. Reject H_o. At least one regression coefficient is not 0.

d. H_o is rejected in all cases if $t < -2.306$ or if $t > 2.306$. Advertising and sales force should be retained, city dropped. (Note that dropping city removes the problem with multicollinearity.)

Predictor	Coef	Stdev	t-ratio	P
Constant	31.13	13.40	2.32	0.049
Adv	2.1516	0.8049	2.67	0.028
Sales	5.0140	0.9105	5.51	0.000
City	5.665	6.332	0.89	0.397

e. The new output is $y' = 25.30 + 2.6187\text{adv} + 5.0233\text{ sales}$

Predictor	Coef	Stdev	t-ratio
Constant	25.30	11.57	2.19
Adv	2.6187	0.6057	4.32
Sales	5.0233	0.9003	5.58

Analysis of Variance

Source	SS	DF	MS
Regression	5462.4	2	2731.2
Error	462.3	9	51.4
Total	5924.7	11	

f.

Observation	Cars	Predicted	Residual
1	127.0	122.7	4.3
2	138.0	139.9	−1.9
3	159.0	153.2	5.8
4	144.0	145.8	−1.8
5	139.0	130.1	8.9
6	128.0	127.5	0.5
7	161.0	161.1	−0.1
8	180.0	178.8	1.2
9	102.0	99.7	2.3
10	163.0	168.5	−5.5
11	106.0	122.7	−16.7
12	149.0	146.0	3.0

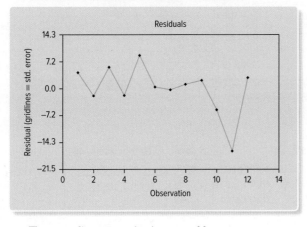

The normality assumption is reasonable.

g. The critical value could be a problem. However, with a small sample the residual plot is acceptable.

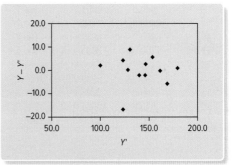

23. a. The regression equation is:

$$y' = 965.3 + 2.865x_1 + 6.75x_2 + 0.2873x_3$$
$$y' = 965.3 + 2.865(220) + 6.75(64) + 0.2873(1500) = \$2\ 458\ 775$$

b. Analysis of Variance

Source	SS	DF	MS
Regression	45510101	3	15170034
Error	12215892	12	1017991
Total	57725994	15	

$F = 15170034/1017991 = 14.902$

H_o is rejected because computed F of 14.9 is greater than the critical value of 3.49. At least one of the regression coefficients is not zero.

c. $H_o: \beta_1 = 0$ $H_o: \beta_2 = 0$ $H_o: \beta_3 = 0$
$H_1: \beta_1 \neq 0$ $H_1: \beta_2 \neq 0$ $H_1: \beta_3 \neq 0$
Reject H_o if $t < -2.179$ or $t > 2.179$

variables	t (df = 12)	p-value
Intercept		
X1	1.810	.0954
X2	0.657	.5236
X3	2.586	.0238

$X_1 = 1.810$ do not reject; $X_2 = 0.657$ do not reject; $X_3 = 2.586$ reject. Both workers and dividends are not significant variables. Inventory is significant. Delete dividends and rerun the regression equation.

d. The regression equation (if we used x_1 and x_3) is:
$$y' = 1134.8 + 3.258X_1 + 0.3099X_3$$

Predictor	Coef	Stdev	t-ratio
Constant	1134.8	418.6	2.71
Workers	3.258	1.434	2.27
Inv	0.3099	0.1033	3.00

Analysis of Variance

Source	SS	DF	MS	F
Regression	45070638	2	22535319	23.15
Error	12655356	13	973489	
Total	57725994	15		

e.

Observation	Profit	Predicted	Residual
1	2800.0	2148.6	651.4
2	1300.0	1445.7	−145.7
3	1230.0	1812.3	−582.3
4	1600.0	1532.9	67.1
5	4500.0	3520.8	979.2
6	5700.0	5920.3	−220.3

(Continued)

Observation	Profit	Predicted	Residual
7	3150.0	1960.0	1190.0
8	640.0	1534.7	−894.7
9	3400.0	4402.7	−1002.7
10	6700.0	6833.4	−133.4
11	3700.0	3539.9	160.1
12	6440.0	5885.9	554.1
13	1280.0	2939.9	−1659.9
14	4160.0	2322.7	1837.3
15	3870.0	3624.0	246.0
16	980.0	2026.2	−1046.2

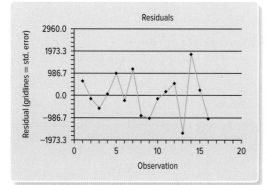

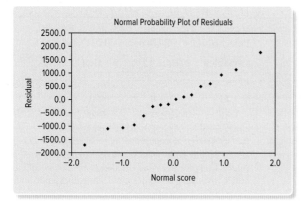

The normality assumption is reasonable.

f.

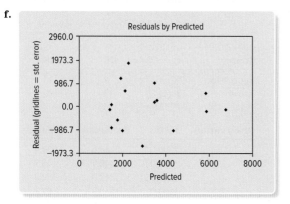

25. a. The correlation of Income and Median Age = 0.721. So there does appear to be a linear relationship between the two.

b. Income is the "dependent" variable.

c. The regression equation is Income = 22 805 + 362 Median Age. For each year increase in age, the income increases $362 on average.

d. Using an indicator variable for Population > 400 000, the regression equation is

Income = 24 865 + 251 Median Age + 6888 Population.

That changes the estimated effect of an additional year of age to $251 and the effect of the population > 400 000 as adding $6888 to income.

e. Notice the p-values are not more than 5%. This indicates that the independent variables are significant influences on income.

Predictor	Coef	SE Coef	T	P
Constant	24865	4552	5.46	0.002
med age	250.5	102.4	2.45	0.050
pop	6888	2501	2.75	0.033

f. The residuals appear normally distributed.

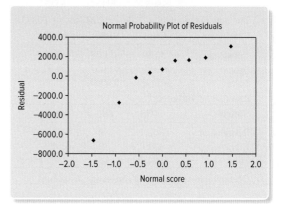

g. The variation is about the same across the different fitted values.

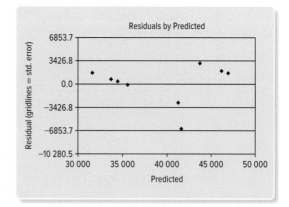

27. a.

	Salary	GPA	Business
Salary	1.000		
GPA	.902	1.000	
Business	.911	.851	1.000

Yes; multicollinearity occurs between GPA and Business (.851)

b. $y' = 23.4474 + 2.7748\text{GPA} + 1.3071\text{Business}$

As GPA increases by one point salary increases by $2775. The average business school graduate makes $1307 more than a corresponding non-business graduate. Estimated salary is $33 079; found by $23 447 + 2775(3.00) + 1307(1).

c. $R^2 = \dfrac{21.182}{23.857} = 0.888$

so, 88.8% of the variation in the y-variable is explained or accounted for, by the independent variables.

d. Since the p-values are less than 0.05, there is no need to delete variables.

Predictor	Coef	SE Coef	T	P
Constant	23.447	3.490	6.72	0.000
GPA	2.775	1.107	2.51	0.028
Business	1.3071	0.4660	2.80	0.016

e. The residuals appear normally distributed.

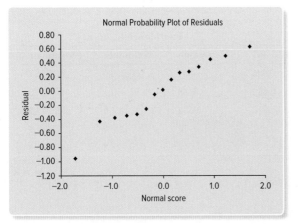

f. The variance is the same as we move from small values to large. So there is no homoscedasticity problem.

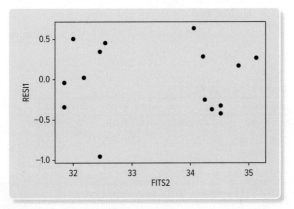

29. a. The regression equation is

Sales $= 1.02 + 0.0829$ Infomercials

Predictor	Coef	SE Coef	T	P
Constant	1.0188	0.3105	3.28	0.006
Infomercials	0.08291	0.01680	4.94	0.000
$S = 0.308675$		R-sq $= 65.2\%$		R-sq(adj) $= 62.5\%$

Analysis of Variance

Source	DF	SS	MS	F	P
Regression	1	2.3214	2.3214	24.36	0.000
Residual Error	13	1.2386	0.0953		
Total	14	3.5600			

b. The global test on F demonstrates there is a substantial connection between sales and the number of commercials.

c.

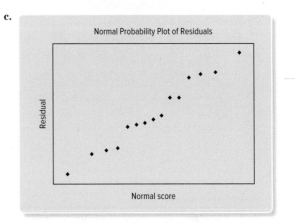

d. The residuals appear to be fairly normally distributed.

31. a. The correlation of Screen and Price is 0.893. So there does appear to be a linear relationship between the two.

b. Price is the "dependent" variable.

c. The regression equation is Price $= -2484 + 101$ Screen. For each inch increase in screen size, the price increases $101 on average.

d. Using "dummy" indicator variables for Sharp and Sony, the regression equation is

Price $= -2308 + 94.1$ Screen $+ 15$ Manufacturer Sharp $+ 381$ Manufacturer Sony

Sharp can obtain on average $15 more than Samsung and Sony can collect an additional benefit of $381.

e. Here is some of the output.

Predictor	Coef	SE Coef	T	P
Constant	−2308.2	492.0	−4.69	0.000
Screen	94.12	10.83	8.69	0.000
Manufacturer_Sharp	15.1	171.6	0.09	0.931
Manufacturer_Sony	381.4	168.8	2.26	0.036

The p-value for Sharp is relatively large. A test of their coefficient would not be rejected. That means they may not have any real advantage over Samsung. On the other hand, the p-value for the Sony coefficient is quite small. That indicates that it did not happen by chance and there is some real advantage to Sony over Samsung.

f. A histogram of the residuals indicates they follow a normal distribution.

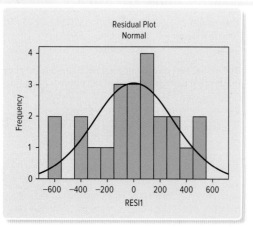

g. The residual variation may be increasing for larger fitted values.

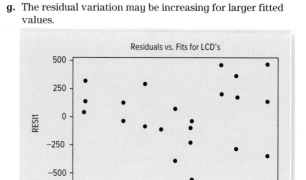

33. a.

Regression output					confidence interval	
variables	**coefficients**	**std. error**	**t (df= 93)**	**p-value**	**95% lower**	**95% upper**
Intercept	−39,826.2	63,708.2	−0.625	.5334	−166,338.0	86,685.7
Number of Bedrooms	−22,566.6	34,591.9	−0.652	.5158	−91,259.1	46,126.0
Full Baths	97,362.9	50,802.9	1.916	.0584	−3,521.6	198,247.5
Total Square Feet	334.5	47.9	6.987	4.15E-10	239.4	429.6
Type	−196,886.9	66,993.3	−2.939	.0042	−329,922.3	−63,851.4

List price = −39 826.2 −22 566.6 Number of Bedrooms + 97 362.9 Full Baths + 334.5 Total Square Feet − 196 886.9 Type

The number of Full Baths and the Total Square Feet have positive coefficients. The others are negative.
We would expect Type to be negative, but not the other variables.

b. R^2 0.730
73.0% of the variation in the y-variable is explained or accounted for, by the independent variables.

c. Correlation Matrix

	List Price	Number of Bedrooms	Full Baths	Total Square Feet	Type
List Price	1.000				
Number of Bedrooms	.640	1.000			
Full Baths	.736	.646	1.000		
Total Square Feet	.813	.846	.755	1.000	
Type	.315	.652	.264	.619	1.000

Strong correlation: Full baths (.736) and Total Square Feet (.813).

Multicollinearity: exists between Bedrooms and Total Square Feet (.846), and Full baths and Total Square Feet (.755).

d. $H_o: \beta_1 = \beta_2 = \beta_3 = \beta_4 = 0$
H_i: Not all β's = 0

p-value	The p-value < .05, so reject the null hypothesis.
1.24E-25	

e.

Regress on output

variables	coeficients	std. error	t (df=93)	p-value
Intercept	−39,826.2	63,708.191	−0.625	.5334
Number of Bedrooms	−22,566.6	34,591.857	−0.652	.5158
Full Baths	97,362.9	50,802.921	1.916	.0584
Total Square Feet	334.5	47.871	6.987	4.15E-10
Type	−196,886.9	66,993.299	−2.939	.0042

$H_o: \beta_1 = 0$
$H_i: \beta_1 \neq 0$
The number of bedrooms is not significant to the model, and should be removed.

f.

Regression output

Variables	coefficients	std. error	t (df=94)	p-value
Intercept	−53,924.1	59,747.5682	−0.903	.3691
Full Baths	92,038.6	49,989.6131	1.841	.0688
Total Square Feet	318.9	41.3781	7.708	1.30E-11
Type	−211,781.7	62,789.7878	−3.373	.0011

Full Baths should also be removed from the equation.

Regression output

variables	coefficients	std. error	t (df=95)	p-value
Intercept	25,442.336	41,888.2426	0.607	.5450
Total Square Feet	378.473	26.1398	14.479	8.98E-26
Type	−257,589.540	58,370.8391	−4.413	2.69E-05

All variables are now significant.

g. The plot appears to be normal.

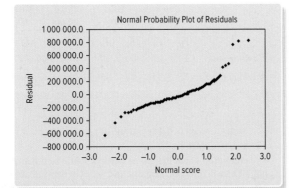

Chapter 14

1. a. 3
  b. 7.815
3. a. Reject H_o if $\chi^2 > 7.815$
  b.
  $$\chi^2 = \frac{(10-20)^2}{20} + \frac{(20-20)^2}{20} + \frac{(30-20)^2}{20} + \frac{(20-20)^2}{20} = 10.0$$
  c. Reject H_o. The frequencies are not equal.
5. H_o: The outcomes are the same. H_1: The outcomes are not the same.
  Reject H_o if $\chi^2 > 9.236$
  $$\chi^2 = \frac{(3-5)^2}{5} + ... + \frac{(7-5)^2}{5} = 7.60$$
  Do not reject H_o. Cannot reject H_o that outcomes are the same.
7. H_o: There is no difference in the proportions. H_1: There is a difference in the proportions.
  Reject H_o if $\chi^2 > 15.086$
  $$\chi^2 = \frac{(47-40)^2}{40} + ... + \frac{(34-40)^2}{40} = 3.400$$
  Do not reject H_o. There is no difference in the proportions.

9. a. Reject H_o if $\chi^2 > 9.210$
  b. $\chi^2 = \frac{(30-24)^2}{24} + \frac{(20-24)^2}{24} + \frac{(10-12)^2}{12} = 2.50$
  c. Do not reject H_o.
11. H_o: The proportions are as stated. H_1: The proportions are not as stated.
  Reject H_o if $\chi^2 > 11.345$
  $$\chi^2 = \frac{(50-25)^2}{25} + \frac{(100-75)^2}{75} + \frac{(190-125)^2}{125} + \frac{(160-275)^2}{275} = 115.22$$
  Reject H_o. Proportions are not as stated.
13. H_o: There is no relationship between the person resides and section read. H_1: There is a relationship.
  Reject H_o if $\chi^2 > 9.488$
  $$\chi^2 = \frac{(170-157.50)^2}{157.50} + ... + \frac{(88-83.62)^2}{83.62} = 7.340$$
  Do not reject H_o. There is no relationship between the person resides and section read.
15. H_o: No relationship between error rates and item type.
  H_1: There is a relationship between error rates and item type.
  Reject H_o if $\chi^2 > 9.21$
  $$\chi^2 = \frac{(20-14.1)^2}{14.1} + \frac{(10-15.9)^2}{15.9} + ... + \frac{(200-199.75)^2}{199.75}$$
  $$+ \frac{(225-225.25)^2}{225.25} = 8.033$$
  Do not reject H_o. There is no relationship between error rates and item type.
  (Computer value = 8.036)
17. H_o: $p_s = 0.50$, $p_r = p_1 = 0.25$
  H_1: Distribution is not as given above.
  $df = 2$ Reject H_o if $\chi^2 > 4.605$.

Turn	f_o	f_e	$f_o - f_e$	$(f_o - f_e)^2/f_e$
Straight	112	100	12	1.44
Right	48	50	−2	0.08
Left	40	50	−10	2.00
Total	200	200		3.52

H_o is not rejected. The proportions are as given in the null hypothesis.

19. H_o: There is no preference with respect to TV stations.
  H_1: There is a preference with respect to TV stations.
  $df = 3 - 1 = 2$ H_o is rejected if χ^2 is greater than 5.991

TV Station	f_o	f_e	$f_o - f_e$	$(f_o - f_e)^2$	$(f_o - f_e)^2/f_e$
CTV	53	50	3	9	0.18
Global	64	50	14	196	3.92
Citytv	33	50	−17	289	5.78
Total	150	150			9.88

H_o is rejected. There is a preference for TV stations.

21. H_o: $p_{ne} = 0.21$, $p_m = 0.24$, $p_s = 0.35$ and $p_w = 0.20$
  H_1: The distribution is not as given.
  Reject H_o if $\chi^2 > 11.345$.

Area	f_o	f_e	$f_o - f_e$	$(f_o - f_e)^2/f_e$
New York State	68	84	−16	3.0476
Ont(exc GTA)	104	96	8	0.6667
GTA	155	140	15	1.6071
Other	73	80	−7	0.6125
Total	400	400	0	5.9339

There is not enough evidence to reject H_o. The geographical distribution of her club members has not changed.

23. H_o: $p_0 = 0.4$, $p_1 = 0.3$, $p_2 = 0.2$, $p_3 = 0.1$
H_1: The proportions are not as given
Reject H_o if $\chi^2 > 7.815$

Applications	f_o	f_e	$(f_o - f_e)^2/f_e$
0	46	48	0.083
1	40	36	0.444
2	22	24	0.167
3	12	12	0.000
Total	120	120	0.694

Do not reject H_o. Evidence does not show a change in the accident distribution.

25. H_o: Level of management and concern regarding the environment are not related.
H_1: Level of management and concern regarding the environment are related
Reject H_o if $\chi^2 > 16.812$
$$\chi^2 = \frac{(15-14)^2}{14} + \dots + \frac{(31-28)^2}{28} = 1.550$$
Do not reject H_o. Levels of management and environmental concerns are not related.

27. H_o: Whether a claim is filed and age are not related.
H_1: Whether a claim is filed and age are related.
Reject H_o if $\chi^2 > 7.815$
$$\chi^2 = \frac{(170-203.33)^2}{203.33} + \frac{(74-40.67)^2}{40.67} + \dots + \frac{(24-35.67)^2}{35.67} = 53.639$$
Reject H_o. Age is related to whether a claim is filed.

29. H_o: $p_0 = 0.55$, $p_1 = 0.28$, $p_2 = 0.17$
H_1: The proportions are not as given
Reject H_o if $\chi^2 > 5.991$

Applications	f_o	f_e	$(f_o - f_e)^2/f_e$
0	220	247.5	3.056
1	158	126	8.127
2	72	76.5	0.265
Total	450	450	11.448

Reject H_o. Young adults differ from the general population.

31. H_o: The proportions are the same H_1: The proportions are not the same
Reject H_o if $\chi^2 > 16.919$

f_o	f_e	$f_o - f_e$	$(f_o - f_e)^2$	$(f_o - f_e)^2/f_e$
44	28	16	256	9.143
32	28	4	16	0.571
23	28	−5	25	0.893
27	28	−1	1	0.036
23	28	−5	25	0.893
24	28	−4	16	0.571
31	28	3	9	0.321
27	28	−1	1	0.036
28	28	0	0	0.000
21	28	−7	49	1.750
280	280			14.214

Do not reject H_o. The digits are evenly distributed.

33. H_o: Gender and attitude toward the deficit are not related
H_1: Gender and attitude toward the deficit are related
Reject H_o if $\chi^2 > 5.991$
$$\chi^2 = \frac{(244-292.41)^2}{292.41} + \frac{(194-164.05)^2}{164.05} + \frac{(68-49.53)^2}{49.53}$$

$$+ \frac{(305-256.59)^2}{256.59} + \frac{(114-143.95)^2}{143.95} + \frac{(25-43.47)^2}{43.47} = 43.578$$

Since $43.578 > 5.991$ you reject H_o. A person's position on the deficit is influenced by his or her gender.

35. H_o: Gender and type of movie are not related
H_1: Gender and type of movie are related
Reject H_o if $\chi^2 > 11.345$

	Action		Documentary		Romantic		Comedy	
Gender	f_o	f_e	f_o	f_e	f_o	f_e	f_o	f_e
Male	75	61.25	50	49	60	75.95	60	58.8
Female	50	63.75	50	51	95	79.05	60	61.2

$\chi^2 = 3.087 + 2.966 + 0.020 + 0.020 + 3.350 + 3.218 + 0.024 + 0.024 = 12.708$

The computed value lies to the right of 11.345, so the null hypothesis is rejected. Gender and type of movie are related. The p-value is 0.0053, which is smaller than the significance level of .01. This confirms the null hypothesis should be rejected.

37. H_o: Loyalty and years of service are not related.
H_1: Loyalty and years of service are related.
Reject H_o if $\chi^2 > 7.815$

	Less 1 year		1–5 years		6–10 years		More than 10 years	
	f_o	f_e	f_o	f_e	f_o	f_e	f_o	f_e
Would remain	10	21	30	27	5	9	75	63
Would not remain	25	14	15	18	10	6	30	42
	35		45		15		105	

$\chi^2 = 5.762 + 8.643 + 0.333 + 0.500 + 1.778 + 2.667 + 2.286 + 3.429 = 25.397$

The computed value lies to the right of 7.815, so the null hypothesis is rejected. Loyalty and years of service are related. The p-value is 0.00001 which is smaller than the significance level of 0.05. This confirms the null hypothesis should be rejected.

39. H_o: There is no difference in the proportion of students who are absent on Fridays.
H_1: There is a difference in the proportion of students who are absent on Fridays.
Reject H_o if $\chi^2 > 9.488$

Days of the Week	f_o	f_e	$(f_o - f_e)^2/f_e$
Monday	11	8.8	0.550
Tuesday	6	8.8	0.891
Wednesday	8	8.8	0.073
Thursday	7	8.8	0.368
Friday	12	8.8	1.164
			3.045

The computed value lies to the left of 9.488, so there is not enough evidence to reject the null hypothesis. There is no difference in the proportion of students who are absent on Fridays.

41. H_o: The proportions are as stated. H_1: The proportions are not as stated.

Reject H_o if $\chi^2 > 9.488$

f_0	f_e	$(f_0 - f_e)^2/f_e$
7	3	5.333
11	8	1.125
16	21	1.190
3	5	0.800
3	3	0.000
		8.449

There is not enough evidence to reject H_o. Proportions are as stated and follow the distribution as seen in Professor Brown's classes in the past.

43. a. H_o: There is no relationship between type and list price.

H_1: There is a relationship between type and list price.

List Price (thousands $)

Type	less than 300	300 to under 500	500 to under 700	more than 700	Total
Apartment	28	21	5	4	58
Town house	8	5	1	0	14
House	4	5	5	12	26
					98

Chi-square Contingency Table Test for Independence

	Less than 400	400 to under 600	600 to under 800	More than 800	Total
Apartment	28	21	5	4	58
Town house	8	5	1	0	14
House	4	5	5	12	26
Total	40	31	11	16	98

29.20	chi-square
6	df
.0001	p-value

Reject H_o. There is an association between the type and list price.

b. H_o: The number of bedrooms and list price are not related.

H_1: The number of bedrooms and list price are related.

List Price (thousands$)

Type	less than 400	400 to under 600	600 to under 800	800 +	Total
1-3 Bedrooms	39	29	8	4	80
4+ bedrooms	1	2	3	12	18
					98

	less than 400	400 to under 600	600 to under 800	more than 800	Total
1-3 Bedrooms	39	29	8	4	80
4+ bedrooms	1	2	3	12	18
Total	40	31	11	16	98

44.46	chi-square
3	df
1.21E-09	p-value

Reject H_o. There is an association between the number of bedrooms and list price.

Chapter 15

1. average 2013–2015: $256 501

		Index
2011	221 933	86.5
2012	227 807	88.8
2013	241 652	94.2
2014	254 481	99.2
2015	273 369	106.6
2016	264 007	102.9
2017	267 068	104.1

3.

		Index
2017	$470 253	152.0
2016	$469 359	151.7
2015	$452 691	146.3
2014	$388 553	125.6
2013	$354 951	114.7
2012	$348 178	112.5
2011	$344 118	111.2
2010	$328 728	106.2
2009	$274 711	88.8
2008	$309 448	100.0

a. List prices have increased by 52% over the period.

b. average = $351 565

		Index
2017	$470 253	133.8
2016	$469 359	133.5
2015	$452 691	128.8
2014	$388 553	110.5
2013	$354 951	101.0
2012	$348 178	99.0
2011	$344 118	97.9
2010	$328 728	93.5
2009	$274 711	78.1
2008	$309 448	88.0

5. a. $P_t = \dfrac{2.69}{2.49}(100) = 108.03$ $P_s = \dfrac{3.59}{3.29}(100) = 109.12$

$P_c = \dfrac{2.79}{1.79}(100) = 155.9$ $P_a = \dfrac{3.79}{2.29}(100) = 165.5$

b. $P = \dfrac{12.86}{9.86}(100) = 130.4$

c. $P = \dfrac{(2.69)(6)+(3.59)(4)+(2.79)(2)+(3.79)(3)}{(2.49)(6)+(3.29)(4)+(1.79)(2)+(2.29)(3)}(100)$

$= 123.1$

d. $P = \dfrac{(2.69)(6)+(3.59)(5)+(2.79)(3)+(3.79)(4)}{(2.49)(6)+(3.29)(5)+(1.79)(3)+(2.29)(4)}(100)$

$= 125.5$

e. $I = \sqrt{(123.1)(125.5)} = 124.3$

7. a. $P_W = \dfrac{0.10}{0.07}(100) = 142.9$ $P_b = \dfrac{0.10}{0.04}(100) = 250.0$

$P_b = \dfrac{0.18}{0.15}(100) = 120.0$ $P_H = \dfrac{0.10}{0.08}(100) = 125.0$

b. $P = \dfrac{0.48}{0.34}(100) = 141.2$

c.

$P = \dfrac{(0.10)(17\,000)+(0.10)(125\,000)+(0.18)(40\,000)+(0.10)(62\,000)}{(0.07)(17\,000)+(0.04)(125\,000)+(0.15)(40\,000)+(0.08)(62\,000)}(100)$

$= 160.9$

d.

$$P = \frac{(0.10)(20000)+(0.10)(130000)+(0.18)(42000)+(0.10)(65000)}{(0.07)(20000)+(0.04)(130000)+(0.15)(42000)+(0.08)(65000)}(100)$$
$$= 160.6$$

e. $I = \sqrt{(160.9)(160.6)} = 160.7$

9. $V = \dfrac{1.87(214)+2.05(489)+1.48(203)+3.29(106)}{1.52(200)+2.10(565)+1.48(291)+3.05(87)}(100) = 93.8$

11. The increase in the CPI is 37.0%, so $600(1.370) = \$822.00$

13. $X = (\$52\,500)/1.362 = \$38\,546.26$ Buying power has decreased ($\$39\,000.00 - \$38\,546.26) = \$453.74$.

15.

Year	Mercury	Mercury	Industry Index
2000	$26 650	100.0	100.0
2005	$31 972	120.0	122.5
2010	$36 382	136.5	136.9
2013	$37 269	139.8	144.9
2016	$39 500	148.2	146.0

The Mercury plant workers received increases slightly less than the industry average with the exception of 2016.

17.

Region	Jan-17	Index
National Average	$470 253	100.0
Vancouver	$878 242	186.8
Calgary	$451 242	96.0
Saskatoon	$335 121	71.3
Toronto	$770 745	163.9
Halifax	$265 237	56.4

The value of home listings is highest in Vancouver, at 86.8% higher than the national average. Halifax is the lowest at 43.6% $(100 - 56.4)$ less than the national average.

19.

Region	Jan-10	Index
National Average	$328 728	100.0
Vancouver	637 637	194.0
Calgary	382 009	116.2
Saskatoon	270 191	82.2
Toronto	409 058	124.4
Halifax	241 968	73.6

The value of home listings is highest in Vancouver, at 94.0% higher than the national average. Halifax is the lowest at 26.4% less than the national average.

21.

Region	Jan-17	Index	
Vancouver	$878 242	158.8	
Calgary	$451 242	81.6	average = $552 933
Saskatoon	$335121	60.6	
Toronto	$770 745	139.4	
Halifax	$265 237	48.0	

The value of home listings is highest in Vancouver at 58.8% higher than the average of Toronto and Saskatoon.

23.

Date	Closing Price	Index
Mar-17	$6.89	20.5
Mar-16	7.69	22.9
Mar-15	11.05	32.9
Mar-14	9.66	28.8
Mar-13	13.03	38.8
Mar-12	13.44	40.0
Mar-11	55.65	165.6
Mar-10	75.25	224.0

Date	Closing Price	Index
Mar-09	54.49	162.2
Mar-08	115.49	343.7
Mar-07	157.50	468.8
Mar-06	98.89	294.3
Mar-05	92.71	275.9
Mar-04	122.4	364.3
Mar-03	19.08	56.8
Mar-02	44.34	132.0
Mar-01	33.60	100.0

The stock increased by 368.8% by Mar 2007 but then started to decline.

The stock as of Mar 2017 is 79.5% less than the Mar 2001 closing price.

25.

Date	Closing Price	Index	
Mar-17	$6.89	6.3	
Mar-16	7.69	7.0	
Mar-15	11.05	10.1	
Mar-14	9.66	8.8	average = 109.16
Mar-13	13.03	11.9	
Mar-12	13.44	12.3	
Mar-11	55.65	51.0	
Mar-10	75.25	68.9	
Mar-09	54.49	49.9	
Mar-08	115.49	105.8	
Mar-07	157.50	144.3	
Mar-06	98.89	90.6	
Mar-05	92.71	84.9	
Mar-04	122.4	112.1	
Mar-03	19.08	17.5	
Mar-02	44.34	40.6	
Mar-01	33.60	30.8	

Mar 2007 was the highest close over the seventeen years.

27. $P_M = \dfrac{2.39}{0.81}(100) = 295.1 \quad P_S = \dfrac{1.49}{0.84}(100) = 177.4$

$P_M = \dfrac{3.79}{1.44}(100) = 263.2 \quad P_P = \dfrac{3.99}{2.91}(100) = 137.1$

29.

$$P = \frac{(2.39)(18)+(1.49)(5)+(3.79)(70)+(3.99)(27)}{(0.81)(18)+(0.84)(5)+(1.44)(70)+(2.91)(27)}(100) = 213.7$$

31. $I = \sqrt{(213.7)(208.1)} = 210.9$

33. $P_R = \dfrac{0.60}{0.50}(100) = 120 \quad P_S = \dfrac{0.90}{1.20}(100) = 75.0$

$P_W = \dfrac{1.00}{0.85}(100) = 117.65$

35. $P = \dfrac{(0.60)(320)+(0.90)(110)+(1.00)(230)}{(0.50)(320)+(1.20)(110)+(0.85)(230)}(100) = 106.9$

37. $I = \sqrt{(106.9)(106.0)} = 106.5$

39. $P_C = \dfrac{0.90}{0.60}(100) = 150.0 \quad P_C = \dfrac{0.69}{0.49}(100) = 140.8$

$P_P = \dfrac{2.99}{1.99}(100) = 150.3 \quad P_P = \dfrac{1.29}{0.89}(100) = 144.9$

41. $P = \dfrac{(0.90)(2000)+(0.69)(200)+(2.99)(400)+(1.29)(100)}{(0.60)(2000)+(0.49)(200)+(1.99)(400)+(0.89)(100)}(100)$
$$= 149.5$$

43. $I = \sqrt{(149.5)(149.3)} = 149.4$

45. $P_{PC} = \dfrac{5.99}{4.99}(100) = 120.0 \quad P_{PL} = \dfrac{0.99}{0.89}(100) = 111.2$

$P_{PP} = \dfrac{1.19}{0.99}(100) = 120.2 \quad P_{PC} = \dfrac{1.79}{1.49}(100) = 120.1$

47. $P = \dfrac{(5.99)(400)+(0.99)(1000)+(1.19)(850)+(1.79)(350)}{(4.99)(400)+(0.89)(1000)+(0.99)(850)+(1.49)(350)}(100)$
$= 118.2$

49. $I = \sqrt{(118.2)(118.2)} = 118.2$

51. $I = \dfrac{1971.0}{1159.0}(0.20) + \dfrac{91}{87}(0.10) + \dfrac{114.7}{110.6}(0.40) + \dfrac{1501}{1214}(0.30)$
$= 1.2305*100 = 123.05$

The economy is up 23.05% from the base year to the current year.

53. February:
$I = \dfrac{6.8}{8.0}(0.40) + \dfrac{23}{20}(0.35) + \dfrac{303}{300}(100) = 0.9950*100 = 99.5$

March:
$I = \dfrac{6.4}{8.0}(0.40) + \dfrac{21}{20}(0.35) + \dfrac{297}{300}(100) = 0.9350*100 = 93.5$

55. 114.6, found by ($19 989/$17 446)(100)
123.1, found by ($21 468/$17 446)(100)
124.3, found by ($21 685/$17 446)(100)
91.3, found by ($15 922/$17 446)(100)
105.3, found by ($18 375/$17 446)(100)
314.2, found by ($54 818/$17 446)(100)

57. a.
$P = \dfrac{\$6.83(1500)+9.35(10)+4.62(250)+6.85(1000)+13.65(30)}{\$6.10(1500)+8.10(10)+4.00(250)+6.00(1000)+12.00(30)}(100)$
$= 113.03$

b.
$P = \dfrac{\$6.83(2000)+9.35(12)+4.62(250)+6.85(900)+13.65(40)}{\$6.10(2000)+8.10(12)+4.00(250)+6.00(900)+12.00(40)}(100)$
$= 112.83$

c. $I = \sqrt{113.03(112.83)} = 112.93$

59. $X = (\$89\ 673)/1.284 = \$69\ 839.$ "Real" salary increased $69 839 − $69 800 = $39.

61. a. $X = \dfrac{1}{128.4}(100) = 0.7788162$

b. $36 000/116.5(100) = $30 901; Simone's purchasing power has increased since 2002.

c. $X = \dfrac{1}{122.8}(109.1) = 0.88844$

d. $45 000/128.4(100) = $35 047; Simone's purchasing power has increased since 2002.

63. a.

PoQo	PtQo	
247 500.00	292 500.00	
25 000.00	35 000.00	
5000.00	7000.00	= 395 250/334 250(100)
21 000.00	25 000.00	
35 750.00	35 750.00	118.2
334 250.00	395 250.00	

(LO 15-3)

b.

PoQt	PtQt	
412 500.00	487 500.00	
31 250.00	43 750.00	= 618 500/525 400(100)
5000.00	7000.00	
18 900.00	22 500.00	117.7
57 750.00	57 750.00	
525 400.00	618 500.00	

c. $\sqrt{(118.2)(117.7)} = 117.9$

65. a.

Year	S&P/TSX	Index	NASDAQ	Index
2001	7833.24	100.0	1950.4	100.0
2002	6772.66	86.5	1335.51	68.5
2003	8293.70	105.9	2003.37	102.7
2004	9246.65	118.0	2175.44	111.5
2005	11 272.36	143.9	2205.32	113.1
2006	12 908.39	164.8	2415.29	123.8
2007	13 778.58	175.9	2652.28	136.0
2008	8987.70	114.7	1577.03	80.9
2009	11 746.11	150.0	2269.15	116.3
2010	13 443.22	171.6	2652.87	136.0
2011	11 955.10	152.6	2605.15	133.6
2012	12 433.53	158.7	3019.51	154.8
2013	13 621.55	173.9	4176.59	214.1
2014	14 632.44	186.8	4736.05	242.8
2015	13 009.95	166.1	5007.41	256.7
2016	15 287.59	195.2	5383.12	276.0

The S&P/TSX increased by 95.2%.
The Nasdaq increased by 176.0%.

b.

Year	S&P/TSX	Index	S&P 500	Index
2001	7833.24	100.0	1148.08	100.0
2002	6772.66	86.5	879.82	76.6
2003	8293.70	105.9	1111.92	96.9
2004	9246.65	118.0	1211.92	105.6
2005	11 272.36	143.9	1248.29	108.7
2006	12 908.39	164.8	1418.3	123.5
2007	13 778.58	175.9	1468.36	127.9
2008	8987.70	114.7	903.25	78.7
2009	11 746.11	150.0	1115.1	97.1
2010	13 443.22	171.6	1257.64	109.5
2011	11 955.10	152.6	1257.6	109.5
2012	12 433.53	158.7	1426.19	124.2
2013	13 621.55	173.9	1848.36	161.0
2014	14 632.44	186.8	2058.9	179.3
2015	13 009.95	166.1	2043.94	178.0
2016	15 287.59	195.2	2238.83	195.0

The S&P/TSX increased by 95.2%.
The S&P 500 increased by 95.0%.

c.

Year	S&P/TSX Venture	Index	NASDAQ	Index
2001	1036.59	100.0	1950.4	100.0
2002	1074.08	103.6	1335.51	68.5
2003	1751.28	168.9	2003.37	102.7
2004	1825.47	176.1	2175.44	111.5
2005	2236.55	215.8	2205.32	113.1
2006	2987.08	288.2	2415.29	123.8
2007	2839.66	273.9	2652.28	136.0
2008	797.02	76.9	1577.03	80.9
2009	1520.72	146.7	2269.15	116.3
2010	2287.85	220.7	2652.87	136.0
2011	1484.66	143.2	2605.15	133.6
2012	1221.3	117.8	3019.51	154.8
2013	931.97	89.9	4176.59	214.1
2014	695.53	67.1	4736.05	242.8
2015	525.66	50.7	5007.41	256.7
2016	762.37	73.5	5383.12	276.0

The S&P/TSX Venture decreased by 26.5%

The Nasdaq increased by 176.0%.

d.

Year	S&P/TSX Venture	Index	S&P 500	Index
2001	1036.59	100.0	1148.08	100.0
2002	1074.08	103.6	879.82	76.6
2003	1751.28	168.9	1111.92	96.9
2004	1825.47	176.1	1211.92	105.6
2005	2236.55	215.8	1248.29	108.7
2006	2987.08	288.2	1418.3	123.5
2007	2839.66	273.9	1468.36	127.9
2008	797.02	76.9	903.25	78.7
2009	1520.72	146.7	1115.1	97.1
2010	2287.85	220.7	1257.64	109.5
2011	1484.66	143.2	1257.6	109.5
2012	1221.3	117.8	1426.19	124.2
2013	931.97	89.9	1848.36	161.0
2014	695.53	67.1	2058.9	179.3
2015	525.66	50.7	2043.94	178.0
2016	762.37	73.5	2238.83	195.0

The S&P/TSX Venture decreased by 26.5%

The S&P 500 increased by 95.0%.

Chapter 16

1. $b = \dfrac{2469 - (721)(15)/5}{55 - (15)^2/5} = \dfrac{306}{10} = 30.6$ $a = \dfrac{721}{5} - 30.6\left(\dfrac{15}{5}\right) = 52.4$

for 2019, $t = 7$; $y' = 52.4 + 30.6t = 52.4 + 30.6(7) = 266.6$

3. a.

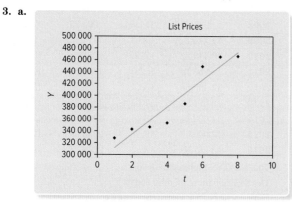

b. $b = \dfrac{8(15\,187\,750) - (3\,156\,831)(36)}{8(204) - (36)^2} = 23\,381.20$

$a = \dfrac{3\,156\,831}{8} - 23\,381.20\left(\dfrac{36}{8}\right) = 289\,388.48$

$y' = 289\,388.48 + 23\,381.20t$

c. Every year, expect the amount to increase by about $23 381.20.

d. 2020($t = 11$) = $546 581.68

e. 2015($t = 6$) = $429 675.68; the predicted value is an estimate while the given value is the actual value.

5. $y' = 1.7143 + 0.75t$; for $t = 9$: $y' = 1.7143 + 0.75(9) = 8.5$

7. a. $y' = -0.0532000 + 0.1104058t$

b. 28.95%, found by 1.28945 −1.0

c. $y' = -0.0532000 + 0.1104058t$ for 2020, $t = 8$

$y' = -0.0532000 + 0.1104058(8) = 0.8300464$

Antilog of 0.8300464 = 6.76

9.

Quarter	Average SI Component	Seasonal Index
1	0.6859	0.6900
2	1.6557	1.6655
3	1.1616	1.1685
4	0.4732	0.4760

Note: Excel/MegaStat answers may be slightly different due to rounding.

11.

t	Estimated pairs (millions)	Seasonal index	Quarterly forecast (millions)
21	40.05	110.0	44.055
22	41.80	120.0	50.160
23	43.55	80.0	34.840
24	45.30	90.0	40.770

13. $y' = 5.1741 + 0.37868t$. The following are the sales estimates.

Estimate	Index	Seasonally Adjusted
10.097	0.6900	6.967
10.476	1.6655	17.447
10.854	1.1685	12.683
11.233	0.4760	5.347

15. a. $y' = 16\,881 - 328t$, assuming the line starts at 15 900 in 1997 and goes down to 10 900 in 2016.

b. 328

c. 8 353, found by 16 881 − 328(26)

17. a.

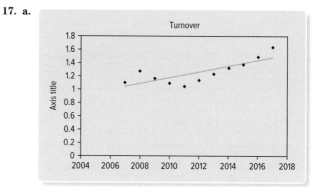

b. $y' = 1.00455 + 0.04409t$

c. for $t = 4, y' = 1.18091$, and for $t = 9, y' = 1.40136$

d. for $t = 16, y' = 1.71$

e. Each asset turned over 0.044 times

19. a.

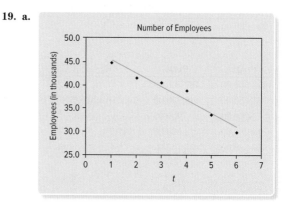

b. $y' = 49.140 - 2.9829t$

c. for 2014, $y' = 40.1913$ and for 2017, $y' = 31.2426$

d. for 2020 $y' = 22.2939$

e. The number of employees decreases at a rate of 2.9829 per year.

21. a. Log $y' = 0.790231 + 0.113669t$

Log $y' = 1.244907$, antilog is 17.575

b. Log $y' = 1.813252$, antilog is 65.05

c. 29.92, which is the antilog of 0.113669 minus 1

d. Log $y' = 2.154259$, antilog is 142.65

23. a.

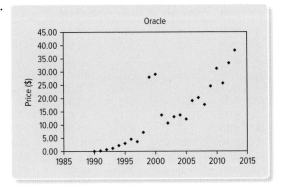

Oracle

The following results are using MegaStat.

b. The equations are $y = -3.1543 + 1.4342t$ and/or log $y' = -0.1100 + 0.0803t$.

The equation using the logarithm appears better because R^2 is larger.

c. log $y' = -0.1100 + 0.0803(7) = 0.4521$; antilog = \$2.83.

log $y' = -0.1100 + 0.0803(12) = 0.8536$; antilog = \$7.14.

d. log $y' = -0.1100 + 0.0803(30) = 2.299$, antilog is \$199.07.

The linear estimate is $y' = -3.1543 + 1.4342 (30) = \$39.87$.

e. The annual rate of increase is 20.3%.

25. a. July 87.5, August 92.9, September 99.3, October 109.1

Month	Total	Mean	Seasonal
July	348.9	87.225	86.777
Aug.	368.1	92.025	91.552
Sept.	395.0	98.750	98.242
Oct.	420.4	105.100	104.560
Nov.	496.2	124.050	123.412
Dec.	572.3	143.075	142.340
Jan.	333.5	83.375	82.946
Feb.	297.5	74.375	73.993
March	347.3	86.825	86.379
April	481.3	120.325	119.707
May	396.2	99.050	98.541
June	368.1	92.025	91.552
		1206.200	

b. Correction = 1200/1206.2 = 0.99486

c. April, November, and December are periods of high sales, while February is low.

27. a.

Seasonal Index by Quarter

Quarter	Average SI Component	Seasonal Index
1	0.5014	0.5016
2	1.0909	1.0913
3	1.7709	1.7715
4	0.6354	0.6356

b. The production is the largest in the third quarter. It is 77.1% above the average quarter. The second quarter is also above average. The first and fourth quarters are well below average, with the first quarter at about 50% of a typical quarter.

29.

Seasonal Index by Quarter

Quarter	Average SI Component	Seasonal Index
1	0.5549	0.5566
2	0.8254	0.8280
3	1.5102	1.5148
4	1.0973	1.1007

a. Note: Excel answers may be different due to rounding.

b. $y' = 7.683 + 0.0023t$

c.

Period	Production	Index	Forecast
21	7.7305	0.5566	4.3028
22	7.7328	0.8280	6.4024
23	7.7351	1.5148	11.7169
24	7.7374	1.1007	8.5163

31.

Seasonal Index by Quarter

Quarter	Average SI Component	Seasonal Index
1	1.1962	1.2046
2	1.0135	1.0206
3	0.6253	0.6297
4	1.1371	1.1451

The regression equation is: $y' = 43.636 + 7.21956t$

Period	Visitors	Index	Forecast
29	253.00	1.2046	304.77
30	260.22	1.0206	265.59
31	267.44	0.6297	168.41
32	274.66	1.1451	314.51

In 2017 there were a total of 928 visitors. A 10% increase in 2018 means there will be 1021 visitors. The quarterly estimates are 1021/4 = 255.25 visitors per quarter.

Period	Visitors	Index	Forecast
Winter	255.25	1.2046	307.47
Spring	255.25	1.0206	260.52
Summer	255.25	0.6297	160.73
Fall	255.25	1.1451	292.28

The regression approach is probably superior because the trend is considered.

33. a. The linear trend line is $y' = 0.4757 + 0.1133 * t$ and the logarithmic trend line is log

$$y' = -0.0834 + 0.0255 * t.$$

b. The equation using the logarithm appears better because R^2 is larger at 0.9168 compared to 0.8907.

c. The years 2018 and 2019 would be coded $t = 24$ and 25, respectively.

For 2018: log $y' = -0.0834 + 0.0255(24) = 0.5286$ and its antilog is 3.38.

For 2014: log $y' = -0.0834 + 0.0255(25) = 0.5541$ and its antilog is 3.58

35. There appears to be a regular increase in the number of tickets sold.

Year	Tickets (thousands)	Three-Year Moving Total	Three-Year Moving Average
2003	5.6		
2004	6.7	19.1	6.4
2005	6.8	20.8	6.9
2006	7.3	21.6	7.2
2007	7.5	21.3	7.1
2008	6.5	20.2	6.7
2009	6.2	19	6.3
2010	6.3	19.7	6.6
2011	7.2	21	7.0
2012	7.5	22.1	7.4
2013	7.4	23	7.7
2014	8.1	23.8	7.9
2015	8.3	24.7	8.2
2016	8.3	25.1	8.4
2017	8.5		

Year	Tickets (thousands)	Five-Year Moving Total	Five-Year Moving Average
2003	5.6		
2004	6.7		
2005	6.8	33.9	6.8
2006	7.3	34.8	7.0
2007	7.5	34.3	6.9
2008	6.5	33.8	6.8
2009	6.2	33.7	6.7
2010	6.3	33.7	6.7
2011	7.2	34.6	6.9
2012	7.5	36.5	7.3
2013	7.4	38.5	7.7
2014	8.1	39.6	7.9
2015	8.3	40.6	8.1
2016	8.3		
2017	8.5		

37. a.

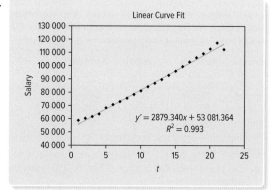

Linear Curve Fit

$y' = 2879.340x + 53\,081.364$
$R^2 = 0.993$

b. $y' = 2879.34t + 53\,081.364$

c. $t = 24$; Predicted $= \$122\,185.52$

d. The average salary has increased by $2879.34 per year over the time period.

39. a.

	I	II	III	IV		
			0.898065	0.52859		
	1.480355	1.108005	0.893401	0.493703		
	1.505646	1.105853				
Total	2.986001	2.213858	1.791466	1.022292		Correct Factor
Mean	1.493001	1.106929	0.895733	0.511146	4.006809	0.998301
Adj	1.490464	1.105048	0.894211	0.510278		
Index	149.0464	110.5048	89.42107	51.02776		

b. The company does most of their business in the winter quarter followed by the spring. The fall quarter has the lowest sales.

41. If sales are the same each month, monthly sales $= (825\,000/12) = \$68\,750$.

For Feb: $68\,750(126.9/100) = \$87\,244$; for Mar: $68\,750(86.3/100) = \$59\,331$.

43. a.

t	Year	Quarter	Units	Seasonal Indexes	Desesonalized Units
1	2014	1	1234	102.89	1199
2	2014	2	1300	101.89	1276
3	2014	3	1225	90.32	1356
4	2014	4	1323	104.89	1261
5	2015	1	1334	102.89	1297
6	2015	2	1234	101.89	1211
7	2015	3	1134	90.32	1256
8	2015	4	1450	104.89	1382
9	2016	1	1511	102.89	1469
10	2016	2	1496	101.89	1468
11	2016	3	1300	90.32	1439
12	2016	4	1545	104.89	1473
13	2017	1	1434	102.89	1394
14	2017	2	1576	101.89	1547
15	2017	3	1356	90.32	1501
16	2017	4	1598	104.89	1523

b. $y' = 1201.0216 + 20.8525t$

c. 20.8525 average units over the time period

d.

t	Predicted
17	1556
18	1576
19	1597
20	1618

Chapter 17

1. $EMV(A_1) = 0.30(\$50) + 0.50(\$70) + 0.20(\$100) = \$70$
$EMV(A_2) = 0.30(\$90) + 0.50(\$40) + 0.20(\$80) = \$63$
$EMV(A_3) = 0.30(\$70) + 0.50(\$60) + 0.20(\$90) = \$69$

Decision: Choose alternative 1

3. *Opportunity loss*

	S_1	S_2	S_3
A_1	$40	$ 0	$ 0
A_2	0	30	20
A_3	20	10	10

5. Answers in $000
$EOL(A_1) = 0.30(\$40) + 0.50(\$0) + 0.20(\$0) = \$12$
$EOL(A_2) = 0.30(\$0) + 0.50(\$30) + 0.20(\$20) = \$19$
$EOL(A_3) = 0.30(\$20) + 0.50(\$10) + 0.20(\$10) = \$13$

7. Expected value under conditions of certainty is $82, found by
$0.30(\$90) + 0.50(\$70) + 0.20(\$100)$ $EVPI = \$82 - \$70 = \$12$

9. Yes, it changes the decision. Choose alternative 2 (answers in $000)
$EMV(A_1) = 0.50(\$50) + 0.20(\$70) + 0.30(\$100) = \$69$
$EMV(A_2) = 0.50(\$90) + 0.20(\$40) + 0.30(\$80) = \$77$
$EMV(A_3) = 0.50(\$70) + 0.20(\$60) + 0.30(\$90) = \$74$

11. a. Answers in ($000)
$EMV(neither) = 0.30(\$0) + 0.50(\$0) + 0.20(\$0) = \$0$
$EMV(1)$ $= 0.30(\$125) + 0.50(\$65) + 0.20(\$30) = \$76$
$EMV(2)$ $= 0.30(\$105) + 0.50(\$60) + 0.20(\$30) = \$67.50$
$EMV(both)$ $= 0.30(\$220) + 0.50(\$110) + 0.20(\$40) = \$129$

b. Choose both

c.

	Opportunity loss		
	S_1	S_2	S_3
Neither	$220	$110	$40
1	95	45	10
2	115	50	10
Both	0	0	0

d. $EOL(neither) = 0.30(\$220) + 0.50(\$110) + 0.20(\$40) = \$129.00$
$EOL(1) = 0.30(\$95) + 0.50(\$45) + 0.20(\$10) = \$53.00$
$EOL(2) = 0.30(\$115) + 0.50(\$50) + 0.20(\$10) = \$61.50$
$EOL(both) = 0.30(\$0) + 0.50(\$0) + 0.20(\$0) = \$0$

e. $EVPI = \$0$, found by $\$129 - \$129$
Certainty $= 0.30(\$220) + 0.50(\$110) + 0.20(\$40) = \$129$

13. The payoff table is as follows in $000

	Recession	No Recession
	S_1	S_2
Production	−$10.0	$15.0
Stock	−5.0	12.0
CD	6.0	6.0

a. Purchase CD

b. Increase production

c. (Answers in $000)
$EMV(Prod.) = 0.20(-10) + 0.80(15.0) = 10.0$
$EMV(Stock) = 0.20(-5) + 0.80(12.0) = 8.6$
$EMV(CD) = 0.20(6) + 0.80(6) = 6.0$
Expand Production

d. $EVPI = [0.20(6) + 0.80(15)] - [10.0] = 13.2 - 10.0 = 3.2$

15. a.

	Event				
Act	10	11	12	13	14
10	$500	$500	$500	$500	$500
11	200	550	550	550	550
12	−100	250	600	600	600
13	−400	−50	300	650	650
14	−700	−350	0	350	350

b.

Act	Expected profit
10	$500.00
11	504.50
12	421.50
13	233.50
14	−31.50

Order 11 mobile homes because expected profit of $504.50 is the highest.

c.

	Opportunity Loss				
Supply	10	11	12	13	14
10	$0	$50	$100	$150	$200
11	300	0	50	100	150
12	600	300	0	50	100
13	900	600	300	0	50
14	1200	900	600	300	0

	Act				
	10	11	12	13	14
Expect. Opp. Loss	$95.50	$91	$174	$362	$627

d. Decision: Order 11 homes because the opportunity loss of $91 is the smallest.

e. $91, found by $595.50 − 504.50 = $91.00 value of perfect information

17. a.

	Event					
Act	41	42	43	44	45	46
41	$410	$410	$410	$410	$410	$410
42	405	420	420	420	420	420
43	400	415	430	430	430	430
44	395	410	425	440	440	440
45	390	405	420	435	450	450
46	385	400	415	430	445	460

b. Expected profits are:

Act	Expected Payoff
41	$410.00
42	419.10
43	426.70
44	432.20
45	431.70
46	427.45

c. Order 44 because $432.20 is the largest expected profit.

d. Expected opportunity loss:

41	42	43	44	45	46
$28.30	$19.20	$11.60	$6.10	$6.60	$10.85

e. Order 44 because the opportunity loss of $6.10 is the smallest. Yes, it agrees.

f. $6.10, found by $438.30 − $432.20 = $6.10 value of perfect information
The maximum we should pay for perfect information is $6.10.

19. a.

	Event			
Option	100	300	500	700
1	$29.99	$39.99	$59.99	$79.99
2	34.99	34.99	44.99	64.99
3	59.99	59.99	59.99	59.99

b. Expected costs are:

Option	Expected Cost	
1	$52.49	found by 0.25(29.99) + 0.25(39.99) + .25(59.99) + 0.25(79.99)
2	44.99	found by 0.25(34.99) + 0.25(34.99) + 0.25(44.99) + 0.25(64.99)
3	59.99	found by 0.25(59.99) + 0.25(59.99) + 0.25(59.99) + 0.25(59.99)

Option 2 is best.

c. Option 1, because 29.99 is lower than 34.99 or 59.99.

d. Option 3, because 59.99 is lower than 79.99 or 64.99.

e.

	Event			
Option	100	300	500	700
1	$0	$5	$15	$20
2	5	0	0	5
3	30	25	15	0

f. Option 2, because 5 is lower than 20 or 30.

g. $EVPI = 44.99 - [0.25(29.99) + 0.25(34.99) + 0.25(44.99) + 0.25(59.99)]$
$= 44.99 - 42.49 = 2.50$

21. $EMV(A_1) = 0.35(\$150) + 0.45(\$170) + 0.20(\$125) = \$154.00$
$EMV(A_2) = 0.35(\$120) + 0.45(\$140) + 0.20(\$180) = \$141.00$
$EMV(A_3) = 0.35(\$85) + 0.45(\$105) + 0.20(\$90) = \$95.00$
Decision: Choose alternative 1

23. **Opportunity loss**

	S_1	S_2	S_3
A_1	$0	$0	$55
A_2	30	30	0
A_3	65	65	90

25. $EOL(A_1) = 0.35(\$0) + 0.45(\$0) + 0.20(\$55) = \$11.00$
$EOL(A_2) = 0.35(\$30) + 0.45(\$30) + 0.20(\$0) = \$24.00$
$EOL(A_3) = 0.35(\$65) + 0.45(\$65) + 0.20(\$90) = \$70.00$

27. Certainty $= 0.35(150) + 0.45(170) + 0.20(180) = \$165$
$EMV(A_1) = 0.35(\$150) + 0.45(\$170) + 0.20(\$125) = \$154.00$
$EMV(A_2) = 0.35(\$120) + 0.45(\$140) + 0.20(\$180) = \$141.00$
$EMV(A_3) = 0.35(\$85) + 0.45(\$105) + 0.20(\$90) = \$95.00$
EVPI $= \$165 - 154 = \$11$

29. Certainty $= 0.5(150) + 0.20(170) + 0.30(180) = \$163.00$
$EMV(A_1) = 0.5(\$150) + 0.20(\$170) + 0.30(\$125) = \$146.50$
$EMV(A_2) = 0.5(\$120) + 0.20(\$140) + 0.30(\$180) = \$142.00$
$EMV(A_3) = 0.5(\$85) + 0.20(\$105) + 0.30(\$90) = \$90.50$
EVPI $= \$163 - 146.50 = \$16.50$

Appendix A

A.2: Solutions to Practice Tests

Practice Test—Chapter 1

Part I

1. Statistics
2. Descriptive statistics
3. Statistical inference
4. Sample
5. Population
6. Nominal
7. Ratio
8. Ordinal
9. Interval
10. Discrete
11. Nominal
12. Nominal

Practice Test—Chapter 2

Part I

1. Frequency table
2. Frequency distribution
3. Bar chart
4. Pie chart
5. Histogram or frequency polygon
6. 7
7. Class interval
8. Midpoint
9. Total number of observations
10. Upper class limits

Part II

1. a. $30
   b. 105
   c. 52
   d. 0.19
   e. $165
   f. $120, $330
   g.

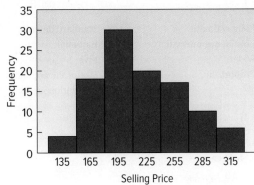

h.

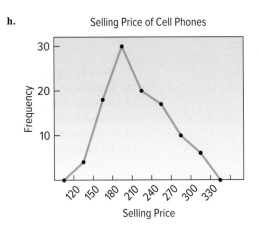

Selling Price of Cell Phones

Practice Test—Chapter 3

Part I

1. Parameter
2. Statistic
3. Zero
4. Median
5. 50%
6. Mode
7. Range
8. Variance
9. Variance
10. Never
11. Median
12. Normal rule or empirical rule
13. Box plot
14. Quartile
15. Percentile
16. Skewness
17. First quartile
18. Inter-quartile range

Part II

1. a. Sample mean $= 508/7 = 72.57$
   b. Median $= 74.00$
   c. Range $= 80 - 54 = 16$
   d. $s = \sqrt{\dfrac{239.714}{7-1}} = 6.32$

2. Weighted mean $= \dfrac{200(\$36) + 300(\$40) + 500(\$50)}{200 + 300 + 500} = \$44.20$

3. $20.88 \pm 2(1.41) = 20.88 \pm 2.82 = 23.70$

4. a. $L_{50} = (11 + 1)\dfrac{50}{100} = 6$; median $= 35$
   b. $L_{25} = (11 + 1)\dfrac{25}{100} = 3$; $Q_1 = 23$
   c. $L_{75} = (11 + 1)\dfrac{75}{100} = 9$; $Q_3 = 91$

d.

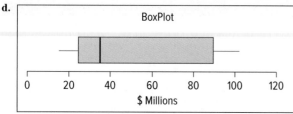

BoxPlot

$ Millions

Practice Test—Chapter 4

Part I

1. Probability
2. Experiment
3. Event
4. Relative frequency
5. Subjective
6. Classical
7. Mutually exclusive
8. Exhaustive
9. Mutually exclusive
10. Complement rule
11. Joint probability
12. Independent

Part II

1. **a.** P (both) $= \left(\frac{5}{20}\right)\left(\frac{4}{19}\right) = 0.0526$

   b. P (at least 1) $= 1 - P$ (neither)
   $$= 1 - \left(\frac{15}{20}\right)\left(\frac{4}{19}\right)$$
   $$= 1 - 0.5526 = 0.4474$$

2. P (at least 1) $= P$ (jogs) $+ P$ (bikes) $- P$ (both)
   $$= 0.30 + 0.20 - 0.12 = 0.38$$

3. $5! = 120$

Practice Test—Chapter 5

Part I

1. Probability distribution
2. Probability
3. One
4. Mean
5. Two
6. Never
7. Equal
8. Binomial
9. 0.075
10. 0.183

Part II

1. **a.** Binomial

   b. $P(x = 1) = {}_{16}C_1 (0.15)^1 (0.85)^{15} = (16)(0.15)(0.0874) = 0.210$

   c. $P(x = 1) = 1 - P(x - 0) = 1 - {}_{16}C_0 (0.15)^0 (0.85)^{16} = 0.9257$

2. **a.** Poisson

   b. $P(x = 3) = \dfrac{3^3 e^{-3}}{3!} = \dfrac{9}{6(20.0855)} = 0.224$

   c. $P(x = 0) = \dfrac{3^0 e^{-3}}{0!} = 0.050$

   d. $P(x = 1) = 1 - P(x = 0) = 1 - 0.050 = 0.950$

3.

Errors Found (x)	P(x)	xP(x)	$(x - \mu)^2 P(x)$
1	20	0.2	0.288
2	50	1	0.02
3	20	0.6	0.128
4	10	0.4	0.324
		2.2	0.76

   a. $\mu = 1(0.2) + 2(0.5) + 3(0.2) + 4(0.1) = 2.2$

   b. Variance = 0.76 (see chart above)

Practice Test—Chapter 6

Part I

1. One
2. Infinite
3. Discrete
4. Always equal
5. Infinite
6. One
7. All of them
8. 0.2764
9. 0.9396
10. 0.0450

Part II

1. **a.** $z = \dfrac{2000 - 1600}{850} = 0.47; P(0 \leq z < 0.47) = 0.1808$

   b. $z = \dfrac{900 - 1600}{850} = -0.82; P(-0.82 \leq z \leq 0.47)$
   $$= 0.2939 + 0.1808 = 0.4747$$

   c. $z = \dfrac{1800 - 1600}{850} = 0.24; P(0.24 \leq z \leq 0.47)$
   $$= 0.1808 - 0.0948 = 0.0860$$

   d. $1.645 = \dfrac{x - 1600}{850}$
   $$x = 1600 + 1.645(850) = 2998$$

Practice Test—Chapter 7

Part I

1. Random sample
2. No size restriction
3. Strata
4. Sampling error
5. Sampling distribution
6. 120
7. Standard error of the mean
8. Always equal
9. Decrease
10. Normal distribution of sample means

Part II

1. $z = \dfrac{11 - 12.2}{2.3/12} = -1.81$

   $P(z < -1.81) = 0.5000 - 0.4649 = 0.0351$

Practice Test—Chapter 8

Part I

1. Point estimate
2. Confidence interval
3. Wider
4. Proportion
5. 95
6. Standard deviation
7. Binomial
8. Five
9. Size of the population
10. Population mean

Part II

1. **a.** Unknown

   b. 9.3 years

   c. $\dfrac{2.0}{\sqrt{26}} = 0.392$

   d. $9.3 \pm 1.708(0.392) = (8.63, 9.97)$

2. $n = \left(\frac{2.33}{0.02}\right)^2 (0.27)(1 - 0.27) = 2676$

3. $0.64 \pm 1.96 \sqrt{\frac{0.64(1 - 0.64)}{100}} = (0.546, 0.734)$

Practice Test—Chapter 9

Part I

1. Null hypothesis
2. Accept
3. Significant level
4. Test statistic
5. Critical value
6. Two
7. Standard deviation (or variance)
8. p-value
9. Binomial
10. Five

Part II

1. $H_0: \mu \leq 90, H_1: \mu > 90$
   $df = 18 - 1 = 17$
   Reject H_0 if $t > 2.567$
   $t = (96 - 90)/\left(12/\sqrt{18}\right) = 2.121$
   Do not reject H_0. We cannot conclude that the mean time in the park is more than 90 minutes.

2. $H_0: \mu \leq 485, H_1: \mu > 485$
   Reject H_0 if $z > 1.645$
   We assume a 0.05 significance level.
   $z = \frac{489.97 - 485}{13.43/\sqrt{25}} = 1.85$
   Reject H_0. The mean weight is more than 485 g.

3. $H_0: p \geq 0.67, H_1: p < 0.67$
   Reject H_0 if $z < -1.645$
   $z = \frac{\frac{180}{300} - 0.67}{\sqrt{\frac{0.67(1 - 0.67)}{300}}} = -2.578$
   Reject H_0. Less than 0.67 of the couples seek their mate's approval.

Practice Test—Chapter 10

Part I

1. Zero
2. z
3. Proportion
4. Population standard deviation
5. Difference
6. t distribution
7. Samples or parameters estimated
8. Paired
9. Independent
10. Dependent samples

Part II

1. $H_0: \mu_1 - \mu_2 = 0; H_1: \mu_1 - \mu_2 \neq 0; df = 14 + 12 - 2 = 24$
   Reject H_0 if $t < 2.064$ or $t > 2.064$
   $s_p^2 = \frac{(14 - 1)(30)^2 + (12 - 1)(40)^2}{14 + 12 - 2} = 1220.83$
   $t = \frac{837 - 797}{\sqrt{1220.83\left(\frac{1}{14} + \frac{1}{12}\right)}} = \frac{40.0}{13.7455} = 2.910$
   Reject H_0. There is a difference in the mean kilometres travelled.

2. $H_0: p_1 - p_2 = 0; p_1 - p_2 \neq 0$
   Reject H_0 if $z < 1.96$ or $z > 1.96$
   $P_c \frac{128 + 149}{300 + 400} = \frac{277}{700} = 0.396$
   $z = \frac{\frac{128}{300} - \frac{149}{400}}{\sqrt{\frac{0.396(1 - 0.396)}{300} + \frac{0.396(1 - 0.396)}{400}}} = \frac{0.054}{0.037} = 1.459$
   Do not reject H_0. There is no difference on the proportion that liked the soap in the two cities.

Practice Test—Chapter 11

Part I

1. F distribution
2. Positively skewed
3. Variances
4. Means
5. Population standard deviations
6. Error or Residual
7. Equal
8. Degrees of freedom
9. Variances
10. Independent

Part II

1. $H_0: \sigma_1^2 - \sigma_2^2 = 0$
   $H_1: \sigma_1^2 - \sigma_2^2 \neq 0$
   $df_1 = 12 - 1 = 11; df_2 = 14 - 1 = 13$
   Reject H_0 if $F > 2.635$
   $F = \frac{(40)^2}{(30)^2} 1.78$
   There is not enough evidence to reject H_0. We cannot conclude there is a difference in the variation of the number of kilometres travelled.

2. **a.** 3
   b. 21
   c. 3.55
   d. $H_0: \mu_1 = \mu_2 = \mu_3$
   H_1: not all treatment means are the same.
   e. Reject H_0
   f. The treatment means are not the same.

Practice Test—Chapter 12

Part I

1. Scatter diagram
2. -1 and 1
3. Less than zero
4. Coefficient of determination
5. t
6. Predicted or fitted
7. Sign
8. Larger
9. Error
10. Independent

Part II

1. a.

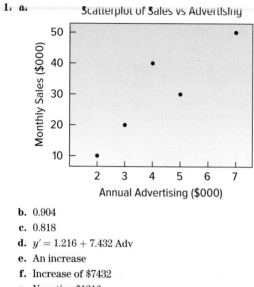

Scatterplot of Sales vs Advertising

(Monthly Sales ($000) vs Annual Advertising ($000))

b. 0.904

c. 0.818

d. $y' = 1.216 + 7.432$ Adv

e. An increase

f. Increase of \$7432

g. Negative \$1216

h. \$34 660, found by: $y' = 1.216 + 7.432 (4.5)$

Practice Test—Chapter 13

Part I

1. Independent variables
2. Least squares
3. Mean square error
4. Independent variable
5. Independent variable
6. Different from zero
7. F distribution
8. t distribution
9. Linearity
10. Correlated
11. Dummy variable

Part II

1. a. Four

b. $y' = 70.06 + 0.42x_1 + 0.27x_2 + + 0.75x_3 + 0.42x_4$

c. $R^2 = 1050.8/1134.6 = 0.926$

d. $s_{e.1234} = \sqrt{4.19} = 2.05$

e. $H_0: \beta_1 = \beta_2 = \beta_3 = \beta_4 = 0$

H_1: not all of the β's are 0.

Reject H_0 if $F > 2.87$

$F = 262.70/4.19 = 62.70$

Reject H_0. Not all the regression coefficients equal zero.

f. $H_0: \beta_1 = 0; \beta_1 \neq 0$; Reject H_0 if $t < -2.086$ or $t > 2.086$

$t = 2.47$. Reject H_0

$H_0: \beta_2 = 0; H_1: \beta_2 \neq 0; t = 1.29$. Do not reject H_0.

$H_0: \beta_3 = 0; H_1: \beta_3 \neq 0; t = 2.50$. Reject H_0.

$H_0: \beta_4 = 0; H_1: \beta_4 \neq 0; t = 6.00$. Reject H_0.

Conclusion. Drop variable 2, and rerun the model.

Practice Test—Chapter 14

Part I

1. Nominal
2. No assumption
3. At least 30 observations
4. Two
5. 6
6. Independent
7. 4
8. The same
9. 9.488
10. Degrees of freedom

Part II

1. H_0: There is no difference between the school district and census data.

H_1: There is a difference between the school district and census data.

Reject H_0 if $\chi^2 > 7.815$

$$\frac{(120 - 130)^2}{130} + \frac{(40 - 40)^2}{40} + \frac{(30 - 20)^2}{20} + \frac{(10 - 10)^2}{10} = 5.76$$

Do not reject H_0. There is no difference between the census and school district data.

2. H_0: Gender and book type are independent.

H_1: Gender and book type are related.

Reject H_0 if $\chi^2 > 5.991$

$$\frac{(250 - 197.31)^2}{197.31} + \cdots \frac{(200 - 187.5)^2}{187.5} = 54.842$$

Reject H_0. Men and women read different types of books.

Practice Test—Chapter 15

Part I

1. Denominator
2. Index
3. Quantity
4. Base period
5. $1992 = 100.0$

Part II

1. a.

Year	Sales	Index	Found by
2013	\$130 000	100.0	(130 000/130 000)*100
2014	145 000	111.5	(145 000/130 000)*100
2015	120 000	92.3	(120 000/130 000)*100
2016	170 000	130.8	(170 000/130 000)*100
2017	190 000	146.2	(190 000/130 000)*100

b. average = 137 500

Year	Sales	Index	Found by
2013	\$130 000	94.5	(130 000/137 500)*100
2014	145 000	105.5	(145 000/137 500)*100
2015	120 000	87.3	(120 000/137 500)*100
2016	170 000	123.6	(170 000/137 500)*100
2017	190 000	138.2	(190 000/137 500)*100

2. a. 108.9, found by: (1100/1010)*100

b. 111.2, found by: (4525/4070)*100

c. 110.2, found by: (5400/4900)*100

d. 132.7, found by: (5400/4070)*100

Practice Test—Chapter 16

Part I

1. Trend
2. Moving average
3. Residual
4. Same

Part II

1. For January of the 5th year, the seasonally adjusted forecast is 70.0875, found by: $1.05(5.50 + 1.25 \times 49)$. For February of the 5th year, the seasonally adjusted forecast is 66.844, found by: $0.983(5.50 + 1.25 \times 50)$.

Appendix B.1

Areas under the Normal Curve

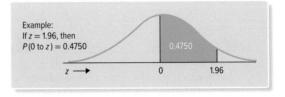

Example:
If $z = 1.96$, then
$P(0 \text{ to } z) = 0.4750$

0.4750

$z \longrightarrow$ 0   1.96

z	0.00	0.01	0.02	0.03	0.04	0.05	0.06	0.07	0.08	0.09
0.0	0.0000	0.0040	0.0080	0.0120	0.0160	0.0199	0.0239	0.0279	0.0319	0.0359
0.1	0.0398	0.0438	0.0478	0.0517	0.0557	0.0596	0.0636	0.0675	0.0714	0.0753
0.2	0.0793	0.0832	0.0871	0.0910	0.0948	0.0987	0.1026	0.1064	0.1103	0.1141
0.3	0.1179	0.1217	0.1255	0.1293	0.1331	0.1368	0.1406	0.1443	0.1480	0.1517
0.4	0.1554	0.1591	0.1628	0.1664	0.1700	0.1736	0.1772	0.1808	0.1844	0.1879
0.5	0.1915	0.1950	0.1985	0.2019	0.2054	0.2088	0.2123	0.2157	0.2190	0.2224
0.6	0.2257	0.2291	0.2324	0.2357	0.2389	0.2422	0.2454	0.2486	0.2517	0.2549
0.7	0.2580	0.2611	0.2642	0.2673	0.2704	0.2734	0.2764	0.2794	0.2823	0.2852
0.8	0.2881	0.2910	0.2939	0.2967	0.2995	0.3023	0.3051	0.3078	0.3106	0.3133
0.9	0.3159	0.3186	0.3212	0.3238	0.3264	0.3289	0.3315	0.3340	0.3365	0.3389
1.0	0.3413	0.3438	0.3461	0.3485	0.3508	0.3531	0.3554	0.3577	0.3599	0.3621
1.1	0.3643	0.3665	0.3686	0.3708	0.3729	0.3749	0.3770	0.3790	0.3810	0.383
1.2	0.3849	0.3869	0.3888	0.3907	0.3925	0.3944	0.3962	0.3980	0.3997	0.4015
1.3	0.4032	0.4049	0.4066	0.4082	0.4099	0.4115	0.4131	0.4147	0.4162	0.4177
1.4	0.4192	0.4207	0.4222	0.4236	0.4251	0.4265	0.4279	0.4292	0.4306	0.4319
1.5	0.4332	0.4345	0.4357	0.4370	0.4382	0.4394	0.4406	0.4418	0.4429	0.4441
1.6	0.4452	0.4463	0.4474	0.4484	0.4495	0.4505	0.4515	0.4525	0.4535	0.4545
1.7	0.4554	0.4564	0.4573	0.4582	0.4591	0.4599	0.4608	0.4616	0.4625	0.4633
1.8	0.4641	0.4649	0.4656	0.4664	0.4671	0.4678	0.4686	0.4693	0.4699	0.4706
1.9	0.4713	0.4719	0.4726	0.4732	0.4738	0.4744	0.4750	0.4756	0.4761	0.4767
2.0	0.4772	0.4778	0.4783	0.4788	0.4793	0.4798	0.4803	0.4808	0.4812	0.4817
2.1	0.4821	0.4826	0.4830	0.4834	0.4838	0.4842	0.4846	0.4850	0.4854	0.4857
2.2	0.4861	0.4864	0.4868	0.4871	0.4875	0.4878	0.4881	0.4884	0.4887	0.4890
2.3	0.4893	0.4896	0.4898	0.4901	0.4904	0.4906	0.4909	0.4911	0.4913	0.4916
2.4	0.4918	0.4920	0.4922	0.4925	0.4927	0.4929	0.4931	0.4932	0.4934	0.4936
2.5	0.4938	0.4940	0.4941	0.4943	0.4945	0.4946	0.4948	0.4949	0.4951	0.4952
2.6	0.4953	0.4955	0.4956	0.4957	0.4959	0.4960	0.4961	0.4962	0.4963	0.4964
2.7	0.4965	0.4966	0.4967	0.4968	0.4969	0.4970	0.4971	0.4972	0.4973	0.4974
2.8	0.4974	0.4975	0.4976	0.4977	0.4977	0.4978	0.4979	0.4979	0.4980	0.4981
2.9	0.4981	0.4982	0.4982	0.4983	0.4984	0.4984	0.4985	0.4985	0.4986	0.4986
3.0	0.4987	0.4987	0.4987	0.4988	0.4988	0.4989	0.4989	0.4989	0.4990	0.4990

Student's *t* Distribution

Confidence interval

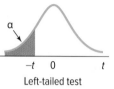

Left-tailed test

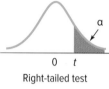

Right-tailed test

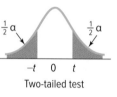

Two-tailed test

	Confidence Intervals, *c*					
	80%	**90%**	**95%**	**98%**	**99%**	**99.9%**
	Level of Significance for One-Tailed Test, α					
df	**0.10**	**0.05**	**0.025**	**0.01**	**0.005**	**0.0005**
	Level of Significance for Two-Tailed Test, α					
	0.20	**0.10**	**0.05**	**0.02**	**0.01**	**0.001**
1	3.078	6.314	12.706	31.821	63.657	636.619
2	1.886	2.920	4.303	6.965	9.925	31.599
3	1.638	2.353	3.182	4.541	5.841	12.924
4	1.533	2.132	2.776	3.747	4.604	8.610
5	1.476	2.015	2.571	3.365	4.032	6.869
6	1.440	1.943	2.447	3.143	3.707	5.959
7	1.415	1.895	2.365	2.998	3.499	5.408
8	1.397	1.860	2.306	2.896	3.355	5.041
9	1.383	1.833	2.262	2.821	3.250	4.781
10	1.372	1.812	2.228	2.764	3.169	4.587
11	1.363	1.796	2.201	2.718	3.106	4.437
12	1.356	1.782	2.179	2.681	3.055	4.318
13	1.350	1.771	2.160	2.650	3.012	4.221
14	1.345	1.761	2.145	2.624	2.977	4.140
15	1.341	1.753	2.131	2.602	2.947	4.073
16	1.337	1.746	2.120	2.583	2.921	4.015
17	1.333	1.740	2.110	2.567	2.898	3.965
18	1.330	1.734	2.101	2.552	2.878	3.922
19	1.328	1.729	2.093	2.539	2.861	3.883
20	1.325	1.725	2.086	2.528	2.845	3.850
21	1.323	1.721	2.080	2.518	2.831	3.819
22	1.321	1.717	2.074	2.508	2.819	3.792
23	1.319	1.714	2.069	2.500	2.807	3.768
24	1.318	1.711	2.064	2.492	2.797	3.745
25	1.316	1.708	2.060	2.485	2.787	3.725
26	1.315	1.706	2.056	2.479	2.779	3.707
27	1.314	1.703	2.052	2.473	2.771	3.690
28	1.313	1.701	2.048	2.467	2.763	3.674
29	1.311	1.699	2.045	2.462	2.756	3.659
30	1.310	1.697	2.042	2.457	2.750	3.646
31	1.309	1.696	2.040	2.453	2.744	3.633
32	1.309	1.694	2.037	2.449	2.738	3.622
33	1.308	1.692	2.035	2.445	2.733	3.611
34	1.307	1.691	2.032	2.441	2.728	3.601
35	1.306	1.690	2.030	2.438	2.724	3.591

	Confidence Intervals, *c*					
	80%	**90%**	**95%**	**98%**	**99%**	**99.9%**
	Level of Significance for One-Tailed Test, α					
df	**0.10**	**0.05**	**0.025**	**0.01**	**0.005**	**0.0005**
	Level of Significance for Two-Tailed Test, α					
	0.20	**0.10**	**0.05**	**0.02**	**0.01**	**0.001**
36	1.306	1.688	2.028	2.434	2.719	3.582
37	1.305	1.687	2.026	2.431	2.715	3.574
38	1.304	1.686	2.024	2.429	2.712	3.566
39	1.304	1.685	2.023	2.426	2.708	3.558
40	1.303	1.684	2.021	2.423	2.704	3.551
41	1.303	1.683	2.020	2.421	2.701	3.544
42	1.302	1.682	2.018	2.418	2.698	3.538
43	1.302	1.681	2.017	2.416	2.695	3.532
44	1.301	1.680	2.015	2.414	2.692	3.526
45	1.301	1.679	2.014	2.412	2.690	3.520
46	1.300	1.679	2.013	2.410	2.687	3.515
47	1.300	1.678	2.012	2.408	2.685	3.510
48	1.299	1.677	2.011	2.407	2.682	3.505
49	1.299	1.677	2.010	2.405	2.680	3.500
50	1.299	1.676	2.009	2.403	2.678	3.496
51	1.298	1.675	2.008	2.402	2.676	3.492
52	1.298	1.675	2.007	2.400	2.674	3.488
53	1.298	1.674	2.006	2.399	2.672	3.484
54	1.297	1.674	2.005	2.397	2.670	3.480
55	1.297	1.673	2.004	2.396	2.668	3.476
56	1.297	1.673	2.003	2.395	2.667	3.473
57	1.297	1.672	2.002	2.394	2.665	3.470
58	1.296	1.672	2.002	2.392	2.663	3.466
59	1.296	1.671	2.001	2.391	2.662	3.463
60	1.296	1.671	2.000	2.390	2.660	3.460
61	1.296	1.670	2.000	2.389	2.659	3.457
62	1.295	1.670	1.999	2.388	2.657	3.454
63	1.295	1.669	1.998	2.387	2.656	3.452
64	1.295	1.669	1.998	2.386	2.655	3.449
65	1.295	1.669	1.997	2.385	2.654	3.447
66	1.295	1.668	1.997	2.384	2.652	3.444
67	1.294	1.668	1.996	2.383	2.651	3.442
68	1.294	1.668	1.995	2.382	2.650	3.439
69	1.294	1.667	1.995	2.382	2.649	3.437
70	1.294	1.667	1.994	2.381	2.648	3.435

Appendix B.2

Student's *t* Distribution *(concluded)*

df	Confidence Intervals, *c*						df	Confidence Intervals, *c*					
	80%	90%	95%	98%	99%	99.9%		80%	90%	95%	98%	99%	99.9%
	Level of Significance for One-Tailed Test, α							Level of Significance for One-Tailed Test, α					
df	0.10	0.05	0.025	0.01	0.005	0.0005	df	0.10	0.05	0.025	0.01	0.005	0.0005
	Level of Significance for Two-Tailed Test, α							Level of Significance for Two-Tailed Test, α					
	0.20	0.10	0.05	0.02	0.01	0.001		0.20	0.10	0.05	0.02	0.01	0.001
71	1.294	1.667	1.994	2.380	2.647	3.433	89	1.291	1.662	1.987	2.369	2.632	3.403
72	1.293	1.666	1.993	2.379	2.646	3.431	90	1.291	1.662	1.987	2.368	2.632	3.402
73	1.293	1.666	1.993	2.379	2.645	3.429	91	1.291	1.662	1.986	2.368	2.631	3.401
74	1.293	1.666	1.993	2.378	2.644	3.427	92	1.291	1.662	1.986	2.368	2.630	3.399
75	1.293	1.665	1.992	2.377	2.643	3.425	93	1.291	1.661	1.986	2.367	2.630	3.398
76	1.293	1.665	1.992	2.376	2.642	3.423	94	1.291	1.661	1.986	2.367	2.629	3.397
77	1.293	1.665	1.991	2.376	2.641	3.421	95	1.291	1.661	1.985	2.366	2.629	3.396
78	1.292	1.665	1.991	2.375	2.640	3.420	96	1.290	1.661	1.985	2.366	2.628	3.395
79	1.292	1.664	1.990	2.374	2.640	3.418	97	1.290	1.661	1.985	2.365	2.627	3.394
80	1.292	1.664	1.990	2.374	2.639	3.416	98	1.290	1.661	1.984	2.365	2.627	3.393
81	1.292	1.664	1.990	2.373	2.638	3.415	99	1.290	1.660	1.984	2.365	2.626	3.392
82	1.292	1.664	1.989	2.373	2.637	3.413	100	1.290	1.660	1.984	2.364	2.626	3.390
83	1.292	1.663	1.989	2.372	2.636	3.412	120	1.289	1.658	1.980	2.358	2.617	3.373
84	1.292	1.663	1.989	2.372	2.636	3.410	140	1.288	1.656	1.977	2.353	2.611	3.361
85	1.292	1.663	1.988	2.371	2.635	3.409	160	1.287	1.654	1.975	2.350	2.607	3.352
86	1.291	1.663	1.988	2.370	2.634	3.407	180	1.286	1.653	1.973	2.347	2.603	3.345
87	1.291	1.663	1.988	2.370	2.634	3.406	200	1.286	1.653	1.972	2.345	2.601	3.340
88	1.291	1.662	1.987	2.369	2.633	3.405	∞	1.282	1.645	1.960	2.326	2.576	3.291

Appendix B.3

Binomial Probability Distribution

n = 1
Probability

x	0.05	0.10	0.20	0.30	0.40	0.50	0.60	0.70	0.80	0.90	0.95
0	0.950	0.900	0.800	0.700	0.600	0.500	0.400	0.300	0.200	0.100	0.050
1	0.050	0.100	0.200	0.300	0.400	0.500	0.600	0.700	0.800	0.900	0.950

n = 2
Probability

x	0.05	0.10	0.20	0.30	0.40	0.50	0.60	0.70	0.80	0.90	0.95
0	0.903	0.810	0.640	0.490	0.360	0.250	0.160	0.090	0.040	0.010	0.003
1	0.095	0.180	0.320	0.420	0.480	0.500	0.480	0.420	0.320	0.180	0.095
2	0.003	0.010	0.040	0.090	0.160	0.250	0.360	0.490	0.640	0.810	0.903

n = 3
Probability

x	0.05	0.10	0.20	0.30	0.40	0.50	0.60	0.70	0.80	0.90	0.95
0	0.857	0.729	0.512	0.343	0.216	0.125	0.064	0.027	0.008	0.001	0.000
1	0.135	0.243	0.384	0.441	0.432	0.375	0.288	0.189	0.096	0.027	0.007
2	0.007	0.027	0.096	0.189	0.288	0.375	0.432	0.441	0.384	0.243	0.135
3	0.000	0.001	0.008	0.027	0.064	0.125	0.216	0.343	0.512	0.729	0.857

n = 4
Probability

x	0.05	0.10	0.20	0.30	0.40	0.50	0.60	0.70	0.80	0.90	0.95
0	0.815	0.656	0.410	0.240	0.130	0.063	0.026	0.008	0.002	0.000	0.000
1	0.171	0.292	0.410	0.412	0.346	0.250	0.154	0.076	0.026	0.004	0.000
2	0.014	0.049	0.154	0.265	0.346	0.375	0.346	0.265	0.154	0.049	0.014
3	0.000	0.004	0.026	0.076	0.154	0.250	0.346	0.412	0.410	0.292	0.171
4	0.000	0.000	0.002	0.008	0.026	0.063	0.130	0.240	0.410	0.656	0.815

n = 5
Probability

x	0.05	0.10	0.20	0.30	0.40	0.50	0.60	0.70	0.80	0.90	0.95
0	0.774	0.590	0.328	0.168	0.078	0.031	0.010	0.002	0.000	0.000	0.000
1	0.204	0.328	0.410	0.360	0.259	0.156	0.077	0.028	0.006	0.000	0.000
2	0.021	0.073	0.205	0.309	0.346	0.313	0.230	0.132	0.051	0.008	0.001
3	0.001	0.008	0.051	0.132	0.230	0.313	0.346	0.309	0.205	0.073	0.021
4	0.000	0.000	0.006	0.028	0.077	0.156	0.259	0.360	0.410	0.328	0.204
5	0.000	0.000	0.000	0.002	0.010	0.031	0.078	0.168	0.328	0.590	0.774

Binomial Probability Distribution *(continued)*

n = 6
Probability

x	0.05	0.10	0.20	0.30	0.40	0.50	0.60	0.70	0.80	0.90	0.95
0	0.735	0.531	0.262	0.118	0.047	0.016	0.004	0.001	0.000	0.000	0.000
1	0.232	0.354	0.393	0.303	0.187	0.094	0.037	0.010	0.002	0.000	0.000
2	0.031	0.098	0.246	0.324	0.311	0.234	0.138	0.060	0.015	0.001	0.000
3	0.002	0.015	0.082	0.185	0.276	0.313	0.276	0.185	0.082	0.015	0.002
4	0.000	0.001	0.015	0.060	0.138	0.234	0.311	0.324	0.246	0.098	0.031
5	0.000	0.000	0.002	0.010	0.037	0.094	0.187	0.303	0.393	0.354	0.232
6	0.000	0.000	0.000	0.001	0.004	0.016	0.047	0.118	0.262	0.531	0.735

n = 7
Probability

x	0.05	0.10	0.20	0.30	0.40	0.50	0.60	0.70	0.80	0.90	0.95
0	0.698	0.478	0.210	0.082	0.028	0.008	0.002	0.000	0.000	0.000	0.000
1	0.257	0.372	0.367	0.247	0.131	0.055	0.017	0.004	0.000	0.000	0.000
2	0.041	0.124	0.275	0.318	0.261	0.164	0.077	0.025	0.004	0.000	0.000
3	0.004	0.023	0.115	0.227	0.290	0.273	0.194	0.097	0.029	0.003	0.000
4	0.000	0.003	0.029	0.097	0.194	0.273	0.290	0.227	0.115	0.023	0.004
5	0.000	0.000	0.004	0.025	0.077	0.164	0.261	0.318	0.275	0.124	0.041
6	0.000	0.000	0.000	0.004	0.017	0.055	0.131	0.247	0.367	0.372	0.257
7	0.000	0.000	0.000	0.000	0.002	0.008	0.028	0.082	0.210	0.478	0.698

n = 8
Probability

x	0.05	0.10	0.20	0.30	0.40	0.50	0.60	0.70	0.80	0.90	0.95
0	0.663	0.430	0.168	0.058	0.017	0.004	0.001	0.000	0.000	0.000	0.000
1	0.279	0.383	0.336	0.198	0.090	0.031	0.008	0.001	0.000	0.000	0.000
2	0.051	0.149	0.294	0.296	0.209	0.109	0.041	0.010	0.001	0.000	0.000
3	0.005	0.033	0.147	0.254	0.279	0.219	0.124	0.047	0.009	0.000	0.000
4	0.000	0.005	0.046	0.136	0.232	0.273	0.232	0.136	0.046	0.005	0.000
5	0.000	0.000	0.009	0.047	0.124	0.219	0.279	0.254	0.147	0.033	0.005
6	0.000	0.000	0.001	0.010	0.041	0.109	0.209	0.296	0.294	0.149	0.051
7	0.000	0.000	0.000	0.001	0.008	0.031	0.090	0.198	0.336	0.383	0.279
8	0.000	0.000	0.000	0.000	0.001	0.004	0.017	0.058	0.168	0.430	0.663

Binomial Probability Distribution *(continued)*

n = 9
Probability

x	0.05	0.10	0.20	0.30	0.40	0.50	0.60	0.70	0.80	0.90	0.95
0	0.630	0.387	0.134	0.040	0.010	0.002	0.000	0.000	0.000	0.000	0.000
1	0.299	0.387	0.302	0.156	0.060	0.018	0.004	0.000	0.000	0.000	0.000
2	0.063	0.172	0.302	0.267	0.161	0.070	0.021	0.004	0.000	0.000	0.000
3	0.008	0.045	0.176	0.267	0.251	0.164	0.074	0.021	0.003	0.000	0.000
4	0.001	0.007	0.066	0.172	0.251	0.246	0.167	0.074	0.017	0.001	0.000
5	0.000	0.001	0.017	0.074	0.167	0.246	0.251	0.172	0.066	0.007	0.001
6	0.000	0.000	0.003	0.021	0.074	0.164	0.251	0.267	0.176	0.045	0.008
7	0.000	0.000	0.000	0.004	0.021	0.070	0.161	0.267	0.302	0.172	0.063
8	0.000	0.000	0.000	0.000	0.004	0.018	0.060	0.156	0.302	0.387	0.299
9	0.000	0.000	0.000	0.000	0.000	0.002	0.010	0.040	0.134	0.387	0.630

n = 10
Probability

x	0.05	0.10	0.20	0.30	0.40	0.50	0.60	0.70	0.80	0.90	0.95
0	0.599	0.349	0.107	0.028	0.006	0.001	0.000	0.000	0.000	0.000	0.000
1	0.315	0.387	0.268	0.121	0.040	0.010	0.002	0.000	0.000	0.000	0.000
2	0.075	0.194	0.302	0.233	0.121	0.044	0.011	0.001	0.000	0.000	0.000
3	0.010	0.057	0.201	0.267	0.215	0.117	0.042	0.009	0.001	0.000	0.000
4	0.001	0.011	0.088	0.200	0.251	0.205	0.111	0.037	0.006	0.000	0.000
5	0.000	0.001	0.026	0.103	0.201	0.246	0.201	0.103	0.026	0.001	0.000
6	0.000	0.000	0.006	0.037	0.111	0.205	0.251	0.200	0.088	0.011	0.001
7	0.000	0.000	0.001	0.009	0.042	0.117	0.215	0.267	0.201	0.057	0.010
8	0.000	0.000	0.000	0.001	0.011	0.044	0.121	0.233	0.302	0.194	0.075
9	0.000	0.000	0.000	0.000	0.002	0.010	0.040	0.121	0.268	0.387	0.315
10	0.000	0.000	0.000	0.000	0.000	0.001	0.006	0.028	0.107	0.349	0.599

n = 11
Probability

x	0.05	0.10	0.20	0.30	0.40	0.50	0.60	0.70	0.80	0.90	0.95
0	0.569	0.314	0.086	0.020	0.004	0.000	0.000	0.000	0.000	0.000	0.000
1	0.329	0.384	0.236	0.093	0.027	0.005	0.001	0.000	0.000	0.000	0.000
2	0.087	0.213	0.295	0.200	0.089	0.027	0.005	0.001	0.000	0.000	0.000
3	0.014	0.071	0.221	0.257	0.177	0.081	0.023	0.004	0.000	0.000	0.000
4	0.001	0.016	0.111	0.220	0.236	0.161	0.070	0.017	0.002	0.000	0.000
5	0.000	0.002	0.039	0.132	0.221	0.226	0.147	0.057	0.010	0.000	0.000
6	0.000	0.000	0.010	0.057	0.147	0.226	0.221	0.132	0.039	0.002	0.000
7	0.000	0.000	0.002	0.017	0.070	0.161	0.236	0.220	0.111	0.016	0.001
8	0.000	0.000	0.000	0.004	0.023	0.081	0.177	0.257	0.221	0.071	0.014
9	0.000	0.000	0.000	0.001	0.005	0.027	0.089	0.200	0.295	0.213	0.087
10	0.000	0.000	0.000	0.000	0.001	0.005	0.027	0.093	0.236	0.384	0.329
11	0.000	0.000	0.000	0.000	0.000	0.000	0.004	0.020	0.086	0.314	0.569

Appendix B.3

Binomial Probability Distribution (continued)

n = 12
Probability

x	0.05	0.10	0.20	0.30	0.40	0.50	0.60	0.70	0.80	0.90	0.95
0	0.540	0.282	0.069	0.014	0.002	0.000	0.000	0.000	0.000	0.000	0.000
1	0.341	0.377	0.206	0.071	0.017	0.003	0.000	0.000	0.000	0.000	0.000
2	0.099	0.230	0.283	0.168	0.064	0.016	0.002	0.000	0.000	0.000	0.000
3	0.017	0.085	0.236	0.240	0.142	0.054	0.012	0.001	0.000	0.000	0.000
4	0.002	0.021	0.133	0.231	0.213	0.121	0.042	0.008	0.001	0.000	0.000
5	0.000	0.004	0.053	0.158	0.227	0.193	0.101	0.029	0.003	0.000	0.000
6	0.000	0.000	0.016	0.079	0.177	0.226	0.177	0.079	0.016	0.000	0.000
7	0.000	0.000	0.003	0.029	0.101	0.193	0.227	0.158	0.053	0.004	0.000
8	0.000	0.000	0.001	0.008	0.042	0.121	0.213	0.231	0.133	0.021	0.002
9	0.000	0.000	0.000	0.001	0.012	0.054	0.142	0.240	0.236	0.085	0.017
10	0.000	0.000	0.000	0.000	0.002	0.016	0.064	0.168	0.283	0.230	0.099
11	0.000	0.000	0.000	0.000	0.000	0.003	0.017	0.071	0.206	0.377	0.341
12	0.000	0.000	0.000	0.000	0.000	0.000	0.002	0.014	0.069	0.282	0.540

n = 13
Probability

x	0.05	0.10	0.20	0.30	0.40	0.50	0.60	0.70	0.80	0.90	0.95
0	0.513	0.254	0.055	0.010	0.001	0.000	0.000	0.000	0.000	0.000	0.000
1	0.351	0.367	0.179	0.054	0.011	0.002	0.000	0.000	0.000	0.000	0.000
2	0.111	0.245	0.268	0.139	0.045	0.010	0.001	0.000	0.000	0.000	0.000
3	0.021	0.100	0.246	0.218	0.111	0.035	0.006	0.001	0.000	0.000	0.000
4	0.003	0.028	0.154	0.234	0.184	0.087	0.024	0.003	0.000	0.000	0.000
5	0.000	0.006	0.069	0.180	0.221	0.157	0.066	0.014	0.001	0.000	0.000
6	0.000	0.001	0.023	0.103	0.197	0.209	0.131	0.044	0.006	0.000	0.000
7	0.000	0.000	0.006	0.044	0.131	0.209	0.197	0.103	0.023	0.001	0.000
8	0.000	0.000	0.001	0.014	0.066	0.157	0.221	0.180	0.069	0.006	0.000
9	0.000	0.000	0.000	0.003	0.024	0.087	0.184	0.234	0.154	0.028	0.003
10	0.000	0.000	0.000	0.001	0.006	0.035	0.111	0.218	0.246	0.100	0.021
11	0.000	0.000	0.000	0.000	0.001	0.010	0.045	0.139	0.268	0.245	0.111
12	0.000	0.000	0.000	0.000	0.000	0.002	0.011	0.054	0.179	0.367	0.351
13	0.000	0.000	0.000	0.000	0.000	0.000	0.001	0.010	0.055	0.254	0.513

Appendix B.3

Binomial Probability Distribution *(concluded)*

$n = 14$
Probability

x	0.05	0.10	0.20	0.30	0.40	0.50	0.60	0.70	0.80	0.90	0.95
0	0.488	0.229	0.044	0.007	0.001	0.000	0.000	0.000	0.000	0.000	0.000
1	0.359	0.356	0.154	0.041	0.007	0.001	0.000	0.000	0.000	0.000	0.000
2	0.123	0.257	0.250	0.113	0.032	0.006	0.001	0.000	0.000	0.000	0.000
3	0.026	0.114	0.250	0.194	0.085	0.022	0.003	0.000	0.000	0.000	0.000
4	0.004	0.035	0.172	0.229	0.155	0.061	0.014	0.001	0.000	0.000	0.000
5	0.000	0.008	0.086	0.196	0.207	0.122	0.041	0.007	0.000	0.000	0.000
6	0.000	0.001	0.032	0.126	0.207	0.183	0.092	0.023	0.002	0.000	0.000
7	0.000	0.000	0.009	0.062	0.157	0.209	0.157	0.062	0.009	0.000	0.000
8	0.000	0.000	0.002	0.023	0.092	0.183	0.207	0.126	0.032	0.001	0.000
9	0.000	0.000	0.000	0.007	0.041	0.122	0.207	0.196	0.086	0.008	0.000
10	0.000	0.000	0.000	0.001	0.014	0.061	0.155	0.229	0.172	0.035	0.004
11	0.000	0.000	0.000	0.000	0.003	0.022	0.085	0.194	0.250	0.114	0.026
12	0.000	0.000	0.000	0.000	0.001	0.006	0.032	0.113	0.250	0.257	0.123
13	0.000	0.000	0.000	0.000	0.000	0.001	0.007	0.041	0.154	0.356	0.359
14	0.000	0.000	0.000	0.000	0.000	0.000	0.001	0.007	0.044	0.229	0.488

$n = 15$
Probability

x	0.05	0.10	0.20	0.30	0.40	0.50	0.60	0.70	0.80	0.90	0.95
0	0.463	0.206	0.035	0.005	0.000	0.000	0.000	0.000	0.000	0.000	0.000
1	0.366	0.343	0.132	0.031	0.005	0.000	0.000	0.000	0.000	0.000	0.000
2	0.135	0.267	0.231	0.092	0.022	0.003	0.000	0.000	0.000	0.000	0.000
3	0.031	0.129	0.250	0.170	0.063	0.014	0.002	0.000	0.000	0.000	0.000
4	0.005	0.043	0.188	0.219	0.127	0.042	0.007	0.001	0.000	0.000	0.000
5	0.001	0.010	0.103	0.206	0.186	0.092	0.024	0.003	0.000	0.000	0.000
6	0.000	0.002	0.043	0.147	0.207	0.153	0.061	0.012	0.001	0.000	0.000
7	0.000	0.000	0.014	0.081	0.177	0.196	0.118	0.035	0.003	0.000	0.000
8	0.000	0.000	0.003	0.035	0.118	0.196	0.177	0.081	0.014	0.000	0.000
9	0.000	0.000	0.001	0.012	0.061	0.153	0.207	0.147	0.043	0.002	0.000
10	0.000	0.000	0.000	0.003	0.024	0.092	0.186	0.206	0.103	0.010	0.001
11	0.000	0.000	0.000	0.001	0.007	0.042	0.127	0.219	0.188	0.043	0.005
12	0.000	0.000	0.000	0.000	0.002	0.014	0.063	0.170	0.250	0.129	0.031
13	0.000	0.000	0.000	0.000	0.000	0.003	0.022	0.092	0.231	0.267	0.135
14	0.000	0.000	0.000	0.000	0.000	0.000	0.005	0.031	0.132	0.343	0.366
15	0.000	0.000	0.000	0.000	0.000	0.000	0.000	0.005	0.035	0.206	0.463

Appendix B.4

Poisson Distribution

					μ				
x	0.1	0.2	0.3	0.4	0.5	0.6	0.7	0.8	0.9
0	0.9048	0.8187	0.7408	0.6703	0.6065	0.5488	0.4966	0.4493	0.4066
1	0.0905	0.1637	0.2222	0.2681	0.3033	0.3293	0.3476	0.3595	0.3659
2	0.0045	0.0164	0.0333	0.0536	0.0758	0.0988	0.1217	0.1438	0.1647
3	0.0002	0.0011	0.0033	0.0072	0.0126	0.0198	0.0284	0.0383	0.0494
4	0.0000	0.0001	0.0003	0.0007	0.0016	0.0030	0.0050	0.0077	0.0111
5	0.0000	0.0000	0.0000	0.0001	0.0002	0.0004	0.0007	0.0012	0.0020
6	0.0000	0.0000	0.0000	0.0000	0.0000	0.0000	0.0001	0.0002	0.0003
7	0.0000	0.0000	0.0000	0.0000	0.0000	0.0000	0.0000	0.0000	0.0000

					μ				
x	1.0	2.0	3.0	4.0	5.0	6.0	7.0	8.0	9.0
0	0.3679	0.1353	0.0498	0.0183	0.0067	0.0025	0.0009	0.0003	0.0001
1	0.3679	0.2707	0.1494	0.0733	0.0337	0.0149	0.0064	0.0027	0.0011
2	0.1839	0.2707	0.2240	0.1465	0.0842	0.0446	0.0223	0.0107	0.0050
3	0.0613	0.1804	0.2240	0.1954	0.1404	0.0892	0.0521	0.0286	0.0150
4	0.0153	0.0902	0.1680	0.1954	0.1755	0.1339	0.0912	0.0573	0.0337
5	0.0031	0.0361	0.1008	0.1563	0.1755	0.1606	0.1277	0.0916	0.0607
6	0.0005	0.0120	0.0504	0.1042	0.1462	0.1606	0.1490	0.1221	0.0911
7	0.0001	0.0034	0.0216	0.0595	0.1044	0.1377	0.1490	0.1396	0.1171
8	0.0000	0.0009	0.0081	0.0298	0.0653	0.1033	0.1304	0.1396	0.1318
9	0.0000	0.0002	0.0027	0.0132	0.0363	0.0688	0.1014	0.1241	0.1318
10	0.0000	0.0000	0.0008	0.0053	0.0181	0.0413	0.0710	0.0993	0.1186
11	0.0000	0.0000	0.0002	0.0019	0.0082	0.0225	0.0452	0.0722	0.0970
12	0.0000	0.0000	0.0001	0.0006	0.0034	0.0113	0.0263	0.0481	0.0728
13	0.0000	0.0000	0.0000	0.0002	0.0013	0.0052	0.0142	0.0296	0.0504
14	0.0000	0.0000	0.0000	0.0001	0.0005	0.0022	0.0071	0.0169	0.0324
15	0.0000	0.0000	0.0000	0.0000	0.0002	0.0009	0.0033	0.0090	0.0194
16	0.0000	0.0000	0.0000	0.0000	0.0000	0.0003	0.0014	0.0045	0.0109
17	0.0000	0.0000	0.0000	0.0000	0.0000	0.0001	0.0006	0.0021	0.0058
18	0.0000	0.0000	0.0000	0.0000	0.0000	0.0000	0.0002	0.0009	0.0029
19	0.0000	0.0000	0.0000	0.0000	0.0000	0.0000	0.0001	0.0004	0.0014
20	0.0000	0.0000	0.0000	0.0000	0.0000	0.0000	0.0000	0.0002	0.0006
21	0.0000	0.0000	0.0000	0.0000	0.0000	0.0000	0.0000	0.0001	0.0003
22	0.0000	0.0000	0.0000	0.0000	0.0000	0.0000	0.0000	0.0000	0.0001

Table of Random Numbers

02711	08182	75997	79866	58095	83319	80295	79741	74599	84379
94873	90935	31684	63952	09865	14491	99518	93394	34691	14985
54921	78680	06635	98689	17306	25170	65928	87709	30533	89736
77640	97636	37397	93379	56454	59818	45827	74164	71666	46977
61545	00835	93251	87203	36759	49197	85967	01704	19634	21898
17147	19519	22497	16857	42426	84822	92598	49186	88247	39967
13748	04742	92460	85801	53444	65626	58710	55406	17173	69776
87455	14813	50373	28037	91182	32786	65261	11173	34376	36408
08999	57409	91185	10200	61411	23392	47797	56377	71635	08601
78804	81333	53809	32471	46034	36306	22498	19239	85428	55721
82173	26921	28472	98958	07960	66124	89731	95069	18625	92405
97594	25168	89178	68190	05043	17407	48201	83917	11413	72920
73881	67176	93504	42636	38233	16154	96451	57925	29667	30859
46071	22912	90326	42453	88108	72064	58601	32357	90610	32921
44492	19686	12495	93135	95185	77799	52441	88272	22024	80631
31864	72170	37722	55794	14636	05148	54505	50113	21119	25228
51574	90692	43339	65689	76539	27909	05467	21727	51141	72949
35350	76132	92925	92124	92634	35681	43690	89136	35599	84138
46943	36502	01172	46045	46991	33804	80006	35542	61056	75666
22665	87226	33304	57975	03985	21566	65796	72915	81466	89205
39437	97957	11838	10433	21564	51570	73558	27495	34533	57808
77082	47784	40098	97962	89845	28392	78187	06112	08169	11261
24544	25649	43370	28007	06779	72402	62632	53956	24709	06978
27503	15558	37738	24849	70722	71859	83736	06016	94397	12529
24590	24545	06435	52758	45685	90151	46516	49644	92686	84870
48155	86226	40359	28723	15364	69125	12609	57171	86857	31702
20226	53752	90648	24362	83314	00014	19207	69413	97016	86290
70178	73444	38790	53626	93780	18629	68766	24371	74639	30782
10169	41465	51935	05711	09799	79077	88159	33437	68519	03040
81084	03701	28598	70013	63794	53169	97054	60303	23259	96196
69202	20777	21727	81511	51887	16175	53746	46516	70339	62727
80561	95787	89426	93325	86412	57479	54194	52153	19197	81877
08199	26703	95128	48599	09333	12584	24374	31232	61782	44032
98883	28220	39358	53720	80161	83371	15181	11131	12219	55920
84568	69286	76054	21615	80883	36797	82845	39139	90900	18172
04269	35173	95745	53893	86022	77722	52498	84193	22448	22571
10538	13124	36099	13140	37706	44562	57179	44693	67877	01549
77843	24955	25900	63843	95029	93859	93634	20205	66294	41218
12034	94636	49455	76362	83532	31062	69903	91186	65768	55949
10524	72829	47641	93315	80875	28090	97728	52560	34937	79548
68935	76632	46984	61772	92786	22651	07086	89754	44143	97687
89450	65665	29190	43709	11172	34481	95977	47535	25658	73898
90696	20451	24211	97310	60446	73530	62865	96574	13829	72226
49006	32047	93086	00112	20470	17136	28255	86328	07293	38809
74591	87025	52368	59416	34417	70557	86746	55809	53628	12000
06315	17012	77103	00968	07235	10728	42189	33292	51487	64443
62386	09184	62092	46617	99419	64230	95034	85481	07857	42510
86848	82122	04028	36959	87827	12813	08627	80699	13345	51695
65643	69480	46598	04501	40403	91408	32343	48130	49303	90689
11084	46534	78957	77353	39578	77868	22970	84349	09184	70603

Appendix B.6

Critical Values of Chi-Square

This table contains the values of χ^2 that correspond to a specific right-tail area and specific number of degrees of freedom.

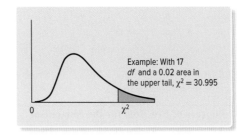

Example: With 17 *df* and a 0.02 area in the upper tail, $\chi^2 = 30.995$

Degrees of Freedom, *df*	Right-Tail Area			
	0.10	0.05	0.02	0.01
1	2.706	3.841	5.412	6.635
2	4.605	5.991	7.824	9.210
3	6.251	7.815	9.837	11.345
4	7.779	9.488	11.668	13.277
5	9.236	11.070	13.388	15.086
6	10.645	12.592	15.033	16.812
7	12.017	14.067	16.622	18.475
8	13.362	15.507	18.168	20.090
9	14.684	16.919	19.679	21.666
10	15.987	18.307	21.161	23.209
11	17.275	19.675	22.618	24.725
12	18.549	21.026	24.054	26.217
13	19.812	22.362	25.472	27.688
14	21.064	23.685	26.873	29.141
15	22.307	24.996	28.259	30.578
16	23.542	26.296	29.633	32.000
17	24.769	27.587	30.995	33.409
18	25.989	28.869	32.346	34.805
19	27.204	30.144	33.687	36.191
20	28.412	31.410	35.020	37.566
21	29.615	32.671	36.343	38.932
22	30.813	33.924	37.659	40.289
23	32.007	35.172	38.968	41.638
24	33.196	36.415	40.270	42.980
25	34.382	37.652	41.566	44.314
26	35.563	38.885	42.856	45.642
27	36.741	40.113	44.140	46.963
28	37.916	41.337	45.419	48.278
29	39.087	42.557	46.693	49.588
30	40.256	43.773	47.962	50.892

Critical Values of the F Distribution at a 5% Level of Significance

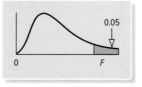

			Degrees of Freedom for the Numerator														
		1	**2**	**3**	**4**	**5**	**6**	**7**	**8**	**9**	**10**	**12**	**15**	**20**	**24**	**30**	**40**
Degrees of Freedom for the Denominator	1	161	200	216	225	230	234	237	239	241	242	244	246	248	249	250	251
	2	18.5	19.0	19.2	19.2	19.3	19.3	19.4	19.4	19.4	19.4	19.4	19.4	19.4	19.5	19.5	19.5
	3	10.1	9.55	9.28	9.12	9.01	8.94	8.89	8.85	8.81	8.79	8.74	8.70	8.66	8.64	8.62	8.59
	4	7.71	6.94	6.59	6.39	6.26	6.16	6.09	6.04	6.00	5.96	5.91	5.86	5.80	5.77	5.75	5.72
	5	6.61	5.79	5.41	5.19	5.05	4.95	4.88	4.82	4.77	4.74	4.68	4.62	4.56	4.53	4.50	4.46
	6	5.99	5.14	4.76	4.53	4.39	4.28	4.21	4.15	4.10	4.06	4.00	3.94	3.87	3.84	3.81	3.77
	7	5.59	4.74	4.35	4.12	3.97	3.87	3.79	3.73	3.68	3.64	3.57	3.51	3.44	3.41	3.38	3.34
	8	5.32	4.46	4.07	3.84	3.69	3.58	3.50	3.44	3.39	3.35	3.28	3.22	3.15	3.12	3.08	3.04
	9	5.12	4.26	3.86	3.63	3.48	3.37	3.29	3.23	3.18	3.14	3.07	3.01	2.94	2.90	2.86	2.83
	10	4.96	4.10	3.71	3.48	3.33	3.22	3.14	3.07	3.02	2.98	2.91	2.85	2.77	2.74	2.70	2.66
	11	4.84	3.98	3.59	3.36	3.20	3.09	3.01	2.95	2.90	2.85	2.79	2.72	2.65	2.61	2.57	2.53
	12	4.75	3.89	3.49	3.26	3.11	3.00	2.91	2.85	2.80	2.75	2.69	2.62	2.54	2.51	2.47	2.43
	13	4.67	3.81	3.41	3.18	3.03	2.92	2.83	2.77	2.71	2.67	2.60	2.53	2.46	2.42	2.38	2.34
	14	4.60	3.74	3.34	3.11	2.96	2.85	2.76	2.70	2.65	2.60	2.53	2.46	2.39	2.35	2.31	2.27
	15	4.54	3.68	3.29	3.06	2.90	2.79	2.71	2.64	2.59	2.54	2.48	2.40	2.33	2.29	2.25	2.20
	16	4.49	3.63	3.24	3.01	2.85	2.74	2.66	2.59	2.54	2.49	2.42	2.35	2.28	2.24	2.19	2.15
	17	4.45	3.59	3.20	2.96	2.81	2.70	2.61	2.55	2.49	2.45	2.38	2.31	2.23	2.19	2.15	2.10
	18	4.41	3.55	3.16	2.93	2.77	2.66	2.58	2.51	2.46	2.41	2.34	2.27	2.19	2.15	2.11	2.06
	19	4.38	3.52	3.13	2.90	2.74	2.63	2.54	2.48	2.42	2.38	2.31	2.23	2.16	2.11	2.07	2.03
	20	4.35	3.49	3.10	2.87	2.71	2.60	2.51	2.45	2.39	2.35	2.28	2.20	2.12	2.08	2.04	1.99
	21	4.32	3.47	3.07	2.84	2.68	2.57	2.49	2.42	2.37	2.32	2.25	2.18	2.10	2.05	2.01	1.96
	22	4.30	3.44	3.05	2.82	2.66	2.55	2.46	2.40	2.34	2.30	2.23	2.15	2.07	2.03	1.98	1.94
	23	4.28	3.42	3.03	2.80	2.64	2.53	2.44	2.37	2.32	2.27	2.20	2.13	2.05	2.01	1.96	1.91
	24	4.26	3.40	3.01	2.78	2.62	2.51	2.42	2.36	2.30	2.25	2.18	2.11	2.03	1.98	1.94	1.89
	25	4.24	3.39	2.99	2.76	2.60	2.49	2.40	2.34	2.28	2.24	2.16	2.09	2.01	1.96	1.92	1.87
	30	4.17	3.32	2.92	2.69	2.53	2.42	2.33	2.27	2.21	2.16	2.09	2.01	1.93	1.89	1.84	1.79
	40	4.08	3.23	2.84	2.61	2.45	2.34	2.25	2.18	2.12	2.08	2.00	1.92	1.84	1.79	1.74	1.69
	60	4.00	3.15	2.76	2.53	2.37	2.25	2.17	2.10	2.04	1.99	1.92	1.84	1.75	1.70	1.65	1.59
	120	3.92	3.07	2.68	2.45	2.29	2.18	2.09	2.02	1.96	1.91	1.83	1.75	1.66	1.61	1.55	1.50
	∞	3.84	3.00	2.60	2.37	2.21	2.10	2.01	1.94	1.88	1.83	1.75	1.67	1.57	1.52	1.46	1.39

Appendix B.7

Critical Values of the *F* Distribution at a 1% Level of Significance

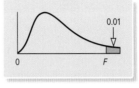

		Degrees of Freedom for the Numerator														
	1	**2**	**3**	**4**	**5**	**6**	**7**	**8**	**9**	**10**	**12**	**15**	**20**	**24**	**30**	**40**
1	4052	5000	5403	5625	5764	5859	5928	5981	6022	6056	6106	6157	6209	6235	6261	6287
2	98.5	99.0	99.2	99.2	99.3	99.3	99.4	99.4	99.4	99.4	99.4	99.4	99.4	99.5	99.5	99.5
3	34.1	30.8	29.5	28.7	28.2	27.9	27.7	27.5	27.3	27.2	27.1	26.9	26.7	26.6	26.5	26.4
4	21.2	18.0	16.7	16.0	15.5	15.2	15.0	14.8	14.7	14.5	14.4	14.2	14.0	13.9	13.8	13.7
5	16.3	13.3	12.1	11.4	11.0	10.7	10.5	10.3	10.2	10.1	9.89	9.72	9.55	9.47	9.38	9.29
6	13.7	10.9	9.78	9.15	8.75	8.47	8.26	8.10	7.98	7.87	7.72	7.56	7.40	7.31	7.23	7.14
7	12.2	9.55	8.45	7.85	7.46	7.19	6.99	6.84	6.72	6.62	6.47	6.31	6.16	6.07	5.99	5.91
8	11.3	8.65	7.59	7.01	6.63	6.37	6.18	6.03	5.91	5.81	5.67	5.52	5.36	5.28	5.20	5.12
9	10.6	8.02	6.99	6.42	6.06	5.80	5.61	5.47	5.35	5.26	5.11	4.96	4.81	4.73	4.65	4.57
10	10.0	7.56	6.55	5.99	5.64	5.39	5.20	5.06	4.94	4.85	4.71	4.56	4.41	4.33	4.25	4.17
11	9.65	7.21	6.22	5.67	5.32	5.07	4.89	4.74	4.63	4.54	4.40	4.25	4.10	4.02	3.94	3.86
12	9.33	6.93	5.95	5.41	5.06	4.82	4.64	4.50	4.39	4.30	4.16	4.01	3.86	3.78	3.70	3.62
13	9.07	6.70	5.74	5.21	4.86	4.62	4.44	4.30	4.19	4.10	3.96	3.82	3.66	3.59	3.51	3.43
14	8.86	6.51	5.56	5.04	4.69	4.46	4.28	4.14	4.03	3.94	3.80	3.66	3.51	3.43	3.35	3.27
15	8.68	6.36	5.42	4.89	4.56	4.32	4.14	4.00	3.89	3.80	3.67	3.52	3.37	3.29	3.21	3.13
16	8.53	6.23	5.29	4.77	4.44	4.20	4.03	3.89	3.78	3.69	3.55	3.41	3.26	3.18	3.10	3.02
17	8.40	6.11	5.18	4.67	4.34	4.10	3.93	3.79	3.68	3.59	3.46	3.31	3.16	3.08	3.00	2.92
18	8.29	6.01	5.09	4.58	4.25	4.01	3.84	3.71	3.60	3.51	3.37	3.23	3.08	3.00	2.92	2.84
19	8.18	5.93	5.01	4.50	4.17	3.94	3.77	3.63	3.52	3.43	3.30	3.15	3.00	2.92	2.84	2.76
20	8.10	5.85	4.94	4.43	4.10	3.87	3.70	3.56	3.46	3.37	3.23	3.09	2.94	2.86	2.78	2.69
21	8.02	5.78	4.87	4.37	4.04	3.81	3.64	3.51	3.40	3.31	3.17	3.03	2.88	2.80	2.72	2.64
22	7.95	5.72	4.82	4.31	3.99	3.76	3.59	3.45	3.35	3.26	3.12	2.98	2.83	2.75	2.67	2.58
23	7.88	5.66	4.76	4.26	3.94	3.71	3.54	3.41	3.30	3.21	3.07	2.93	2.78	2.70	2.62	2.54
24	7.82	5.61	4.72	4.22	3.90	3.67	3.50	3.36	3.26	3.17	3.03	2.89	2.74	2.66	2.58	2.49
25	7.77	5.57	4.68	4.18	3.85	3.63	3.46	3.32	3.22	3.13	2.99	2.85	2.70	2.62	2.54	2.45
30	7.56	5.39	4.51	4.02	3.70	3.47	3.30	3.17	3.07	2.98	2.84	2.70	2.55	2.47	2.39	2.30
40	7.31	5.18	4.31	3.83	3.51	3.29	3.12	2.99	2.89	2.80	2.66	2.52	2.37	2.29	2.20	2.11
60	7.08	4.98	4.13	3.65	3.34	3.12	2.95	2.82	2.72	2.63	2.50	2.35	2.20	2.12	2.03	1.94
120	6.85	4.79	3.95	3.48	3.17	2.96	2.79	2.66	2.56	2.47	2.34	2.19	2.03	1.95	1.86	1.76
∞	6.63	4.61	3.78	3.32	3.02	2.80	2.64	2.51	2.41	2.32	2.18	2.04	1.88	1.79	1.70	1.59

Degrees of Freedom for the Denominator

Pronunciation Key

Chapter 3

SYMBOL	MEANING	PRONUNCIATION
μ	Population mean	*mu*
Σ	Operation of adding	*sigma*
ΣX	Adding a group of values	*sigma X*
$\overline{X}$	Sample mean	*X bar*
$\overline{X}_w$	Weighted mean	*X bar sub w*
GM	Geometric mean	*GM*
ΣfX	Adding the product of the frequencies and the class midpoints	*sigma fX*
σ^2	Population variance	*sigma squared*
σ	Population standard deviation	*sigma*
s^2	Sample Variance	*s^2*
s	Standard Deviation	*s*
CV	Coefficient of Variation	*CV*
sk	Pearson's Coefficient of Skewness	*sk*
ΣfX^2	Sum of the product of the class midpoints squared and the class frequency	*sigma fX squared*
L_p	Location of percentile	*L sub p*
Q_1	First quartile	*Q sub 1*
Q_3	Third quartile	*Q sub 3*

Chapter 4

SYMBOL	MEANING	PRONUNCIATION
$P(A)$	Probability of A	*P of A*
$P(\sim A)$	Probability of not A	*P of not A*
$P(A \text{ and } B)$	Probability of A and B	*P of A and B*
$P(A \text{ or } B)$	Probability of A or B	*P of A or B*
$P(A\|B)$	Probability of A given B has happened	*P of A given B*
$_nP_r$	Permutation of n items selected r at a time	*Pnr*
$_nC_r$	Combination of n items selected r at a time	*Cnr*
$n!$	Product of all positive integers $\leq n$	*n factorial*

Chapter 7

SYMBOL	MEANING	PRONUNCIATION
$\mu_{\overline{X}}$	Mean of the sampling distribution of the sample mean	*mu sub X bar*
$\sigma_{\overline{X}}$	Population standard error of the sample mean	*sigma sub X bar*
$s_{\overline{X}}$	Estimate of the standard error of the sample mean	*s sub X bar*
$\sigma_{\overline{p}}$	Population standard error of the sample proportion	*sigma sub p bar*

Chapter 8

SYMBOL	MEANING	PRONUNCIATION
$\sigma_{\overline{X}}$	Standard error of the sample means	*sigma sub X bar*
σ_p	Standard error of the population proportion	*sigma sub p*
s_p	Standard error of the sample proportion	*s sub p*
$s_{\overline{X}}$	Sample standard deviation of the sample means	*s sub X bar*

Chapter 9

SYMBOL	MEANING	PRONUNCIATION
H_0	Null hypothesis	*H sub zero*
H_1	Alternative hypothesis	*H sub one*

Chapter 10

SYMBOL	MEANING	PRONUNCIATION
p_c	Pooled proportion	*p sub c*
s_p^2	Pooled sample variance	*s sub p squared*
$\overline{X}_1$	Mean of the first sample	*X bar sub 1*
$\overline{X}_2$	Mean of the second sample	*X bar sub 2*
$\overline{d}$	Mean of the difference between dependent observations	*d bar*
s_d	Standard deviation of the difference between dependent observations	*s sub d*

Chapter 11

SYMBOL	MEANING	PRONUNCIATION
SS total	Sum of squares total	*S S total*
SST	Sum of squares treatment	*S S T*
SSE	Sum of squares error	*S S E*
T_c^2	Column totals squared	*T sub c squared*
n_c	Number of observations in each treatment	*n sub c*
MSE	Mean square error	*M S E*

Chapter 12

SYMBOL	MEANING	PRONUNCIATION
$\sum xy$	Sum of the products of x and y	*Sum xy*
ρ	Coefficient of correlation in the population	*Rho*
y'	Estimated value of y	*y prime*
S_e	Standard error of estimate	*S sub e*
r^2	Coefficient of determination	*r square*

Chapter 13

SYMBOL	MEANING	PRONUNCIATION
b_1	Regression coefficient for the first independent variable	*b sub 1*
b_k	Regression coefficient for any independent variable	*b sub k*
$s_{e \cdot 12 \cdots k}$	Multiple standard error of estimate	*s sub e 1,2 $\cdots$ k*
R^2	Coefficient of multiple determination	*R squared*

Chapter 14

SYMBOL	MEANING	PRONUNCIATION
χ^2	Probability distribution	*ki square*
f_o	Observed frequency	*f sub oh*
f_e	Expected frequency	*f sub e*

Chapter 15

SYMBOL	MEANING	PRONUNCIATION
p_0	Base period of a value	p sub 0
p_1	Given or selected period of a value	p sub 1
p_t	Current period of a value	p sub t

Chapter 17

SYMBOL	MEANING	PRONUNCIATION
$EMV(A_i)$	Expected monetary value of decision alternative, i	EMV A sub i
$P(S_j)_{,} S_j)$	Probability of states of nature	P S sub j
$V(A_i, S_j)$	Value of payoffs resulting from combination of decision alternative and a state of nature	V A sub i, S sub j
$EOL(A_i)$	Expected opportunity loss for a particular decision alternative	EOL A sub i
$R(A_i, S_j)$	Regret or loss for a particular combination of a state of nature and a decision alternative	R A sub i, S sub j

Formulas

Chapter 3 Describing Data: Numerical Measures

- Population mean

$$\mu = \frac{\sum x}{N}$$

[3–1]

- Sample mean

$$\bar{x} = \frac{\sum x}{n}$$

[3–2]

- Weighted mean

$$\bar{x}_w = \frac{w_1 x_1 + w_2 x_2 + w_3 x_3 + \ldots + w_n x_n}{w_1 + w_2 + w_3 + \ldots + w_n}$$

[3–3]

- Geometric mean

$$GM = \sqrt[n]{(x_1)(x_2)\ldots(x_n)}$$

[3–4]

$$GM = \sqrt[n]{\frac{\text{Value at end of period}}{\text{Value at beginning of period}}} - 1$$

[3–5]

- Range

$$\text{Range} = \text{Maximum value} - \text{Minimum value}$$

[3–6]

- Mean deviation

$$MD = \frac{\sum |x - \bar{x}|}{n}$$

[3–7]

- Population variance

$$\sigma^2 = \frac{\sum (x - \mu)^2}{N}$$

[3–8]

- Population standard deviation

$$\sigma = \sqrt{\frac{\sum (x - \mu)^2}{N}}$$

[3–9]

- Sample variance, deviation formula

$$s^2 = \frac{\sum (x - \bar{x})^2}{n - 1}$$

[3–10]

- Sample variance, direct formula

$$s^2 = \frac{\sum x^2 - \frac{(\sum x)^2}{n}}{n - 1}$$

[3–11]

- Sample standard deviation, direct formula

$$s = \sqrt{\frac{\sum x^2 - \frac{(\sum x)^2}{n}}{n - 1}}$$

[3–12]

- Chebyshev's theorem

$$1 - \frac{1}{k^2}$$

- Coefficient of variation

$$CV = \frac{s}{\bar{x}}(100)$$

[3–13]

- Pearson's coefficient of skewness

$$sk = \frac{3(\bar{x} - \text{Median})}{s}$$

[3–14]

- Location of a percentile

$$L_p = (n + 1)\frac{P}{100}$$

[3–15]

- Arithmetic mean of grouped data

$$\bar{x} = \frac{\sum fx}{n}$$

[3–16]

- Median, grouped data

$$\text{Median} = L + \frac{\frac{N}{2} - f_c}{f}(i)$$

[3–17]

- Standard deviation, grouped data

$$s = \sqrt{\frac{\sum fx^2 - \frac{(\sum fx)^2}{n}}{n - 1}}$$

[3–18]

Chapter 4 A Survey of Probability Concepts

- Classical probability

$$\frac{\text{Probability of}}{\text{event happening}} = \frac{\text{Number of favourable outcomes}}{\text{Number of possible outcomes}}$$

[4–1]

- Multiplication formula

$$\text{Total number of arrangements} = (m)(n)$$

[4–2]

- Permutation formula

$${}_nP_r = \frac{n!}{(n - r)!}$$

[4–3]

- Combination formula

$${}_nC_r = \frac{n!}{r!(n - r)!}$$

[4–4]

- Special rule of addition

$$P(A \text{ or } B) = P(A) + P(B)$$

[4–5]

- Complement rule

$$P(\sim A) = 1 - P(A)$$

[4–6]

- General rule of addition

$$P(A \text{ or } B) = P(A) + P(B) - P(A \text{ and } B)$$

[4–7]

- Special rule of multiplication

$$P(A \text{ and } B) = P(A)P(B)$$

[4–8]

- General rule of multiplication

$$P(A \text{ and } B) = P(A)P(B \mid A)$$

[4–9]

Chapter 5 Discrete Probability Distributions

- Mean of a discrete probability distribution

$$\mu = \sum [xP(x)]$$

[5–1]

- Variance of a discrete probability distribution

$$\sigma^2 = \sum [(x - \mu)^2 P(x)]$$

[5–2]

- Binomial probability distribution

$$P(x) = {}_nC_x P^x (1 - p)^{n - x}$$

[5–3]

- Mean of a binomial distribution

$$\mu = np$$

[5–4]

- Variance of a binomial distribution

$$\sigma^2 = np(1 - p)$$

[5–5]

- Hypergeometric distribution

$$P(x) = \frac{({}_SC_x)({}_{N-S}C_{n-x})}{{}_NC_n}$$

[5–6]

- Poisson distribution

$$P(x) = \frac{\mu^x e^{-\mu}}{x!}$$

[5–7]

- Mean of a poisson distribution
$$\mu = np \qquad [5\text{--}8]$$

Chapter 6 Continuous Probability Distributions

- Mean of the uniform distribution
$$\mu = \frac{a+b}{2} \qquad [6\text{--}1]$$

- Standard deviation of the uniform distribution
$$\sigma = \sqrt{\frac{(b-a)^2}{12}} \qquad [6\text{--}2]$$

- Uniform distribution
$$P(x) = \frac{1}{b-a} \quad \text{if } a \le x \le b \text{ and 0 elsewhere} \qquad [6\text{--}3]$$

- Standard normal value
$$z = \frac{x-\mu}{\sigma} \qquad [6\text{--}4]$$

Chapter 7 Sampling Methods and the Central Limit Theorem

- Standard error of the mean
$$\sigma_{\bar{x}} = \frac{\sigma}{\sqrt{n}} \qquad [7\text{--}1]$$

- Finding the z-value of $\bar{x}$ when the population standard deviation is known
$$z = \frac{\bar{x} - \mu}{\sigma/\sqrt{n}} \qquad [7\text{--}2]$$

- Sample proportion
$$\bar{p} = \frac{x}{n} \qquad [7\text{--}3]$$

- Standard error of the proportion
$$\sigma_p = \sqrt{\frac{p(1-p)}{n}} \qquad [7\text{--}4]$$

- Find the z-value of $\bar{p}$ when the population proportion is known
$$z = \frac{\bar{p} - p}{\sqrt{\frac{p(1-p)}{n}}} \qquad [7\text{--}5]$$

Chapter 8 Estimation and Confidence Intervals

- Confidence interval for the population mean with σ known
$$\bar{x} \pm z \frac{\sigma}{\sqrt{n}} \qquad [8\text{--}1]$$

- Confidence interval for the population mean with σ unknown
$$\bar{x} \pm t \frac{s}{\sqrt{n}} \qquad [8\text{--}2]$$

- Confidence interval for a population proportion
$$\bar{p} \pm z \sigma_p \quad \text{where } \sigma_p = \sqrt{\frac{p(1-p)}{n}} \qquad [8\text{--}3]$$

- Standard error of the sample proportion
$$s_p = \sqrt{\frac{\bar{p}(1-\bar{p})}{n}} \qquad [8\text{--}4]$$

- Confidence interval for a sample proportion
$$p \pm z \sqrt{\frac{\bar{p}(1-\bar{p})}{n}} \qquad [8\text{--}5]$$

- Standard error of the sample mean, using a correction factor (known σ)
$$\sigma_{\bar{x}} = \frac{\sigma}{\sqrt{n}} \sqrt{\frac{N-n}{N-1}} \qquad [8\text{--}6]$$

- Standard error of the sample mean, using a correction factor (unknown σ)
$$s_{\bar{x}} = \frac{s}{\sqrt{n}} \sqrt{\frac{N-n}{N-1}} \qquad [8\text{--}7]$$

- Standard error of the sample proportion, using a correction factor
$$s_p = \sqrt{\frac{\bar{p}(1-\bar{p})}{n}} \sqrt{\frac{N-n}{N-1}} \qquad [8\text{--}8]$$

- Sample size for estimating the population mean
$$n = \left(\frac{z\sigma}{E}\right)^2 \qquad [8\text{--}9]$$

- Sample size for the population proportion
$$n = p(1-p)\left(\frac{z}{E}\right)^2 \qquad [8\text{--}10]$$

Chapter 9 One-Sample Tests of a Hypothesis

- z test statistic
$$z = \frac{\bar{x} - \mu}{\sigma/\sqrt{n}} \qquad [9\text{--}1]$$

- Testing a mean, σ unknown
$$t = \frac{\bar{x} - \mu}{s/\sqrt{n}} \qquad [9\text{--}2]$$

- Test of hypothesis, one proportion
$$z = \frac{\bar{p} - p}{\sigma_p} \qquad [9\text{--}3]$$

- Test of hypothesis, one proportion
$$z = \frac{\bar{p} - p}{\sqrt{\frac{p(1-p)}{n}}} \qquad [9\text{--}4]$$

Chapter 10 Two-Sample Tests of Hypothesis

- Variance of the distribution of differences in means
$$\sigma^2_{\bar{x}_1 - \bar{x}_2} = \frac{\sigma_1^2}{n_1} + \frac{\sigma_2^2}{n_2} \qquad [10\text{--}1]$$

- Two-sample test of means—known σ
$$z = \frac{\bar{x}_1 - \bar{x}_2 - (\mu_1 - \mu_2)}{\sqrt{\frac{\sigma_1^2}{n_1} + \frac{\sigma_2^2}{n_2}}} \qquad [10\text{--}2]$$

- Pooled sample variance
$$s_p^2 = \frac{(n_1 - 1)s_1^2 + (n_2 - 1)s_2^2}{n_1 + n_2 - 2} \qquad [10\text{--}3]$$

- Two-sample test of means—unknown σ
$$t = \frac{\bar{x}_1 - \bar{x}_2 - (\mu_1 - \mu_2)}{\sqrt{s_p^2\left(\frac{1}{n_1} + \frac{1}{n_2}\right)}} \qquad [10\text{--}4]$$

- Paired t test
$$t = \frac{\bar{d} - \mu_d}{s_{d/\sqrt{n}}} \qquad [10\text{--}5]$$

- Two-sample test of proportions
$$z = \frac{\bar{p}_1 - \bar{p}_2 - (p_1 - p_2)}{\sqrt{\frac{p_c(1-p_c)}{n_1} + \frac{p_c(1-p_c)}{n_2}}} \qquad [10\text{--}6]$$

- Pooled proportion
$$p_c = \frac{x_1 + x_2}{n_1 + n_2} \qquad [10\text{--}7]$$

Chapter 11 Analysis of Variance

- Test statistic for comparing two variances

$$F = \frac{s_1^2}{s_2^2}, s_1^2 > s_2^2 \qquad [11\text{--}1]$$

- SS total

$$\sum (x - \overline{x}_G)^2 \qquad [11\text{--}2]$$

- SSE

$$\sum (x - \overline{x}_c)^2 \qquad [11\text{--}3]$$

- SST $\qquad$ SST = SS total − SSE $\qquad$ [11–4]

- Confidence interval for the difference in treatment means

$$(\overline{x}_1 - \overline{x}_2) \pm t \sqrt{\text{MSE}\left(\frac{1}{n_1} + \frac{1}{n_2}\right)} \qquad [11\text{--}5]$$

Chapter 12 Linear Regression and Correlation

- General form of linear regression equation

$$y' = a + bx \qquad [12\text{--}1]$$

- Slope of the regression line

$$b = \frac{n(\sum xy) - (\sum x)(\sum y)}{n(\sum x^2) - (\sum x)^2} \qquad [12\text{--}2]$$

- Y-intercept

$$a = \frac{\sum y}{n} - b\frac{\sum x}{n} \qquad [12\text{--}3]$$

- Standard error of estimate

$$S_e = \sqrt{\frac{\sum (y - y')^2}{n - 2}} \qquad [12\text{--}4]$$

- Computation formula for the standard error of estimate

$$S_e = \sqrt{\frac{\sum y^2 - a(\sum y) - b(\sum xy)}{n - 2}} \qquad [12\text{--}5]$$

- Confidence interval for the mean of y, given x

$$y' \pm tS_e \sqrt{\frac{1}{n} + \frac{(x - \overline{x})^2}{\sum (x - \overline{x})^2}} \qquad [12\text{--}6]$$

- Prediction interval for y, given x

$$y' \pm tS_e \sqrt{1 + \frac{1}{n} + \frac{(x - \overline{x})^2}{\sum (x - \overline{x})^2}} \qquad [12\text{--}7]$$

- Correlation coefficient—conceptual form

$$r = \frac{\sum (x - \overline{x})(y - \overline{y})}{(n - 1)s_x s_y} \qquad [12\text{--}8]$$

- Correlation coefficient

$$r = \frac{n(\sum xy) - (\sum x)(\sum y)}{\sqrt{[n(\sum x^2) - (\sum x)^2][n(\sum y^2) - (\sum y)^2]}} \qquad [12\text{--}9]$$

- t-test for the coefficient of correlation

$$t = \frac{r\sqrt{n - 2}}{\sqrt{1 - r^2}} \text{ with } n - 2 \text{ degrees of freedom} \qquad [12\text{--}10]$$

- Coefficient of determination

$$r^2 = \frac{\text{Explained variation}}{\text{Total variation}}$$
$$= \frac{\sum (y' - \overline{y})^2}{\sum (y - \overline{y})^2} \qquad [12\text{--}11]$$

$$r^2 = \frac{\text{SSR}}{\text{SST}} = 1 - \frac{\text{SSE}}{\text{SST}} \qquad [12\text{--}12]$$

- Standard error of estimate

$$S_e = \sqrt{\frac{\text{SSE}}{n - 2}} \qquad [12\text{--}13]$$

Chapter 13 Multiple Regression and Correlation Analysis

- General multiple regression equation

$$y' = a + b_1 x_1 + b_2 x_2 + \cdots + b_k x_k \qquad [13\text{--}1]$$

- Multiple standard error of estimate

$$S_{e \cdot 12 \cdots k} = \sqrt{\frac{\sum (y - y')^2}{n - k - 1}} \qquad [13\text{--}2]$$

- Coefficient of multiple determination

$$R^2 = \frac{\text{SSR}}{\text{SS total}} \qquad [13\text{--}3]$$

- Global test

$$F = \frac{\text{SSR}/k}{\text{SSE}/[n - k - 1]} \qquad [13\text{--}4]$$

- Testing individual regression coefficients

$$t = \frac{b_i - 0}{s_{b_i}} \qquad [13\text{--}5]$$

Chapter 14 Chi-Square Applications

- Chi-square test statistic

$$\chi^2 = \sum \left[\frac{(f_o - f_e)^2}{f_e}\right] \qquad [14\text{--}1]$$

- Expected frequency

$$f_e = \frac{(\text{Row total})(\text{Column total})}{\text{Grand total}} \qquad [14\text{--}2]$$

Chapter 15 Index Numbers

- Simple index

$$P = \frac{P_t}{P_0} \times 100 \qquad [15\text{--}1]$$

- Simple average of the price indexes

$$P = \frac{\sum P_i}{n} \qquad [15\text{--}2]$$

- Simple aggregate index

$$P = \frac{\sum P_t}{\sum P_0} \times 100 \qquad [15\text{--}3]$$

- Laspeyres price index

$$P = \frac{\sum p_t q_0}{\sum p_0 q_0} \times 100 \qquad [15\text{--}4]$$

- Paasche price index

$$P = \frac{\sum p_t q_t}{\sum p_0 q_t} \times 100 \qquad [15\text{--}5]$$

- Fisher's ideal index

$$\text{Fisher's ideal index} = \sqrt{(\text{Laspeyres index})(\text{Paasche index})} \qquad [15\text{--}6]$$

- Value index

$$V = \frac{\sum p_t q_t}{\sum p_0 q_0} \times 100 \qquad [15\text{--}7]$$

- Real income

$$\text{Real income} = \frac{\text{Money income}}{\text{CPI}} \times 100 \qquad [15\text{--}8]$$

- Using an index as a deflator

$$\text{Deflated sales} = \frac{\text{Actual sales}}{\text{An appropriate index}} \times 100 \qquad [15\text{--}9]$$

- Using an index to find purchasing power

$$\text{Purchasing power of dollar} = \frac{\$1}{\text{CPI}} \times 100 \qquad [15\text{--}10]$$

Chapter 16 Time Series and Forecasting

- Linear trend equation

$$y' = a + bt \qquad [16\text{--}1]$$

- The slope

$$b = \frac{n\sum ty - (\sum y)(\sum t)}{n\sum t^2 - (\sum t)^2} \qquad [16\text{--}2]$$

- The intercept

$$a = \frac{\sum y}{n} - b\left(\frac{\sum t}{n}\right) \qquad [16\text{--}3]$$

- Log trend equation

$$\log y' = \log a + \log b(t) \qquad [16\text{--}4]$$

- Correction factor for adjusting quarterly means

$$\text{Correction factor} = \frac{400}{\text{Total of four means}} \qquad [16\text{--}5]$$

Chapter 17 An Introduction to Decision Theory

- Expected monetary value

$$\text{EMV}(A_i) = \sum \left[P(S_j) \times V(A_i, S_j) \right] \qquad [17\text{--}1]$$

- Expected opportunity loss

$$\text{EOL}(A_i) = \sum \left[P(S_j) \times R(A_i, S_j) \right] \qquad [17\text{--}2]$$

- Expected value of perfect information

EVPI = Expected value under conditions of certainty

   − Expected value under conditions of uncertainty   [17–3]

Index